D1716904

Exploring World History

GLOBE BOOK COMPANY

Exploring World History

Sol Holt

John R. O'Connor

SOL HOLT

Sol Holt has made many contributions to social studies education over the course of his professional career. He has been a social studies teacher in the New York City high schools, served as social studies department chairman for twenty-five years, trained hundreds of teachers in social studies methods, and been author or coauthor of texts in geography, economics, and history.

JOHN R. O'CONNOR

John O'Connor taught social studies for many years before becoming a principal in the New York City school system. He is widely known for his lectures and articles on reading skills in the social studies. In addition to this book, John O'Connor has coauthored other Globe textbooks: *Exploring United States History, Exploring American Citizenship, Unlocking Social Studies Skills,* and *Exploring the Urban World.* He has edited Globe's *Exploring American History, Exploring A Changing World,* and *Exploring the Non-Western World.*

Acknowledgments for photographs begin on page 682.
Acknowledgments for printed matter begin on page 684.
Photo Editor: Adelaide Garvin Ungerland.
Illustrations, Maps, and Charts: Mel Erikson.

Cover photograph: Temple of Luxor, Egypt, Hypostyle Hall built by Amenophis III, 18th Dynasty, and Colossus of Ramses II.

ISBN: 0-87065-025-4

Copyright © 1987 by Globe Book Company, Inc.
190 Sylvan Ave., Englewood Cliffs, NJ 07632

Published simultaneously in Canada by Globe/Modern Curriculum Press.
Printed in the United States of America   4   5   6   7   8   9   0

CONTENTS

Unit I: What Was Life Like in the Earliest Civilizations?

Unit II: What Do We Owe to the Ancient Greeks and Romans?

V

LIST OF MAPS

ORIGINAL SOURCES

TOPICAL CONTENTS

UNIT I

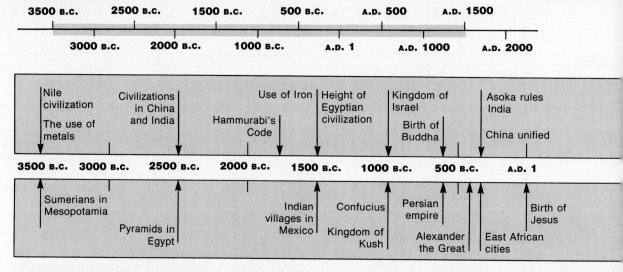

| 3500 B.C. | 2500 B.C. | 1500 B.C. | 500 B.C. | A.D. 500 | A.D. 1500 |

| 3000 B.C. | 2000 B.C. | 1000 B.C. | A.D. 1 | A.D. 1000 | A.D. 2000 |

| Nile civilization | Civilizations in China and India | | Use of Iron | Height of Egyptian civilization | Kingdom of Israel | Asoka rules India |
| The use of metals | | Hammurabi's Code | | | Birth of Buddha | China unified |

| 3500 B.C. | 3000 B.C. | 2500 B.C. | 2000 B.C. | 1500 B.C. | 1000 B.C. | 500 B.C. | A.D. 1 |

| Sumerians in Mesopotamia | | | | Indian villages in Mexico | Confucius | Persian empire | Birth of Jesus |
| | | Pyramids in Egypt | | | Kingdom of Kush | Alexander the Great | East African cities |

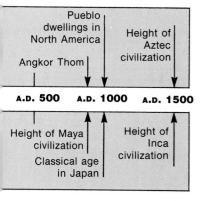

Pueblo
dwellings in
North America

Angkor Thom

Height of
Aztec
civilization

A.D. 500   A.D. 1000   A.D. 1500

Height of Maya
civilization

Classical age
in Japan

Height of
Inca
civilization

What Was Life Like in the Earliest Civilizations?

**A wall painting in an ancient Egyptian tomb
shows a man and a woman tending their fields.**

1

INTRODUCTION A:
Before Written History

DID EARLY PEOPLE LEAVE TRACES?

1. Perhaps you have been on a picnic recently. When you arrived at the picnic grounds you were probably able to tell if there had been others there before you. Different things might have been left behind which showed that people had been there. There may have been scraps of food, a knife, even a smoking fire. You may have even been able to tell how many people had been there. You may have figured out what they had eaten for lunch from the things they had left behind. In other words, you may have discovered certain things about the people who had come before you by the *traces* they had left.

2. People in battle are very careful not to leave traces behind them when they leave their camp. If the enemy should come by the camp, the traces will tell them many important things. A single empty shell will tell the enemy the kind of weapons the people were carrying. Tracks and tire marks will give the enemy an idea of the equipment the soldiers had. We can tell a great deal about people by discovering even small traces of them.

3. The people who lived on earth thousands of years ago (ancient people) left traces. Like skilled detectives, we can put together these small clues and discover how ancient people lived. Some people make the study of the earliest human beings their life's work. These scientists, called *archaeologists* (ark-ee-OLL-o-jists), dig in the ruins of ancient buildings and towns. They look for bones of humans and for objects the ancient people used. Even today, archaeologists are finding the remains of ancient people and cities. When bones and skeletons are found, they are studied by *anthropologists* (an-throh-POLL-oh-jists). These scientists can learn from these bones how people lived. *Geologists* (jee-OLL-oh-jists) study the rock in which traces of life have been found. Geologists can tell how long it took the rock to form. Using this information, they can decide how many years ago the bones or weapons were buried.

HOW DID PEOPLE LIVE AND LOOK IN THE STONE AGE?

4. Human beings probably appeared on the earth from 500,000 to 1,000,000 years ago. The period of time from the earliest traces of people on earth to about 10,000 years ago is known as the *Stone Age*. We call it this because people made most of their tools out of stone during this period. At different times during the Stone Age, great masses of ice, called *glaciers*, moved south from the Arctic region. In North America, the glaciers at one time reached as far south as the Ohio River. Much of Europe and Asia was also covered with ice. The great ice

masses pushed rocks in front of them, smoothing off mountain tops and filling the valleys. The ice melted from time to time. Then the waters from the melting ice cut out valleys and formed rivers and lakes.

5. Human beings had a hard time keeping alive during the time of glaciers. Some people and animals moved south to where there were no glaciers. Others went to live in caves. Scientists say that about 12,000 years ago the last ice blanket began to melt. Today, glaciers are still found in the polar regions of the earth. The icebergs of the North Atlantic Ocean are pieces of ice that have broken off from northern glaciers.

6. Archaeologists have discovered remains of the earliest humans in Europe, Asia, and East Africa. These people probably lived from 30,000 to 1,000,000 years ago. They are often called *prehistoric* people because they lived before history was written down. People of 70,000 years ago seem to have been short and heavy with large heads and long, dangling arms. They lived in caves and used weapons made of stone and wood. Humans who lived about 20,000 years ago were much more like the human beings of today. They were taller than earlier humans, had smaller heads, and walked upright. Dressed in modern clothes, they might have looked much like people of today. Like the humans before them, they lived in caves. They painted on the cave walls. Many of their paintings were of the animals of their time, such as reindeer, wild horses, buffalo, and huge elephants known as *mammoths* (MAM-oths).

7. Ancient people lived before farming was developed. They moved about in search of berries and vegetables and hunted wild animals in order to eat. Because they sometimes traveled in groups, it was necessary for them to learn how to speak. So *language* began. People learned to make sounds that would have meaning for others. Fire was the great discovery of these people. How they discovered it we do not know. But it is very important, since people could use fire to protect themselves against the

Cave paintings such as this one show the interest early humans had in art and beauty. It would suggest that Stone Age life involved more than just obtaining food and shelter.

cold. They could also use it to scare away wild animals. Still later, people learned that they could improve the flavor of meat by cooking it over flames. Fire was the most important discovery of the Stone Age.

8. Then, about 10,000 years ago, Stone Age people learned to improve their weapons and tools. They still made them out of stone, but now they polished them. Polishing made the cutting edges sharper and more useful. The hammers we use today are shaped like those of the Stone Age people of 10,000 years ago. Humans became so good at making their own tools that they managed to make needles of bone, which they used to sew together animal skins for clothing.

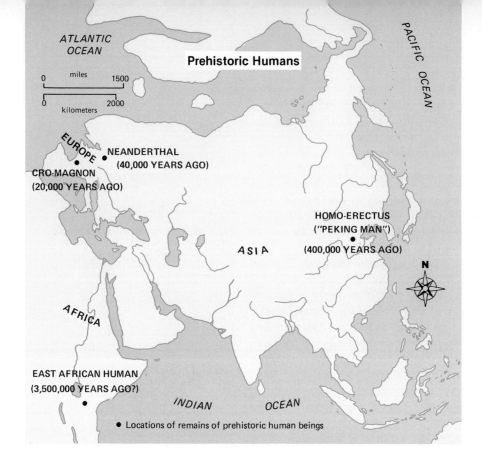

ATLANTIC OCEAN

PACIFIC OCEAN

Prehistoric Humans

miles
0   1500
0   2000
kilometers

EUROPE

•NEANDERTHAL
(40,000 YEARS AGO)

CRO-MAGNON
(20,000 YEARS AGO)

HOMO-ERECTUS
("PEKING MAN")
•
(400,000 YEARS AGO)

ASIA

N

AFRICA

EAST AFRICAN HUMAN
(3,500,000 YEARS AGO?)

INDIAN   OCEAN

• Locations of remains of prehistoric human beings

HOW DID SETTLEMENTS BEGIN?

9. Two discoveries greatly changed the life of ancient people. One was the domestication (taming) of animals. The other was farming. Earlier, Stone Age humans had to keep hunting for animals, because wild animals ran away. But when they learned to tame animals, they could keep the animals with them. Dogs were probably the first animals to be domesticated. As people moved from place to place in search of grass for their animals, dogs were used to guard the herds. But thanks to the domestication of animals, people did not have to find new hunting lands so often. They did not have to move their houses and families as many times as before.

10. As people began to farm, they wandered even less. For now they could grow food for themselves and their animals and settle down for a longer time in one place. In fact, they could not go far from their homes, for they had crops to watch. And since they were going to stay in one place for a while, they built homes that would last longer. More and more people came to areas of fertile land (land on which crops could grow) and settled there. Village life began to take the place of wandering tribal life.

11. The wandering tribes were usually led by a chief. Once people settled near each other in large numbers, it was necessary to form a larger kind of government. There was a need to make rules about the ownership of land. So people joined together to form governments to protect their precious lands. Humans had not yet learned to write. Nor would they have had time to write even if they had known how to. But they did think, and they worried. They believed that there were many gods; that is, pow-

4

This painting shows a scene following a successful hunt. What in the picture shows that animals provided more than just food?

ers higher than themselves. They thought that some of these gods were helpful and others were harmful. They buried their dead and often buried weapons and food with them.

HOW DID METALS AID EARLY PEOPLE?

12. Metal was discovered about 6,000 years ago. Probably by accident, people found that they could make things out of copper by first heating it until it was soft enough to shape. Later, copper was combined with tin to make bronze. From then on, humans could make tools and weapons with sharper points and edges. With these, they could do better work, and the things they made would last longer. When people started to become fond of metal trinkets, trade began.

13. If fire was the most important discovery of humans, the wheel may have been the greatest invention. It was invented sometime during the Age of Metals. The wheel made it

possible for people to carry heavier loads over greater distances. It made trade with neighbors easier. Two-wheeled carts (chariots) were used in warfare. Four-wheeled wagons were pulled by donkeys, oxen, or cows over short distances. The wheel is as important to people today as it was 8,000 years ago.

The horse in cave paintings is similar to domestic horses today. Why was the taming of animals an important advance for early peoples?

14. In earliest times, most trade was done with one's neighbors. Then people learned to use rafts and boats hollowed out of logs. Now they could trade with villages hundreds of miles away. As trade spread, ideas were carried to distant areas. Many people throughout the ancient world found out how metal tools were made. People also learned to use the wind to push sailboats upstream against the river current. They then built larger boats with huge oars. These oars could speed boats along when there was no wind.

15. The human race had done many things by the time it invented writing and began to record history. People had learned to use fire and animals and the soil in order to survive. They had learned new methods of transportation. They had begun to exchange ideas with people who lived a distance away. Soon they would communicate through a written language.

Testing Your Vocabulary _____

Choose the correct answer.

1. *Glaciers* may be best described as
   a. small pieces of ice floating in water.
   b. huge masses of ice.
   c. soil that has been washed away by moving water.
2. A *domesticated* animal is best described as one that
   a. has been tamed.
   b. is useful in the forest.
   c. has hide that can be made into leather.
3. A person who studies the age of ancient rocks is known as
   a. a geologist.
   b. an anthropologist.
   c. an archaeologist.

Understanding What You Have Read _____

1. The main idea of paragraphs 4 and 5 is
   a. the making of tools in the Stone Age.
   b. life at the time of the glaciers.
   c. how valleys, rivers, and lakes were formed.
   d. everyday life in a cave.
2. In which paragraph do you find facts about
   a. the meaning of *geologist?*
   b. early people's use of fire?
   c. the meaning of *bronze?*
   d. people's ability to sail upstream by boat?
3. The taming of animals was important in the early days of civilization because
   a. animals came close to the villages.
   b. people could keep useful animals for a long time.
   c. food had to be grown to feed the animals.
4. The wheel was one of the greatest inventions because
   a. it has not changed since its invention.
   b. it led to the discovery of fire.
   c. it enabled goods to be carried to distant places more easily.

5. During the early Stone Age, people lived in caves because they
   a. needed shelter for their animals.
   b. found minerals to make tools.
   c. wanted protection from the cold.
6. Fire was important to ancient people because
   a. it gave them protection against wild animals and the cold.
   b. it was used for sending signals from one tribe to another.
   c. it burned away forests and gave them a place to farm.
7. There was little village life in the Stone Age because
   a. people had not yet learned to raise their own crops and they had to keep moving to find food.
   b. groups of people were always at war with each other.
   c. people were busy painting pictures on their cave walls.

Tell whether these statements are true or false. If a statement is false, change the words in italics to make it true.

1. An *anthropologist* studies the bones of ancient people.
2. We know something about people of the Stone Age because we have discovered *traces* of their way of life.
3. In North America, glaciers once reached as far south as *Texas*.
4. A *geologist* is a scientist who studies rocks in which traces of early civiliza-tions have been found.
5. *Horses* were probably the first animals to be tamed.
6. Stone Age people painted pictures of *animals* on the walls of caves.
7. Bronze is a metal made by mixing tin and *lead*.
8. The continent of *Asia* had many glaciers.

Arrange these events in the order in which they took place:

1. trade with distant places begins
2. the discovery of bronze
3. the use of fire is discovered
4. written history starts
5. glaciers cover much of the northern part of the earth
6. the taming of animals develops
7. people learn to grow crops

Developing Ideas and Skills

SOURCES OF INFORMATION

You have read on page 2 that historians are like detectives as they look for information about the past. Fossils, paintings, and buried cities are the things they study to learn about prehistoric people, who left no written records. If we want to know about prehistoric people, we might try to see for ourselves some of these *firsthand sources of information,* such as fossils and paintings. Since most of us cannot easily do this, we must use *secondhand information,* such as photographs and books.

Most of us get our information about the past from history books. Historians (people who write history) may depend upon earlier historians for information. Or they may look at other written records from the past. We can see that people's ability to write has helped us learn history. The use of language gives us information that we could not get from human remains, tools, and statues uncovered from long ago.

There are many sources of information. You have already learned about firsthand sources, which we call *original sources.* An excellent original source is a record of events written by a person who actually took part in them. Those who saw something happen and wrote about it are among our best sources of information.

Very often, however, there are two eyewitnesses to the same event. They may give completely different accounts of what they saw happen. Did you ever hear two witnesses to a fight tell who started it? Do you always agree with the umpire in a baseball game? Historians face this kind of problem when they study different accounts of the same event and try to decide which is the correct one. They must know which sources are most reliable.

For example, let us imagine that you wanted to learn about two astronauts in orbit around the moon who are having trouble with the oxygen system in their spacecraft. Some of the sources of information about this event would be these:

1. the report of the astronauts from the spacecraft;
2. the report of the space controllers on the ground in touch with the astronauts;
3. a discussion of the trouble on television;
4. a report by a friend who tells you what he heard about the trouble;
5. a newspaper story of the trouble in the spacecraft.

Which of these is the best source of information? Which is the next best source? Which source is the poorest? Can you give reasons why several people seeing the same event will give different accounts of what happened?

AIM: What geographic features influence the way people live?

INTRODUCTION B:

Geography Influences History

HOW DOES GEOGRAPHY AFFECT HISTORY?

1. News stories remind us of the methods people use to improve their environment—their surroundings. We come upon a newspaper headline like HOUSTON, AN AIR-CONDITIONED CITY, and read a story about how the working climate of a city has been changed by air conditioning. Another headline announces: GIANT DAM CONTROLS FLOODS ON THE NILE RIVER, and the story reports that a regular flow of water for crops is now possible. CANAL GIVES RUSSIA AN INLAND WATERWAY—trade and travel are improved. PIPELINE THROUGH ALASKA IS FINISHED—oil resources are brought to places that lacked them before. All of these developments will help to change people's lives. History is often the story of people changing their lives by changing the geography of their land. Geography and history are closely linked.

2. How does geography affect the way people live? We can begin to answer this question by a study of early civilizations. You will learn in Unit 1 that they were most often located in fertile river valleys. Rivers provided water for raising crops and livestock. They made travel and trade easier. People came to live together along the rivers. Larger communi-

ties developed around them. The earliest cities of history were located along the waterways of Africa and Asia. You will also learn about some early civilizations in different parts of the world. The geography of each had a great effect on its history.

3. Nearness to large bodies of water affects the history of people and nations. Seas and oceans often keep people apart. But sometimes they have brought them together. The soil was poor for the ancient Phoenicians, who lived along the eastern coast of the Mediterranean (med-i-ter-RAIN-ee-an) Sea. So they made the

An early city in Africa. Why were cities often located on rivers?

sea the center of their lives. They became great sailors and traders. The Greeks, too, used the same sea to trade with the people of Asia and Africa. Two oceans border the United States. At first, the oceans kept this nation isolated; that is, apart from other countries. Later, the oceans became busy paths of trade with other people. For hundreds of years, the sea tended to isolate Japan also. But those same waters helped to make it a world power, because Japan developed a powerful navy.

Ancient ships were propelled by wind and rows of oars pulled by hand. What were the advantages of sea travel?

HOW DOES THE SURFACE OF LAND AFFECT HISTORY?

4. The *topography* (tah-POG-ra-fee) of a region often helps to decide its history. The word *topography* means the surface of the land—the rivers, lakes, plains, deserts, and mountains. In Unit I, you will learn that deserts tend to separate people. But deserts can also protect them. Deserts east and west of the Nile River in Africa protected the ancient civilization of Egypt. The great Sahara Desert, which covers much of North Africa, kept the people of Central Africa isolated for centuries. The Gobi Desert, in Asia, protected China from invaders from the north for hundreds of years.

5. Mountains often have the same effect as

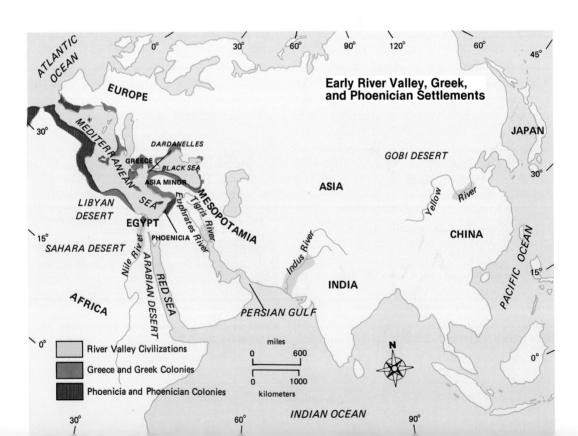

Early River Valley, Greek, and Phoenician Settlements

River Valley Civilizations

Greece and Greek Colonies

Phoenicia and Phoenician Colonies

miles
0   600

0   1000
kilometers

deserts. They separate people. Ancient Greece had many cities. They were called city-states because they were like separate countries. Kept apart by mountains, they could not unite under one government. For the same reason, it took China a long time to become a united country. In the Middle East, mountains helped the people of Afghanistan to hold off invaders for centuries. Many wars have been fought in the lands around Switzerland, in Europe. But Switzerland has usually been able to remain neutral, or to avoid taking sides. The reason? The highest mountains in Europe are in Switzerland.

A desert village in Africa. Give at least two reasons to support the statement that "deserts can be protective."

Mt. Sinai is located in the Sinai Peninsula. It was the site of many important religious events in ancient Jewish history.

HOW DOES GEOGRAPHIC LOCATION AFFECT HISTORY?

6. Where a country or region is located on the earth has an important effect on its history. For example, ancient people who lived around the Mediterranean Sea or the Indian Ocean were near other settlements. Their location allowed them to exchange goods and ideas with other peoples. Some regions have *strategic* (stra-TEE-jic) importance. That means they are important places in time of peace or war. For example, Turkey lies on both sides of the Dardanelles, which is a narrow body of water that separates Asia from Europe. This region has been called "the crossroads of the world." At one time, a large amount of trade between Europe and Asia passed through the Dardanelles. This narrow body of water is important to many nations.

7. In past centuries, the most powerful nations of the world have been located north of the equator. Nations south of the equator have been far removed from busy trade routes. Some have become important in world affairs only in this century. Some lands south of the equator were settled by Europeans only within the last

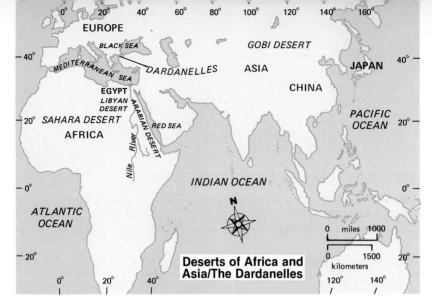

Map labels:
0° 20° 40° 60° 80° 100° 120° 140° 160°

EUROPE

BLACK SEA

GOBI DESERT

MEDITERRANEAN SEA — DARDANELLES   ASIA   JAPAN

40°   40°

EGYPT   CHINA

LIBYAN DESERT

SAHARA DESERT   RED SEA   PACIFIC OCEAN

20°   ARABIAN DESERT   20°

AFRICA

Nile River

INDIAN OCEAN

N

0°   0°

ATLANTIC OCEAN

0   miles   1000

Deserts of Africa and Asia/The Dardanelles

20°   0   1500   20°

kilometers

0°   20°   40°   120°   140°

200 years. The first European colony in Australia was begun in 1788. Narrow pieces of land often become important because they connect trade routes. World history has been changed by the building of the Panama and Suez canals. They were built across narrow strips of land. These canals make it no longer necessary for ships to travel thousands of miles around continents.

WHAT OTHER GEOGRAPHIC FACTORS AFFECT HISTORY?

8. Climate, too, will affect a people's history. The earliest civilizations developed in mild climates. Extremes of heat and cold may delay the growth of a nation. For example, much of the Soviet Union lies within the coldest parts of the north. Many of its rivers flow into the frozen Arctic Ocean. It has few ports on important trade routes. Part of the Soviet Union's history is a story of its attempts to get ports on warm water. Another example of the effect of climate is Brazil. It is almost as large as the United States. It has thousands of miles of navigable rivers (ships can travel on them). But almost half the country is a tropical rain forest. The heat and wetness of such a land make progress and development difficult. Would Brazil be one of the leading powers of the world if it had a different location or climate?

9. Natural resources—soils, minerals, gas, oil, forests, water—also affect the growth of civilizations. Fertile soil along rivers made farming possible in early civilizations. The silks and spices of Asia attracted traders and brought Europe and Asia into contact with each other. Coal, iron, and oil helped to speed the growth of the United States. Some nations of the Middle East have political power today because of their vast oil resources. Of course, a natural resource of any kind has no value until people put it to use. People, too, are resources. With their ideas, skills, and talents, people decide how resources shall be used. People plan the paths that nations follow. People also change those paths according to their needs. History, then, is the story of people and their environment.

10. In paragraph 1, you read headlines that showed how people of today have changed their surroundings. They tackled problems created by geography. People try to improve their surroundings and to make better use of natural resources. They have been successful in these tasks many times, and in many places. They have learned to live and work under conditions of extreme heat and cold. They have found ways to create substitutes for goods they need but do not have. They have even begun to learn how to live in a new environment that is beyond the earth.

12

Testing Your Vocabulary _____

Instructions under "Developing Ideas and Skills" will help you to understand how to recognize the meanings of words and terms from *clues.*

Understanding What You Have Read _____

1. The main idea of paragraphs 6 and 7 is that
   a. some nations have become powerful only in the last few years.
   b. canals are important waterways.
   c. the Mediterranean Sea was the center of early trade routes.
   d. the location of a country has an effect upon its history.

2. In which paragraph do you find facts about
   a. people as resources?
   b. the importance of the location of Turkey?
   c. the location of earliest civilizations?
   d. the effect of deserts on the history of a people?

3. One reason why the earliest civilizations were located along river valleys is that
   a. the valleys could not be invaded by an enemy.
   b. tame animals were found along the rivers.
   c. the rivers provided water for growing crops.

4. Which of these groups has most often served to separate people?
   a. rain forests and rivers
   b. mountains and deserts
   c. canals and mountains

5. The Dardanelles, which separate Europe from Asia, have been important in world history mainly because they
   a. have served as a trade route for many nations.
   b. are located among the world's richest oil fields.
   c. have been the center of the earliest civilizations.

6. One reason why ancient Greek cities did not unite under one government was that
   a. rivers in Greece were not used for trade.
   b. a large part of Greece was desert.
   c. mountains tended to separate Greek cities from one another.

7. The history of the Soviet Union has been affected by geographic factors mainly because
   a. it has few warm-water ports.
   b. it has many deserts and mountains.
   c. most of it lies within a region of heavy rainfall.

Tell whether you agree or disagree with the following statements. Which paragraphs in the chapter helped you to decide?

1. Oceans can isolate people or bring them together.
2. The Mediterranean Sea was used by ancient people to trade and exchange ideas.
3. People have not yet learned how to live in extreme heat and cold.

4. Most early civilizations were located along river valleys.
5. The use of natural resources is of little importance to a nation's growth.
6. Mountains have often been a factor in protecting people from invasion by unfriendly people.

Developing Ideas and Skills

FINDING MEANINGS THROUGH CLUES

As you read *Exploring World History,* you will find some words, terms, or expressions that you may not recognize. Sometimes it is easy to tell the meaning of a word from the way it is used in a sentence. Often there will be clues to the meaning of words. It is important that you recognize some of these common clues.

Let us look at some of the difficult or unfamiliar words in "Geography Influences History" and find the clues that tell us what they mean.

In the first sentence of paragraph 1, the dash is used to bring in a phrase that suggests the meaning of *environment.* The sentence tells us that people have found ways "to improve their environment—their surroundings."

The phrase *that is* is another important word clue. In the ninth sentence of paragraph 3, the meaning of the word *isolated* is explained by the words that follow *that is.* These words are "apart from other countries."

Near the end of paragraph 5, we come upon the word *neutral.* The clue to the meaning of *neutral* is *or.* This little word is used here to say that *to avoid taking sides* is another way of saying *to remain neutral.*

A parenthesis may also be used to show word meanings. Paragraph 8 contains a parenthesis after *navigable rivers.* The words in parenthesis explain that *navigable rivers* means "rivers that ships can travel on."

Often the meaning of a word is explained in a nearby sentence. The word *topography* appears at the start of paragraph 4. The second sentence of the paragraph tells us "The word *topography* means the surface of the land . . ." The word *strategic,* in paragraph 6, is also defined in the sentence that follows it. This sentence tells us that strategic places are "important places in time of peace or war."

There are other clues, too. A comma often helps us to figure out word meanings. We could say that "A person is isolated, kept apart from others." The meaning of the word may be given in the sentence in which it is used. The sense of the paragraph may be a clue. The word *called* sometimes hints at a word's meaning. For example, "Priests *called* Brahmans were the highest caste." The word *called* tells us that Brahmans were a caste, or social class, of priests.

In your study you will often be asked to give the meanings of words or terms. Also, you must often know the meanings of special words if you are to understand important facts of history. Remember the clues that may help you.

1. a dash   —
2. the words *that is*
3. the word *or*
4. a parenthesis   ( )
5. a comma   ,
6. the sentence before the word in question
7. the sentence after the word in question
8. the definition in a sentence
9. the word *called*
10. the sense of the whole paragraph

AIM: How did a great civilization develop in Egypt?

CHAPTER 1

Egypt: Gift of the Nile

HOW DID A RIVER AID EGYPT'S GROWTH?

1. When ancient people learned to farm, they looked for fertile land to live on. The valleys close to rivers had fertile farm land and a good supply of water. Travel on rivers was easy and cheap. So the first great civilizations in the world grew up by river valleys. In this unit, you will learn about these great river-valley civilizations of the ancient world. You will find that a large number of people live in these river valleys now.

2. An ancient writer said, "Egypt is the gift of the Nile." The mighty Nile River meant life to the Egyptians 6,000 years ago and it still does today. The Nile rises in the mountains of Central Africa and Ethiopia. Its waters pass through 3,000 miles of mountains and swampland in Africa before they enter Egypt. The great civilization of Egypt was built along the last 600 miles of the river's course to the Mediterranean Sea.

3. Each summer the Nile flooded. The precious water covered land for 8 to 10 miles on each side of the river, making it fertile. Egyptian farmers could grow wheat, barley, and cotton near the river. Fields farther from the river were made fertile by means of irrigation (a man-made water system). During the dry seasons, the Egyptians built mud holes

along the banks of the river, each one higher than the other. A bucket attached to a turning pole brought water from one level to the next. After it reached the highest level, the water ran off into irrigation ditches. This system of buckets and poles was called a *shadoof* and is still used for irrigation in Egypt today.

4. The geography of their land helped the Egyptian people develop their great civilization. The deserts, mountains, and waters kept enemies out. The land both east and west of the Nile River is desert. The great Sahara Desert to the west covers an area about the same size as the United States. Beyond the eastern desert are mountains that border the Red Sea. In the south, where the Nile begins, are the mountains of Central Africa. To the north is the Mediterranean Sea. Since ships could not travel far in ancient times, only the bravest of adventurers would dare to sail far out on the Mediterranean to invade Egypt. Not having to worry about frequent foreign invasions, the Egyptians could use all their energy to build their great culture.

HOW WERE THE EGYPTIANS GOVERNED?

5. By bringing the people together, the Nile River helped to bring them under one government. At first, each village along the river had its own government. Since river travel was easy, people of different villages were able to meet and trade with one another. Sometimes they fought. Because they were not cut off from one another, groups of villages could unite to form large governments. These governments, in turn, joined others, until there were just two very large governments—that of Upper Egypt and that of Lower Egypt. Finally, about 3200 B.C., a ruler named Menes united Upper and Lower Egypt into one kingdom. As head of the kingdom he was named the *pharaoh* (FAIR-oh). He was called pharaoh, for he and his people believed that he was a god and it was not right to call him by his own name. Menes, and each pharaoh after him, had complete power over the people. The pharaohs claimed they owned the land. There were times when they did, indeed, control all of Egypt's land. Farmers rented their land from the pharaoh, paying for it with the crops they raised.

Tanti and his wife, a pharaoh of the 5th dynasty. This dynasty was part of the Old Kingdom, which lasted from 2664–2155 B.C.

6. Several classes of people lived in Egypt. The upper class was made up of landlords. They had great power at those times when the pharaohs could not control the land themselves. Another class was made up of priests, who were in charge of the temples. Since religion was so important in Egyptian life, the priests had great power, also. A third class was made up of government officials. They collected taxes, kept records, and checked on building and irrigation projects. Of special importance were scribes. These were the record keepers. They helped the government operate in an orderly way. Many worked for wealthy landlords, who valued their services greatly. Skilled artisans (AR-tis-zuns) were yet another class. They made copper and bronze ornaments, wooden objects, and pottery. They even invented a type of paper, called papyrus (pah-PY-rus). Stonecutters and masons decorated the pyramids.

7. Most Egyptians were peasants. Men and women farmed the land. It was the peasant families that produced the grains which filled the pharaohs' storehouses. They dug the ditches and worked on the great temples. They also paid the heaviest taxes. The building of the pyramids and other kinds of hard work were done by slaves. They were usually people who had been captured in war. Some slaves became house servants of nobles. They could gain their freedom and work toward a position in government. But for most slaves, life was short and unhappy. They were often whipped, allowed to go hungry, and made to work until they were exhausted.

8. Women were greatly respected in ancient Egypt, but they were expected to obey their husbands. They were allowed to own property and run their own businesses. Many were advisors to their husbands. One woman, named Hatshepsut, became queen, taking power after the death of her husband. She is best known for her interest in mining, trade, and the building of temples. She was the first great woman ruler that we know about.

9. Many of the great works of the Egyptians were the result of their religious beliefs. The Egyptians believed in many gods. They were among the first people to believe in a life after death. They thought that a person's spirit lived on in the dead body. Therefore, they tried to preserve the dead body. They treated it with spices and wrapped it in linen cloth. A body preserved this way is called a *mummy*. The Egyptians believed that people who lived good lives would be rewarded after death. People who lived bad lives would be punished.

10. Pharaohs were rich enough to make great preparations for their lives after death. They had great tombs, called pyramids, built for themselves. The pyramid was a symbol of the power of the pharaoh. Food and drink were put in the pyramid because it was believed that the dead person's spirit ate and drank. The walls were painted with pictures of the great deeds of the pharaoh. Some personal belongings were placed in the tomb, so pharaohs could be prepared for life in the next world. The great pyramids were made of solid blocks of stone. The greatest pyramid is that of Khufu, sometimes called Cheops (KEE-ops). Each side of this pyramid is longer than two football fields! It is believed that 5 million men worked for 20 years on this pyramid alone. We have learned a great deal about pyramids with the discovery of the tomb of Tutankhamen (too-tangk-Ah-men), or King "Tut," in 1922. King Tut's mummy was found in a coffin of solid gold.

11. The Egyptians also built temples. The most famous is the one to the god Amon (AH-mom), at Karnak. The entrances to many temples were lined with statues of gods. Each has the head of a man and the body of a lion. Such a statue is called a *sphinx* (ss-finks). The Egyptians also built obelisks (AH-bel-lisks). These

Back of the throne of King Tutankhamen (1361–1352 B.C.). What does this scene tell you about Egyptian life?

were tall columns, each made of one piece of stone, weighing as much as 1,000 tons.

12. Of all the ancient river-valley peoples, the Egyptians left one of the best records of their history. They painted pictures on the walls of tombs and temples. They also developed a system of writing, called hieroglyphics (hi-roh-GLIF-iks). This is a kind of writing in which pictures or symbols are used instead of words. Writing was done with a pen made from bushes growing along the Nile River. The Egyptians wrote on papyrus. From this we get the word paper. One of the most famous works of the Egyptians is the *Book of the Dead*. This is a collection of wise sayings and advice on what to do in life and after death in order to please the gods.

13. The floods of the Nile meant life to the

The sphinx guards two pyramids. Why do you think the Egyptians made the sphinx with the body of a lion and the head of a man?

Egyptians. The floods covered the land with fertile soil each year. The Egyptians, therefore, kept records of the times that the river flooded. As a result, they were able to develop the first calendar. This calendar had 12 months of 30 days each. Five days were added at the end of the 12th month, making 365 days in the year. This calendar is a remarkable feat for so early in history.

14. Like other ancient peoples, Egyptians thought that magic cured some diseases. They believed that sickness was the work of evil spirits. Yet their work with mummies shows that they knew a great deal about the human body. They developed cures for some diseases that show a surprising knowledge of medicine. They even set up medical centers in some temples.

15. A study of all the achievements of the Egyptians would take much time. They used their time and skills to make great advances in government, religion, education, mathematics, and science. Their ideas spread to those whom they conquered or with whom they traded.

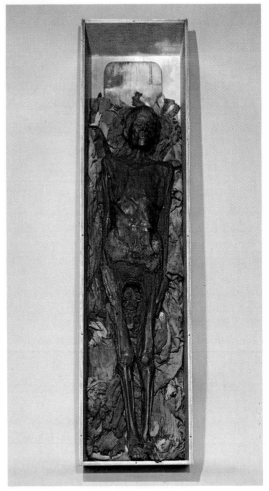

The Egyptian mummies have lasted to the present time. This mummy is of Ameniriirt. He ruled during the 25th Dynasty, 750–656 B.C.

18

HOW YEARS ARE NUMBERED

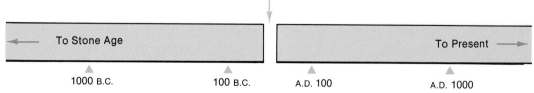

BIRTH OF CHRIST

| ← To Stone Age | To Present → |

▲ 1000 B.C.   ▲ 100 B.C.   ▲ A.D. 100   ▲ A.D. 1000

Testing Your Vocabulary

Choose the correct answer.

1. An *artisan* would most likely
   a. dig irrigation ditches.
   b. make bronze vases.
   c. collect taxes.
2. If Egyptians worked on a *shadoof*, they might have
   a. made paper-like material for writing.
   b. cut stones for pyramids.
   c. helped get water from the Nile.
3. In *hieroglyphics*, each word is shown by a
   a. picture or symbol.
   b. series of straight lines.
   c. group of dots in different shapes.

Understanding What You Have Read

1. The main idea of paragraph 4 is that
   a. the Nile was important to the Egyptians.
   b. few people dared to sail the Mediterranean Sea.
   c. the Sahara Desert covers most of North Africa.
   d. the geography of Egypt contributed to Egyptian civilization.
2. In which paragraphs do you find facts about
   a. the best-known Egyptian system of writing?
   b. the irrigation system of ancient Egypt?
   c. the work of peasants?
   d. the reason why the dead were preserved as mummies?
3. During dry seasons, Egyptian farmers were able to grow wheat and cotton because of
   a. heavy rains in Central Africa.
   b. the knowledge of how to rotate crops.
   c. water for irrigation from the Nile.
4. The Egyptians took great care in burying their pharaohs because they believed that
   a. a person's spirit lived after death.
   b. the body never died.
   c. their rulers deserved this care.
5. The pyramids and temples that the Egyptians built show
   a. that the Egyptians depended a great deal on the Nile River.
   b. the great power of the farmers.

c. the importance of religion to the Egyptians.
6. Many achievements of the Egyptians are important because
   a. they let peasants live more comfortable lives.
   b. we have come to use the Egyptian system of writing.

c. their ideas influenced other people in the ancient world.
7. We know that the Egyptians must have had a good knowledge of mathematics because they
   a. buried their dead.
   b. were able to build the pyramids.
   c. knew the causes of many diseases.

Tell whether these statements are true or false. If a statement is false, change the words in italics to make it true.

1. The *Sahara* is the great desert of North Africa.
2. The Nile River flows in a *southerly* direction.
3. *Hatshepsut* was a great woman ruler in Egypt.
4. Record-keeping in ancient Egypt was a job for *scribes*.
5. Pharaoh was a name given to Egyptian *landlords*.
6. *Slaves* were considered to be the lowest class of people in ancient Egypt.
7. The Egyptians worshipped *many gods*.
8. Many ornaments of ancient Egypt were made of *bronze and copper*.
9. Most of the great civilizations of the ancient world grew up along *the shores of rivers*.
10. The Egyptians learned to make use of the dry land near the Nile by means of *irrigation*.

Match the explanations in the second column with the terms in the first column.

1. sphinx
2. *Book of the Dead*
3. mummy
4. obelisk
5. Karnak
6. papyrus

a. location of temple to the God Amon
b. paintings on the walls of pyramids
c. statue with the head of a man and the body of a lion
d. material used to write upon
e. tall, heavy column of stone
f. collection of wise sayings
g. dead body wrapped in linen

Developing Ideas and Skills

USING A MAP

Study the map on page 21 carefully. Then decide whether the following statements are true or false.

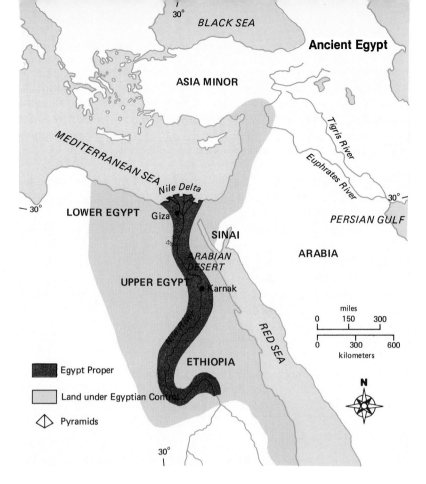

Ancient Egypt

1. The Nile River flows into the Red Sea in the north.
2. The Arabian desert lies between the Red Sea and the Persian Gulf.
3. The distance from the Nile Delta to the Egyptian city of Karnak is about 500 miles.
4. There is only a land passage from the Mediterranean Sea to the Red Sea.
5. The pyramids were built in the southern part of Egypt.
6. There is no outlet from the Black Sea to the Mediterranean Sea.

FINDING THE MAIN IDEA

You have probably noted that one of the first questions you are asked after you have read each chapter is to find a *main idea*. One paragraph, a group of paragraphs, or the entire chapter will each have a main idea. Sometimes you will be asked to choose a good title for part of a chapter, or for the whole chapter. If you are able to give such a title for the selection you have read, you will show that you understand the main idea of the selection. To be able to find the main idea or most important thought of what has been written is a necessary skill. It is a skill that you should develop in all your reading as well as in your work in social studies.

Some main ideas are easy to find. The idea is clearly given in the paragraph. Often, it is in the first sentence. But it can be in the last sentence, too, as a summary of the paragraph. In fact, it can be in any sentence or it may not be stated directly at all. However, since all the sentences of the paragraph are about one main thought, you should be able to get the main idea from reading the paragraph.

In paragraph 4, we discover why the deserts, mountains, and water of Egypt tended to keep the people free from fear of invasion. You will find the main idea stated in the first sentence, "The geography of their land helped the Egyptian people develop their great civilization."

In paragraph 5, the main idea is also stated in the first sentence, "By bringing the people together, the Nile River helped to bring them under one government." All the sentences tell how the first governments developed and how all parts of Egypt were united under the Pharaoh.

After reading paragraph 14, you will see that most of the sentences describe ancient Egyptian knowledge of the human body. The idea may not be found in a single sentence, yet it is clear that the main idea is that the Egyptians knew something about, and were interested in, the human body. The main idea might be, "The Egyptians knew a great deal about the human body."

Throughout your reading, keep in mind the goal of finding the main idea or ideas. This skill is the basis of many other social-studies skills: taking notes, making a summary of your notes, making an outline, and finding evidence to support your judgments.

FINDING MEANINGS THROUGH CLUES

See if you can use your knowledge of word clues to figure out the meanings of these words and terms in "Introduction A: Before Written History":

Paragraph 3 *archaeologist*—what clue helped you?
Paragraph 1 *traces*—what clue helped you?
Paragraph 4 *glaciers*—what clue helped you?
Paragraph 13 *chariots*—what clue helped you?

AIM: How did a great civilization grow in the valley of the Tigris and Euphrates Rivers?

CHAPTER 2

Mesopotamia: Land of the Two Rivers

WHY DID PEOPLE SETTLE NEAR WATER?

1. If you live in a large city, you are probably near a body of water. People very often try to live near water. To ancient people, water meant food. Farming was good on the moist, fertile soil along river banks. Water meant trade, because the goods people needed could be shipped by river. At about the same time that Egyptian civilization developed along the Nile, another civilization was growing on the land between the Tigris and Euphrates Rivers. This land was called Mesopotamia which means "Land Between the Rivers." Today, it is called Iraq. The Tigris and Euphrates Rivers flow south through desert land toward the Persian Gulf. Near the gulf, the plain is very fertile. Irrigation is necessary, however, because there is little rainfall.

2. The history of Mesopotamia is the story of different peoples who lived in the valley because it had fertile land. The most important were the Sumerians, the Assyrians, and the Chaldeans (KAL-DEE-ans). To the west of Mesopotamia is desert. Whenever the wanderers of the desert felt the need for water and fertile

soil, they moved toward the Tigris and Euphrates valley. Unlike the mountains of Egypt, those of Mesopotamia could not keep out invaders. One after another, tribes entered the valley and conquered other tribes. Some of the tribes remained and became part of the civilization around the rivers.

This is a painting by Peter Brueghel of the Tower of Babel. The tower was a ziggurat built near Babylon, in Mesopotamia. Babel is the Hebrew name for the city.

WHAT WAS MESOPOTAMIAN CIVILIZATION LIKE?

3. Unlike Egypt, Mesopotamia did not have stone. Buildings were made of bricks formed of dried clay. These brick buildings have not lasted through the centuries, as the stone buildings of Egypt have. However, ruins of walled cities and of temples called *ziggurats* (ZIG-oo-rats) have been found many feet below earth. Ziggurats were built with steps on the outside that could be used to climb to the top. The Sumerians had worshipped their gods from mountain tops before they came to Mesopotamia. Since there were no mountains in the valley, they built high temples to look like mountains. They climbed the steps to the top and worshipped there.

4. The people of Mesopotamia were great builders. They built the "Hanging Gardens of Babylon" on the roofs of the ruler's palace. The Hanging Gardens were one of the wonders of the ancient world. The Assyrians built a great viaduct. A viaduct is a long bridge made up of many short bridges held up by towers. It can carry water, or it can carry a road over rivers and valleys. The Assyrians' viaduct carried water to their city from mountains 50 miles away. Their bridge was made of millions of blocks of stone brought from Egypt or the valley of the Indus River in India.

5. The early Sumerians of Mesopotamia developed a system of writing. It was called *cuneiform* (kew-NEE-a-form), or wedgeshaped writing. Marks were made in soft clay with a pointed stick called a stylus. When the clay dried and hardened, the marks made by the stylus remained. Since the end of the stylus formed a triangle, it left marks in the shape of a wedge. Cuneiform was different from Egyptian hieroglyphics. In cuneiform, each symbol was a different wedge shape which stood for a sound. In hieroglyphics, each symbol was a picture which stood for a word. We have found clay tablets from ancient Mesopotamia recording laws and

The hanging Gardens of Babylon. Why do you think they were called one of the wonders of the ancient world?

information about medicine.

6. The different peoples of Mesopotamia did not believe in a life after death. Only the gods, they thought, lived forever. The people of each city worshipped their own gods, who they believed protected them. New tribes entering the valley brought beliefs in new gods. Religion was important in Mesopotamia. By using magic, rulers would try to find out what the gods wished or planned to do. No important change was made within the land nor any battle begun before the ruler communicated with the gods. Like the Egyptians, the Mesopotamians built great temples to their gods.

WHAT KINGDOMS RULED IN MESOPOTAMIA?

7. The first important people in Mesopotamia were the Sumerians, who began to rule about 3500 B.C. The Sumerians developed cuneiform writing, used carts with wheels, and developed the first known code of laws. They were the first people to divide the day into 24 hours, the hour into 60 minutes, and the minute into 60 seconds.

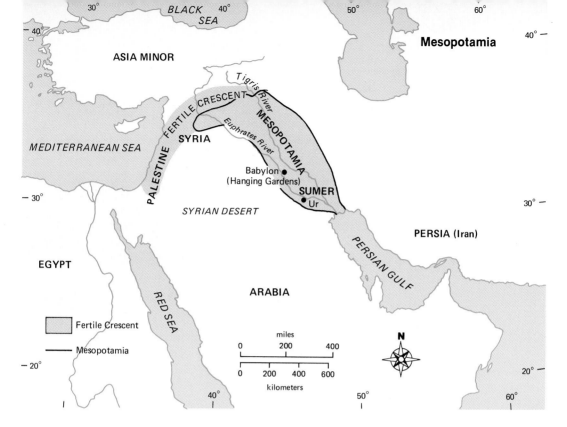

Mesopotamia

ASIA MINOR

BLACK SEA

MEDITERRANEAN SEA

FERTILE CRESCENT

Tigris River

Euphrates River

MESOPOTAMIA

SYRIA

PALESTINE

Babylon
(Hanging Gardens)

SUMER
Ur

SYRIAN DESERT

PERSIA (Iran)

PERSIAN GULF

EGYPT

ARABIA

RED SEA

Fertile Crescent

Mesopotamia

miles
0   200   400

0   200   400   600
kilometers

N

8. The Sumerians were conquered about 2100 B.C. by people from Syria. These people established their kingdom at Babylon, a city on the Euphrates River. The most famous of the kings of Babylon was King Hammurabi (Ha-moo-RA-be). He formed a code of laws that was written on clay tablets. Hammurabi's Code was one of the first written sets of laws. Writing the laws was most important, for then people who read the laws could not mistake what they were. But Hammurabi's Code was a harsh set of laws (page 28). Tablets on which the code was written were found about 60 years ago. They have helped us to know a great deal about the life of the people of Mesopotamia.

9. The fierce Assyrians conquered Mesopotamia about 900 B.C. The Assyrians were a feared people, for they burned and robbed wherever they went. They destroyed armies. They used weapons made of iron and wore copper and iron helmets. The people they captured were often tortured and made slaves. But the Assyrians were also great builders. They built

roads to connect the lands they conquered. They also made carvings of figures on flat rocks. One of the Assyrian rulers gathered a library of more than 20,000 clay tablets containing stories about the people of Mesopotamia.

10. In spite of their fighting ability, the Assyrians were also conquered. About 530 B.C., the Persians, under their ruler Cyrus, invaded Mesopotamia. It was then Persia's turn to build an empire in the valley. The Persians conquered Asia Minor, Syria, Palestine, and Egypt. Their empire made up an area about half the size of the United States today. The roads the Persians built linked all parts of the empire.

11. The Persian rulers knew how to run their government. They divided the empire into parts called provinces. A governor was placed in charge of each province. In this way the Persians could control far points of the empire better than if one ruler tried to govern all of it. The Persians set up a money system. Coins of gold and silver were used by all people throughout the Persian lands. There was an-

25

Persepolis was the greatest city of ancient Persia. It was built in 528 B.C. and destroyed by Alexander the Great in 330 B.C.

other reason for the success of the Persians. Their kings allowed the different conquered people to keep their own religions and speak their own languages. But even this vast empire came to an end. Alexander the Great of Greece conquered the Persians and ended their empire after they had ruled Mesopotamia for 200 years.

Testing Your Vocabulary

Choose the best answer.

1. A *viaduct* may be used to
   a. carry a road over a valley.
   b. find the length of a day or a year.
   c. raise heavy stone into place in a building.

2. *Cuneiform* writing is
   a. written on paper.
   b. a series of pictures.
   c. shaped like wedges.

3. The *ziggurats* of the ancient Mesopotamians were
   a. pointed sticks.
   b. temples with steps on the outside.
   c. brick buildings that could last for many centuries.

4. Persian governors were put in charge of *provinces*. A province is
   a. a government building.
   b. an area in which all people practice the same religion.
   c. a part of a larger area.

Understanding What You Have Read _____

1. The purpose of paragraphs 1 and 2 is to describe
   a. how invaders caused trouble.
   b. transportation along the Euphrates River.
   c. why tribes settled in the Tigris-Euphrates valley.
   d. differences between Mesopotamia and Egypt.

2. In which paragraphs do you find facts about
   a. the buildings in Mesopotamia?
   b. cuneiform writing?
   c. the meaning of the word *Mesopotamia*?
   d. the Code of Hammurabi?

3. We know what kind of buildings the early people in the Tigris-Euphrates valley built because
   a. paintings of buildings have been found on walls of caves.
   b. some temples are still standing.
   c. we have found ruins of buildings below the ground.

4. Hammurabi's Code was important because it
   a. was one of the first sets of written laws.
   b. established the kingdom of Sumer in Mesopotamia.
   c. ended fighting in the Tigris-Euphrates valley.

5. The chief reason for settlements along the Tigris and Euphrates Rivers was that
   a. the soil there was fertile.
   b. this valley was in the middle of the east-west trade routes.
   c. many minerals could be found nearby.

6. We know that the people of Mesopotamia were religious because
   a. their beliefs were the same as those of the people of Egypt.
   b. their great buildings were temples to their gods.
   c. they treated prisoners with mercy.

7. A reason for the success of the Persian empire was that the Persians
   a. gained great wealth from ancient Egypt.
   b. allowed conquered people to keep their own religion and language.
   c. conquered Greece.

Agree or disagree. From your reading of Chapter 2, tell whether you agree or disagree with these statements. Give reasons for your answers.

1. A visitor to ancient Egypt and Mesopotamia would have found that life was much the same in both places.
2. Egyptian buildings lasted longer than those of the Tigris and Euphrates valley.
3. The use of clay was important to the people of Mesopotamia.
4. The desert had little effect on the life of the people in Mesopotamia.

5. The Egyptians and the Sumerians had the same system of writing.
6. The religious beliefs of Egypt and those of Mesopotamia were the same.
7. The people of Mesopotamia believed that the wishes of their gods were important.
8. The Assyrians gave little to the culture of Mesopotamia.

Using Original Sources

The following is adapted from Hammurabi's Code of Laws, written on clay tablets about 1700 B.C. Read the Code carefully. Then see if you can answer the questions that follow.

Hammurabi's Code of Laws

If a man offers as a bribe grain or money to the witnesses, he shall himself bear the punishment passed in that case. . . .

If a man rents a field for cultivation and does not perform the work required in the field, he shall give the owner of the field grain on the basis of the next field . . .

If a builder builds a house for a man and does not make the construction firm, and the house which he has built collapses and causes death, that builder shall be put to death . . .

If a man, in a case, utters threats against the witnesses or does not prove the testimony he has given, if that be a case involving life, that man shall be put to death . . .

If one man strike another man in a quarrel and wound him, he shall swear: "I struck him without intent," and he shall be responsible for the physician . . .

If a man destroys the eye of another man, they shall destroy his eye . . . If a son strike his father, they shall cut off his fingers. . . .

Do you agree or disagree with the following statements about Hammurabi's Code? Give reasons for your answers.

1. The Code said that witnesses who lie in court will receive whatever punishment the accused person would have received if found guilty.
2. The Code recognized that a person may hurt another by accident.
3. The Code was concerned only with court cases.
4. The Code ordered respect for one's parents.
5. The Code said that judges should show mercy in their sentences for crimes.
6. Honesty in business was ordered by the Code.
7. A lazy person would not be punished by the Code.

AIM: How did the early Phoenicians, Hebrews, and Hittites contribute to our way of life?

CHAPTER 3

Other Peoples of the Middle East

WHAT EARLY CIVILIZATIONS BEGAN IN THE AREA OF THE FERTILE CRESCENT?

1. Although the earliest civilizations developed in valleys near rivers, people soon moved to places near other bodies of water. One of these places was the land east of the Mediterranean Sea. This area is generally dry. But there is a narrow strip of land along the shores of the Mediterranean which is good for farming. This strip of fertile soil and the fertile Tigris-Euphrates valley form an area shaped like a quarter moon. The area curves around the northern end of the Arabian desert. Because of its shape and fertility, the area is called the *Fertile Crescent*. (See map, page 25.)

2. Two other peoples who had a great influence on our way of life built civilizations in the Fertile Crescent. These were the Phoenicians (Fin-NISH-ans) and the Hebrews. Because they lived along important trade routes, they were often invaded and conquered. Their lands were not so fertile as the valleys of the Nile or the Tigris-Euphrates. Therefore, many of their people made a living in ways other than farming. Many Phoenicians turned to the sea and became great sailors. The Hebrews raised sheep in the dry valleys and on mountainsides.

HOW DID PHOENICIAN CULTURE SPREAD?

3. Because they were good sailors, the Phoenicians became successful traders. Forests of cedar grew on the mountains of Lebanon behind their lands. The Phoenicians used this wood to build ships. Even the Egyptians knew what great carpenters the Phoenicians were. From their port cities of Sidon (SY-don) and Tyre (TY-er), Phoenician traders sailed their ships throughout the Mediterranean Sea. Some

Phoenicians trading with early Britons. Why were the Phoenicians successful traders?

sailed through the Strait of Gibraltar into the Atlantic Ocean. Phoenician sailors were known even along what are now the coasts of Spain and Great Britain. As they traded their wood products and cloth, they established colonies along the coasts of the Mediterranean. The city of Carthage, in North Africa, was their most famous colony. The Phoenicians traded not only by sea. They led caravans into Mesopotamia and returned with silver and tin. They developed a purple dye, and their robes dyed with it were much in demand.

4. One of the most important contributions of the Phoenicians was their *alphabet*. The Phoenician system of writing contained 22 signs—all consonants, no vowels. Because the Phoenicians traveled so far, their alphabet spread throughout the Mediterranean world. The Greeks, for example, took the alphabet and used it. In fact, the word *alphabet* comes from the first Greek letters, *alpha* and *beta*. Later, the Romans took the alphabet from the Greeks. Still later, the nations of western Europe copied it from the Romans.

Phoenician	Greek	Roman	English
ꓕ	ᐱ	A	A
ꓹ	ß	B	B
Ψ	F	F	F
ꟲ	N	N	N
w	Ƹ	S	S
X	Ꝉ	T	T

WHAT CONTRIBUTIONS OF THE HEBREWS INFLUENCED LATER CULTURE?

5. The ancient Hebrew people lived in the area known as Palestine. The Mediterranean Sea lay to the west. The Hebrews were often under the control of more powerful kingdoms nearby. According to the Bible, about 2000 B.C., Abraham, the founder of the Jewish people, led his people from Mesopotamia into the land of Canaan, or Palestine. Other Hebrews, called Israelites, lived east of Palestine, and some lived in Egypt. The pharaohs of Egypt made slaves of the Israelites, who longed for freedom. About 1300 B.C., the Israelites were led by Moses out of Egypt toward the Promised Land—Palestine. This journey was called the *Exodus,* or going away. They joined with other Hebrews and reached Palestine about 1000 B.C.

6. The Israelites and the Hebrew followers of Abraham joined to form the kingdom of Israel. Saul was its first king. He was followed by David. David had been a hero in the defeat of the Philistines, a neighboring people who had tried to keep the Israelites from reaching Palestine. Solomon, the son of David, ruled Palestine at the height of its glory. He is known for his wisdom. Today, we still use the expression "as

A re-creation of Solomon's temple.

wise as Solomon." Solomon built a magnificent temple in Jerusalem and formed an army that brought safety and glory to Israel.

7. In order to pay for his temples and other luxuries, however, Solomon and his son forced the poor people to pay very heavy taxes. When Solomon died, the people rose up against the government. The kingdom then was split into two parts. Both parts, now weak, were overrun by invaders from Mesopotamia. The Persians and the Romans also entered Palestine. About 100 B.C., the Hebrew people were forced to leave Palestine. In the centuries that followed, they moved to all parts of the world. Not until nearly 2,000 years later did the Jewish people return to their homeland. In 1948, the state of Israel was set up in an area that had been part of Palestine.

8. The great gift of the Hebrews was their religion. The Hebrews were the first people to practice a religion based on belief in one god. Belief in a single god is called *monotheism*

This painting of Moses by Rembrandt shows him breaking the tablets of the law. How does art help you interpret history?

(MON-oh-thee-ism). The Hebrew god was not like the gods of ancient Egypt or Mesopotamia. He was believed to be all-knowing, all-powerful, all-just, and eternal. He made the world and all that is in it. Humans, the Hebrews believed, were created in the image of God. This belief gave people great dignity.

9. The Hebrews believed that God had given them rules to live by. These rules are the Ten Commandments. When the people broke God's law, prophets spoke out against them and reminded them of God's will. The story of the Hebrews is contained in the Old Testament of the Bible. Some of the major figures of the Old Testament are women. However, the Hebrews did not think of women as the equals of men. In this, the Hebrews were like other ancient peoples. Yet the Old Testament of the Bible makes it clear that the Hebrews had respect for good wives. Many of the religious ideas of the Hebrews were carried over into Christianity. As we shall later see, Christianity began in Palestine.

WHAT DISCOVERY OF THE HITTITES STARTED THE IRON AGE?

10. The land of Asia Minor (where modern Turkey now is) was another important land of ancient trade. (See map, page 33.) This land connected Europe and Asia. The Hittites were a powerful people in Asia Minor before 1200 B.C. They were outstanding horsemen. Their use of horses and chariots in battle gave them an advantage over their neighbors. They also learned the secret of heating iron to make it pure. When Hittite power ended, about 1000 B.C., this secret was learned by other people, and the use of iron spread to other lands. Iron was stronger than bronze, and there was more of it than the copper and tin that make up bronze. So iron took the place of bronze as the chief metal for tools and weapons. Thus, the Iron Age began.

Testing Your Vocabulary

Choose the correct answer.

1. If monotheism means the belief in *one* God, which of these words would you think means rule by *one* person?
   a. anarchy
   b. monarchy
   c. aristocracy

2. An example of an *exodus* might be
   a. the departure of many people from Europe to live in the United States.
   b. a Bible reading.
   c. the freeing of slaves.

Understanding What You Have Read

1. The purpose of paragraph 2 is to describe
   a. ports of the Mediterranean.
   b. great sailors of the ancient world.
   c. the Fertile Crescent.
   d. the civilizations of the Phoenicians and the Hebrews.

2. In which paragraph do you find facts about
   a. sheep-raising by the Hebrews?
   b. the Hittite secret of making iron pure?
   c. the Phoenician invention of the alphabet?
   d. the early rulers of Israel?

3. The early Hebrews had a great influence on our civilization because of their
   a. belief in one God.
   b. use of horses and wheeled carts.
   c. use of wood in architecture.

4. The people of Israel found it difficult to keep their freedom probably because they
   a. were usually surrounded by powerful neighbors.
   b. had poor leaders in their early history.
   c. were far from trade routes.

5. Farming was not so important in Phoenicia and Palestine because
   a. forests provided the people with their greatest wealth.
   b. these areas had valuable iron resources.
   c. these areas had little fertile land.

6. Although the alphabet of the Phoenicians had no vowel sounds, it is important to us because
   a. it was the first known system of writing.
   b. it was an idea of the Egyptians, and the Phoenicians spread it throughout the world.
   c. it was passed on to people who later formed our modern alphabet.

7. Iron replaced bronze as the most useful metal because
   a. iron was more valuable.
   b. there was more iron than copper and tin.
   c. iron was useful in pottery.

Developing Ideas and Skills

USING A MAP

Study the map on page 33 carefully. Choose the correct answer.

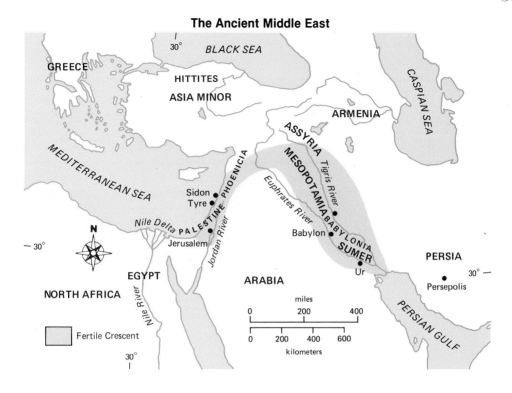

The Ancient Middle East

1. All of the following are parts of the Fertile Crescent EXCEPT
   a. Babylonia
   b. Phoenicia
   c. Egypt

2. The large body of water at the eastern tip of the Fertile Crescent is the
   a. Mediterranean Sea
   b. Persian Gulf
   c. Red Sea

3. All of these people bordered the Mediterranean Sea EXCEPT the
   a. Hebrews
   b. Phoenicians
   c. Hittites

4. All of these rivers are part of the Fertile Crescent EXCEPT the
   a. Tigris River
   b. Nile River
   c. Euphrates River

5. The two most important rivers of the Fertile Crescent flow into the
   a. Persian Gulf
   b. Mediterranean Sea
   c. Black Sea

Using Original Sources

The Armenians (Ar-MEEN-ee-ans) lived north of the Assyrians, between the Black and Caspian seas. In this selection, the Greek historian Herodotus describes how the Armenians traded with the city of Babylon along the Euphrates River. What does it tell you about trade in this region about 400 years B.C.?

Herodotus Describes Trade on the Euphrates

The boats which came down to Babylon are round and made of skins. The frames, which are of willow, are cut in the country of the Armenians, and on these, which serve for hulls, a covering of skins is stretched outside. Thus the boats are made, without either stem or stern, quite round like a shield. They are then entirely filled with straw, and their cargo is put on board. Their chief freight is wine, stored in casks, made of wood of the palm tree. They are managed by the men who stand upright in them, each plying an oar. Each vessel has a live donkey on board; those of a larger size have more than one. When they reach Babylon, the cargo is landed and offered for sale; after which the men break up their boats, sell the straw and the frames, and loading their donkeys with the skins, set off on their way back to Armenia.

1. What is the meaning of the word *casks*?
2. Why does each boat have a donkey on board? How are the donkeys used?
3. Why aren't the boats saved to return to Armenia?
4. Why are the skins returned to Armenia?

TURNING POINTS

Technology

The Middle East: Chariots

A great step in the development of civilization was taken when the chariot was invented. The earliest chariots had four wheels and were pulled by oxen. They first appeared in Mesopotamia in about 3500 B.C. Until that time, freight was loaded onto people and animals. The chariot made it possible to transport goods faster and over greater distances. It also improved communication between towns.

The first war chariot was probably used by the Hittites in about 1800 B.C. Ancient wall drawings show the Hittites in battle against the Egyptians. The war chariot was a two-wheeled vehicle pulled by one or two horses. A small platform held two or three people. One person directed the horses. Arrows and spears flew from the hands of the other warriors. The chariots raised clouds of dust as they rolled across battlefields at great speed.

In time, chariot racing became a popular sport. It was enjoyed at special events held by the ancient Greeks and Romans. Crowds of people came to these events to root for their favorites. Great cheers rose from the stadium in much the same way as they do at car races today.

Critical Thinking

1. How would warriors with chariots have an advantage over rivals who had none?
2. In what ways could the chariot have helped ancient towns to develop?

AIMS: What were early civilizations in India and Southeast Asia like? What religions developed in India and Southeast Asia?

CHAPTER 4

India and Southeast Asia: Home of Ancient Cultures

WHERE DID THE CULTURE OF INDIA BEGIN?

1. We know Asia today as a region where hundreds of millions of people live. China now has almost a billion people. India has almost 650 million people. These two nations have the largest populations in the world. Great numbers of Chinese and Indian people live in crowded river valleys. Their ancient civilizations began in these fertile river valleys about 5,000 years ago. In Southeast Asia, river valleys gave birth to the Khmer (KMUR) civilization.

2. India is located in the southern part of Asia. It is part of a large peninsula shaped like a triangle. A peninsula is land surrounded by water except for a small part that is attached to the mainland. This peninsula is about half the size of the United States. Today it includes three countries—India, Bangladesh, and Pakistan. In the north, the giant Himalaya Moun-

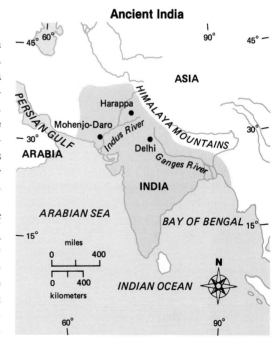

Ancient India

tains, the highest mountains in the world, separate India almost completely from the rest of Asia. The Himalaya Mountains extend to the southwest, too. With water on three sides of the land and mountains on the north side, the early Indian people could live with little fear of invasion. There were passes in the mountains, however, and some invaders were able to get through to the river valleys. The snow and rain from the northern mountains fed the waters of the Indus and Ganges rivers of India. (See map, page 35.) Large numbers of people were able to live in the valleys of these rivers.

WHAT TRACES DID THE EARLY PEOPLE OF INDIA LEAVE?

3. Not until this century did we learn about the great ancient civilizations along the Indus River of India. Archaeologists have uncovered the remains of two great cities along the Indus River, Mohenjo-Daro (mo-HEN-jo DAW-ro) and Harappa (hur-RA-puh). These were well-planned cities, whose streets were built exactly in squares. The people who lived in these cities were probably peaceful, for few traces of weapons have been found.

4. Probably the people of the Indus River valley traded with Mesopotamia or Egypt at some time. They made metal bracelets and necklaces. They grew wheat, barley, and cotton and raised cattle, goats, and sheep. They knew how to irrigate land for farming. Their cities had modern systems of sewerage. Some homes even had bathrooms with tile floors. Mohenjo-Daro and Harappa disappeared about 2000 B.C. We have not yet discovered why. They may have been destroyed by flood or conquered by an invading tribe.

5. The Indo-Aryans came to India from Persia about 1500 B.C. They settled in the Indus River valley. They moved on to the Ganges River valley, where they conquered the people living there. The Indo-Aryans used horses and chariots. Bows and arrows were their chief weapons. They divided the land they settled into states and put a ruler called a rajah (RAH-jah) in charge of each section.

WHAT DID HINDUISM AND BUDDHISM TEACH?

6. Religion was important in the lives of the Indo-Aryan people. The religion that developed among them lives on in India today. The Indo-Aryans believed that their god, Brahma, was the source of life. The priests, called Brahmans, were the best educated of all the Indo-Aryans. They developed a rich literature which included poems and legends. The books containing this literature are called the *Vedas*. The Indo-Aryan language was called *Sanskrit*. Scholars today are able to understand it.

7. These Indo-Aryans developed the *caste* system of India. In the caste system, people are born into a certain social class. No one may marry a person from another caste, and it is almost impossible to move up to a higher caste. The occupations people have, or the jobs they perform, are decided by the caste to which they belong. Nobody may do the work that is meant for members of a different caste. The Brahmans made up the highest caste. The nobles and the warriors were in the next caste. Then came the skilled workers and those who took part in trade. The fourth caste, which had the largest number of people, was made up of servants, those who worked for others. And in the lowest caste were the *untouchables*. These were slaves, captured prisoners, and those who had been dropped from other castes. The untouchables did all the work that the others would not do. They lived in the most miserable conditions. In modern times, the Indian government ended the caste system, but some people still hold to it. The customs that people have formed over thousands of years are hard to change.

8. The religion of the Indo-Aryans is called *Hinduism*. It teaches that life is largely

Testing Your Vocabulary

Choose the correct answer.

1. *Sanskrit* is the name given to
   a. the language of the ancient Indo-Aryans.
   b. the caste system.
   c. the great books of the Hindus.
2. A good meaning for the word *caste* would be
   a. a life of suffering.
   b. a social class.
   c. an old custom.
3. In paragraph 9 we learn that the name *Buddha* means *the enlightened one. Enlightened* here means
   a. generous.
   b. wise.
   c. happy.

Understanding What You Have Read

1. The purpose of paragraph 7 is to describe
   a. the caste system of India.
   b. the spread of Buddhism in Asia.
   c. the meaning of rebirth.
   d. the importance of religion in India.
2. In which paragraph do you find facts about
   a. the populations of different countries in Asia?
   b. the disappearance of the ancient city of Harappa?
   c. the kinds of people who were untouchables?
   d. the temple of Angkor Wat?
3. Hindus do not believe in killing animals because
   a. their diet is largely fish and vegetables.
   b. they think that the life of an animal is sacred.
   c. milk is needed to feed the millions of people.
4. The idea that a person could never rise to a better caste was accepted in India probably because it was believed that
   a. a person's place in life was a reward or punishment for the way in which he or she had lived in an earlier life.
   b. priests and landowners could not do heavy work.
   c. slavery was a necessary part of Hindu life.
5. The people of early India had little contact with the people of China or of the west because
   a. continual fighting among the villages kept the people busy.
   b. India is almost completely surrounded by water and mountains.
   c. the rivers of India were not suited for transporting goods.
6. Most of India's people were crowded into river valleys because
   a. invading tribes forced them to crowd together to protect themselves.
   b. valleys had stone for buildings.
   c. fertile land was found near the rivers.
7. India has had difficulty ending the caste system because
   a. people have been practicing this custom for thousands of years.
   b. it is a belief of the Buddhists.
   c. the untouchables wish to continue it.

From your reading of Chapter 4, tell whether you agree or disagree with the following statements. Give reasons for your answers.

1. In early India, there were some rich people, but the great mass of people were poor.
2. France claimed much of Southeast Asia because of French explorations there.
3. "Untouchables" could rise above their caste by marrying persons of a higher caste.
4. Buddhists pray and study apart from the busy world.
5. We get much information about India from the Vedas.
6. People of India today are allowed to follow only the Hindu religion.
7. Early Indians built high temples to honor their gods.
8. The largest number of people in India are crowded along the Ganges River valley.

Developing Ideas and Skills

WRITING AN OUTLINE

In order to review what we have read, it is a good idea to make notes in our notebook as we read. The best way to do this is by using an outline. An outline is an orderly list of main ideas and subtopics. Subtopics are facts that support or develop a main idea. There are two keys to good outlining. The first key is to find the main idea or ideas of each chapter. The second is to see how facts are used to develop each main idea.

Having read Chapter 4, you can see that there are four main ideas in the chapter. They are:

1. *The Geography of India.* Paragraphs 1 and 2 are about the size and population of India and its river valleys and mountains.
2. *The Early Settlements of India.* Paragraphs 3, 4, and 5 tell us something about the earliest known settlements in ancient India. We learn about the crops the people raised, how they farmed, what their cities were like, and how invaders conquered the land.
3. *The Religions of Ancient India.* Paragraphs 6, 7, 8, and 9 tell something about the early religions of India. We learn about the Hindus and Buddhists, their holy writings, their caste system.
4. *The Khmer Civilization of Southeast Asia.* Paragraphs 11, 12, 13, and 14 tell us about the discovery of Khmer cities and what their ruins tell us of the Khmer people.

If you had taken notes in the way described, you would have written down what the chapter is about. But you would not have written the same words that are in the chapter. In making the outline, we first write the main ideas; that is, what the chapter is about. Beneath each main idea we list subtopics; that is, the facts that we want to remember. Read the outline on the next page to see how the chapter is divided into main ideas and subtopics.

Ancient India and Southeast Asia

(Main Idea)	A. The Geography of India
(Subtopic)	1. Most people were crowded into river valleys.
(Subtopic)	2. It is a peninsula about half the size of the United States.
(Subtopic)	3. The Himalaya Mountains separate India from the rest of Asia.
(Subtopic)	4. Invaders could come into river valleys only through mountain passes.
(Main Idea)	B. Early Civilization in India
(Subtopic)	1. Cities had irrigation and sewerage systems.
(Subtopic)	2. People traded, grew crops, raised cattle.
(Subtopic)	3. Later, Indo-Aryans conquered the land around the Ganges.
(Main Idea)	C. The Religions of India
(Subtopic)	1. The Brahmans were well educated. They had a system of writing (Sanskrit) and wrote works of literature (Vedas).
(Subtopic)	2. In the caste system, people were divided according to social classes.
(Subtopic)	3. Today, most people in India are Hindus. All life is sacred to the Hindus, and they believe in rebirth.
(Subtopic)	4. Buddhism began in India and spread to China, Japan, and Southeast Asia.
(Main Idea)	D. The Khmer Culture
(Subtopic)	1. The Khmer civilization was located in Southeast Asia. Its religion and language came from India.
(Subtopic)	2. The temple of Angkor Wat, built to honor the god, Vishnu, was the greatest of Khmer temples.
(Subtopic)	3. We do not know what happened to the Khmer city of Angkor Thom.

An outline can be a great help to remembering what you read. This is a simple outline. Your outline can be longer or shorter. An outline is both a summary of a chapter and a listing of your notes on the chapter. During your work in world history, you will have the chance to write simple outlines of chapters, source materials or reports. Remember this plan: first find the main ideas of the chapter; then fill in the details that belong under each main idea.

REVIEWING WORD MEANINGS THROUGH CLUES

Tell the meaning of each word listed below, from Chapter 4. Tell also the clue in the text that helped you figure out its meaning.

peninsula, paragraph 2   *untouchables*, paragraph 7
rajah, paragraph 5   *Buddha*, paragraph 9
Brahman, paragraph 6   *reign*, paragraph 10

AIM: How did the Chinese civilization begin?

CHAPTER 5

China: Where a Great Civilization Began

HOW DID THE GEOGRAPHY OF CHINA AFFECT ITS EARLY SETTLEMENT?

1. If there were slogans for each of the ancient civilizations, the slogan for China might be "We outlived them all!" In China, a land about the size of Canada, traces of a civilization older than that of Egypt or Mesopotamia have been found. Chinese civilization is known to have existed 4,000 years ago. And it still goes on today.

2. The geography of China made it possible for a civilization to develop early. The Yellow and Yangzi (YANG-see) Rivers meant hundreds of fertile valleys. Transportation was good along the rivers. China has more good soil and rainfall than Egypt or the Fertile Crescent. Yet the geography of China is not the same all over the land. Southeastern China, which is on the Pacific Ocean, has a climate like the states of South Carolina and Georgia. Here there is plenty of rain and good soil. Northern China, with great plains, has less rainfall. Half of China is covered with highlands. Since mountains divide the land in many places, the early Chinese lived in small, separate villages. Many village people never saw people from outside their own village. The people of China, therefore, have always differed among themselves in their customs and ideas.

3. The Chinese people probably knew less of the outside world than the people of any of the other early civilizations. The eastern border of China is the Pacific Ocean. High mountains cut off China on the south and west from other peoples. Only in the north is there an opening

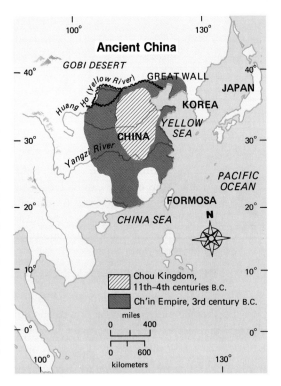

Ancient China

GOBI DESERT

Huang Ho (Yellow River)

GREAT WALL

JAPAN

KOREA

YELLOW SEA

CHINA

Yangzi River

PACIFIC OCEAN

FORMOSA

CHINA SEA

N

▨ Chou Kingdom, 11th-4th centuries B.C.

■ Ch'in Empire, 3rd century B.C.

miles
0   400

0   600
kilometers

for invaders. Wanderers from the north often did invade China, but they did not seem to change Chinese life. Conquerors came, but the quiet and gentle farm life of the people went on. Europeans did not visit China until about the 13th century.

WHAT IS KNOWN ABOUT THE EARLY CHINESE?

4. We do not know how many people lived in ancient China. Those who study Chinese history believe that the population of China was greater than that of ancient Egypt, Mesopotamia, or India. Farming is, and has always been, the chief work of the Chinese people. The peasants of ancient China worked the soil in spite of invasions, wars, and floods. The people did not think very much about the world outside China. They were happy with their life and thought that they lived the best way possible.

A bronze statue of the Kuan-Yin T'ang Dynasty, A.D. 618–907. The fine detailed art from ancient China suggests a highly developed civilization. Give reasons to support that statement.

The Great Wall of China. It was built about 228–210 B.C. and winds for 1400 miles over mountains, rivers, and valleys. Why do you think it is considered one of the wonders of the world?

5. To the Chinese people, the family had the greatest importance. Children were taught to be obedient to their parents. Older people were especially honored. Ancestor worship (devotion to family members who had died) was a part of the life of the ancient Chinese family. Whatever a person did brought either honor or dishonor to the family. The oldest male in the family ruled family life. Women had a lesser role. When a girl married, she went to live with her husband's family. Yet women worked along with men in the fields, and did the household work too. They were treated with respect by their husbands.

6. The Chinese learned to use bronze and iron much later than the Mesopotamians. Writing, too, developed later than in other civilizations. The Chinese language is one of the hardest to learn. It is made up of thousands of symbols. Each symbol is a different word. And any one word may have different meanings, depending upon the way in which it is spoken. The earliest buildings were made of wood; so they have not lasted through the centuries. Canals and dikes were built to protect the precious water supply. The Great Wall, built across the northern border of China to keep out invaders, is one of the wonders of the world.

43

HOW DID DYNASTIES RULE CHINA?

7. Because the ancient Chinese lived in separate villages it was not easy to unite them under one government. At first, each city-state, or small group of villages, ruled itself. Then, about 1700 B.C., *dynasties*—in which each father passed down the ruling power to his son— gained control of China. One of the early dynasties was the Chou (JOU) family. Chou leaders began a system of *feudalism* (FYOOD-uh-liz-um) about 1000 B.C. Under this system, all land was controlled by the Chou family. Lords were given parts of the land. Lords ruled over their own lands, were loyal to the Chou family, and fought for it. The lords, in turn, gave smaller pieces of land to peasants, who paid high taxes in exchange. The lords lived very well in their fine homes, some with tiled floors. The poor lived in mud huts and raised rice, chickens, and a few cattle.

8. The Chou dynasty was one of the great periods in early Chinese history. Silk had already been grown in China. Now it was produced in larger amounts. Fine vases of bronze and jade were made. Iron tools were produced. Chinese workers made fine wood carvings. But there was little order or peace. The city-states fought each other. In the middle of this disorder, a great religious leader arose: Confucius (kun-FYOO-shus).

9. Confucius tried to show his people the path to peace. At the age of 22, he became a great teacher. He continued to preach his ideas until his death, 50 years later. Confucius taught that people should lead useful lives and not worry about death. The greatest problems that humans have, Confucius believed, was that they wanted too much. He taught the Chinese to lead good, moral lives. People should respect their elders. Children should listen to the advice of their parents. His lessons can be summed up in the "golden rule": "Do unto others as you would have them do unto you."

10. Another religious leader, named Lao-tse (LOW-DZOO), also tried to find a way to end the wars among the people. Lao-tse believed that people should not worry too much about their problems, because nothing in this world is of great importance. We should therefore accept life as we find it and enjoy the wonderful earth on which we live.

11. Although the teachings of Confucius and Lao-tse were accepted by many, they did not stop the wars and disorders in China. About 300 B.C., the Ch'in (CHIN) dynasty took control of the city-states of China and ruled by force. The Ch'in dynasty ruled more of China than had any of the earlier emperors. The Ch'in wanted the Chinese to forget their old ways and give all their loyalty to the ruling family. So they tried to rid the land of old ideas. Books containing the ideas of Confucius were burned. But it was not long before the Ch'in dynasty was overthrown. Another dynasty, the Han, ruled for the next 400 years.

Testing Your Vocabulary

Choose the best answer.

1. A *dynasty* refers to
   a. rule of land by one person.
   b. ownership of land by a few people.
   c. a series of rulers from the same family.

2. The best meaning for *symbol* (paragraph 6) is
   a. a letter of the alphabet.
   b. a sign standing for a word.
   c. a secret code.

Understanding What You Have Read

1. A good title for paragraphs 9 and 10 might be
   a. Religious Leaders in Early China
   b. Emperors Who Wanted Peace
   c. Respect for Ancestors
   d. Ending Wars Among the Cities

2. In which paragraph do you find facts about
   a. the coming of Europeans to China?
   b. the population of ancient China?
   c. the difficulty of learning the Chinese language?
   d. the teachings of Confucius?

3. An early civilization developed in China because
   a. people moved from Mediterranean lands in search of good trade routes.
   b. Chinese river valleys provided fertile soil and transportation.
   c. strong leaders ended warfare among the Chinese people.

4. For thousands of years, China had little to do with the outside world for each of these reasons EXCEPT
   a. its geography kept it separated from other lands.
   b. the interests of the Chinese people did not lead them outside their villages.
   c. trade was impossible, for the Chinese had few things to trade.

5. The Chinese language is difficult because
   a. only the educated people speak it.
   b. it has thousands of different symbols, each with a different meaning.
   c. it cannot be written on paper or stone.

6. China was overrun by invaders several times because
   a. the Chinese people were not unified enough to fight against the invaders.
   b. there were no mountains to keep out invaders.
   c. religious leaders taught the people not to fight against invaders.

7. The Chou dynasty is important in Chinese history because
   a. the Chou rulers built the Great Wall.
   b. this period marked the beginning of the Iron Age.
   c. fine silks, wood, and jade products were produced.

Developing Ideas and Skills

USING A TIME LINE

Since history is the story of events that happen at different times, it is necessary to learn some dates when we study history. Knowing exact dates is often not necessary. It is more important to have an idea of the general period of time in which an event took place than to know the exact date. We should know the correct order of general periods of history. We should know which event took place first and which events followed. An important aid in learning the order of events is a *time line.*

A time line may cover hundreds or thousands of years, or it may cover shorter periods of time, such as 10 or 20 years. In speaking of long periods of time, it is easier to use special terms for those periods than to tell exact numbers of years. When we study world history, which covers so many years, it is important that we use these special terms correctly. A few of them are listed on page 46.

An *age* usually means a long period ot time, as in the *Ice Age,* the *Iron Age,* the *Middle Ages.*

A *century* means 100 years.

A *decade* means 10 years.

B.C. means Before Christ.

A.D. is the abbreviation of Anno Domini, which is Latin for "in the year of our Lord"; that is, after the birth of Christ.

On the following time line, all the events take place before the birth of Christ. The year of the birth of Christ is the central point we use in deciding dates. When we speak of dates before the birth of Christ, we use the letters "B.C." after the number of the year. When we speak of dates after the birth of Christ, we often use the letters "A.D.," but it is not always necessary to do so. Also, we place the "A.D." before the year number. The higher the number of a year before the birth of Christ, the earlier that date is. The higher the number of a year after the birth of Christ, the later that date is. In other words, 20 B.C. came before 10 B.C., but A.D. 20 came after A.D. 10.

Study the time line carefully. Then see if you can answer the questions that follow it by using the information it presents.

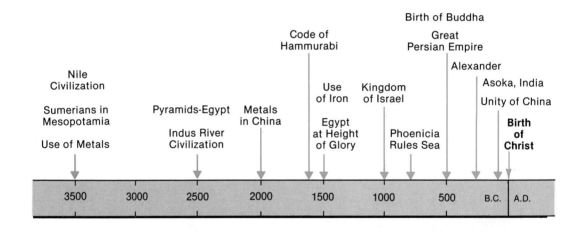

1. Tell the order in which these periods of history occur:
   a. The time of the kingdom of Israel
   b. The time of the Persian Empire at its height
   c. The beginning of civilization along the Indus River
   d. The period of Phoenician sea power

2. Which of these leaders lived first?
   a. Alexander
   b. Buddha
   c. Hammurabi

3. Which two events took place at about the same time?
   a. Writing the Code of Hammurabi and building the pyramids in Egypt.

b. Birth of Buddha and the time of the Persian Empire at its height.

c. Beginning of civilization along the Indus River and the time of the king-dom of Israel.

4. About what year was the Code of Ham-murabi prepared?

5. Were metals used first in China or in Egypt?

6. Could the Phoenicians have known about the use of iron?

7. Which reached the height of its power first, the Egyptian kingdom or the Persian Empire?

8. How many years after the beginning of Indian civilization did Asoka rule?

USING A MAP

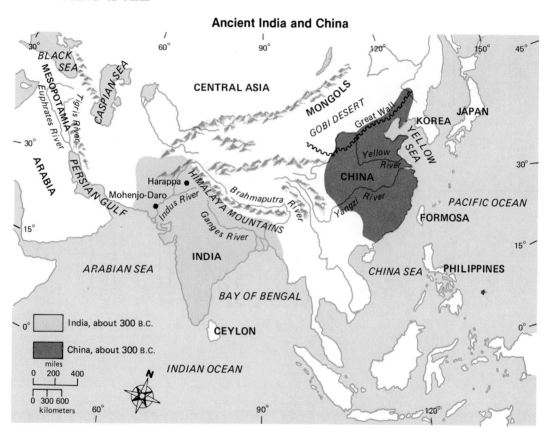

Ancient India and China

Study the map carefully. Then decide whether these statements are true or false.

1. Great river valleys are found both in India and in China.

2. Invaders on horseback could enter China anywhere along its eastern border.

3. It was difficult to travel by land from China to India.

4. It was possible for traders to travel from Mesopotamia to China by an all-water route.

5. By seeing where Mongol tribesmen lived, we know that they were outstand-ing sailors.

Using Original Sources

The following poem is by a woman named Hsu Shu. She lived in the second century A.D. Literature can often let us see how differently people lived in the past. But it can also show us similarities between the lives of people who lived centuries ago and the lives of people today. After reading the poem, think about the differences and similarities between the woman of the poem and a woman of today whom you know. Then answer the questions.

To My Husband

Hapless am I!   *hapless = luckless*
In sickness I came here.
I am lingering within these doors   *lingering = staying, unwilling to go*
For, though time passes, I remain uncured.
I neglect attention to you;
I break the laws of love and duty.
Now you, sir, to obey orders,
Have gone to the far-off capital.
Long, long will be our separation,
And there is no way to tell you my thoughts.
Expecting your return I am all eagerness.
And waiting for you, I stand about aimlessly.
My thoughts of you are knotted in my heart;
In sleep I think of your radiant countenance.   *countenance = face*
You have gone far away;
Your separation from me is daily lengthening.
Would that I had wings,   *would = I wish*
That I might fly after you.
Oft do I moan, and deep do I sigh,
And tears wet my coat.

1. How would you describe the feelings expressed in this poem? What real-life situation has caused them?
2. Suppose that you had not been told that this poem was by a Chinese woman of the second century. What is said in the poem that might make you guess that the poem was from the past, and from a culture different from our own?
3. How is the life of the speaker different from the life of a typical wife of today? How is it similar?
4. Would a poem to her husband by a 20th-century woman have to be much different from Hsu Shu's poem? (Give reasons for your answer.)

AIM: How did Japan develop a rich culture in a small area?

CHAPTER 6

Japan: How a Civilization Grew on Small Islands

WHAT WAS EARLY JAPANESE SOCIETY LIKE?

1. A dream of some people is to live on an island, at least for a time. An island gives us a feeling of being alone. It is peaceful and quiet. The island keeps us apart from the troubles of the world. Thousands of years ago, an island would tend to isolate its people from busy civilizations on continents. This was true of early Japan. Its hundreds of islands stretch for 1,500 miles from north to south. The nearest continental land is Korea, 100 miles away. China lies 500 miles to the west. Japan has four main islands, and mountains cover much of them. There is little land for farming and few minerals. From Japan's earliest years, its people have found that the sea would fill some of their needs. Rice has always been the main food crop of Japan.

2. No one knows when people first settled in Japan. The earliest Japanese may have been the Ainu (EYE-noo). They probably came from the mainland of Asia. When others came to Japan, the Ainu were pushed farther north. People from northern Asia came to Japan

Japanese temple in Kyoto. How does this picture suggest the description of peace and quiet?

through Korea. These people and people from Pacific islands took the place of the Ainu. The first written record of the Japanese came to light in the 3rd century A.D. These are Chinese records. They tell of a tomb culture in Japan, of people who built great mounds as burial places for their leaders. These records also noted that the rulers of Japan were sometimes women.

3. Japanese society was divided into clans in this early period. A clan is a group of families related to each other. Warriors of the nobility were the leaders of the clans. Each clan had its own god. The god was believed to be the founder of the clan. The clan members' ancestors were worshipped as well. Clans fought each other for power. The head of the strongest clan was called *emperor* or *empress*. About A.D. 500 the head of the Yamoto clan declared himself emperor. He was Japan's first emperor.

4. *Shintoism*, or Shinto, was the religion of early Japan. The word *Shinto* means *way of the gods*. It is a simple religion that respects the forces of nature. There are few rules to follow and no holy books. At first, it grew out of the worship of nature. Later, it developed other features. Shintoism teaches its followers to worship plants, birds, sunsets, mountains, waterfalls—nature's gifts to people. Each of these wonders of nature has a god or spirit. The most important is the sun goddess. The emperor of Japan is believed by many Shintoists to be her descendant. Ancestors are also honored. A Shinto family will call upon ancestors for help in trying to live good lives.

HOW DID THE CHINESE AFFECT JAPANESE CIVILIZATION?

5. Japan borrowed much from Chinese culture. Chinese writing was used in Japan before A.D. 500. The Japanese used the symbols in Chinese writing to jot down their own speech sounds. In time, their own system of writing developed. A calendar and new religions also came from China. The teachings of Confucius and Buddha were introduced into Japan. Buddhism spread quickly there. Buddhist monasteries were built by members of royal families. (A monastery is a living place for monks. These are

Empress Jingu ruled Japan in the third century. During this time Japan was ruled by clans. The emperor or empress was the head of the leading clan. Explain how the rule of clans was related to ancestor worship.

people who want to carry on a religious life.) One ancient Japanese monastery is still standing at Nara (nah-RAH), a city in central Japan. It has the oldest buildings in the world made of wood. Students from Japan also went to China to learn about arts, science, and government. The Japanese used what they learned from the Chinese to develop their own way of life.

6. Japanese rulers admired the Chinese system of one central government. Several Japanese rulers tried to break the power of the great clans to give the emperor more power. To do this, a capital was set up at Nara in 710. It was later moved to the site of the present city of Kyoto (kee-OH-toh). The emperor ruled from there. But large clans still ruled some parts of the country.

7. The few centuries after Nara became the capital city are called the classical age of Japan. Works of art of a new kind were displayed in many great temples. Most often these were statues of Buddha in wood and bronze. Artists began to develop their own styles, free of Chinese influence. The same was true of writers. Tales took the place of poetry as the favorite form of literature. Most stories were written by women of the royal court. The most famous story, the novel *The Tale of the Genji*, (JEN-jee) is the work of Lady Murasaki (moo-rah-SAH-kee). It tells of life in the emperor's court about the year 1000. It has been called one of the world's great books. Women of noble birth in Japan were expected to be talented in music and painting as well as in writing.

8. By the end of the 12th century, the power of the central government had been weakened. The large clans could not be controlled. Emperors still tried to rule, but they had little power. Clans formed their own armies and fought each other. In 1192, Yoritomo (yoh-ree-TOH-moh), the leader of the most powerful clan, was named *shogun* (SHOH-gun), or supreme military governor, by the emperor. He became the leader of the emperor's army. Japan now had a military government. Yoritomo divided the country into provinces and named a governor for each. Most often the governor was a large landowner. The shogun became the real head of government. The emperor held the title of ruler, but he was ruler in name only. Government by shoguns lasted in Japan for 700 years.

9. Large landowners and lords of estates formed private armies to protect their lands. These armies were made up of hired soldiers. These professional warriors were the *samurai* (SAM-moor-eye). They were given land by the lords in return for the protection they provided. In some ways, the samurai were like the knights of Europe in the Middle Ages. (See page 144.) The position of samurai was inherited. Land was, also. The samurai had their own strict code of conduct, although it was not written. They

Samurai warrior. The armor is made of iron. Notice that he carries two swords. The long blade is covered with fur when it is not in use. Compare him with the knights of the Middle Ages.

were expected to be brave, to be loyal to their lord, to put up with pain, and to show neither anger nor joy. To be captured or to be disloyal was to lose one's honor. In either case, a warrior was expected to commit *seppuku* (seh-POO-koo), or suicide. Women in a samurai household were likewise expected to be obedient and loyal to their lords.

Testing Your Vocabulary

Choose the best answer.

1. In a *monastery* you would expect to find
   a. people living a religious life.
   b. warriors learning to fight on horseback.
   c. members of the royal court.
2. A *shogun* would most likely
   a. try to divide large estates among poor people.
   b. write poetry.
   c. direct armies in war.
3. A *clan* is a
   a. group of related families.
   b. part of a large territory.
   c. a god who watches over one family.
4. *Samurai* became famous as
   a. writers of novels.
   b. warriors.
   c. people who developed the Japanese language.

Understanding What You Have Read

1. The main idea of paragraph 5 is that
   a. a calendar was introduced into Japan from China.
   b. Chinese culture gave much to Japanese culture.
   c. Buddhism spread slowly throughout Japan.
   d. the Japanese borrowed little from other cultures.

2. In which paragraph do you find facts about
   a. the meaning of Shintoism?
   b. the earliest Japanese people?
   c. women writers of the royal court?
   d. the meaning of *seppuku*?

3. Because mountains cover much of the Japanese islands, the Japanese people
   a. started trade with China 3,000 years before the birth of Christ.
   b. turned to the sea to make a living.
   c. used the mountains as tombs for their leaders.

4. One reason for the weakness of the Japanese emperors was that
   a. many land-holding clans had too much power.
   b. the language used by emperors was not understood by the people.
   c. Japan was often invaded by armies from mainland Asia.

5. When we think of Japan's religions, calendar, system of writing, and central government, we might well remember that
   a. much of Japanese culture came from China.
   b. Japan's culture was never influenced by other lands.
   c. Japan's culture was created mostly by warriors.

6. One of the reasons why the shogun became the real ruler of Japan was that
   a. shoguns received their education in China.
   b. the shoguns had defeated enemies of Japan in several long wars.
   c. powerful clans could not be controlled by the emperor.

7. The Japanese love of gardens and nature may be traced to their early belief in
   a. seppuku
   b. Shinto
   c. ancestor worship

Tell whether these statements are true or false. If a statement is false, change the word in italics to make it true.

1. The belief that every thing and every force of nature (mountains, waterfalls, sunsets, and so on) has a god is part of the religion called *Shintoism.*

2. *Hinduism* is a religion that came to Japan from China.

3. The people who came to Japan from northern Asia most likely came by way of *Korea.*

4. Bravery, loyalty, and honor were part of the code of conduct of the *samurai.*

5. The period of great Japanese literature, painting, and sculpture is called the *classical* age.

6. Japanese emperors set up a capital at *Tokyo* in A.D. 710.

7. Japan's first shogun was *Murasaki.*

8. The earliest written records of Japanese civilization were written in *Chinese.*

9. Government by shogun in Japan lasted for nearly *700* years.

10. Great *poetry* was written by women of the royal Japanese court.

Developing Ideas and Skills

USING A MAP
Study the map. Then answer the following questions.

1. What are the four main islands of Japan?

2. People in Hokkaido might have some differences in their way of life from people in Kyushu. Why?

3. The latitude of London, England, is 51°, north; that of Memphis, Tennessee, is 35°; that of Miami, Florida, is 25°. Which of these cities is about the same distance from the equator as Tokyo?

4. People from the Philippines probably traveled to Japan and settled there early in its history. About how far did they have to travel?

5. On which island did most of the important events in early Japanese history take place?

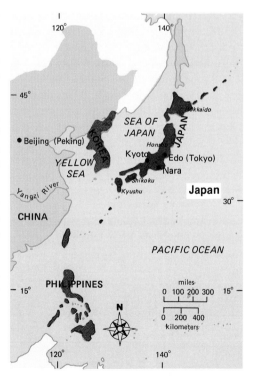

AIM: What early civilizations developed south of the Sahara Desert?

CHAPTER 7

Africa: Where Powerful Civilizations Grew

WHEN DID EARLY AFRICAN CIVILIZATIONS DEVELOP?

1. African culture existed long before European explorers of the 15th century first came upon the continent. For thousands of years there had been little contact between Europe and Africa south of the Sahara Desert. There are good reasons why this land was little known for so long. For one thing, the great Sahara Desert separates the coast of North Africa from the grasslands and rain forests to the south. (This desert covers most of northern Africa.) Also, much of the heart of Africa is uncomfortably hot and wet to Europeans. There are few

Louis and Mary Leakey dig in Tanzania for bones and tools of early humans.

good harbors along the coast. And only a few rivers can bring travelers inland.

2. Some of the most important findings about early African people, and about the earliest human beings, have come from three British anthropologists. They are Louis and Mary Leakey and their son, Richard. While searching in Tanzania, Mary Leakey found a humanlike skull that is thought to be 1.8 million years old. In Kenya, Richard Leakey found the skull of a humanlike creature that may be nearly 3 million years old. In 1974, in Ethiopia, an American anthropologist, Donald Johanson, found the remains of a 3.5-million-year-old female being that resembles modern human beings. She is known as Lucy. It seems that people who looked like men and women of today appeared in Africa a very long time ago.

3. The writings of ancient peoples help us to know more about them. But there are no written records of African civilizations, except for those found in Egypt. Egyptians, as we have learned, had a system of writing. The records they kept have helped us to know a great deal about their early kingdoms. But there were other kingdoms in Africa at the time of the

pharaohs. They left no written records. Much of what we know of these kingdoms we have learned only in the last century. As a result of the findings of anthropologists, it is now believed that the earliest humans may have first appeared in East Africa. Also, there probably were civilizations in the Sahara region of Africa as early as 4000 B.C. It is thought that these civilizations came to an end when the water supply dried up. Perhaps these people moved farther east, toward the Nile River.

4. In West Africa, near Jos, Nigeria, miners have found the remains of an ancient settlement. It has been named the Nok culture. This black civilization was at its height about 1000 B.C. The people were farmers who used stone tools in their work. The Nok culture had fine artists. They made beautiful clay sculptures. Samples of some of their work have been found.

Nigerian bronze head. Sculpture was a highly developed art form in early Africa.

The same kind of sculpture has also been found farther south, along the coast of West Africa.

WHAT POWERFUL KINGDOMS AROSE SOUTH OF THE ANCIENT EGYPTIANS?

5. In ancient times, African kingdoms appeared along the Nile River, south of Egypt. One of these was the kingdom of Kush. Kushites had been forced to hand over gold and slaves as tribute to the pharaohs. Piankhi (pee-AN-kee), leader of the Kushites, planned for years to end the rule of Egypt over his people. When he felt the time had come, he led his people northward. They captured towns along the way. About 750 B.C., Piankhi captured the Egyptian city of Memphis. The Egyptians were forced to surrender. He returned to Kush with vast treasures of gold and silver. The Kushites continued to rule Egypt for almost 100 years. Queens as well as kings ruled the Kushite lands. When the Assyrians united with Egypt, they put an end to Kushite rule. The capital of Kush was moved farther south to Meroë (MER-o-ee). Here an even more powerful civilization developed.

6. Large amounts of iron have been found near Meroë. The people of Kush had tools and weapons of iron. There are no signs that they used copper or bronze. Kushites may have gone straight from a Stone Age to an Iron Age way of life. People farther south in Africa also used iron tools. Most likely, the iron came from the mines of Meroë. Gold, ivory, and slaves were sent through Meroë on the Nile River along trade routes across the Sahara.

7. The highlands of Ethiopia lie southeast of Kush. One of ancient Ethiopia's important cities was Axum (AK-soom). The Axumites were traders. They carried their goods both by land and by sea. No one is sure how far they traveled from their homeland. It is believed, however, that they traded with the people of Egypt, of Mesopotamia, and even of India. Axum became powerful enough to invade and conquer Kush about 300 B.C.

WHAT EARLY BLACK CULTURES EXISTED IN AFRICA SOUTH OF THE SAHARA?

Ruins of Zimbabwe. These are among the most remarkable remains of early African civilizations. Within the walls is a Conical Tower that may have been used for religious ceremonies.

8. Cities existed along the eastern coast of Africa about 2,000 years ago. These cities were chiefly trading centers. Ships came to them from across the Indian Ocean. Goods from East Africa were exchanged for goods from lands in Asia, probably India. Stories of this trade have been found in an ancient Egyptian guidebook on sailing the Indian Ocean. The guidebook was written a few years after the birth of Jesus.

9. European explorers in Africa in the 19th century found traces of an ancient black people south of the Sahara. These people lived in kingdoms much like those of the pharaohs of Egypt. In Zimbabwe (zim-BAH-bway), many caves have pictures that show life as it was thousands of years ago. Pictures of elephants, snakes, and people were painted in bright colors made from berry juice. Hidden from the sun, the colors are almost as bright today as when they were painted. Also in Zimbabwe, formerly known as Rhodesia, are the stone ruins of the early Zimbabwe culture. Huge stones show where buildings once stood. A great temple made of 15,000 tons of stone still stands. This temple was the work of black Africans of the Iron Age.

10. We never stop learning about the earliest civilizations on earth. In Africa, south of the Sahara, we have learned slowly, partly because there have been few written records. Nevertheless, we are beginning to realize how great and important were the ancient cultures in Africa. The last hundred years have given us our greatest knowledge of ancient Africa. Who knows what stories may be uncovered during the next hundred years?

Testing Your Vocabulary _____

Choose the best answer.

1. An anthropologist is a scientist who
   a. studies the history of African people.
   b. studies the bones of ancient people.
   c. tests chemicals in a laboratory.
2. When people *pay tribute* to another people, they
   a. show their thanks for favors received.
   b. give a gift as a sign of friendship.
   c. give something to keep from being attacked or punished.

Understanding What You Have Read

1. The main idea of paragraph 9 is that
   a. great stone ruins have been found in Zimbabwe.
   b. cave paintings are still colorful.
   c. traces of ancient people have been found in Zimbabwe.
   d. Africans had an early Iron Age.

2. In which paragraph do you find facts about
   a. the findings of the anthropologist Mary Leakey?
   b. the traders of ancient Ethiopia?
   c. the remains of the Nok culture?
   d. early cities along the eastern coast of Africa?

3. Little is known of ancient kingdoms in Africa (except for Egypt) because
   a. there are no written records.
   b. the Nile is the only important river in Africa.
   c. the earliest remains of humans have been found in Egypt.

4. The Kushites were unusual in that
   a. they made paintings that have lasted for thousands of years.
   b. they used iron for tools without ever having used copper or bronze.
   c. their kingdom was located in eastern Africa.

5. Piankhi wanted to conquer Egypt because
   a. his people had been forced to give wealth to Egypt for many years.
   b. Egypt's iron supply meant power for the Kushites.
   c. Egypt had stopped Kushite trade with people on the Mediterranean Sea.

6. We know there were cities along the coast of East Africa long ago because
   a. there are stone ruins of docks dating from 2,000 years ago.
   b. there are ruins of palaces of Egyptian pharaohs.
   c. an ancient guidebook for sailors tells about these cities.

7. Some believe that the earliest humans first appeared in Africa because
   a. writings in the pyramids tell us so.
   b. iron tools have been discovered in Africa.
   c. human bones found in Africa are the oldest ever found by archaeologists.

Match the descriptions in the right column with the names of places in the left column. (One of the descriptions cannot be used.)

1. Nok
2. Tanzania
3. Meroë
4. Sahara
5. Axum
6. Zimbabwe

a. where ancient bones were found by Mary Leakey
b. called the city of gold
c. Nigerian culture noted for clay sculpture
d. culture that built great stone temples
e. important city of ancient Ethiopia
f. city in ancient Kush that had large amounts of iron
g. great desert of North Africa

Developing Ideas and Skills

USING A MAP

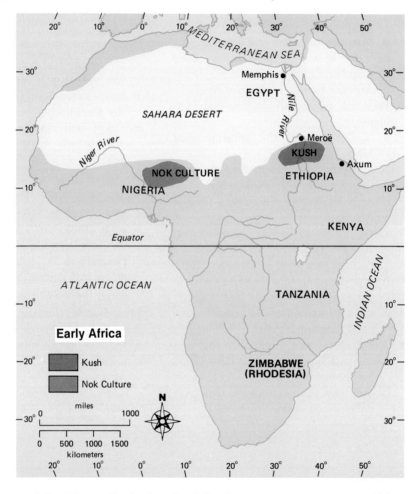

Study the map carefully. Then tell whether the following statements are true or false.

1. The Zimbabwe culture was located south of the equator.
2. The Sahara Desert takes up most of the southern part of Africa.
3. Cultures that traded across the Indian Ocean would most likely have been located in eastern Africa.

4. Ethiopia, Kush, and Egypt were all located near the waters of the Nile River.

5. One could travel by water from Rhodesia to Egypt.

6. The Nok and Zimbabwe cultures were located along the east coast of Africa.

AIM: How did early American Indian civilizations develop?

CHAPTER 8

American Indians: First in the New World

WHO WERE THE FIRST PEOPLE TO COME TO NORTH AMERICA?

1. We all now know that America was not discovered first by Europeans. There were already people living in America when Columbus reached it, in 1492. These native Americans were called Indians by the Spanish newcomers. The Spanish believed they had reached India. Some early explorers found traces of highly developed Indian civilizations. As early as 1500 B.C., Indians in Mexico had gathered in villages. They had learned to farm the land. At this time, ancient Egypt was at the height of its power.

2. Native Americans (American Indians) most likely came to North America from Asia. It is believed that 25,000 years ago Asia and North America were connected by land. Today, a narrow body of water, the Bering Strait, separates Asia from Alaska. These early Americans moved slowly south. A small number remained in what is now Alaska, Canada, and the United States. When Columbus first reached America, 90 percent of all Native Americans were living in Central and South America. The oceans kept these early American people apart from Europe, Asia, and Africa. In the Americas, rivers and mountains kept people apart. Because of this, different Native American groups developed different languages and cultures.

3. Wherever Native Americans lived, they made use of the land as they found it. For example, the Inuit (IN-oo-it), or Eskimos, hunted wolves, deer, and seal in the frozen north. These gave them food, clothing, and tools. Other Native Americans lived in warmer regions in what is now the United States. Some roamed across the plains to hunt for animals as food. Others raised corn and squash. About 1,000 years ago, the Cahokian (kah-HOH-kee-un) Indians built over a hundred huge mounds near what is now East St. Louis, Illinois. Homes and temples stood on them. The largest of these mounds may be the largest structure made of earth in the world. It is known as Monk's mound. The southwest was the home of Pueblo tribes. These Native Americans lived in homes of stone or sun-dried bricks called *adobe* (ah-DOH-bee) in Spanish. In Chaco Canyon, New Mexico, remains of huge structures where thousands lived have been found. Their stone walls contain hundreds of rooms. One writer has called it the "largest apartment house in America before 1900." About the year A.D. 1000, the residents of the area left. There are no signs of battle. Why everybody left is still a mystery.

4. Unlike the early Asian civilizations, the important civilizations of America did not develop around river valleys. The Mayans (MAH-yuns) lived on the Yucatan (yoo-kah-

TAN) peninsula of modern Mexico and in Central America. They lived in a hot climate and had to fight against the jungle. Most of them were farmers who worked with simple tools. They practiced a kind of agriculture called *stick farming*. In this system, a clearing was made in the jungle. Then holes were dug with wooden sticks, and crops were planted. When the jungle grew back in the clearing, the farmers simply moved to another clearing. Stick farming is still done in the jungles of Central and South America and Africa today.

WHAT WERE THE ACHIEVEMENTS OF THE MAYANS OF MEXICO?

5. The Mayans, like other American Indians, did not have a potter's wheel or wheeled carts. Nor did they use animals to pull their heavy loads or do their work. Yet they built cities whose streets were paved with stone. Stone buildings and monuments to their gods show the Mayan ability as builders.

6. Like all the ancient civilized people, the Mayans were religious. Their greatest buildings were pyramids, which they used as religious temples. Stairs took the worshippers to the tops of the pyramids, and offerings to the gods were made on altars. The Mayans did not bury their dead in their pyramids, as did the ancient Egyptians. They used their temples for prayer and offerings. Very often, human beings were killed on the altars as offerings to the gods.

7. The priests were the best educated Mayans. Besides being priests, they were scholars in many fields. The Mayans invented a system of arithmetic based on the number 20. Their calendar was more exact than any yet developed in other ancient civilizations. Using a remarkable system of mathematics, they figured out that a year was made up of 365 days.

WHO WERE THE AZTECS?

8. On a lake island where Mexico City now stands, the *Aztecs* built their capital city of Tenochtitlán (Tan-oak-teh-TLAN). The Aztecs were more warlike than the Mayans. The Aztecs had conquered neighboring tribes and controlled almost all of southern Mexico by the time the first Spanish explorers arrived. Tenochtitlán was the center of their empire. Roads connected this island capital with the lands south of the city. Drawbridges connected it with the lands across the water.

9. Most Aztecs were farmers. Corn and potatoes, unknown to the people of Europe at that time, were their chief crops. The Aztecs were good crafts workers who made things out of gold, silver, and copper. Neither they nor any of the other American Indians knew about bronze or iron.

10. The Aztecs worshipped many gods. They guided their lives by their religious beliefs. The Aztecs practiced human sacrifice more than other peoples. Prisoners of war and slaves were often killed upon their temple altars. When a new temple was finished about 1500, more than 20,000 people were sacrificed on its altars. The Spanish conquerors were surprised that the Aztec religion was so bloody, while their city was so beautiful.

Here, a modern man performs a sacrificial dance before the Altar of Sacrifice in Chichen Itza. The sculpture dates back to the early Mayan cultures.

WHAT KIND OF CULTURE DID THE INCAS BUILD IN THE MOUNTAINS?

11. The *Incas*, who lived in the Andes Mountains of Peru, Ecuador, and Bolivia, developed a civilization even greater than that of the Aztecs. The climate of the Andes was cooler than the climates in which the Mayans or the Aztecs lived. The Incas were skilled people. They learned to farm their hilly lands with the help of irrigation. On the mountainside, they built terraces, level plots of land set one above another, like steps. The government owned all the land, and gave the people plots of land to farm. Corn and potatoes were the chief crops.

12. Although they lived in a mountainous country, the Incas were united by their government and their fine roads. The ruler was called the Inca. Governors were in charge of each part of the empire. Roads and bridges were built through the mountains and across valleys and rivers. These roads, connecting all parts of the Inca empire, were probably the best in the world at that time. Inca buildings showed how highly skilled the people were. Stones, cut and polished, fit together perfectly. Today we can see ruins of the Inca cities. The ancient capital city at Cuzco, in Peru, is one of the most famous ruins.

13. Despite their great network of highways and bridges, the Incas did not know about the use of the wheel. Runners carried messages to all parts of the kingdom. The runners worked in relays and never seemed to get tired. Messages could be sent more than 1,000 miles within a week. The llama, a woolly mountain animal, was sometimes used to carry heavy loads. But most carrying was done by human beings. Before the New World was discovered by Europeans, the Incas were the only American Indians to use animals to do work.

14. Like other Indian peoples, the Incas believed in many gods. The sun god was the most important god of their religion. They believed that their emperor, the Inca, was descended from the sun god. The Incas built temples and offered sacrifices to their gods. But they rarely sacrificed humans. They had a great deal of gold and silver. It was this gold and silver that the Spanish conquerors were seeking when they came to Peru, shortly after 1500. The Inca civilization was highly developed. There were doctors, dentists, jewelers, and clothing makers among the people. The Incas had a simple calendar, not nearly so accurate as those of the Mayans and Aztecs. They had no system of writing. Instead they used strings of different colors to send messages.

SUMMARIZING ANCIENT CIVILIZATIONS

15. In your study of the great civilizations of the ancient world, you have probably noted some important ways in which these civilizations were alike or different. You have learned that farming was the chief work of the people

The ruins of Machu Picchu give evidence of a highly developed culture. What in the picture supports that statement?

of all these civilizations. All ancient people were deeply religious. Usually they believed in many gods. The Hebrews were the first people to believe in one god. All built great monuments or temples. The civilizations of Native Americans began much later than those of ancient Egypt, Mesopotamia, India, and China. Until Columbus came to America, in 1492, the Indians did not know about the use of bronze, iron tools, or the wheel.

Testing Your Vocabulary

Choose the best answer.

1. A *sacrifice*, as used in this chapter, may best be described as
   a. a way of getting rid of goods and animals.
   b. belief in a religious idea.
   c. an offering to the gods.

2. In paragraph 11, the word *terraces* means
   a. an outdoor living area, near a house.
   b. a flat roof on a house.
   c. step-like plots of land for planting crops.

3. In paragraph 13, the *"network of highways"* means a set of roads that were
   a. large and costly.
   b. spread out in all directions.
   c. narrow and poorly built.

Understanding What You Have Read

1. A good title for paragraphs 8 through 10 might be
   a. The Sun God of the Americas
   b. Religions of the American Indians
   c. The Civilization of the Aztecs
   d. Indians of North America

2. In which paragraph do you find facts about
   a. the Aztec practice of sacrificing humans?
   b. the Inca use of the llama to do work?
   c. the Mayan development of an exact calendar?
   d. the building skills of the Incas?

3. Spanish explorers were surprised by the Aztec civilization because
   a. they found the same crops that were being grown in Europe.
   b. the Aztec buildings and cities were very beautiful.
   c. the Aztecs had learned to use iron tools.

4. By the time European explorers came to America,
   a. Native Americans were using wheeled carts to trade with each other.
   b. most Native Americans were living in Central and South America.
   c. Native Americans in North America had begun to use one language.

5. The Incas did not use wheels because
   a. they did not know about them.
   b. they did not need them for the work they did.
   c. wooden wheels did not last long on the rough roads.

6. Spanish conquerors were interested in the Indian civilizations in America mainly because
   a. they could sell the fine Indian cotton and silk goods in Europe.
   b. the Indians could direct them to the riches of the plains of North America.

c. the Indians had a great deal of gold and silver.

7. The American Indians were like the people of the early civilizations of Asia and Africa in that

a. they all guided their lives by their religious beliefs.

b. they all used the same kinds of tools and methods of transportation.

c. they began at about the same time.

Developing Ideas and Skills

USING A MAP

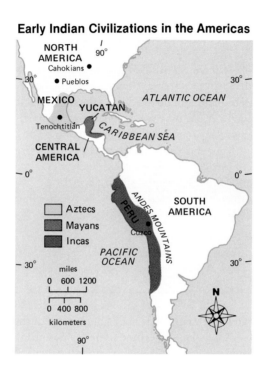

Early Indian Civilizations in the Americas

Study the map carefully. For each statement, write **T** in your notebook if the statement is correct; write **F** if the statement is not correct; write **N** if there is not enough information on the map to help us decide whether or not the statement is correct.

1. Tenochtitlán was the center of the Mayan civilization.
2. Spanish explorers traveled around the tip of South America to reach Peru.
3. The civilizations shown here were the only large Indian groups in the Americas.
4. The Inca empire lay along a coast.
5. The people of the three Indian civilizations in Central and South America traded with one another.
6. All of these civilizations were located along the western coast of America.
7. Only the Incas lived in South America.
8. The Incas lived in a larger area than the Aztecs or the Mayans.

Summary of Unit I

A few of the most important ideas, events, and facts in this unit are listed below. Can you add any others?

1. Where people live influences the way they live.
2. Knowledge of the past is based upon remains, written records, stories, and legends which have been handed down through the centuries.
3. The first great civilizations developed along river valleys.
4. The taming of animals and the beginning of farming were the two chief reasons why early people were able to settle in one place.
5. The Code of Hammurabi is important because it was the first written code of laws.
6. Religious beliefs have often been a strong force in determining how ancient people lived.
7. As time passed, ideas and goods were exchanged between some early civilizations. Each civilization borrowed something from others.
8. The Chinese and Japanese civilizations developed at different times, but both were isolated from the civilizations of the Middle East.
9. The history of African civilization has been made known to us only recently, largely because there are few written records.
10. Native American civilizations did not know of some of the discoveries and inventions of ancient Asian and African cultures.

Making Generalizations

It is important to know many facts about the history of the world. But by themselves, facts have little value. They do not become useful to us until we can put them together—until we can see larger patterns and draw conclusions based on a number of facts. We know, for example, that the early Mesopotamian civilization was founded near rivers. This is a fact. We also know that both the early Egyptian and the early Chinese civilizations were located near rivers. From these statements, we can see a pattern. We can express it in a sentence: Several early civilizations began near rivers. We call this broader statement a *generalization*. We can then ask: Why was this true? Why wasn't it true of the Incas? Is it true of cultures developing today? Thus our generalization has opened up avenues to understanding more about the history of human kind.

There is a danger in making generalizations. We can make generalizations that are not accurate. For example, you may have heard someone say: "Everyone likes to dance." You know this statement is not true. There are some people who do not like to dance. It would be more accurate to say: "Many people like to dance." In the example in the first paragraph, we could not say: "All early civilizations began along rivers." Why would this not be an accurate statement?

In each of the following exercises, read the three factual statements. Then make one accurate generalization based on those statements.

A. Factual statements:
1. The Egyptians lined their temples with statues of their gods.
2. The Hebrews developed a religion based on a belief in one God.
3. The Mayans offered human sacrifices to please their gods.
Generalization:

B. Factual statements:
1. The Incas developed their great civilization high in the mountains of South America.
2. Mesopotamian civilization developed around fertile river valleys.
3. The Phoenicians, great sailors and traders, settled along the Mediterranean Sea.
Generalization:

TURNING POINTS

Culture

Asia: Uncovering the Past

Sometimes it takes hard work and many years to uncover the remains of an ancient world. This is the case with the tomb of the Chinese emperor Shi Huang-di.

Shi died in 210 B.C. According to historians of early China, 700,000 laborers worked for over 36 years to build the emperor's burial chamber. The story of his tomb was passed down through ancient writings and tales. People wondered if the tomb was real or just a legend. In 1974, the mystery was solved when a well digger accidentally discovered the site. Soon afterward, a team of workers began to explore the tomb. What they found was truly amazing.

There is an army of warriors guarding the tomb. Each warrior is six feet tall and is made of clay. No two look alike. Some look fierce. Others seem to be smiling. Royal war chariots were also found. Each one is pulled by four full-size clay horses. The soldier's weapons had been treated with chemicals to preserve them. After 22 centuries, most of the swords are still unbroken.

The burial site spreads out over 21 square miles. Some people think that as many as 30,000 figures may be there. There also are stories of a fabulous jeweled coffin. In years to come, more will be known about Shi, his tomb, and the people he ruled.

Critical Thinking

1. What can you tell about the skills of the ancient Chinese people?
2. What do such preparations for death suggest about Shi's beliefs about life after death?

UNIT II

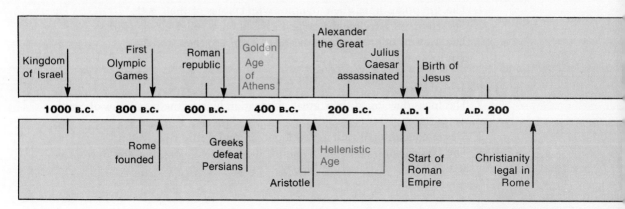

3500 B.C.	2500 B.C.	1500 B.C.	500 B.C.	A.D. 500	A.D. 1500
3000 B.C.	2000 B.C.	1000 B.C.	A.D. 1	A.D. 1000	A.D. 2000

Kingdom of Israel

First Olympic Games

Roman republic

Golden Age of Athens

Alexander the Great

Julius Caesar assassinated

Birth of Jesus

| 1000 B.C. | 800 B.C. | 600 B.C. | 400 B.C. | 200 B.C. | A.D. 1 | A.D. 200 |

Rome founded

Greeks defeat Persians

Aristotle

Hellenistic Age

Start of Roman Empire

Christianity legal in Rome

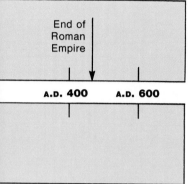

End of
Roman
Empire

A.D. 400   A.D. 600

What Do We Owe to the Ancient Greeks and Romans?

**A temple from ancient Greece overlooks the
Mediterranean Sea.**

67

AIM: How did geography play a part in the early development of ancient Greece?

CHAPTER 1

Greece: Land by the Sea

WHAT KIND OF CIVILIZATION DEVELOPED IN CRETE?

1. When we want to cross a small stream it is good to find a place in the water where there are several stones. We can then step from one stone to another to reach the opposite side. These "stepping stones" connect the shores of the stream. Throughout history, people have used stepping stones or connecting points to travel from one place to another. The island of Crete, in the Mediterranean Sea, and the smaller islands of the Aegean (ih-JEE-un) Sea are examples of some historic stepping stones.

2. Crete is close both to Greece and to Egypt. (See map, page 10.) Not long ago, ruins of an ancient civilization were uncovered on Crete. This civilization dates back to 3000 B.C. The ruins of the city of Knossos (NOS-us), the capital, showed that the city had great palaces. There were paintings on walls, plumbing in homes, and even pipes carrying drinking water. This was a rich civilization. The people of Crete traded with Egypt, Asia Minor, and the lands of Asia near the Mediterranean. (Cretans appear in paintings found on the walls of ancient Egyptian monuments.) The paintings of the ancient Cretan people tell us much about their life. Because their land was not very fer-

tile, the Cretans turned to the sea for a living. They traded olive oil, pottery, and bronze goods for the copper, gold, and silver found in other parts of the ancient world.

Decorated doorway from the palace of Knossos in Crete. What can you tell about the culture of Crete from this picture and the one on page 69?

HOW DID CRETAN CULTURE SPREAD TO GREECE?

3. Greece was still wild and unsettled when Cretan civilization was at its height. Early invaders from the north found that the land in Greece was not fertile. Mountains covered much of Greece, and the soil in the valleys was not good for farming. Trade, therefore, rather than farming, became important to the early people of Greece. They traded with Crete. Soon, they borrowed the customs and habits of the Cretans, as well as their system of writing. The Greeks built their tombs in the style used in Crete. They even painted on the walls of their buildings as did the Cretans. Cretan culture became part of Greek culture.

4. In ancient Greece, as in other civilizations, geography played an important part. Greece is a peninsula. It is small and mountainous. It has many smaller peninsulas. Everywhere, it seems, water is near. At its widest part, Greece is but 100 miles across. It was natural, therefore, for a growing Greek population to move to nearby islands. Some moved to Asia Minor, Sicily, and Italy. As a result, Greeks came into contact with the people of Phoenicia, Egypt, and Syria. As we saw, Greeks took their alphabet from the Phoenicians.

5. Trade is important in spreading customs and learning. Greek customs and learning began to spread throughout the Mediterranean world. Trade with the people living near the Aegean Sea and then with Asia Minor brought

This photo of the palace of Knossos shows the columns and ornate walls surrounding the courtyard.

the Greeks into contact with the city of Troy, about 1200 B.C. The Greeks attacked this city in Asia Minor and defeated its army. The story of the battle of Troy and what happened afterward was made famous by the Greek poet Homer in *The Iliad* and *The Odyssey*.

6. Mountains and waters divided Greece into many small parts. It was not easy, therefore, for people to unite under one rule. City-states, separate towns like those in Mesopotamia, developed. The city-states were small. Compared with cities of today, they had few people. In 750 B.C., most Greek city-states had no more than 5,000 people. The city-states were independent of one another. Each had its own government. Not all the governments were of the same kind.

The story of the Trojan horse is famous. According to the myth, the Greek soldiers hid in the wooden horse. Once inside the walls of Troy, they rushed out and captured the city.

WHAT MADE ATHENS A DEMOCRACY?

7. Two of the most famous Greek city-states were Athens and Sparta. Athens was ruled sometimes by kings, called tyrants, and sometimes by small groups of aristocrats, men of noble birth. But ancient Athens is best remembered for another kind of government: democracy. The free citizens of Athens were the government. About 590 B.C., Solon (SOH-lon), one of ancient Greece's great rulers, gave a group of Athenian citizens the power to pass laws. Later rulers gave the people even greater freedom.

8. Athens had what we would call a *direct democracy.* All citizens could vote on laws. The United States, Great Britain, and Canada have *representative democracies.* That is, citizens elect representatives who pass the laws. Because ancient Athens had a small population, it was possible for all males to take part in passing laws. In the United States, there are millions of citizens. It is not possible for all of them to take part in passing laws, so they elect representatives. Only males were citizens of Athens. Women, slaves, and people born in other cities were not allowed to become citizens. There were always more non-citizens than citizens in Athens. Ancient Athens did not have what we would call a complete democracy.

9. All citizens of Athens were members of the General Assembly, which made the laws. As Athens grew, this meant that several thousand men might vote on such matters as spending money or declaring war. This was too large a number to gather at one time. Therefore, a Council of Five Hundred was chosen by lot among the citizens. The council divided itself so that there was always one group on duty. It chose its own officers. But all citizens had a chance to serve their city in different ways. The Athenians believed that every citizen was able to take part in running the government. Moreover, it was the duty of every citizen to take such a role.

10. All citizens of Athens were expected to serve on juries in court cases. Jurors were paid well so they could leave their work while they served on a jury. A jury might have from 201 to 501 members. The number was made large on purpose. It was felt that in this way no one could bribe enough jurors to change a decision. The more serious a case was, the more jurors were needed for it. As many as 1,000 jurors served on some cases.

11. Athenians loved their city. They tried to work, study, and improve themselves for the good of Athens. Each citizen received two years of military training. This insured that the city would be properly protected in time of danger.

HOW DID SPARTA DIFFER FROM ATHENS?

12. In spirit, the city-state of Sparta (see map, page 73) was quite different from Athens. Spartans were more warlike people. They, too, made slaves of the people they conquered. Later, they forced neighboring people to work as slaves for them. Spartan slaves were called *helots* (HEL-uts). Because their lives were so miserable, helots were always ready to revolt. This may be one reason why Sparta had to be a strong military state.

13. The Spartan government was run by a small group of men. They controlled the lives of the Spartan people. Today we would call such a government a *totalitarian* government. All of life in Sparta centered on the military. Every male baby was examined to see if he was completely healthy. If he was not, or seemed to be weak, he was taken to a mountainside and left to die. For if a boy could not become a good soldier, he was thought to be of no use to Sparta.

14. At the age of 7, boys were sent to community training centers. Here they lived separated from their parents until they were 30. The training of young Spartans was tough. They ran, wrestled, swam, and fought. They were beaten so they would learn to endure pain. In battle, a Spartan soldier was expected to win or die. Girls, too, received athletic training. But this ended with marriage.

15. Spartans had little time for art, literature, or philosophy. Sparta's chief concern was war. No ideas from Athens or other city-states were allowed to enter Sparta. Trade was discouraged, for trade brings ideas. It is amazing what the Spartans did to make trade difficult. Instead of using gold coins as other Greeks did, Spartans used heavy iron bars for money. With such money, not many citizens could carry a pocketful of change.

Testing Your Vocabulary

Choose the best answer.

1. *Aristocrats* are
   a. people of noble birth.
   b. rulers who have complete power.
   c. those who make changes in government.
2. In a *totalitarian* government
   a. all people vote and anyone can hold office.
   b. no trade with other people is allowed.
   c. people's lives are controlled by the rulers.
3. *Helots* in Sparta were
   a. soldiers.
   b. doctors.
   c. slaves.

Understanding What You Have Read

1. The main idea in paragraph 4 is that
   a. Greece is small and mountainous.
   b. the development of Greece was influenced by the country's geography.
   c. Phoenicia influenced Greece.
   d. the early Greeks moved to nearby islands.
2. In which paragraph do you find facts about
   a. contact between Greece and Crete?
   b. the workings of the jury system in Athens?
   c. the training of young boys in Sparta?
   d. Spartan ideas on trade?
3. It was difficult for Greek people to become united because
   a. they had different religious beliefs.
   b. mountains made communication between city-states difficult.
   c. fertile farm land kept the Greeks tied to their own little plots of land.
4. Small, separate city-states developed in ancient Greece because
   a. Greek travelers in Egypt had seen city-states.
   b. its geography made it difficult for large groups of people to live together.
   c. Greeks from different cities worshipped different gods.
5. One of the reasons why the Greeks traded a great deal with Asia Minor was that
   a. their land was so poor for farming that the Greeks had to become traders rather than farmers.
   b. Asian iron was needed to make Greek weapons.
   c. cities of Asia Minor had defeated the Greeks.
6. One way in which the democracy of ancient Athens differed from democracy as we know it today is that
   a. trial by jury was not allowed.
   b. not everyone in Athens could become a citizen.
   c. the General Assembly did not represent the people of the city.
7. Another way in which democracy in ancient Athens was different from democracy in the United States today is that
   a. citizens and non-citizens made laws in Athens.
   b. both men and women took part in making laws in Athens.
   c. all citizens took a direct part in making laws in Athens.

For each of the following statements, write *A* in your notebook if the statement is about Athens only; write *S* if it is about Sparta only; write *B* if the statement is about *both* Athens and Sparta.

1. All citizens served on juries.
2. Only good soldiers were important to the city.
3. A great deal of trade was carried on.
4. Life centered on the military.
5. Citizens took turns in holding government office.
6. All persons were expected to be loyal to their city.
7. It was a totalitarian state.
8. It was a direct democracy.
9. Defeat in battle was a disgrace to a soldier.
10. The citizens were interested in art, literature and philosophy.

Developing Ideas and Skills

USING A MAP

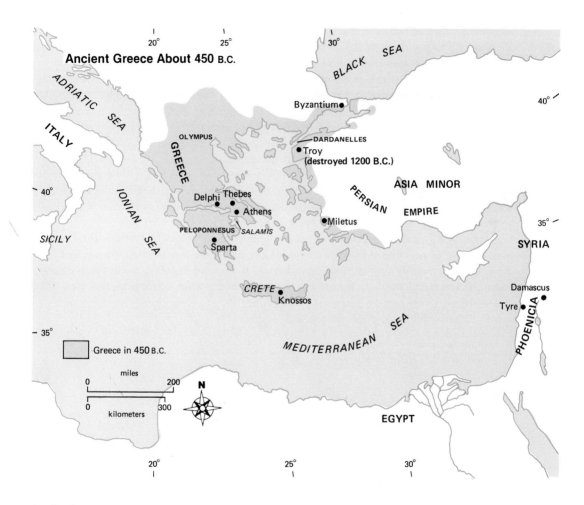

Ancient Greece About 450 B.C.

Study the map carefully. Then tell whether these statements are true or false.

1. Few important Greek cities were located in northern Greece.
2. Athens and Sparta were both located on the peninsula called the Peloponnesus (pel-uh-puh-NEE-sus).
3. Neither Athens nor Sparta was a seaport.
4. The Greeks controlled parts of Asia Minor in 450 B.C.
5. The Greeks controlled the water route from the Mediterranean Sea to the Black Sea.
6. Mount Olympus is located near the important Greek cities.
7. Some Greeks settled on the island of Crete.

Building Your Vocabulary

Many English words are made up of parts of words from other languages. Some of the words we hear, speak, or read every day are made up of *prefixes* and *roots* that have come down to us from ancient Greek. A prefix is one or more letters placed at the beginning of a word stem to make up a word. For example, the word *semicircle* is formed by placing the prefix *semi-* at the beginning of the stem *-circle-*. The prefix *semi-* means *half;* so the word *semicircle* means *half a circle.*

A root is a basic word, or word stem, that other words come from. For example, *-log-* is a Greek root meaning either *study* or *word.* From it we get many English words. We saw three of these words in Chapter 1 of the Introduction: *anthropologist, archaeologist,* and *geologist.* Each refers to somebody who *studies* something. An anthropologist studies the ways of life of human beings. An archaeologist usually studies the remains of their culture. A geologist studies the history of the earth.

If you learn just a small number of Greek prefixes and roots you will be able to figure out the meanings of many hundreds of new or hard English words. In the chapters that follow, you will have the opportunity to learn some of these word parts. You will be able to practice using them to build up your vocabulary. But let's start now.

The Greek prefix *mono-* means *one, single,* or *alone.* The Greek root *-theo-* means *god.* In the chapter "Other Peoples of the Middle East," we learned that the ancient Jews were the first people to practice monotheism. If you did not know what *monotheism* meant, you would be able to figure it out from knowing what its parts meant. Now take this sentence: *Other peoples practiced polytheism. Poly-* is a Greek prefix meaning *many* or *much.* What would you guess *polytheism* means?

a. human sacrifice
b. belief in a life after death
c. belief in many gods
d. ancestor worship

The letter *a-* is a Greek prefix meaning *no, not, without.* In the sentence *Some people accept atheism,* what do you think the word *atheism* means?

a. belief in two gods
b. communism
c. belief that there is no God
d. belief that God is good

Recall what the prefix *mono-* and what the root *-log-* mean. What does the word *monologue* mean in the sentence *The comedian's act was one long monologue?*

a. a talk by one speaker
b. conversation between two speakers
c. pantomime
d. a story performed by a puppet

Can you think of any other words that begin with the prefix *mono-,* meaning *one, single,* or *alone?*

AIMS: How did the Greek city-states unite to defeat their enemies? How was Greek culture spread to other lands?

CHAPTER 2

Unity and Victory; Division and Defeat

WHAT DID THE CITY-STATES HAVE IN COMMON?

1. The Greek city-states were much like a family. Although they were separated from each other, all were Greek. They shared a pride in being Greek. They worshipped the same gods. The Greeks felt their gods were much like humans. Their gods were part of one great family. Zeus (ZOOS) was the father of the gods. Athena was the goddess of wisdom. Apollo was the god of music and poetry. Ares was the god of war. (Later, the Romans worshipped the Greek gods. But they gave Roman names to the gods. The family of Greek gods was believed to live on top of Mount Olympus, in northern Greece.

2. The Greek gods were different from the gods of other people we have studied. The Greeks thought it was possible to ask questions of their gods. Both the answers the gods gave and the places where they gave them were called *oracles*. The oracles were spoken by priests and priestesses who had received answers from the gods. Often the answers were not clear but clouded in mystery. So those people who asked a question had to figure out as best they could the meaning of what was spoken. However, the gods often advised people to do everything in moderation; that is, to take a middle road between too much and too little. The most famous oracle was in the city of Delphi.

3. To honor Zeus, father of gods, the Greeks held athletic contests. These began in 776 B.C. They were held at the foot of Mount

The battle of Salamis was a great victory for Greece against its Persian enemies.

Olympus and were called Olympic games. Men from each of the city-states met every four years and took part in different events. They raced, jumped, and threw the discus and javelin. Horse and chariot races were part of the program. Winners at the games were looked up to as heroes and received special awards. The Olympic games were important beause they helped to unite the Greek people. Today's Olympic games are also held every four years. Nations from all over the world take part. The modern Olympics are based on the early Greek games.

WHAT WERE THE RESULTS OF THE PERSIAN WARS?

4. Like members of a family, the city-states sometimes did not get along with one another. Their disputes, at times, led to war. But no matter how much members of a family may quarrel, they seem to unite and help each other when threatened. That is what happened when Darius, the emperor of Persia, threatened Greece. The Greek city-states in Asia Minor were conquered by Darius, despite help from other Greek cities, including Athens. Finally, Darius decided to invade Greece itself. Again, the Greek cities joined together to defeat the enemy.

5. Persia tried to invade Greece in 492 B.C., but a storm destroyed the Persian fleet. The Persians returned in 490 B.C., landing at Marathon, north of Athens. The Spartans were celebrating a feast at this time. So the Athenians met the Persians alone. The brave men of Athens routed the Persian army. Darius was forced to return to Persia. The Greek victory at Marathon is one of the great battles of world history. Thanks to it, Greek civilization survived. The news of the victory was brought to Athens by a runner who raced the entire way, more than 25 miles. The modern marathon race gets its name from that event.

6. For ten years, Greece was at peace. Then Xerxes (ZURK-seez), son of Darius, sent a Persian army into Greece once more. The Persians crossed from Asia to Europe over the Dardanelles, the strait that separates the two continents. (See map, page 12.) The Persian navy attacked Greece. The Spartans under Leonidas met the Persians in the northern mountains. For three days, the Spartans held back the large Persian army at a mountain pass called Thermopylae (thur-MOP-uh-lee). Then a traitor told the Persians of a way around the pass. The Spartans were overcome. Trapped, they fought until the last man died. The Persians then marched on to Athens and burned the city. However, in a naval battle at Salamis (SAL-uh-mis), the ships of Athens defeated the Persian fleet. The Persians returned to their homeland. The next year, a combined Greek army defeated the Persian land force. Thus, the threat of Persian power was ended.

7. The Greeks now decided that they had to be united to protect themselves from invaders. They formed a league of city-states called the Delian (DEE-lee-un) League. The headquarters was located on the Greek island of Delos (DEE-los). Athens gave the most money and troops to the league of city-states. Soon it became the most powerful member of the

Battle of Thermopylae 480 B.C.

league. All of Greece became little more than an empire of Athens. Athenian power and trade spread across the Aegean Sea. Great wealth poured into Athens. The city began a period of great cultural growth. Historians call this period the Golden Age of Greece.

HOW DID WARS PUT AN END TO THE GOLDEN AGE OF ATHENS?

8. Pericles was the leader of Athens during its great age of power and glory, from 460 to 429 B.C. Great temples were built. *Sculptors* made statues showing the Greek idea of beauty. *Dramatists* wrote plays that were produced in outdoor theaters. Historians wrote the story of Greek cities for the first time. Scientists and philosophers studied and taught. The Golden Age of Greece was the greatest civilization that had developed up to that time. You will read about many of the famous works of Athenians in Chapter 3.

9. War between Athens and Sparta brought an end to the Golden Age. Small Greek cities had begun to fear the growing power of Athens. They asked Sparta to help them. In 432 B.C., Sparta declared war on Athens. The wars between the two cities lasted for thirty years. Many cities were ruined. During the wars, a plague broke out and spread through Athens. Thousands, including Pericles, died. Finally, Sparta was able to conquer Athens. It then tried to control all of Greece just as Athens had done. New wars broke out, and Sparta was defeated by other cities. Soon there was no city powerful enough to lead the other city-states. Once again, Greece was disunited and weak.

HOW DID ALEXANDER HELP TO SPREAD GREEK POWER AND CULTURE?

10. To the north of Greece lies a province called Macedonia. Philip, ruler of Macedonia,

Bronze statues such as this one of Athena flying her owl show the beauty and skill of Greek art. The statue is less than six inches in height, yet the artist has achieved great detail.

saw the weakness of Greek cities and decided to conquer them. Demosthenes (dih-MOS-thuh-neez), the great orator of Athens, warned the Greeks that Philip was about to attack. But the Greeks had already lived through too much war. They were unable to unite against their enemy. Philip invaded the Greek peninsula with a well-trained army. His soldiers were protected with iron armor. Their catapults hurled stones against the Greek volunteers and over walls. Their battering rams broke down the walls of Greek cities. By 346 B.C., Philip was master of Greece.

11. Philip was followed as ruler by his 20-year-old son, Alexander. As a young boy, Alexander had been taught by the great Greek philosopher Aristotle. As a result, Alexander grew to love Greek art, drama, and ideas. But he is best remembered as a soldier. He conquered so much land in Europe, Asia, and Africa that he became known as Alexander the Great.

12. Alexander defeated the Persians in Asia Minor. Next, he freed Egypt from Persian rule. Crossing the Tigris and Euphrates rivers, he made himself king of Persia. His march eastward continued to the Indus River, in India. But his soldiers refused to go any farther. They feared that Alexander had come to love Persian culture and had forgotten he was Greek. Alexander returned to Persia with his homesick troops. He died suddenly in Persia after a short illness. He was 33 when he died.

13. Winning battles and conquering lands were not Alexander's only successes. Wherever he went, he brought Greek customs and learning. He founded cities that became centers of culture for hundreds of years. Alexandria, in Egypt, and Antioch, in Asia Minor, were two of these cities. Alexander brought together the cultures of East and West. Trade increased between Greece and Persia. People moved from Greece to Asia Minor. The cultures of Greece and Persia were mixed. This mixture produced a new type of culture, and the Hellenstic Age began.

14. Alexander's empire was the largest the world had known. No one was prepared to rule this vast territory after his death. It was finally divided into three parts. Each section was ruled by one of his generals. Two hundred years of disorder followed. Then the Romans came, and Greek culture was spread to the lands of the western Mediterranean Sea.

Testing Your Vocabulary

Choose the best answer.

1. An *oracle*, as used in paragraph 2, is
   a. one who tells what the future will be.
   b. a god.
   c. a message from the gods.
2. Philip of Macedonia used *a machine that hurled stones over city walls*. It was called a
   a. sling.
   b. catapult.
   c. battering ram.
3. A *marathon* race is one that
   a. is run in relays.
   b. brings bad news.
   c. covers a long distance.
4. *Dramatists*
   a. plan warfare.
   b. make statues.
   c. write plays.

Understanding What You Have Read

1. A good title for paragraph 9 is
   a. Spartan Bravery
   b. Athens, Leader of Greece
   c. The Rise and Fall of Sparta
   d. Pericles, Leader of the Golden Age
2. In which paragraph do you find facts about
   a. the beginning of the Olympic games?
   b. the reasons why Athens and Sparta went to war?
   c. Alexander's love of Greek culture?
   d. The meaning of Hellenistic Age?
3. The Delian League, an organization of Greek city-states, was set up in order to

   a. make Athens the leading Greek city-state.
   b. end wars among the city-states.
   c. protect city-states against attack from Persia.
4. Philip of Macedonia was able to conquer the Greek city-states because
   a. Persian rule had weakened the Greeks.
   b. Alexander was fighting in Asia and could not send his armies to help against Philip.
   c. the city-states had been weakened by war and could not unite.

Developing Ideas and Skills

USING A MAP

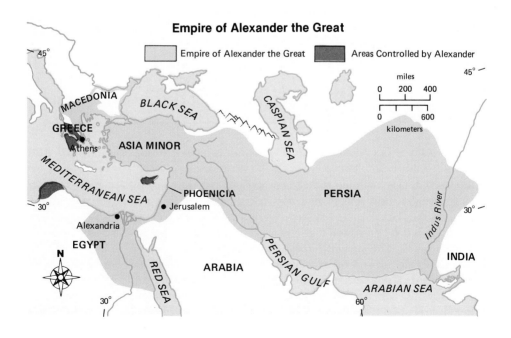

Empire of Alexander the Great

Empire of Alexander the Great   Areas Controlled by Alexander

Study the map carefully. Then tell whether the statements are true or false.

1. Not all of India was part of Alexander's empire.
2. Territories of both the Hebrews and the Phoenicians were part of Alexander's empire.
3. Alexander's homeland, Macedonia, was in Asia Minor.
4. Alexander's empire went mainly south and west of Macedonia.
5. Alexander's empire was near all the important water routes of the Middle East.

Using Exact Language

In reading history or in discussing ideas in class, you may find expressions that mean different things to different people. For example, if we said, "*In ancient times*, persons accused of crimes were proven to be innocent," what would be meant by *in ancient times?* What period of time are we talking about? When did *ancient times* begin and end?

You can test this in class. Ask the other members of your class to join you in writing down the years you think of when you read such expressions as these:

many years ago	in the Middle Ages
recently	in the days of knighthood
a few centuries ago	in modern times
early in Greek history	in the 5th century

After you have written down your dates, compare them with those of your classmates. Do you all agree on the meaning of these frequently used expressions? How much difference is there in the dates you gave from those of your classmates?

Do you now see why, in the study of history and in class discussions, we are often asked to remember a few *exact* dates?

Building Your Vocabulary

A suffix is one or more letters added on to a root to make up a word. The word *dramatist,* for example, ends with the Greek suffix *-ist.* In this word, *-ist* means *doer.* A dramatist does something; namely, makes dramas. This suffix can also mean *believer.* That is its meaning in the word *monotheist.* A monotheist is one who believes in one god.

Another Greek suffix that appears in a great many English words is *-ism.* One of its meanings is *belief in something.* The word *polytheism* ends with this suffix. It means *belief in many gods.* The ancient Greeks were polytheists.

Give at least two words ending in the suffix *-ism* that you came upon in early chapters of this book. (Hint: two of them refer to religions that began in India.)

Now let's see whether knowing what the suffix *-ism* means can help you to figure out the meaning of a difficult word. In the sentence *Confucianism spread throughout China,* the word *Confucianism* means

a. the family of Confucius.
b. the followers of Confucius.
c. belief in what Confucius taught.
d. the sayings of Confucius.

The letters -zo- make up a Greek root meaning *animal*. With this in mind, answer the following question. A zoologist is

a. a fear of animals
b. a person who studies animals.
c. a disease caught from animals.
d. a home for animals.

TURNING POINTS

Culture

The World: History Through Stories

The history of a civilization is part of its culture. How is this history passed on? Today, we have many methods of recording the history of our time. There are books, tapes, films, and other methods. In ancient times there were storytellers. They told and retold tales of great heroes and their battles. These stories, or oral histories, became part of the memories of those who heard them. The Greek poet Homer had heard legends about the war between the Greeks and the people of Troy. The battles had been fought hundreds of years before his time. Homer retold these stories in the form of poems. In time, they were written down in the *Iliad* and *The Odyssey*.

There are other civilizations whose histories were passed down in stories. In Africa the *griots*, or storytellers, would retell the histories they had heard as children. Their ability was highly valued by the community. When people came together to celebrate a wedding or a successful harvest, they would listen to the griot's stories. These stories bound the community together in celebration of its past. The history of Africa is now part of written history. Historians have gathered much of it from men and women who repeated the griot's stories.

Critical Thinking

1. What qualities do the storytellers of Greece and the griots of Africa have in common?
2. In what ways do you think the stories of storytellers are different from what you read in a history book? In what ways do you think they are the same?

AIM: What were some important contributions of the Greeks to civilization?

CHAPTER 3

The Greeks Built a Remarkable Society

WHAT WAS GREEK CULTURE LIKE?

1. We know that trade and war helped to spread Greek civilization thousands of miles. What kind of culture was Greek culture? What great things did the Greeks do? During the Golden Age of Pericles, the people of Athens built one of the most beautiful buildings in the history of the world. This was the Parthenon, a temple dedicated to Athena, the goddess of wisdom. A statue of Athena, made by Phidias (FID-ee-us) was in the center of the temple. The Parthenon is located on the Acropolis (uh-KROP-uh-lis), a hill overlooking the city. It is made of white marble, and the stones fit to-gether perfectly. Evenly spaced columns surround the building. Its simple, balanced style became a model for some of our own finest government buildings. The Lincoln Memorial, for example, in Washington, D.C., is modeled after the Parthenon.

2. The Greeks thought that the human body was beautiful. They loved to carve statues representing it. Greek sculpture is known for its simple, graceful style. Greek sculptors tried to show the ideal human figure. Each part of the body was shaped as perfectly as possible. Greek statues were usually of athletes, gods, and goddesses. "The Discus Thrower," by Myron, is one of the most famous and beautiful Greek sculptures of an athlete.

A model of the Parthenon. Why do you think later civilizations built so many public buildings in this architectural style?

A Roman imitation of Myron's "Discus Thrower." Why do you think that this statue is one of the most admired works of art in the world?

3. Among the Greeks of the Golden Age of Athenian culture were the first historians. Herodotus (hir-ROD-uh-tus) is called the "father of history." He is the author of the first written history, the story of the Persian wars. He traveled throughout Egypt and Asia Minor. There he learned about the invasions of the Persians and the customs of the places he visited. In his history, he describes those customs that make the story interesting. Not all of his stories, however, are based on fact. Another historian, Thucydides (thoo-SID-i-deez), wrote of the wars between Athens and Sparta. His history is a careful and accurate account of these wars.

4. Drama was an important part of life in Athens. It was more than just entertainment. It was something like a community festival. (Women, however, did not act in the plays.) In fact, drama grew out of religious celebrations.

These were held in honor of the god Dionysus (dy-uh-NY-sus). Greek theaters were outdoors. The audience sat in semicircular rows of seats. The seating area was cut out of a hillside that overlooked the stage. The audience saw three plays called tragedies. A tragedy is a play in which the main character undergoes great suffering. The suffering may be caused by fate, a power that controls the future. Or it could be caused by a weakness in character. Usually these plays warned the audience not to be too sure of their luck. Sometimes they taught that human beings should not try to get more than ordinary life can give. After the three tragedies came a comedy. Greek comedies poked fun at human weaknesses. The three greatest dramatists of Athens were Aeschylus (ES-kuh-lus), Sophocles (SOF-uh-kleez), and Euripides (yoo-RIP-i-deez). Their plays are still performed today.

5. Also among the Greeks were the world's first great *philosophers*. Philosophy is the search for knowledge, truth, and wisdom. The great Greek philosophers tried to find out the meaning of things. Their ideas are still studied today. The three most famous are Socrates (SOK-ruh-teez), Plato (PLAY-toh), and Aristotle (AR-i-stot-ul).

6. Socrates lived about 400 B.C. He tried to teach the people around him to think and to understand. His method was to ask questions. When he got an answer, he would ask another question. These back-and-forth talks between Socrates and another person are called dialogues. "Know thyself," Socrates always told his students. But he became unpopular with powerful people in Athens. They thought that he was weakening the government by teaching the young to think for themselves. At last, he was put on trial and sentenced to death. Although he could have escaped, Socrates refused to break the law. He accepted the death sentence. He died by drinking poison made from a plant called hemlock.

7. Plato was a pupil of Socrates. Much of

Many Greek dramas are still performed today. This is a scene from *Oedipus Rex,* by Sophocles.

what we know about Socrates comes from the writings of Plato. Plato wrote dialogues in which Socrates is the main speaker. In some of these dialogues, Socrates expresses his own ideas. In others, Plato expresses *his* own ideas through Socrates. One of his greatest dialogues is the *Republic*. This is about the ideal state and how it would be governed. Plato's ideas about how people should live and what society should be like have been studied for over 2,000 years.

8. Aristotle studied under Plato and founded his own school. He was also the teacher of Alexander the Great. Aristotle was concerned with all areas of knowledge. Thanks to the notes his students kept, we know many of his ideas about art, nature, the universe, and human life. Our civilization has gotten from Aristotle many of its ideas about how to think correctly. The science of reasoning that Aristotle developed is called *logic*. Not only are Plato and Aristotle the greatest Greek philosophers, but they are also two of the most impor-

tant thinkers who have ever lived.

9. The Greeks were scientific. They tried to find reasons for the things that happened around them. Hippocrates (hih-POK-ruh-teez) is called the "father of medicine." He was probably the first to think of medicine as a science, and not as magic. He looked for the causes of diseases in nature. He turned to science for cures. He believed that a doctor should build up a patient's strength through good diet and other sensible methods. Today, new doctors take the Hippocratic oath. The oath calls upon doctors to practice medicine honorably and only for the cure of the sick.

10. The Greeks made important discoveries in mathematics and physics. Euclid (YOO-klid) set down the principles of geometry. Thales (THAY-leez) discovered how to tell when there would be an eclipse of the sun. Modern students of physics still study the teachings of Archimedes (ar-kuh-MEE-deez). He first explained the principle of the lever, by which we are able to move heavy objects. It was he who said, "Give me a place to stand with a lever long enough, and I will move the world."

ARE GREEK ACHIEVEMENTS ALIVE TODAY?

11. From ancient Greece came many important achievements. The Greeks were curious about life and its meaning. They thought about politics and about ways to improve government. In Athens, there was a democracy in which people enjoyed freedom as they never had before. Greek scientists showed people how to study the world around them in order to discover the truth about it. Greek writers and artists gave the world an idea of beauty as something simple and graceful. People today still look to ancient Greece, despite some of its weaknesses, as a model of civilization. Many of our ideas and ideals are based on the ideas and ideals of ancient Greece. Ancient Greek culture lives on as inspiration to us.

Testing Your Vocabulary _____

Choose the best answer.

1. When people argue logically, they
   a. speak loudly and clearly.
   b. use proper reasoning.
   c. have prepared themselves well.
2. Fate is
   a. weakness of character.
   b. a power that controls the future.
   c. the struggle to get more than ordinary life can give.
3. A tragedy is a play
   a. that pokes fun at the leaders of government.
   b. in which the main character undergoes great suffering.
   c. that is about people in an imaginary
   land.

Understanding What You Have Read _____

1. A good title for paragraphs 5 through 8
   might be
   a. What the Ancient Greeks Talked
   About
   b. The Death of Socrates
   c. Greek Education
   d. Three Great Minds
2. In which paragraphs do you find facts
   about
   a. the Greek temple called the Parthenon?
   b. Greek knowledge of mathematics
   and physics?
   c. ancient Greek drama?
   d. the meaning of philosophy?
3. Most plays by Greek dramatists were
   serious plays because
   a. the people of Athens had little to be
   happy about.
   b. Greeks thought deeply about life.
   c. slaves played most of the parts in the
   plays.
4. Aristotle is sometimes called the most
   brilliant man of the ancient world because he
   a. knew so much in many areas of
   knowledge.
   b. was Alexander's teacher.
   c. was the leader of Athens in its golden
   age.
5. Hippocrates is called the "father of
   medicine" because
   a. his oath is taken by our nurses today.
   b. he discovered how blood circulates in
   the body.
   c. he thought of medicine as science,
   not as magic.

Tell whether these statements are true or false. If the statement is false, change the words in italics to make it true.

1. Philosophy means *love of music.*
2. Greek plays were presented *outdoors.*
3. *Thucydides* was a philosopher who
   taught by asking questions.
4. The most beautiful building in ancient
   Athens was the *Temple of Zeus.*
5. Alexander was a pupil of *Aristotle.*

Match the items in the second column with the people in the first column.

1. Herodotus
2. Socrates
3. Plato
4. Aristotle
5. Archimedes
6. Hippocrates
7. Sophocles

a. known as the "father of medicine"
b. called the "father of history"
c. teacher and philosopher sentenced to death
d. writer of tragedies
e. philosopher who wrote on science, politics, and logic, among other things
f. told when there would be an eclipse of the sun
g. explained the principle of the lever
h. philosopher who wrote on the ideal state in the *Republic*

Developing Ideas and Skills

USING SOURCES OF INFORMATION

When you go to a club meeting in school, you listen first to the reading of the *minutes* of the last meeting before you start new business. The minutes are a record of what the club did at the last meeting. They are, therefore, a *source of information* about the club. People, organizations, and governments keep records as a future source of information.

Some important sources of historical information are described below:

A *log* is kept by the captain of a ship or aircraft. In the log are written the important events of the journey. The log of Christopher Columbus is our best source of information about his voyages.

A *journal* is much like a log. It is often the record of the daily events of a legislature, or lawmaking body. James Madison kept a journal of the Philadelphia Convention that drew up the United States Constitution, in 1787. From his journal, we have learned how the Constitution was written.

A *diary* is kept by one person. It is a record of the writer's own experiences. Many famous people have kept diaries. Some have been made public and can be read by anyone. From these diaries we are able to learn the thoughts of some of our public officials on important events.

Letters of famous people also tell us their thoughts on important events. Letters of presidents and generals have been made public long after these people died.

Histories are in themselves good sources of information. From the Greek historians we have obtained most of our knowledge about the wars the Athenian people fought. It is often necessary to read several histories of the same event to get at the truth. For a history may be written by persons who have opinions of their own about the event and do not give all sides of the story.

Documents, or official papers, are good sources of information. Our Declaration of Independence and the Bill of Rights are two famous documents of American history.

Newspapers give us the details of events of the day. One must be careful about newspapers. A newspaper may slant the news so that its readers will believe what the newspaper wants them to believe.

Throughout this book, you will come to different examples of sources of information. You will be asked to examine them. You will be asked questions that will help you to improve your skill in getting information from sources. You will learn to find out for yourselves the truth about events of the past and present.

Check yourself on using the best sources of information by answering these questions.

A. Which would be the best source for learning how the ancient Egyptians used the Nile River?
  1. a newspaper story about the Nile today in your Sunday newspaper
  2. a movie based on the life of an Egyptian pharaoh
  3. the hieroglyphics on a stone found near the Nile River and telling about the river

B. Which would be the best source for learning what were ancient Egyptian beliefs about life after death?
  1. a story in a French newspaper on the history of the pyramids
  2. the paintings and writings on the walls of an Egyptian temple
  3. a world history written by an Englishman about 1750

Using Original Sources

How does a historian decide what is truth when writing history? Thucydides, the ancient Greek historian, tells of his method in the following (adapted) paragraph.

Thucydides on Writing History

I have described nothing but what I either saw myself, or learned from others of whom I asked the most careful and particular questions. The task was a long and hard one, because eyewitnesses of the same occurrences have different accounts of them. They remembered or were interested in the actions of one side or the other. And very likely the strictly historical character of my writing may be disappointing to the ear. But I shall be satisfied if what I have written is thought useful by the kind of reader I keep in mind. I mean the person who desires to be shown a true picture of the events that have happened and the events like them that may be expected to happen in the future.

1. Is this paragraph an original or a secondary source?
2. How did Thucydides try to make his history accurate?
3. Why is an eyewitness not always reliable?
4. What did Thucydides mean by the statement "the strictly historical character of my writing may be disappointing to the ear"?
5. Thucydides believed that history can give people a picture of events that may happen in the future. Do you agree with his belief? Why, or why not?

AIM: What was the everyday life of the early Greeks like?

CHAPTER 4

How People Lived in Greece

HOW DID THE GREEKS SPEND THEIR LEISURE TIME?

1. You may wonder how the great works of the Greeks helped them in their daily lives. We must ask ourselves this question, for today we live in a world where great inventions and discoveries are constantly being made. We have machines that do our work. We have more time to enjoy life than ever before. We want more comfortable homes, time for travel, and quick transportation. To the ancient Greeks, comfort was not a goal of life. The Greeks thought and created for the love of beauty.

2. Greece has a warm and sunny climate. In ancient Athens, most citizens raised grain and olives on their farms. The wealthy had others work for them. The men of Athens spent much time outdoors. The markeplace was the chief meeting place. People went there in the morning to hear the latest news and to argue.

3. Women in Athens were rarely seen, even when there were guests in the home. They did not go with their husbands on visits to friends. They served meals, but did not sit at the dinner table with the men. Women were not citizens. They could not own property or take part in making laws. A woman in Athens with talent had little chance to use it. Pericles, how-

The Agora, or marketplace, of Athens. This model shows how it might have looked. The long, roofed row of columns on the left was called the Stoa of Attalus.

ever, brought a woman from Asia Minor to his home. He could not marry her, for she was not from Athens. But she invited to his home writers, artists, and thinkers to study and exchange ideas. In Sparta, however, women were honored. They were the mothers of Spartan soldiers and matched them in courage. They worked in the fields along with their husbands.

4. Greek homes were made of sun-dried brick. They were dark inside. The patio was outside and received sunlight. Homes were simple and had little furniture. The Cretan people, who came before the Greeks, had a sewerage system. The ancient Greeks did not. They disposed of garbage by throwing it into the street.

The patio of a Greek home. What does this picture tell you about Greek life?

Walkers had to be careful as they went to the marketplace. They might be covered with garbage by the time they got there. Greeks ate with their fingers, for they had no utensils.

5. The purpose of Greek schools was to develop a boy's mind and body. Education for boys began at about the age of seven. Schools were private. Education was not easy, for it was expected that a boy would work hard to become a useful citizen. He went to the gymnasium where he worked and studied all day. He ran and wrestled, and studied music and public speaking. Even when his schooling was finished for the day, a Greek boy stayed at the gymnasium with his friends. For this was the center of his life. In Sparta, as you have learned, education was harsh. Girls received no education, except in Sparta.

HOW DID CITIZENS DIFFER FROM SLAVES?

6. Greek farmers worked in fields near the city. Some farmers worked alongside their slaves. Small shopkeepers carried on trade in the Greek cities, except in Sparta, using coined money. Masons built the great buildings. Craftsmen turned out leather goods, armor, and spears. Miners brought great stones from distant quarries for buildings and theaters. Most ancient Greeks, however, did not care whether or not they gained great fortunes. They tried to earn enough money to pay for their basic needs. But their greater interest was in their city and their government.

7. Not everyone in ancient Greece was considered a free citizen. Slavery was a part of Greek life. During the Golden Age, more than one-third of the 300,000 people in Athens were slaves. Slavery in Greece was different from slavery in the United States before the Civil

Terracotta vase from the 6th century B.C. The figures show women drawing water from a public fountain. Above, warriors battle.

War. In ancient times, many slaves were people who had been captured in war. Thus, Persians or Egyptians might be Greek slaves. Slaves did much of the household work, because most Greek citizens disliked such work. Slaves also worked on farms and in mines. Some were even teachers.

8. The Greek gods played an important part in the life of the people. Festivals, such as the Olympic games, were held in honor of the gods. The Greeks thought of their gods as being much like human beings except that the gods did not grow old or die. Because the Greek gods seemed human, the people feared them less. Offerings were made to the gods at mealtimes. The people tried to keep the gods happy. They believed that if the gods were pleased they would do what the people wished. Unlike the people of other ancient civilizations, the Greeks did not have many priests.

Testing Your Vocabulary

Choose the best answer.

1. A *gymnasium* in ancient Greece was a place for
   a. play and study.
   b. military training.
   c. the study of crafts.

2. *Utensils*, as used in paragraph 4, means
   a. towels and napkins.
   b. equipment for eating, such as knives and forks.
   c. tables and chairs.

Understanding What You Have Read

1. A good title for paragraph 5 is
   a. Sunny Greece
   b. The Marketplace
   c. Education in Greece
   d. Home Life of the Greeks
2. In which paragraph do you find facts about
   a. women's place in Greek life?
   b. the kinds of work done by slaves?
   c. the religious beliefs of the Greeks?
   d. Greek homes?
3. Men spent a large part of their time in the marketplace because
   a. men could not sit at the dinner table at home with women.
   b. it was the only place where men could talk freely.
   c. it was a good place to talk and hear the news.
4. The Greeks made offerings to their gods because
   a. they wanted the gods to do what they asked of them.
   b. their priests demanded the offerings.
   c. they lived in great fear of their gods.
5. Boys in Athens were educated chiefly to prepare them
   a. for work in a particular trade.
   b. to be useful citizens in all ways.
   c. to be warriors.
6. Which of these were found in most Greek homes?
   a. A finely furnished eating room
   b. Running water
   c. An outdoor patio
7. Women were not equal to men in Athens because women
   a. could not live with their husbands.
   b. did all the farming and trading.
   c. could not be citizens of the city.

Developing Ideas and Skills _____

MAKING AN OUTLINE

Below are three headings or main ideas for an outline of Chapter 4. In your notebook, write in sub-topics where blanks appear. A few sub-topics have been written to guide you.

Life in Ancient Greece

A. Everyday Life at Home
   1. Men spent much time in the marketplace.
   2. _____
   3. _____
   4. _____
B. Occupations
   1. Farmers worked their fields near the city.
   2. _____
   3. _____
   4. _____
C. Education and Religion
   1. Religious festivals were held in honor of the gods.
   2. _____
   3. _____
   4. _____

DRAWING INFERENCES

To infer is to draw a conclusion. The conclusion may be based on facts and information. Or it may be based on hints. Below are ten statements. Infer which of them are true and which are false. Base your inferences on the facts, information, and hints in Chapter 4.

1. Greek homes were not heated during the winter.
2. An ancient Greek might spend more time thinking about the meaning of life than thinking about ways of making money.
3. The education of young men in Athens was very similar to the education of young men in Sparta.
4. Greek mothers probably gave their daughters all the education the daughters received.
5. Greeks wore heavy woolen clothing, carefully fitted.
6. Greek women probably held important government jobs.
7. The Greeks believed that their gods had sad and joyful experiences.
8. Physical training was an important part of the education of Greek boys.
9. The father of the Greek family did all the repairs around the home.
10. Free public schools were supported by the government in all Greek cities.

Using Original Sources

The following passage is from a book written by Thucydides, an ancient Greek historian. He quotes a speech of Pericles', the great leader of Athens. This speech was made at the funeral of Athenian soldiers killed in the war between Athens and Sparta. The quotation has been adapted for use in this book.

Pericles' Speech to the Athenians

. . . We do not copy our neighbors but are an example to them. It is true that we are called a democracy, for the government of the city is in the hands of the many and not the few . . . Neither does poverty keep a person from taking part in the government, but a man may do good for his country whatever his condition is. . . . A spirit of honor and respect shows through our public acts; we do not do wrong, because we have respect for the authorities and for the laws. . . .

And we have not forgotten to provide relief from work for our tired spirits; we have regular games and festivals throughout the year; our homes are beautiful and elegant; and the delight which we feel in all these things helps to get rid of sadness.

Our city is thrown open to the world, and we never send away a foreigner or stop him from seeing or learning anything about us . . . for we are lovers of the beautiful, yet simple in our tastes, and we improve the mind without loss of manliness. We use wealth not for talk, not to boast, but when there is real use for it. To admit poverty is no disgrace; the true disgrace is doing nothing to avoid it. . . .

Choose the correct answers, based on the passage you have just read.

1. An Athenian did not do wrong because he
   a. feared cruel punishment.
   b. respected the law and authorities.
   c. was watched by the secret police.
2. The feeling that the Athenian got daily from his games, sacrifices, and home was one of
   a. sadness.   b. weariness.   c. delight.
3. Pericles believed that
   a. only a few people should participate in the city government.
   b. only the poor should not take part in government.
   c. citizens should be active in the government of Athens.
4. The Athenians
   a. welcomed visitors to their city.
   b. showed only their best side to visitors.
   c. were tricky in their dealings with foreigners.
5. According to Pericles, a city's wealth should be used
   a. to show one's greatness.
   b. to fool one's enemies.
   c. for useful things.

Choose the word or expression closest in meaning to the italicized word in each of the following sentences.

1. When we write and when we speak, we should avoid *verbiage*.
   a. a lot of useless words
   b. lies
   c. words

2. The cultures of ancient Israel, Greece, and Rome are three *antecedents* of modern culture.
   a. things that came before
   b. enemies of
   c. things that happened at the same time

3. Numerous arguments between the players and the referee *protracted* the game to three hours.
   a. shortened
   b. complicated
   c. drew out

4. Sometimes it is better for a fighting force to *circumvent* the enemy than to attack them directly.
   a. surrender to
   b. go around in order to avoid
   c. retreat from

TURNING POINTS

Culture

Europe and the Middle East: Christian Catacombs

The early Christians needed hiding places. To escape persecution by the Romans, they often observed their religious practices in secret. This could be done in the catacombs. They dug the catacombs from soft rock in areas that were close to Rome and other cities.

The Christians buried their dead and held funeral services in the catacombs. According to Roman law, all burial places were sacred. The Christians were safe in these dark passageways.

The Christians also used the catacombs as chapels. They decorated the walls and ceilings with pictures. These pictures show scenes from Bible stories. Other pictures reflect the Christian belief in an afterlife.

By the early 400s the Christians no longer needed to hide. Christianity had become the accepted religion of the Roman Empire. In the centuries that followed, people forgot about the catacombs. They lay untouched until 1578, when they were accidentally rediscovered. Catacombs have also been found in other parts of Italy, as well as in Egypt, Syria, and Tunisia. These were used by ancient people to bury their dead, long before the Christians dug catacombs for *their* purposes.

Critical Thinking

1. How can art help us to learn about history?
2. Why were the catacombs forgotten for centuries?

UNIT III

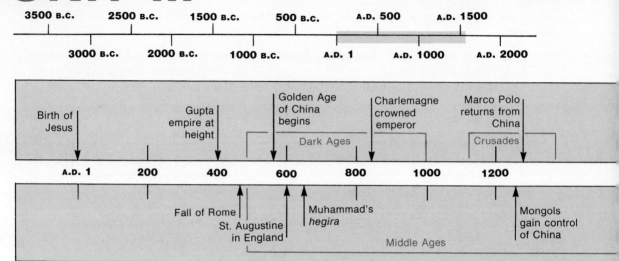

3500 B.C.		2500 B.C.		1500 B.C.		500 B.C.		A.D. 500		A.D. 1500	
	3000 B.C.		2000 B.C.		1000 B.C.		A.D. 1		A.D. 1000		A.D. 2000

	Birth of Jesus		Gupta empire at height		Golden Age of China begins		Charlemagne crowned emperor		Marco Polo returns from China

Dark Ages

Crusades

A.D. 1	200	400	600	800	1000	1200

Fall of Rome

St. Augustine in England

Muhammad's *hegira*

Middle Ages

Mongols gain control of China

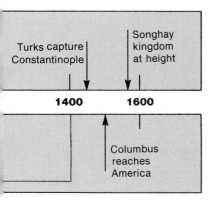

Turks capture
Constantinople

Songhay
kingdom
at height

1400   1600

Columbus
reaches
America

How Did People Live during the Middle Ages?

This prince of medieval India used a lively elephant for transportation.

AIM: How did the Eastern (Byzantine) Empire of Rome develop its own culture and spread it into Europe?

CHAPTER 1

Byzantium Keeps Culture Alive

WHY DID CONSTANTINOPLE BECOME THE CAPITAL OF THE EMPIRE?

1. Rome fell in A.D. 476. But Roman culture did not disappear. The Eastern Roman Empire (also called the Byzantine Empire) carried on the culture of the Romans. The emperor Constantine had divided the Roman Empire into two parts. This division remained after his death. There were two rulers of the empire. One was in Rome; one was in Constantinople.

2. The Eastern Roman Empire was attacked from many sides. But it was able to defend itself ably for nearly a thousand years. Constantinople was its center. For hundreds of years it was one of the world's great cities. When Rome fell, Constantinople stood and kept the name and culture of the Roman Empire alive.

3. Constantinople was a good place for a capital. It was located on the straits between the Aegean and Black seas. (See the map below.) The city is on a peninsula, with water

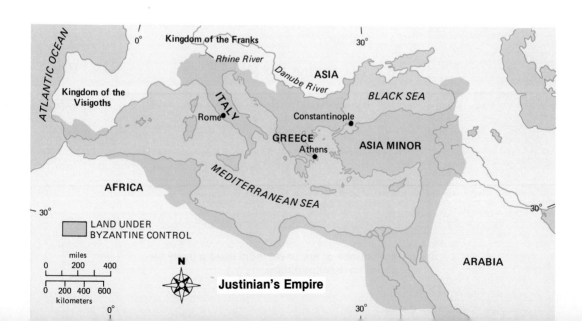

LAND UNDER BYZANTINE CONTROL

Justinian's Empire

on three sides. On the mainland side, a protecting wall had been built. The city was a natural defense for one of the waterways linking Asia and Europe. It was the home of a million people, a city of great wealth. There were great buildings, churches, and palaces. People of all kinds came to the city. There were merchants, artists, teachers, beggars, and even criminals.

WHAT WAS BYZANTINE CULTURE LIKE?

4. The rulers of the Byzantine Empire were *autocrats*. An autocrat is one who rules with complete power. Emperors of Byzantium made the laws and collected taxes. They commanded the army and navy. They spent the money of the empire as they wished. Emperors were not chosen by the people. Each emperor picked the one who was to follow him.

5. Justinian was one of the greatest of the eastern emperors. He ruled for almost 40 years. His reign ended in A.D. 565. For twenty-five of those years, he was co-ruler with his wife, Theodora. They shared the power of the throne. Theodora's courage saved her husband when mobs threatened to storm the palace and overthrow him. She founded hospitals and convents. During their co-rule, they got back lands that barbarian tribes had taken. Persian attempts to seize the whole empire were stopped short before they reached Constantinople. One of the great works of Justinian was a code of laws. It arranged all the laws that existed into one body of laws. The Justinian Code was written in Latin. It became the law of the East.

6. Greek was the language of the Eastern Empire. In the 11th century, the Catholic Church of the East broke away from the Roman Catholic Church. It became known as the Greek Orthodox Church. The patriarch of Constantinople was its leader, in place of the pope. The Eastern Church began to follow different practices from those of the Church of Rome. Its

priests, for example, were allowed to marry.

7. There was great beauty in Byzantine art and architecture. One of the most famous churches is that of Saint Sofia, in Constantinople. It is still standing. Giant domes were used in churches all over the Eastern Empire. Inside churches, walls and ceilings were done in *mosaics*. These are pictures made of small, colored pieces of stone. Artists made *icons*, or pictures of saints. These were also done in mosaics of many colors. Homes and churches had icons. Artists, too, made copies of Greek and Roman writings. They decorated them with gold lettering and tiny colored paintings.

HOW DID BYZANTINE CULTURE SPREAD TO EUROPEAN COUNTRIES?

8. The culture of the East met the culture of the West in Constantinople. The city became rich from its trade. Merchants came to Constantinople from nearby lands to buy and sell. Africa, Europe, and Asia shared in the trade of the city. Nearby were the mines of Eastern Europe and the grain fields of Egypt. Silk was introduced by missionaries returning from China.

St. Sofia, Constantinople, Turkey. Compare the architecture of this church with that of Notre Dame on page 148. How are they alike? How are they different?

It became the city's leading product and brought it great wealth. Woolens, armor, silver, gold, and perfumes were offered for trade. The West traded its grain, salt, and fish in return. The gold coins of the Byzantines were of great value in other lands. They were a symbol of Byzantine wealth.

9. The Byzantine way of life spread to southern Russia. The Byzantines traded with the people of the Russian city of Kiev. Ideas and goods from Byzantium brought new ideas to the early Russian settlers. The results of the spread of ideas can be seen in eastern Europe today. The Russian language uses some Greek letters. Many of their old and beautiful buildings are in the Byzantine style. Greek Orthodox Christianity is the religion of millions of Russian people and others in eastern Europe.

10. When the Crusaders of Europe went east in the 11th and 12th centuries, they saw Constantinople for the first time. (You will study about the Crusaders in Chapter 7.) They found the east to be very different from their homelands. Many were attracted to it and stayed. The Crusaders captured Constantinople for a short time, but the city won back its rule. In time, wars and heavy taxes weakened the power of the Byzantine Empire. Constantinople was finally captured by the Ottoman Turks,

An icon from a Byzantine church in Bulgaria. How does this picture support the statement that "Byzantium kept culture alive"?

in 1453. This event marked the end of the city's influence. But the city had done its work. It kept alive Greek and Roman culture, and passed it on to later peoples.

Testing Your Vocabulary

Choose the best answer.

1. If a person has an *icon*, he would likely
   a. use it to copy writings.
   b. put it in an important place in his home.
   c. paint with it.
2. An *autocrat* is one who
   a. rules with complete power.
   b. collects taxes.
   c. is interested in art, architecture, and literature.
3. *Mosaics* were made chiefly of
   a. tile or stone.
   b. copper or bronze.
   c. silver or gold.

Understanding What You Have Read

1. A good title for paragraphs 8 and 9 might be
   a. Businessmen of Constantinople
   b. Byzantine Trade and Its Results
   c. Greek Traditions in Eastern Europe
   d. Russian Settlements in Europe

2. In which paragraph do you find facts about
   a. the population of Constantinople?
   b. Justinian and the Theodora?
   c. the religion of most Russians today?
   d. icons in Byzantine churches?

Choose the correct answer or answers. In each of the following five questions, one, two, or all three answer choices may be correct.

1. Constantinople was a good location for the capital of the Eastern Roman Empire because
   a. its waterways connected Europe and Asia.
   b. it controlled the Mediterranean Sea.
   c. it was protected on all sides.

2. Justinian was one of the greatest of the eastern Roman emperors because he
   a. brought all Roman laws together into one code.
   b. was able to get back some of the territory lost by the Romans.
   c. led a Crusade to the Holy Land.

3. Constantinople became a trading center because
   a. its location enabled it to receive goods from both East and West.
   b. it could get minerals and grains.

   c. it had magnificent buildings and palaces.

4. Many of the ideas and customs of Eastern Europe today can be traced to the Byzantine Empire because
   a. Russian sailors traded in the Mediterranean.
   b. missionaries from Rome entered Russia in the 5th century.
   c. early Byzantine traders brought their customs to Russia.

5. Which of these are results of Byzantine civilization?
   a. The Latin language began to be used in eastern churches.
   b. Greek and Roman ideals were saved for later civilizations.
   c. Roman law continued to be followed in the East.

Select the item, either a, b, or c, that does not belong with the others in the group.

1. *Geography of Constantinople*
   a. is a peninsula
   b. on a strait
   c. has many mountains

2. *Architecture in Constantinople*
   a. churches
   b. raceways for chariots
   c. palaces

3. *Byzantine Culture*
   a. Latin
   b. mosaics
   c. icons

4. *Byzantine Trade*
   a. gold coins
   b. pottery from Asia
   c. export of silk

5. *Greek Orthodox Church*
   a. led by the pope
   b. priests could marry
   c. Greek language used

6. *Constantinople after A.D. 500*
   a. captured by Persians
   b. captured by Turks
   c. captured by Crusaders

Developing Ideas and Skills _____

SKIMMING

When we look for information, it is not always necessary for us to read every word on every page of a book to find what we want. When we look for a telephone number, for example, we *skim* through the pages of the directory. Instead of reading every name on the page we look over the whole page at once to see what is on it.

We can skim in many ways. One way is to look quickly over the page for key words or key sentences. If we wanted information about farming, for example, we would look quickly down the page for words such as *agriculture, crops, fields,* and *growing season.* Any of these words would tell us that there probably is something on the page about farming.

If we are trying to find out what is in a whole book, we can skim through *the table of contents.* The chapter titles tell us what kind of information it has and on which pages different topics may be found.

In *skimming* this book, we can use another method. We might look at the first sentence in each paragraph. The first sentence can tell you what the paragraph is about. Then you can decide if you should read the rest of the paragraph for more information.

Let us try *skimming* Chapter 2 of this unit. *Don't read the chapter. Just read the first sentence of each paragraph. Then, close your book* and see what information you found about the chapter. You will find that the first sentences give you this information.

Muhammad was a prophet of God, Allah.

Muhammad believed that he was chosen by Allah to preach.

The holy book, the Koran, contains the sayings of Muhammad.

Islam controlled the lives of Muslims.

The Muslims tried to get others to accept their religion.

There was no force strong enough to stop the Muslim movement.

In a short time, the Muslim empire spread from Spain to India.

Many civilizations were brought together under the Muslim empire.

The Muslims borrowed part of the Roman style in their buildings.

The Arabs gained knowledge from the Indians and Chinese.

The Muslim world kept growing after Muhammad's death.

You have gained quite a bit of information about Muhammad and his religion simply by reading the opening sentence of each paragraph. You also know in which paragraphs you might look for more information about particular topics.

Suppose you were trying to answer the following questions. In which paragraph would you read further?

Were there any Muslims in Europe?

What were some of the contributions of the Muslims?

Why did Muhammad's religion spread?

What are the religious beliefs of the Muslims?

Did Muslim buildings use the Roman arch?

AIM: How did the religion of Muhammad influence many people in the East and the West?

CHAPTER 2

The World of Muhammad's Followers

HOW DID THE RELIGION OF ISLAM BEGIN?

1. "There is no God but Allah and Muhammad is his prophet." This is the prayer of the religion called Islam, practiced by the followers of Muhammad. Muhammad was born in the city of Mecca, in Arabia, about A.D. 570. His parents died when he was very young, so he lived with his uncle. As a boy, he spent much of his time watching the caravans that came through Mecca on their way to India and Asia Minor. He became a camel driver himself. Later, he married a widow who had hired him to work in her own caravan business.

2. When he was about 40 years of age, Muhammad began to believe that he had been chosen by Allah to preach a new way of life. He took from the Jewish and Christian religions the belief that there was only one god. Muhammad taught that Moses and Jesus were prophets of the one god. However, he was the greatest prophet since he was born at a later time. There were many in Mecca who believed in Muhammad's teachings. There were others who would not accept the faith of Islam. Muhammad made enemies and was forced to leave the city of Mecca for Medina, also in Arabia, in A.D. 622.

This event is known as the *Hegira,* or the flight. The calendar of Islam begins in the year 622.

3. Muhammad's teachings are written in the *Koran,* the holy book of Islam. Muslims, as believers of Islam are called, have several important duties. They must pray five times a day. Each time they pray, they must face the holy city of Mecca. There are no priests or clergy in Islam. A person in the community has the duty of calling the people to prayer. During one month of the year Muslims must fast (not eat) every day from sunrise to sunset. Fasting helps the faithful to understand what it is like to be

The Alhambra is a group of buildings built in the 13th & 14th centuries in Spain. This building, the Court of the Lions, shows the influence of Muslim culture.

poor. In this way, Muslims are taught to be kind to the poor and to slaves. During their lives, Muslims must make a pilgrimage, a holy journey, to Mecca. Muslims believe in one God. They are not allowed to make statues or holy pictures. They must be honest in their business dealings and try to spread the religion of Islam.

4. The religion of Islam governed the way people lived in Muslim communities. The rulers, *caliphs* (KAY-lifs), it was believed, carried out the wishes of Allah. When a ruler was overthrown, it was believed that he had disobeyed the orders of Allah. Men were able to work, study, and gain wealth and positions in government. Women could not. In Islam, women were respected, but they were not men's equals. A man could have four wives. A woman could have only one husband. Muslim women could own property. But they had to cover their faces with a veil when leaving their house. At home, a Muslim woman had to stay in her room or rooms.

HOW DID ISLAM SPREAD AS FAR AS EUROPE AND INDIA?

5. Muhammad's followers felt that they had to try to make people of other religions become Muslims. They called their wars "holy wars" and brought the teachings of Muhammad to the people they conquered. Conquered people had to pay taxes to their Muslim rulers. This must have caused many people to become Muslims, for those who practiced the Muslim religion did not have to pay taxes. The Muslims were tough desert fighters and good horsemen. A Muslim believed that if he died for his beliefs in battle he would enter paradise right away. So the religion of Islam spread all over southwestern Asia. Only eight years after the death of Muhammad, his followers had conquered Syria, Mesopotamia, and Palestine. Persia and Egypt were conquered in the next ten years. Later the Muslim push to the east brought the religion of Islam first to India and then to China.

6. The Muslim faith also moved south and west. It could not be stopped. The power of Rome had long since gone. All of North Africa as far as Morocco fell to Muslim forces. North African Muslims, called Moors, crossed into Spain and conquered it in 715. Next they moved into southern France. But, the Muslim advance came to an end. At Tours in 732, the Moors were defeated by Charles Martel, the leader of the Franks. The spread of Muslim power was stopped. The Battle of Tours was an important event in Western history. The Muslim defeat at Tours ended a threat to the Christian Church in Western Europe, except for Spain. The Moors returned to Spain, where they stayed in power until 1492.

7. A little over a century after Muhammad's death, the Muslim empire reached from Spain in the west to India in the east. It was controlled by many different caliphs. These caliphs were autocrats, having complete power. The people could not choose their own caliphs or make their own laws. Although there was no single ruler for the Muslim empire, the people were united for several reasons. The religion of Islam, in which all the people believed, was their strongest tie. In addition, all Muslims knew the Arabic language. Educated people had to learn to read the Koran, which was written in Arabic.

HOW DID MUSLIM CULTURE JOIN THE EAST AND WEST?

8. In the Muslim world, the cultures of Persia, Egypt, and Mesopotamia were brought together. Goods were traded with Asia, Africa, and Europe. The products of Asian and African lands were brought to the Western world. The city of Baghdad (in the country which is today called Iraq) became the center of Muslim culture in Asia. Cordova in Spain was the European center of Muslim learning and trade.

9. In architecture, the Muslims borrowed many Roman practices but changed them to suit their own needs. The *mosque,* or Muslim church, was the most important building in a city. The Muslims used the Roman arch, changed into the shape of a horseshoe in their mosques. The dome of a mosque looked like a bulb. Reaching upward were slender, pointed towers. Most Muslim works of art were made up of lines in lacelike patterns. This is because the Koran forbids the making of statues or paintings of animals or human beings. *Tapestries,* materials with woven designs, decorate the walls of Muslim buildings. Muslim craftsmen also made beautiful works with glazed tile.

10. From the people of India and China, the Muslims learned chemistry and mathematics. They translated books on these subjects into the Arabic language. The works of Aristotle, the Greek philosopher, were translated into Arabic and brought to Europe. Since the Muslim empire was so large, the people learned about the new drugs and ideas in medicine of different parts of the world. From India came the system of using Arabic numbers (1, 2, 3, 4, etc.), the system we use today. Roman numbers (I, II, III, IV, etc.) had been used until then. The Muslims used many words which we have

The Mosque of Omar in the old city of Jerusalem.

added to our own language, such as *algebra, alcohol, almanac, coffee, sofa, magazine, traffic,* and *zero.*

11. For hundreds of years after the death of Muhammad, the Muslim world grew. Muslim traders spread their religion wherever they traveled. The important trade routes of the world from East to West were at one time controlled by the Muslims. First, the Muslim world circled the Mediterranean Sea. Later, it surrounded the Indian Ocean as well. Modern Pakistan, for example, is an Islamic nation. Trade also brought Muslims and their culture to the East Indies (modern Indonesia) and modern Malaya. Islam also spread south into Central Africa. Many African blacks became Muslims. Today, more than 550 million people practice the religion of Islam.

A detail from the Alhambra. Why are most Muslim buildings decorated with lace-like lines instead of paintings or statues?

Testing Your Vocabulary

Choose the best answer.

1. A *mosque* is to a Muslim as
   a. a synagogue is to a Jew.
   b. an arch is to a Roman.
   c. an obelisk is to an Egyptian.
2. When persons make a *pilgrimage*, they
   a. give food to the poor.
   b. journey to a holy place.
   c. try to change somebody else's religion.
3. A *caliph* may also be called
   a. an artist.
   b. a governor.
   c. a trader.

Understanding What You Have Read

1. The purpose of paragraphs 2 and 3 is to describe
   a. the early life of Muhammad.
   b. the flight of Muhammad.
   c. the teachings of Muhammad.
   d. how Islam and Christianity are alike.
2. In which paragraph do you find facts about
   a. the meaning of the Hegira?
   b. the Battle of Tours?
   c. the centers of Muslim civilization in Asia and Europe?
   d. the role of Muslim women?
3. A reason for the rapid spread of Islam was that
   a. the Persian Empire accepted the teachings of Muhammad.
   b. the followers of Muhammad believed that it was their duty to change people to the religion of Islam.
   c. the Muslim rulers were democratic.
4. The Battle of Tours is considered to be an important battle in the history of the world because
   a. it ended barbarian invasions in Asia.
   b. it brought more trade between Europe and Africa.
   c. it ended the spread of Islam in Western Europe.
5. Muslim civilization was important because
   a. ideas of the East and West were mixed and spread throughout the world.
   b. Muslim law became the basis of justice in Europe.
   c. great works of Muslim art and architecture were copied by the Romans and Greeks.
6. A reason why early Muslim civilization is important today is that
   a. it started the belief in one God.
   b. it set up trade routes from Asia to Europe that still exist.
   c. it gave us our modern system of numbers.
7. The Muslim people were drawn close together by
   a. the same religion and trade.
   b. the travels of Muhammad and other prophets.
   c. a strong government with one powerful ruler.

Developing Ideas and Skills

USING A MAP

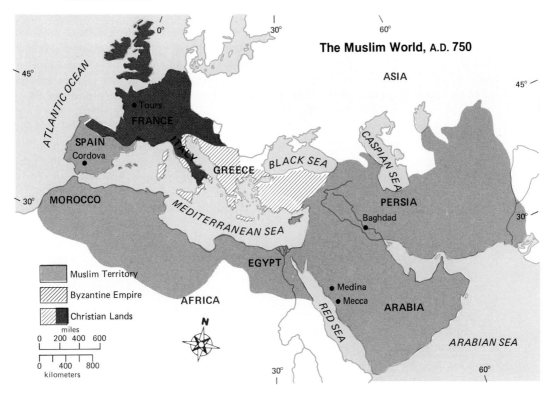

The Muslim World, A.D. 750

Study the map on page 135 carefully. Then decide whether the statements are true or false.

1. Muslim conquests included parts of Alexander's empire and parts of the Roman Empire.
2. Only a small part of the Muslim world was located in the Middle East.
3. Islam did not reach Italy.
4. From Arabia, where it began, Islam spread to both north and west.
5. Spain was the only European country under Muslim influence in A.D. 750.

Using Original Sources

The Koran is the holy book of Islam. In it, Muhammad tells what has been revealed to him by Allah. These revelations are called *Suras*. Here is one part of the Koran. What does it tell you about this new religion of the 7th century?

The Koran

And fight for the cause of God against those who fight against you.

And kill them wherever ye shall find them, and put them out from whatever place they have ejected you; for disputes within a country are worse than blood-shed: yet attack them not at the sacred Mosque, unless they attack you therein; but if they attack you, slay them. Such is the reward of those who do not believe Islam.

Fight therefore against them until there be no more civil discord, and the only worship be that of God: but if they stop, then let there be no hostility save against the wicked. (Sura 186, 187, 189)

1. What were good Muslims supposed to do if others opposed their religion?
2. What was to be the reward of those who did not follow Islam?
3. How did Muhammad suggest that disputes within a country could be ended?
4. Using these few sentences as a guide, what do you think would be the relationship between Muslims and Christians and Jews?
5. Is this selection a primary or secondary source?

TURNING POINTS

Culture

The Middle East: Jerusalem

Judaism, Christianity, and Islam are all religions which teach that there is only one God. Much of their history comes together in the ancient city of Jerusalem. The city today has many places that are sacred to each religion.

One sacred place in Jerusalem is the Dome of the Rock. It is holy to those who believe in the teachings of Islam. Muslims come to this shrine to pray beneath its great, golden dome. Beautiful mosaics cover its walls. Some contain graceful Arabic writings that spell out verses from the Koran. Beneath the dome itself is a huge rock. The Muslims believe that this is the place from which Muhammad rose to heaven.

Not far from the Dome of the Rock is the Western Wall, Judaism's most holy place. The wall is all that is left of the Temple of Solomon. This place of worship was destroyed by the Romans in A.D. 70. Jews come to this wall to pray and to mourn the destruction of the Temple.

Jerusalem is also the home of the Church of the Holy Sepulcher. It is built in the place where Christians believe Jesus may have been entombed. Christians come here to pray. The Church is lit with many candles.

A walk through the streets of Jerusalem is a journey through the history of three major religions. Their beliefs have had a lasting effect on the world.

Critical Thinking

1. What are two things that Judaism, Christianity, and Islam have in common?
2. Why do you think people want to visit the holy places of Jerusalem?

AIM: How did the fall of the Roman Empire affect European life and culture?

CHAPTER 3

Barbarians Sweep over Europe

HOW DID INVASIONS AFFECT EUROPE?

1. People need law and order. They want to feel safe in their homes and outside. History shows us that people have used different ways to find the peace and safety they want. During the early centuries of the Roman Empire, there was peace. It was a forced peace, for no one was strong enough to oppose the power of the Roman armies. But at least the people were safe. The downfall of Rome meant the end of law and order. In Europe, there was little law and order for almost 1,000 years, until our modern nations were born.

2. Barbarian tribes (peoples outside the Roman Empire who lived in a rough, uncivilized way) had taken turns invading the empire of Rome. Small parts of the empire had been conquered by tribes even before the city of Rome fell and the whole empire ended. These tribes were not used to city life. They were fighting peoples. If they were not at war with the same enemy, they were fighting one another. Each tribe was ruled by its own chief. Its people lived in mud huts and hunted and fished for a living. They could not read or write and had no schools. They were wanderers who easily grew tired of living in the same place.

The pope crowned Charlemagne Roman Emperor of the west in A.D. 800. This act established the tradition of a close connection between religion and the state.

3. After the barbarians conquered Rome, Roman culture did not end completely. The customs of the Romans mixed with the customs of the invaders. But the barbarians were not the great builders that the Romans had been. Soon,

roads and bridges broke down. Travel became unsafe, for there were no Roman legions to protect travelers. Trade among towns almost stopped. Towns became smaller and farther apart. Many of the duties that had once been carried out by the government were taken over by the Church.

4. Several barbarian tribes conquered Europe. The *Franks* gained control of Gaul, which had been part of Rome since the time of Julius Caesar. Other tribes, the *Angles* and the *Saxons,* crossed into Britain. When the Roman soldiers left Britain to defend the city of Rome, the Angles and Saxons were able to conquer Britain. Italy was conquered first by the *Ostrogoths* and later by the *Lombards.*

5. Of all the tribes, the Franks were probably the most important. In the 5th century, Clovis, a Frankish leader and a Christian, gained control of Gaul. (Gaul was made up of France, Belgium, the Netherlands, and western Germany.) The Frankish kings protected the Church and its property. The Church, in turn, supported the Frankish kings. The power of the Franks reached its height during the reign of Charles, who had been elected to rule. Charles is known as *Charlemagne,* which means Charles the Great. Charles ruled the kingdom of the Franks for 44 years.

HOW DID WESTERN EUROPE CHANGE UNDER CHARLEMAGNE?

6. Charlemagne himself could not read or write as a boy. Yet he believed in education. He set up a palace school where children of his court studied for service in the Church and in government. To this school came the greatest teachers of Europe. One of them was a famous Englishman, Alcuin. Charlemagne also set up monasteries. A monastery is a place where holy men gather to live a life of work and prayer.

7. Charlemagne felt it his duty to spread the Christian faith. He led his armies against any people who were not Christians. During his reign, Charlemagne was almost always at war with the tribes that attacked his borders. He went far into Europe to defeat other tribes. In all his conquests, he was able to convert defeated peoples to Christianity. He helped the pope fight the Lombards and gave to the pope land in Italy that became known as the Papal States. In 800, while Charlemagne was on a visit to Rome, the pope crowned him Roman Emperor of the West.

8. Charlemagne was popular with his people. Under him there was, for a while, a strong government in most of Western Europe. But his death led to the breakup of the Frankish empire. It soon became clear that the Frankish kingdom had become strong because of Charlemagne's wisdom. Charlemagne's son, Louis, was a weak ruler. Upon his death, Louis' three sons divided the empire among themselves. One received most of Germany. A second son received most of what is now France. The third son was given Italy, Belgium, Holland, and a strip of land between Germany and France, called Alsace-Lorraine.

WHAT CAUSED THE DARK AGES?

9. New invasions followed the breakup of Charlemagne's lands. The most feared of all the invaders were the Northmen, or Vikings. They were fierce warriors who sailed south from Norway in their fast, strong ships. They raided towns and cities along the western coast of Europe. At night, they would invade a town, stealing what they could and destroying what they could not take with them. The Vikings seemed to be everywhere. They seized rich prizes from England, Ireland, France, and the lands along the Mediterranean Sea. They set up a colony on Iceland, in the northern Atlantic Ocean.

10. One of the boldest of the Vikings was Eric the Red. He sailed westward from Norway across the Atlantic and set up a colony in

Greenland. His son, Leif Ericson, went even farther. On a voyage from Norway to Greenland, he was blown off course. He sighted a distant shore. Landing there, he found an unknown country that had warmer weather than the northern lands he had come from. He named the new country Vinland, because of the grapes he found. Leif was really somewhere on the coast of North America. In 1965, Yale University published a map showing Vinland in North America. The map was said to have been made in 1440, fifty years before Columbus's voyage to the New World.

11. When the Frankish empire fell, many rulers from the different tribes began to fight one another for power in Europe. There was no united government to bring order. People wanted protection from the barbarians and robbers that roamed over Europe. So families crowded together within the walls of towns. Or they lived on the lands of a landowner called a lord. Here they farmed for the lord in exchange for protection. This new way of life was called *feudalism* and it spread over Europe. The years 500–1000, in which government was weak, men lived in fear, and feudalism began, are called the Dark Ages.

Leif Ericson sighting an unknown land; what did he call the new land?

Testing Your Vocabulary

Choose the best answer.

1. When we speak of the *reign* of a king or queen, we refer to
   a. the time in which they actually rule the kingdom.
   b. the weather and geography of their kingdom.
   c. the clothes that are proof that they are rulers.

2. A *century* means
   a. 20 years.
   b. 50 years.
   c. 100 years.

Understanding What You Have Read

1. The purpose of paragraph 3 is to describe the
   a. mixture of Roman and barbarian customs.
   b. way in which the towns in Europe grew farther apart.
   c. reasons why trade in Europe ended.
   d. wars between the tribes of Europe.

2. In which paragraph do you find facts about
   a. the barbarian tribes' homes and way of life?
   b. which tribes conquered Gaul and all of Britain?
   c. the crowning of Charlemagne as Roman emperor?
   d. the Viking founding of a colony in Iceland?

In each of the next five questions, one, two, or all three answer choices may be correct.

1. The 500-year period after the Fall of Rome has been called the Dark Ages because
   a. Roman and Greek ideas were spread throughout Europe.
   b. people had little to do with one another.
   c. barbarians roamed over Europe making life unsafe.
2. Charlemagne is famous in the history of Europe because he
   a. believed in education.
   b. developed a strong government at a time when there was little unity in Europe.
   c. defeated tribes that threatened the Church.
3. Charlemagne's empire broke up shortly after his death because
   a. there were no schools to teach his followers his ideas.
   b. the pope stopped supporting the Christian kings.
   c. his son and grandsons were weaker rulers than he.
4. The breakup of Charlemagne's empire resulted in
   a. the rise of democratic nations in Western Europe.
   b. new interest in education and learning.
   c. wars among many people for control of small areas of land.
5. Vikings hold an important place in world history because they
   a. set up colonies in Iceland and Greenland.
   b. published maps of their explorations.
   c. broke the power of tribes along the Mediterranean Sea.

Tell whether these statements are true or false. If a statement is false, change the words in italics to make it true.

1. Holy men worked and prayed in the *palace school.*
2. France was once part of a territory called *Gaul.*
3. The tribe that ruled France was called the *Franks.*
4. *Clovis* was a ruler of the Franks who set up a palace school.
5. When the Roman Empire fell, many duties of government were taken over by the *Church.*
6. Charlemagne was crowned Roman emperor by the *pope.*
7. Fierce warriors from Norway who set up a colony in Greenland were called the *Magyars.*
8. The Dark Ages lasted for almost *1,000* years.
9. The religion that Charlemagne practiced was *Christianity.*
10. The Papal States were given to the Pope by *the last Roman emperors.*

Developing Ideas and Skills _____

USING A MAP

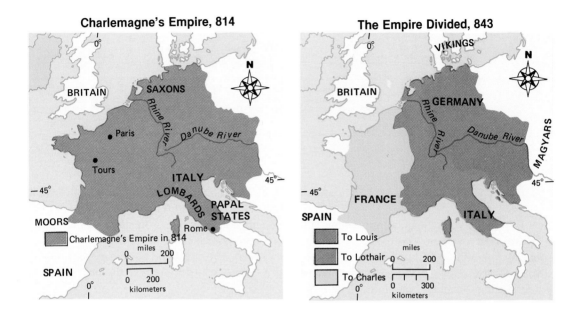

Charlemagne's Empire, 814

The Empire Divided, 843

Study the maps carefully. Then decide whether these statements are true or false.

1. When Charlemagne's empire was divided, part of Spain was added to France.
2. The overall size of the empire had increased by 843.
3. Charlemagne's empire included part of present-day Germany.
4. The Papal States were part of France.
5. Barbarian tribes had moved near the borders of the empire by 843.

AIM: How did different classes of people live in Europe in the Middle Ages?

CHAPTER 4

Manor Life: Castles and Huts

WHAT WAS FEUDALISM LIKE?

1. When a young man helps a young lady with her coat or opens the car door for her, someone might say, "Chivalry is not dead." Such a saying refers to the time of chivalry, when dashing knights rode horses, had fine manners, and showed uncommon respect for women. Chivalry was practiced during the Middle Ages of Europe. But not everyone was a knight and led an exciting, romantic life. Only a few were able to do so. Most people lived very dull lives with little to change or brighten the routine of daily living. The Middle Ages is also called the age of *feudalism.*

2. Every civilization has an *economic* system. This is the way people earn a living and get the things they need. *Feudalism* was the social and economic system of the people of Europe during the Middle Ages. Under feudalism, a person farmed a piece of land for a richer, more powerful person in return for protection. The *fief,* or piece of land, was at the heart of the feudal system. A lord who owned a large piece of land might divide it among ten people. The ten would then give the lord part of their crops or lend men to fight in the lord's army. The ten might, in turn, divide their land among poor farmers who would work the land.

In return, the farmers would get the safety that their lords and knights could give them. But the exchange of work for protection was not really fair. The poor farmer, called a *serf,* had to stay on his land. A serf could not move from it even if a different lord took over the fief.

HOW DID THE LORDS LIVE?

3. The lord's house was the most important building on the *manor,* the land belonging to the lord. Around the lord's home were the homes of the poor serfs in the village and the fields and pasture land. On a large manor, the lord lived in a castle. If the lord was not so rich, he lived in a large house. The house or castle was usually built on a hill, making it possible for the lord to see bands of wandering robbers or noblemen who might try to overthrow him.

4. A castle was as much a fort as a home. A high tower was both a lookout post and a place to live. Around the stone castle was a wall of stone or wood. Around this wall was a canal filled with water. This canal was called a moat. To get across the water to the castle, one had to go over a drawbridge, which could be raised to keep people out. One large room inside the castle was used as a meeting place and a dining

room. Although it had a fireplace, neither this room nor any other was comfortably heated. There were no knives or forks for meals, not even for the noble family. Meat was sliced with a sword and eaten with the fingers. So, although the nobleman's castle was much better than the mud huts of the serfs, it was still cold, damp, and uncomfortable.

5. The fief was a plot of land farmed by the peasant families. Crops were grown there for the villagers and the lord of the manor. A good fief grew enough food to feed everyone, including the soldiers hired by the lord. The more fighting men on the manor, the stronger was the lord of that manor. A person who had a fief was a *vassal* of the lord who gave it to him. The vassal owed loyalty. A lord who had vassals might himself be a vassal of a more powerful lord. Some lords had few vassals and small manors, while others were rich and powerful.

HOW DID THE SERFS LIVE?

6. The serfs lived in a village outside the castle walls. Their homes were huts of mud or

Knights in combat. The knights protected the manor. Combat skills were important and knights began training at early ages. They were usually of noble birth.

wood with roofs of straw. They had one room, with a dirt floor. All members of the family slept on mats on the floor. Windows were openings in the wall covered with oiled paper. Sickness was usual among these poor families. Children often died at an early age or were crippled by sickness early in life. Most serfs farmed, but some worked in mills, grinding wheat and rye. Another might be the blacksmith. Since serfs could not leave their land, children usually did the same work as their parents.

7. The lord's fief was divided into strips so that one person would not have all the fertile soil. Even so, peasant families worked together in tilling the soil and harvesting the crops. The lord sometimes gave his serfs tools and oxen, but very often they had to pull their own wooden plows through the soil. These people knew nothing about modern methods of rotating crops, so a three-field system was used for farming. Two fields were planted in rye, wheat, oats, or barley. The third field was left to *lie fallow*, or unplanted, so the fertility of its soil would come back. Thus, each field would grow crops in two years out of three. The animals of all the serfs were fed on the same pasture land.

8. Not only did serfs have to remain on the land, but they had to follow other rules as well. For the use of the lord's tools or mill they paid the lord part of their crops. There was no money, and so all payments were made in goods. Serfs could not marry without the lord's consent. The meals of a serf's family were simple: pork or duck, wine, bread, and cheese. The serfs, therefore, had few rights and few amusements. The peasant family gave its work and its life to the lord. The lord, in return, offered land, protection, and order.

9. Men, women, and children shared work in the fields. Women had few rights under law in the early Middle Ages. For example, a woman could not appear in court alone. A male relative had to appear with her. Husbands had complete control over their wives. Yet, women were often called on to carry out the same duties as men. When husbands were away from home fighting, women took over the affairs of the land. They bought supplies, kept accounts, and took charge of the defense of the castle.

WHAT RULES DID KNIGHTS FOLLOW?

10. For the sons of nobles, life was different from that of the serfs. Sons of nobles had chances to become knights. At the age of seven, a boy could begin training as a *page* or a helper to another noble. He would learn the manners and customs of the noble family. When a boy was fourteen, he could become a *squire*. Then he was able to carry and care for the weapons of the lord. At the age of 21, after he had proven his ability to ride and use his weapons properly, he became a knight.

11. Chivalry, or the rules of behavior for knights, gave the Middle Ages a romantic side. According to the rules of chivalry, knights were to be courteous and brave. They were to be helpful to women and to any person in trouble. They were to be courteous to knights whom they defeated in tournaments. Since these rules were for nobles only, the knight's treatment of his serfs was often cruel and thoughtless.

Besides combat, knights were supposed to follow strict rules of conduct.

Testing Your Vocabulary _____

Match the explanations in the second column with the terms in the first column.

1. feudalism
2. fief
3. vassal
4. manor
5. Middle Ages
6. squire
7. serf

a. the noble's estate and the lands around it that he owned
b. a peasant who could not leave the land on which he farmed
c. a young man of noble birth training to become a knight
d. the holder of a fief who owed loyalty to a lord
e. the economic system of the Middle Ages
f. a piece of land under the feudal system
g. the period of history from the year 500 until the year 1500

Understanding What You Have Read _____

1. The purpose of paragraph 4 is to describe
   a. how the lord spotted his enemies.
   b. the furniture in a castle.
   c. the homes of noble families in the Middle Ages.
   d. methods of protecting lands from robbers.

2. In which paragraphs do you find facts about
   a. the economic system of feudalism?
   b. the training of a boy to be a knight?
   c. the three-field system of agriculture?
   d. the moat that surrounded a castle?

3. The Middle Ages are sometimes called the "Age of Chivalry" because
   a. bands of robbers roamed over Europe.
   b. castles were turned into forts.
   c. knights had fine manners and helped people in trouble.

4. The three-field system of farming was used to grow crops because it
   a. brought new kinds of work for many villagers.
   b. saved the fertility of the soil that was farmed.
   c. divided land equally among the peasants of the village.

5. Villages were established near a castle because
   a. the farmer was forced to stay on his land.
   b. people needed the protection of the noble and his knights.
   c. fiefs were divided among peasant farmers.

6. Disease and sickness spread quickly on the manor because
   a. most people worked together on farms.
   b. buildings were crowded together so that they almost touched each other.
   c. houses were cold and there were no doctors to care for the poor.

7. Knights were important because they were
   a. trained to defend the manor.
   b. skilled craftsmen.
   c. highly educated people.

Developing Ideas and Skills _____

A. FINDING PROOF OF STATEMENTS

Tell whether the following statements are true or false. Which paragraph in this chapter helped you make your decision?

1. Peasant farmers often moved from village to village in order to make a better living.
2. Nobles gave an example of fine dinner manners in their castle life.
3. Few people on the manor had much entertainment or fun.
4. All the lands belonging to the lord made up the manor.
5. All lords lived in large, expensive, and beautiful castles.
6. Nobles' castles were warm and comfortable to live in.
7. Bread and cheese were common foods of serfs' families.
8. Knights were kind and helpful to both nobles and serfs.
9. Many lords were also vassals of other lords.
10. Not all peasants were farmers.

B. STUDYING A DRAWING

Look at this drawing of a medieval manor. Then decide whether the statements are true or false.

1. Each serf lived on his own small farm.
2. All people of the manor lived inside the castle walls.
3. The castle was located on the highest point of the land.
4. Rapids in the stream provided power to run the village mill.
5. The largest single piece of land was used for pasture.

AIMS: What caused the rise of towns in Europe during the Middle Ages? How did the growth of towns result in greater industry and trade?

CHAPTER 5

Town Life in the Middle Ages

HOW DID TOWNS BEGIN TO GROW?

1. Today, nearly three-fourths of the people of North America and Europe live in cities. In ancient times there were cities also. Athens and Rome were large cities, for example. But life in cities and even large towns almost disappeared from Europe after the Fall of Rome. As the barbarians took over Europe, people rushed to feudal manors for protection. The number of towns became smaller and there were fewer people. So there was little town life in Europe for several hundred years after the Fall of Rome. Then, towns started to spring up again during the Middle Ages. A change was taking place. Europe was moving out of the Dark Ages.

2. One reason for the growth of towns was that there were fewer barbarian invasions. Another reason for the new towns was that the number of people increased. It was not possible for everyone who wanted work to find it on the manor. The feudal system had finally brought some order and safety to Europe. People began to think about matters other than living on manors and defending themselves. So towns sprang up. People had settled near castles for protection against barbarians and roaming bands of thieves. Many towns were simply the villages that had surrounded the castle. They became larger, and grew to be towns.

3. Other towns sprang up near monasteries. Towns also developed where main roads crossed. Such crossroads were good places for merchants to meet, trade goods, and set up shops. Or towns began near rivers, because rivers provided easy and cheap transportation. Other towns were located along the sea, near good harbors or fishing ports.

4. Where large numbers of people gathered, they had to depend on one another for the goods and services they needed. Barbers, tailors, carpenters, metal workers—people with many different skills gathered in the towns. They traded their own products or services for those of others.

5. Crowds always bring problems. The problems of the towns and cities of the Middle Ages seem to have been as great as the problems facing our cities today. Houses, three and four stories high, were jammed together. The upper levels of these houses reached out over the streets. Houses on one side of the street almost touched the houses on the opposite side. As a result, the streets were dark. Since garbage was dumped in the streets, the streets were very dirty. A heavy rain was often the only means of garbage removal.

6. Most towns were surrounded by walls, which the people had built because of their fear of robbers. Darkness also brought fear. Few dared to walk the streets at night, for police protection was unknown. Because houses were made of wood, fires were common. When a fire broke out, it spread quickly through the crowded towns, easily leaping from one house to another across the narrow streets. Poor sanitation conditions and a lack of clean water meant that sickness spread quickly. Because getting pure water was a problem, most townspeople drank wine or beer at meals.

7. The cathedral, or main church, was the most important building in the medieval town. Any town that had a cathedral was usually called a city. It was thought that the beauty and size of the cathedral showed how religious the people were. People were proud of their cathe-

drals and each town tried to build a more magnificent cathedral than its neighboring town. At first, cathedrals were built in the Roman style of architecture. Then a new style, called Gothic, began. The name *Gothic* was given to the style by those who believed that only a Goth or a barbarian could like this style. The Gothic cathedral was a large, heavy building. It had high towers and pointed arches.

WHY WERE GUILDS IMPORTANT?

8. One of the important parts of town life were the *guilds*. A *merchant guild* was an organization of people in the same kind of business. Business people joined together in guilds to protect their interests. In time of need, such as the death of a guild member, the guild cared for the families of its members. Sometimes, guild members combined their money to buy goods that they all needed from foreign lands. To keep

The Cathedral of Notre Dame and the Cathedral of Chartres are among the most famous examples of Gothic architecture. Compare this style of architecture with that of the Mosque of Omar on page 133.

others from setting up the same businesses, the guilds made sure that only members of the guild were allowed to open shops and sell goods.

9. Just as people in business formed merchant guilds, skilled workers formed *craft guilds*. There was a guild for each different trade. Craft guilds protected their members. But they also protected the people who bought their product. Buyers could be sure that the guild product was of the highest quality. The guilds decided the price of goods and nobody could charge a higher or a lower price. Since the Church did not approve of businesses' charging too much, the prices were usually fair. The trades of people of the Middle Ages form many of our names today: taylor, carpenter, miller, smith, potter (one who makes vases and bowls), mason (one who works with stone), tanner (leather worker), fletcher (maker of bows and arrows), and many others.

10. A young man worked hard to become a member of a craft guild. He had to become an expert in his craft or trade. As a young man, he began to learn his trade by working for a *master*. He swept floors and ran errands for the master. He was then called an *apprentice*. Sometimes he was paid for his services, and sometimes he was not. In a few years, he could become a *journeyman*. Then he could be paid for his work. As a journeyman, he hired himself out to work with a master of a trade. Then he had to make a *masterpiece*, or sample of his work. This sample had to be approved by other members of the guild. Finally, if he had the money to set up his own shop, he could become a master and a member of the guild. Only the real expert became a guild member.

11. Women could not join guilds. As in the early Middle Ages, their lives were controlled by their husbands. In many ways, women's roles in family life were as important as those of their husbands. They cared for the children, directed the servants, and made cloth. Nearly all women knew how to spin thread and weave it into cloth. Women could inherit land or a business.

Some owned shops and carried on their husbands' trades after their deaths.

12. The guild system made it difficult for a person to begin a trade or earn much money. It did mean, however, that buyers got the best quality in goods. It also meant that the members of guilds received fair pay for their work. In short, the guilds controlled the goods bought and sold within a town. Guilds were therefore able to make much money. Much of the power of the town government was backed by the wealth of the guilds. Their money was often used in building churches and hospitals in the town.

HOW DID TRADE AFFECT TOWNS?

13. Town fairs offered both business and pleasure for the townspeople. People came from all over the surrounding countryside to buy and sell their goods and take part in dancing, wrestling, and games of chance. Acrobats and jugglers performed their tricks for the visiting crowds. At first, fairs were held only on holy days and lasted one day. But as they became more popular, they went on for several days. The largest fairs took place in towns and cities along the leading trade routes. At the big fairs,

Merchants brought their goods to markets such as the one shown in this picture. How did these markets bring wealth to the towns and cities?

goods were brought from many parts of the world. One could find silks, spices, and rugs from the East; furs from the colder parts of Europe; woolens from Belgium. Fairs also provided a chance for the people to exchange news and ideas.

14. Towns brought trade, and trade meant wealth for the towns. The townspeople found that they could use their wealth to gain more freedom for themselves. For example, the land on which towns were built was usually owned by nobles. With their money, the townspeople could buy the rights to run their own affairs. The rights that the people got were written in a *charter*, a contract between the noble and the town. As the towns gained more voice in government, they began to coin their own money, collect tolls at the town gates, and tax their people. In this way they could better carry on the business of government. Of course, not all towns had the same amount of freedom. As a result, some merchants moved to towns that offered them greater opportunities and more freedom.

Testing Your Vocabulary

Choose the best answer.

1. A *craft guild* may be compared with a modern-day
   a. university.
   b. union of skilled workers.
   c. corporation.
2. An *apprentice* is
   a. a beginner in his trade.
   b. in business for himself.
   c. a teacher of others.
3. When a group is given a *charter*, it
   a. gets the right to make or sell a product.
   b. is given enough money to begin a business.
   c. gets an agreement allowing it to do certain things.

Understanding What You Have Read

1. A good title for paragraphs 9 and 10 is
   a. Power in Town Governments
   b. Where Some of Our Names Come From
   c. Union of Merchants
   d. How Craft Guilds Worked

2. In which paragraph do you find facts about
   a. the development of towns near main roads.
   b. the architecture of cathedrals.
   c. what happened at fairs.
   d. the duties of an apprentice.

3. All of these were important reasons for the growth of towns in the Middle Ages EXCEPT
   a. a growth in population meant that there was not enough work for all people on the manors.
   b. barbarian invasions became fewer in number.
   c. lords gave protection to people within castle walls.

4. Merchant guilds were formed to
   a. give people lower prices for their goods.
   b. protect buyers against poorly made goods.
   c. protect shopkeepers from outsiders who wanted to work in the same trade.

5. Craft guilds did not allow their members to

a. receive a fair price for the work that they did.

b. buy goods in foreign lands.

c. produce poor work.

6. Townspeople were able to govern themselves more because

a. they used their new wealth to buy certain rights from lords.

b. kings had taken power from nobles and granted the townspeople rights.

c. serfs revolted and demanded rights when they moved to the towns.

7. Fairs were held chiefly to

a. celebrate religious holidays.

b. trade goods.

c. buy and sell serfs.

Tell whether you agree or disagree with the following statements, giving reasons for your answers.

1. The building of cathedrals was an expression of religious faith.
2. Townspeople began to gain more voice in their government.
3. In time, women outnumbered men as members of guilds.
4. Towns began to spring up quickly a few years after the Fall of Rome.
5. Gothic cathedrals had the same style of architecture as the buildings of Rome.
6. One of the benefits of feudalism was that it brought some order to Europe.
7. In a town of the Middle Ages, the wealthy people probably spent their evenings at the theater or taking walks.
8. When a large number of people settle in one place, trade among them usually results.
9. Most town homes of the Middle Ages were built of stone.

Developing Ideas and Skills

MAKING AN OUTLINE

Below are three headings for an outline of Chapter 5. Sub-topics are also listed. Write the letter of the best heading for each sub-topic.

Headings
A. Town Life in the Middle Ages
B. The Guild System
C. Trade Among Towns

Sub-topics
1. Large fairs took place on leading trade routes.
2. Merchants and skilled workers built churches and hospitals.
3. A masterpiece had to be approved by a master craftsman.
4. Sickness and fires were frequent.
5. All merchants charged the same price for the same goods.
6. Cathedrals were the centers of attention.
7. Buyers could be sure that goods sold were of the highest quality.
8. Houses were close together, reaching out into the street.
9. Sanitation conditions were poor.
10. Merchants moved to towns where there was greater freedom.
11. Travel on streets at night was not safe.
12. Tolls were collected at town gates.

AIM: Why did the Church become so important in the lives of Europeans during the Middle Ages?

CHAPTER 6

The Medieval Church in People's Lives

WHAT POWERS DID THE CHURCH HAVE?

1. Today, one-fourth of the people of the United States and Canada are members of the Roman Catholic Church. The rest of the people are members of other religious groups. During the Middle Ages, almost everyone in Western Europe was Catholic. Rulers, lords, and serfs alike were Catholic. They lived and died under the protection and authority of the Church. The people drew comfort from their religion. They needed this comfort to withstand the troubles of life at that time. They believed there was happiness after death for those who had led good lives. This belief was important for the poor serfs. There were no national ties (as we know them) to bring people together. They were united by their belief in the same religion.

2. The pope is the head of the Catholic Church. He follows in the steps of Peter, the first bishop of Rome. During the Middle Ages, the pope had great power. Since all rulers in Europe were Catholic, they obeyed the pope. This meant that the Church controlled matters of politics as well as religion. Below the pope were those who reached the people directly:

the bishops and priests. The Church was an important landowner, controlling large territories. Some Church officials were vassals, holding fiefs like any other lord. The people paid a *tithe*, or sum of money, to support the Church. In this way, the Church gained more wealth and bought more land.

3. The Church had ways of punishing those who disobeyed it. The punishment was the same for rulers as it was for common people. The pope could *excommunicate* a person. This meant that the person was cut off from the Church. People who were excommunicated found that no Christian was allowed to have anything to do with them. If the person was a noble, his subjects might revolt. The Church's punishment for a large group of people was called an *interdict*. That is, the pope would close all churches in a certain region. No religious ceremonies were allowed to take place.

4. The Church was involved in all the activities of its members. It kept the only records of births, marriages, and deaths. To try to keep peace among nobles at war, the Church forbade fighting from Thursday evening until Monday morning, and also on holy days. This period of peace was called the "truce of God." The

Church also had a say in business life. It ordered guilds to charge fair prices for their goods. It preached that greed for riches was wrong.

WHAT DID MONASTERIES CONTRIBUTE TO SOCIETY?

5. The *monastery* was an important part of life in the Middle Ages. Monastery life had actually begun hundreds of years earlier. Holy people, called hermits, had gone into the mountains or forests to live alone, away from the sinfulness and troubles of the world. These hermits spent their lives in work and prayer. In time, hermits came together in groups to live away from the world. They were called *monks*. About the year 500, St. Benedict set up rules for monks and founded a monastery in Italy in which they could live and pray. Soon monastery life spread over Western Europe. Women called nuns also lived apart from the world.

6. Monks took vows of poverty, obedience, and chastity. That is, they promised God that they would keep no goods or money, obey those above them, and never marry. Monks spent each day in work and prayer. Since the monks spent their lives working, the idea of work suddenly became noble. You remember that the rich in Rome thought they were too good to work. Only the poor did what had to be done around the house and in the city. Now, however, the monks, the holiest and the best educated people in Europe, were hard workers.

7. The monks were good farmers. They showed the serfs the use of the three-field system in farming. But not all the monks farmed in the monastery fields. Many spent their time copying the valuable writings of the past. Since most people of the time could not read or write, the monks alone kept alive the great written culture of the past. Very often, priests and monks were the only educated people to be found in an entire region. Sometimes monks taught the village children in monastery schools or set up libraries. Monasteries were also used as hospitals and resting places for travelers.

8. Only a few people in Europe knew how to read and write. Even rulers were often uneducated. Only great rulers like Charlemagne of France and King Alfred of Great Britain were interested in education and culture. Since even the rich were uneducated, peasant farmers could not be blamed for their lack of interest in learning. Besides, they had to spend all their time plowing, planting, and harvesting in order to earn a living. Nearly all education was run by the Church. Monastery schools taught Latin, grammar, music, and astronomy.

9. Missionaries as well as monks spread the teachings of the Church. Starting in 597, St. Augustine of Canterbury, a missionary, preached Christianity in England. Later, St. Patrick spread the teachings of the Church to Ireland. St. Boniface converted the barbarian tribesmen of Germany to Christianity. A group of missionaries led by a Spanish monk, St. Dominic, walked barefoot across Europe, preaching.

Monks at work designing a new church. Name at least three different tasks taking place in the picture.

The picture above shows monks copying manuscripts. The picture on the right shows a completed page. Imagine copying a whole book by hand and illustrating each page as you go!

His followers were known as Dominicans. They still form one of the large teaching and missionary orders of the Catholic Church.

10. One of the greatest figures of the Middle Ages was St. Francis of Assisi. He turned from a life of wealth, into which he was born, to live a life of poverty as a missionary. During the early years of the 13th century, he traveled about Europe. He taught the importance of loving one's neighbor and caring for the poor. Francis loved the birds and animals, for they were also God's creatures. His followers were known as Franciscans.

Spiritual men like St. Francis of Assisi were often subjects in paintings. The artist tried to emphasize the goodness of the man and often showed him in "heavenly" scenes.

Testing Your Vocabulary

Choose the best answer.

1. When a *tithe* was paid, people
   a. paid their yearly tax to their lord.
   b. gave part of their goods to a monastery.
   c. gave part of their income to the Church.
2. When a *truce* is declared, it means that
   a. fighting is stopped.
   b. no church services are held for a certain period of time.
   c. a vow is taken.
3. Paragraph 5 states that some women lived "apart from the world." Here *the world* means
   a. the planet earth.
   b. crowded cities.
   c. society with all its sinfulness, cares, and nonreligious concerns.

Understanding What You Have Read

1. The main idea of paragraph 7 is that
   a. hermits spent their lives alone in prayer.
   b. monks were educated people who preserved the culture of the past.
   c. monks did many kinds of work.
   d. monks were farmers.
2. In which paragraph do you find facts about
   a. St. Patrick's missionary work in Ireland?
   b. Christians paying part of their income to the Church?
   c. the pope's power over rulers in religious matters?
   d. St. Benedict's rules for monks?
3. The pope's excommunication of the ruler of a country was important because it meant that
   a. the ruler's subjects might revolt.
   b. the ruler immediately lost all the territory he had conquered in other lands where the Church had power.
   c. no religious ceremonies were allowed in the ruler's territory.
4. The Church was important in the Middle Ages for all these reasons EXCEPT
   a. the Church encouraged scientific experiments.
   b. the Church helped stop wars among nobles on holy days.
   c. almost everyone, rich and poor, was a member of the Catholic Church.
5. St. Francis of Assisi is thought to be one of the world's noblest men because he
   a. became one of the great popes of the Middle Ages.
   b. set down rules to be followed in all monasteries.
   c. gave up a life of wealth to preach love of one's neighbor.
6. The fact that monks worked as well as prayed was important because
   a. little farming was done except in monasteries.
   b. the monks made the idea of work noble.
   c. they earned money to pay for the costs of government.
7. The work of the monks was important for all of these reasons EXCEPT
   a. they set up some schools for village children.

b. they taught better methods of farming.

c. they organized workers into guilds.

8. Monks did all of these EXCEPT
   a. copied valuable literary works of the past.
   b. gave shelter to travelers.
   c. were members of guilds.

9. Monks took all these vows except
   a. poverty.
   b. justice.
   c. obedience.

10. All of these were taught in monastery schools EXCEPT

a. Latin.
b. engineering.
c. music.

11. Missionaries of the Middle Ages included all these EXCEPT
    a. St. Paul.
    b. St. Dominic.
    c. St. Boniface.

12. All of the following were features of the Catholic Church in the Middle Ages EXCEPT
    a. it owned land.
    b. it kept records.
    c. it set down rules for trading with foreign lands.

Developing Ideas and Skills

KNOWING IMPORTANT TERMS

In social studies, there are terms that you will see again and again. Three of these important terms are:

political—this term has to do with government or politics.

social—this term has to do with the way people live together.

economic—this term has to do with money, business, and earning a living.

Political conditions, then, refer to the workings of government, how people govern themselves and how they are governed by others.

Social conditions refer to the customs that people have: their clothes, their use of leisure time, their interests.

Economic conditions refer to the wages that people are paid for their work, the goods they make and sell, and what they are able to buy or trade.

Look at the following list of features of European life in the Middle Ages. Read each statement carefully. Then decide what term you would give to each: political feature, social feature or economic feature. Some statements may require more than one term.

1. Vassals ruled their land, but they were ruled by other vassals.
2. Rulers had little power, and this power became even less as the nobles became more important.
3. The people of a manor tried to grow or make everything, so that they did not have to depend upon others for food or clothing.
4. In the Middle Ages, there was only one Christian Church and it guided the way people lived.
5. There were few good roads and much fighting, so that trade almost disappeared.
6. The serfs farmed the lands of the manor but got no wages for their work.
7. The fall of the Roman Empire caused

people to gather together in small groups, each with its own ruler.

8. Few people had an education. Only priests, monks, and a few nobles were able to read and write.

9. Life in the Middle Ages was difficult and neither nobles nor serfs had fun.

10. Merchant guilds brought together merchants who combined their wealth to buy goods from foreign lands.

LEARNING ABOUT THE PAST THROUGH ART

Look at this painting carefully. Then answer the questions below.

1. What does this painting from the Middle Ages show?
2. Name the things that look familiar to you. Point out the things that you cannot name.
3. What do you think the man and woman are doing?
4. Imagine you could go back in time to the real-life scene of this painting. How would the life going on around you be like life as you know it today? How would it be different?
5. What might be going on outside the room shown in the painting?
6. What would the man and woman of the painting think when they met you?

CHAPTER 7

The Church's Power over Kings and Nobles

WHY DID POPES AND RULERS DISAGREE?

1. You remember that Charlemagne had been crowned emperor by the pope. Otto the Great, a German ruler, was also crowned Holy Roman Emperor by the pope. These acts gave the pope a great deal of power. It seemed that a person could not become a ruler unless the pope agreed. As a result, many rulers became jealous of the Church. This brought serious conflicts between the Church and the nobles.

2. An easy way for nobles to prove their loyalty to the Church was to grant land to Church officials. So the Catholic Church became one of the large landowners of the Middle Ages. Bishops and priests became feudal lords. They therefore owed loyalty to the nobles from whom they had received the land. But as bishops and priests, they also owed loyalty to the Church. Who, then, would choose a new bishop when one died? Would it be the noble who owned the bishop's land and was his lord? Would it be the Church, who was in charge of religious matters? Who really had the power to put Church officials into office and to *invest* (furnish) them with the power of their position? This question became known as the argument over the right of *investiture*. During the 12th

century, popes spoke out against the rulers' power of investiture.

3. Finally, Pope Gregory VII forbade the investiture of Church officials by kings and lords. Later, Gregory said that he would take away the powers of any ruler who disobeyed his orders. Henry IV, the Holy Roman Emperor, did not like this order. He declared that Gregory was no longer pope. Gregory, in turn, told the people of Germany that they did not have to obey King Henry. The nobles, who did not like Henry, revolted against him. The serfs and townspeople were afraid of being excommunicated. They also turned against him. Henry had to go to Italy to ask forgiveness from the pope. Pope Gregory forced him to wait outside in the snow for three days before granting him pardon. The pope thus showed that he had more power than the king. In 1122, a final agreement was reached. It was agreed that the Church would choose its own bishops. Emperors and kings were, in return, given the right to give land to Church officials and control non-religious matters in that land.

4. These were not the only conflicts that showed the power of the Church in the Middle Ages. In the 13th century, King John of England did not accept a bishop whom the pope had chosen. So Pope Innocent III excommunicated the king. Then, the Church brought to trial religious groups that did not agree with its teachings. Many people were sentenced to death for *heresy*, or disagreeing with long-accepted beliefs of the Church. In the 13th century, the pope and Church had its greatest power over the affairs of people.

WHY DID THE CRUSADERS FAIL TO CAPTURE THE HOLY LAND?

5. An example of the power of the Church was the Crusades. The term *Crusade* comes from the Latin word *crux* meaning *cross*. The cross was the symbol worn by the Crusaders. The Crusades were holy wars whose aim was to get back the Holy Land, Palestine, from the Turks. In 1071, the Seljuk (SEL-jook) Turks had captured Jerusalem. Christian pilgrims on their way from Europe to Jerusalem were sometimes attacked by the Turks, who were Muslims. Muslim forces were also trying to get control of Constantinople, the capital of the empire. The Byzantine emperor asked the pope for help against the Muslims. At a Church Council in 1095, Pope Urban called on all Christians to defeat the Turks and get back the Holy Land.

6. The Pope's call was answered by thousands in Europe. Most of the Crusaders were deeply religious people. They were moved by their religious beliefs to go to, and fight for, the Holy Land. Other people had different reasons for joining the Crusades. There were knights who went for love of adventure and kings who

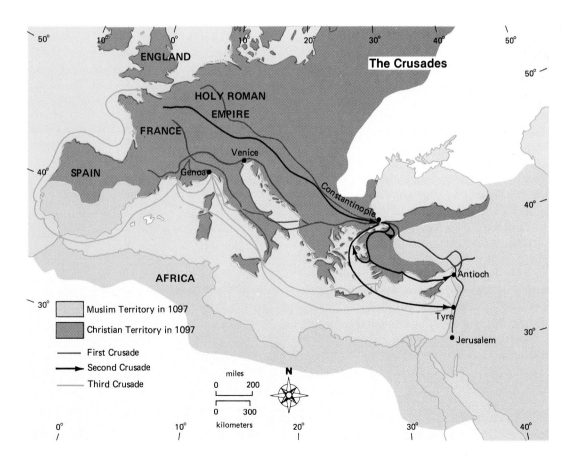

went looking for glory. There were criminals who went to escape punishment and debtors who wished to escape their debts. There were lords who hoped to win land from the Muslims. Even runaway children went along. Whatever their reasons, thousands of people joined the Crusades.

7. The early Crusaders were hardly ready for the dangers they were to meet. The first attempt at a Crusade was led by Peter the Hermit and Walter the Penniless. Death and disease caused their followers to give up and return home. Nobles from France, Italy, and Germany then led the first Crusade. The Crusaders captured Jerusalem in 1099. In a second Crusade, however, Christian leaders began to disagree among themselves. Thus weakened, they again lost Jerusalem to the Muslims.

8. The third Crusade was led by three rulers of Europe: Richard the Lion-Hearted, of England; Philip II, of France; and Frederick Barbarossa, of Germany. With leaders like these, how could the Crusaders fail to get back the Holy Land? But the Christians met up with many troubles. Frederick drowned in Asia Minor. Philip and Richard could not agree, and Philip returned to Europe. Richard continued on, but could not capture Jerusalem. He did, however, reach an agreement with the Muslim ruler. From then on, Christians were allowed to go on their pilgrimages to Jerusalem in safety.

9. Some Crusades led to unexpected results. Once the Crusaders turned against their fellow Christians, the Byzantines. The Crusaders owed money to merchants in Venice. These merchants had helped pay for the Crusades. Instead of wanting to be paid back in money, the merchants asked the Crusaders to attack Constantinople. This city was Venice's rival in trade. The Crusaders agreed, and Christians fought against Christians. The pope begged them to stop, but they would not. Constantinople was captured by the Crusaders. It stayed under the control of the West for fifty years and never got back the greatness it once had.

HOW DID THE CRUSADES CHANGE EUROPEAN LIFE?

10. In 200 years of Crusades, the Christians did not get back the Holy Land. But the Crusades had other results, ones that were felt in many ways and in many places. Those Europeans who reached the Holy Land tasted new foods: sugar, lemon, rice, coffee, and spices. Spices were to become very important to Europeans. Spices kept meat and other foods from spoiling at a time when there were no iceboxes or refrigerators. New goods also were brought back to Europe: silk, muslin, mirrors, and rugs. The richer people of Europe found that these things made their lives much more comfortable and wanted more of them. So the Crusades brought about new trade between Europe and Asia Minor. Europeans also wished to learn about Muslim discoveries in medicine, science, and mathematics.

11. Great cities arose along the Mediterranean Sea as a result of the Crusades. The Mediterranean was the main route of trade between

The Turkish ruler, Mehmed II, built this castle in 1452 shortly before capturing Constantinople.

Europe and the East. The Italian cities of Venice and Genoa became leading seaports. Ships sailed to and from Venice, bringing goods into Europe. These goods were shipped to more distant ports and cities in Europe. Merchants in Venice who had sold goods to the Crusaders became rich. So did bankers in Venice who had lent money to the Crusaders.

12. The Crusades led to the end of feudalism. Serfs who left the manors to fight in the Crusades found a better life and did not return. Others who had left the manors returned to the towns and cities instead, hoping for a better life. The nobles lost power. Many had borrowed money or sold their serfs to join the Crusades. Now, with the nobility weakened, kings were able to control more territory. Along with the power of kings, the power of the Church grew also.

13. No longer were Europeans happy with the life they had lived. Stories of the Crusaders caused people back home to want new kinds of goods. There was a new interest in travel. As people traveled more, the trade of goods and ideas grew even more, and the crusading spirit did not die out. Later, Christians in Europe felt the crusading wish to convert the people in far-off Asia to Christianity.

Testing Your Vocabulary

Choose the best answer.

1. *Investiture* means
   a. the power to excommunicate.
   b. the power to make a person a Church official.
   c. the right of the Church to take the land of another.
2. Persons who were guilty of *heresy*,
   a. did not believe in one of the long-established teachings of the Church.
   b. were Church officials who were vassals of a lord.
   c. were nobles who granted land to the Church.

Understanding What You Have Read

1. The main idea of paragraphs 3 and 4 is that:
   a. the people of Germany revolted against their king.
   b. the Church showed its power over kings.
   c. King Henry IV argued with the pope.
   d. troubles between popes and emperors were ended.
2. In which paragraph do you find facts about
   a. the types of people who went on the Crusades?
   b. the Crusade led by Richard the Lion-Hearted?
   c. reasons why the Crusades began?
   d. the meaning of *investiture?*
3. Popes and rulers argued about the
   a. rights of Muslims in the Holy Land.
   b. right to choose Church officials.
   c. right of monks to teach in village schools.
4. Pope Urban called for a Crusade when
   a. Constantinople fell to the Persians.
   b. the Turks kept Christian pilgrims from going to the Holy Land.

c. traders from Italy were attacked in Asia Minor.

5. One reason for the failure of the Crusades was that
   a. there were few who were willing to join the Crusades.
   b. leading bishops of Europe fought against one another.
   c. the Crusaders were not ready for the hardships and dangers they met.

6. All of these were results of the Crusades EXCEPT

a. Muslims were driven out of the Holy Land.
b. trade grew between the people of Europe and Asia.
c. the nobles lost power.

7. A reason for the weakening of feudalism after the Crusades was that
   a. lords had fought one another during the Crusades.
   b. the power of the Church was weakened.
   c. many serfs who had left the manors did not return.

Developing Ideas and Skills

USING SOURCES OF INFORMATION

There are many original sources you might use to find the information you want. But there are also sources of valuable information that are not original or firsthand. These sources are made up of facts put together by experts who have looked at original sources. The following are four sources that you will probably use often.

An *atlas* is a book of maps. An atlas often has an index that lists the names of every place shown on the maps. Maps may show things besides the location and boundaries of places. They may show the differences in weather in different places, amount of rainfall, the crops grown, the minerals mined, the population, or the religions.

An *almanac* is a book of useful facts and figures about different topics such as countries, sports, or entertainment. Almanacs usually come out every year. Facts about nations and people you may wish to learn are in an almanac. The index of one of today's almanacs shows such topics as these: positions of the moon, pay of army officers, amount of paper printed in the United States, airplane speed records, and volcanoes in Mexico.

An *encyclopedia* is a book or series of books that discuss topics listed in alphabetical order. The topics in an encyclopedia cover almost every subject you can imagine. Most of the articles are written by experts. Our best encyclopedias are in many volumes or books. The following is a sample of the items in a leading encyclopedia:

Hellenism (Greek life and culture)
Hellespont (the ancient name for the Dardanelles near Turkey)
Helmets (heavy hats worn for protection in war or sports)
Helots (slaves of ancient Sparta)

Textbooks are the source of information that students use most. In learning about social studies, you will be interested in books about geography, politics, and economics. One of your main jobs is choosing the right books for your needs. Books that cover a long period of time cannot give you as much information about an event as those covering a smaller period of years. Note the difference in these textbooks:

History of the World—a book with this title would cover the history of humanity for at least 6,000 years.

Ancient History—this book would be about only the ancient world, a period of about 4,000 years.

History of Ancient Greece—this book would be limited further to about 800 years in ancient times.

Greece in the Golden Age—this book would be an even shorter period, about 70 years.

You have a choice of hundreds of books in which to look for information. *Skim* the tables of contents of different books. See which of the books you have chosen include the information you want. Select the book that suits your needs best.

Which would be the best book in which to find the following?

1. A map of the Holy Land
2. The number of Muslims and Christians today
3. A summary of the results of the Crusades
4. The names of the popes in the last 50 years
5. A short discussion of the life of King John of England
6. A map showing the straits near Constantinople
7. A description of clothing worn by Crusaders

Using Original Sources

Many of the Crusaders were poor. They found a different kind of life and often a more comfortable life in the Middle East. One Crusader describes how many felt.

A Crusader Describes the Middle East

We who were once Westerners have become like Asians. He who was once Roman or Frank is now a Gallilean, or a man of Palestine. Whoever once lived in Rheims or Chartres finds himself a citizen of Tyre or Antioch.

Already we have forgotten places of our birth. Some of us in this country have homes and servants which belong to them. Someone else has married a wife who is not his country woman—a Syrian, an Armenian, or even a Muslim who has received the grace of Baptism.

One cultivates vines, another fields. They speak different languages and are already capable of understanding all of them. Confidence in each other has drawn us together. In truth it is written, "The lion and the ox eat from the same manger."

Whoever was once a stranger is now a native. The pilgrim has become a citizen. To those who had nothing but a small piece of land, God has given a village; those who were poor, God has made rich. Why should anyone go back to the West when the East is so kind to him?

1. What did the Crusader like about the Middle East?
2. What is the Crusader referring to when he says that he is a citizen of Tyre or Antioch?
3. What does the writer mean when he says that the lion and the ox eat together? Who is the lion? Who is the ox?
4. Name several benefits the Crusaders found in their travels to Asia.

AIM: What progress was made in India, China, and Japan during the Middle Ages?

CHAPTER 8

Asia During the Middle Ages

WHAT WAS INDIA'S GOLDEN AGE?

1. Europe did not stand apart from the rest of the world in the Middle Ages. Many of the goods that were wanted in Europe after the Crusades came from Asia. Europe and Asia were more closely linked as trade between them grew. As a result of trade, the period of European exploration and discovery began.

2. After its early settlements, India suffered a series of invasions from the West. Alexander had reached India about 325 B.C. Its people were not united for hundreds of years thereafter. It was northern India that suffered most from invasions. Southern India is a highland region. Invaders found it more difficult to conquer.

3. From the 4th to the 6th century A.D., India enjoyed a period of great glory. It was a golden age under the Gupta Dynasty. Northern India was united. Universities, perhaps the first in the world, were founded. Poetry and literature were written in *Sanskrit*, the early Hindu language. A system of numbers was introduced by Hindu mathematicians. The zero, decimals, and *pi* (the Greek letter standing for the ratio of

a circle's circumference to its diameter) were part of their system. These ideas were later brought to Europe by Arab traders. For years it had been supposed that Arabs had first developed these ideas. Steel, soap, and glass were produced by skilled workers in India. Gupta culture was carried east to China, to Burma, and even to the island of Java.

HOW DID INVASIONS AFFECT INDIA'S PROGRESS?

4. The Huns, a barbarian tribe of central Asia, invaded India in the 5th century. The Gupta rulers were defeated. The unity of northern India was ended. Then, Muslim traders came from the west. India had silks, jewels, and spices that Crusaders had seen in their travels to the Holy Land. More Muslims came. Northern India was invaded a dozen times. A Muslim empire was set up at Delhi in 1206.

5. The Muslims were not barbarians. But they tried to convert the Hindus of India by force and terror. Hindus were heavily taxed. Their statues, idols, and temples were destroyed. Religious leaders were killed. Hinduism was not uprooted. But it was the beginning of many religious wars to come. Conflict between Hindus and Muslims in India has lasted to this day.

6. The Muslim empire weakened and again India was invaded. This time Mongols came from central Asia. In 1526 their leader, Baber, united more of India than had ever been united before. Early in the Mongol reign, Hindu had greater freedom of religion. Special taxes on Hindus were ended. Another golden age for India began. Akbar, son of Baber, was the greatest of the Mongol rulers. Nearly all of India came under his control. Taxes were reduced and schools were started. Christian missionaries were invited to come to India.

7. A grandson of Akbar built the famous Muslim temple, the Taj Mahal, as a tomb for his wife. It has a dome of marble. Precious stones decorate its walls. Thousands of workers toiled for a dozen years to finish the tomb. This and other great buildings cost huge sums of money. Taxes became heavier and the poor became poorer. Later rulers attacked the Hindus once more. India was invaded in the 16th and 17th centuries, this time by European powers. Divided by invasions and wars within the country, India was not strong enough to resist. Europeans took control of India. India did not rid itself of foreign rule until 1947.

WHAT PROGRESS WAS MADE IN CHINA'S GOLDEN AGE?

8. While Europe was still in the Dark Ages, there was a golden age in China, too. From the 6th to the 13th century, China achieved great things in trade, art, and education. China's borders reached to India, in the southwest, and to Manchuria and Mongolia in the north. Great ships and caravans carried silk, spices, jewels, and works of art to Arab traders of the West. In return, incense and ivory were brought eastward to China.

9. The Chinese had improved their farming methods. Large cities grew up. Changes in

Although the Taj Mahal was built in the 16th century and the pyramids of Egypt were built in 3000 B.C., both structures were tombs. Compare the reasons for building each structure.

farming produced enough food to feed the growing city population. Terraces were built on hillsides to protect good soil. The Chinese rotated crops to keep the soil fertile, as monks had done in Europe. Tea became important in Chinese trade. The Chinese invented gunpowder, but it was used chiefly in firecrackers. Once gunpowder came into use in Europe, feudalism there was doomed. The walls of castles were no defense against a foe that used cannons and gunpowder.

10. China also had a golden age in art and literature. Chinese paintings showed scenes of great beauty. Sculptors made statuettes (small statues) of animals. These later became one of the highest forms of Chinese art. Skilled workers turned out fine silks, which Moslem traders eagerly sought. Pottery and fine porcelain dishes were highly valued. The works of Buddhist poets were translated into Chinese.

HOW DID MONGOL INVASION AND RULE AFFECT CHINESE LIFE?

11. China's golden age was ended by the Mongols, the horsemen of central Asia. The

Mongols were probably the world's finest horsemen. They lived on horseback and could ride for days without rest or food. Genghis Khan (1162–1227) was the great Mongol conqueror. His forces moved in many directions. They rode into northern China and Korea. After the death of Genghis Khan, his sons continued to spread Mongol power. At one time, the Mongol empire reached into Persia and Mesopotamia, and even as far west as Russia and Poland.

12. China held off the Mongols until 1279. Then it fell to Kublai Khan, grandson of Genghis. Peace and order were restored to China. Trade between East and West was at its greatest. Roads were built and harbors were improved. Chinese caravans crossed Asia, linking Asia with Europe. Gunpowder and block printing made their way to Europe.

13. During the reign of Kublai Khan, Marco Polo visited China. Marco was the son of a trader of Venice. He traveled to China with his father and stayed there for twenty years. Kublai Khan took a liking to Marco and made him governor of a city. When he returned to Europe in 1295, Marco Polo wrote about the glories of China under the Mongols. He told

Marco Polo before Kublai Khan. What does this picture tell you about Marco Polo's attitude toward Kublai Khan?

exciting stories of the wealth of Kublai Khan. Europe had already showed a taste for Chinese goods. Now, the tales of Marco Polo made Europeans want to trade with Asia more than ever before.

14. It is likely that Marco Polo admired the Mongol rulers more than the Chinese people did. The Chinese never grew to like the foreigners who had invaded their land. Yet, for almost 100 years, Kublai Khan and his successor ruled in China. During their rule, long dry spells and floods hurt the crops of Chinese farmers. In time, the people revolted against the Mongols and drove them out. Then, the strong rulers of the Ming Dynasty took control of China. A period of even greater trade between China and Europe began.

HOW DID EVENTS IN CHINA AFFECT JAPAN?

15. The Mongols took another step after they went into China and Korea. It led to Japan. Kublai Khan demanded that Japan surrender. The demand was turned down. The Mongols put together a great force to invade Japan. They were turned back by violent storms that destroyed the Mongol forces. The Japanese believed the storms were brought on by some supernatural force. They called them *Kami Kazi*—divine wind. During the fight against the Mongols, Japan had built a large number of ships. They were now used to trade with China. By 1500, Japan was also trading with other parts of Asia.

16. The war with the Mongols was costly. The rule of the shogun was weakened. Other powerful lords and the emperor, too, challenged the shogun's rule. A new shogun family came to power in 1338. But the fighting among lords did not stop. Peace did not come for another 200 years. Then the shogun, Tokugawa (toh-ku-GAW-wah) took over leadership of Japan. He tried to restore order by isolating

Japan from outsiders once more. Not until the 16th century did Europeans come to Japan. Then, traders from Portugal arrived. A few years later, Christian missionaries came to try to convert the Japanese people.

17. In spite of the political disorders in Japan, this was a time of economic growth.

Farmers had learned to make good use of Japan's limited amount of farmland. Two or more crops of rice were raised each year. Hillsides were terraced for growing wheat. Towns sprang up near harbors and around castles. Tea was cultivated and became a major product in Japanese trade.

Testing Your Vocabulary _____

Choose the best answer.

1. *Sanskrit* is the name of the
   a. highlands of southern India.
   b. holy book of the Hindu religion.
   c. ancient Hindu language.
2. Chinese artists of the Chinese golden age made *statuettes.* These were
   a. stained-glass windows.
   b. small carved figures
   c. pictures of saints made out of small colored tiles.

Understanding What You Have Read _____

1. The main idea of paragraphs 4 through 6 is that
   a. the Gupta Dynasty ended with the invasion of the Huns.
   b. India was ruled for a time by Muslims.
   c. a golden age in India followed rule by the Mongols.
   d. India was invaded or ruled by outsiders for more than 1,000 years.
2. In which paragraph are these facts found:
   a. a part of India was bothered little by invaders?
   b. Arabic numerals were brought to Europe?
   c. the Mongols spread their power all over Asia?
   d. the Mongols tried to invade Japan?
3. The period of the Gupta rulers in India is known as a golden age because
   a. the Crusades brought new trade between Europe and India.
   b. the Hindus made great progress in literature and mathematics.
   c. Mongols treated the Hindus fairly.
4. Muslim rule in India caused troubles that have lasted to the present day because the Muslims
   a. were barbarians.
   b. asked Christian missionaries to come to India.
   c. tried to destroy the Hindu religion.
5. One of the achievements of the Mongols in India was the
   a. building of the Taj Mahal.
   b. successful defense of India against European powers.
   c. introduction of Arabic numerals.
6. Marco Polo's stories of his travels were

important because they

a. led Europeans to attack the Mongol empire.

b. made Europeans eager to get the riches of the East.

c. caused revolts of peasants against

their lords.

7. A reason for economic growth in Japan in the Middle Ages was that

a. strong shoguns kept order.

b. Japan was isolated from Asia.

c. farming methods were improved.

Choose the item that does not belong with the others in each group.

1. Chinese civilization:
   a. Arabic numerals
   b. gunpowder
   c. porcelain dishes
2. Hindu civilization:
   a. Arabic numerals
   b. printing
   c. decimal system
3. Chinese farming:
   a. rotation of crops
   b. terracing
   c. use of iron plows
4. History of India:
   a. Muslims b. Romans c. Huns
5. Rulers of India:
   a. Gupta   b. Akbar   c. Soong
6. Japan in the Middle Ages:
   a. Shoguns
   b. Tokugawa
   c. Genghis Khan
7. Goods traded from Asia:
   a. fish   b. silk   c. tea

Developing Ideas and Skills

USING A MAP

Study the map. Then answer the questions on page 169.

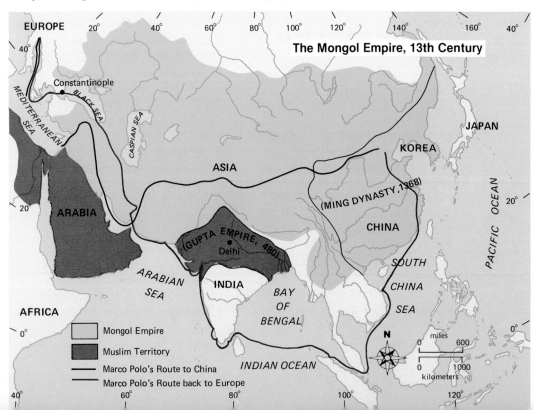

The Mongol Empire, 13th Century

Using the map as a guide, tell whether the following statements are true or false.

1. The Mongol empire included a part of Europe and all of Southeast Asia.
2. Marco Polo would have first visited India on his journey to China.
3. Marco Polo's route home from China was longer in miles than his route to China.
4. The Mongol empire could not have had ports on both its western and eastern borders.
5. Both the Black Sea and the Caspian Sea were entirely inside the Mongol empire.

Using Original Sources

Read the following description of the Mongols (here called Tartars) by Marco Polo. Then see if you can answer the questions that follow.

Marco Polo's Description of the Mongols

The Tartars drink mare's milk prepared in a way that makes it seem like white wine, and good to drink . . . . Their garments are mostly of cloth of gold and silk, lined with rich skins like sable and ermine. Their arms are bows and arrows and swords and axes; but they rely mostly on their bows, for they are excellent archers, the best that are known in the world. And on their backs they wear armour of leather that has been boiled and is very strong. They can endure more work than any other people; for often, when it is necessary, they will go for a month, taking no meat with them, except the mare's (horse's) milk they live on. . . . And for their horses they have no need to carry either barley or straw or oats, for they graze on the grass in the fields as they go and are very obedient to their masters. And when it is needful, they will remain on horseback all night fully armed. And their horses can go on grazing all the time. There are no people on earth who can so endure great pains and great discomfort, who have fewer wants to satisfy, and are better at conquering lands and kingdoms.

Choose the correct answer.

1. The chief weapons of the Tartars were their
   a. swords b. spears c. bows.
2. The leather worn by the Mongols had been
   a. tanned b. dried c. boiled.
3. For the Mongols, Marco Polo had great
   a. respect b. love c. dislike.
4. The chief food of the Mongols was the milk of the
   a. cow b. horse c. goat.
5. When it was necessary, the Mongols would sleep
   a. on grassy fields
   b. on horseback
   c. in tents.
6. The Mongols probably got their food, except milk, chiefly by
   a. hunting b. farming c. fishing.
7. Which of these words describes the Mongols as seen by Marco Polo?
   a. obedient b. brave c. tireless
   d. helpless e. strong f. lazy
   g. greedy h. alert

AIM: What kinds of civilizations existed in West Africa between the 8th and 17th centuries?

CHAPTER 9

Black Rulers of West Africa

WHAT BLOCKED TRADE TO WEST AFRICA?

1. Europeans had traded with the people of Africa along the Mediterranean Sea for centuries. Ancient Rome had fought wars with the North African city of Carthage 200 years before the birth of Jesus. Yet the Romans did not explore Africa below the Sahara. This great desert blocked the way to the middle of Africa. The blacks of West Africa were little touched by outsiders for thousands of years. Yet there were organized kingdoms in Africa during the Middle Ages in Europe.

2. The camel helped change the course of history in West Africa. About the 3rd century A.D., camels were brought to north Africa by the Berbers. The Berbers were a desert tribe. The camel made it possible to cross the Sahara Desert. Arab traders began to cross the Sahara with their camel caravans to trade with black tribes about A.D. 400. The trade continued to grow until the 7th century. The Arabs brought with them their books, their written language, and the Muslim religion. Many of the black people were converted to the religion of Islam. We owe much of what we know about the early African kingdoms to Arab writers.

3. Early Arab traders also wanted slaves. Slavery was as much a part of life in West Africa as it had been in ancient Egypt, Greece, and Rome. White traders made slaves of blacks. On the other hand, blacks were also slaves of other black tribes. Anyone who was captured in war or who was a "foreigner" from another tribe might be made a slave. Chiefs of black tribes sold slaves to traders. However, more than slaves were traded. The black kingdoms held riches in gold. Other important trading products were salt and ivory. For these, the Arabs exchanged beads and cloth.

HOW WAS WEST AFRICA RULED?

4. One of the earliest African kingdoms south of the Sahara was the black kingdom of Ghana. It began in the 8th century (at the time of Charlemagne) and lasted for 300 years. Most of the people worked at farming or sheepherding. Others were spinners or weavers and made beautiful cloth for the rich. Coined money was unknown. Gold was wound up like wire and used for money. Trade was carried on with surrounding peoples. Goods from Ghana were known in places as far away as Baghdad.

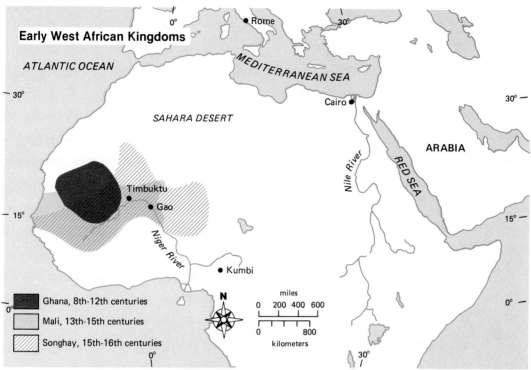

Early West African Kingdoms

ATLANTIC OCEAN

MEDITERRANEAN SEA

SAHARA DESERT

- Rome

Cairo ●

ARABIA

Nile River

RED SEA

Timbuktu ●

● Gao

Niger River

● Kumbi

N

■ Ghana, 8th-12th centuries

▨ Mali, 13th-15th centuries

▨ Songhay, 15th-16th centuries

miles
0 200 400 600

0   800
kilometers

5. The kingdom of Ghana was ruled by an all-powerful king. Arab writers described the wealth of the kingdom of Ghana. They told of the king's horses that were dressed in gold and watchdogs that wore collars of gold and silver. An army of nearly 200,000 soldiers stood behind the power of the ruler. But fierce Muslim warriors captured Ghana in the 11th century. Although the empire of Ghana continued on, it became weaker and weaker. In 1240, its capital city of Kumbi was destroyed by people from the nearby empire of Mali.

6. The Mali kingdom had many great rulers. Mali kings converted to Islam. Perhaps the greatest of all Mali rulers was Mansa Musa. He controlled territory in West Africa about the size of Western Europe. In his land were great gold mines. The wealth of Mali was built on gold, ivory, cattle, and cotton. Taxes also helped pay the expenses of the kingdom. The wealth of the Mali court became famous throughout Africa and the Middle East.

7. A good Muslim, Mansa Musa made a pilgrimage to Mecca. This was not easy, for Mecca lay 2,000 miles away, beyond the Sahara Desert. Few kings in Europe were as wealthy as this Mali ruler. It was reported that there were 60,000 people in his caravan to the holy city. 500 servants marched ahead of Mansa, each carrying a bag of pure gold. Each of 80 camels carried 300 pounds of gold. Along the way, Mansa gave away gifts of gold in the towns through which he passed.

8. In Egypt and Arabia, the Mali travelers met learned men. These scholars and teachers became friends of the emperor. When Mansa returned to Mali, a Muslim architect went with him. The architect tore down the mud huts of Mali and put up buildings in the Muslim style. Mosques were built and Mansa had a magnificent palace built for himself. But Mansa, a good emperor, was also known for his kindness and help to the poor. He died in 1337, at the age of 25.

This map, drawn in 1375, shows the routes of Mansa Musa. What do the figures tell you about the way Mansa Musa traveled?

9. After Mansa Musa's death, conflicts among different parts of his kingdom caused the downfall of Mali rule. In its place, the black kingdom of Songhay rose to power. The Songhay empire may well have been the greatest of the black African empires. Led by its warrior king, Sunni Ali, it conquered neighboring tribes. Sunni Ali then led his armies westward from Gao (gah-OH) taking Timbuctu and other cities along the Niger (NY-jer) River. About the time that Columbus sailed to America, the Songhay empire reached its greatest height. Songhay withstood attacks from Berber groups but finally fell in 1596 to Moroccans.

10. Askia the Great was the ruler of the Songhay at the height of its power. Askia was a good Muslim. He made the Koran, the holy book of Islam, the law of West Africa. He did special favors for Muslim schools and mosques. Askia also made a pilgrimage to Mecca, carrying with him a large amount of gold. He took many scholars with him to meet and talk with the scholars of the Muslim world. Under Askia, scholars, teachers, and philosophers held an important place in the kingdom. After his death, no strong ruler followed. The Songhay empire went the way of the black African empires before it.

11. The early history of West Africa, then, is the history of three kingdoms: Ghana, Mali, and Songhay. They had courts, cities, armies, and governments such as were set up in Europe some years later. Trade brought African culture to Europe and to the East. The Africans were skilled in basket-making, woodwork, pottery, and weaving. They were good artists and crafts workers. When the black people of West Africa were brought as slaves to the New World, America, they had behind them a long history and culture.

Testing Your Vocabulary

Choose the best answer.

1. A *pilgrimage* is
   a. a sacrifice.
   b. a journey to a sacred place.
   c. an offering of gold.

2. An *architect* is
   a. a person who studies old bones.
   b. one who plans buildings.
   c. a ruler of a country.

Understanding What You Have Read

1. A good title for paragraphs 6 through 8 is
   a. Learned Men of the East
   b. Trade of Ghana
   c. The Mali Kingdom
   d. Gold Mines of West Africa

2. In which paragraph do you find facts about
   a. the goods traded between Arabs and Africans?
   b. the pilgrimage of Mansa Musa?
   c. the rule of Askia?
   d. the beginning of Arab trade with black kingdoms?

3. The Romans were not interested in going to the middle of Africa to trade because
   a. they were always stopped by the Arabs.
   b. there seemed to be no way to cross the Sahara Desert.
   c. they had been defeated by Carthage.

4. Early Arab traders helped change the culture of West Africa by
   a. showing the black people how to farm.
   b. offering gold for clothing.
   c. bringing their written language, books, and religion.

5. Much of what we know about early black African kingdoms comes from
   a. Arab writers.
   b. Greek historians.
   c. the Koran.

6. Both the Mali and Songhay kingdoms fell because
   a. stronger Hindu armies conquered them.
   b. rulers wasted the wealth of the empires.
   c. conflicts began after the deaths of strong rulers.

7. One of the reasons why the early blacks of West Africa were important is that they:
   a. contributed to the culture of the New World.
   b. brought slavery to Africa.
   c. brought Muslim culture to North Africa.

Complete the statement in your notebook.

1. Northern Africa is separated from central and southern Africa by the _____ Desert.
2. Great black kingdoms were found chiefly in _____ Africa.
3. In the Mali kingdom, new buildings were in the _____ style.
4. Askia was ruler of the _____ kingdom.
5. Early kingdoms of West Africa were located near the _____ River.
6. The Muslim religion was brought to the black kingdoms by the _____.
7. The empire of _____ reached its heighth about the time that Columbus made his voyages to America.
8. The first of the great black African kingdoms was _____ .
9. The chief way of travel across the Sahara Desert was _____ .
10. The _____ brought camels to North Africa.

Developing Ideas and Skills

USING A TIME LINE

Study the time line below. Then answer the questions that follow it.

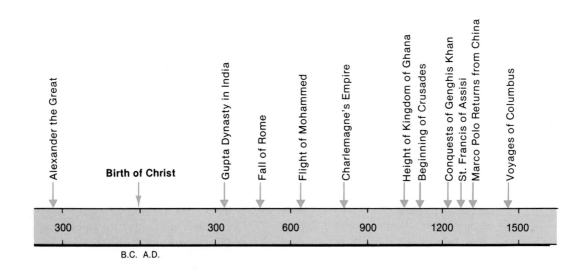

1. Which of these events happened before the reign of Charlemagne?
   a. The flight of Muhammad
   b. The beginning of the Crusades
   c. The kingdom of Ghana reached its peak

2. Which two events took place within 100 years of each other?
   a. Gupta Dynasty and the birth of Christ
   b. The flight of Muhammad and the reign of Charlemagne
   c. The start of the Crusades and the Kingdom of Ghana at its peak.
3. Which two people lived at about the same time?
   a. Francis of Assisi and Genghis Khan
   b. Christopher Columbus and Marco Polo
   c. Alexander the Great and Jesus
4. About how many years passed between the conquests of Alexander the Great and those of Genghis Khan?
   a. 1,200 years
   b. 1,500 years
   c. 1,800 years
5. When the golden age in India was ending
   a. Charlemagne was crowned Holy Roman Emperor.
   b. Rome fell.
   c. the Crusades were beginning.

Using Original Sources

How good a detective are you? Read the following passage (translated and adapted for this text) about the African kingdom of Mali. It was written more than 600 years ago by Ibn Battuta, an Arab trader. Then, see if you can answer the questions on page 176.

The Kingdom of Mali

Among the admirable qualities of these people, the following are to be noted:

1. The small number of acts of injustice that one finds there; for the blacks are of all people those who hate injustice.
2. The complete and general safety one enjoys throughout the land. The traveler has no more reason than the man who stays at home to fear bandits or thieves.
3. The blacks do not take away the goods of white men of North Africa who die in their country, not even when there are big treasures. They deposit them . . . among the whites until those who have a right to the goods present themselves and take possession.
4. They make their prayers on time . . . and punish their children if they should fail in this . . .
5. The blacks wear fine garments on Fridays. If by chance a man has no more than one shirt or a soiled blouse or coat, at least he washes it before putting it on to go to public prayer.
6. They are eager to learn the Koran by heart. Those children who neglect this are put in chains until they have memorized the Koran.

Do you agree or disagree with these statements? Give reasons for your answers.

1. Blacks of the Mali kingdom knew how to read.
2. Most people of Mali were believers in Christianity.
3. The Malis were unfriendly to strangers and travelers.
4. Mali children were punished if they did not study their lessons.
5. The Malis wore bright-colored clothes on all occasions.
6. It was dangerous to travel alone in the kingdom of Mali.

Summary of Unit III

A few of the most important events and facts described in this unit are listed below. Can you add any others?

1. Constantinople, on the straits leading to the Black Sea, was the capital of the Byzantine empire. It was a center of trade between East and West for centuries after the Fall of Rome.
2. The followers of Muhammad spread their religion and culture from India to North Africa and into Spain within a few hundred years.
3. Charlemagne of France developed a strong government at a time when there was little unity in Europe.
4. Feudalism was the way of life in Europe from the Fall of Rome to the beginning of modern times.
5. Towns grew in Europe as the barbarian invasions stopped and trade expanded.
6. The Catholic Church had great power over rulers and their people during the Middle Ages. Almost everyone in Europe was a member of the Catholic Church.
7. The Crusades did not result in the capture of the Holy Land. But they brought Europeans into contact with new ideas and new products.
8. While Europe was going through the Dark Ages, India was enjoying a golden age.
9. The travels of Marco Polo made Europeans interested in the civilization of China.
10. Great black kingdoms existed in West Africa at the time when Europe was in the Middle Ages.

Making Generalizations

In each of the exercises on page 177, read the three factual statements. Then make one accurate generalization based on those statements.

A. Factual Statements:
1. The Muslims drew much of their knowledge of chemistry and mathematics from the Chinese.
2. The Muslims adopted the Arabic system of numbers from India.
3. In their buildings, the Muslims used the Roman arch.
Generalization:

B Factual Statements:
1. As a result of the Crusades, some European nobles lost power, thus weakening the feudal system.
2. The Crusaders were introduced to new goods and a new way of life in the Middle East.
3. As a result of the Crusades, cities along the Mediterranean grew into rich seaports.
Generalization:

TURNING POINTS

Culture

Africa: Timbuctu

Timbuctu, founded around A.D. 1100, was once a famous city. People thought of it as the richest place in the world. In many ways it was.

Timbuctu is near the southern edge of the Sahara Desert, not far from the Niger River. Because of its location, it was known as the "meeting point of camel and canoe." The camel caravans of Arab traders carried goods to Timbuctu from North Africa. Salt was a particularly valuable item. People need salt in their diets, and western Africa had none. Canoes from the south brought gold, ivory, and slaves up the Niger River to Timbuctu. These were traded for the Arab goods from the north. Merchants became wealthy and the city grew.

Timbuctu also became known as a city of Muslim learning. Scholars came to its great university, called Sankore (sahn-KOH-ray), to study history, law, and the ways of Islam. People traveled from all over the Muslim world to use the city's large libraries. Askia the Great was a strong supporter of learning. When he ruled, he made Timbuctu the capital of the Songhay empire.

After the Songhay empire fell, Timbuctu was controlled by a series of different groups. Its influence and wealth declined. Today, the city is a small town of about 9,000 people in the nation of Mali.

Critical Thinking

1. Why was Timbuctu considered a prize by the different groups that conquered it?
2. In what ways is location important to the growth of a city?

UNIT IV

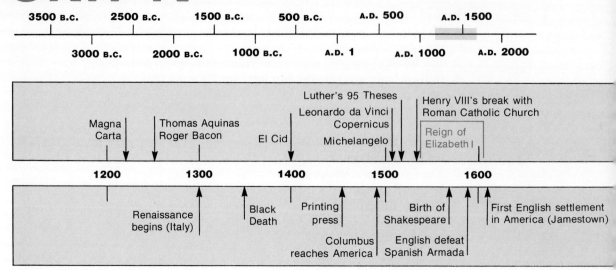

3500 B.C.	2500 B.C.	1500 B.C.	500 B.C.	A.D. 500	A.D. 1500
3000 B.C.	2000 B.C.	1000 B.C.	A.D. 1	A.D. 1000	A.D. 2000

Magna
Carta

Thomas Aquinas
Roger Bacon

El Cid

Luther's 95 Theses
Leonardo da Vinci
Copernicus
Michelangelo

Henry VIII's break with
Roman Catholic Church

Reign of
Elizabeth I

1200	1300	1400	1500	1600

Renaissance
begins (Italy)

Black
Death

Printing
press

Columbus
reaches America

Birth of
Shakespeare

English defeat
Spanish Armada

First English settlement
in America (Jamestown)

1700

How Did Modern Europe Spring from the Past?

Early sailors depended on the position of the stars to judge their location on the open seas.

179

CHAPTER 1

Learning in the Middle Ages

DID THE GROWTH OF TOWNS INFLUENCE LEARNING?

1. People are schooled in different things. Some people study a trade, such as printing or carpentry. Others study academic subjects, such as mathematics or English. Still others cannot go to school: they learn by doing. In Europe, after the Fall of Rome, there was little interest in learning, art, or literature. As the barbarians swept over Europe, keeping alive was the main goal in life. Except for the monks and clergy (church officials, such as priests), few people were educated. In fact, few could read or write.

2. The growth of towns brought a new interest in learning. For when people lived together in cities with walls, they felt safe. They had more time to think about education. As people traded with one another, they learned from one another. Interest in art was reborn. Since religion was the most important part of people's lives, cathedrals and churches showed best the people's artistic feeling and skill. Stained-glass windows in churches were beautiful. Woodworkers spent long hours carving religious scenes on the pews in cathedrals. Sculptors carved statues of saints out of stone. Even

Stained glass windows from the Notre Dame Cathedral. Why was there a rebirth of interest in the arts during the Middle Ages?

monks copying books in monasteries added colorful pictures of the events described.

WHAT KIND OF SCHOOLS WERE SET UP?

3. Schools were set up in towns. Education in these schools was not free, but it was not very expensive. Private schoolmasters, paid by a lord, might be teachers. However, nearly all teachers were priests or monks. Students were usually taught only reading, writing, and arithmetic. Those who planned to go to a university studied Latin.

4. Education was usually for boys only. The daughter of a lord was taught music, needlework, and manners by the lord's private schoolmaster. Sometimes she was taught to read. Poor girls received no education, except training in taking care of the home. Girls who joined a convent to become nuns had the best chance of getting an education. In convents, girls were taught to read so that they could read prayer books. Girls in convents also produced fine needlework.

HOW DID UNIVERSITIES DEVELOP IN EUROPEAN CITIES?

5. The university was the most important development in education in the Middle Ages. In Bologna, Italy, a group of students who wanted to study law gathered together and hired teachers. This was one of the first European universities. In Paris, a number of teachers started a university. Other universities were begun in Heidelberg, Germany, and at Oxford and Cambridge, in England.

6. At first, universities had no buildings and few classrooms. Classes met wherever they could. Whatever rooms could be found often had no desks or blackboards. Sometimes students sat on the floor and wrote notes as the

The University at Oxford. Why was academic learning difficult during the Middle Ages?

teacher talked. In cold weather, note-taking was quite a problem. Rooms were not heated and hands froze. Often the teacher read from a book and the students just listened. If a student had a good memory, he might do very well. Usually, each class had only one book, which had been copied by hand by monks in a monastery. Books were done in many colors and were very expensive. If a university had a library, it might have just one copy of a book. It would be chained to a shelf, so nobody could take it.

7. Because many of the students studied to be priests, religion and Latin were important subjects. Universities also taught law, philosophy, and medicine. In their classes, students read the works of ancient Roman writers. They

were taught logic: the science of correct reasoning. But they were also taught that reason should be based on some authority. The authority of the Church was the most important. But the authority of the ancient thinkers of Greece and Rome was also very important. When a student finished his studies, he became a bachelor of arts. If he studied some more, he could become a master of arts. Finally, with more study, the student could become a doctor of law, theology, or medicine. Only a doctor could be a teacher in a university. Most of the doctors who taught were priests or monks.

8. Many great men taught in the Middle Ages. *Peter Abelard* had so many students that he is considered the founder of the University of Paris. He showed how the Greek philosopher Aristotle's way of thinking could be used in connection with the beliefs of Christianity. Another great teacher was *Saint Thomas Aquinas*. His philosophy, which also closely followed Aristotle's, is today the official philosophy of the Catholic Church. He showed that human reason and religious faith were both gifts of God. After his death he was made a saint. *Roger Bacon*, of England, taught the value of observation and experience when seeking the truth. He also taught the value of knowing Hebrew and Greek when studying the Bible and Aristotle.

9. St. Thomas Aquinas and Roger Bacon were men of the 13th century. By the time the 14th century began, some important changes were taking place in European culture. Writers had begun to write about nonreligious matters. Many of the new writers were not priests. Men became interested in natural science, art, literature. This period of change is called the Renaissance (REN-ih-sans). *Renaissance* means *rebirth* or *revival.* In Europe, an interest in studying human life and the world as the ancient Greeks had studied them was reborn. Also, ancient Greek literature long lost to Western Europe was being rediscovered.

10. The great changes took place all over

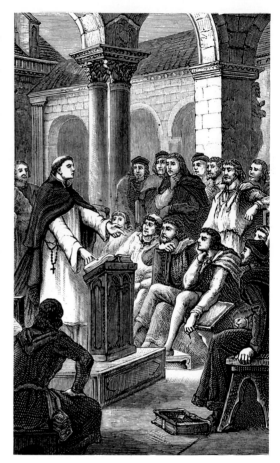

Saint Thomas Aquinas teaching eager students. Why was his philosophy so important?

Europe. But they began in Italy. The Crusaders had brought great wealth to Italian cities. Venice and Genoa were centers of trade. Merchants in Milan and bankers in Florence had become rich by lending money to the Crusaders. Italy was the home of ancient Rome. Thus, the ideas and glory of Rome were close by, waiting to be reborn. Skilled artists and learned men lived in Italy. The Catholic Church, the center of learning in the Middle Ages, was based in Italy. It was natural for the Renaissance to begin here. We are going to learn more about the rebirth of learning elsewhere in Europe in Chapter 2.

Testing Your Vocabulary

Choose the best answer.

1. In education, a *doctor* is one who
   a. teaches science and medicine.
   b. continues study after becoming a master of arts.
   c. has studied for the priesthood.

2. To learn by *experiment* means to
   a. be a scientist.
   b. depend upon the advice of experts.
   c. discover facts or test ideas by working with what can be observed.

Understanding What You Have Read

1. A good title for paragraph 6 is
   a. The Universities of the Middle Ages
   b. Taking Notes in the University
   c. Religion in the University
   d. Studying the Greek Masters

2. In which paragraph do you find facts about
   a. the education of girls?
   b. stained-glass windows in cathedrals?
   c. the ideas of St. Thomas Aquinas?
   d. subjects studied in the universities?

3. There was little education in Europe after the Fall of Rome because
   a. few people were intelligent enough for education.
   b. the growth of trade kept people busy with other matters.
   c. staying alive was the main goal in life.

4. Monks or other clergy ran the schools because
   a. education in the Middle Ages was not free.
   b. there were no buildings to house schools.
   c. they were usually the only educated people.

5. In the universities, a student had to support his ideas by
   a. presenting his opinion in flowery, poetic language.
   b. showing that his opinion was based on a respected authority.
   c. showing that his opinion was useful to society.

6. Changes in learning began about the 14th century because
   a. free public education had begun in most large cities of Europe.
   b. universities had been set up in many cities.
   c. people became interested in matters other than religion.

7. A girl of the Middle Ages might receive some education if she
   a. lived near a university.
   b. joined a convent.
   c. was able to study in Italy.

Tell whether the statements are true or false. If a statement is false, change the words in italics to make it true.

1. Thomas Aquinas used the works of *Socrates* as a basis for his religious beliefs and teachings.

2. In the universities, students read the works of *Roman* writers.

3. A teacher who said that students should prove their statements by experimentation was Roger Bacon.

4. Most cathedrals had statues of saints carved out of *wood.*

Developing Ideas and Skills

WRITING AN OUTLINE

Below are topics and some subtopics for an outline of Chapter 1 of Unit IV. In your notebook, fill in the rest of the outline.

Learning in the Middle Ages

A. Reasons for New Interest in Learning
  1. The growth of towns brought people together.
  2. _____
  3. _____
B. Schooling for Boys and Girls
  1. Schools were run by monks and priests.
  2. _____
  3. _____
C. The Universities in the Middle Ages
  1. They had few rooms or books.
  2. _____
  3. _____

Using Original Sources

A doctor in Spain wrote to his sons at a university in 1315. The letter below tells us some of the beliefs of educated people during the Middle Ages. After reading these lines from the doctor's letter, see if you can answer the questions that follow.

A Medieval Doctor's Advice

Beware of eating too much and too often, especially during the night. Avoid eating raw onions in the evening . . . because they dull the intellect and the senses. . . . Avoid all foods . . . such as milk and fresh cheese except very rarely . . .

Don't eat many nuts except rarely and following fish. I say the same of meat and fruit, for they are bad and difficult to digest.

Avoid sleeping on your back except rarely. . . . Don't go straight to bed on a full stomach but an hour after the meal . . . walk about for a bit after a meal, at least around the square, so that the food may settle in the stomach . . .

. . . wash the head, if you are accustomed to wash it, at least once a fortnight (two weeks) with hot lye and in a place sheltered from draughts on the eve of a feast day toward nightfall. Then dry your hair with a brisk massage; afterwards do it up; then put it in a bonnet or cap . . .

Also, in summer, in order not to have fleas or not to have more of them, sweep your room daily with a broom and do not sprinkle it with water, . . . but you may spray it occasionally with strong vinegar, which comforts the heart and brain . . .

Singing, too, exercises the chest. And if you will do this, you will have healthy limbs, a sound intellect and memory, and you will avoid rheum (running eyes and nose).

Do you agree or disagree with these statements about the doctor's letter to his sons?

1. The doctor was worried about the problem of digesting food after a meal.
2. During the Middle Ages, a young man might wash his hair many times a week.
3. All the suggestions made by the doctor are made by doctors today.
4. The doctor probably thought that singing is good for the memory.
5. Doctors in the Middle Ages thought that onions, nuts, and cheese were healthful.
6. Fleas were a problem for students living in the university.

TURNING POINTS

Technology

The World: Papermaking

Monks were important caretakers of learning during the Middle Ages. In the silence of their monasteries, they slowly and carefully copied books onto sheets of paper. The paper that monks used—and the kind we use today—was first developed by the Chinese.

In ancient times, the Chinese wrote by carving letters onto pieces of bone. Later, their emperors had stories of important events written on bronze jars. Sometimes the stories were carved on stone. The earliest books were written on strips of bamboo or on pieces of silk. The silk had the advantage of being light in weight. However, it was very expensive. A less expensive material was needed.

The earliest paper was made in China about A.D. 100. Tree bark, hemp, and rags were boiled and then pounded together into a loose pulp. A glue made from plants was added. Then the mixture was placed over a fine screen. The liquid part passed through the screen. Whatever remained was dried into a kind of paper. This art of making refined paper spread throughout Asia. It was brought to Egypt in about A.D. 700 by Arab traders. Before this, the Egyptians had used papyrus. In the 12th century, papermaking was brought to Europe by the Moors, who conquered Spain.

Critical Thinking

1. What advantages does paper have over earlier materials on which people wrote?
2. Identify one important way that traders and soldiers affected history.

AIM: How did the writers and artists of the Renaissance affect education after 1300?

CHAPTER 2

Artists and Writers Find a New Style

The *Mona Lisa,* by Leonardo da Vinci. Why do you think the woman's smile has been a favorite topic for discussion among art lovers?

WHY DID EDUCATORS COPY THE WORKS OF THE ANCIENTS?

1. A boy who wants to be a baseball player copies the movements of a professional player. A person who wants to sing may imitate the style of a popular singer. When we wish to become skilled at something, we usually copy one who has achieved greatness in that field. The beginning of the Renaissance (about 1300) was a period in which Europeans copied or imitated the art, literature, and culture of the ancient Greeks and Romans. In this way they themselves made great advances in these areas.

2. The imitation of the ancients was started largely in the universities during the Middle Ages. You recall that students had to support their ideas with the works of ancient writers. This resulted in an interest in all the works of the ancients. Writers, artists, and thinkers of the Middle Ages began to imitate writers, artists, and thinkers of ancient times.

Unfortunately, Europeans often did not know the difference between what was good in the ancients' work and what was poor. If an idea was old enough, or was Greek or Roman, it was thought to be correct and it was copied.

HOW DID ROMANCE LANGUAGES DEVELOP?

3. Latin was the language used by educated people during the Middle Ages. Books were written in Latin. But because peoples were kept apart by mountains and other natural barriers, they developed their own ways of speaking. The language spoken by the common people of a particular region is called a *vernacular.* These new languages all came from Latin, the language of the Romans. They are therefore called Romance languages. The Romance languages are French, Spanish, Italian, Portuguese, and Romanian. During the Renaissance, writers began to use the vernacular as well as Latin. At the same time, there developed a new interest in human life and things of the world. Those who turned their attention to human affairs were called *Humanists.* Humanists wrote in the language of their own countries while encouraging the study of Latin and Greek (classical studies).

4. During the Renaissance, many stories were about the lives of the saints. Many plays had religious themes. The Italian poet Dante Alighieri wrote *The Divine Comedy* in Italian. *The Divine Comedy* tells of Dante's imaginary journey through Hell and Purgatory to Paradise. Later, Chaucer, an Englishman, wrote his *Canterbury Tales* in English. These were stories, some serious, some funny, told by people on a pilgrimage. Today you will find the English language in which Chaucer wrote hard to understand. This is because English during the Middle Ages was not like the English we speak today. But for a long time Latin was still the language of educated people. Petrarch, a great Italian poet and one of the first great humanists, wrote in both Italian and Latin.

WHAT DID PRINTING DO FOR LEARNING?

5. One of the most important inventions of the Renaissance was the printing press. It was invented by Johann Gutenberg, a German, about the year 1450. Before the printing press was invented, the only books were those hand-copied by monks. Few people had such books or were able to read them. Now, many copies of a book could be printed, and in every language. Because of the printing press, learning spread to all parts of Europe. The printing press meant not only more books but also more work. For

Detail from *David,* by Michelangelo. How does this statue support the statement that "Europeans imitated Greek and Roman culture?"

now there was a new profession: printing. And as the number of books grew, so did the number of people who were able to read them.

6. As more books were printed, there grew a need for cheaper paper. The Egyptians had used pressed reeds of the papyrus plant for their writing. Later, *parchment*, made from the skins of calves and sheep, was used. Both were expensive. The Chinese had known how to make paper for more than a thousand years. Now, traders brought this knowledge to Europe. Once paper became easier and cheaper to make and books were printed, ideas spread more easily than before.

WHO WERE SOME OF THE GREAT RENAISSANCE ARTISTS?

7. Artists of the Renaissance showed creativity in painting and sculpture. Their paintings were more lifelike than the paintings of the Middle Ages had been. There was a naturalness to the faces and figures of people shown in Renaissance works. Scenes of the countryside showed depth, width, and height. Rich families in Italian cities supported young artists with money. Nobles were *patrons*, or supporters, of the arts. One of the best known of these families was the Medici, of Florence. The homes of ruling families were often centers of culture. Wives of city-state rulers were educated. They studied music and languages. Their lives were spent surrounded by fine art and in the great libraries of the time.

8. One of the greatest artists and thinkers of the Renaissance was Leonardo da Vinci. He was a painter, an engineer, and a scientist. In fact, many great men of the Renaissance had many different interests. *The Last Supper* and the *Mona Lisa* are two of Leonardo's most famous paintings. Leonardo wrote a book about anatomy, the study of the human body. He even tried to invent a machine that would fly.

9. Michelangelo was another great Renaissance artist. He was a sculptor, painter, arch-

The *Madonna of the Chair,* by Raphael. How does this painting reflect Raphael's "quiet style"?

itect, and poet. Michelangelo was asked by the pope to paint scenes on the walls and ceiling of the Sistine Chapel, in the Vatican. For four years, Michelangelo worked on scenes from the Bible, such as the *Creation of the World* and the *Last Judgment.* His statues of Moses and David and his Pietá are among the world's greatest sculptures. As an architect, he helped design St. Peter's Church in Rome.

10. Raphael, along with da Vinci and Michelangelo, was a painter of Florence. His painting, the *Madonna of the Chair* is an example of his quiet style. In Venice, the painter, *Titian,* worked with brilliant colors. Deep red-brown was his favorite. From his paintings, we get the word *titian,* meaning red-brown.

11. Renaissance architects copied the styles of ancient Roman and Greek buildings. Buildings with arches, domes, and columns took the place of the Gothic buildings of the Middle Ages. St. Peter's Church in Rome is an example of the architecture of the Renaissance. This

Self-Portrait as a Young Man, by Rembrandt von Rijn. How is this painting more lifelike than those from the Middle Ages on pages 149 and 157?

giant cathedral was not finished for centuries. Its dome, designed by Michelangelo, is 400 feet above the floor of the church.

12. Artists and writers in other parts of Europe also created great works. Rubens, Van Dyck, and Rembrandt, of Holland, painted scenes of everyday life. Rembrandt also painted portraits, or studies of people. Velasquez and El Greco were leading Spanish artists. The Renaissance also produced great writers. Erasmus, a Dutch writer, was a humanist who traveled all over Europe. He was a man of great culture and wisdom. His writings poked fun at people who blindly followed custom, instead of using reason. Sir Thomas More, of England, is famous for his book *Utopia*. The book tells what life could be like in a perfect land. The word *utopia* is now used to mean an imaginary, perfect society. Cervantes, of Spain, wrote *Don Quixote*. This book is one of the great works of literature. It pokes fun at a person's desire for greatness and at the knight's code of chivalry.

Testing Your Vocabulary

Choose the best answer.

1. Many famous documents have been written on *parchment*, which is
   a. the skin of sheep.
   b. paper made from rags.
   c. an expensive paper made from an Egyptian plant.
2. Throughout history writers and philosophers have imagined different kinds of *utopias*. A utopia is a
   a. perfect society.
   b. foreign country.
   c. home in the country away from the crowded city.
3. A person who is "titian-haired" would be a
   a. blonde.
   b. brunette.
   c. redhead.

Understanding What You Have Read

1. The main idea of paragraphs 3 through 6 is that
   a. writers began to use the language of the people.
   b. Romance languages came from Latin.
   c. writers became famous.
   d. there were reasons why people read.

189

2. In which paragraph do you find facts about
   a. the Chinese knowledge of making paper?
   b. the works of Michelangelo?
   c. the architecture of the Renaissance?
   d. the invention of the printing press?

3. Many writers did not choose to write in their own language because
   a. most people spoke Latin.
   b. their native language was too difficult to read.
   c. Latin was the "official" language of educated people.

4. Leonardo da Vinci is called a "man of the Renaissance" because he
   a. disagreed with the Church.
   b. painted in the stiff style of the Middle Ages.
   c. had many different interests.

5. The humanists were so named because they
   a. paid for the education of young artists.
   b. were interested in human affairs and the world around them.
   c. wrote books on the anatomy of the human body.

6. Renaissance painters and sculptors were supported by
   a. monks and priests.
   b. the universities in large cities.
   c. wealthy families in Italy.

7. The importance of Gutenberg's invention was that
   a. more books could be printed and more people could read them.
   b. Europeans learned how to make paper.
   c. running a book shop became a profitable business.

Match the names in the first column with the descriptions in the second column.

1. the Medici
2. Dante
3. Leonardo da Vinci
4. Gutenberg
5. Raphael
6. Erasmus
7. Michelangelo
8. Rembrandt
9. Chaucer
10. Cervantes

a. inventor of the printing press
b. designer of the dome of St. Peter's Church
c. a family of Florence that helped young artists
d. Spanish artist who used gloomy colors
e. author of the *Canterbury Tales*
f. Austrian painter of scenes of everyday life
g. writer of *The Divine Comedy*
h. painted the *Madonna of the Chair*
i. painted *The Last Supper*
j. Dutch humanist
k. Spanish author of *Don Quixote*
l. Dutch painter of famous portraits

Developing Ideas and Skills

KNOWING SOURCES OF INFORMATION

A. Choose the best answer.

1. To find out if a world-history book has a chapter on Renaissance art, you should read the
   a. first chapter
   b. table of contents
   c. end-of-chapter summaries
2. If you wanted to know the size and area of a country in Europe, you would look in
   a. a text on European history
   b. an almanac
   c. a text on government
3. To find a page in a text which tells you about the writings of Chaucer, you would use the
   a. index
   b. title page
   c. bibliography
4. To find a complete biography of Michelangelo, you would look in
   a. an almanac
   b. a world-history textbook
   c. an encyclopedia
5. To find the boundaries of a country, you would use an
   a. atlas
   b. almanac
   c. encyclopedia

B. Read the following list of sources. If the item is an *original* source, write **O** on your paper. If it is a *secondary* source, write **S.**

1. The diary of a member of the Medici family of Florence.
2. *Genghis Khan and the Mongol Horde,* a biography by Harold Lamb.
3. The stories of Marco Polo, covering his life in China under Kublai Khan.
4. Michelangelo's sketches for designing St. Peter's Cathedral.
5. *A History of the Popes,* by Farrow.
6. Pericles' speech at a funeral of soldiers of Athens.
7. Diagrams used by Johann Gutenberg in making his printing press.
8. A recent newspaper feature story about the importance of Gutenberg's invention.
9. A radio broadcast of a play about the invention of gunpowder.
10. The notebook of a 13th-century monk, writing about building a church.

AIM: How did the discoveries of the Renaissance lead to scientific progress?

CHAPTER 3

Scientists Learn about the World

WHY WERE DISCOVERIES IMPORTANT?

1. You have seen on television or heard stories in which people were lost in a forest. In their wandering, they had lost their sense of direction. They did not know the route to follow to find a familiar road or landmark that would lead them to safety. One of the group, however, had a compass. It enabled them to locate their position and tell the direction to follow to lead them out of danger. The compass is a simple little instrument. But it led the group from the darkness of being lost back to safety.

2. In much the same way, scientific discoveries led Europe from the Middle Ages to modern times. The works of painters, writers, and sculptors were all important in bringing a new way of thinking to Europe. But they were not alone in bringing Europe to modern times. Scientific discoveries and inventions during the Renaissance changed Europe as well. In some cases, Europe learned ideas and methods that the Chinese, Arabs, and others had known for a great many years. Much of the learning grew out of the scholarly writings of the Middle Ages.

WHAT WERE SOME EFFECTS OF THE DISCOVERIES IN MATHEMATICS?

3. Before the Renaissance, the Roman system of numbers was used by the people of Europe. In the Roman system, numbers were written thus: I, II, V, X (1, 2, 5, 10). Dealings with Moslem traders brought the Arabic system to Europe. About year 1200, Arabic numbers began to replace the old Roman system of counting. In Roman counting, there was no zero. Arabs counted in numerals from one (1) to nine (9) and zero (0). When numerals were combined with zero, any number could be written: 30; 300; 3,000 . . . etc. Now, using the Arabic system made bookkeeping easier and more accurate. Distances could be measured more easily. The numbers of people could be counted more accurately. Buying and selling were easier, and merchants could keep exact records of their sales. Today, we still use the Arabic system of numbers.

4. The use of the compass, known in China for centuries, was discovered by Europeans during the Renaissance. The compass made it possible for sailors to cross unknown seas.

They no longer had to stay within sight of land when taking a long voyage. Scientists found a way to measure distances of objects during the Renaissance. In the Middle Ages, people used sundials and hourglasses filled with sand to tell time. Now they learned to tell time more exactly. By 1500, clocks that could tell time accurately had been made. Soon clocks were small enough so that they could be carried by anyone.

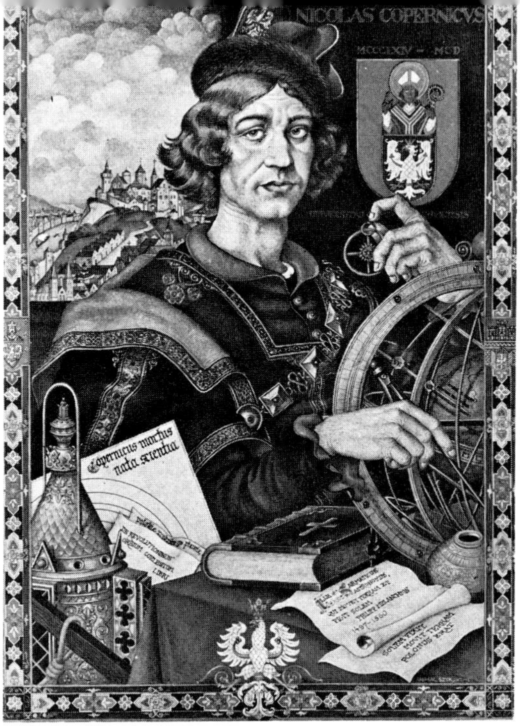

Copernicus in his study. Why do you think people did not want to believe that the earth revolved around the sun?

HOW DID EXPERIMENTS AID PROGRESS?

5. Earlier, in the Middle Ages, Roger Bacon had tried to teach students to experiment and test ideas. Most people of this time did not listen to Bacon's teachings. Most people did not trust new ideas. They seemed to be happy with what they already knew and accepted old ideas without proof. But during the Renaissance, people began to experiment and investigate. They wanted to find out new things about the world around them. In 1543, a Polish astronomer, Copernicus, argued that the sun—not the earth—was the center of the universe, and the earth revolved around the sun. Before then, most people believed that the universe was as the 2nd-century astronomer Ptolemy (TOL-uh-mee) had described it. Ptolemy thought the earth was at the center of the universe, with the sun, moon, stars, and planets revolving around the earth. Copernicus's ideas were at first laughed at and rejected, but are now seen as the basis of modern astronomy.

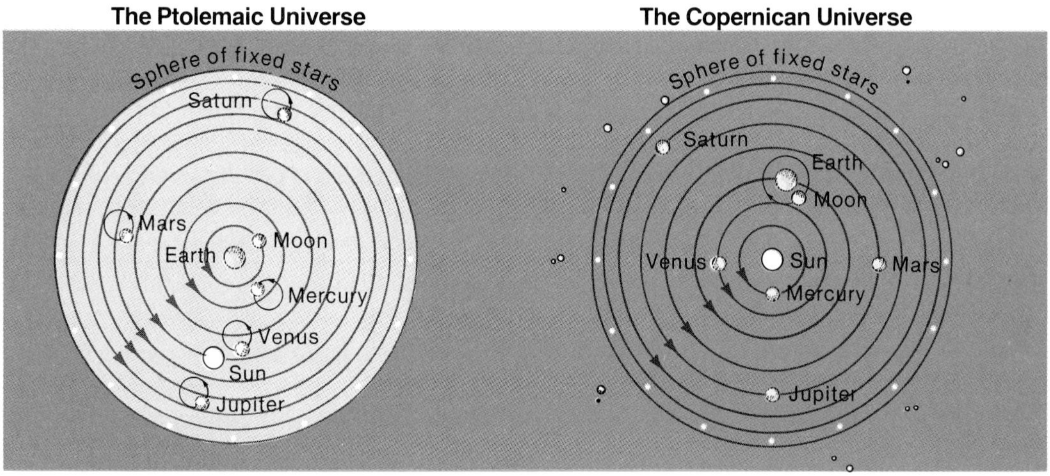

6. Galileo, of Italy, experimented with the motion of objects. He did not agree with Aristotle that objects of different weights fell at different speeds. Galileo dropped objects of different weights from a tower we know as the Leaning Tower of Pisa. He observed that they all reached the ground at the same time. In this way he proved his new idea. Galileo also studied the motion of objects hung from a rope. He thus learned how the pendulum of a clock works. He was able to make a pendulum that counted seconds, minutes, and hours. Galileo also improved the telescope. With it, he studied the heavens. Using his telescope he was able to prove Copernicus's view that the sun is the center of our system of planets.

7. You have already read that the Chinese invented gunpowder. In Europe, Roger Bacon had experimented with gunpowder. Bacon even explained how to make it. Gunpowder changed warfare in Europe. Feudal lords could no longer feel completely safe behind the stone castles or wooden walls that had protected them for centuries. Rulers who were able to buy gunpowder gained more power. As kings became powerful, nobles became weaker. Feudalism was moving slowly but surely toward its end.

8. Changes took place in Europe during the Renaissance. But the effects of the Renaissance were not felt in the same way all over Europe. Nor did the new interest in learning affect the lives of all people in the same way. For many men and women, new ideas made

Galileo experimenting with the speed of falling bodies. What did he prove? How were his ideas different from those of Aristotle?

them curious about the world around them. For others, the Renaissance was no different from the Middle Ages. There was still a class of nobles with special privileges. There were still common people who farmed their land as their families had done for years. There were city dwellers who bought and sold goods. And there were women, who, except for a few, were not allowed to enter a "man's world."

Testing Your Vocabulary

Choose the best answer.

1. An *astronomer* is most interested in
   a. accurate methods of keeping time.
   b. studying the heavens.
   c. testing soils and rocks.

2. The *universe*, as used in paragraph 5, is
   a. the earth and all things in space.
   b. the sun and the stars.
   c. the source of the earth's light.

Understanding What You Have Read

1. The main idea of paragraph 6 is that
   a. discoveries of scientists were not accepted.
   b. experiments helped scientists to form new ideas.
   c. Galileo studied objects in motion.
   d. for a long time people were happy with what they already knew.
2. In which paragraph do you find facts about
   a. the use of Arabic numerals?
   b. Galileo's experiments with falling objects?
   c. the results of the use of gunpowder?
   d. the importance of the compass?
3. As a result of the use of Arabic numbers
   a. Europeans began to trade with the Muslim world.
   b. more records were kept than ever before.
   c. clocks were invented.
4. The use of the compass helped sailors to tell
   a. how far away other ships were.
   b. their distance from land.
   c. in which direction they were heading.
5. The use of gunpowder played an important part in the history of Europe because it
   a. helped to end the power of feudal lords.
   b. weakened the power of rulers.
   c. increased trade between the Muslims and Europe.

Using Original Sources

Lodovico, a Renaissance ruler of the city of Milan, advertised for military engineers, architects, sculptors, and painters. In this letter, Leonardo da Vinci (see page 188) asked for work and told of all his talents. What kinds of work did he think he could do?

Leonardo da Vinci Looks for Work

I have extremely light and strong bridges, easily carried, and with them you may chase after and, at any time, flee from the enemy, and others that cannot be destroyed by fire, easy to lift and place. I also have a method for destroying those of the enemy.

I know how, when a place is attacked, to take water out of the trenches, and make bridges and covered ways and ladders.

I have plans for making cannons, very easy to move, with which to hurl small stones in the manner almost of hail.

I will make covered chariots, safe and unattackable . . . And behind these, infantry could follow quite unhurt.

In time of peace I believe I can give perfect satisfaction, the equal of any other in architecture and in guiding water from one place to another.

I can carry out sculpture in marble, bronze, or clay, and also I can do in painting whatever may be done, as well as any other.

1. Which of these modern things was NOT mentioned by Leonardo in his letter?
   a. tanks in warfare
   b. building of canals
   c. use of submarines
2. Most of the things Leonardo said he could do were concerned with
   a. war.
   b. buildings.
   c. sculpture.
3. Leonardo da Vinci has been called a "Renaissance man," which means an all-round man. Does his letter help to prove or disprove this title?
4. Do you think the things mentioned by Leonardo would interest the ruler of Milan? Why?

TURNING POINTS

Technology

The World: Clocks

A teacher in Peru starts a class *on time*. A traveler in Nigeria boards a plane *on time*. A television reporter in India goes on the air *on time*. To be on schedule, everyone at the school, at the airport, and at the T.V. station must know what time it is. They must all be able to divide the day into hours and minutes and seconds. They must all do this in the same way. They need a language they all understand. The instrument they all use for this purpose is the clock.

Since ancient times, people have tried to measure time. Two of the first clocks—the sundial and the water clock—were invented by the Egyptians. The sundial measures time by casting a shadow from a stick onto a dial that marks off the hours of the day. Early water clocks measured time with buckets that were marked off at intervals.

The first mechanical clocks appeared around A.D. 1000. Some say these clocks were first used in China. Others believe they were first used in Europe. The early European mechanical clocks were powered by falling weights. They were unreliable and they were large. Because of their size, they could only be kept in public places, such as the towers of city halls and churches.

For centuries, scientists, inventors, and craftspeople worked to make clocks smaller. In time, clocks could be kept in homes, put on ships, or carried around. They also became more accurate. By the 1700s the pendulum clock had become accurate to about one second a day. By the end of the 1800s, timepieces were accurate to within a hundredth of a second. The 20th-century world of split-second timing was here.

Critical Thinking

1. What would be some disadvantages of measuring time with a sundial?
2. What are some reasons that accurate timekeeping is so important today?

AIM: How did England become a powerful nation under strong rulers?

CHAPTER 4

England is United

HOW DID EARLY KINGS UNITE ENGLAND?

1. Those on whom we depend for something we need will have some power over us. For, if we do not please them, they may not give us what we need. In the early Middle Ages, rulers depended on the military support of nobles. Rulers had little power. They were weaker than the nobles on whom they depended for help. The invention of gunpowder helped to change this condition. A monarch's firearms and cannons could defeat the nobles' horsemen and destroy their castle walls. Rulers, therefore, gained power over nobles.

2. Merchants and townspeople also helped rulers to gain more power. Trade brought wealth to town merchants so that they could now give money to their rulers. Both merchants and common people wanted to end the wars among nobles that made trade difficult. Under one ruler, laws could be the same everywhere. Traders and merchants would be able to travel more safely. The same money could be used throughout the entire country. This would help trade. Most people wanted to be ruled by a single monarch, even one with complete power. They thought this much better than being governed by rival lords who were always fighting with each other. People wanted order and safety. So the townspeople helped rulers by giving them money to buy firearms and cannons.

3. One of the first nations to become united under one ruler was England. Although it was an island, Britain had been invaded several times. The Romans had conquered Britain and ruled it for almost 500 years. When the Romans left, Angles and Saxons (German tribes) settled in England. An Anglo-Saxon king, Alfred the Great, had stopped an invasion by the Danes about the year 800. This brought some unity to England.

4. In 1066, a stronger invader came. William, the Duke of Normandy, crossed into Brit-

Many centuries before England became unified under one ruler, different peoples lived there. Stonehenge is among the most famous remains of these ancient peoples. No one is sure what Stonehenge was; it is one of history's unsolved mysteries.

ain from France. The Normans were descendants of the Northmen who had settled in France. They were Christians who spoke French and had French customs. William defeated the English at the Battle of Hastings. He became ruler of Britain. The mixture of the French language of Normandy with the Anglo-Saxon language of Britain developed into the English language that is spoken in Britain and the United States today.

5. William the Conqueror, as he was called, controlled the nobles in his new kingdom. He was able to keep all large landowners far apart so they could not join forces and cause him trouble. William was, in fact, the lord of all England. His rule was really feudalism under a king. But there was peace in the land. William's government kept records of people, land, and animals. These famous records are called the Domesday Book. With these records, fairer taxes were collected.

HOW WAS THE KING'S POWER LIMITED?

6. About 100 years after the rule of William the Conqueror, King Henry II ruled England. Henry began some practices that democracies follow today. Henry appointed judges who traveled all over England. In each town, they asked respected men to tell them about crime in their villages. Then, townspeople helped the judges decide the cases. From this developed the jury system—the system by which a group of people decide a case. In Henry's time, Church officials were not affected by the jury system. The Church had its own courts and tried its own cases.

7. King John, Henry's son, was a different kind of ruler. His cruel nature caused him trouble. John had plotted against his brother and murdered his cousin to become king. He had quarreled with the pope. Thus, both the Church and the nobles were his enemies. When he ordered people to pay heavy taxes to support his

wars, the nobles revolted. In order to remain king, John had to sign the Magna Carta (Great Charter), in 1215. This is an important document in the history of English-speaking people. Under the Magna Carta, John was not allowed to levy (set) taxes without the approval of nobles. A nobleman could not be put in prison unless he was found guilty by a jury of nobles.

8. The power of English rulers over nobles had grown for 200 years. Now, through the Magna Carta, the monarch's power was limited by law. Monarchs could no longer put into prison those they disliked, for trial by jury was required. Rulers could no longer levy taxes whenever they needed money for war. The nobles now had control of money. The nobles, therefore, now had to agree to a war before the monarch could wage it. Large landowners and clergymen formed a council to approve of the monarch's decisions. This group of nobles in England came to be known as the Great Council. Later, small landowners and merchants formed a separate, lower branch of the council. The council of nobles was called the House of Lords. The lower council grew into the House of Commons. These two councils became the Parliament. It is the law-making body of England. English rulers were the first in Europe to unite a nation by taking power from the nobles. Now, the power of the ruler was limited by these same nobles.

9. During much of the 14th and 15th centuries England fought in many wars. First came the Hundred Years' War with France. It was caused by an argument over who was to be ruler of France. The old king had died with no children to inherit his throne. English kings, who owned a great deal of land in France, said that they had the right to the French throne. War broke out and English armies invaded France. France was saved when a young peasant girl named Joan of Arc (page 203) led the French army to victory. After losing the Hundred Years' War, England was torn apart by civil wars. These were fought by two rival English families who both wanted the English throne. This bloody warfare, called the War of the Roses, was won by the House of Tudor. Henry Tudor became king. The Tudor family ruled England from 1485 to 1603.

HOW DID THE TUDORS RULE ENGLAND?

10. The most powerful of the Tudor monarchs was Henry VIII, who ruled from 1509 to 1547. He was a skillful, hot-tempered king with a strong desire for power. Henry VIII disliked the power of the Church. When he wished to be divorced from his wife, Catherine, the pope would not agree. So Henry announced the end of the marriage himself. He then broke away from the Catholic Church and set up a Church of England with himself as its head. He appointed his own bishops and took away Catholic property. Any English people who opposed Henry were thrown into prison or killed. Thus, England broke away from the Catholic Church, which had been the church of the English people for over 1,000 years.

11. Religious arguments went on in England. When Henry's daughter, Mary, married King Philip of Spain, she brought the Catholic religion back to England. As queen, she punished her father's followers who had accepted the Church of England. In 1558, another of Henry's daughters, Elizabeth, came to the throne. Queen Elizabeth I is regarded as one of the greatest rulers in English history. During her 45 years as ruler of England, she led her nation to a place of great power and importance in Europe.

12. Queen Elizabeth was not a Catholic. The Church of England became the official English Church once more. Except for attacks on Spanish ships, England was at peace under Elizabeth. Sir Francis Drake, an Englishman, sailed around the world. Later, he led a fleet that defeated a great Spanish armada of 132 ships sent to invade England. England's trade and wealth grew. The first trading post in India was set up. Wool became an important product in trade. As a result, much farm land was turned into pasture for sheep. This forced many farmers to leave their land and crowd into the cities. Elizabeth taxed wealthy merchants to pay for the needs of the poor in the cities.

13. Elizabeth brought peace and prosperity to most of her people. Under her leadership, the English people developed a feeling of pride in their country. England had defeated its enemy, Spain. British trade had spread throughout the world. Its queen was respected abroad and admired by her people. Its literature flourished. During the reign of Elizabeth, William Shakespeare, one of the greatest writers of all time, wrote many of his finest plays.

Queen Elizabeth I of England. Why was she popular with the English people?

William Shakespeare by an unknown artist. Name at least three of his plays.

Testing Your Vocabulary _____

Choose the best answer.

1. When monarchs *levy* a tax, they
   a. make people pay it.
   b. make it greater than it was.
   c. set it aside.
2. The *Parliament* of England does the

same work as the political body in the United States called
   a. Congress.
   b. the Supreme Court.
   c. the President's Cabinet.

Understanding What You Have Read _____

1. The main idea of paragraphs 7 and 8 is that
   a. King John had many enemies.
   b. England limited the power of its monarchs
   c. the Great Council became the House of Lords.
   d. trial by jury is an old English practice.
2. In which paragraph do you find facts about
   a. England's part in the Hundred Years' War.
   b. King Henry VIII's break with the Catholic Church?
   c. The Norman invasion of England?
   d. Alfred the Great's unification of England?
3. Trial by jury was a result of King Henry II's
   a. asking nobles for advice.
   b. sending judges all over England.
   c. keeping a record of all land owned by nobles.
4. William the Conqueror's reign was important because during this period
   a. there was complete democracy in

France.
   b. French and English customs and languages were mixed in England.
   c. civil war broke out in England.
5. Merchants wanted the country run by one ruler rather than by many nobles because
   a. rulers were very democratic.
   b. rulers did not like to levy taxes.
   c. under one ruler, laws would be the same all over a country.
6. The reign of Queen Elizabeth I was considered a great one because
   a. England defeated Spain and became a great sea power.
   b. England fought wars with several European countries and won them all.
   c. Elizabeth returned England to the Catholic religion.
7. The Hundred Years' War was the result of
   a. a disagreement over the collection of taxes.
   b. a disagreement over who would become king of France.
   c. Henry VIII's divorce from Catherine.

Tell whether these statements are true or false. If a statement is false, change the words in italics to make it true.

1. The English council of nobles was later called the *House of Lords*.
2. Henry VIII was a *Norman* king of England.

3. In the Hundred Years' War, England fought against *France.*

4. William Shakespeare wrote his plays during the reign of *King Henry II.*

5. The *Magna Carta* limited the power of the English ruler.

6. At the Battle of Hastings, in *1215,* the French defeated the English.

7. The English, under *Sir Francis Drake,* defeated the Spanish Armada.

8. William the Conqueror and his followers were *Vikings.*

9. The Church of England was set up by *King John.*

10. The French and Anglo-Saxon languages were mixed to become the *English* language.

Developing Ideas and Skills

USING A TIME LINE

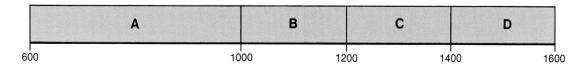

Complete the time line in your notebook by writing the *letter* of the correct time period for each event listed below.

1. William the Conqueror invaded England
2. Queen Elizabeth I ruled
3. Danes invaded England
4. Henry VIII broke with the Catholic Church

5. Alfred the Great ruled England
6. The Battle of Hastings was fought
7. The jury system began
8. The Magna Carta was signed by the king

AIM: How did France become a powerful nation?

CHAPTER 5

A National Spirit Grows in France

HOW DID ROYAL POWER GROW?

1. The other countries of Europe did not become unified so quickly as England. In France, the power of the nobles lasted longer than in England and kept any one ruler from gaining control. In Spain, unity was slowed under the Muslims, who ruled parts of the country until 1492. Italy and Germany were divided into many small states ruled by nobles. Rivalry among these small states held back unity until the late 19th century. The longer it took countries to become united, the longer it took them to become democratic.

2. In France, there had been some unity under Charlemagne. But his empire broke up after his death. It had been divided into three parts. None of these three parts became large enough, important enough, or unified enough to become a nation. Feudalism continued, with different lords ruling different parts of France. Lords elected their own leaders, who became known as kings. In 987, a group of lords around Paris elected Hugh Capet as their king. He was king, however, only to the lords who elected him. Only they obeyed him. The other lords looked on the king as just another noble ruling an area of land. In the rest of France, feudal lords continued to have power.

Tapestry of Joan of Arc before the Chateau Chignon in 1428. Joan of Arc tried to drive the English out of France. Her deeds contributed to the spirit of nationalism in France.

3. Hugh Capet was the first of a long line of kings who ruled until the Hundred Years' War. In time, these French kings gained control over more and more territory. There were several reasons for this. Many nobles left France to fight in the Crusades. While they were gone, the king took their lands. Kings had the support of the city merchants who helped them in their wars against the feudal lords. Another reason was the end of the practice of dividing a king's land among all of his sons. When a Capet king died, his eldest son became king and got all his

land. The new king was no longer elected by the nobles. Still another reason for the increasing power of the Capet kings was the growing importance of the city of Paris. This great trading center was the heart of France. The wealth of Paris helped support the kings.

4. Later kings of France gained more power. Philip Augustus, 1180–1223, took away English territory in France. King John of England was too weak to fight back. Whenever he could, Philip Augustus took land from the feudal lords. He appointed tax collectors and other officials who would obey him alone. These were usually townspeople. The lords were not given important jobs, and in this way they lost more power.

5. Philip's grandson, Louis IX, became a saint of the Roman Catholic Church. This had not happened often: a king becoming a saint! In those days, when kings were often cruel, it was rare to find one as kind as Louis IX. His courage made him popular with his people. Louis led Crusades. He wanted justice for all his people. He set up royal courts and invited people to come and tell him their problems.

6. France had no Magna Carta and made slow progress toward democracy. In order to get new taxes, King Philip the Fair founded the French Estates-General. Although this body met with the king, it had little power. Certainly, it had much less power than the English Parliament. In the course of time, it was called together only when the king needed it. Usually, it did little more than support the king. There were three Estates in the Estates-General. Each one represented a different class of people in France. The First Estate was the clergy; the Second was the nobility; the Third was the merchants and large landowners.

7. Philip the Fair did not like the power of the Church. He fought the clergy, going so far as to take Church property. This was 200 years before Henry VIII of England did the same thing. At one time, a French pope was elected. He lived at Avignon, in southern France.

HOW DID THE HUNDRED YEARS' WAR INCITE A NATIONAL SPIRIT?

8. The Hundred Years' War with England nearly ruined all of France. The two countries did not fight during all of those hundred years. But even when there was no organized warfare, roving bands of thieves ran through the French countryside and cities. The French were finally able to drive out the English. But they suffered greatly and much of their property was destroyed. Good farmland was ruined, as were cities. In the middle 1300's, a sickness called the bubonic plague, or Black Death, swept over Europe and Asia, killing about half the people within 20 years.

9. Out of the war with England came a national spirit in France. Heroes and stories of courage inspired the French. One of the greatest of heroines was a young farm girl, Joan of Arc. Joan said that she heard voices telling her to lead her people against the English in France. She took charge of the French armies

The Plague Pit. The plague killed so many people that normal funerals were not possible. Death carts such as this came through the towns daily to take away the dead.

and led them to several victories. In her most important battle, she drove the British from the French city of Orleans. A year later, she was captured by the English. Condemned to death for being a witch, she was burned at the stake. Later, she was named a saint by the Roman Catholic Church.

10. The Hundred Years' War caused the nobles in France to lose power. All the people were now afraid of invasions. As a result, the Estates-General let the king raise money to pay

for an army to defend France. Having a national army, the king could easily defeat feudal lords who threatened him. Louis XI made France one of the strong nations of Europe. The French court became famous in Europe for its wealth and luxury. Nobles came there, hoping to win the favor of the king. The tables were now turned. Earlier, the middle class had supported the king against the nobles. Now, the nobles supported the king against the middle class.

Testing Your Vocabulary

Choose the best answer.

1. A *plague* is best defined as
   a. a deadly sickness that spreads quickly.
   b. a group of swift-riding, armed horsemen.
   c. violent winds caused by very warm weather.

2. The word *court*, as used in "French court" (paragraph 10), means
   a. the large courtyard surrounding the palace.
   b. the ruler and his followers.
   c. the place where trials are held.

Understanding What You Have Read

1. The main idea of paragraph 3 is that
   a. many nobles of France joined the Crusades.
   b. Paris became a great trading center.
   c. Capet kings spread their power over a large territory.
   d. Capet kings ruled for several hundred years.

2. In which paragraph do you find facts about
   a. the division of Italy and Germany into many states?
   b. the setting up of the Estates-General?
   c. the election of a French pope?
   d. the effects of the Hundred Years' War on France?

3. The Estates-General had little power in France because
   a. the clergy had no voice in it.
   b. it did not meet with the king.
   c. it could meet only when the king

wanted to call it together.

4. The Hundred Years' War helped develop a national spirit in France because
   a. it destroyed French farmland.
   b. French heroes inspired the people.
   c. France recovered from the Plague.

5. A reason why French kings gained power over the nobles was that
   a. money was voted to raise a national army.
   b. French kings had led Crusades.
   c. the nobles caused France to lose the Hundred Years' War.

6. All of these are examples of how little national unity there was in Europe EXCEPT
   a. Spain was partly occupied by the Muslims until the 15th century.
   b. Italy was divided into small states.
   c. In France, kings continued to gain power throughout the Middle Ages.

Developing Ideas and Skills

TELLING FACT FROM OPINION

Tell whether each of the following is a statement of fact or a statement of opinion.

1. Merchants would have gained more democracy if they had supported nobles against monarchs.
2. The power of the nobility lasted longer in France than in England.
3. Although he had faults, Philip the Fair did more for France than any ruler before him.
4. The Hundred Years' War kept France from becoming the strongest nation in Europe.
5. Much of France was ruined by the Hundred Years' War.
6. Wars cannot be stopped no matter what the leaders of nations may do.

Using Original Sources

Joan of Arc, a French peasant girl, believed she was sent by God to rid her nation of English troops and have Charles VII crowned King of France. In 1429, with a small group of soldiers, she drove the English from Orleans, a city north of Paris. The king was crowned. But Joan was captured and put on trial by the English for witchcraft and heresy. She was found guilty and was burned at the stake. Twenty-five years later, the Church withdrew the charges against her. In 1919, she was made a saint of the Catholic Church. The following document is taken from the *Proceedings of the Condemnation of Joan of Arc*. It was presented as evidence against her at her trial in 1431.

Letter sent by Joan of Arc to the English during the siege of Orleans.

King of England, and you, Duke of Bedford, who call yourself Regent of France . . . listen to the King of Heaven. Give to the Maid, who is sent here by God, the King of Heaven, the keys of all the fair towns which you have taken and violated in France. She has come here in God's cause to reclaim the royal blood. She is ready to make peace, on condition that you leave France and pay for what you have taken. And as for you, archers, men-at-arms, gentlemen, and others who remain before the city of Orleans, go with God to your country; and if you do not, know of the Maid who will soon come to you, to your great ruin. King of England, if you do not do this, I am the war captain, and wherever I shall find your people in France, I shall make them leave, whether they want to or not; and if they will not do so I shall have them killed. I am sent here by God, King of Heaven, to throw you out of France.

1. What reasons did Joan give for driving the English out of France?
2. What demands did Joan make of the English king?
3. What did Joan mean by writing "to reclaim the royal blood"?
4. What in her letter shows the change in attitude between loyalty to a feudal lord and loyalty to one's country?

AIM: What problems faced other European nations in becoming united?

CHAPTER 6

National Unity Comes Slowly in Europe

HOW DID THE MOORS BRING PROGRESS TO SPAIN?

1. Spain's history was different from that of the rest of Europe. Spain is a peninsula—land surrounded on three sides by water. Also, the high and rugged Pyrenees Mountains separate Spain from France on the fourth side. So Spain is separated from the rest of Europe. It is only eight miles from Africa, across the Strait of Gibraltar. These facts of geography help to explain the story of Spain in the history of Europe. While most of Europe was in cultural darkness during the Middle Ages, Spain was enjoying the learning and culture of the Moors (Muslims).

2. Many different people came to Spain and left behind a part of their culture. Ancient Phoenicians and Greeks had trading posts in Spain. Colonists from the African city of Carthage founded Barcelona, Spain's large northeastern seaport. The Romans came to Spain and stayed for 600 years. Two Roman emperors were Spanish. The Romans built roads, bridges, and aqueducts, many of which can still be seen. They brought their religions and the Latin language. Spanish is one of the languages based on Latin. The Visigoths came when the Romans left and set up a Christian kingdom in Spain that lasted until 711.

3. Early in the 8th century, the Moors crossed into Spain from Africa. For the next 800 years, they controlled Spain. The Moors were part Arab and part North African. They brought with them the religion of Islam and the culture of the East. They pushed the Christians back to the northwest. Spain was split into many small kingdoms, which the Muslims ruled.

4. When most Europeans had forgotten the learning of ancient Greece and the Middle East, those in Moorish Spain were studying it. Cordova, the Moorish capital in Spain, was a large city when London and Paris were still only villages. The Moors set up schools and libraries. They asked Jewish and Muslim scholars to come to Spain to teach and study. The Moors made great contributions to science, medicine, and astronomy. Their beautiful palaces and mosques can still be seen in Cordova and Granada. Moorish traders brought rugs, silks, tile, and jewels to Spain. Farmers grew such crops as rice, cotton, lemons, and oranges.

5. In the 11th century, Christian kings in northern Spain began to push back Muslim rulers. Spain's great folk hero, Rodrigo Díaz de Vivar, known as El Cid, was a vassal of the King of Castile. By 1400, El Cid and his forces had captured Cordova. The kingdom of Castile then controlled central Spain. The kingdom of Aragon won back the east. The Moors were then

Interior of the Grand Mosque of Cordova. This Mosque was built in Spain before Charlemagne ruled in France and about the time the Anglo Saxon king Alfred the Great brought some unity to England.

limited to the area around the city of Granada, in the south. When Ferdinand of Aragon married Isabella of Castile, Spain was united. In 1492, Granada was captured.

6. Ferdinand and Isabella forced non-Christians to leave Spain. They wanted Spain to be completely Christian. Spaniards with Jewish or Moorish ancestors left. This meant the loss of many teachers and businessmen who had given Spain a high degree of culture and prosperity. Ferdinand and Isabella turned their attention to the New World. They hoped their explorers would find riches there.

WHY DID ITALY REMAIN DIVIDED?

7. Italy did not become a unified nation until late in the 19th century. In the 1400s, there were as many as 12 different states in Italy. Some were city-states, such as Venice and Florence. Then there were the Papal States, governed by the pope, which were in central Italy. There was also the kingdom of Naples, in the south. Italian nobles wanted to keep control of their own land. Many times the different parts of Italy were the battlefields for other powers. France and Spain often fought each other for control of the Italian peninsula. Thus Italy stayed divided while other parts of Europe were becoming modern unified nations.

WHAT CAUSED THE BREAKUP OF THE HOLY ROMAN EMPIRE?

8. Germany, too, was a divided land until late in the 19th century. During the Middle Ages, the German states tried to bring back the glory of the old Roman Empire. Otto the Great named himself Holy Roman Emperor in 962. The word *holy* was used to show that the empire was a Christian one. The Holy Roman Empire was hardly Roman. It was really a group of German-speaking states, plus some Italian land. There was little unity in this empire. When the emperor went to Italy to keep order, the feudal lords in Germany revolted. When he returned to the German states, the Italian lands revolted.

El Cid ordering the execution of the Muslim leader Ahmed. His adventures were told in an epic poem written 40 years after his death. How do you think epic poems contributed to a spirit of nationalism?

9. In 1438, a member of the Hapsburg family became Holy Roman Emperor. The Hapsburgs continued to rule until 1806. One of the Hapsburgs was Emperor Charles V (1519–1558). His influence was felt all over Europe. Charles was, on his mother's side, the grandson of Ferdinand and Isabella. Thus, he became ruler of Spain. He also ruled all the Spanish colonies in America. From his father, he inherited all the Hapsburg lands. Among these were the Netherlands and Belgium, as well as the German and Italian states. It was said that Charles's titles alone would have filled several pages.

10. The energy and ability of Emperor Charles V were amazing. He fought the Turks who had overrun Hungary. He fought against France in Italy and Germany. He helped to arrange the peace between Catholics and Protestants in Germany. But all his wars, his titles, and his power could not unite the German people. Finally, he gave up the throne and divided his empire. His brother Ferdinand ruled the Hapsburg lands in central Europe. His son, Philip, ruled Spain, the Netherlands, and parts of Italy.

HOW DID RUSSIA FREE ITSELF FROM THE MONGOLS?

11. In Russia, early settlements were made by tribes of Slavs. In the 9th century, a Norseman, Rurik, set up his rule in the north and later moved south to the city of Kiev (KEE-ef), in the Ukraine. Christianity was introduced into Russia by the Byzantines. When the Mongols swept over Asia and Europe, Kiev fell to them. Mongol rule lasted in Russia for about 200 years. During this period, Muscovy, a region lying to the east of Kiev, became an important political center. The prince of Muscovy threw off the rule of the Mongols in the 15th century. Under Ivan the Great, Muscovy extended its rule westward. Within 100 years, it had gained control over nearly all of Russia.

Testing Your Vocabulary

Choose the best answer.

1. The word *prosperity* as used in paragraph 6 means
   a. economic success.
   b. education.
   c. training.

2. *Moors* are
   a. conquerors from Asia.
   b. barbarian tribes.
   c. Muslims of Northwest Africa.

Understanding What You Have Read

1. A good title for paragraphs 3 and 4 might be
   a. Small Kingdoms of Spain.
   b. The City of Cordova.
   c. Palaces and Mosques.
   d. The Moors in Spain.

2. In which paragraph do you find facts about
   a. the boundaries of Spain?
   b. city-states of Italy?
   c. the land ruled by the Hapsburg emperors?

d. El Cid, the Spanish national hero?

3. Ferdinand and Isabella forced the Moors out of Spain because
   a. they wanted Spain to be completely Christian.
   b. the Moors had given little to Spanish culture.
   c. the Moors had ruined fertile farm land in southern Spain.

4. The Holy Roman Empire lost much of its influence because
   a. there was no Holy Roman Emperor.
   b. there was little unity among the many German states.
   c. Monarchs who ruled the empire were little known in Europe.

5. All of these are reasons why Italy remained divided until the 19th century EXCEPT
   a. there was a wide variety of religious beliefs among the people.
   b. more powerful nations tried to control parts of Italy.
   c. nobles of Italy wanted to keep control of their lands.

6. Spain finally became a unified nation when
   a. Christians in northern Spain united.
   b. the kingdoms of Aragon and Castile were joined together.
   c. the Moors came to Spain.

7. Russia played a small part in European affairs in the Middle Ages because
   a. its great rulers kept to themselves.
   b. Christianity had not yet come to Russia.
   c. it was continually being conquered and ruled by different groups.

A. Match the names in the first column with the descriptions in the second column.

   1. Ferdinand
   2. Otto the Great
   3. Charles V
   4. Rurik
   5. El Cid

   a. Norseman who ruled part of Russia
   b. Spanish hero, important in freeing northern Spain
   c. Holy Roman Emperor of the 10th century
   d. Prince of Muscovy
   e. King of Aragon and King of Spain
   f. Hapsburg emperor with much territory in Europe

B. Match the names in the first column with the descriptions in the second column.

   1. Cordova
   2. Kiev
   3. Papal States
   4. Gibraltar
   5. Barcelona

   a. largest of the German states
   b. Moorish capital of Spain
   c. territory in Italy governed by the popes
   d. Russian city controlled by the Norsemen in the 9th century
   e. Spanish seaport, founded by Carthage
   f. area where strait separates Spain from North Africa

Developing Ideas and Skills _____

USING A MAP

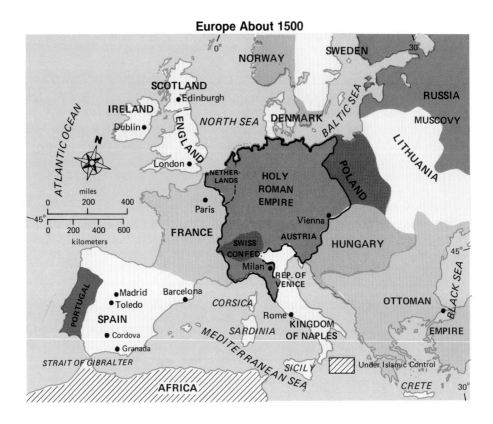

Europe About 1500

Study the map carefully. Then choose the correct answers.

1. A present European country that does *not* appear on this map is
   a. Belgium.
   b. Portugal.
   c. Denmark.

2. A modern nation that in 1500 was a group of smaller states was
   a. Italy.
   b. France.
   c. the Netherlands.

3. Which of these states of Europe had almost the same boundaries in 1500 as it has today?
   a. Lithuania
   b. Hungary
   c. Portugal

4. The Holy Roman Empire included all of these EXCEPT
   a. the Netherlands.
   b. Poland.
   c. Austria.

5. Greece (not shown on the map) in 1500 was part of
   a. Hungary.
   b. the Ottoman Empire.
   c. the Holy Roman Empire.

AIM: How did the desire to carry on trade with the East lead to Europe's greater knowledge of the world?

CHAPTER 7

Europe Looks for New Trade Routes

WHY WERE THE OLD TRADE ROUTES UNSATISFACTORY?

1. We often have strange ideas about places we have never seen. The same was true of Europeans in the early 15th century. They traded with Asia, but they knew almost nothing about it. Marco Polo's travels had given them some idea of the East's riches. Arab traders brought precious goods from the lands east of Persia. But few Europeans had been to India or China. Almost as little was known about the lands below the Sahara Desert, in Africa. Europeans had never seen the Americas or the Pacific Ocean. Some geographers accepted the idea that the world was round, but not most people. To the average person of that time, the Atlantic Ocean went just so far, and then one dropped off the edge of the flat earth.

2. Goods coming from the East were carried over different routes before they arrived in Europe. Spices, for example, were brought by Arab traders from China to India by caravan. Then they were taken by boat to the Persian Gulf and up the Euphrates River. A camel caravan took them to Constantinople, Alexandria, or an eastern Mediterranean port. If the ships sailed from India to the Red Sea, their cargo was then carried by caravan across the desert to Alexandria. There Italian merchants from Venice and Genoa picked up the spices and jewels and brought them to Europe. Finally, the goods were sent on to the other trading cities of Europe. Goods from the East had to be loaded and unloaded many times along the way. The cost of goods was high because of the risk and because many workers had to be paid for their work. When spices reached Europe, they were 20 times their original cost in Asia.

3. The wealth of many Italian cities depended upon trade. There were dangers along the trading routes. If anything happened to close these routes, the traders of the Italian cities might be ruined. Such an event finally did happen. The Ottoman Turks swept over Asia Minor and conquered Constantinople in 1453. Europeans now had the added danger and costs of passing through the territory of the unfriendly Turks. The Turks could make traders pay for the use of the routes. A new way had to be found to keep up the profitable trade with Asia.

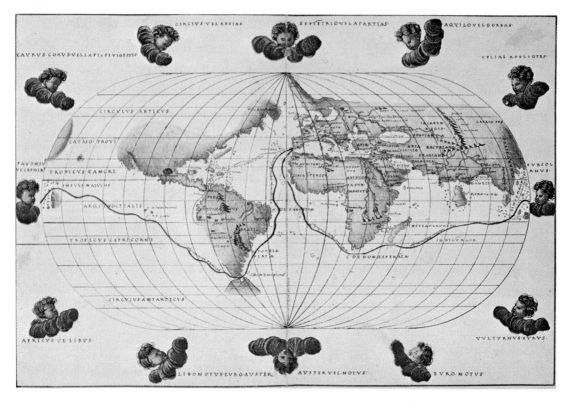

This map from the late Renaissance shows the Western Hemisphere. How did the period of exploration help make maps more accurate?

WHO SEARCHED FOR A NEW ROUTE?

4. Spain and Portugal had long hoped to take away some of the Italian cities' trade. In the late 1400s, Prince Henry of Portugal began the search for a new route to India. This route would take ships around Africa. No one had used such a route before. In fact, no one knew where the southern end of Africa was. Prince Henry started a school for navigators. He collected maps and valuable instruments such as compasses. His sailors began looking for the southern end of Africa by exploring its west coast. They sailed a little bit farther south each time. After the death of Prince Henry, the search continued. In 1488, Bartholomew Diaz, a Portuguese explorer, lost sight of land on his voyage far south along the coast of Africa. When he saw land again, he was on the other side of Africa. He then realized that he had rounded the southern tip of Africa.

5. Ten years later, Vasco da Gama sailed around the southern tip of Africa and reached India. He returned with goods whose value was 60 times the cost of his voyage. This was the kind of profit for which the Portuguese rulers were looking. The new route was thousands of miles longer than the old but it was much more profitable. The Portuguese kingdom set up trading posts along the route of da Gama's voyage. The Portuguese tried their best to keep the route a secret from the rest of Europe.

6. Christopher Columbus, born in the trading city of Genoa, Italy, believed that the earth was round. He knew that if the earth was

Vasco da Gama discovered a trade route around the tip of Africa. Why did the Portuguese try to keep the route a secret from the rest of Europe?

round, he could reach India by sailing west. Columbus did not know of the American continents that would stand in his way. For years, he tried to find someone who would believe him. Finally, Queen Isabella of Spain decided to take a chance. She gave him three ships and men for his trip. We have all read of Columbus's courage in crossing the unknown Atlantic. His voyage took a little more than two months. He landed at an island in the Bahamas. He named this island San Salvador. He went on to Cuba and then returned to Spain. Columbus believed he had landed in India. Frustrated, he returned to Europe without the treasure he had expected to find in the East.

7. Columbus made four trips to the New World. He explored the Caribbean Islands and the northern coast of South America. But he found no treasure. He was disappointed with his voyages and felt that he was a failure. He did not realize that he had found new continents, the Americas. At first the Spanish believed that America was just a useless land blocking the way to the East. They did not think much of Columbus's discoveries. Portugal had already found a new route to the riches of the East. Spain had not.

8. Spain's search for a new route did not end. Vasco de Balboa, sailing for Spain, crossed the Isthmus of Panama and discovered the Pacific Ocean. But he did not find a water route to the East. England sent an Italian sailor, John Cabot, across the Atlantic in 1497. Cabot reached the northeastern coast of North America. He found the great fishing grounds near Newfoundland. But he found no treasure of jewels, gold, silver, or spices.

9. In 1519, Ferdinand Magellan, a Portuguese navigator sailing for Spain, started on a voyage westward. He found the southern route

Columbus arriving in San Salvador. Where did Columbus think he had landed?

around South America and came to the Pacific Ocean. Sailing west, he landed in the Philippine Islands, where he was killed in a fight with the people there. His sailors continued around Africa and back to Spain. They had completely circled the world, proving that the world was round. But the route they took was too long to be useful.

10. France sent an Italian sailor, Giovanni da Verrazano, to the New World in 1524. He searched for but could not find a passage through the American continent. Then, Jacques Cartier, also sent by the French, sailed up the St. Lawrence River. Cartier thought that this river might be a route to the Pacific Ocean. For the Dutch, Henry Hudson, in 1609, sailed up the river that today bears his name. He, too, hoped that the waterway would lead him through to the westward side of America. He returned to North America the following year, this time sent by England. On this voyage he went farther north, entering Hudson Bay. Hudson was still looking for a passage to the East. He died without finding it.

11. There is little doubt that the desire for the goods of the East changed history. The search for trade routes to the East went on for more than 150 years. During this time, many discoveries were made about America. They added to people's knowledge of the world. Some explorers brought riches to their countries. For a short time, Spain and Portugal were the richest nations in the world. In the next chapter we will see some of the results of the discoveries and explorations of the 15th and 16th centuries.

Testing Your Vocabulary

Choose the correct answer.

1. In paragraph 4, to be *frustrated* means being
   a. happy about a situation.
   b. unhappy because things didn't work out the way you wanted them to.
   c. curious about finding something out.

Understanding What You Have Read

1. A good title for paragraphs 2 and 3 might be
   a. Eastern Trade Routes.
   b. Loading and Unloading Caravans.
   c. The Ottoman Turks Capture Constantinople.
   d. Venice and Genoa, Centers of Trade.

2. In which paragraph do you find facts about
   a. the profits of Vasco da Gama's voyage?
   b. the discovery of the Pacific Ocean?
   c. the reasons for the high cost of goods in eastern trade?

d. European knowledge of the world in the 15th century?

3. Cartier and Hudson explored the New World hoping to find
   a. good fishing waters.
   b. fertile land.
   c. a water passage to Asia.

4. Vasco da Gama's voyage to India was important to Portugal because
   a. it started schools for navigators sailing around Africa.
   b. it was the beginning of a cheaper way to get goods from the East.
   c. Portugal was now Spain's rival for trade with India.

5. Columbus made his first voyage to America after

   a. Vasco da Gama reached India.
   b. Hudson found Hudson Bay.
   c. Constantinople was captured by the Turks.

6. Magellan's voyage is important because it
   a. proved that the world is round.
   b. brought great profits to Spain.
   c. showed that there was an easy route to Asia.

7. The trading wealth of the Italian cities was in danger in 1453 because
   a. Spain found a route to the Pacific.
   b. Vasco da Gama reached India.
   c. Constantinople was captured by the Ottoman Turks.

Choose the correct answer. Tell which of the three choices for each statement is correct.

1. In the early 1400s, Europeans
   a. knew much about Asia.
   b. knew little of Asia although they traded with it.
   c. sent ships from Venice all the way to China.

2. An important city along the trade routes from the East was
   a. Constantinople.
   b. Barcelona.
   c. Paris.

3. All of these were problems in transporting goods from the East to Europe EXCEPT
   a. the high cost.
   b. unfriendly people along the routes.
   c. the demands of the bankers of Venice.

4. A school for navigators was started by
   a. Magellan.
   b. Ferdinand and Isabella.
   c. Prince Henry of Portugal.

5. The first nation to profit from exploration was
   a. Portugal.

   b. Spain.
   c. France.

6. Many explorers sent by Spain, France, and England were
   a. Italian.
   b. Greek.
   c. Dutch.

7. Whose explorations took place first?
   a. Magellan's
   b. Hudson's
   c. Cabot's

8. The Philippines were claimed by
   a. England.
   b. Spain.
   c. France.

9. The only one of these explorers to explore North America was
   a. Cartier.
   b. Magellan.
   c. Balboa.

10. In the early period of exploration the richest countries were
    a. France and England.
    b. Portugal and Spain.
    c. Portugal and France.

Developing Ideas and Skills _____

USING A MAP

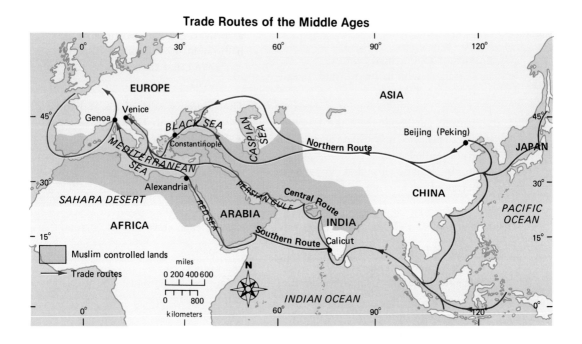

Trade Routes of the Middle Ages

Study the map above carefully. In your notebook, write **T** if the statement is true; write **F** if the statement is false; write **N** if there is not enough information on the map to help you decide whether or not the statement is correct.

1. The important trade routes from the East met in the Mediterranean Sea.
2. More goods were carried over the northern than the southern route.
3. No trade routes reached Japan.
4. The northern route from China was a land route all the way to the Black Sea.
5. No trade routes passed through Muslim lands.
6. More goods went east from Genoa than from Venice.
7. Italian cities were the chief ports of trade for goods arriving in Europe from Asia.

Early Voyages of Discovery

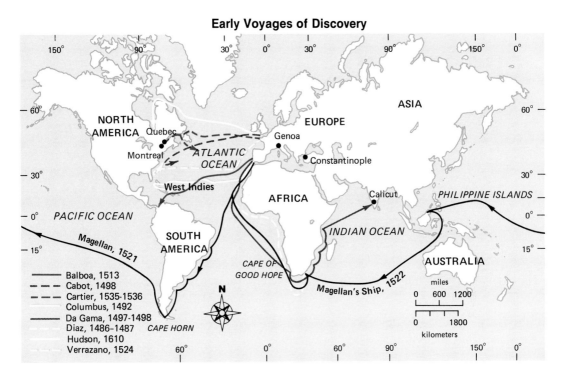

Study the map carefully. Then choose the correct answer.

1. The explorer who reached the Philippine Islands was
   a. Magellan.
   b. Cabot.
   c. Hudson.

2. All of these explorers reached the coast of North America EXCEPT
   a. Cabot.
   b. Cartier.
   c. Magellan.

3. Which of these men made the earliest voyages?
   a. Da Gama
   b. Magellan
   c. Columbus

4. Two explorers who rounded the southern tip of Africa were
   a. Hudson and Cartier.
   b. Da Gama and Diaz.
   c. Cabot and Columbus.

5. The busiest exploration route shown on the map is the
   a. North Atlantic Ocean.
   b. Indian Ocean.
   c. Pacific Ocean.

AIM: How did the race for colonies result in changes among the nations of Europe?

CHAPTER 8

The Search for Colonial Wealth

WHY WAS PORTUGAL THE FIRST TO BEGIN EXPLORATIONS?

1. By the end of the 15th century, there were some strong nations in Europe. Portugal and Spain, however, were the only nations ready to look for a new route to reach the riches of the East. France and England were weak after a hundred years of fighting each other. Then England was torn by civil war for 30 years more. Neither Germany nor Italy was united. Only Spain and Portugal had the wealth and opportunity to explore. Their explorations turned out to be of great importance to the people of Europe.

2. Vasco da Gama, of Portugal, had been the first to find an all-water route to India. Portugal then set up trading posts on important waterways. A few Portuguese soldiers manned posts on the Red Sea, the Persian Gulf, and the Strait of Malacca (which links the Indian Ocean and the South China Sea). Their main purpose was to protect the trade routes. Colonists did not try to settle in these far-off lands. In time, Portugal lost all but a few small areas in India to other nations. Brazil, in South America, had been claimed by Pedro Cabral, a Portuguese explorer, in 1500. It was the only important colony that Portugal was able to hold.

3. This was a glorious age for Spain as well as for Portugal. Hernando Cortéz had conquered the Aztec civilization in Mexico. Francisco Pizarro had conquered the Incas in Peru. From Mexico and Peru, the Spanish took great riches in gold and silver. Hernando De Soto found the Mississippi River. Francisco Coronado explored the southwestern part of North America. Gold and silver were Spain's chief in-

Francisco Pizarro. For what country did he explore and what were his accomplishments?

terests in America. But Spanish adventurers and traders also came to its colonies. Missionaries arrived and taught the Indians. Many of the Indians were converted to Christianity. A "New Spain" grew up in the land south of what is now the United States. The riches of the New World colonies made Spain wealthy and powerful.

4. Spain's period of glory lasted for about a century. The riches of the New World had been spent almost as fast as Spain had taken them. More wealth was lost by Spain when English ships raided Spanish treasure ships leaving South America. To stop these English raids, King Philip of Spain built a great fleet of warships. It became known as the Armada. The Spanish Armada sailed into England's coastal waters in 1588. In a great naval battle, the smaller and lighter English ships were able to damage the heavier Spanish vessels. A violent storm finished what the English ships had begun. The Spanish navy was badly defeated. Many of its great warships were sunk. Spain was never able to recover from this loss. England, on the other hand, became the great sea power.

The Spanish Armada. Why did Spain think the Armada could not be defeated?

WHAT OTHER NATIONS JOINED THE RACE?

5. French explorers gained land for France in North America. Jacques Cartier discovered the St. Lawrence River in 1534. Samuel de Champlain founded the city of Quebec in 1608. He went on to explore and claim land around the Great Lakes for France. Father Jacques Marquette and Robert LaSalle gained for France the territory along the Mississippi River. In time, a long line of French fur-trading posts reached through the center of North America. But not many people wanted to live there. The weather in much of the French territory was very cold. In addition, there was no gold or silver to be found. France let only Catholics come to the French colonies. So the number of settlers never grew as it did in the neighboring English colonies.

6. England made its first permanent settlement in America in 1607 at Jamestown, Virginia. The colony of Jamestown had hard times at first. When they found that they could earn money from planting and trading in tobacco, however, the colonists became rich. In 1620, English settlers arrived in Massachusetts. By 1733, there were 13 English colonies along the Atlantic coast of North America. Although the area was not so large as the French area, there were ten times more people in the English settlements. The colonies were closer together, too, so that it was easier for them to keep up relations with one another.

7. Shortly after 1600, the Dutch entered the race for colonies. Dutch ships were heavy and slow, but they could carry large cargoes of goods. The Dutch became famous shipbuilders. Their ships were found in ports all over the world. The Dutch East India Company was formed. It soon took control of the East Indies islands from Portugal. From the East Indies, the Dutch brought coffee, rubber, sugar, and spices to the cities of Europe. In America, the Dutch founded a colony in 1623 at New Amsterdam

(later New York). They lost it to the English about forty years later.

WHAT WERE SOME OF THE RESULTS OF COLONIZATION?

8. The different countries needed money to pay for their voyages to far-off lands. In Europe, trading companies were formed. In a trading company, a group of people, rather than a single person, shared the cost of the voyages. Each person in the group gave a sum of money for the voyage. Each person became known as a shareholder or stockholder in the company. If the voyage or the colony made a profit, each shareholder made a profit. The trade in sugar from the West Indies, in spices and coffee from the East Indies, and in tobacco from Virginia made large profits for the shareholders of trading companies.

Jacques Marquette and Louis Joliet explored the Mississippi River in search of a way through North America to Asia. In the process they discovered that the Mississippi River flowed into the Gulf of Mexico, not the Pacific Ocean.

9. Countries and trading companies set up colonies chiefly to get riches for themselves. The desire for wealth led nations to explore distant lands. This brought many benefits to the people of Europe. New products and goods became known and used: potatoes, corn, rice, tea, cotton, tobacco, silks, and spices. European towns grew into cities as trade grew. Banks became more numerous. Banks were needed as safe places to keep profits and to borrow money to pay for voyages. A middle class arose in the cities of Europe. The middle class was made up of merchants, bankers, and business people. These people were called the middle class because they were neither as rich as the landowning lords nor as poor as peasants or farmers.

10. From the search for riches and glory in far-off lands came many evils. The worst of the evils was the slave trade. Slavery had existed in Europe and Africa before Columbus's first voyage. But once colonies were begun in the New World, the slave trade grew quickly. Spain and Portugal brought the first blacks from West Africa to work on plantations in the New World. Slave-trading posts were established along the west coast of Africa by all nations. Africans were taken from their homes and chained together for shipment. Then they were loaded into overcrowded boats for the trip to the New World. Those who survived the voyage were sold as pieces of property to whoever offered the most money.

11. There is no way of knowing the number of blacks who were brought from Africa to the Americas. Probably as many died on the way as arrived safely. There was no protest from Europe against this horrible evil until the late 18th century. The harm done to black people by the slave trade cannot be truly measured.

12. Europeans looked differently on the people of Asia than on the Indians of North America or the Africans. The people of Europe respected the cultures of India and China. But the people of India and China had little interest in Europe. Asians felt that the goods of Europe were not as valuable as their own products.

13. At first the Chinese would not let the Portuguese even enter China. Later, they let them set up trading posts. The Japanese let a Catholic missionary, Francis Xavier, enter Japan in 1549. A century later, there were conflicts between the Christians and Japanese rulers. Thousands of Christians were killed. The English had more success in India. Trade had begun along the west coast of India in 1612. In less than 50 years, the British were trading in the city of Bombay. Thus, colonies and trade changed the history of Europe, Africa, Asia, and America in the 16th and 17th centuries.

Testing Your Vocabulary _____

Choose the best answer.

1. The term *New Spain* refers to
   a. Spanish colonies in the New World.
   b. changes in Spain as a result of explorations.
   c. the beginnings of democratic changes by Spanish rulers.
2. The *stockholders* of a 17th-century company were those who
   a. traded with the colonies.
   b. owned a share, or part, of the company.
   c. bought the goods sold by the company.
3. A nation is involved in a *civil war*, the war is
   a. over the rights of the common people.
   b. between people of the same nation.
   c. between two kings of different countries.

Understanding What You Have Read _____

1. A good title for paragraph 9 is
   a. Exploring Distant Lands.
   b. Exploration Brings Changes to Europe.
   c. New Products for Europe.
   d. Rise of the Middle Class.
2. In which paragraph do you find facts about
   a. colonial trading companies?
   b. the bringing of slaves to the New World?
   c. European ideas about India and China?
   d. French settlements in America?
3. Spain and Portugal led in the search for a new route to the East because
   a. England was not interested in trade with far-off lands.
   b. France had been torn by civil wars.
   c. no other European nations had the wealth and opportunity to spend on voyages of exploration.
4. Spain's power began to decline as a result of
   a. the defeat of the Spanish Armada by England.
   b. Portuguese claims to South America.
   c. the arrival of English settlers in America.
5. English colonies in North America
   a. were farther apart from one another than French colonies.

b. had more people than French colonies.

c. covered a greater area than French colonies.

6. All of these were results of the founding of colonies by European nations EXCEPT

a. the parent countries gained wealth.

b. new goods were more widely used.

c. the middle class lost power.

7. Trading companies were formed because

a. rulers wanted to control the colonies.

b. it was good business for individuals to "pool" their money in such a company.

c. bankers lent money only to shareholders.

Complete the following chart in your notebooks. You may remember some of the information from your study of American history.

Discovery and Exploration

Explorer	Country	Discovery
1. Vasco da Gama	Portugal	A route to India around Africa.
2. John Cabot	England	_____
3. Christopher Columbus	Spain	_____
4. Ferdinand Magellan	_____	_____
5. Jacques Cartier	_____	_____
6. Henry Hudson	_____	_____
7. Hernando De Soto	_____	_____
8. Hernando Cortez	_____	_____
9. Francisco Pizarro	_____	_____
10. Samuel De Champlain	_____	_____
11. Robert LaSalle	_____	_____

Choose the correct answer.

1. The only important colony in the New World held by Portugal for a long time was

a. India.

b. Brazil.

c. South Africa.

2. All of these river valleys were claimed by France EXCEPT the valley of the

a. St. Lawrence River.

b. Mississippi River.

c. Hudson River.

3. The first slaves were brought to the New World to the colonies of

a. France.

b. Holland.

c. Spain.

4. All of these were members of the middle class EXCEPT

a. nobles.

b. bankers.

c. merchants.

5. In the middle of the 17th century, England had won important trading areas in

a. China.

b. India.

c. Japan.

Developing Ideas and Skills _____

USING A MAP

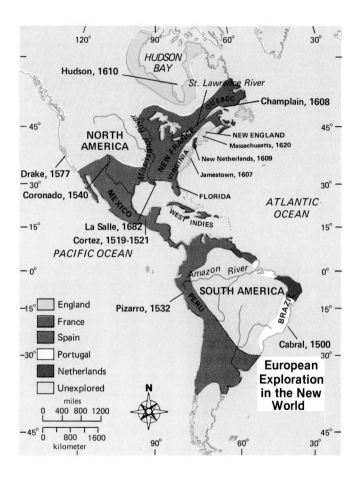

Study the map carefully. Tell whether these statements are true or false. If a statement is false, change the words in italics to make it true.

1. Coronado explored the southwestern part of North America for *Spain*.
2. The English settled mainly in *North America*.
3. The greatest amount of territory in the New World was held by *France*.
4. Hudson Bay was claimed by *the Netherlands*.
5. The only nations to claim land along the Pacific Coast were *Spain* and *France*.
6. A large part of the center of both North and South America was *unexplored* in the 17th century.
7. French settlements were largely in *South America*.
8. Most of Brazil was claimed by *Spain*.

Using Original Sources

Below is part of an account of Ferdinand Magellan's voyage. It was written by Antonio Pigafeta, one of Magellan's crew. The events in this account took place in the Philippine Islands shortly before Magellan was killed in a fight with Philippine tribesmen. Read the passage and then try to answer the questions that follow it.

Magellan's Meeting with the Filipinos

. . . on Friday, we showed these people a shop full of our merchandise, at which they were very much surprised. For metals, iron, and other large merchandise, they gave us gold. For the other, smaller articles, they gave us rice, swine [hogs], goats, and other food. . . .

On Sunday morning, April fourteen [1521], forty men of us went ashore, two of whom were completely armed and preceded [went before] the royal banner. When we reached the land, the artillery was fired. . . . The captain [Magellan] and the king sat down on chairs of red and violet velvet, the chiefs on cushions, and the others on mats. The captian told the king through the interpreter that he thanked God for inspiring him to become a Christian; and that he would more easily conquer his enemies than before. . . . The captain told the king that he was going back to Spain, but that he would make him the greatest king of these regions. . . . A large cross was set up in the middle of the square. The captain told them that if they wished to become Christians, as they had declared . . . they must burn all their idols and set up a cross in their place. . . . Five hundred were baptized before Mass.

Do you agree or disagree with these statements? Give reasons for your answers.

1. This story is probably taken from a log kept by Pigafeta.
2. Magellan told the king that he would be able to defeat his enemies if he became a Christian.
3. Magellan expected to return to Spain.
4. When Magellan went ashore on this Sunday morning, he believed he would be attacked by the king and his men.
5. Spanish explorers were interested in spreading Christianity.
6. The king could offer the Spanish explorers little that they wanted.
7. Magellan and his men allowed the people to keep their idols after they had become Christians.
8. Only a few of the Filipinos decided to become Christians.

AIM: How did the need for changes in the Catholic Church lead to the start of new Christian religions?

CHAPTER 9

Protestant Religions Are Formed

WHY DID SOME PEOPLE WANT CHANGES IN THE CHURCH?

1. The term *Christian* today usually means a Protestant or a Catholic. But at the beginning of the 16th century in Western Europe, Christians were members of the Catholic Church. At this time, people began to revolt against the Church. There had been attacks on the Church from time to time before this. But few people seemed to wish to leave the Church. Before the century was half over, there were other Christian churches besides the Catholic Church. These were called Protestant. How did these new religions come to be?

2. There is no simple explanation for the Protestant Reformation. Many Christians felt that the clergy had become too interested in worldly or non-religious affairs. Others did not like the wealth of the Church. Peasants who were very poor did not want to give a *tithe* ($\frac{1}{10}$ of their money) to the Church. They felt that this was making the clergy rich. Rulers wanted their people to be loyal to them first, rather than to the Church. Merchants who wanted to charge high interest rates on loans did not like the Church to stop them. In addition, the invention of the printing press gave more people the

Martin Luther burning the Pope's order for his excommunication. Luther was an important leader of the Reformation.

chance to read. People began to read works by writers who spoke against the power of the Church.

WHO LED THE PROTESTANT REVOLT?

3. The desire for reform, or change and improvement, in the Catholic Church began before 1500. John Wycliffe of England had pro-

tested against the wealth of the clergy in the 14th century. John Hus, in the 15th century, was burned at the stake for preaching *heresy*. Heresy is a religious opinion or teaching that goes against the established beliefs of a religion. A person who holds heretical ideas is called a *heretic*. The Dutch humanist Erasmus had protested against the behavior of some churchmen. But until the 16th century, most rulers had backed the Catholic Church. They helped to put down those who protested against it. Now, however, it was different. Some rulers and peasants backed those who taught ideas different from those of the Catholic Church.

4. Martin Luther was the most important figure of the Reformation. Luther was a monk who taught religion at the University of Wittenberg, in Germany. He did not like some of the practices of the Catholic Church. One of these was the system of *indulgences*. An indulgence was a pardon for a sin. It was granted by the Church to those who made some sacrifice of something they wanted. Luther saw that indulgences were being sold to those who gave money to the Church. In 1517, he posted on the door of a church in Wittenberg a list called the 95 Theses. These were statements of his beliefs. Luther did not want to leave the Church. He felt, rather, that he could correct what he believed was wrong with it.

5. Luther preached that people could save themselves by faith alone. They did not need the help of the Catholic Church. He told people to read and study the Bible for themselves and not depend upon priests. The pope was angry with Luther's 95 Theses. Luther was brought to trial before Church leaders. He was found guilty and was excommunicated (denied Church membership) in 1521. Luther burned the pope's order of excommunication in public. He was backed by many German princes who wanted Church lands and did not like the way money was sent from Germany to Italy for the pope. In this way the Protestant Lutheran Church was formed. It was called Protestant

because of the protest made by Luther's followers to the order of the pope.

6. Many peasants became Lutherans. They hoped that their lords, having become Lutherans, might treat them better if they changed religions, too. When they did not get better treatment, some peasants revolted against their princes. They went back to their old religion. But Luther did not back the peasants in their revolt. He thought that a prince or lord had the right to decide the religious affairs of the people on his land. He told the princes to crush the revolt, and they did. For years there was fighting and bloodshed in the German states. Finally, in 1555, peace came. The result of this was that the people were forced to follow the religion of their ruler from then on.

7. All those who protested against Church practices were called Protestants. Another leader of Protestant change was John Calvin.

John Calvin. His teachings eventually gave rise to the branch of Protestantism called Presbyterian.

He had fled from France to Switzerland because he was persecuted in his homeland. Calvin believed that what happened to a person during his life was decided beforehand by God. People could do nothing to change their lives. This belief is known as *predestination.* Calvin also believed that churches should be run by ordinary people in their towns. He felt that church ceremonies should be simple. His Sunday sermons were long, and preachers of Calvinism talked for hours. His followers gave up bright clothes, dancing, and other kinds of entertainment.

8. Calvin's teachings spread to Holland and England as well as to Switzerland. In England, his followers became known as *Puritans.* It was this religious group that settled in the early New England colonies. Protestant ideas also spread into Scandinavia and France. In England, they became the Church of England, although the Puritans remained a separate Protestant group. On page 199 you learned how King Henry VIII had broken with the pope and founded a new national church. The Church of England kept many practices of the Catholic Church, but it did not accept the pope as its head.

HOW DID THE CATHOLIC CHURCH RESPOND?

9. As a result of the Protestant Reformation the Catholic clergy decided it was time to end the abuses of their Church. A Church council met at Trent in 1545. It lasted 18 years. At this council, Catholic teachings were restated. The sale of indulgences was stopped. Bishops and priests were ordered to live in their own parishes and spend their time in spiritual work. A new edition of the Bible was published. Some sermons were now allowed to be given in the local language.

10. A new Catholic religious order, or group, was formed. The Society of Jesus, or Jesuits, was founded by Ignatius Loyola, a former Spanish soldier and a priest. The Jesuits were teachers and missionaries. Through their efforts, much of Europe kept the Catholic faith. They taught in Poland, the Netherlands, Ireland, and England. Jesuit missionaries went to teach in India and China and among the Indians in North and South America. Their spirit and ability led to their being called "Soldiers of the Church."

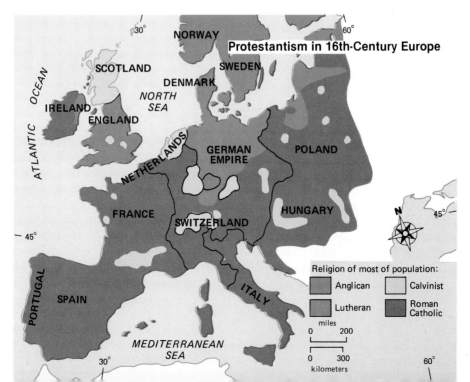

Protestantism in 16th-Century Europe

Religion of most of population:
Anglican
Calvinist
Lutheran
Roman Catholic

11. One of the unfortunate results of this period was the growth of religious *intolerance*. Intolerance means not allowing beliefs different from one's own to exist. Intolerance of the religious beliefs of others was not new in Western Europe. But for the first time there were Christians of different beliefs fighting one another. Rulers of Western Europe wanted every person in their countries to have the same religion. Courts of the Catholic Church, known as the *Inquisition*, punished those suspected of heresy. Thousands of Jews and Christians who were judged to be heretics were condemned to death. Even Ignatius Loyola, later made a saint, was put in prison twice. In England, France, and Germany religious differences brought bloody massacres. Religious persecution drove many people to start new colonies in America.

Testing Your Vocabulary

Choose the best answer.

1. Martin Luther wrote the 95 Theses. *Theses* are
   a. plans for a new religion.
   b. statements of ideas or beliefs.
   c. quotations from the Bible.
2. A person who practices *intolerance*
   a. wants changes.
   b. does not respect the beliefs or opinions of others.
   c. has ideas different from others in the community.
3. The term *Reformation* in this chapter refers to
   a. efforts to bring back the glory of the feudal states.
   b. efforts to relive the past.
   c. efforts to change conditions in the Catholic Church.

Understanding What You Have Read

1. The main idea of paragraphs 9 through 11 is that
   a. there were many changes in the Catholic Church and in Europe as a result of the Protestant Reformation.
   b. Jesuit missionaries taught in many countries in Europe and Asia.
   c. the Council of Trent gave new orders to the clergy.
   d. the people of Europe were forced to follow the religion of their ruler.
2. In which paragraph do you find facts about
   a. the beliefs of John Calvin?
   b. the posting of the 95 Theses?
   c. the work of the Council of Trent?
   d. the results of intolerance?
3. Martin Luther did *not* support peasant revolts against rulers because he
   a. thought that rulers had the right to decide the religion of their people.
   b. did not want another conflict with the pope.
   c. wanted to take away Church lands.
4. All of these are reasons for the Protestant Reformation EXCEPT
   a. Rulers were worried that their people were more loyal to the Church than to them.
   b. many Christians felt that the Church was too interested in worldly affairs.
   c. the Jesuits spread Catholic teaching throughout the world.
5. Peasants followed Martin Luther's

break with the Church because

a. they were loyal to their princes.

b. they hoped to get better treatment from their princes.

c. Luther wanted them to revolt.

6. Revolts in the German states were ended by the agreement that

a. the people would follow the religion of their rulers.

b. people could read and interpret the Bible for themselves.

c. church ceremonies would be made more simple.

7. Among the changes in the Catholic Church that followed the Protestant Reformation was that

a. churches were to be organized by the people in each town.

b. the sale of indulgences would be stopped.

c. Catholics would no longer have to obey the pope.

Developing Ideas and Skills

USING A TIME LINE

Below is a time line that covers the periods in Unit 4. Use it to answer the following questions.

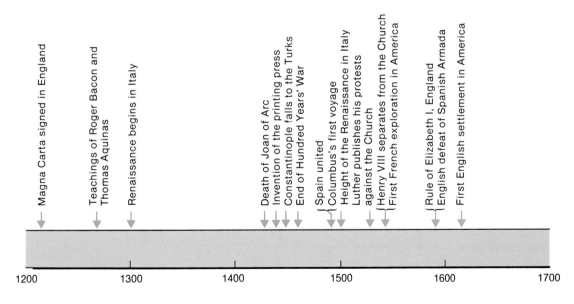

A. Choose the correct answer.

1. Which of these events took place at the earliest time?

a. Elizabeth I ruled England.

b. The Hundred Years War finally came to an end.

c. The printing press was invented.

2. Which of these events took place in the *15th century?*

a. Constantinople fell to the Turks.

b. The French explore in North America.

c. The Renaissance starts in Italy.

3. The Renaissance lasted for a period of over
   a. 50 years.
   b. 100 years.
   c. 200 years.
4. In what century did the Hundred Years War begin?
   a. the 13th
   b. the 14th
   c. the 15th
5. Which of these countries first sent explorers to America?
   a. Spain
   b. France
   c. England
6. Which of these pairs includes events that took place about 100 years apart?
   a. The teachings of Roger Bacon–the beginning of the Renaissance
   b. Spain was united–Elizabeth I ruled England
   c. France began to explore in America–the English defeat the Spanish Armada

B. Still using the time line on page 229, answer *Yes* or *No* for each of the following. Give reasons for your answers.

7. Could Sir Francis Drake have studied sailing with Christopher Columbus?
8. Did the success of Joan of Arc end the Hundred Years War?
9. Were countries of Europe exploring the New World at the same time Italian artists were painting their masterpieces?
10. Could the works of St. Thomas Aquinas have been bought as books by many people shortly after they were written?

Summary of Unit IV _____

A few of the most important events and facts described in this unit are listed below. Can you add any others?

1. During the Middle Ages, there was a rebirth of interest in learning throughout Western Europe.
2. The invention of the printing press and the use of native languages in writing brought more books to more people who could read them.
3. National unity came earlier to England than to other countries of Europe.
4. England led Europe in the movement toward democratic government through the Magna Carta, the jury system, and the beginnings of Parliament.
5. Spain was united when the Moors were defeated, but there was a decline in religious tolerance. Many people who had brought culture to Spain were forced to leave.
6. During the Middle Ages, Italy and Germany were groups of small states rather than unified nations.
7. Spain and Portugal were the first nations to gain success and riches in the search for a new route to the Far East.

8. The search for a different route to the East went on for more than 150 years. During these years important discoveries and explorations were made.
9. The beginning of the slave trade was an evil of the period of exploration. It brought untold injury to the black people.
10. The desire for change in the Catholic Church led to the Reformation in which new Christian religions, called Protestant, were formed.

Making Generalizations

After each generalization below, provide two additional supporting statements from your reading of Unit IV.

A. Generalization: The Renaissance was marked by numerous artistic and scientific achievements.
   Supporting statements:
   1. Michelangelo painted the ceiling of the Sistine Chapel.
   2.
   3.

B. Generalization: Religion can be a force in unifying a nation.
   Supporting statements:
   1. Strong loyalty to Christianity helped the Spanish to unite to drive out the Moors.
   2.
   3.

C. Generalization: Religion can be a source of conflict and disunity.
   Supporting statements:
   1. When Henry VIII broke with the Roman Catholic Church, religious arguments flared in England.
   2.
   3.

D. Generalization: The period of exploration and discovery resulted in both benefits and evils.
   Supporting statements:
   1. Exploration added to Europe's knowledge of the world.
   2.
   3.

UNIT V

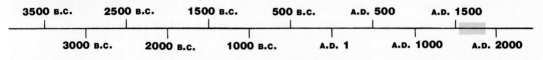

3500 B.C.	2500 B.C.	1500 B.C.	500 B.C.	A.D. 500	A.D. 1500
3000 B.C.	2000 B.C.	1000 B.C.	A.D. 1	A.D. 1000	A.D. 2000

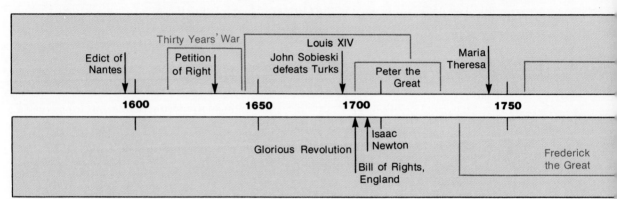

Thirty Years' War

Louis XIV
John Sobieski
defeats Turks

Maria
Theresa

Edict of
Nantes

Petition
of Right

Peter the
Great

1600	1650	1700	1750

Glorious Revolution

Isaac
Newton

Bill of Rights,
England

Frederick
the Great

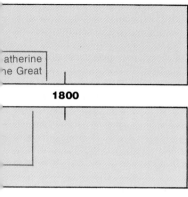

How Did Governments Change in Europe?

This playground in an 18th-century French garden was a good place to spend a pleasant afternoon.

233

AIM: How were the people of England able to gain civil and other rights from their rulers?

CHAPTER 1

England Seeks Self-Government

WHAT CONFLICTS LED TO A CIVIL WAR?

1. Often a person who visits his or her home after a long time away from it will not recognize the old neighborhood. It has changed. To the visitor, the old neighborhood does not look like the place it once was. This is what people who lived in Europe in 1500 would have experienced if they could have returned to Europe in 1600.

2. Europe had gone through a rebirth of learning during those years. Inventions and discoveries had changed the ideas of Europeans. Trade had grown. Europe had become interested in the newly discovered lands in the Americas. Cities had sprung up. A middle class of merchants and skilled artisans had begun to take power away from landowning nobles. Common people were beginning to show more loyalty to their monarch than to their lord. The Protestant Reformation had caused the Catholic Church to lose some of its power.

3. These changes helped the rulers of countries gain power. By the 16th century Europe was ruled by absolute monarchs who had complete power. The absolute monarch could be found in the countries of Western Europe: England, France, Spain, Portugal, and Holland.

Other states did not have absolute rulers. Russia and Poland were not yet united into national states. Their rulers had little control over the nobility. Italy and Germany were still groups of small states. Southeastern Europe was under the rule of the Ottoman empire. Nationalism, which is the spirit of loyalty to, and pride in, one's own country, came much later for these people than for the people of Western Europe.

4. English rulers had less power than other monarchs of the time. The Magna Carta, signed in 1215 (see page 198) put limits on the power of English monarchs. As the monarch's advisers became powerful, they grew into a Parliament. Parliament was soon able to keep rulers from taxing the people unless Parliament agreed. Between 1600 and 1700, English rulers and Parliament tried to gain power over each other.

HOW DID CROMWELL RULE ENGLAND?

5. James I became king of England after Queen Elizabeth I. He said he had a *divine right* to rule. This meant that he believed he had been chosen by God to rule. Thus, an insult to the king was a crime against God. James persecuted Protestants who were not members of the

Church of England as well as Puritans. As a result, many people left England. Neither the people nor Parliament liked James as king. Once, when he needed money, James dismissed Parliament and called another to back him up. But this new Parliament did not give him the money he wanted.

6. Charles I, James's son, also had trouble with Parliament. He dismissed it over and over again. At one time, he ruled for 11 years without any Parliament. He, too, persecuted the Puritans. He formed special courts to punish anyone who did not like his laws. In 1628, when Charles needed money, Parliament refused to vote for more taxes until he signed the *Petition of Right*. Charles had to sign this agreement. It said that he could never again levy taxes without the agreement of Parliament.

7. Charles's troubles were not over. He again dismissed Parliament, hoping to get back the power over it he had lost. When a revolt broke out in Scotland, he had to call Parliament back into session to get the money he needed for his army. The angry Parliament stayed in session for 20 years. The conflict between it and the king grew worse. It led to a civil war. On the side of the king were the *Cavaliers*, made up of Anglicans and nobles. On the other side were Parliament, the Puritans, and small landowners. These were called *Roundheads* because they cut their hair short, unlike the style at court. Oliver Cromwell became leader of the Roundheads and defeated the king. Charles I was taken prisoner and executed.

WHY DID ABSOLUTE POWER FADE?

8. After Charles's execution, in 1649, England was ruled as a *commonwealth* until 1660. The word *commonwealth* then meant a government in which representatives of the people held supreme power. During this period there was no king of England. Oliver Cromwell ruled as Lord Protector. Although he was an able

Oliver Cromwell ruled from 1649 to 1658. Why did Cromwell lose the backing of the people?

man, Cromwell slowly lost the backing of the people. Many who had been against Charles I were not sure they had acted rightly. Executing a king was an act that many people were sorry about later. In addition, Cromwell dismissed Parliament and ruled as a dictator. He passed laws favoring the Puritans. He decided that life in England should be led according to the ideas of John Calvin (page 226), with little joy or entertainment. When Cromwell died in 1658, his son became ruler. He was not as able as his father. Then Parliament asked the son of the executed Charles I to become king.

WHAT WAS THE GLORIOUS REVOLUTION?

9. Charles II was welcomed to England. The king was restored to the throne. This period is called the *Restoration*. The Restoration

was a lively and carefree period in English history. Everywhere people were happy about the return to "normal" life. Charles II was a Catholic, but he kept it a secret until his death. When Charles II died, his brother, James II, became king. James II was also a Catholic. He placed Catholics in high positions in the government. When a son was born to James, the people of England saw that there would be a long line of Catholic kings. They did not want this to happen. Parliament, therefore, asked William and Mary of Orange, who were Protestants, to take the throne. James II fled from England, and William and Mary began to rule in 1688. This change in rulers is known as the Glorious Revolution. It was a revolution without bloodshed or violence.

10. The Glorious Revolution meant that Parliament became the strongest power in England. From this point on, Parliament could decide who should become ruler of England. It could also decide whom English rulers should marry. In 1689, Parliament passed the *Bill of*

The coronation of Charles II marked the beginning of the Restoration. Although the king was restored to power, did parliament become weak? Why or why not?

William and Mary being offered the English crown. Why is their acceptance of the English throne called the "Glorious Revolution"?

Rights, which outlined the rights of the English people. According to the Bill of Rights: (1) the ruler could not tax the people or raise any army without the consent of Parliament; (2) people could appeal to the ruler if they felt they were being treated unfairly; (3) those accused of crimes were given jury trials; (4) unfairly high bail and unusual punishments were forbidden. (The founders of the United States used ideas from the English Bill of Rights when they wrote the American Bill of Rights.)

11. Another result of the Glorious Revolution in England was the Toleration Act. This granted freedom of worship to Protestants who were not members of the Church of England. Still, only members of the Church of England could hold office. Catholics were not granted this right until 1829; nor did Jews gain the right to hold most government positions for a number of years. Yet, at the beginning of the 18th century, the English had more freedom than the other peoples of Europe. They had control over their taxes. They had civil liberties then unknown in the rest of Europe.

Testing Your Vocabulary

Choose the best answer.

1. The opposite of an *absolute* ruler is
   a. an aristocrat.
   b. a ruler elected by a few nobles.
   c. a democratic ruler.

2. *Nationalism* is
   a. interest in the poor.
   b. belief in old customs.
   c. loyalty to one's country.

Understanding What You Have Read

1. A good title for paragraphs 6 and 7 is
   a. The Death of Charles I
   b. Victory for the Roundheads
   c. Troubles of Charles I
   d. The Petition of Right

2. In which paragraph do you find facts about
   a. the rule of kings by "divine right"?
   b. the Glorious Revolution?
   c. the English Bill of Rights?
   d. English government under Oliver Cromwell?

3. The Restoration is given its name because
   a. religious freedom was restored to England.
   b. the English monarch was restored to the throne.
   c. Parliament restored taxes on nobles.

4. Many Puritans left England during the rule of James I because
   a. James had dismissed Parliament.
   b. they were not allowed to follow their own religion.
   c. their lands were ruined in the war with Scotland.

5. Many rulers of Europe said that they ruled by divine right because they
   a. believed that God had chosen them to rule the people.
   b. were all of the same religion.
   c. were chosen by the church.

6. The chief cause of the civil war in England in the middle of the 17th century was the
   a. struggle for power between Parliament and Charles I.
   b. struggle for power between James I and Charles I.
   c. execution of Charles I.

7. The coming of William and Mary to the throne of England in 1688 is known as the Glorious Revolution because
   a. the dictator Cromwell was overthrown.
   b. Protestant kings began to rule England.
   c. the change in rulers was made without bloodshed or violence.

In your notebooks, write the letters of each group of events in the order in which the events took place.

1. a. Magna Carta
   b. Bill of Rights
   c. Petition of Right

2. a. The Restoration
   b. Rule of Charles I
   c. Dictatorship of Cromwell

3. a. War between the Cavaliers and Roundheads
   b. William and Mary become rulers of England
   c. The beginning of the Church of England

Developing Ideas and Skills

WRITING AN OUTLINE

Below is part of an outline of the important ideas in chapter 1 of unit V. In your notebook, fill in the rest of the outline.

The Power of English Rulers in the 17th Century

A. Reasons for the Rise of Absolute Rulers in Europe
   1.
   2.
   3.
B. Threats to the Rights of the English people
   1. Kings dismiss Parliament.
   2.
   3.
C.
   1. King John signs the Magna Carta, 1215.
   2. Charles I signs the Petition of Right, 1628.
   3.
   4.

Using Original Sources

In this chapter you learned that Charles I went out of his way to make trouble for the Puritans. In the following selection, Charles issues a declaration concerning entertainment on Sundays. Puritans believed that there should be no sports or entertainment on Sunday.

Charles I on Sunday Entertainment

Our dear father of blessed memory [Charles' father, James I] in his return from Scotland found that his subjects were not allowed lawful recreations upon Sundays after evening prayers ended and upon holydays. He thought that if these times were taken from them, those who work all week would have no recreations at all to refresh their spirits. He published a declaration to all his loving subjects concerning lawful sports to be used at such times.

Our pleasure is that after the end of divine service our good people should not be discouraged from any lawful recreation such as dancing, either men or women; archery for men; leaping, vaulting, or any other such harmless recreation. Also women shall be allowed to carry rushes to the church for decorating it, according to their custom; but we do here say that unlawful games, such as bear and bull baitings, are not allowed on Sundays, and at all times law forbids the lower class of people from bowling.

Answer the following using the information in the passage.

1. Charles I allowed men and women to
   a. dance on Sunday.
   b. decorate their churches.
   c. hunt wild animals.
2. Charles continued to forbid
   a. dancing by children.
   b. archery.
   c. bowling.
3. From this selection you can tell that
   a. Charles I was a Puritan.
   b. Charles I disagreed with his father.
   c. Charles I felt that some recreation on Sunday was harmless.
4. What does the selection tell you about the kinds of recreation people enjoyed in England in the early 1600s?
5. How do you think Puritans reacted to this declaration?

TURNING POINTS

Government

The World: The Power to Govern

Every nation has some form of government. Governments differ according to their laws and how those laws are upheld. Important questions for all governments are: Who has the power to govern? How was that power acquired? What are the rights of the people being governed? You saw how the answers to these questions changed in England at the end of the 17th century.

One kind of government is a monarchy. Under this system, one person rules. Hatsheput, a pharaoh who ruled ancient Egypt, was a monarch. So, too, was Osei Tutu, a 17th-century king who ruled the Ashanti people of Africa. Monarchs usually gain their power because they are members of a royal family. For instance, Charles I became king of England because he was the son of King James. Many rulers of the past strengthened their positions of power by claiming to be chosen by God. In Europe, this was called Divine Right. In China, a similar idea was called the Mandate of Heaven. This meant that a ruler was given a mandate, or order, by heaven to govern. If a ruler was cruel, however, he would lose the mandate.

Another kind of government that is led by one person, or by a small group of people, is a dictatorship. The leader of a dictatorship usually gains and keeps power by force. The dictator controls the government as well as the nation's military forces and resources. The people in a dictatorship have few rights.

In another kind of government, the people have some of the power. The power to rule is agreed upon by both the people and their leaders. This is known as a democracy. Usually, the power to govern in a democracy is determined by an election.

Critical Thinking

1. Give two ways in which a dictatorship and a democracy differ.
2. If the powers of an ancient Chinese ruler and a dictator were threatened, how would they defend their right to govern?

AIM: How did the rulers of France gain absolute power?

CHAPTER 2

In France, the Sun King

HOW DID EARLY FRENCH KINGS GAIN POWER?

1. No one could mistake the plan of French kings to rule without help from their people. For 200 years, France was ruled by the Bourbon family of kings. Henry IV, first of the Bourbon kings, said plainly that he did not expect to be disobeyed by his people. Louis XIV, who ruled for 72 years, said the same. When the powers of the English rulers were being limited by Parliament, the French had no power over their rulers.

2. Earlier in the history of France, French kings had enjoyed less power than English rulers. Religious wars among noble families kept France from being united under one ruler during most of the 16th century. Many French people became Protestants, called Huguenots. French kings, who were Catholic, looked upon the Huguenots as a threat to their power and persecuted them. In Paris alone several thousand Huguenots were murdered in 1572. Then there was a struggle for power. This ended in victory for Henry IV, who became king in 1589.

3. Henry IV was a popular king. Although he was a Catholic, he issued the Edict of Nantes, in 1598. This gave the Huguenots freedom of worship and the right to hold government office. Henry IV built roads and helped to improve farming. During his rule, Samuel de Champlain, the explorer, came to America. He helped France set up a claim to much land in North America. Henry IV's son, Louis XIII, followed him to the throne at the age of 9. Since the new king was a child, France was actually run by the king's ministers, or advisers. The most important of the king's ministers was Cardinal Richelieu, who was clever and strong. He led France for 20 years, carefully gaining power for the king.

4. To gain more power for the king, Richelieu chose government officials from the middle class. This weakened the power of the nobles. Those who spoke out against Richelieu were sent to prison or executed. The Estates-General, the French parliament, was not allowed to meet. Although the Huguenots were allowed to worship as they pleased, other rights were taken away from them. Under Richelieu's leadership, France backed the Protestants in the Thirty Years' War. He did this to weaken the power of Spain and Austria. Richelieu led France well, and Louis XIII was liked by most of his people.

HOW DID LOUIS XIV RULE FRANCE?

5. The king whose royal power was greater than the power of any other ruler in Europe in the 17th century was Louis XIV. Louis was 5 years old when he came to the throne, and he was king for 72 years—from 1643 to 1715. In his youth, the nation was run by Cardinal Mazarin. Mazarin weakened further the power of the nobles. Through war with Spain, the French extended their land to the Pyrenees Mountains in Spain.

6. When Louis XIV was old enough to rule by himself, he took power without trouble. Louis loved his role as king and absolute ruler. He is reported to have said, "I am the State." He would have liked to handle all the affairs of France by himself. But it would have been impossible. He turned over his money problems to his financial minister, Jean Colbert.

7. Colbert began an economic system called *mercantilism*. Mercantilism is based on the idea that a country's wealth is measured by how much gold and silver it has. A nation becomes wealthy by selling as much as it can to other countries and receiving gold and silver in return. It buys as little as possible from other countries so that it will not have to give away its own gold and silver. Colbert felt that French colonies should send to France goods that France could sell to other nations for gold and silver. He put tariffs, or taxes, on goods coming into France from other countries, so French people would not buy too much. Other nations with colonies followed Colbert's plan and began to practice mercantilism.

8. Louis XIV made France the leading nation of Europe. But in doing so, he fought in war after war, spent large amounts of money, and persecuted the Huguenots. He ended the Edict of Nantes, thus closing Huguenot churches. Many Protestants left France. Since many Huguenots were merchants and skilled crafts workers, these policies, in time, weakened France. They helped bring about the downfall of French kings late in the 18th century.

9. At Versailles (vur-SY), about 12 miles from Paris, Louis built a magnificent palace. It was here that he held his court. Nobles and rich landlords crowded the royal court, hoping to gain the favor of the "Sun King," as Louis was called because of the brilliance of his court. Some performed services for the king, such as combing his hair or drying him after a bath. Lavish entertainment at court cost much money. At Versailles, Louis XIV was further removed than ever from the common people and their problems.

10. Louis XIV had a strong army and he used it. But the nations of Europe did not want to see one nation among them become too powerful. They wished to keep a *balance of power;* that is, to have all nations of about equal power.

King Louis XIV of France. How does this picture show the wealth of his reign?

The palace at Versailles remains today as a symbol of great wealth and a museum of many works of art.

This policy of balance of power has been followed by European nations throughout the 20th century. When Louis invaded the Spanish Netherlands (which is Belgium today) in 1667, England, Holland, and Sweden joined against him. When he attacked the Dutch to get revenge, many helped to open the Dutch dikes to flood the land in front of the French troops. In 1689, a group of nations fought against France when Louis XIV tried to take a German state along the Rhine River. In 1701, he tried to place his grandson on the Spanish throne. The War of the Spanish Succession followed, in which France gained very little. In the fighting that went on in the American colonies, Louis also met with defeat. The war for a French empire in the colonies ended in 1697.

11. The Treaty of Utrecht (1713) ended the War of the Spanish Succession. The terms of the treaty affected the future of Europe. The grandson of Louis XIV was allowed to remain as King of Spain. It was agreed, however, that Spain and France could never unite to form one country. The Netherlands and Spain's claims in Italy were given to Austria. French claims in America, Newfoundland, and the Hudson Bay region were given to England. Louis XIV had fought four wars and had spent huge sums of money. He had persecuted Protestants. Yet France was hardly stronger at his death than it had been when he became king 72 years earlier. Louis warned his great grandson not to follow his example. But if his advice was heard at all, it was quickly forgotten.

Testing Your Vocabulary

Choose the best answer.

1. The policy of *mercantilism*.
   a. increased trade between the colonies and foreign countries.
   b. allowed a nation to get goods from its colonies and sell these goods.
   c. caused nations to buy as much as they could from other countries.
2. A *balance of power* in world affairs means that nations
   a. seek colonies to find gold and silver.
   b. form close friendships with their neighboring countries.
   c. equal one another in power.
3. A king's *minister*, as used in this chapter, is a
   a. member of the clergy.
   b. person whose job is to make sure the king is comfortable.
   c. person chosen to be an adviser to the king.

Understanding What You Have Read

1. The main idea of paragraph 10 is that
   a. the French had a large and well-trained army.
   b. Louis XIV fought many wars but gained few victories.
   c. European nations fought with their colonies.
   d. the Dutch defeated the French forces.
2. In which paragraph do you find facts about
   a. the ways in which Cardinal Richelieu served Louis XIII?
   b. the treatment of the Huguenots in the 16th century?
   c. the terms in the Treaty of Utrecht?
   d. the life of the nobles at the palace at Versailles?
3. The nations of Europe joined to stop King Louis XIV because
   a. they did not want one nation to become too powerful.
   b. they feared the friendship between England and France.
   c. French ideas of liberty threatened their own power.
4. Cardinal Richelieu supported the Protestants in the Thirty Years' War because
   a. the French kings were Protestant.
   b. Protestant princes had offered to help France against England.
   c. a victory for the Protestant forces would weaken Austria and Spain.
5. Through the efforts of Colbert, French colonies were established
   a. as a home for the Huguenots.
   b. to bring gold and silver to France.
   c. as a means of ending English control in America.
6. All of these were policies of Louis XIV EXCEPT
   a. spending large amounts of money to help the poor.
   b. bringing more wealth to the king.
   c. persecuting the Huguenots.
7. All of these were part of the treaty ending the War of the Spanish Succession EXCEPT
   a. England gained the Strait of Gibraltar.
   b. France gained more colonies in America.
   c. Spain lost territory to Austria.

In your notebook, next to each statement, write **E** if it applies to England only; write **F** if it applies to France only; write **B** if it applies to both England and France. Use the information in chapters 1 and 2 to answer these questions.

1. Religious persecution was carried out.
2. The same king ruled for 72 years.
3. The monarch's power was limited in the 17th century.
4. Territory in America was lost.
5. A revolution without bloodshed was successful.
6. A king had the richest court in Europe.
7. The king was overthrown in the 17th century.
8. There was no king or queen for 11 years in the 17th century.
9. Catholic monarchs ruled in the 17th century.
10. Monarchs ruled with absolute power.

Using Original Sources

What was Louis XIV of France really like? Saint-Simon (san-see-MAWN), a nobleman of Louis's court and a writer of memoirs, lived during the last 40 years of the reign of Louis XIV. Here he describes some of the character traits of the "Sun King."

Louis XIV: The Sun King

He was the very figure of a hero with proportions such as a sculptor would choose to model; a perfect face and the grandest air. He was as dignified and majestic in his dressing gown as when dressed in robes of state, or on horseback at the head of his troops.

He excelled in all sorts of exercise—the ability to speak well and listen with quick understanding.

Louis XIV's vanity was without restraint. It colored everything and convinced him that no one even approached him in military talents and in government. Hence those pictures in the gallery at Versailles which disgust every foreigner; those opera prologues that he himself tried to sing; the sickening compliments that were continually offered to him in person and which he swallowed with unfailing relish. Hence his distaste for all merit, intelligence, education, and, most of all, for all independence of character and sentiment in others and, above everything else, a jealousy of his own authority.

1. What characteristics do you think made people respect Louis XIV and follow him?
2. Why do you think Louis XIV had a "distaste for merit, intelligence, education and independence" in others?
3. How does this description of Louis XIV show one of the disadvantages of monarchies?

AIM: How did Russia and its rulers come to play a leading role in European affairs?

CHAPTER 3

Russia Becomes a Modern Nation

HOW DID GEOGRAPHY AFFECT EARLY RUSSIAN DEVELOPMENT?

1. When we read a newspaper we see that different events are going on in many countries at the same time. We sometimes forget this in studying world history. Thus, when England was having its Glorious Revolution, Louis XIV was ruler of France. At the same time, German states were gaining importance in the politics of Europe. Peter the Great came to the throne of Russia. Events in one country often affect events in another country. We are going to learn how Russia grew in power under Peter and Catherine the Great, who followed him some years later.

2. Geography has played an important role in the history of Russia. The country is largely a vast plain covered with forests and swamps. The Russian plain in the 17th century reached from Poland on the west to the Ural Mountains on the east. It was crossed by many rivers, making transportation of goods easy. The earliest settlers in Russia were Slavs, who wandered over the plains. The lowlands made it easy for settlers to move about. But it also made it easy for invaders to enter Russia from all sides. Mongols, or Tartars, came from the east

Peter the Great supervising the building of St. Petersburg. It was the first Russian city built in imitation of Western European cities and was Russia's first port city.

and Turks from the south. Vikings and Swedes entered from the north, and Poles and Germans from the west.

3. In the 8th and 9th centuries, the Vikings invaded the plains of Russia. Kiev became the Viking center of trade along the Dnieper (NEE-pur) River. The city of Novgorod

(NAWV-guh-rut) was a Viking trading center in the north. In the 13th century, the Mongols came from the east. They ruled Russia for almost 300 years. Traders built a fort, called a *kremlin*, at Moskva (we call it Moscow today), and a city grew up around it. In time, Moscow became a feudal state, like those in Western Europe. The people of Moscow borrowed their customs and ideas partly from the Byzantine culture of Constantinople and partly from the Mongols of Asia.

4. In the late 15th century, Ivan III of Moscow became independent of the Mongols. His power grew. Ivan captured Novgorod and also gained a trading center in the north. He became known as Ivan the Great. He was the first ruler of modern Russia.

5. It was Ivan's grandson who first used the title of Czar (ZAR). The title is taken from the Roman title of *Caesar*, or emperor. Ivan IV, the Czar, defeated the Mongols and took their lands along the Volga River. Ivan started out as a good ruler, but after a serious illness he appeared to become insane. From then on, he was known as Ivan the Terrible. He destroyed the town of Novgorod and killed its citizens when he believed they were plotting against him.

WHAT WAS LIFE LIKE FOR SERFS?

6. The peasants in Russia lived under some of the worst conditions found in all of Europe. All children born to peasants were serfs forever. With such a dark future facing them, thousands of serfs ran away from their landlords. They were hunted down and, if captured, horribly punished. Many of them were sent to work in the mines of Siberia. The Russian serfs' lives were hard. Summers in Russia were short, and the farm work had to be done quickly. Winters were long. The serfs spent much of their time in their dreary homes on the plains and in the forests. Their religious faith saved them from despair. Although life was hard, they believed in a reward for their troubles after death.

HOW DID PETER THE GREAT MODERNIZE RUSSIA?

7. The Romanov family came to power in Russia in 1613. The greatest of the Romanovs was Peter the Great. He became king when he was only 17 years old and ruled Russia for the next 36 years (1689–1725). Peter wanted to make his country like the nations of Western Europe. He talked to the merchants who came to Moscow and learned of Western customs and machines. He traveled in the West and brought Western ideas home with him. He forced the Russian people to wear Western clothes and to follow Western customs. He even made them smoke tobacco. Men were forced to cut off their beards, and women were encouraged to spend time out of their homes and take part in gala parties such as were common in France. Trade and industry grew during Peter's reign.

This picture shows Peter the Great as a ship's carpenter's apprentice. He often traveled in the West disguised as a commoner.

Hospitals and schools were built, but the schools were for the children of nobles only.

8. Peter the Great built a large army and navy and used them to add to Russia's land. Russia's borders had no ice-free water outlets for shipping. A war against the Turks gave Peter control, for a time, of land on the northern edge of the Black Sea (see map, p. 249). This gave Russia an outlet to a warm-water port—a port that would not freeze up during the cold Russian winter. Then Peter wanted a "window on the West," too. For 20 years he fought a war with Sweden, which was then a powerful nation. In the end, Peter got what he wanted: an outlet on the Baltic Sea.

9. Peter was a giant of a man who was respected by all. But he was stubborn and often cruel. He built a new capital at St. Petersburg (today called Leningrad) on the Gulf of Finland. More than 100,000 men worked on it. Many died from sickness or cold. Yet nothing was allowed to stand in the way of the completion of the capital. When his palace guards revolted, Peter executed more than a thousand of them. Peter placed the Russian Church under his own control. He also weakened the power of the nobles. He ordered that a person could no longer become a noble simply by birth but rather through service to the czar. The serfs, whose lives were like those of slaves, found no relief under Peter's rule.

10. Peter the Great died in 1725, after having made Russia one of the leading nations of Europe. Another outstanding ruler continued Peter's work in making Russia a force in European affairs. This was Catherine II, known as Catherine the Great. She ruled from 1762 to

Catherine the Great of Russia. Name at least three achievements of her reign.

1796. Catherine came to the throne after her husband was murdered. She educated herself chiefly through reading the works of writers of Western Europe. She was an intelligent woman. She exchanged letters with Europe's leading thinkers. She wrote plays, fairy tales, and school books for children. Under Catherine, nobles and merchants were given greater freedom. Many nobles came to the royal court as they did in Western Europe. The serfs, however, were treated cruelly. What few rights they had were reduced further.

11. Catherine wanted the Russian people to be proud of their nation. She tried to make Russia more European. She fought wars with her neighbors as Peter the Great had done. Together with Prussia and Austria she helped to divide Poland. This pushed Russia's borders farther west. Then, the Turks were driven from the land north of the Black Sea. Now Russia was close to reaching the goal of many of its monarchs—control of Constantinople. By the end of Catherine's reign, Russia was the largest country in Europe.

Testing Your Vocabulary _____

Choose the best answer.

1. The headquarters of the Soviet Union today is called the Kremlin. A *kremlin* is
   a. an office building

b. a trading center.
c. a fort.

2. The phrase *"window on the West"* (par-

agraph 8) refers to
a. a showplace city for western visitors.
b. an outlet for shipping on the western border.
c. the new capital at St. Petersburg.

3. The title of *Czar*, used by Russian rulers, means
a. emperor.
b. divine right.
c. prince.

Understanding What You Have Read

1. A good title for paragraphs 7 through 9 is
a. Revolt after Revolt.
b. Peter the Great.
c. Travels of a Czar.
d. Waterways in the South and West.
2. In which paragraphs do you find facts about
a. the earliest settlers in Russia?
b. the founding of Moscow?
c. the life of the serfs in Russia?
d. the education of Catherine the Great?
3. Invaders were common in early Russian history because
a. the large rivers of Russia flow into the Black Sea.
b. much of Russia was made up of forests and swamps.
c. much of Russia was made up of lowlands.
4. Peter the Great helped the Russian people by
a. building hospitals and schools.
b. giving serfs a chance to get an education.
c. starting the first parliament in Russian history.
5. One of the reasons why Peter the Great had little trouble with his people was that he
a. held little power himself.
b. was powerful and often cruel.
c. was supported by the town guilds.
6. Russia was always interested in a port on the Black Sea because
a. Russia needed ports in the West.
b. Russia needed ports that are not frozen part of the year.
c. the Black Sea was part of the direct shipping route from England to India.
7. Catherine the Great differed from Peter the Great in that she
a. gave some freedom to nobles and merchants.
b. disliked the customs of Western nations.
c. did not fight wars with her neighbors during her rule.

Choose the correct answer.

1. When Peter the Great ruled Russia, the ruler of France was
a. Cardinal Richelieu.
b. Louis XIV.
c. Henry IV.
2. All of the following invaded territory which is now part of Russia EXCEPT
a. the Vikings.
b. the Mongols.
c. the Saxons.
3. An old and important city for trade along the Dnieper River was
a. Kiev.
b. Moscow.
c. St. Petersburg.
4. In order to gain a port on the Baltic Sea, Peter the Great fought a long war with

a. France.
b. Sweden.
c. Poland.

5. In order to gain a port on the Black Sea, Russia had to defeat the
   a. Swedes.
   b. Vikings.
   c. Turks.

6. Russia took part of Poland and moved its borders farther west during the reign of
   a. Ivan the Terrible.
   b. Peter the Great.
   c. Catherine the Great.

7. Serfs were sent to the mines of Siberia
   a. as punishment for running away.
   b. because of their religious beliefs.

c. because they would not accept Western ideas.

8. Peter the Great has been called the greatest of the
   a. Romanovs.
   b. Bourbons.
   c. Tudors.

9. Peter the Great's chief contribution to Russian life was
   a. bringing Western ideas to Russia.
   b. the building of the capital at St. Petersburg.
   c. trade with the Far East.

10. The people of Moskva borrowed customs from the Byzantines and the
    a. Poles.
    b. Mongols.
    c. French.

Developing Ideas and Skills

USING A MAP

Study the map on page 249 carefully. Choose the correct answer.

1. The city of Kiev is located on which body of water
   a. Volga River
   b. Black Sea
   c. Dnieper River

2. Russia in 1800
   a. included Sweden.
   b. extended to the Caspian Sea.
   c. included all of Poland.

3. From Moscow to the western border of Russia is chiefly
   a. a region of mountains.
   b. a plain.
   c. an area of lakes.

4. Czar Peter's "window on the West" was the
   a. Baltic Sea.
   b. Dnieper River.
   c. Black Sea.

5. An important city along the Black Sea is
   a. St. Petersburg.
   b. Moscow.
   c. Odessa.

Using Original Sources

The following is a description of Peter the Great, written by a bishop who met Peter on his visit to London in 1697 and 1698.

Bishop Brunet's Description of Peter the Great

Peter came this winter over to England, and stayed some months among us; I waited on him, and was ordered, both by the King and the Archbishop and bishops, to attend upon him, and to offer him such informations of our religion and constitutions as he was willing to receive. . . . He is a man of very hot temper, very quickly inflamed . . . he wants not in ability, and he has a larger measure of knowledge than might be expected from his education, which was very indifferent . . . he has mechanical talents, and seems to be born rather a ship carpenter than a great prince: this was his chief study and exercise when he stayed here: He made much with his own hands, and made all about him work at the models of ships. . . . He was indeed determined to encourage learning and to polish his people, by sending some of them to travel in other countries, and to draw strangers to come and live among them. He is determined, but understands little of war . . .

He went from here to the court of Vienna, where he planned to have stayed some time, but he was called home sooner than he had intended (the discovery of a plot among those he had trusted most) . . . on this occasion, he let loose his fury on all whom he suspected; some hundred of them were hanged all round Moscow, and it was said that he cut off many heads with his own hand, and [was] so far from . . . showing any sort of tenderness that he seemed delighted with it. How long he is to be the scourge of that nation, or of his neighbours, God only knows. . . .

Choose the correct answer, on the basis of the information given in the selection.

1. The education of Peter the Great would best be described as
   a. based on philosophy and religion.
   b. limited and informal.
   c. equal to that of the best scholars of Europe.

2. Peter the Great showed that he was
   a. able to make things himself.
   b. aware of the problems of Russian serfs.
   c. interested in how English schools were run

3. Peter stayed in England for
   a. several months.
   b. a few days.
   c. almost two years.

4. Peter's stay in Vienna was cut short because he
   a. became ill.
   b. hurried home to put down a revolt.
   c. wanted to bring with him students from Western Europe.

TURNING POINTS

Government

Europe: The Peasants of Russia

During the 1700s, peasants made up a large majority of the Russian population. At least 75 percent of the people in the country were peasants. Most of them lived in communities that were governed by wealthy landowners. According to Russian law at that time, peasants could not own any property. It belonged to their masters. The law also forbade them from moving to other parts of the country.

The daily life of the Russian peasants was terribly hard. During the long, bitterly cold winters, they struggled to keep warm. Their houses rarely had heat or running water. In the summer, the peasants worked for as much as 18 hours a day. They tilled the land, harvested crops, and threshed grain. Most of them had only bread and soup to eat. The soup was usually made from potatoes or cabbage. Meat was seldom available. In some places, peasants were allowed to have meat once a year—on Easter.

No matter how hard they worked, the peasants were almost always in debt. They had to pay heavy taxes to the government. They also were taxed by their masters. Their struggle for existence was tiring. They worked day after day only to raise money to buy food for their families and to pay taxes.

In 1861, the peasants were freed. They were granted the right to own property. They also gained the right to move elsewhere if they wished. In many other ways, however, their lives remained the same. Major changes in Russia were to come later.

Critical Thinking

1. Describe how a Russian peasant might have felt in 1861.
2. What generalization can you make about the political power of Russian peasants during the 1700s? Support your answer with two details.

AIM: How was Eastern Europe affected by wars in the 17th and 18th centuries?

CHAPTER 4

Unity and Disunity in Eastern Europe

HOW WELL DID THE HAPSBURGS RULE THE AUSTRIAN EMPIRE?

1. While the German states remained weak, Austria had become a power in Europe in the 15th and 16th centuries. Austria's monarchs had, for some time, been the rulers of the Holy Roman Empire. This was made up of a large number of separate states. It included many people who spoke different languages. They practiced different religions, too. The Hapsburg family of Austria ruled this large and mixed empire. Through many marriages, the Hapsburgs gained land and power throughout Europe.

2. The position of Holy Roman Emperor, however, was little more than a title. Austrian rulers really had no empire. After the Thirty Years' War (1618–1648), the Hapsburgs had lost control of many of the smaller German states. The Ottoman Turks in the east threatened Austria. The Turks had captured Constantinople in 1453. By the middle of the 17th century, they controlled territory in Asia, Africa, and most of southeastern Europe. In 1683, the Turks tried to capture the Austrian capital of Vienna. With the help of the Polish king, John Sobieski, Austria turned back the Turks. Later Austria was able to add Hungary to its empire.

3. Austria's chief rival in Europe was France. Louis XIV tried to place his grandson on the Spanish throne and end Hapsburg rule in Spain. Austria went to war against France. After the war, Austria won from Spain part of Italy and the area now called Belgium.

4. In 1740, one of the greatest of the Hapsburg rulers came to the throne of Austria. Maria Theresa, at the age of 23, was a brilliant leader. Like those who came before her, Maria Theresa was an absolute monarch. But she was an *enlightened* ruler; that is, she was kind and wise. Maria Theresa showed interest in the common people. She helped the peasants, improved education, and carefully watched the wealth of her empire. Shortly after Maria Theresa came to power, Austria fought a war with Prussia over the territory of Silesia. Prussia was one of the large German states. The other nations of Europe took sides in the war. France and Prussia were *allies;* that is, they were on the same side. After 8 years of war, Prussia kept Silesia.

5. Maria Theresa was followed as ruler by her son, Joseph II. He was an *enlightened despot.* This is to say, he was both wise and all-powerful. He freed the serfs and ended the death penalty for certain crimes. He let the Protestants worship freely, something his

Maria Theresa of Austria. Compare this portrait with those of Oliver Cromwell, Louis XIV, and Catherine the Great. How does each reflect the culture of his or her country?

mother had not allowed. Joseph II tried to make all the people of his empire Austrian in manners and customs. But this was impossible. The Austrian empire was made up of too many different cultures.

WHAT WARS DID PRUSSIA WAGE?

6. During the 18th century, Prussia became Austria's rival for leadership among the German states. Several rulers helped bring Prussia to a position of leadership in Europe. Frederick I, the first king of Prussia, invited to Prussia the Huguenots who had fled from France. Many came. They did much to develop farming and industry. Frederick William I, who followed Frederick I as ruler, built up a power-

ful Prussian army. It became the best-trained military force in Europe. Prussia had a higher percentage of its population in the army than any of the other leading nations of Europe.

7. Frederick the Great (Frederick II) became King of Prussia in 1740. (This was the same year that Maria Theresa came to the throne in Austria.) Frederick, like Maria Theresa, was an enlightened ruler. He loved the arts, theater, and philosophy. He invited to Prussia many of the great European thinkers of his time. Frederick involved Prussia in many wars. He invaded Silesia in 1740 and started a war with Austria. He also led Prussia in the Seven Years War (1756–1763), which was fought in Europe, America, and India. With England as his only major ally, Frederick held off the combined armies of Austria, Spain, and France. Although Prussia gained no land as a result of this war, it became an important power in Europe. In 1772, allied with Austria and Russia, Frederick took part of Poland.

WHY WAS POLAND DIVIDED?

8. Poland, like Prussia and Austria, is located on the great plain of northern Europe. It has no natural defenses. It has always been sur-

Frederick the Great's flute concert at San-Souci. During this period in Europe, the nobility supported, or were patrons of, the arts. How does this explain why many paintings were of nobles and music was written for the nobility?

rounded by enemies eager to overrun and take control of its land. Many times in Poland's history, only its great cavalry (troops on horseback) kept it from being conquered. The Polish people are largely Slavic and mostly Catholic. They used Latin as the basis of their alphabet. Their Slavic neighbors in Russia, on the other hand, belong to the Greek Orthodox Church. The Russians took the Greek alphabet as the basis of their written language.

9. The fertile soil of their plains made the Poles a farming people. Most were peasants who worked on land owned by nobles. Poland was still a feudal state when trade and industry began in Western Europe. In 1800, it was almost 500 years behind its western neighbors in development. Although Poland had a king, the nobility made certain that he had little power. In the Polish congress, the vote of one noble could defeat a new law.

10. One of Poland's greatest kings was John Sobieski. It was he who answered the call of the Holy Roman Emperor and helped drive the Turks from Vienna. It was unfortunate for Poland that there were few kings like him. Polish hopes of growing into a strong independent nation were shattered when Poland was invaded and divided by its neighbors three times before 1800. For more than a hundred years thereafter, Poland as a nation disappeared from the map of Europe.

The Prussians attack a Church used as a fortress during the Seven Years' War.

WHO RULED SOUTHEASTERN EUROPE?

11. In the 17th century, southeastern Europe was under the control of the Ottoman Turks. The Turks were Muslims. Under Muslim rule, Christians were allowed to worship as they wished, but they were taxed heavily. The Turks had some great leaders, but too few to lead a powerful empire for hundreds of years. Sultan after sultan ruled in luxury. The Turks, however, were always a threat to Austria. Worried about Turkish power, the Austrians could never give their complete attention to France, on the west, or to the Protestants, in the north.

Testing Your Vocabulary _____

Choose the best answer.

1. Rulers would be called *enlightened* if they
   a. ruled with absolute power.
   b. were concerned about the people in their kingdoms.
   c. carried on military campaigns.
2. A *sultan* is the title of a
   a. leader of the Austrian army.
   b. ruler of a Muslim country.
   c. wealthy Muslim landlord.
3. The Polish *cavalry* were
   a. peasant volunteers.
   b. natural defenses.
   c. troops on horseback.

254

Understanding What You Have Read _____

1. A title for paragraph 7 might be
   a. Enlightened Rulers.
   b. The Rise of Prussia.
   c. The Seven Years' War.
   d. Frederick the Great.
2. In which paragraph do you find facts about
   a. feudalism in 17th-century Poland?
   b. Poland's king, John Sobieski?
   c. Austria's chief rival in Europe?
   d. Maria Theresa's rule of Austria?
3. Austria was unable to turn all its attention to stopping the rise of Prussia because
   a. it was threatened by the Ottoman Turks in the east.
   b. Poland had tried to capture its capital city.
   c. Russia had advanced on its eastern border.
4. One of the reasons why Poland was unable to shake off feudalism in the 17th century was that
   a. rulers had too little political power.
   b. rulers had too much power.
   c. it was necessary to trade with the Ottoman Turks.
5. Poland was always surrounded by enemies because
   a. its land had no natural means of defense.
   b. its rulers fought wars against almost every country in Europe.
   c. it was a Protestant nation surrounded by Catholic nations.
6. Emperor Joseph II of Austria is said to have been an enlightened ruler because he
   a. trained the largest army in Europe.
   b. broke the rising power of Prussia.
   c. allowed freedom of religion.
7. The power of the Ottoman Turks began to weaken because
   a. they did not allow Christians to practice their religion.
   b. they had weak leaders who devoted themselves to luxury.
   c. they spent all their gold and silver buying the products of Europe.

Match the descriptions in the second column with the items in the first.

A.
1. Prussia
2. Austria
3. Russians
4. Poland
5. Ottoman Turks

a. ruled the lands of southeastern Europe
b. land ruled by Hapsburg emperors
c. Slavic people who used the Greek alphabet as the basis of their language
d. country continually divided by other European powers
e. country with the strongest army in Eastern Europe

B.
1. John Sobieski
2. Maria Theresa
3. Joseph II
4. Frederick I

a. freed the serfs in Austria
b. known as the first King of Prussia
c. enlightened queen of Austria
d. Polish king who helped defeat the Turks at Vienna

Developing Ideas and Skills

USING A MAP

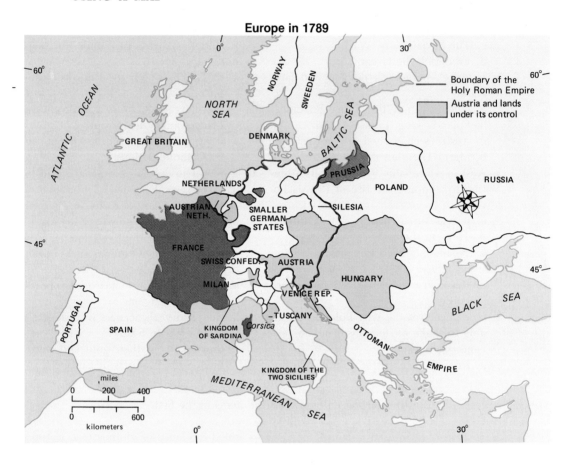

Europe in 1789

Study the map carefully. Then tell whether these statements are true or false.

1. The Ottoman Empire covered part of southeastern Europe.
2. All of Austria's territory lay within the Holy Roman Empire.
3. Italy was divided into a number of states.
4. Much of Germany was under the control of France.
5. Great Britain had no large possessions on the mainland of Europe.
6. Prussian lands extended to the border of Russia.
7. Russia controlled the entrances to the Black Sea.

CHAPTER 5

Wars of Absolute Rulers

WHAT WERE THE RESULTS OF THE THIRTY YEARS' WAR?

1. You may have heard the expression "Might makes right." In the age of absolute rulers, many thought this was true. The idea seemed to be "If I have power, I can do what I want." Rulers did not care so much about justice as they did about gaining land, power, and wealth. Strong nations attacked weaker neighbors. Nations changed their allies without thought of friendship, religion, or family ties. Friends became enemies and enemies became friends. We are going to see how this attitude led to wars in the 17th and 18th centuries.

2. The Thirty Years' War, 1618–1648, started in the kingdom of Bohemia, a small state under Hapsburg rule. A group of Protestant nobles did not want another Catholic king on the throne of Bohemia. They chose a Protestant prince as their ruler. The Hapsburg emperor, who was a Catholic, sent an army into Bohemia and defeated the nobles. Bohemia became part of Austria. The war continued. The issue of religion was forgotten in the fight for power that followed.

3. The Protestants looked for help from the north. Denmark came to their aid, but it

was also defeated by the Hapsburg forces. In 1630, Sweden joined the Protestant forces. Catholic France entered on the side of the Protestants. The defeat of the hated enemy, Austria, was more important to France than religion at this point. The war dragged on until 1648. In that year, the nations, tired of fighting, signed a peace treaty.

4. The 30 years of fighting brought many important results. German princes still had the power to choose the religion of their people. Thus, Protestants were allowed to worship in German states having Protestant rulers. Holland became an independent country for the first time. France gained the territory of Alsace, along the Rhine, which before had been a German state. The power of the Hapsburgs was weakened.

5. The Thirty Years' War was one of the most terrible in all history. More than one-third of the German people died in battle or from disease. Villages and towns were destroyed. Bands of soldiers entered towns and stole or burned everything in sight—not once, but many times. Much of Germany's valuable farmland was ruined. It would seem that Europe would be so tired of wars that it would not let them happen again. But later generations did

The massacre of Magdeburg by the Catholic forces of Emperor Ferdinand during the Thirty Years' War. The Swedish king Gustavus Adolphus entered the war on the side of the Protestants in 1630, but was too late to stop the destruction of Magdeburg.

not remember the war's horrors. New and ambitious rulers came to power. The seeds of new wars were planted.

WHY DID MORE YEARS OF WAR FOLLOW IN EUROPE?

6. Louis XIV led France into four wars. England, Holland, and Sweden usually fought against him. Louis XIV's wars were fought in the French and English colonies also.

7. The War of Austrian Succession took place after Maria Theresa became ruler of Austria. Maria Theresa's father had got most of the rulers of Europe to accept his daughter as ruler of the Hapsburg empire. As soon as Maria Theresa came to the throne, however, they forgot this. France and Spain joined with Prussia to fight against Austria, England, and Holland. This war went on for eight years. Maria Theresa learned that her "friends" were not to be trusted.

8. After the war, Maria Theresa planned her revenge against Prussia. She was able to gain many allies. She even had her old enemy, France, join her. But Prussia did not wait until Austria was ready. Prussia invaded Maria Theresa's empire and the Seven Years' War began. Only England was on Prussia's side. But the armies of Prussia under Frederick the Great were strong. Then the friendships that Maria Theresa had made so carefully began to fall apart. The Seven Years' War brought little change of territory in Europe. Prussia, however, became a leader in European affairs.

WHY DID ENGLAND AND FRANCE FIGHT WARS IN AMERICA AND INDIA?

9. While Europe was at war, Great Britain and France were fighting for control of North America. France claimed a large area, from the St. Lawrence River to the Great Lakes and the Mississippi Valley. But there were few settlers in French territory and they had few rights. Part of the profits from their rich fur trade was taken by the king in France. English colonies, on the other hand, had many settlers and were close together along the Atlantic coast. They were able to govern themselves, for the most part.

10. When both Great Britain and France claimed the Ohio River Valley, in 1754, war broke out. It is known as the French and Indian War. France first took the lead. But the English had more men and more supplies. The English capture of the French fort of Quebec ended the war, in 1763. France lost Canada to the English and gave the Louisiana Territory to Spain.

11. The English-French rivalry also went on in India. Portugal had lost all but a small part of its Indian land. When Mongol control of India weakened, French and English trading companies tried to become friendly with local Indian rulers. France slowly became important in southern India. Then an English leader, Robert Clive, arrived in India. He joined the military service of the British East India Trading Company. Clive set about to defeat the Indian rulers who were friendly with the French. When more than 100 English were killed by an Indian leader, Great Britain wanted revenge.

12. Clive defeated an Indian force 20 times larger than his own. By the time the Seven Years' War was ending in Europe, in 1763, Great Britain was almost in full control of India. It had become the leading sea power in the world. The French were deeply in debt from their wars. Their once-powerful place among the nations of the world had begun to slip badly. France waited for a chance to strike back at Great Britain, the enemy that had defeated it. The revolt of the English colonies in America in 1775 gave it that chance.

Robert Clive examining enemy lines at the Battle of Plassey in 1757. He led 3,200 troops against 50,000 Indians and won!

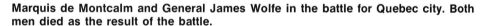

Marquis de Montcalm and General James Wolfe in the battle for Quebec city. Both men died as the result of the battle.

Testing Your Vocabulary _____

Choose the best answer.

1. *Might makes right* (paragraph 1) means that
   a. the powerful can do what they want and insist that it is good.
   b. revenge is often good.
   c. powerful kings are very often great men.
2. An *ally* may be compared with
   a. a teammate.
   b. an enemy.
   c. a scholar.
3. In paragraph 5, *generation* refers to a
   a. half-century.
   b. group of people born about the same time.
   c. time of war.

Understanding What You Have Read _____

1. A good title for paragraphs 9 through 12 is
   a. The American Fur Trade
   b. Robert Clive, Hero in India
   c. France Loses Territory in Two Continents
   d. England Takes Canada
2. In which paragraph do you find facts about
   a. the French-English war in the American colonies?
   b. the results in Germany of the Thirty Years' War?
   c. the beginning of the Thirty Years' War?
   d. Robert Clive's arrival in India?
3. The Thirty Years' War began as a result of
   a. France's defense of Protestants in Germany.
   b. a conflict over the choice of a ruler for Bohemia.
   c. Sweden's attack on Austria.
4. All of these were results of the Thirty Years' War EXCEPT
   a. the Holy Roman Empire became the most powerful force in Europe.
   b. German rulers could choose the religion of their people.
   c. Holland became independent.
5. As a result of the Seven Years' War in America.
   a. France gained a hold on the Ohio River Valley.
   b. England gained control of Louisiana.
   c. France lost Canada to England.
6. As a result of Robert Clive's work in India
   a. French trading companies gained control of northern India.
   b. England gained almost full control of India.
   c. England and Portugal began to share trade with Indian princes.
7. One of the weaknesses of French colonies in North America was that
   a. they were crowded close together.
   b. there was little unity, since each colony governed itself.
   c. they had few people.

Match the description in the second column with the country in the first column.

1. Sweden
2. Canada
3. Germany
4. Holland
5. Bohemia
6. Austria

a. German state that caused the start of the Thirty Years' War
b. became independent after the Thirty Years' War
c. suffered greatest ruin during Thirty Years' War
d. a center of French-English struggle for control
e. took Louisiana from France in 1763
f. secured the help of France in the Seven Years' War
g. joined Protestant forces for a time in the Thirty Years' War

Developing Ideas and Skills

USING A TIME LINE

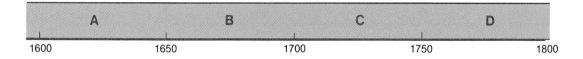

For each of the events listed, write in your notebook the letter of the period of time in which that event took place.

1. The Thirty Years' War was fought
2. The Glorious Revolution took place in England
3. The Romanovs came to power in Russia
4. The reign of King Louis XIV of France ended
5. France lost territory in North America to England
6. Frederick the Great came to power in Prussia
7. John Sobieski stopped the Turks at Vienna
8. The rule of Oliver Cromwell in England came to an end
9. Maria Theresa came to the throne of Austria
10. England gained complete control of India

AIM: How did the people of Europe live in the time of absolute rulers?

CHAPTER 6

The People of the 18th Century

WHAT POWERS DID MONARCHS HAVE?

1. Almost two centuries of wars had done little to change the lives of most of the people of Europe. By the end of the 18th century, only a few countries had become more democratic. England was not yet a democracy. But at least some English people had a voice in government. The power of the English ruler had been limited and people had gained some civil rights. In Holland and Switzerland, there were also gains in democracy. This was not true, however, in the rest of Europe.

2. The power of rulers in most countries was absolute. They still claimed to govern by divine right. Monarchs waged wars and spent money as they wished. Nobles and common people had little to say about their government. Rulers often punished people without trial. They forced all those living in their countries to follow their own religion. Even enlightened monarchs had complete power. Unfortunately, there were very few wise rulers. It was no wonder that educated people began to speak openly against their governments.

HOW DID THE RICH AND POOR DIFFER?

3. Different social classes divided the people of every land, including England. Nobles lived in great homes on large estates. In spite of their wealth, however, they had little to say in their governments. They served their ruler and, in turn, had servants themselves. The nobles spent their time in hunting, dancing, and entertaining their ruler at court.

4. The peasants were chiefly farmers. Their life and work were much the same as they had always been. Even farming methods had changed very little in Europe. Fields were ro-

Musicians play for a gathering of the nobility. Young Wolfgang Amadeus Mozart is at the piano.

tated so that each year one-third of the land was left unfarmed. Wooden plows were used to turn over the soil. Only a small harvest was the reward for all the hard work. In England, however, some farm improvements were made. Fertilizer began to be used. English farmers rotated their crops so that no field was left unused. Different crops were planted, and food was stored for cattle over the winter. English farmers began to fence in their land. They learned scientific ways of raising a better breed of cattle.

5. Most serfs had been freed in England, France, and Holland. But serfdom still existed in much of Europe. Serfs were taxed by rulers, by the nobles, and by the Church. They paid for their monarch's wars and for their courts. They had no voice at all in government. After taxes were paid, peasants had little left for themselves. Most of them had barely enough to eat. Bread was the most common food. Meat was a luxury. Homes were often one-room huts covered with grass.

6. Peasant women worked along with their husbands in the fields. Few people in power cared about the problems of the poor. Women of poor families learned to spin, sew, and cook. That was their education. No women were bankers, but in England some were merchants. Many of these merchants were widows who carried on the business of their husbands. (In 1690, the average life span was 32 years.) The education that girls of good families received from nuns or private tutors was as good as the education most men of wealth received. These girls were taught music, Latin, and religion. A few women rose to power and governed nations. Among them were Isabella of Spain, Elizabeth in England, and Catherine in Russia. A ruler of Milan once said about his wife, who ruled while he was at war, "I have more confidence in her than in my whole army." So, a few fortunate women could rule nations. But most other women had fewer rights than those held by the poorest of men.

7. In towns and cities, the middle class had sprung up as trade grew. The middle class was made up of merchants, people in business, and bankers. More trade caused villages to grow into towns and towns to grow into cities. By 1750, the city of London had a million people, and Paris, Vienna, and Lisbon were all large cities. The walls that had once protected the towns had since been torn down. Houses spread out into the countryside. Streets were wider than before and were often paved. Oil lamps lit the streets at night. Middle-class people were not as poor as the peasants, but they were not as rich as the nobles.

8. In the cities, industry and trade were carried on. Products from the New World were in demand: furs, tobacco, cotton, rice, sugar, gold, and silver. From Asia came spices, jewels, and tea. The British, French, and Dutch had many ships. Their port cities were busy loading and unloading goods to and from the colonies. The merchants, bankers, and shopkeepers, who carried on this trade, along with doctors and lawyers, were the backbone of the middle class. These were the people who read and discussed laws and religion in the coffee houses, which became popular meeting places. These were the people who wanted to share in running their government. By the end of the 18th century, they began to ask for it.

WHAT CULTURAL ADVANCES WERE MADE?

9. The 17th and 18th centuries were eras of gifted artists and writers. There were many great men in literature, music, and science. The court of Louis XIV was the center of a new burst of culture called the *enlightenment*. French literature and art were highly valued everywhere. Only the nobles, however, were able to enjoy the new cultural works. Rulers liked to show off their wealth in works of art and architecture. Public buildings had rows of

columns, in imitation of classical Greece and Rome. The inside walls of buildings were often covered with murals (large wall paintings).

10. From France and England came great writers. Molière, in France, wrote satires, or comedies about the behavior of nobles at the French court. English writers such as John Milton and Alexander Pope wrote great poetry. Milton's *Paradise Lost*, a long religious poem, is one of the great works of world literature. Other English writers, such as Jonathan Swift and Joseph Addison, wrote satires poking fun at the foolishness of society.

The picture on the right by William Hogarth is called *The Enraged Musician*. Explain the title in terms of 18th century life. *Gulliver's Travels* was a satire by Swift. Below, Gulliver is in the land of the giants.

11. Most music of this period had a religious background. German composers wrote memorable religious works. George Frederick Handel composed works for choral singing. His most famous work is *The Messiah*, performed by both singers and instruments. Wolfgang Amadeus Mozart wrote every kind of musical work. By the time he was 18 years of age, he had composed 200 different works. He was indeed a great genius. The master of the organ, Johann Sebastian Bach, wrote beautiful religious music.

12. Important discoveries were made in science. In the early 17th century, William Harvey discovered how the blood circulates through the body. When the microscope was invented some years later, it proved Harvey's ideas to be correct. Near the end of the 17th century, Isaac Newton, an English mathematician, considered by some the greatest scientist ever, discovered the principles of the law of gravity. This discovery is one of the most important of man's achievements in science. The Frenchman, René Descartes, made new discoveries in mathematics. In 1764, James Watt, an Englishman, developed a steam engine. This simple invention modernized transportation. It also helped start an Industrial Revolution.

264

Testing Your Vocabulary

Choose the best answer.

1. French and English writers of the 18th century wrote *satires*. Satires are
   a. long stories that criticize kings and queens.
   b. plays that tell about the life of the common people.
   c. writings that poke fun at the foolishness of society.

2. The term *composer* usually refers to
   a. architecture.
   b. music.
   c. literature.

Understanding What You Have Read

1. The main idea of paragraph 2 is that
   a. there were few wise rulers in Europe.
   b. in most European countries, the rulers had absolute power.
   c. democracy had made great progress all over Europe.
   d. more people were educated than ever before.

2. In which paragraph do you find facts about
   a. products from the New World that Europeans wanted?
   b. the education of peasant women?
   c. the discovery of the circulation of the blood?
   d. improvements made in farming in England?

3. By the 18th century none of these had changed much EXCEPT
   a. farming methods.
   b. the power of monarchs.
   c. the size of towns.

4. Middle-class people, rather than the poor, would probably be the leaders of movements to better conditions because they

a. were better educated.
b. were unsuccessful traders.
c. had the same privileges that the nobles had.

5. By the 18th century, England had become more democratic than the rest of Europe in that
   a. English composers were very famous.
   b. the English had gained some rights, and the powers of the rulers had been limited.
   c. England had larger cities than other European countries.

6. Johann Sebastian Bach and George Frederich Handel were famous
   a. musicians.
   b. poets.
   c. painters.

7. One of the reasons for the growth of large cities was that
   a. writers and scientists crowded into cities to carry on their work.
   b. town walls had been torn down, giving people more room in which to live in the cities.
   c. the invention of the steam engine made it easier to move to cities.

Tell whether the following statements about Europe in the 18th century are true or false. If a statement is false, change the words in italics to make it true.

1. Modern scientific methods of farming were first used by farmers in *France.*
2. Merchants, *bankers,* and doctors were all members of the middle class.
3. Tea and spices were products of the *New World* that Europeans wanted.
4. The court of the *English* rulers was known as the richest in Europe.
5. The luxuries of monarchs were paid for mainly by taxes on *serfs.*
6. *The Messiah* was composed by George Frederick Handel.
7. Artists and musicians performed their skills for the pleasure of the *nobles.*
8. *William Harvey* discovered the circulation of the blood.
9. The great music of the 17th and 18th centuries centered around *political* ideas.
10. By the end of the 18th century, most serfs had been freed in *Austria,* France, and Holland.

Developing Ideas and Skills

KNOWING IMPORTANT TERMS

In the following exercise, some features of European life in the 18th century are listed. Read each feature carefully. Then write in your notebook whether it is an *economic,* a *social,* or a *political* feature of life in Europe at the time. (Review the meaning of these terms.)

1. Several nations had great women rulers.
2. Nobles lived in great mansions while serfs lived in misery.
3. Nobles spent much time in hunting and entertainment.
4. Farmers in England had learned how to rotate their crops.
5. Serfs had to pay taxes to the monarch, lord, and Church.
6. Artists and writers gathered in the French court, the richest court in Europe.
7. Only in England had people gained certain civil rights.
8. French and English ports were kept busy loading goods for distant lands.
9. Enlightened rulers tried to understand the needs of their people.
10. The rise of towns and cities brought about a growth of trade.

Summary of Unit V

A number of the most important events and facts mentioned in this unit are listed below. Can you add any others?

1. Absolute rulers controlled almost all of Europe in the 17th and 18th centuries. King Louis XIV of France ruled by "divine right."
2. In England, the power of the monarch had been limited before the 18th century.

3. Under Oliver Cromwell, England was a republic, but Cromwell's government was unpopular, and the people returned the king to the throne.
4. Enlightened rulers may have understood the problems of their people, but they did little to improve their lives.
5. The events that took place in Europe affected America and Asia.
6. Peter the Great brought Western ideas to Russia and made his country a power in Europe.
7. Poland, which is on the plains of northern Europe, was not easily defended. It was divided by its neighbors three times before 1800.
8. Large nations of Europe felt that a *balance of power* was the best way to keep peace. If all the nations were equally powerful, none would be strong enough to make war on another.
9. Absolute rulers fought war after war in the 17th and 18th centuries. The Thirty Years' War stands out as one of the most terrible in history.
10. The lives of most people in Europe were hardly changed in the 17th and 18th centuries. People still lived and worked as their ancestors had done hundreds of years before.

Making Generalizations

In each of the following, make one accurate generalization based on the three factual statements given.

A. Factual statements:
   1. Nobles in England forced King John to sign the Magna Carta.
   2. Charles I was forced by Parliament to sign the Petition of Right.
   3. Parliament passed the Bill of Rights after King James II was forced to flee from England.
   Generalization:

B. Factual statements:
   1. England was united under powerful rulers while Germany was but a group of small states.
   2. English kings and queens had their powers limited at the same time that French rulers had absolute power.
   3. Russia was ruled by Mongol invaders while the English had their own monarchs.
   Generalization:

C. Factual statements:
   1. From 1618 to 1648 several European countries were involved in The Thirty Years' War.
   2. In the 17th and 18th centuries, England and France fought several wars in many parts of the world.
   3. Peter the Great, Czar of Russia (1689–1725), fought for 20 years with Sweden to win a port on the Baltic.
   Generalization:

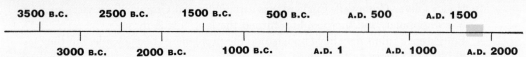

UNIT VI

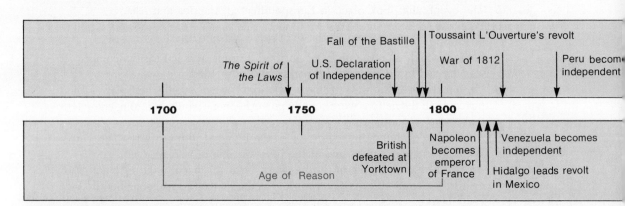

3500 B.C.	2500 B.C.	1500 B.C.	500 B.C.	A.D. 500	A.D. 1500
3000 B.C.	2000 B.C.	1000 B.C.	A.D. 1	A.D. 1000	A.D. 2000

Fall of the Bastille

Toussaint L'Ouverture's revolt

The Spirit of the Laws

U.S. Declaration of Independence

War of 1812

Peru becomes independent

1700   1750   1800

British defeated at Yorktown

Napoleon becomes emperor of France

Venezuela becomes independent

Hidalgo leads revolt in Mexico

Age of Reason

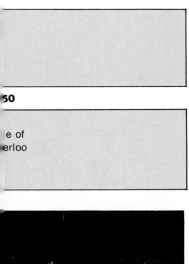

How Did the Idea of Liberty Advance in Modern Times?

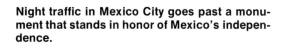

Night traffic in Mexico City goes past a monument that stands in honor of Mexico's independence.

269

AIM: How did the writers of the 18th century prepare the way for revolutions against absolute rulers?

CHAPTER 1

The Age of Reason Brings New Ideas

HOW DID SCIENCE LEAD TO AN AGE OF REASON?

1. At the beginning of the Renaissance, in the 14th century, Europeans looked with great admiration on the works of Greek and Roman writers, artists, and thinkers. They could not improve on these works, they believed. But educated people of the 18th century had a different outlook. They looked ahead, rather than to the past. They looked for future improvements in the lives of men and women of all social and economic classes.

2. When people change their ways of thinking about one matter, they often change them about other things, too. One change often brings others. By the 18th century, scientists had discovered that there were natural laws that governed what happened on earth. Some thinkers began to believe that government and society might also follow such natural laws.

3. Scientists became popular even with monarchs and nobles. It became fashionable for some rulers and nobles to pay for the work of scientists. Some even gave them places to work. Scientists believed in testing ideas and reasoning. Their work carried over into government. Their ideas caused people to question the wis-

dom of old laws and the rules by which society was governed. During the 18th century, some people began to accept as true only what they could reason for themselves. What they could not understand by reasoning, they would not believe. Thus, the 18th century is often called "The Age of Reason."

WHAT WERE THE IDEAS OF LOCKE AND VOLTAIRE?

4. Writers of the 17th and 18th centuries wrote about the rights of people. John Locke, of England, in the late 17th century stated that people have natural rights. These are rights that all people are entitled to simply by being human. They have these rights because they are born with them. Among these rights, Locke wrote, are those of life, liberty, and ownership of property. Locke said that governments cannot take away these rights. Governments are formed to protect the rights of citizens. If a government does not protect the natural rights of its people, then the people can put an end to that government and form another. Thomas Jefferson used many of Locke's ideas in writing the American Declaration of Independence.

Voltaire, author and philosopher. In what ways would Voltaire be considered a leader?

5. Perhaps the best known writer of the 18th century was the Frenchman Voltaire (vol-TAIR). He gave up being a lawyer to become a political writer. Voltaire's strongest attacks were against the Catholic Church. He felt that the Church taught people to accept some ideas without using their reason. Voltaire was jailed for his writings and sent away from Paris. He lived in England for a few years. He admired the English form of government. Many royal courts of Europe also welcomed Voltaire. For a time, he was a favorite of Prussia's Frederick the Great and Catherine the Great of Russia.

6. Voltaire was popular, partly because of his great wit. Whenever he was questioned, he would come up with a clever answer. Much of the middle class agreed with his attacks on the Church and government. Throughout his life, he fought for the rights of people who were harmed because of their political or religious beliefs. But he did not believe in democratic government. He did not think that the masses of people had the wisdom to rule themselves. He believed in enlightened rulers who understood the people's needs and cared for them. His most well-known work is the story *Candide*.

HOW DID OTHER WRITERS PREPARE THE WAY FOR REVOLUTION?

7. Another French writer, Montesquieu (MON-tes-kyoo), was a lawyer and a judge. His most famous work was the *Spirit of the Laws*. Like Voltaire, Montesquieu spent several years in England, and he liked the English system of government. He approved of parliament's limiting the powers of the monarch. Montesquieu said that no one form of government is better than any other if both serve the people well. Montesquieu believed that the powers of government should be divided. One branch of government should make the laws. Another should decide how the laws are to be applied. A third branch should enforce the laws. This idea is

How did Montesquieu influence the writing of the United States Constitution?

known as *separation of powers*. Montesquieu's ideas were known by the men who wrote the Constitution of the United States. They were careful to divide the powers of the federal government among the President, the Congress, and the courts.

8. Jean Jacques Rousseau (roo-SOH) was a Frenchman whose writings helped to bring on the French Revolution. Rousseau spent his life wandering throughout Europe. Although he saw evil in the world, Rousseau thought that people were born good. Only terrible conditions under which some people lived made them evil. Rousseau believed that people formed governments when they needed laws to guide them. Bad governments were the cause of some of the terrible conditions under which people lived. If these conditions were corrected, Rousseau said, people would be good. He felt that governments should serve the people. If a government did not serve the people, then the people had the right to take the power away from the government. And since governments are made up of people, people must be educated.

9. There was also in France a group of people who published an encyclopedia. They were called the Encyclopedists. This encyclopedia was more than a book of facts. In it were the latest ideas about government and religion. Denis Diderot (deed-ah-ROH) was the editor. He and his co-workers labored more than 20 years on this work. When finished, there were 28 volumes. The Encyclopedists spoke out

Denis Diderot. How do the works of the men described in this chapter support the statement that they were part of the Age of Reason?

against the Catholic Church and the governments of the time. They favored political liberty, religious freedom, and the use of reason by all people. When the first volumes of their work were published, the French government burned them. It had also burned the works of Voltaire, hoping to keep the people from reading them.

10. Can writers alone bring about changes in the conditions of the people in Europe? Can writers alone cause a revolution? Only a few people in Europe, of course, were able to read and write at this time. But those who could read were members of the middle class as well as of the clergy and nobility. The middle class was able to do something about the evils of European governments and society. But writers alone did not cause the revolts that followed. They gave birth to the ideas of the revolution. Action followed ideas, and action took place first in America. You will read about this in the next chapter.

Testing Your Vocabulary

Choose the best answer.

1. The opposite of *private property* is
   a. property owned by the government.
   b. property not yet paid for.
   c. land in the city.
2. In paragraph 2, laws by which *society* is governed are mentioned. *Society* re-

fers to
   a. life under a king.
   b. a country where religion plays a major part in the life of the people.
   c. a very large group of people sharing the same culture.

3. Most governments have several *branches*. A *branch* in this sentence means
   a. a division or part.
   b. a philosopher.
   c. part of a tree.

Understanding What You Have Read _____

1. The main idea of paragraph 10 is that
   a. writers were most popular with the middle class.
   b. few people were able to read the works of the thinkers of the Age of Reason.
   c. writers would not change the minds of too many people.
   d. writers introduced the revolutionary ideas that would later result in action.

2. In which paragraph do you find facts about
   a. John Locke's ideas about government and the rights of citizens?
   b. the meaning of the term *Age of Reason?*
   c. the idea of the separation of powers of government?
   d. Voltaire's early profession?

3. Voltaire was popular with the middle class because he
   a. admired the English government.
   b. attacked the Church and the governments of the time.
   c. favored a democratic government.

4. Many political writers went to England because
   a. only in England were all people allowed to vote.
   b. England treated members of all religions equally.
   c. they were persecuted for their writings in France.

5. An idea of John Locke's that the writers of the Declaration of Independence used is that
   a. there should be no national religion.
   b. there should be three branches of government.
   c. all people have natural rights which governments cannot take away.

6. Works of some of the writers of the Age of Reason were burned because they
   a. attacked the power of the governments then existing in Europe.
   b. spoke in favor of the power of the nobles.
   c. believed in the idea of a national Protestant Church.

7. Rousseau favored education because he believed that
   a. educated people cause revolutions.
   b. only educated people could govern themselves well.
   c. people could not understand their religion if they were not educated.

Tell whether you agree or disagree with the following conclusions, giving reasons for your answers

1. Voltaire was popular with monarchs who ruled by divine right.
2. Scientists became important people in Europe in the 18th century.
3. Writers during the Age of Reason tried to bring back the power of the Church and the acceptance of the Church's ideas.

4. John Locke's ideas developed out of the ideas of Thomas Jefferson in the Declaration of Independence.
5. Popular writers of the Age of Reason were welcomed only by the rulers of England.
6. Most of the writers of the Age of Reason

believed in the idea that governments were formed to serve the people.
7. Members of the middle class were leaders in furthering revolutionary ideas.
8. Roger Bacon would probably have agreed with most of the writers of the Age of Reason.

Developing Ideas and Skills

MAKING A CHART

The following chart is about the *Age of Reason.* In your notebook, fill in the missing items.

Writer	Country	Important Ideas
Locke	England	1. Every person has natural rights which governments cannot take away. 2. _____
Voltaire	_____	1. _____ 2. _____
Montesquieu	_____	1. No one form of government is better than any other.
_____	France	1. People are naturally good, but social and political conditions make people evil. 2. The people must be educated.
Diderot	_____	1. _____

Some Results of the Age of Reason:
1. _____
2. _____

AIM: How were the American colonists able to free themselves from England's rule?

CHAPTER 2

The American Colonies Revolt

WHY DID THE SPIRIT OF FREEDOM GROW IN THE COLONIES?

1. "Absence makes the heart grow fonder" is an old saying. Very often it is true. For the English people in Colonial America, however, absence from the parent country had an opposite effect. During their 150 years of settlement in America, the colonists had drawn further and further away from Great Britain. The people who had settled in America in the 17th century had found a life very different from the one they had known in England. To the colonists, England seemed very far away. Few of them had ever even been there.

2. Before 1763, Great Britain had paid little attention to its colonies in America. It had been busy with wars in Europe and civil wars at home. The laws that Parliament passed to control the colonies were hardly enforced. The American settlers had begun to make their own laws. By 1763, an elected assembly made the laws in each colony. Americans felt they were quite able to govern themselves.

3. Great Britain defeated the French for control of North America in 1763. Then Great Britain began to tighten its control of the colonies. The colonists, however, did not feel they

The 13 Colonies

needed the protection of English troops. The British government had other ideas. It began to enforce trade laws that had not been enforced before. The colonies were not allowed to sell to foreign countries any goods that were also made in England. The trade of the colonies had to be carried on in British ships. This made the colonists angry. They *smuggled* goods; that is, they brought them in secretly. King George III sent troops to America to stop the smuggling. British troops were allowed to enter any home and search it. British soldiers were also allowed to live in the homes of American colonists, whether or not the colonists wanted the soldiers.

4. The British Parliament then passed new tax laws. Some of the revenue from taxes was to be used to pay for the troops sent to the colonies. When the colonies protested, some taxes were repealed, or canceled. But the tax on tea remained, and colonists could buy tea only from Great Britain. The colonists felt they were being taxed without their consent. In 1773, colonists boarded British ships in Boston harbor and dumped their cargoes of tea overboard. As a result of this "Boston Tea Party," Great Britain closed the port of Boston to all trade.

5. Delegates from each of the colonies met in Philadelphia in 1774. They were not then thinking about separation from England. They wanted justice. They believed they were being taxed unfairly. They felt there was no one in Parliament who represented the colonies and spoke for their interests. Protests were sent to the British king, and the American delegates agreed to meet again the following year. Before that meeting could take place, fighting broke out between British troops and the colonists near Boston.

6. Despite the fighting, not everyone in the colonies wanted freedom from Great Britain. Many did not want a war. These people were still loyal to the king. But they wanted the king to allow them their rights as British subjects. George III, however, would not listen to

the protests from his American subjects. He insisted that the colonists had to be punished. As far as he was concerned, they were traitors. So the fighting, which had begun near Boston, broke out again.

7. The meeting of the colonial leaders became known as the Continental Congress. The Congress felt that the American colonies had to be free of British rule. Thomas Jefferson was chosen to write a statement of independence. His Declaration of Independence was issued on July 4, 1776. In it Jefferson stated that it was the duty of a people to change its government if that government took away its rights. The statement listed 27 complaints against the king. The colonies were ready to do whatever was necessary to win their freedom.

How did European thought influence the writing of the U.S. Constitution?

WHY WERE THE AMERICAN COLONISTS SUCCESSFUL?

8. When the American Revolution began, British troops were well trained. The British navy was the strongest in the world. What is more, the colonists were divided in their feeling about war with Great Britain. A great many, including most of the wealthy, remained loyal to the king. On the other hand, the Americans were fighting on their own land and defending their own homes. The British had to move supplies across thousands of miles of ocean. And, as the war dragged on, Americans won the support of England's old enemies. These were France, Holland, and Spain. Finally, the American troops were led by an able general, George Washington.

9. Washington led a small, poorly trained colonial army. His men did not have the supplies they needed to fight well. Often, they were not paid. Washington was forced to retreat many times after battles. But he carefully guarded his army. He rarely fought the British in an open battle. He was successful in fighting a war of "hit and run." He would strike at the British forces and then retreat inland. This would draw the British away from their base of supplies near the seacoast.

The winter at Valley Forge is remembered as an heroic period in American History. Why?

General Cornwallis of the British army surrendered to General Washington at Yorktown.

10. Because he managed his forces with skill, Washington kept the Americans from losing the war. After the British were defeated at the Battle of Saratoga (1777), the French began to help the Americans. Later, Holland and Spain entered the war against their old enemy, Great Britain. France wanted revenge for the loss of Canada to Great Britain some years earlier. It was the French fleet that helped Washington trap the British at Yorktown. This battle forced the British to surrender and end the war.

HOW DID THE AMERICAN REVOLUTION WEAKEN THE POWER OF ABSOLUTE RULERS IN EUROPE?

11. The American Revolution lasted six long years. In 1783, the peace treaty was signed at Paris, France. Under this treaty, Great Britain recognized the 13 colonies as an independent nation. The boundaries of the new nation extended from the Atlantic Ocean to the Mississippi River. As a result of the American Revolution, Great Britain was deeply in debt. Perhaps even more important was the fact that the Americans had openly revolted against their king, and had won their freedom. The defeat of King George III weakened the power of absolute rulers all over Europe. The fight for liberty in America gave hope to people everywhere who were treated unfairly by their rulers. Those who wanted a better life took courage from the deeds of the Americans.

277

Testing Your Vocabulary

Choose the best answer.

1. To *repeal* a law is to
   a. pass it.
   b. end it.
   c. add more ideas to it.
2. *Smuggled goods* are those that have been
   a. brought into a country secretly, without being taxed.
   b. taxed before entering the country.
   c. captured by the enemy.

Understanding What You Have Read

1. A good title for paragraph 8 is
   a. British and Colonial Strengths at the Outset of the War.
   b. Why the American Colonies Won the Revolution.
   c. Fighting Begins in Massachusetts.
   d. The Power of the British Navy.

2. In which paragraph do you find facts about
   a. the announcement of the Declaration of Independence?
   b. American dislike of British troops in the colonies?
   c. the colonial leaders who met at Philadelphia in 1774?
   d. French help to the Americans in their fight for independence?

3. Many colonists felt they were able to govern themselves because every colony had
   a. a system of public education.
   b. experience in making its own laws.
   c. representatives in the British Parliament.

4. A reason why the British government had not enforced laws to control the colonies was that
   a. the colonists had been loyal to Great Britain.
   b. the British government had been concerned with other problems in Europe.
   c. the British government knew the colonies could govern themselves.

5. The colonies disliked the tax on tea because
   a. tea was used at every meal.
   b. Great Britain sent its worst tea to America.
   c. they were being taxed by Parliament without their consent.

6. The British army had the problem of
   a. keeping its men together.
   b. outnumbering the Americans.
   c. getting supplies.

7. All of these were important results of the American Revolution EXCEPT
   a. a revolt by the people of Great Britain followed the American Revolution.
   b. American success gave the hope of freedom to people in many parts of the world.
   c. the power of absolute rulers was further weakened.

Using Original Sources

The Treaty of Peace officially ending the American Revolution was signed at Paris in 1783. Independence was actually won, however, when the English general, Lord Cornwallis, surrendered at Yorktown, Virginia, in 1781. This is part of the description of that surrender as told by James Thacher, a doctor in the service of the American army.

British Troops Surrender at Yorktown

At about twelve o'clock, the combined army was arranged and drawn up in two lines extending more than a mile in length. The Americans were drawn up in a line on the right side of the road, and the French occupied the left. At the head of the former, Washington took his station, attended by his aids. The French troops, in complete uniform, displayed a military and noble appearance. The Americans, though not all in uniform nor their dress so neat, yet exhibited an erect soldierly air.

It was about two o'clock when the captive army advanced through the line formed for their reception. Everyone was prepared to gaze on Lord Cornwallis, but he disappointed the onlookers. Pretending to be ill, he made General O'Harra his substitute as leader of the army. This officer was followed by the conquered troops in a slow and solemn step.

The royal [British] troops showed a decent and neat appearance. But in their line of march we saw a disorderly and unsoldierly conduct. Their step was irregular, and their ranks frequently broken.

Some of the officers appeared to be exceedingly chagrined [upset] when giving the word "ground arms," and many of the soldiers showed a sullen [angry, but silent] temper, throwing their arms on the pile with violence as if determined to break them.

1. Americans felt that the war for independence had been won at the Battle of Yorktown. Do you think the British had the same feeling?
2. The writer said that Lord Cornwallis pretended to be ill. Do you think this is a statement of fact or an opinion? What other reason could Lord Cornwallis have for not appearing at the surrender?
3. What is meant by the order to "ground arms"? Why do you think the British officers felt "chagrined" when they gave that order?
4. Put yourself in the place of a doctor with the British army watching the same scene. Now describe the same scene through his eyes.
5. How might Washington and his soldiers have felt as the British army passed before them?

AIM: How did the Spanish colonies in Latin America win their freedom?

CHAPTER 3

Independence in Latin America

WHAT IS LATIN AMERICA?

1. "Death to bad government!" That was the cry of Father Miguel Hidalgo as he led the peasant revolt in Mexico in 1810. This cry was heard throughout Latin America from 1800 to 1825. By 1825, nearly all of the Latin American people had shaken off European rule. Once having gotten rid of bad European governments, however, the Latin American countries often set up bad governments of their own. Although they gained independence, the people of Latin America did not gain freedom. In this chapter, we will see how this came to be.

2. Latin America is the area south of the United States. It runs from Mexico to the tip of South America. It includes the islands of the Caribbean Sea. This area was settled by the Spanish, Portuguese, and French. Since all of their languages come from Latin, we call this area Latin America. It is more than twice the size of the United States. But there are areas where few people live. Giant rain forests cover much of the northern part of South America. The Andes Mountains run from the northern end of the continent to the southern end. Early settlements were made mainly along the coasts. Because of the geography of Latin America, there was always little unity among the people.

General Simón Bolívar was one of the great leaders of independence in Latin America. He fought for Colombian independence and has been called the George Washington of South America.

WHAT SOCIAL CLASSES EXISTED?

3. A class system developed early in Latin American history. At the top of the social ladder were the European-born white people. Most had been placed in the colonies by the rulers of Europe. They held the highest positions in colonial government and in the Church. Another group were *creoles*. They were descendants of Europeans, but were born in the Latin American colonies. Their social position was lower than that of European-born people, and they were often jealous of them. Creoles often owned large estates and were merchants or mine owners. In general, the leaders of the revolutionary movements in Latin America were creoles. Some had been to Europe and had read the works of Locke, Voltaire, and Rousseau. People in the Latin American colonies were forbidden by their European rulers to read about the American and French Revolutions. But colonists who went to Europe spread the word when they returned.

4. Another group were the *mestizos* (meh-STEE-zohs), who were part European and part Indian. Mestizos were chiefly farmers. Still lower on the social ladder were the Indians. They worked on the estates and in the mines. At the bottom of the social ladder were the blacks. They had been brought to Latin America as slaves to work on plantations. Blacks made up a large part of the populations of the Caribbean islands and Brazil.

5. Most of Latin America was controlled by Spain. Brazil, however, was a Portuguese colony. The colony of Haiti, in the Caribbean Sea, was French. The rulers in Spain, Portugal, and France had little interest in the people in their colonies. They wanted only the gold, silver, and other treasures to be found there. Treasures from the Spanish colonies were shipped to Europe only in Spanish ships. This meant more business for European shipmakers and sailors. Goods grown or made in Spain could not be produced in the colonies. This forced the colonies to pay high prices for goods they could have made themselves more cheaply. Colonists had almost no self-government. They were taxed heavily. The poorer people often paid higher taxes than the wealthy did.

6. Revolts began in Latin America when Napoleon I, the French emperor, made his brother king of Spain. The Spanish colonists felt no loyalty to this Frenchman. But these early revolts did not last long. When Napoleon's empire fell, the rightful king of Spain returned to power. He tried to tighten his control of the colonies in Latin America. But the desire for freedom was burning strongly now, and it could not be put out.

HOW DID EARLY REBELS SUCCEED IN HAITI AND MEXICO?

7. The first successful revolt in Latin America took place in a French, rather than a Spanish, colony. Nine out of ten people on the French island of Haiti were black slaves. In 1794, Toussaint L'Ouverture (too-SAHN loo-ver-TYOOR) led a successful revolt against French rule. He was an educated slave who had read the works of Voltaire and Rousseau. Fol-

Toussaint L'Ouverture was influenced by the writings of Voltaire and Rousseau, yet he was captured by the French. What do you think this says about France's attitude toward the French colonies in America?

lowing the revolution, he set up a republic and put an end to slavery. Napoleon I, who was then in power in Europe, sent an army to restore French rule. Toussaint L'Ouverture was captured and taken to France, where he died in prison. Fighting went on in Haiti, but the French were finally driven out. A republic was again set up in Haiti in 1804.

8. In Mexico, Father Miguel Hidalgo led a revolt of Indian and mestizo farmers. The rebels had little chance against trained Spanish soldiers. They were easily defeated, and Father Hidalgo was shot. Some years later, however, the creoles led a revolt and captured Mexico City. Mexico declared its independence from Spain in 1821.

HOW DID OTHER SPANISH COLONIES WIN INDEPENDENCE?

9. One of the early leaders of the freedom movement in South America was Francisco Miranda, of Venezuela. Miranda encouraged the idea of revolt in Latin America. He declared independence for Venezuela in 1811, but he was defeated by the Spanish. After Miranda had died in prison in Spain, Simón Bolívar took up the revolutionary work Miranda had begun. Bolívar has been called "the George Washington of South America." Bolívar, a creole, gave his life and fortune to gain independence for the Spanish colonies. He first marched from Venezuela into Colombia. Here, he surprised the weaker Spanish forces. Having defeated them, he returned to Venezuela. There he won another victory, thus bringing independence to Colombia and Venezuela.

10. In the southern part of Latin America, the freedom movement was led by José de San Martín. San Martín had been a member of the Spanish army. He left Spain to take the lead in the fight of the Spanish colonies. In 1816, San Martín freed Argentina. He then decided to free the people in Chile and Peru, across the Andes Mountains. His march across the mountains has been compared with Hannibal's march

across the Alps to attack ancient Rome. San Martín freed Chile. He then entered Peru, declaring the independence of that colony.

11. Spanish forces remained in Peru, however. San Martín knew they had to be defeated if Peru was to keep its independence. In a meeting with Bolívar, San Martín decided to let his forces join Simón Bolívar and finish the job they had begun. Bolívar defeated the Spanish armies. Peru gained its independence in 1824. San Martín and Bolívar together freed eight Spanish colonies. Only a few islands remained part of the Spanish Empire in Latin America. Cuba and Puerto Rico were the most important of these islands.

WHY WAS DEMOCRACY HARD TO ACHIEVE?

12. Most of the new Latin American nations became republics, which were democracies. They wrote constitutions like that of the United States, giving rule to all the people. But their government could not remain democratic for long. For it is almost impossible to have a government run by the people when only a few of them can read and write. Most of the people were still very poor. The social class system of the old colonies remained. Unlike the colonists in the United States, most Latin American people had little experience in self-government. They had not yet learned to be loyal to their new republics. Poor roads, mountains, deserts, and jungles also kept the people from becoming unified.

13. Under these conditions, it was easy for a strong leader with an armed force to gain control of the government. The leader who controlled the army was able to rule. The history of Latin America, therefore, is the history of strongmen, dictators who ruled their countries with an iron hand. When a dictator died or was overthrown, another usually took his place. Latin America had defeated Spain and won its independence. But during the 19th century, most of the people had gained little freedom.

Testing Your Vocabulary

Choose the best answer.

1. The *creoles* made up a social class in Latin America. Creoles are people
   a. of mixed Spanish and Indian ancestry.
   b. of mixed black and white ancestry.
   c. of European descent, born in the colonies.
2. *Independent but not free* means for the Latin American
   a. having freedom to live in a democracy.
   b. having freedom from Spanish rule, but enjoying few liberties.
   c. having freedom from the parent country, but being forced to work for rich landowners.

Understanding What You Have Read

1. A good title for paragraph 5 is
   a. Products of Latin America
   b. Open Revolt Begins
   c. Treasures of Spain
   d. How Spain Controlled Its Colonies
2. In which paragraph do you find facts about
   a. the revolt in Mexico led by Father Hidalgo?
   b. why the new Latin American republics could not set up democracies?
   c. San Martín's march across the Andes Mountains?
   d. the meaning of *mestizo?*
3. Few early settlements were made in the middle of South America because
   a. this area is twice the size of the United States.
   b. enough rainfall is found only along the eastern coast.
   c. the geography in this area made living difficult.
4. Creoles led revolutionary movements partly because they
   a. were jealous of the power of European-born people.
   b. held the highest positions in colonial governments.
   c. were loyal to Napoleon.
5. All of these caused problems for the new republics in Latin America EXCEPT
   a. disagreement between Bolívar and San Martín.
   b. few people were able to read and write.
   c. the people had little experience in governing themselves.
6. Simón Bolívar is called "the George Washington of South America" because he
   a. was asked by a congress of Spanish colonies to organize an army.
   b. was a rich plantation owner.
   c. led the fight for independence in Latin America.
7. Dictators were able to grab power in Latin America because
   a. democracy cannot work unless the people are able to read and write.
   b. none of the new nations had written constitutions.
   c. people had a deep loyalty to their newly freed country.
8. People who are of mixed Spanish and Indian ancestry are called
   a. mestizos.
   b. Incas.
   c. peons.

*Developing Ideas and Skills*_____

USING A MAP

Study the map on page 285 carefully. Then tell whether these statements are true or false.

1. San Martín was a leader in freeing the southern part of Latin America.
2. Bolívar and San Martín joined forces in the city of Caracas.
3. Brazil was not a part of Spain's territory.
4. Father Hidalgo led the fight for freedom in Mexico.
5. Spanish territory in 1800 included land that is now part of the United States.
6. Haiti was one of the Spanish lands that revolted.
7. Bolívar's march to freedom led him into Mexico.

TURNING POINTS

Government

Latin America: Josefa Ortiz de Domínguez

In the early 1880s, the people of Mexico were still under the rule of Spain. Many Mexicans were growing resentful. They wanted to govern themselves. A brave woman played an important role at this time.

Josefa Ortiz de Domínguez was born in Mexico City in 1768. Josefa was educated at school, which was unusual for girls in those days. In 1791 she married. Her husband was the mayor of a city in Mexico. He had been appointed by the King of Spain.

Josefa, along with most other Mexicans, objected to Spanish rule. They looked forward to the day when their country would be free. As the mayor's wife, she often heard about matters that concerned the Spanish government. She became an important link to the people who were making plans to fight for independence. She passed on to them information she thought would be helpful to their cause. She took great risks.

One day, Josefa heard that the goverment knew about the rebels' plans. Government forces were being sent to stop the revolutionary movement. She got word to the rebel leaders that they should not wait any longer to act. They decided to move at once. When the government discovered what Josefa had done, she was imprisoned for three years. In time, however, freedom from Spain was won.

The Mexican people celebrate their independence every year. Josefa is remembered on that day, along with the other great heros of the time.

Critical Thinking

1. Why would people object to being ruled by a government that was very far away?
2. What do you think would have happened if Josefa had not gotten word to the rebels of the government's plans?

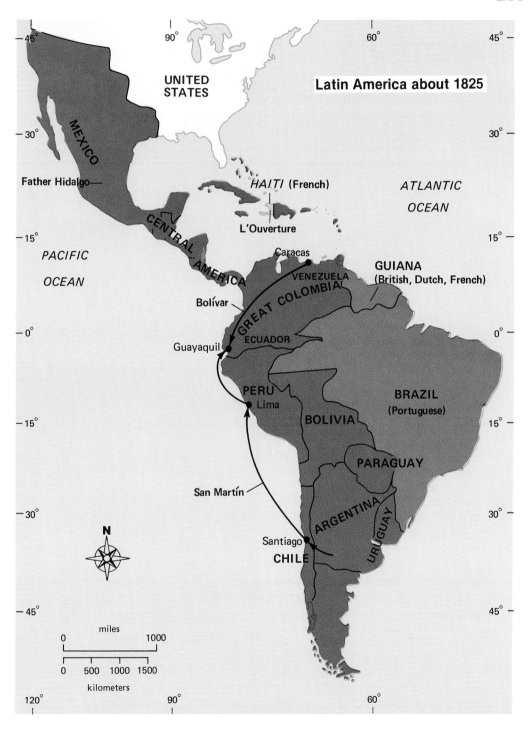

Latin America about 1825

UNITED STATES

MEXICO

Father Hidalgo

CENTRAL AMERICA

PACIFIC OCEAN

HAITI (French)

L'Ouverture

ATLANTIC OCEAN

Caracas

VENEZUELA

GUIANA (British, Dutch, French)

Bolívar

GREAT COLOMBIA

Guayaquil

ECUADOR

PERU

Lima

BOLIVIA

BRAZIL (Portuguese)

PARAGUAY

San Martín

ARGENTINA

URUGUAY

Santiago

CHILE

N

miles
0   1000

0   500 1000 1500
kilometers

90°   90°   60°
120°

AIM: What conditions led to revolution in France in the 18th century?

CHAPTER 4

Revolution in France

WHAT PROBLEMS FACED LOUIS XVI?

1. King Louis XVI, of France, was a well-meaning ruler. He wished to serve his people. But he was not the same kind of man as his ancestor, Louis XIV. If Louis XVI had been given a choice, he might have chosen to be something other than king of France. He did not know how to rule well. He changed his mind too often in order to please his ministers and his queen. His wife, Marie Antoinette, was an Austrian, the daughter of Maria Theresa. She loved being queen. To the French people, she appeared to be snobbish, proud, intolerant, and a spender of money. Worse still, she was an Austrian, and Austria was an old enemy of France.

2. Louis XVI had many problems. Before he came to the throne, France had many debts. These debts grew in number during Louis's reign. The nobles were becoming wealthier while the peasants—the majority of the people—could not better their lives. The nobles and clergy still had their old powers and privileges. They did not have to pay taxes on property, even though they owned half the land in France. Peasants had to work without pay on bridges, roads, and other public works. The growing middle class, also, was beginning to complain about the favored position of the nobles and clergy. It felt that the clergy and nobility should give up their unfair privileges.

3. Conditions were no worse in France than in other countries of Europe. Yet in France they caused a bloody revolution. Why was this so? For one thing, France had a growing middle class. It is from the middle class that the leaders

Marie Antoinette. Why was she disliked by the French people?

of revolutions usually come. In France, they were the ones who wished to rid the nobles and clergy of their special privileges. Another reason was that France was the home of men such as Voltaire and Rousseau. They had introduced revolutionary ideas. Also, France had helped the American colonies in their fight for independence from Great Britain. America's success led many French people to believe that they, too, could overthrow their king and gain freedom as the Americans had.

WHAT REFORMS DID THE FRENCH PEOPLE WANT?

4. By 1789, Louis XVI had so many debts that he needed more tax money to pay them. But when he ordered new taxes, the courts would not sign his order. Louis was forced to call together the Estates-General to approve the taxes he wanted. The Estates-General was a lawmaking body set up years before. But it did not have much power. It had not met in France for 175 years. The Estates-General had three "estates," or groups. The First Estate was made up of the clergy. The Second Estate was made up of the nobility. The Third Estate included the peasants, the middle class, and all others not in the first two estates. The people represented by the Third Estate outnumbered the other two groups by 80 to 1. But each estate voted as a group, so that there were only three votes altogether. And since the clergy and nobility agreed, the Third Estate usually lost by a 2–1 vote. In 1789, the Third Estate had enough of this unfair system. They refused to meet until it was changed so that the majority of the people could have a real voice in their government.

5. A few enlightened members of the clergy and nobility joined the Third Estate in their demands for reform. The king finally agreed to the new voting system. This was the first big step in changing the government of France. The Estates-General became a National Assembly in which voting was by individuals, not by groups. This gave control to the middle and lower classes. Many of the nobles did not like these changes, which threatened their privileges. They left the country. They were called *émigrés* (EM-ih-grays). From outside France, they tried to get rulers of other European nations to help them in stopping the reforms within France. The émigrés tried to overthrow the National Assembly by working with their friends who had stayed in France.

HOW DID MOB ACTION START THE REVOLUTION?

6. King Louis XVI then made a serious mistake. He gathered a force around him at his palace at Versailles. The people of Paris saw this move as a threat to the National Assembly. They became angry and banded together. This large group of angry people—a mob—included city workers, the unemployed, and those in Paris who saw a chance to riot and steal. On July 14, 1789, the mob captured the Bastille (bas-TEEL), a prison for those who had spoken

Why was the taking of the Bastille by the revolutionaries especially violent?

against the king. The prisoners of the Bastille were freed. Rioting then spread to the country-side. Homes and lands of nobles were raided and burned. Absolute rule had come to an end in France. Since then, Bastille Day has been celebrated as a national holiday in France.

7. Disorder continued. In October, hundreds of women marched on the royal palace at Versailles. Lafayette, who was in charge of the National Guard, saved the royal family from harm. But the marchers forced the rulers to return to Paris with them. As they made their way to Paris, the crowd shouted, "We have the baker and the baker's wife and the baker's boy—now we will have the bread." King Louis XVI and Marie Antoinette were now practically prisoners of the people of Paris.

WHAT REFORMS DID THE NATIONAL ASSEMBLY MAKE?

8. The National Assembly passed laws freeing the serfs in France. They ended almost all the privileges of the nobility and the clergy. They ended all special taxes. The Assembly wrote the Declaration of the Rights of Man, listing the ideals of the revolution. "Men are born and remain free and equal in rights," said the Declaration. It said that no one could be sent to prison without a trial. No one could be punished for his or her religious beliefs. It gave freedom of speech and of the press to all citizens.

9. The National Assembly weakened the power of the Catholic church. Church lands were taken and sold to peasants. Religious orders were ended and monasteries were closed. The Assembly ordered that priests and bishops be elected by the people. The great majority of the clergy refused to obey the new laws. They became an important group opposed to the revolution.

10. The National Assembly drew up a constitution for France. This constitution al-

Louis XVI saying farewell to his family. Why was he considered a weak ruler?

lowed the king to keep his throne, but it greatly limited his powers. The king could no longer, for example, refuse to sign any law passed by the Assembly. The constitution set up a legislative assembly, which was to make laws for France. Laws were to be the same all over France. Not everyone, however, had the right to vote for the lawmakers of the legislative assembly. Only those who could pay certain taxes were given the right to vote. Since the middle class had gained in numbers and wealth, it was now in control of France.

Testing Your Vocabulary

Choose the best answers.

1. Émigrés are people who
   a. are traitors.
   b. want to try to change their govern-ment.
   c. run away from their homeland.

2. The *reign* of King Louis XVI refers to his
   a. years of rule.
   b. weakness in governing.
   c. taxes he collected.

Understanding What You Have Read

1. A good title for paragraphs 6 and 7 is
   a. The Storming of the Bastille
   b. The March to Versailles
   c. Rioting Against the Nobles
   d. The People of Paris Take Control

2. In which paragraph do you find facts about
   a. the people who belonged to the Third Estate?
   b. the Declaration of the Rights of Man?
   c. problems facing King Louis XVI in 1789?
   d. Marie Antoinette?

3. The Third Estate wanted reforms in the Estates-General because
   a. there were more nobles than mem-bers of the clergy in the Estates-Gen-eral.
   b. the Third Estate had by far the most members but no more voting power than either of the other estates.
   c. the Estates-General had not met in 175 years.

4. One of the reasons why Marie Antoinette was disliked by the French people was that she
   a. was an Austrian.
   b. led the movement to change the Es-tates-General.
   c. was on the side of the middle class.

5. Most members of the clergy did not favor the reforms of the National As-sembly because
   a. no religious freedom was allowed.
   b. the power of the Church was weak-ened.
   c. the king was overthrown.

6. The fall of the Bastille is important in French history mostly because
   a. prisoners were freed.
   b. it ended freedom of speech.
   c. it marked the end of absolute rule.

7. Most leaders of the French Revolution were from the middle class because
   a. merchants had good reasons for dis-liking Austrian rulers.
   b. middle-class people owned most of the property in France.
   c. many middle-class people were edu-cated and paid heavy taxes, but had few rights.

In your notebook, write the word or words that best complete each statement.

1. The French Revolution began in the year _____.

2. The nobility and _____ enjoyed special privileges in France before the revolution.

3. The _____ _____, called together in 1789, had not met in 175 years.

4. In the Estates-General there were _____ estates.

5. As a result of reforms in the Estates-General, a new body called the _____ _____ was formed.
6. The palace of the king of France was located a few miles from Paris at _____ .
7. The new constitution set up a _____ _____ to make laws for France.
8. "Men are born and remain free and equal in rights" is a statement from the _____ .
9. A country that was long an enemy of France and the homeland of Marie Antoinette was _____ .
10. The mob that marched to Versailles was made up of the workers and unemployed people living in the city of _____ .

Developing Ideas and Skills

GETTING THE MEANING OF A CARTOON

Look carefully at the cartoon below. It appeared in 1789, the year the French Revolution began. Try to figure out exactly what is shown in it. Since the cartoon is about things treated in this chapter, you should review the chapter, looking for events and facts that can help you to figure out the meaning of the cartoon. When you have thought about the cartoon for a while, answer the questions below.

1. Who or what does the blindfolded man in chains represent?
2. Who or what does each of the other men stand for? How do you know?
3. What point was the cartoonist making by showing the three upright men riding on top of the chained man?
4. What facts and events of the chapter you have just studied are brought to mind by the cartoon?
5. What is the message of the cartoon?
6. Why do you think someone might decide to express such a message in a cartoon instead of in words?

Using Original Sources

The following are parts of three significant statements of liberty from three different countries. Read them carefully. Then answer the questions that follow on page 292.

Bill of Rights, England, 1689

The pretended power of suspending [ending] of laws . . . by [the king's] authority without consent of Parliament is illegal. . . . It is the right of the subjects to petition the king. . . . The levying of money for . . . the use of the crown . . . without grant of Parliament . . . is illegal. The raising and keeping of a standing army within the kingdom in time of peace unless it be with the consent of Parliament is against the law. The speech and debates . . . in Parliament ought not to be . . . questioned in any court or place out of Parliament. . . . Excessive bail ought not to be required, nor excessive fines imposed, nor cruel or unusual punishments inflicted.

Bill of Rights, United States, 1791
(from the Constitution, Amendments 1–9)

Congress shall make no law respecting [having to do with] establishment of religion, or prohibiting the free exercise thereof; or abridging [taking away] the freedom of speech or of the press . . . and to petition the government . . .

No soldiers shall, in time of peace, be quartered in any house, without the consent of the owner . . .

Nor shall [any person] be compelled . . . to be a witness against himself . . .

The accused shall enjoy the right of a speedy and public trial by an impartial jury . . . ; to be confronted with witnesses against him . . . ; Excessive bail shall not be required, nor excessive fines imposed, nor cruel and unusual punishments inflicted.

Declaration of the Rights of Man, France, 1789

Men are born free and remain equal in rights. . . . Law is the expression of the general will. Every citizen has a right to participate personally or through his representative in its [the law's] formation. . . . All citizens, being equal in the eyes of the law . . . no person shall be accused, arrested, or imprisoned except in the cases and according to the forms prescribed by law. No one shall be disquieted [attacked] on account of his opinions, including his religious views . . . every citizen may speak, write, and print with freedom, but shall be responsible for such abuses of this freedom as shall be defined by law.

Choose the correct answer.

1. The English and American Bills of Rights are almost exactly alike in their statements about
   a. freedom from search.
   b. the right of assembly.
   c. bail and punishment.
2. All of these statements
   a. show the beliefs of kings and presidents of the time.
   b. list principles to be followed.
   c. were part of court decisions.
3. Which document states that a person may not abuse his freedom of speech?
   a. the American Bill of Rights
   b. the English Bill of Rights
   c. the Declaration of the Rights of Man.
4. Which document says the most about the rights of a person accused of a crime?
   a. the American Bill of Rights
   b. the English Bill of Rights
   c. the Declaration of the Rights of Man.

TURNING POINTS

Culture

Europe: The Salons of Paris

During the 1700s, many new ideas spread across Europe. These ideas centered on the importance of knowledge and the dignity of human beings. Many of these ideas were introduced and discussed in the *salons* of Paris.

The salons were really the living rooms of some influential women in Paris. Once or twice a week these women invited guests to casual gatherings in their homes. The guests included writers, artists, musicians, and leading *philosophes* (philosophers). These people spent hours talking about philosophy, religion, the arts, literature, and government.

The women who ran the salons were intelligent and curious. They had a gift for bringing people together. They created a setting in which ideas could flow. Some of these women were also writers. A few were scientists. Others made contributions by encouraging young artists and writers.

One of the liveliest salons was held by Madame Geoffrin. Some of the most famous philosophers in France attended regularly. One was Denis Diderot, who was working on his encyclopedia. Many of the people who wrote articles for Diderot's encyclopedia were also guests at Madame Geoffrin's. It is said that the leaders of other countries sent representatives to her salon to keep up with the latest ideas.

Critical Thinking

1. Do you think the salons were good places for writers of the encyclopedia? Explain.
2. Based on what you have read, how do you think the salons influenced the French Revolution?

AIM: What changes in France resulted from the revolution?

CHAPTER 5

The French Making Lasting Changes

WHY WAS THE KING DEPOSED?

1. If only revolutions could end at a certain point, much bloodshed would not take place. But history shows us that once such movements are well under way, they are difficult to stop. The National Assembly, set up at the start of the French Revolution, had begun needed reforms. It had announced a Declaration of Rights. It had ended almost all special privileges for the clergy and nobles. It had written a new constitution which set up a legislative assembly to make laws. These were all good changes. Meanwhile, the king remained on the throne. Many people felt that there would never be true equality and liberty in France as long as there was a king or queen. In addition, peasants and other members of the lower class felt that they had gained little from the revolution so far. They saw that the middle class had gained new power. They wished the revolution to go on until they, too, had bettered their condition.

2. Those who felt that the king should be removed wanted to set up a republic in France. King Louis XVI did something that helped to further this point of view. Louis and Marie Antoinette tried to escape from France to join friends among the émigrés. They were discov-

ered, captured, and returned to Paris. It looked as though the king and queen were afraid of, and not interested in, the people. They wanted only to rule with absolute power, surrounded by the nobility.

3. Austria (Marie Antoinette's homeland) and Prussia were looked upon as enemies of the revolution. Their rulers were afraid that the revolutionary ideas of France would spread to

In what ways did Louis XVI's execution at the guillotine show the feelings of the French people?

their own countries. So they welcomed the émigrés of France and gave them military help. These two nations also demanded that Louis XVI be given back his full powers as King of France. The French legislative assembly, believing that Austria was about to attack France, declared war on both Austria and Prussia.

4. French armies met with defeat at almost every turn. Louis XVI, who was known to be in touch with people in Austria and Prussia, was blamed for the French defeats. When foreign armies invaded France, the angry Paris mob stormed the palace and took the king and queen as prisoners. The legislative assembly then decided to remove the king from his throne. They called a convention, or meeting, to set up a republic. The National Convention was made up mainly of people who belonged to the working class.

5. In 1792, the National Convention met and set up the French Republic. It also raised new armies to fight the foreign armies on French soil. The Convention wished to put down those who opposed the revolution. It set up a Committee of Public Safety to help it control the nation and further the revolution. A few months later, it brought King Louis XVI to trial as a traitor. He was found guilty and sentenced to death. In January 1793, he was beheaded by the guillotine. Marie Antoinette met the same fate ten months later.

WHAT IMPORTANT REFORMS FOLLOWED THE REIGN OF TERROR?

6. The members of the National Convention believed that anyone who did not favor the revolution was an enemy of France. The Committee of Public Safety, therefore, began to put to death all those who were thought to be against the revolution. This period is called the Reign of Terror. It is said that more than 10,000 people were killed during the Reign of Terror,

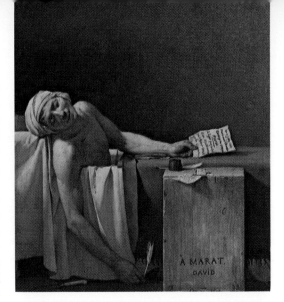

During the Reign of Terror many violent incidents occurred. This painting by David shows Marat, a revolutionary, stabbed to death while taking a bath.

which lasted more than a year. Priests and nobles were executed simply because they were members of the old privileged classes. The guillotine was the most popular means of execution. No one was safe from it. Robespierre (robz-pee-AIR) was the chief leader of the Reign of Terror. For a time, he was the most popular man in France. But when other leaders began to fear that they would be the next ones to be executed, they turned against Robespierre. He was led to the guillotine and beheaded. After this, life became calmer in France. At the same time, the French began to gain victories over their foreign enemies. The Reign of Terror came to an end.

7. The National Convention lasted until 1795. Despite its period of terror, it made important reforms. All males were given the right to vote. Black slavery in the French colonies was ended. Large estates which had been owned by nobles were broken up. This land was sold to the peasants at low prices. The metric system of weights and measures was begun in France. The Convention also drew up a new constitution. This constitution gave control of the government to five men, called directors.

294

The Directorate lasted until 1799. In that year Napoleon Bonaparte overthrew the government and became the ruler of France.

WHAT FREEDOMS DID THE FRENCH PEOPLE GAIN?

8. In a revolution, people sometimes go to extremes in showing their dislike of the old ways of living. The Reign of Terror was an example. Violence and extremism became part of the revolution. But the French people tried to erase the traces of the old way of life in other ways, too. They created a new calendar. The date of the revolution, 1789, was the Year One. They named months for seasons of the year. They ended titles of nobility. Instead, everyone was to be called "citizen." Even playing cards could no longer show kings, queens, or nobles. The style of dress was changed as long trousers took the place of knee breeches. Most of these changes lasted for only a short time.

9. The revolution also brought lasting and important changes. "Liberty, Equality, Fraternity" had been the slogan of the revolution. *Liberty* was achieved as all people gained freedom of speech, of religion, of the press, and of assembly. *Equality* was furthered as the nobility and clergy lost their special privileges. Every man became equal before the law. Slavery was ended. *Fraternity* means a feeling of unity and brotherhood among people of the same nation. The revolution brought national unity to France. But France did not become peaceful, even after six years of bloodshed. It became harder than ever to keep order. Ambitious new leaders in the army saw in this disorder an opportunity to gain power. One of these leaders was Napoleon Bonaparte.

Testing Your Vocabulary

Choose the best answer.

1. *Extremists* led the Reign of Terror. Extremists are
   a. those who want to settle differences in a calm, peaceful manner.
   b. those who sometimes use violence to gain what they want.
   c. traitors to the government.

2. During the French Revolution *fraternity* meant
   a. the brotherhood of all French people.
   b. freedom of speech.
   c. equality of all French people before the law.

Understanding What You Have Read

1. The main idea of paragraph 7 is that
   a. the Reign of Terror ended.
   b. the National Convention made important reforms.
   c. a Directory was established.
   d. the National Convention lasted only a short time.

2. In which paragraph do you find facts that tell about
   a. Robespierre?
   b. the French people's attitude toward Austria and Prussia?
   c. the changes in style of dress during the Revolution?
   d. the execution of Louis XVI and Marie Antoinette?

3. European rulers outside France fought against the French Revolution because they
   a. disliked the power of Marie Antoinette.
   b. feared that the spirit of revolt might spread throughout Europe.
   c. wanted to overthrow Catholic rule in France.

4. All of these were important results of the French Revolution EXCEPT
   a. lands taken from nobles were sold to peasants at low prices.
   b. freedom of speech and religion were gained by all Frenchmen.
   c. it was decided that the head of the government would be elected by all adults.

5. France declared war on Austria because
   a. Austria had invaded France.
   b. the French people believed that Austria was about to attack them.
   c. Marie Antoinette had returned to her homeland to seek help from the Austrian king.

6. The Reign of Terror was caused partly by the
   a. desire to rid France of all enemies of the revolution.
   b. desire to set up a republic.
   c. breaking up of large estates of the nobility.

Developing Ideas and Skills

CHRONOLOGY

Do you know the order of events? Choose the correct answer.

1. If the Age of Revolutions lasted from 1776 to 1825, it would be correct to say that it lasted
   a. three decades.
   b. about half a century.
   c. a generation.

2. Which of these statements is *true?*
   a. Thomas Jefferson could not have known about the French Revolution.
   b. King Louis XVI and Simón Bolívar lived at the same time.
   c. The French people knew about the success of the American Revolution.

3. How soon after the end of the American Revolution did the French Revolution begin?
   a. less than 10 years
   b. a little over 20 years
   c. nearly 50 years

4. Which of these events took place at the same time as the French Revolution?
   a. the Glorious Revolution in England
   b. the independence movement led by Toussaint L'Ouverture
   c. the writing of the American Declaration of Independence

Arrange the events in each lettered group in the order in which they took place.

A. the French Revolution
   the American Revolution
   the revolts in South America

B. Independence movements led by
   Father Hidalgo
   Simón Bolívar
   Toussaint L'Ouverture

C. the English Bill of Rights
   the Declaration of Independence
   the Declaration of the Rights of Man

D. Governments in France
   Estates-General
   National Convention
   National Assembly

AIM: How did the rule of Napoleon Bonaparte in France affect Europe and the world?

CHAPTER 6

Napoleon, Europe's New Master

HOW DID NAPOLEON BECOME DICTATOR?

1. Napoleon Bonaparte was to become master of Europe. He was born on the island of Corsica, off Italy, in 1769. When he died on the island of St. Helena 52 years later, a Frenchman said of him, "He was as great as man can be without virtue." Napoleon changed the course of European history. But he was not always honest in the means he used to reach his goals.

2. Napoleon married Josephine, a woman of high social position. His marriage no doubt helped his career. People first started paying attention to him when, as a young army officer, he defended the National Convention against the Paris mob. As a result, he was put in charge of the French armies in Italy and Austria. In a short time, Napoleon defeated both Austria and Sardinia. With this success, he became a national hero. Then he invaded Egypt, hoping to cut off England's trade route to India. The French fleet was defeated by Lord Nelson, however, at the Battle of the Nile.

3. Napoleon's troubles in Egypt might have caused a weaker man to worry. Napoleon, however, saw the problems that the French directors were having at home. For while Napoleon was off fighting in Egypt, the French armies had lost the European land they had won

Why do you think the French were ready for a strong leader like Napoleon after the years of the revolution?

earlier. The people blamed their leaders. Napoleon's hour had come. He returned quickly to France, overthrew the Directorate, and became ruler of France. Although France supposedly remained a republic, Napoleon actually ruled as dictator.

4. As dictator, Napoleon began to carry out great reforms for France. He set up the Bank of France and made sure that all people were taxed fairly. He built bridges, roads, and beautiful buildings. Under his rule, a system of public education under government control was begun in France. Another lasting achievement was in the field of law. He ordered that all French law be organized into one system. It was called the Code Napoleon. The code of laws was based on the ideas of the French Revolution, such as equality for all citizens. It is still used in France. It is also the basis for laws in Germany, Italy, and (within the United States) the state of Louisiana.

5. Wherever Napoleon's armies went, they spread ideas of liberty and equality. Napoleon also made important religious changes. He restored the Catholic religion as the state religion of France. He returned Church buildings taken away during the revolution. In this way, Napoleon regained the favor of the clergy, who had strongly opposed the revolution. Yet Napoleon was not a deeply religious man. He did what he thought would help to keep him in power. As he said, "I am a Muhammadan in Egypt. I am a Catholic in France." Napoleon's reforms within France and his military victories made him popular with the people. So in 1804 he took the title of Emperor, making himself absolute ruler. The French people thought they had seen the last of absolute rule in 1789. Now, 15 years later, they seemed happy to have Napoleon as absolute dictator.

6. Napoleon went on to wage war with more success than Europe had ever seen before. Great Britain joined with Austria, Prussia, and Sardinia to try to stop him. Together they failed. Napoleon defeated Austria and captured the city of Vienna. He defeated the Prussian and Russian armies and took land from Prussia. He conquered Italy and the Netherlands. He joined the smaller German states into a Confederation of the Rhine, and he made himself ruler of the Confederation.

7. Napoleon made his relatives and friends rulers of defeated nations. Thus, what he could not rule personally, his family controlled. He made allies of friendly countries which had not tried to stop him. Partly to become friendly with Austria, Napoleon divorced Josephine and married Maria Louisa. She was the daughter of the Hapsburg ruler of Austria. By 1807, Napoleon had defeated all his enemies except for Great Britain. He controlled the continent of Europe.

WHAT MISTAKES HURT NAPOLEON?

8. Napoleon saw Great Britain as his most important enemy. The English had taken away

Josephine being crowned queen. Compare the court of Napoleon with the court of Louis XVI. How are they alike? How are they different?

the French colonies in America and India. The British navy was the greatest in the world. In 1805, Admiral Horatio Nelson defeated the French fleet at the Battle of Trafalgar. This naval battle kept Napoleon from invading England. He decided that he could defeat the English in another way. England's wealth and success were based upon the export of its products. To destroy England, Napoleon decided to ruin its trade. He ordered that no nation in Europe could buy English goods. This system of not trading with England was known as Napoleon's *Continental System.* Since all the nations of Europe were either controlled by or allied with Napoleon, they had to follow the system.

9. The Continental System certainly hurt England. But it also hurt the rest of Europe. Europe wanted the goods England had to sell. Many countries began to smuggle in English goods. The French army patrolled the coasts, but they were not able to stop the British ships from coming into Europe. Then, in return, England ordered European countries not to trade with France. The English seized American ships bound for Europe, which they believed were on their way to French ports. These actions led to the War of 1812 between Great Britain and the United States.

10. The attempt to stop trade between Great Britain and Europe was one of the reasons for Napoleon's downfall, because the rest of Europe was opposed to it. Another mistake was Napoleon's attack on Russia. Earlier, Russia had been France's ally. Then Russia decided to end this alliance and buy British goods. Napoleon could not allow this. He raised an army of 600,000 men and invaded Russia in the summer of 1812.

HOW WAS NAPOLEON DEFEATED?

11. The Russians put up little defense against the invading French army. But as the Russian armies retreated, they burned their crops and their villages behind them. The French could get no supplies or food. Their supply lines became longer and harder to defend. The French army was slowed so that it did not reach Moscow until October, 1812. Then they found that the city had been burned by the Russians. They could find no food or shelter. There was no Russian government to conquer. The French army was forced to return home. As it began its slow retreat, the bitterly cold Russian winter came upon it. Thousands of French soldiers starved or froze to death. By the

Napoleon retreats. Why do you think Napoleon was such a popular leader?

time Napoleon reached Germany, there was little left of his once all-powerful army.

12. Given new hope by Napoleon's defeat, the rest of Europe joined against him. England and its allies finally defeated the French army at the Battle of Leipzig, in Germany. In the spring of 1814, the foreign forces entered Paris and Napoleon was finished—or so it seemed. He was sent into exile on the island of Elba, off the coast of Italy. But, as the victorious nations argued about their next move, Napoleon escaped from Elba and returned to France. His march to Paris in 1815 was a triumph. Soldiers sent to stop him joined him instead. Quickly raising an army of 200,000 men, Napoleon set out to destroy his enemies once more.

13. One hundred days later, at the Battle of Waterloo, in Belgium, the English and Prussian forces defeated Napoleon for the last time. The Duke of Wellington led the English forces at this historic battle. Napoleon was sent into exile once more, this time to the island of St. Helena. He died there six years later.

14. How should we judge Napoleon? He was a dictator whose word was law. During his reign, the people of France had no voice in their government. They had no freedom of speech and thus could not criticize him. But Napoleon was respected and admired by many. He was skillful in handling people and government affairs. He made important reforms in law, religion, and finance. He kept some of the reforms of the revolution. Farmers had their own land. The middle class had gained political power. All men had freedom of religion. Through Napoleon the ideals of the French Revolution—liberty, equality, and fraternity—were spread throughout Europe.

Testing Your Vocabulary

Choose the best answer.

1. Napoleon was *exiled* to Elba and St. Helena. To be exiled is to be
   a. forced to become a citizen of another country.
   b. forced to leave the country in which one was born and has lived.
   c. forced to live on an island.

2. The word with the nearest meaning to *triumph* is
   a. defeat.   b. amusement.   c. victory.

Understanding What You Have Read

1. The main idea of paragraphs 8 and 9 is that
   a. England's navy was too powerful for Napoleon to defeat.
   b. Napoleon's Continental System tried to ruin England's trade.
   c. smuggling was a common practice.
   d. Napoleon was ambitious.

2. In which paragraph do you find facts about
   a. Napoleon's reforms in law and religion?
   b. Napoleon's retreat from Russia?
   c. Napoleon's taking the title of Emperor?
   d. the effects of the Continental System on Europe?

3. England was saved from invasion by France because
   a. Prussian troops arrived in France.

b. the French decided to invade Russia instead.

c. Admiral Nelson won a naval victory at Trafalgar.

4. Napleon's Continental System failed for all of these reasons EXCEPT

a. European nations needed English goods.

b. smaller German states formed a Confederation.

c. the French fleet could not stop the smuggling that went on.

5. Napoleon invaded Egypt because

a. he wanted to cut off England's trade route to India.

b. the Egyptian king asked France for help against the English who were

invading his country.

c. French sailors trying to end smuggling were stopped by the Egyptian navy.

6. Napoleon's failure to defeat Russia was caused partly by

a. the Russians' destroying their own property.

b. the large number of people in the Russian army.

c. the arguments among Napoleon's generals.

7. All of the following were achievements of Napoleon EXCEPT the

a. Code Napoleon.

b. Bank of France.

c. Declaration of the Rights of Man.

Match the events in the second column with the places in the first column.

1. Corsica
2. Egypt
3. St. Helena
4. Germany
5. Waterloo

a. the Battle of Leipzig
b. Napoleon's exile
c. the Continental System
d. final defeat of Napoleon
e. Lord Nelson's victory over the French.
f. Napoleon's birth.

In your notebook, under the heading "Napoleon's Activities" list those activities of Napoleon that are included below.

1. Destroyed English sea power.

2. Made France a republic.

3. Tried to ruin England's trade with Europe.

4. Brought the smaller German states together in one confederation.

5. Defeated all the major nations of Europe except England.

6. Lost the support of the French when he was defeated in Russia.

7. Started a system of government-controlled public schools.

8. Won the English colonies in America.

9. Made the Catholic religion the state religion of France.

10. Spread the ideas of the French Revolution throughout Europe.

Developing Ideas and Skills

USING A MAP

Study the map on page 302 carefully. Then choose the correct answer for the statements that follow.

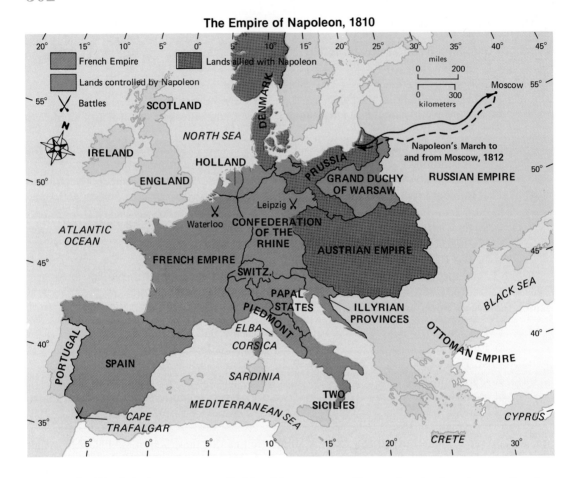

The Empire of Napoleon, 1810

1. All of these were controlled by Napoleon EXCEPT
   a. Russia.   b. Spain.   c. Holland.

2. Under Napoleon, German states were gathered together under the name of the
   a. Grand Duchy of Warsaw.
   b. Confederation of the Rhine.
   c. Austrian Empire.

3. A part of Europe NOT allied with Napoleon was
   a. Denmark.   b. Austria.   c. Sweden.

4. England was
   a. controlled by Napoleon.
   b. not controlled by Napoleon.
   c. allied with Napoleon.

5. Comparing the empire of Napoleon with Europe in 1789 (page 256), the Grand Duchy of Warsaw had taken the place of
   a. Norway.   b. Saxony.   c. Poland.

Summary of Unit VI _____

Some of the most important events and facts discussed in the unit are listed on page 303. Can you add any others?

1. The authors of the Declaration of Independence and the United States Constitution knew about the ideas of John Locke, Montesquieu, and other political writers of Europe.
2. The American Revolution did not begin until England began to tighten its control of the American colonies.
3. The American colonists won their freedom despite England's great advantages in the Revolutionary War.
4. Simón Bolívar and José de San Martín were two outstanding leaders of the independence movement in South America.
5. Having gained their independence, the Latin American people were not able to end problems of poverty, illiteracy, and class differences.
6. The growing middle class in France was well educated. They became the leaders of the French Revolution.
7. The French Revolution began as a movement to end the absolute power of the king and the special privileges of the nobility and clergy.
8. The events of the French Revolution led France into wars with other European nations. These wars lasted for almost 25 years.
9. The French Revolution brought many lasting reforms to France. It spread ideas of equality and liberty throughout Europe.
10. Napoleon Bonaparte became almost complete master of Europe. As dictator, he made important reforms in France.

Supporting Generalizations

After each generalization below, provide two additional supporting statements from your reading of Unit VI.

1. Generalization: Ideas often play an important role in revolutions.
   Supporting statements:
   a. John Locke's writings influenced thinkers in the British colonies when he wrote that governments cannot take away the natural rights of their citizens.
   b.
   c.
2. Generalization: Events in one part of the world often influence events in other parts of the world.
   Supporting statements:
   a. The success of the American Revolution encouraged the Spanish colonies in Latin America to seek independence.
   b.
   c.
3. Generalization: Revolutions do not always bring about desirable results.
   Supporting statements:
   a. One immediate result of the French Revolution was the Reign of Terror.
   b.
   c.

UNIT VII

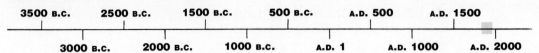

| 3500 B.C. | | 2500 B.C. | | 1500 B.C. | | 500 B.C. | | A.D. 500 | | A.D. 1500 | |
| 3000 B.C. | | 2000 B.C. | | 1000 B.C. | | A.D. 1 | | A.D. 1000 | | A.D. 2000 | |

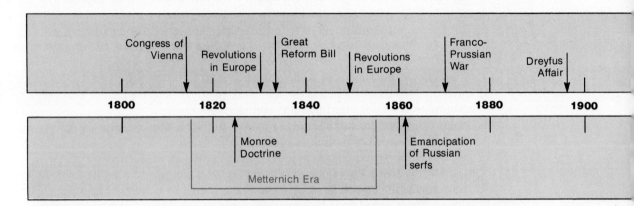

Congress of
Vienna

Revolutions
in Europe

Great
Reform Bill

Revolutions
in Europe

Franco-
Prussian
War

Dreyfus
Affair

1800   1820   1840   1860   1880   1900

Monroe
Doctrine

Emancipation
of Russian
serfs

Metternich Era

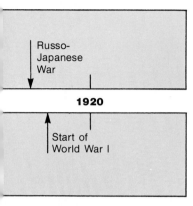

Russo-
Japanese
War

1920

Start of
World War I

How Did Democratic Ideas Grow and Spread?

A 19th-century Hungarian artist painted this scene of people enjoying music at home.

305

AIM: How did the Congress of Vienna change the map of Europe?

CHAPTER 1

The Leaders of Europe Meet

WHY DID EUROPEAN LEADERS MEET AT VIENNA?

1. After every war the hearts of people are filled with the hope that an age of peace and happiness is at hand. So it was after the wars of Napoleon. The people of Europe were hopeful that a better time had come. They believed that the leaders of Europe, who were meeting at the Congress of Vienna (1814–15), would bring them this peace. How mistaken and disappointed they were to be!

2. The Congress of Vienna was set up to solve the problems brought on by the French Revolution and Napoleon's wars. But like so many peace conferences, it turned out to be a meeting of clever but selfish leaders. The most important man at the Congress was Prince Metternich, of Austria. Other leaders present were Charles Talleyrand, of France, and Lord Castlereagh (KAS-ul-ray) and the Duke of Wellington, of Great Britain. Two kings were also present. They were Czar Alexander I, of Russia, and King Frederick William III, of Prussia. These men were all clever statesmen. They wished to get as much as possible for their own countries.

3. Czar Alexander was perhaps the only leader who was interested in the future peace of Europe. He wanted to set up a Holy Alliance to

The Congress of Vienna lasted for ten months and included lavish balls, hunts, and musicales. Beethoven conducted the first performance of his "Seventh Symphony" for the occasion.

bring Christian ideals into European affairs. The members of the Holy Alliance would rule their people with justice, charity, and peace. To please the Czar, the other nations agreed to join the Holy Alliance. But they did not take it seriously. The leaders at the Congress of Vienna had not come to talk about peace. They had come to get as much territory as possible for their own nations.

WHAT WERE THE RULES OF LEGITIMACY AND COMPENSATION?

4. Under the leadership of Prince Metternich, the Congress of Vienna agreed to follow two rules in settling Europe's problems. These were the rules of *legitimacy* and *compensation*. Legitimacy meant that all rulers who had been overthrown by Napoleon would return to their thrones. Compensation meant that the nations that had lost land to Napoleon but had helped defeat him would be paid back with territory.

5. The Congress of Vienna went about returning rulers or members of their families to their old thrones. Thus, Louis XVIII, brother of the executed Louis XVI, became king of France. A king from the House of Orange was returned to the throne of Holland. The Braganza rulers returned to Spain. The Hapsburg princes got back the Italian states they had ruled before Napoleon's conquests. By returning rulers to their thrones, the Congress of Vienna turned its back on the ideas of democracy and government by the people. These were ideas that the French Revolution had spread all over Europe. But the Congress was afraid of revolution. The powers of its leaders were threatened by revolution. So it decided to wipe out the revolutionary ideas of liberty and self-government.

6. According to the principle of compensation, Great Britain received the colonies of Ceylon, Malta, and part of South Africa. Russia was given Finland and a large part of Poland. Holland was given Belgium. Austria was repaid with the Italian provinces of Lombardy and Venetia. Sweden was given Norway.

7. The leaders at Vienna were not interested in the wishes of the people. No one asked the Belgians if they wanted to be part of Holland. No one asked the Poles or Finns if they

Metternich called the French Revolution a "disease which must be cured." What do you think he meant?

wanted to be part of Russia. People who became citizens of a country against their wishes usually felt no loyalty to their new nations. Thus the Congress of Vienna destroyed another idea spread by the French Revolution. This was the feeling of *nationalism*, or pride in one's own country.

HOW DID THE METTERNICH SYSTEM DESTROY MANY NEW FREEDOMS?

8. In almost every case, the Congress of Vienna followed the principles of legitimacy and compensation. These destroyed the ideas of democracy and nationalism. Would the people of Europe stand for this? They had learned a great deal from the French Revolution. Metternich knew that they would not be happy with his changes. But he was a clever man. Metternich made careful plans to put down any rebellions against the political order which the Congress of Vienna had set up.

9. Metternich first formed a Quadruple Alliance. This was a union of four great powers: Prussia, Great Britain, Austria, and Russia. Great Britain soon left it. But France took Britain's place. The purpose of the Quadruple Alliance was to keep peace in Europe. It was also supposed to make sure that the agreements reached at the Congress of Vienna were followed. The members of the alliance held meetings to discuss ways of preventing revolutions. If a revolution did break out anywhere in Europe, they sent their armies to put it down.

10. After the Congress of Vienna, Metternich also set up a system of spies. These spies were to report all people who spoke out against governments. Spies were put in schools, colleges, and clubs. They were sent to public meetings to report revolutionary speeches. Those who might be leaders of revolutions were arrested, jailed, exiled, or killed. A system of *censorship* was also begun. Printed articles and books were checked to see whether they criticized the government. Newspapers and even novels were censored. Metternich did his best to make sure that no democratic or nationalist ideas would be spread.

11. Metternich used a system of censorship, spies, and armed force to achieve his goals. These methods became known as the Metternich System. They were copied by the rulers of France, Russia, and Prussia. Even Great Britain was affected by Metternich's ideas. The British Parliament in 1819 passed the "Six Acts." These limited freedom of speech and assembly. New demands for democracy and reform of the British government were put down.

Testing Your Vocabulary

Choose the best answer.

1. Metternich's idea of *legitimacy* meant
   a. returning rulers to their thrones.
   b. listening to the wishes of the common people.
   c. punishing Napoleon for his crimes.
2. The idea of *compensation* followed at the Congress of Vienna meant
   a. paying the generals who defeated Napoleon.
   b. asking France to pay for damages caused by Napoleon.
   c. repaying countries that helped to defeat Napoleon.
3. When Metternich *censored* newspapers and books, he
   a. made sure that statements criticizing the government did not appear in print.
   b. added his own ideas.
   c. chose the editors.

Understanding What You Have Read _____

1. The purpose of paragraphs 5 through 7 is to explain
   a. the reasons for Napoleon's defeat.
   b. the results of the Metternich System.
   c. the reason why the Holy Alliance was formed.
   d. the principles followed by the Congress of Vienna.
2. In which paragraphs do you find facts about
   a. the meaning of legitimacy and compensation?
   b. the members of the Quadruple Alliance?
   c. the return of French rulers to their throne?
   d. the meaning of the Metternich System?
3. The Congress of Vienna followed the principle of legitimacy because
   a. it was a democratic idea.
   b. they wanted old rulers to return to their thrones in Europe.
   c. it would make France powerful again.
4. Belgium was united with Holland at the Congress of Vienna in order to
   a. make the Belgians happy.
   b. follow the idea of nationalism.
   c. repay Holland with territory.
5. Metternich started his system of spies and censorship because he wanted to
   a. stamp out democratic ideas.
   b. encourage manufacturing and industry.
   c. punish the people of France.
6. The Czar of Russia wanted to form a Holy Alliance because it would
   a. be useful in stopping revolutions.
   b. help the pope in Rome.
   c. bring Christian ideals back to Europe.
7. Great Britain was given Ceylon and Malta at the Congress of Vienna because Britain
   a. wanted to give the people of these colonies independence.
   b. had helped to defeat Napoleon.
   c. planned to send explorers to these places.

Tell whether the following statements are true or false. If a statement is false, change the words in italics to make it true.

1. Belgium was united with *Holland* at the Congress of Vienna.
2. The Duke of Wellington represented *Russia.*
3. Russia received Finland and part of *Poland.*
4. A *Triple Alliance* was organized at the Congress of Vienna.
5. The leaders at the Congress of Vienna believed in the principles of legitimacy and *nationalism.*
6. The Congress of Vienna returned Louis XVIII to the throne of *Prussia.*
7. The leading person at the Congress of Vienna was *Czar Alexander I, of Russia.*
8. The giving of Norway to Sweden followed the principle of *compensation.*
9. *France* received Ceylon and Malta at the Congress of Vienna.
10. The Hapsburg princes were given back the Italian states by the *Congress of Vienna.*

Developing Ideas and Skills

USING A MAP

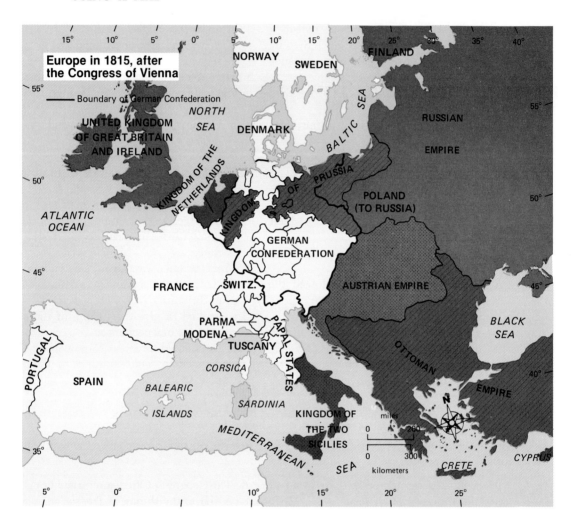

Europe in 1815, after the Congress of Vienna

—— Boundary of German Confederation

Based on what you have read in this chapter, write in your notebook the name of

1. The country whose throne King Louis XVIII was given by the Congress of Vienna.
2. The area that was given to Sweden by the Congress of Vienna.
3. The country represented by the Duke of Wellington and Lord Castlereagh at the Congress of Vienna.
4. The country of which Prince Metternich was the leader.
5. The country to whom Belgium was given by the Congress of Vienna.

AIM: How did Prince Metternich put down revolutions and stop the spread of ideas after the era of Napoleon?

CHAPTER 2

Freedom Is Put Down

WHY DID THE SPIRIT OF REVOLUTION CONTINUE TO GROW?

1. Ideas are like living things. Once they get started, they continue to grow. Two important ideas had been planted in Europe by the French Revolution. These were the ideas of democracy and nationalism. To the people of Europe, democracy meant freedom and self-government. Nationalism meant the pride people felt when united by a common language and history. It also meant their loyalty to the place where they lived.

2. For more than thirty years Prince Metternich tried to put down these ideas in Europe. But they continued to grow, first in one country and then in another. A revolutionary movement would start in one city or area. The armies of the Quadruple Alliance would crush it. Soon another revolt would begin. It, too, would be suppressed. Sometimes a revolution was successful. Most of the time it was not. Europe swayed back and forth from revolution to suppression. This period became known as the Metternich Era.

3. An early threat to the Metternich System came from the United States. You will recall that in 1819 and earlier, the Spanish colonies in South America had rebelled (page 280).

They won their independence. American leaders thought that the Quadruple Alliance wanted to help Spain get back her American colonies. The United States wanted its Latin American neighbors to keep their independence. So, in 1823, President Monroe, of the United States, gave Europe a warning. It was called the Monroe Doctrine. The Monroe Doctrine warned European nations to stay out of the affairs of all American countries.

4. England, which was a member of the Quadruple Alliance, had been carrying on a good trade with Latin America. It felt that if Spain got back control of the area, it would lose this trade. So England sided with the United States. The Quadruple Alliance, weakened by the loss of British support, had to accept the Monroe Doctrine. The Alliance felt also that European affairs needed all their attention. So it did not try to get back Spain's colonies in America. But while the Metternich System was weakened in America, it was not yet weakened in Europe.

WHY DID NEW REVOLUTIONS BREAK OUT ALL OVER EUROPE?

5. Revolutions against the Metternich System broke out all over Europe. A revolution in

President Monroe at the birth of the Monroe Doctrine. Why was it important?

Spain against King Ferdinand VII in 1820 was put down by the armies of the Quadruple Alliance. Revolutions in the Italian states of Piedmont and Naples against Austrian rulers also failed, in 1821.

6. A revolution in Greece, however, had a different result. Greece was part of the Turkish empire. The Greek people were ruled, against their wishes, by the sultan of Turkey. In 1821, they rebelled. The Quadruple Alliance had promised to put down such revolutions. The members of the Alliance, however, who ruled Christian countries, did not like the Moslem government of Turkey. Rather than help to put down the revolt, many European nations came to the aid of the Greeks with arms and money. After eight years of fighting, Greece won its independence, in 1829.

7. New revolts sprang up all over Europe in 1830. Uprisings began in France, Belgium, Poland, and many of the German and Italian states. In France, Charles X, the new king, had wiped out all the democratic gains of the French Revolution. He allowed no freedom of speech, of the press, or of religion. He ended the Chamber of Deputies. This was the parliament which had been elected by the people. When the people of Paris began to riot in 1830, Charles was forced to leave the country. The French people then chose Louis Philippe as their new ruler. This is known as the July Revolution.

8. The July Revolution in France was caused by the suppression of democracy. But the revolution in Belgium in 1830 was caused by the spirit of nationalism. The Congress of Vienna had joined Belgium to Holland. But the Belgians wanted to be independent. They were different from the Dutch of Holland. The Belgians spoke either French or Flemish, or both. But the people of Holland spoke only Dutch. Most Belgians were Catholic. The Dutch were mainly Protestant. Most Belgians were merchants and manufacturers. The Dutch were farmers. These differences and national pride brought on the Belgian uprising. Belgium declared its independence. Soon Holland and the other nations of Europe accepted Belgium as an independent nation.

9. A nationalist revolt in Poland, however, failed. Most of Poland had been given to Russia at the Congress of Vienna. In 1831 the Polish people started an uprising. They wished to become independent. But Czar Nicholas I, of Russia, put down the Polish revolt with great cruelty. Uprisings in the German and Italian states were also crushed at this time.

The French people revolted again in 1848. The Second French Republic was set up. How did this affect the rest of Europe?

WHAT BROUGHT THE METTERNICH SYSTEM TO AN END?

10. How much longer could the Metternich System hold back democracy and nationalism in Europe? It continued for 33 years (1815–48) after the Congress of Vienna. Then violence again broke out all over Europe. It began in 1848 with a new uprising in France. The workers of Paris became tired of the dishonest and undemocratic government of King Louis Philippe. They started a short but bloody revolution. Thousands of workers lost their lives. Louis Philippe escaped from France. The Second French Republic was set up. (The First French Republic had been set up during the French Revolution.)

11. Political leaders said, "When France sneezes, all Europe catches cold." Uprisings in France always stirred up revolutions in other parts of Europe. News of the French revolt spread throughout Europe in 1848. Revolts started in Austria, Hungary, Prussia, and in many of the Italian states. Some of these uprisings were for more self-government. Some were for national independence. Others were caused both by democratic and by nationalistic desires.

12. When revolution broke out in Austria, Metternich's home in Vienna was set on fire by rioters. Metternich hid in a laundry wagon and then escaped to England. The Austrian army, however, was able to crush the revolt. It also put down the uprisings in Hungary and in the

This cartoon shows Metternich fleeing from Austria after the revolution of 1848. Why do you think the cartoonist portrayed him with such a long nose?

Italian states. In Prussia, the uprising began when the king broke his promise to grant a constitution. This uprising failed. Indeed, most of the revolutions of 1848 failed. But the Metternich System had come to an end. As the smoke of the last 1848 uprising cleared, Europe stood at the beginning of a new era of democracy and nationalism.

Testing Your Vocabulary

Choose the best answer.

1. The spirit of *nationalism* in Europe meant
   a. the desire to get the right to vote.
   b. the hope of people having the same history and customs to become a united nation.
   c. the desire of nations to gain colonies.

2. When Metternich *suppressed* revolts in Europe he
   a. agreed to let the rebelling people have self-government.
   b. tried to capture the leaders of the revolts.
   c. used force to stop the uprisings.

Understanding What You Have Read

1. A good title for paragraphs 7 through 9 would be
   a. How the Greeks Won Their Independence.
   b. Why the Metternich System Failed.
   c. Revolutions in Europe in 1830.
   d. How the Belgians Won Their Independence.

2. In which paragraphs do you find facts about
   a. the ideas spread in Europe by the French Revolution?
   b. the revolution in Belgium?
   c. the end of the Metternich System?
   d. the purpose of the Monroe Doctrine?

3. The Greek revolution against the Turkish sultan succeeded because
   a. the Quadruple Alliance favored a Moslem Government for Greece.
   b. the Quadruple Alliance helped the Turks with money.
   c. European nations helped the Greeks with arms and money.

4. The French people started the July Revolution against King Charles X in 1830 because he
   a. did not allow freedom of speech, of the press, or of religion.
   b. started a war of conquest.
   c. formed an alliance with Russia.

5. The United States announced the Monroe Doctrine because
   a. it did not want Spain to get back her American colonies.
   b. Spain had agreed to help the United States.
   c. the United States had colonies in South America.

6. The Belgians did not want to belong to Holland because
   a. the Dutch ruled the Belgians with absolute power.
   b. the Belgians wanted to be part of France.
   c. the Belgians and Dutch had different languages, religions, and economic interests.

Tell whether you *agree* or *disagree* with the following statements, giving reasons for your answers.

1. The Metternich System failed partly because people will generally fight for freedom.
2. The French Revolution helped to spread the idea of nationalism.
3. The Monroe Doctrine helped American nations to remain independent.
4. The many revolutions in France showed that the people were not ready for self-government.
5. The Belgians and the Dutch would have learned to live under one government if they had tried a while longer.
6. The Polish people were cruelly treated by the Russians when the revolution in 1830 was suppressed.
7. Whenever the French had a revolution in the 19th century, people of other countries also revolted.
8. During the Metternich era, nationalist uprisings in the German and Italian states were successful.

Developing Ideas and Skills

USING A TIME LINE

Examine this time line carefully. Copy it in your notebook, adding the number of each event below its correct arrow. There may be more than one number below an arrow.

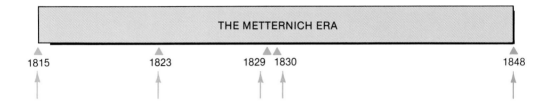

THE METTERNICH ERA

1815   1823   1829 1830   1848

1. Metternich fled from Austria.
2. Congress of Vienna met.
3. United States announced the Monroe Doctrine.
4. Charles X was overthrown in France.
5. Greeks won independence from Turkey.
6. Belgium declared its independence from Holland.
7. King Louis Philippe left France because of a revolution.

Using Original Sources

Prince Metternich was chief minister of Austria for almost forty years. After the Congress of Vienna (1815), he set up a system to suppress all liberal ideas and all democratic movements. In a secret note to Czar Alexander I, of Russia, in 1820, he explained his ideas.

Metternich's Note to Czar Alexander I

. . . The revolutionary seed has entered into every country and spread, more or less. It was greatly developed under the rule of the military despotism of Bonaparte. . . . It followed that the revolutionary spirit could in Germany, Italy, and later on in Spain easily hide itself under the cover of patriotism. . . .

It is mainly the middle classes of society that this moral decay has affected, and it is only among them that the real heads of the party are found. For the great mass of the people it has no attraction. . . . We are convinced that society can no longer be saved without strong and vigorous actions on the part of the governments still free in their opinions and actions. . . .

> The monarchs will fulfill the duties given to them by Him who, by entrusting them with power, has charged them to watch over the keeping of justice, and the rights of all, to avoid the paths of error and walk firmly in the way of truth. . . . Union between the monarchs is the basis of the policy which must now be followed. . . . In short, let the great monarchs strengthen their union, and prove to the world that if it exists it promotes what is good and protects the political peace of Europe. . . .

Choose the best answer for each of the following questions.

According to this note, Metternich believed that

1. the leaders of revolutionary movements were generally from
   a. the middle class.
   b. the peasants.
   c. the nobility.

2. monarchs may rule by
   a. right of election.
   b. right of victory in battle.
   c. divine right.

3. to stop revolutions, rulers should
   a. build up industries.
   b. give the people the right to vote.
   c. form alliances with one another.

TURNING POINTS

Government

Latin America: Princess Isabel of Brazil

At the end of the 19th century, several important changes were taking place in Brazil. One very important change was brought about with the help of Princess Isabel.

Princess Isabel was the daughter of Dom Pedro II, who was the emperor of Brazil. Because she was in line for the throne, Isabel took her responsibilities very seriously. She often helped her father with matters that affected the country. Among her concerns was the well-being of the poor people of Brazil.

In 1888, Dom Pedro II was on a visit to Europe. Princess Isabel was acting as empress while he was away. During this time, the Brazilian parliament met. They were considering a bill that would free all the slaves in the country. Like her father, Isabel was in favor of the bill. She believed that slavery was wrong and should be outlawed.

Isabel led the fight to free the slaves. When the bill was presented to her, she signed it at once. On May 13, 1888, the bill passed. The news was announced to the public. The people of Brazil cheered and paraded through the streets of the city.

Critical Thinking

1. From the article, do you think that most Brazilian people were in favor of or against the bill that freed the slaves?
2. Do you think that Dom Pedro respected and trusted his daughter? Explain.

CHAPTER 3

Democracy Grows in England

HOW DID DEMOCRACY BEGIN IN ENGLAND?

1. When mountain climbers go from one peak to another, they must cross the valley in between. The countries of Europe climbed two political mountain peaks in the 19th century. The first was the French Revolution (1789–1799). From it they learned the ideas of liberty and democracy. The second was the period after 1848, when they began to use these ideas. Between these peaks was the political valley. This was the Metternich Era (1815–48), when democratic ideas were suppressed.

2. The second peak was the age of reform in Europe that followed the Metternich Era. During this time of reform (1848–1914), ideas of democracy grew stronger in Great Britain, France, and Italy. In other countries, such as Germany, Austria, and Russia, the ideas of democracy were still put down by absolute rulers.

3. In England, the birthplace of modern democracy, the Magna Carta brought the first gains in self-government to the people. Hundreds of years before the French Revolution, the nobles of England gained certain rights from their ruler. They did this by forcing King John to sign the Magna Carta, in 1215. The Magna Carta limited the ruler's power. It gave the nobles certain rights. In the 17th century, Parliament passed the Petition of Right, the Habeas Corpus (HAY-bee-us KOR-pus) Act, and the Bill of Rights. The Petition stated that no taxes could be levied without Parliament's consent. The Habeas Corpus Act held that no one could legally be put into prison without first being given a fair trial. And the Bill of Rights made Parliament the strongest political power in Great Britain.

WHAT UNDEMOCRATIC CONDITIONS CONTINUED IN ENGLAND?

4. At the beginning of the 19th century, Great Britain had made gains in democratic government. Englishmen had gained personal liberties. Parliament, rather than the king, passed the laws. But there were still many weaknesses in the English government. Members of Parliament were not paid. Thus, only wealthy landowners could become lawmakers. Only men with a certain amount of property had the right to vote. Craftsmen, farmers, businessmen, workers, and women could not vote. In addition, voting was not secret. Many people were afraid to vote as they really wished. Dishonest men running for office could easily pay people to vote for them.

5. Delegates to Parliament were elected from areas called boroughs. At first, the number of representatives from each borough had been based on the number of people living there. But these numbers had not been changed as the population changed. As a result, some boroughs with few people sent many representatives to Parliament. They were called "rotten boroughs." But new factory cities, such as Birmingham and Leeds, had gained large populations. Yet they had no delegates at all in Parliament. Also, members of Parliament had to belong to the Church of England. Catholics, Jews, and other Protestants, therefore, could not be elected to Parliament.

WHAT REFORMS WERE FINALLY MADE?

6. When the French Revolution began, in 1789, hopes were high that democratic reforms would come to England. But the bloodshed of the French Reign of Terror frightened the British ruling class. They would allow no reforms in England. The ideals of the French Revolution, however, could not be held back forever. Demands for reform in England grew stronger as

memories of the Reign of Terror faded. The Industrial Revolution in England had created new social classes. These included businessmen, factory owners, and factory workers. They too wanted to have a voice in their government. In 1832, Lord John Russell introduced a famous law in Parliament. It is known as the Great Reform Bill.

7. The Great Reform Bill lowered the amount of property that a man had to own in order to vote. This meant that farmers who rented their land could vote. The middle class of merchants, factory owners, and businessmen also gained the right to vote. Farmers and factory workers, however, gained little from the bill. The Great Reform Bill gave the factory cities of England more representatives in Parliament. It ended the "rotten boroughs" by taking away their representatives. The Bill almost brought on civil war. The wealthy landowners strongly opposed it. The famous British war hero, the Duke of Wellington, was the leader of the opposition. But the Bill was finally passed. Thus, the modern age of democratic reform began in England.

8. The Reform Bill of 1832 was the first step. The English people now found it easier to make other reforms. In 1838, English workers began a drive for reform called the Chartist Movement. It lasted ten years. The Chartists, as

The wealthy had beautiful homes in the English countryside.

What can you tell about life in a large factory town from this picture?

they were called, wanted all males to be able to vote. They wanted voting to be made secret. They also hoped to give men who did not own property the right to serve in Parliament. They wanted members of Parliament to be paid. Most of the Chartists demands were later made into law. The movement in England began at about the same time that revolutions against the Metternich System were going on all over Europe. In the United States President Andrew Jackson had brought about a new era of democracy.

9. The British Conservative Party included many rich landowners. Even they saw that peaceful reform was better than revolution. So the leader of their party, Benjamin Disraeli (diz-RAY-lee), introduced a second Reform Bill. It was passed by Parliament in 1867. The new law gave male city workers the right to vote. In 1872 Parliament passed the Secret Ballot Act. It allowed voting to be secret.

10. In 1884, William E. Gladstone, the leader of the Liberal Party, backed the third Reform Bill. This law gave male farm workers the right to vote. After World War I, most women thirty years of age or over got the right to vote. Finally, in 1928, Parliament passed a law giving the right to vote to all men and women over the age of 21. Thus Parliament, using peaceful methods, brought about one of the chief goals of democracy. It gave every British citizen the right to vote.

Although his first speech to parliament was not received well, Disraeli became the leader of the Conservative Party. He was responsible for establishing important social legislation.

Testing Your Vocabulary

Choose the best answer.

1. The *reforms* demanded by the Chartist movement were
   a. lists of candidates for Parliament.
   b. changes in government and voting regulations.
   c. religious beliefs.

2. The Secret *Ballot* Act of 1872 provided for secrecy
   a. in forming political parties.
   b. in sending demands of factory workers to Parliament.
   c. in voting.

Understanding What You Have Read

1. A good title for paragraphs 4 and 5 is
   a. The Struggle Between King and Parliament.
   b. The Unification of Great Britain.
   c. Weaknesses in British Government before the Nineteenth Century.
   d. How the Government in Great Britain Works.
2. In which paragraph do you find facts about
   a. women in England gaining the right to vote?
   b. the Chartist movement?
   c. the passing of the Reform Bill of 1832?
   d. the signing of the Magna Carta?
3. England has been called the birthplace of modern democracy because
   a. the middle class gained the vote in the 17th century.
   b. the power of the ruler was limited, for the first time, by the Magna Carta.
   c. the ruler was forced to give the vote to the peasant farmers.
4. "Rotten boroughs" were unfair because
   a. industrial cities had more representatives than country districts.
   b. they had small populations but many representatives in Parliament.
   c. political leaders in these boroughs were dishonest.
5. The Chartist movement was important because
   a. most of its democratic demands were later made into law.
   b. it was the first movement based on socialist ideas.
   c. it favored the large landowners of England.
6. The reform movement in 19th-century England was held back for many years because
   a. British rulers opposed anything that would give the nobles more power.
   b. British businessmen and merchants felt it would make the farmers too powerful.
   c. the British ruling class remembered the French Reign of Terror.
7. At the beginning of the 19th century England was more democratic than most other European countries because
   a. women in England had the right to vote.
   b. voting was done in secret.
   c. laws were passed by Parliament instead of by order of the ruler.

Match the *causes* in the first column with the *results* in the second column.

Causes	Results
1. the Chartist movement	a. Disraeli's Reform Bill passed
2. French Reign of Terror	b. property ownership no longer needed for membership in Parliament
3. city workers demand right to vote	c. Magna Carta signed
4. Rotten Boroughs	d. Great Reform Bill passed
5. King John's struggle with nobles	e. political reforms held back in England

Developing Ideas and Skills

MAKING A CHART

Using the information in this chapter, complete the following chart in your notebook on Steps in British Democracy.

Law	Date	Gains in Democracy
1. Great Reform Bill	1832	_____
2. _____	1867	Gave vote to city workers
3. Secret Ballot Act	____	_____
4. Third Reform Bill	____	_____

Using Original Sources

In the early 19th century the British took an important step to make their government more democratic. The Great Reform Bill was introduced in Parliament in 1831. One of its most important parts aimed at putting an end to "rotten boroughs." For many months the members of Parliament argued about the bill, until it was finally passed (1832). The following is part of a speech given in Parliament by Lord John Russell in which he asked that the reform bill be passed.

Debate over the Great Reform Bill

Now suppose that a foreigner . . . were told that in this most wealthy, most civilized, and most free country, the representatives of the people . . . were chosen only every six years, would he not be very curious and very anxious to hear in what way that operation was performed? . . . Would not such a foreigner be much astonished [surprised] if he were taken to a green mound and informed that it sent two members to the British Parliament? . . . if he were shown a stone wall, and told that it also sent two members to the British Parliament? . . . He would be still more astonished were he to go into the northern part of the country, and were to see flourishing [growing successfully] towns, containing immense [huge] manufactories [factories] . . . and be informed that these places sent no representatives to Parliament. He would be still more astonished . . . [in] Liverpool for instance . . . [to] see bribery prevail [take place] to the greatest extent; he would see men openly paid for their votes.

Tell whether the following statements are true or false. If a statement if false, change the words in italics to make it true.

According to this speech, Lord John Russell said:
1. Members of Parliament were elected *every year.*
2. Many British cities sent no representatives to *Parliament.*
3. Dishonesty in elections was common in the city of *Liverpool.*
4. Some small boroughs had more *representatives* in Parliament than large cities.
5. Most factory towns were in *southern* England.

TURNING POINTS

Government

The World: The Influence of English Law

Australia. India. Guyana. Jamaica. Canada. The United States. These are all different countries that are spread across the world. They are united, however, in one important way. They share features of a legal system that was developed in England.

According to the English system, certain rights of the individual are protected by law. Such rights include the right to own property. Another is the right of a person accused of a crime to have a fair trial. Because England's legal system held these rights to be important, English colonies often developed in democratic ways.

Before the English came to Guayana and Jamaica, people accused of crimes did not have a right to a trial in a court of law. English law made sure that they did have this right. Before the British came to India, women did not have the same right to own property as did men. English law ordered that Indian women should have many of the same rights as men. Also, Indian law did not have a way for people to choose how to give away their property after death. English law introduced the practice of writing a will. With wills, people could decide exactly to whom they wanted to leave their property.

One of the most important rights provided by English law is the right of *habeas corpus. Habeas corpus* is a Latin phrase meaning "you are ordered to have the body." It means that a person cannot be held in prison without the approval of the courts. This made it less possible for a ruler to have someone jailed without the approval of the courts. This right is part of the legal systems of Australia, India, Guyana, Jamaica, Canada, and the United States. Because of the influence of English law, all of these countries have developed legal systems that provide their citizens with basic democratic rights.

Critical Thinking

1. How did the English legal system lead to the growth of democracy in India?
2. How did the right of *habeas corpus* limit the powers of a ruler?

AIM: How does the British parliamentary system of government work?

CHAPTER 4

Freedom under the British Government

HOW DID THE BRITISH RULERS LOSE THEIR POWER?

1. The United States and Great Britain are two very important democratic countries in the world today. The governments of most other democratic nations are based on the government of one or the other. If we know how the British and United States governments work, therefore, we can understand the governments of almost all free nations. The British government is one of the oldest democratic governments. It is almost seven hundred years old. But there have been changes within it many times.

2. The British ended the absolute rule of their kings and queens with two revolutions. One revolution took place in 1649, when King Charles I was beheaded. The other was the Glorious Revolution. It took place in 1688, when King James II was forced to leave England. Since then, the English have tried to keep revolutions from happening. They would rather have laws passed by Parliament than have more bloodshed. In modern times, therefore, democratic reforms have come to England through *evolution,* or slow change, rather than through revolution, or sudden change.

3. Great Britain has had a king or queen for many centuries. But today the monarch, a queen, has practically no power. She "reigns"; that is, she is recognized as the head of state. But she does not "rule." The queen or king still has the power to pass or veto (turn down) laws. But no British king or queen has dared to veto a law of Parliament since 1707. The king or queen of Great Britain serves mainly as a symbol of the unity of the nation. The most important power in the British government is not the king or queen, but Parliament.

English Houses of Parliament. Describe the difference between political evolution in England and political revolution in France.

Queen Elizabeth II. What is the role of the monarchy in British government today?

WHAT ARE PARLIAMENT'S POWERS?

4. Parliament is the lawmaking body of England. It meets every year and has unlimited power. England has no written constitution. Therefore all acts of Parliament are the law of the land. Also, no English court can say a law is unconstitutional. Like the Congress of the United States, the British Parliament is made up of two branches. They are the House of Lords and the House of Commons. The members of the House of Lords hold their office for life. They are appointed by the king or queen. Some of them have the right to pass their seats on to their children. The House of Commons is the more important branch of Parliament. Its members are elected by the people, usually every five years. Sometimes an election is called before five years are up.

5. Before 1911, the House of Lords and the House of Commons had equal power in passing a law. Both houses had to pass a bill before it could become a law. But an act passed in 1911 took away most of the lawmaking power of the House of Lords. In 1909, the House of Lords had vetoed a law that levied heavy taxes on rich landowners. The House of Commons decided it was time to end the power of the House of Lords. It asked the king for help. The king agreed. He threatened to appoint more nobles to the House of Lords. The new nobles would vote to end the veto power of the Lords. The threat worked.

6. The Parliament Act was passed in 1911. Under this law, the House of Lords gave up most of its lawmaking power. Under the Parliament Act, the House of Lords could hold up the passage of money bills for only 30 days. It could hold up the passage of all other bills for no more than two years. In 1949, this was changed to one year. Thus, the House of Lords, by its own vote, lost its power to veto bills. Today, all it can do is hold up the passing of laws for a short time. The House of Commons has supreme power in the government of England.

HOW DO THE BRITISH PRIME MINISTER AND CABINET RULE ENGLAND?

7. There are usually two main political parties in Parliament. From the party that has a majority of the members of the House of Commons, a prime minister is chosen. The prime minister becomes the head of government. He or she, in turn, chooses a cabinet. It is a group of people who will help the prime minister lead Parliament. The prime minister and cabinet introduce the laws. They see to it that laws that have been passed are carried out. If a prime minister or cabinet member introduces a bill, it is usually passed. If it is not, the prime minister and the cabinet may have to resign.

8. Thus the prime minister and the cabinet

must act according to the wishes of the House of Commons. This is called *ministerial responsibility*. If they have to resign, a new prime minister and cabinet will be chosen. This is usually done by holding new elections. Again, the party getting a majority of the seats in the House of Commons chooses the new prime minister and cabinet. The king or queen always accepts the new prime minister and the cabinet as "His or Her Majesty's government."

9. The governments of Great Britain and of the United States are both democratic. But they are quite different. The United States government is a *congressional* government. The British government is a *parliamentary-cabinet* government. In the United States, the president is elected by the people. In England, the people elect the members of the House of Commons, which then chooses the prime minister. The president of the United States must follow the wishes of the people. The prime minister of England must follow the wishes of the House of Commons.

10. In the United States, the president and Congress are separate. Presidents do not make laws. They *enforce* laws, or see to it that they are carried out. In Great Britain, the prime minister and the cabinet both help make and enforce the laws. The citizens of both countries

Margaret Thatcher was made prime minister of England in 1979.

are given their civil rights by a Bill of Rights. Both countries have two major political parties. The two major parties in Great Britain today are the Conservative Party and the Labor Party. The two major parties in the United States are the Republican and Democratic Parties.

Testing Your Vocabulary

Choose the best answer.

1. When presidents of the United States *enforce* a law, they
   a. introduce it in Congress.
   b. make sure that it is carried out.
   c. discuss its advantages and disadvantages with the cabinet.

2. The British king or queen has no *veto* power over laws. This means that he or she
   a. cannot keep them from being passed.

   b. cannot enforce them.
   c. cannot introduce them into Parliament.

3. The *cabinet*, an important part of the British government, is
   a. a supreme court.
   b. a group of members of the House of Lords.
   c. a group of people who work with the prime minister.

325

Understanding What You Have Read _____

1. The purpose of paragraphs 7 and 8 is to explain
   a. the British cabinet system.
   b. the powers held by the British king or queen.
   c. the Glorious Revolution in England.
   d. the British constitution.

2. In which paragraphs do you find facts about
   a. ministerial responsibility in the British government?
   b. the Parliament Act of 1911?
   c. what the queen of England stands for today?
   d. the names of English political parties today?

3. The British king or queen "reigns but does not rule" because he or she
   a. opens all meetings of Parliament.
   b. has his or her picture on all postage stamps.
   c. heads the state but has no voice in lawmaking.

4. British courts cannot declare laws unconstitutional because
   a. judges are appointed by the monarch
   b. there is no written constitution.
   c. Parliament can force judges to resign.

5. The prime minister is the most important person in the British government because he or she
   a. holds office for life.
   b. can veto laws.
   c. leads the majority party in Parliament.

6. The British Parliament Act of 1911 resulted in
   a. a sharp loss of power by the House of Lords.
   b. a growth in the number of members in Parliament.
   c. reform of the British cabinet system.

7. The House of Commons is the most important branch of the British Parliament because
   a. it has more members than the House of Lords.
   b. it is the oldest branch of the government.
   c. it has almost all of the lawmaking power.

In your notebook, complete the following statements by filling in the correct word or group of words.

1. The two branches of the British Parliament are the House of Lords and the _____ .

2. The head of the British government is the _____ .

3. The House of Lords lost most of its lawmaking power when the _____ was passed in 1911.

4. The members of the House of Lords are appointed by the _____ .

5. The president of the United States is elected to office by the people. The prime minister of Great Britain is chosen by the _____ .

6. The two major political parties in Great Britain today are the Conservative Party and the _____ .

7. The British revolution that forced King James II to leave England is known as the _____ .

8. "He or She reigns but does not rule." This refers to the British _____ .

9. Unless a special election is called, a member of the House of Commons serves for _____ years.

10. The House of Lords can hold up passage of a money bill for no longer than _____ .

Developing Ideas and Skills

UNDERSTANDING DIAGRAMS

Examine the following diagrams of the United States and British governments. Then answer in a few sentences the question that follows them. (You might wish to first review paragraphs 7-10.)

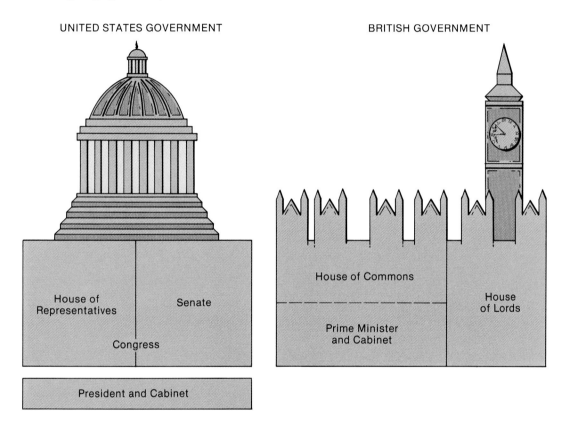

Question: What important differences between the two governments are shown in these diagrams?

AIM: How did the French government come to be what it is today?

CHAPTER 5

The French Change Their Government

WHY HAS THE FRENCH GOVERNMENT CHANGED SO OFTEN?

1. Two hundred years ago, the government of England was a parliamentary democracy. It is the same today. Two hundred years ago France was ruled by an absolute king. Since then, France has had four revolutions, six kings, and five republics. Why has the government of France had so many changes? One of the reasons is that many of the French rulers of modern times refused to allow democratic reforms. The people revolted to gain democracy.

2. France's many wars have also kept its government from becoming strong. German armies have invaded France three times in a single century. The first time was the Franco-Prussian War (1870–71). The second was World War I (1914–18). The third was World War II (1939–45). In the Franco-Prussian War and in World War II, the French were defeated. Defeat in a war usually meant the end of whichever government was then in power. The history of France since the revolution of 1789 has been a story of many sudden changes.

3. We have already read about the French Revolution that began in 1789 (page 286). We have also read about the short revolutions for reform in France in 1830 and 1848, during the Metternich Era. After the revolution of 1848, Louis Philippe, the French king, was forced to leave the country. A Second French Republic was formed. The people elected as their president Louis Napoleon. He was the nephew of Napoleon Bonaparte. The name Napoleon was a magic word to the people of France. The new Napoleon, like his uncle, wanted to be an emperor, not a president.

4. Louis Napoleon made himself Emperor Napoleon III in 1852. Thus, the Second French Republic ended and the Second Napoleonic empire began. The people of France agreed to this. Like his uncle, Napoleon III wanted to make France great by winning military victories. Napoleon III, however, was not the brilliant military leader his uncle had been. First he tried to set up a "puppet government" in Mexico. He put a ruler of his choice on the Mexican throne. This ruler, Maximilian, was Napoleon III's "puppet" because Napoleon could tell him what to do. Maximilian was an Austrian archduke. The Maximilian affair ended in failure, however. The Mexican people revolted and overthrew Maximilian.

5. The Franco-Prussian War began in

1870 when Napoleon III argued with Prussia. The French armies were badly defeated. Napoleon III was taken prisoner. When news of this defeat reached France, a short uprising began. The Second French Empire came to an end. A Third French Republic was set up in 1871. This Republic was supposed to last only a short time, until a king of France could be chosen. But rivalry between two royal families kept either one from gaining the throne.

HOW DID LATER FRENCH REPUBLICS GOVERN?

6. The Third Republic was supposed to be a temporary one. Yet it lasted almost seventy years, until 1940. It turned out to be one of the steadiest governments of modern France. It ended when the Nazi armies of Germany conquered France during World War II. The Third French Republic had many difficult problems or crises. The Boulanger (boo-lan-ZHAY) Affair, for example, almost ended the Third Republic in 1889. General Georges Boulanger of the

French army tried to take control of the government, but he failed.

7. The famous Dreyfus (DRY-fus) Affair, in 1894, was a more serious crisis. Captain Alfred Dreyfus, of the French army, was accused of helping Germany. He was found guilty of being a traitor. It was later proven that high French army officers had accused Dreyfus falsely in order to cover up their own treason. In a new trial Dreyfus was found innocent. He was given back his rank in the army. The Third French Republic also lived through the crisis of World War I. In this war, the French armies stopped the Germans from capturing Paris. But in World War II, the armies of Nazi Germany took Paris. They conquered all of France, thus ending the Third French Republic, in 1940.

8. After World War II, when the Germans had been defeated, a Fourth French Republic (1946–58) was set up. It failed to work well or last very long because of rivalry among many political parties. You will recall that the United States and Great Britain have always had two main political parties each. The French, however, had many parties during the Fourth Re-

Maximilian was executed by troops of the Mexican Republic in 1867 after Napoleon III was forced to withdraw his troops from Mexico.

The court decision declaring Dreyfus innocent established civil authority over military authority.

public. Sometimes there were as many as 12 or 15 different political parties. Because of this, no single political party could get a majority of the votes in the Fourth Republic.

9. In order to pass laws, several small parties would have to join together. They could then form *blocs*, which could control a majority of the votes. But these blocs never lasted long. In the twelve years of the Fourth French Republic more than twenty different cabinets were formed and then overthrown. The average life of each cabinet was about six months. Blocs and cabinets could not hold together long enough to pass important laws. France was always in the middle of a political crisis.

HOW DOES THE FIFTH REPUBLIC WORK?

10. In 1958, General Charles de Gaulle, a hero of World War II, asked the French people to accept a new constitution. The people of France agreed. Thus began the Fifth French Republic. It is still the government of France today. The Fifth French Republic is made up of a president and a premier (prime minister). It also has a national assembly of two houses: a chamber of deputies and a senate. Under the French constitution and its amendments, the French president is elected by the people for seven years. Charles de Gaulle, the first president, resigned in 1969.

11. Under the Fifth French Republic, the president has many powers. The president appoints the premier. (In England, the prime minister is chosen by Parliament.) The French president can end the national assembly after one year and call for new elections. In a crisis, the president can assume the powers of a dictator. The national assembly can pass laws only on certain matters. All other matters are decided by the president.

12. France still has many parties. These do not cause the political crises that they did in the

Charles de Gaulle. How is the power of the French president like the power of the British prime minister? How are they different?

past, however. This is because the president is elected for seven years and also chooses the premier. So there is always a head of government. Under the Fifth Republic, France is a democracy. Freedom of speech, of the press, and of religion, and the right to vote, are given to all. The president and the national assembly are elected by the people. The president of France, however, has far more power than the British prime minister or the president of the United States. Is it wise to give so much power to one person? How long will the Fifth French Republic last? Only time will answer these questions.

Testing Your Vocabulary

Choose the best answer.

1. France has had five different republics. A *republic* is a government in which
   a. people do not have the right to vote.
   b. the people rule through their representatives and leader.
   c. there is a supreme court that makes legal decisions.
2. Napoleon III set up a *puppet* ruler in Mexico. Such a ruler is
   a. a dictator.
   b. a foreigner.
   c. a leader who obeys another, more powerful leader.
3. The Third French Republic was supposed to be *temporary*. This meant
   a. it was to last for a short time only.
   b. it was to be the permanent government.
   c. it was to be run by an elected president.

Understanding What You Have Read

1. A good title for paragraphs 3 through 5 is
   a. How the French Government Works.
   b. De Gaulle's Political Reforms.
   c. The Rise and Fall of Napoleon III.
   d. Crises of the Third French Republic.
2. In which paragraphs do you find facts about
   a. the Maximilian Affair in Mexico?
   b. the Dreyfus Affair?
   c. the Fifth French Republic?
   d. blocs and cabinets in the Fourth French Republic?
3. France's many changes in government were partly caused by
   a. its two-party system.
   b. the lack of a strong French middle class.
   c. its many wars, especially with Germany.
4. France's change in government in 1871 was caused by
   a. the beginning of World War I.
   b. the fall of Metternich.
   c. the end of the Franco-Prussian War.
5. The French people wanted Napoleon III as their ruler mainly because
   a. he reminded them of Napoleon I.
   b. he controlled a powerful army.
   c. he promised to set up a more democratic government.
6. To choose a premier in France
   a. the national assembly votes for the premier.
   b. a two-party system elects the premier.
   c. the president appoints the premier.
7. The Dreyfus Affair in France was of national importance because
   a. it showed there was treason in the army.
   b. it led to French defeat in the Franco-Prussian War.
   c. high government officials were removed from office.

Developing Ideas and Skills

TELLING FACT FROM OPINION

Which of the following statements are *facts* and which are *opinions?*

1. Before de Gaulle came to power in France, the government changed a number of times.
2. Captain Dreyfus was found guilty of being a traitor but was later declared to be innocent.
3. The Fifth Republic of France is more democratic than the Third Republic was.
4. The French people get tired of any government that lasts too long and try to change it.
5. The many parties of France have in the past been the cause of political crises.
6. The government of France includes a president and a premier.
7. France and Germany will always be enemies because they have a boundary in common.
8. Napoleon III was not as clever as Napoleon I.
9. The Dreyfus Affair showed that the Third Republic of France was very weak.
10. The French government is more democratic than the British government.

Using Original Sources

In 1871, the French people set up their Third Republic. It was rocked by many crises. One of the most famous was the Dreyfus Affair (see page 329). In 1894, Captain Alfred Dreyfus, a French officer and a Jew, was sentenced to life imprisonment for being a traitor. Later he was given a new trial and found innocent. One of the men who helped to get him a new trial was the French writer Emile Zola. This is Zola's famous letter to the President of France.

I Accuse

I accuse General Mercier of sharing in one of the greatest acts of injustice of the century! I accuse General Billet of hiding the proof of Dreyfus' innocence to protect the army from disgrace! I accuse General Gense of sharing in this same crime! I accuse three handwriting experts hired by the army of making false reports! I accuse the War Office of a plot with the newspapers to fool the public and cover up their own crimes. Finally, I accuse the War Office of injustice for calling a man guilty on the basis of secret papers! I accuse the War Office of hiding this unlawful trick! I accuse them of protecting the guilty! I accuse them of a crime against justice and the people of France!

1. Dreyfus' trial rocked the country. Can you point to any trials in your country's history that have rocked the country? Explain.
2. Emile Zola was imprisoned for writing this letter. Do you think you would risk punishment in order to correct an injustice such as this?
3. Many people felt that the reason Dreyfus was found guilty was because he was Jewish. Name other examples of discrimination because of religion.

AIM: **How did conditions in Russia lead to a revolution?**

CHAPTER 6

The Czars Rule with an Iron Hand

WHAT POWERS DID THE CZARS HAVE?

1. Great Britain and France are small in size. Russia is the largest nation in the world. Why, then, do we spend so much time describing the history of Great Britain and France, and so little time describing the history of Russia? The reason is that today's ideas of freedom and democracy developed mainly in Great Britain, France, and the United States. In Russia there was little growth of democracy. Russia lived under absolute rulers—czars or czarinas—until 1917. Since then, it has lived under communist dictators.

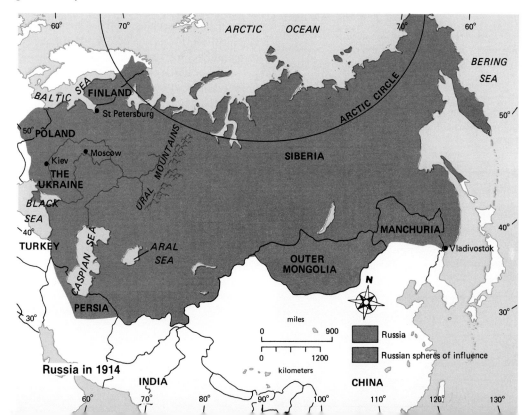

Russia in 1914

2. The French Revolution put an end to absolute rule in France. But Russia had no revolutions in the 17th, 18th, or 19th century. When Louis XVI was absolute ruler of France, just before the French Revolution, Catherine the Great was the absolute ruler of Russia. A century later, France had gone through four revolutions; Russia had gone through none. It was still led by absolute rulers. In other words, Russia's government did not really change for three centuries. But revolution finally came in 1917. Nicholas II turned out to be the last czar.

3. Before 1917, there was no free parliament in Russia to pass laws. The czar made the laws. He appointed government officials to enforce them. A powerful secret-police force made sure that no one started a movement for reform. Under the czars, Russians had very little freedom of speech or freedom of the press. People who dared speak out against the power of the czar were arrested. They would then be exiled to a Siberian prison camp or executed.

WHAT RIGHTS DID THE PEOPLE LACK?

4. Those who were against the rule of the czars had to plan in secret. A number of secret clubs were formed in the cities of Russia. Some of these secret groups wanted to reform Russia slowly. Others wanted fast reform, through revolution. Terrorist groups also met in secret. They believed that the only way to change Russia was to murder the czar and his officials. During the 19th century, many government leaders were murdered by terrorists. In 1881, Czar Alexander II was murdered.

5. The same class differences found in France before the French Revolution could be found in Russia under the czars. The privileged classes in Russia were the nobility and clergy. The nobles owned most of the land. They held all the important government jobs. Most Russians were peasant farmers—serfs. They worked the land of the nobility. Most were very poor. They had no hope of improving their condition. In the late 19th century, a factory working class slowly began to grow in Russian cities. But industrial workers were very few in number.

WHAT REFORMS DID THE CZARS MAKE?

6. The czars practiced a policy of *Russification.* All nationalities living in Russia were to speak, dress, and act like Russians. Poles, Finns, Latvians, and Lithuanians were among those forced to give up their own culture and become Russified. Unfair treatment of Jews was practiced by the czarist government. Jews were not allowed to own land. They could not study in universities or do business in certain trades. Sometimes the czar's officials carried out the organized murder of Jews. This led many Russian Jews to move to the United States at the end of the 19th century.

7. During the 19th century, the spirit of democracy and nationalism grew strong in Western Europe. The czars realized that they, too, would have to make some changes in Russia. Changes were usually made after the Russian armies were defeated in a war. Then the czars would use the reforms to make the people forget the war. After Russia's defeat in the Crimean War (1853–56), for example, unrest began

Czar Nicholas II with his family and officers. Describe Russian life under the rule of the Czars.

to grow among the serfs. To quiet them, Czar Alexander II passed his Edict of Emancipation, in 1861. This order freed all the serfs in Russia. But the freed serfs had no farmland. The czar then organized peasant groups, called *mirs*, which could buy land from the nobles. But the prices were very high. Still, the freeing of the serfs was genuine reform.

8. Absolute rule and the hard life of the Russian people went on. New movements for reforms were cruelly put down, especially after Czar Alexander II was murdered in 1881. Then the Russian navy and army were badly defeated in the Russo-Japanese War (1904–05). Their failure was caused mainly by poor training and dishonesty in the government. The result was that a small revolution took place in 1905. The revolution failed. But it frightened Czar Nicholas II. To quiet the people, he ordered the setting up of a Russian parliament. It was called the *duma*. This was the first time that a parliament had ever been called together in Russia.

This picture is a Bolshevik poster showing the Czar, priest, and rich man riding over the bodies of the workers.

WHAT FINALLY ENDED THE ABSOLUTE RULE OF THE CZARS?

9. This Russian duma was elected by the people. It was supposed to pass laws. When the danger of revolution was over, however, Czar

Nicholas II changed his mind. He let the duma meet, but he took away all its powers. Thus, the absolute rule of the czars did not change. The Russian czars were able to keep power in spite of defeat in two wars. But defeat in a third war finally put an end to their rule. This defeat came in World War I.

Testing Your Vocabulary

Choose the best answer.

1. Under the policy of *Russification*
   a. a captured German might have to serve in the Russian army.
   b. a Polish person living in Russia would be forced to speak Russian rather than Polish.
   c. the power of the church was taken away.
2. When Russian serfs were *emancipated* in 1861, they

   a. were free to leave the land and their masters.
   b. could vote in elections.
   c. could leave Russia.
3. The rulers of Russia before 1917 were called *czars* or *czarinas*. They were
   a. limited dictators.
   b. kings or queens who reigned but did not rule.
   c. all-powerful rulers.

Understanding What You Have Read

1. A good title for paragraphs 3 through 6 might be
   a. Russian Defeat in World War I.
   b. The Russian Revolution of 1917.
   c. Life in Russia under the Czars.
   d. Terrorist Groups in Russia.
2. In which paragraphs do you find facts about
   a. Czar Alexander II's death?
   b. the Russification policy of the czars?
   c. the freeing of Russian serfs?
   d. the Russo-Japanese War?
3. Czarist rule came to an end in Russia when
   a. the nobles forced the czar to sign a charter of reform.
   b. Russian armies were defeated in World War I.
   c. the serfs were freed.
4. We say that the rule of the czars was absolute because
   a. they inherited their thrones.
   b. their powers were limited by a constitution.

c. they made all the laws.

5. The nobility was the most powerful class in czarist Russia because it
   a. led the Russian armies.
   b. owned most of the land and held most government positions.
   c. controlled most factories and industries.
6. Czar Alexander II freed the Russian serfs in 1861 because
   a. they were restless and he knew some reforms were necessary.
   b. the Communists forced him to do so.
   c. Lincoln had just freed the slaves in the United States.
7. Czar Nicholas II gave the people a duma (parliament) because
   a. England and France both had parliaments.
   b. the landowners were becoming disloyal.
   c. he wanted to avoid another revolution.

Developing Ideas and Skills

USING A TIME LINE

Important changes in Czarist Russia usually followed a Russian defeat in war. Three wars are shown on the time line. In your notebook, indicate which event listed below followed each war.

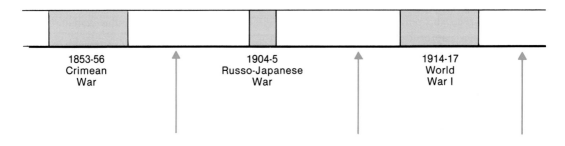

| 1853-56 Crimean War | 1904-5 Russo-Japanese War | 1914-17 World War I |

a. Meeting of first Russian duma.   b. Emancipation of the serfs.   c. Communist Revolution.

Summary of Unit VII ───────────────────────────

Some of the more important events and facts presented in this unit are listed below. Can you add any others?

1. The Congress of Vienna put down the ideas of nationalism and democracy that the French Revolution had made popular.
2. The Congress of Vienna used the ideas of legitimacy and compensation to take away the changes made by Napoleon I.
3. Great Britain was the first major nation to gain a democratic government.
4. British democracy developed slowly through changes in laws made by Parliament.
5. Under the British system of government, Parliament has the most power.
6. The government of Great Britain is called a parliamentary-cabinet system.
7. Since the Napoleonic era, the government of France has been changed several times by wars and revolutions.
8. The present government of France is a democratic republic in which the president has great power.
9. Until the Revolution of 1917, Russia was ruled by czars with absolute power.
10. Since the end of the Revolution of 1917, Russia has been ruled by a Communist dictatorship.

Making Generalizations ────────────────────────

After each generalization below, provide two additional supporting statements from your reading of Unit VII.

A. Generalization: Attempts to suppress popular ideas, such as the Metternich System, often lead to revolution.
   1. Unsuccessful revolutions occurred in Spain in 1820 and 1821.
   2.
   3.

B. Generalization: In the 19th century, democratic reforms were brought about in several European countries.
   1. In 1861, Czar Alexander II freed the Russian serfs.
   2.
   3.

C. Generalization: Some democratic reforms have taken place without violent revolutions.
   1. The Great Reform Bill, extending the right to vote to many Englishmen, was passed by Parliament in 1832.
   2.
   3.

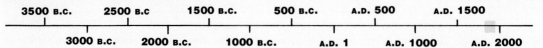

3500 B.C. 2500 B.C 1500 B.C. 500 B.C. A.D. 500 A.D. 1500

3000 B.C. 2000 B.C. 1000 B.C. A.D. 1 A.D. 1000 A.D. 2000

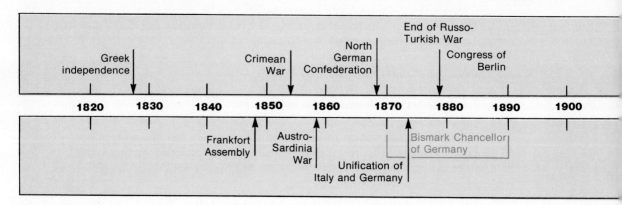

Greek
independence

Crimean
War

North
German
Confederation

End of Russo-
Turkish War

Congress of
Berlin

1820   1830   1840   1850   1860   1870   1880   1890   1900

Frankfort
Assembly

Austro-
Sardinia
War

Unification of
Italy and Germany

Bismark Chancellor
of Germany

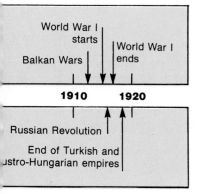

World War I
starts

Balkan Wars

World War I
ends

1910   1920

Russian Revolution

End of Turkish and
ustro-Hungarian empires

How Did Ideas of Nationalism Grow and Spread?

**The spires of a Muslim mosque rise high above
the busy port of Istanbul in Turkey.**

339

AIM: What does nationalism mean and why is it important?

CHAPTER 1

Nationalism Changes Europe

WHAT IS NATIONALISM?

1. When we see our country's flag in a parade, we salute it as it passes by. When we attend school assemblies, we sing our national anthem. We do these things because we are proud of our country. We respect its leaders and are loyal to its ideals. The feeling of loyalty to a country is called patriotism. Nationalism is like patriotism. But nationalism is more of a political force.

2. What makes a people nationalistic? Usually, it is pride in things they all share. These things include their language, history, culture, and ethnic background (nationality). When people want the best for their own nation, they are being nationalistic. Today, the spirit of nationalism is found in most countries of the world.

3. During the Middle Ages, people did not know of nationalism, or loyalty to a nation. They were loyal to a king, a lord, or a military leader—not to a nation. Then, at the end of the Middle Ages, the system of feudalism began to die out. The power of the nobles grew weaker. Nations such as England, France, Spain, and Portugal became united, each under one ruler. In each of these nations, the people spoke the same language. They followed the same customs and had the same history. It was then that feelings of nationalism arose. People became loyal to their country as well as to their rulers.

The Arch of Triumph in France is a symbol of national spirit. This sculpture appears on the outer walls of the arch. How does it show the spirit of nationalism?

HOW DID THE SPIRIT OF NATIONALISM CHANGE EUROPE?

4. A strong spirit of nationalism did not develop in Europe until the time of the French Revolution, in the late 18th century. During the revolution, the king and queen of France were executed. The people of France shifted their loyalty from their monarchs to their country. They made a new national flag. A stirring national anthem was composed. When French armies went out to fight, they carried their flag and sang their anthem. They were fighting for their country, not for their rulers. Thus the spirit of modern nationalism was born.

5. Under Napoleon I, the armies of France fought all over Europe. Wherever they went, they brought the spirit of nationalism. Italians became Italian nationalists. Germans became German nationalists. Poles became Polish nationalists. Napoleon was finally defeated. One of the most difficult problems that faced Prince Metternich was to wipe out this spirit of nationalism that Napoleon had spread. But nationalism could not be destroyed. It grew stronger and stronger in Europe. In the Italian states there appeared many Italian patriots. They wanted to form a single Italian nation. The same thing happened in the German states. German patriots wanted to be united into a single German nation.

6. The spirit of nationalism caused a different result in the Austrian Empire. The Austrian Empire was made up of many different nationalities. It included Hungarians, Romanians, Czechs, and others. Each one of these nationalities hoped to break away from Austria and form its own independent nation. The same was true of the Turkish Empire. It included such different nationalities as Greeks, Bulgarians, Romanians, and Serbians. In some places, therefore, the goal of nationalists was to unite people into a single nation. In other places, their aim was to break up large empires into smaller nations. In the following chapters we shall see how the spirit of nationalism changed the map of Europe in the 19th century. It changed the map of the whole world in the 20th century.

Royal Mounted Police celebrate Canada Day, the national holiday that celebrates Canadian independence. Canada gained independence from Britain in 1867, but it is still a member of the Commonwealth.

NATIONALISM—GOOD OR EVIL?

7. Has the spirit of nationalism been a good thing? You will have to judge for yourself. The spirit of nationalism caused many new, independent nations to be formed. Because of their national pride these nations developed their own literature, art, and music. They built schools and universities. They helped their scientists and scholars. They built homes and industries. Since the end of World War II, nationalism has changed the history of the world. More than ninety new independent nations have been formed.

WHAT ARE THE EVILS OF NATIONALISM?

8. But there is another side to the story of nationalism. Countries with a strong spirit of nationalism have often been too eager to go to war to defend their national honor. This desire has led to *militarism:* the building of large armies and navies. Thus, nationalism has led to many wars in Europe. In the middle of the 19th century, nationalism also led to a race for colonies. The nations of Europe thought that they would gain greater glory and power if they had colonies. This movement was called *imperialism.* Both nationalism and imperialism were basic causes of World War I and World War II.

9. In some countries, nationalism led some people to think that their nationality was better than other nationalities. The Nazis, a political group in Germany during the 1930's and 1940's, said the Germans were a master race. Adolf Hitler, their leader, convinced his followers that other peoples were inferior. This idea finally led to the slaughter of millions of Europeans. (We shall learn more about Hitler and the Nazis in later chapters.)

Testing Your Vocabulary

Choose the best answer.

1. The spirit of *nationalism* refers to a feeling of
   a. dislike for people who speak a different language.
   b. loyalty to a king or queen.
   c. patriotism and loyalty to a nation.
2. A *nationality* is a group of people having the same
   a. customs, language, and history.
   b. religious and business interests.
   c. belief in democratic ideas.
3. *Imperialism,* which grew out of a spirit of nationalism, is
   a. the desire to possess colonies.
   b. rule by a dictator.
   c. freedom of speech and freedom of press.
4. *Militarism* is the desire to
   a. let generals run the government.
   b. get colonies through the use of force.
   c. have large military forces defend the nation.

Understanding What You Have Read _____

1. A good title for paragraphs 8 and 9 would be
   a. The Meaning of Nationalism
   b. The Spread of Nationalism Throughout Europe
   c. The Evils of Nationalism
   d. The Unification of Germany and Italy
2. In which paragraphs do you find facts about
   a. the spread of nationalist ideas by Napoleon's armies?
   b. the effect of nationalism in the Austrian and Turkish Empires?
   c. the time when England, France, and Spain became national states?
   d. Hitler's use of German nationalism?
3. The spirit of nationalism did not exist during the age of feudalism because
   a. feudal lords suppressed all nationalist feelings.
   b. people were loyal to a monarch or lord, rather than to a country.
   c. the Catholic Church did not like the idea of nationalism.
4. Nationalism developed in the German and Italian states after 1815 because
   a. Metternich liked the idea.
   b. newspapers and books carried the idea of nationalism to the common people.
   c. nationalistic ideas had been spread by Napoleon's wars.
5. Nationalism helped bring about imperialism because some people thought that colonies
   a. would always be loyal to the controlling country.
   b. brought more glory and power to a nation.
   c. helped spread nationalistic feelings.
6. Hitler's nationalist ideas were a threat to the entire world because they included the belief that
   a. the German people were a master race.
   b. the United States was Germany's main enemy.
   c. Germans should move to other countries.
7. Nationalist ideas were a threat to the Austrian empire because
   a. the many different nationalities in Austria began to seek independence.
   b. they brought a large number of foreigners to Austria.
   c. they caused Austria to go to war with Germany.

Tell whether you *agree* or *disagree* with each of the following statements. If you disagree, change the words in italics to make a statement with which you agree.

1. *Imperialism* as we know it today began during the French Revolution.
2. The spirit of *nationalism* can often be found in music, art, and literature.
3. Nationalism can develop in a country with a *democratic* form of government.
4. England and France became unified nations *before* Germany and Italy.
5. Nationalism was one reason why the *Austrian Empire* was destroyed.
6. The feeling of pride and loyalty to a nation is called *democracy*.
7. During the Middle Ages, people were loyal *to a lord or ruler*, rather than to a nation.
8. Napoleon's armies spread the idea of *nationalism* in Europe.
9. Prince Metternich tried to wipe out the spirit of *legitimacy*.
10. Nationalism is an idea that can be found *only among the people of Germany*.

Developing Ideas and Skills

UNDERSTANDING A CARTOON

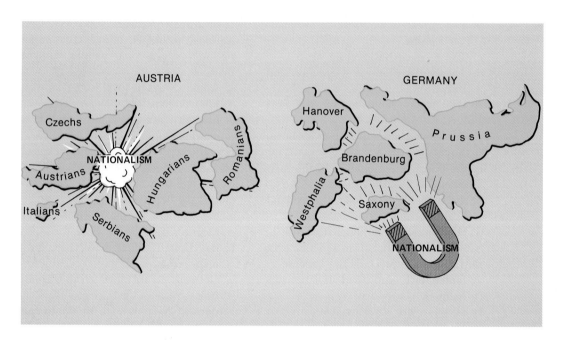

Study the two cartoons. Then answer the questions below:

1. What is the meaning of the explosion shown in the cartoon on the left?
2. What is the meaning of the magnet in the other cartoon?
3. What would be good titles for these two cartoons?

AIM: How did the many German states become a single German nation?

CHAPTER 2

The Germans Unite Their Country

HOW DID THE GERMANS CATCH THE FEVER OF NATIONALISM?

1. Nations are like people. Some are young, some are old, and some are in-between. Such modern countries as Ghana and Bangladesh are less than 50 years old. But Great Britain and France are more than 500 years old. Most of us think of Italy and Germany as older nations. Actually, they became united countries only about a century ago. When Abraham Lincoln was president of the United States, there were still no nations on the map of Europe called Italy or Germany. Instead, there were a number of small Italian states and many German states. These states were ruled by princes, dukes, and other nobles.

2. Italians and Germans caught the fever of nationalism from France in the 19th century. They began to talk about a united Italy and a united Germany. But it was Napoleon I who took the first real step, without even meaning to do so, in uniting Germany. His armies took control of many German states. At that time, there were about 300 German states. Some of these, like Prussia, were large. Others were very small. They were part of the old Holy Roman Empire. The Holy Roman Empire was almost one thousand years old. But it no longer had any meaning. It was neither holy nor Roman nor an empire. It was only an organization of states that had little to do with one another.

3. After Napoleon defeated Austria, he broke up the Holy Roman Empire. He formed a Confederation of the Rhine in 1806 by joining many German states together. This Confederation decreased the number of German states from more than 300 to fewer than 100. But Napoleon's Confederation of the Rhine did not include Prussia or Austria. They were the largest German states. The Congress of Vienna lowered the number of German states to 38. It joined them together in an organization called the German Confederation.

4. German writers and thinkers began to teach nationalistic ideas in the 19th century. Among the important thinkers was Georg Hegel, a great philosopher. Followers of his ideas were leaders in the movement to unite Germany. They pointed out that Germans shared the same language, the same customs, and the same history. They were a real nation. Therefore they should be one united German nation. Writing about German nationalism was easy. But making Germany into one nation took years of struggle.

Georg Hegel, philosopher. How did his writings contribute to the spirit of nationalism in Germany?

one large united Germany. If Germany became a single nation, they would lose their land and power.

6. Prussia was the largest and most powerful German state. It wanted to unite Germany under Prussian leadership. In 1818, Prussia organized many of the German states into a tariff union. Members of the tariff union could trade with one another without paying tariffs (taxes) on imported goods. This brought prices down. All Germans benefited from this union. It made them realize what a good idea it would be to have one German nation.

7. After the fall of Metternich, in 1848, German nationalist leaders met in the city of Frankfort. At this Frankfort Assembly they agreed to form a union of German states. They asked the king of Prussia to be their leader. But the Prussian king refused the crown because he was afraid of Austria. So the plan failed. But the movement for German unification continued. Otto von Bismarck, the prime minister of Prussia, became the new leader of German unification. Bismarck was called the "Iron Chancellor" because he was a strong leader. He decided on a policy of "blood and iron." This meant that he planned to use military force and war, if necessary, to unite Germany.

WHAT FORCES BLOCKED GERMANY'S UNIFICATION?

5. What kept the German people apart? Three main blocks stood in their way: France, Austria, and the ruling nobles of German states. France did not want a united German nation. A strong united nation on its border would be a threat to France. Austria was also afraid. A united Germany would threaten it, too. In addition, Austria feared that its own nationalities (Hungarians, Romanians, Czechs, and others) would want to become independent when they saw the Germans united. Finally, the ruling princes of the small German states did not want

HOW DID BISMARCK UNIFY GERMANY?

8. Bismarck had to defeat those who stood in the way of German unity. These were the German princes, Austria, and France. To do so, Bismarck sent the Prussian armies into three successful wars. In the first war, Prussia defeated Denmark. The next war was with Austria, in 1866. It was called the Seven Weeks' War because it was so short. Prussia quickly and easily crushed the Austrian armies, who were not prepared for war. Austria's power over German affairs ended with its defeat. Prussia then set up the North German Confederation

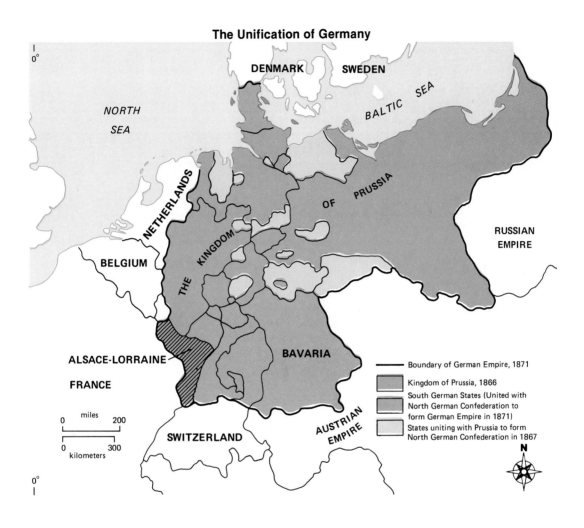

The Unification of Germany

Legend:
- Boundary of German Empire, 1871
- Kingdom of Prussia, 1866
- South German States (United with North German Confederation to form German Empire in 1871)
- States uniting with Prussia to form North German Confederation in 1867

(1867) of German states. Prussia was, of course, the leading member of this Confederation. The states of southern Germany were not included, however. Prussia's military victories showed the German princes and nobles that it would be wise to join with Prussia.

9. Bismarck next turned his attention to France. Napoleon III, who was then emperor of France, was eager for a war with Prussia. He hoped to destroy Prussia's growing power and make himself more popular at home in France. The Franco-Prussian War of 1870–71 turned out to be a total defeat for France. Its armies were forced to surrender. Napoleon III was

Bismarck concluding the treaty at Frankfort, which ended the Franco-Prussian War in 1871. Why was this an important step in the unification of Germany?

Proclamation of William I as emperor of the German empire.

captured, and the victorious German armies entered Paris. The Treaty of Frankfort ended the war. Under this treaty Germany took from France Alsace-Lorraine. This was French land on the border between France and Germany. France was also forced to give Prussia a large sum of money to pay for the war.

10. Following the German victory, Bismarck held an historic meeting at Versailles, near Paris. At this meeting Bismarck joined the states of southern Germany to the North German Confederation. A single new nation—the German Empire—was formed. King William of Prussia became Emperor William I of Germany. Germany was finally unified. A new and powerful nation now made its entrance on the stage of world history. How would it affect the future of Europe and the world?

Testing Your Vocabulary

Choose the best answer.

1. A *philosopher* is a person who
   a. is mainly interested in politics and government.
   b. studies and writes history books.
   c. looks for the truth about human life and the world.
2. The German states formed a *tariff* union. Tariffs are

   a. taxes on imports and exports.
   b. boundaries between states.
   c. claims on colonies.
3. Bismarck was called the "iron chancellor" of Prussia because he was
   a. the king.
   b. the most powerful leader of the state.
   c. the minister of foreign affairs.

Understanding What You Have Read —————

1. The main idea of paragraphs 8 and 9 is that
   a. Napoleon I played an important part in unifying Germany.
   b. Austria was against German unification.
   c. Bismarck united Germany by winning wars.
   d. the Franco-Prussian War was a disaster for France.

2. In which paragraphs do you find facts about
   a. why France and Austria were against German unification?
   b. what the Holy Roman Empire was in the 19th century?
   c. the beginning of the German Empire?
   d. thinkers who wanted German unity.

3. France was against the unification of Germany because
   a. many French people lived in the German states.
   b. many Germans lived in France.
   c. a united Germany would be a threat to France.

4. Bismarck's policy was called one of "blood and iron" because Bismarck
   a. wanted to build up the German steel industry.
   b. favored war as a way of unifying Germany.
   c. wanted to get the iron mines of Alsace-Lorraine from France.

5. Prussia was the leader of the movement to unify Germany because it was
   a. the strongest of the German states.
   b. the oldest of the German states.
   c. the most democratic of the German states.

6. Napoleon III of France was eager for a war with Prussia because he wanted to
   a. help Austria.
   b. raise his popularity at home.
   c. get back Alsace-Lorraine.

7. The Frankfort Assembly of 1848 was a failure because
   a. Metternich vetoed its plans for a united Germany.
   b. France threatened to start a war with Prussia.
   c. the King of Prussia did not want to become king of a united Germany.

Tell whether the following statements are true or false. If a statement is false, change the words in italics to make it true.

1. Germany was completely unified after the *Seven Weeks' War.*

2. The princes of the small German states opposed the unification of *Germany.*

3. *Prussia* was the largest of the German states before they were unified into one country.

4. The *Holy Roman Empire* was formed by Napoleon I.

5. The policy of "blood and iron" was started by *Hegel.*

6. The German *tariff union* showed the people the value of German unification.

7. Austria and *Spain* were against German unification.

8. The North German Confederation was organized after the *Seven Weeks' War.*

9. The Franco-Prussian War was a major victory for *France.*

10. When *Abraham Lincoln* was president of the United States, there was still no united German nation in Europe.

Developing Ideas and Skills _____

UNDERSTANDING A DRAWING

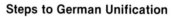

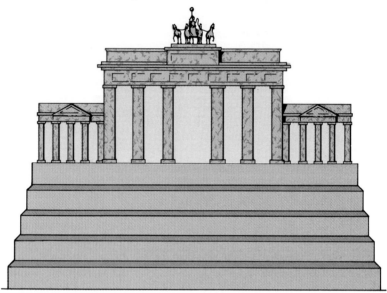

The following events were steps in the unification of Germany:

  a. Tariff Union
  b. Franco-Prussian War
  c. North German Confederation
  d. Confederation of the Rhine
  e. German Confederation

Copy only the steps of the drawing in your notebook. Put the events listed in their proper order on the steps. The earliest event should go on the bottom step.

AIM: How did the Kaisers rule Germany before World War I?

CHAPTER 3

Germany Becomes Autocratic

WHAT POWERS DID THE KAISERS HAVE?

1. If you say the name Adolf Hitler, some older people might shiver with horror. Hitler became dictator of Germany in 1933. This was about sixty years after Germany was united. Hitler was one of the strangest and cruelest men in history. But many Germans of his time thought he was a great man. We often study a criminal's childhood to understand why he became a criminal. So we must study the history of Germany. We will try to understand why many Germans accepted Hitler's inhuman ideas and made him their leader.

2. Germany was united by Bismarck, who used "blood and iron" to do so. Bismarck found that force and war worked well in uniting Germany. So, he also used force to run the government of Germany. The government of the new German nation was set up in 1871. It seemed democratic, but it was not. It had a constitution. It had a legislature to pass laws. All men could vote. But these things were like a good-looking cover on a cheap book. The German government was actually not democratic. It was very *autocratic*. An autocratic government is one that is ruled with absolute power by one person.

3. At the head of the German empire was

the kaiser. Great Britain and Russia also had monarchs. But the kaiser of Germany was not like either of them. The German kaiser had more power than the ruler of Great Britain who was merely a symbol of unity. But he had less power than the czar of Russia. The kaiser led the nation's armed forces. He chose the chancellor who was the prime minister in Germany. The chancellor and his cabinet had to follow the wishes of the kaiser alone. The chancellor could be removed from office by the kaiser at any time. In Great Britain, the prime minister and the cabinet were elected by the House of Commons. They followed the wishes of the House of Commons only.

4. Germany had a parliament, or legislature, with two branches. These were called the *Bundesrat* and the *Reichstag*. Members of the Bundesrat were appointed by the German states. The number of delegates from each state depended upon the state's size. Members of the Reichstag were elected by the people. Unlike the Parliament of Great Britain or the Congress of the United States, the German legislature had very little power. It could not choose the chancellor. It could not pass laws. It could only put off the passage of laws for a while. The kaiser, through his chancellor, decided what laws should be passed.

5. Prussia, the largest state in Germany,

controlled the German government. This was the result of two things. In the first place, the king of Prussia was the man who became kaiser of Germany. Naturally he favored Prussia. The kaiser chose the chancellor. He chose a Prussian. In the second place, Prussia had the largest number of votes in the Bundesrat. Prussia could therefore block any moves to change the constitution. It could also stop the passage of most laws it did not want.

HOW WAS BISMARCK ABLE TO RUN GERMANY AS HE WISHED?

6. Otto von Bismarck united Germany in 1871. For almost twenty years after this he was chancellor of Germany. Bismarck was the kaiser's closest adviser. He decided what laws should be passed and what policies should be followed. Germany had little democracy under Bismarck.

7. Under Bismarck, Germany became rich. It was one of the leading nations of the Industrial Revolution, which you will learn about in a later chapter. German business was good. There were jobs in the cities, and farmers had rich harvests. Scientists and businessmen developed new industries based on chemistry and electricity. They built great steel mills and manufacturing plants. Under Bismarck all parts of the nation began to use the same kind of money. He organized the German railways into a single system.

8. Many non-German people were living in Germany as a result of the wars that had united the country. Danish people lived in Schleswig. There were French people in Alsace-Lorraine. Polish people lived in eastern Germany. These minority groups wanted to keep their own customs and languages. But Bismarck believed that all people living in Germany should think, talk, and act like Germans. He was even against the ties that German Catholics had to the pope.

German ironworks in 1895. Why was manufacturing important to the growth of Germany?

9. Bismarck passed laws which treated minority nationalities unfairly. He started a program to weaken the power of the Catholic Church in Germany. In all that he did, Bismarck had one main idea in mind. The strength of Germany must come first.

10. To end social unrest among workers, Bismarck had the Reichstag pass the first social-insurance laws in Europe, in 1878. Under these laws, workers received government insurance for old age, sickness, and accidents. With these ideas of social insurance for workers, Germany was far ahead of all other countries. Great Britain, for example, did not pass an old-age insurance law until 1908. The United States did not pass its Social Security Act until 1935.

WHY DID THE NEW KAISER DISMISS BISMARCK?

11. William I, the first kaiser of Germany, let Bismarck run the country. Bismarck, known as the "iron chancellor," was not only very clever but also very popular. In 1888, however, a new ruler, Kaiser William II, came to the throne of the German Empire. The new kaiser decided to be his own strong ruler. Bismarck was then removed as chancellor. The fate of Germany now rested in the hands of the ambitious William.

Kaiser William I (left); Kaiser William II (right). Compare the influence of Bismarck on both rulers.

12. The new kaiser thought that Germany should be a leader in world affairs. Like Bismarck, he believed that military power was good for the country. So he set up a large peacetime army. He ordered military service for all men. With its military power, Germany entered the race for colonies. It tried to compete with Great Britain and France for colonies in Asia and Africa. This led to unfriendly relations among the rival nations. These unfriendly relations were among the things that led to World War I.

Testing Your Vocabulary

Choose the best answer.

1. The German government before World War I is called *autocratic* because
   a. few people could vote.
   b. there was no constitution.
   c. it was ruled with absolute power by the kaiser.
2. The German Empire had a *legislature* of two branches. A legislature
   a. sets up tariffs to protect businessmen.
   b. makes the laws for a country.
   c. is a secret police force.
3. Germany followed a policy of *militarism*. Under this policy it
   a. tried to grab colonies away from France.
   b. set up a large army.
   c. took away most of the chancellor's power.

Understanding What You Have Read

1. A good title for paragraphs 8 and 9 is
   a. German Imperialism.
   b. The German Government Before World War I.
   c. The Struggle Against the Church in Germany.
   d. Bismarck's Policies Toward Minority Groups.
2. In what paragraph do you find facts about
   a. social insurance in the German Empire?
   b. Bismarck's dismissal as chancellor?
   c. the power of the Bundesrat and Reichstag?
   d. the race for colonies in Asia and Africa?
3. Bismarck was removed as chancellor because
   a. he opposed the kaiser's policy of militarism.
   b. he did not like social insurance laws.
   c. Kaiser William II wanted power for himself.
4. Prussia controlled the government of the German Empire because
   a. Prussia had a majority of the votes in the Reichstag.
   b. the king of Prussia was also the kaiser of Germany.
   c. a majority of the German people lived in Prussia.
5. The government of the German Empire was not democratic because:
   a. there was no constitution.
   b. the kaiser and his chancellor had almost unlimited power.
   c. the legislature did not represent the people.

Using Original Sources

As chancellor, or prime minister, of Prussia, Bismarck was the real builder of a unified German nation. He knew what he wanted to do, and he explained how he was going to do it. The passage below is from a speech before the Prussian parliament on September 20, 1862. What does it tell you about Bismarck's methods?

Iron and Blood

Germany is looking to Prussia, not for liberty but for power. Some German states may be looking for freedom. But that is not the goal of Prussia. Prussia must build up her power and keep it ready for the right moment. We have already missed some good chances to act. Since the Congress of Vienna, Prussia has not been satisfied with her borders. The great questions of the day are not decided by speeches and majority votes. That was the mistake we made in the past. The great questions of the day are decided by iron and blood.

1. What did Bismarck think of the democratic process ("majority votes") of allowing the people to decide important questions?
2. What did he mean by the phrase "iron and blood" in the last sentence?
3. How did Bismarck feel the German people had been treated by other nations?

Developing Ideas and Skills _____

UNDERSTANDING A CARTOON

This famous cartoon appeared in English newspapers and magazines when Kaiser William II dismissed Bismarck as chancellor of Germany. As used here, the word *pilot* refers to the person who steers a ship.
Which letters in the cartoon refer to the following:

_____ Bismarck
_____ Kaiser William II
_____ The German Empire

Why is *Dropping the Pilot* a good title for this cartoon?

TURNING POINTS

Culture

The World: Olympic Games

The first Olympic Games took place in 776 B.C. in ancient Greece. They were held every four years to honor the Greek gods and goddesses. Winners of the contests received crowns of leaves and were treated as heroes. In 1875, the ruins of the original Olympic stadium were discovered. A Frenchman, Pierre de Coubertin, suggested that the Olympic Games be held again. He believed that international sports competition would promote world peace. The modern games began in 1896.

For the most part, the Olympics have fulfilled de Coubertin's belief. The organizers of the games emphasize the fact that individuals, not countries, win medals. They keep no record of how many medals are won by each country during the games.

Still, some people like to compare the performances of athletes. People from nations that have political differences usually feel proud when their country's performance is rated higher than another's. The Olympic spirit, however, is supposed to be one of international cooperation. Most athletes respect each other's efforts. The people who watch share in the excitement of the competition. There are gasps of admiration as a well-trained athlete scores a perfect 10. The crowd appreciates the skill of the performance. The nationality of the athlete should not matter.

Critical Thinking

1. In what ways can feelings of nationalism be expressed during Olympic Games?
2. In recent times, some countries decided not to participate in the Olympics because of political differences. Do you think de Coubertin would have approved? Explain.

AIM: How did the Italian states finally become unified?

CHAPTER 4

The Italians Unite Their Country

WHAT THREE FORCES BLOCKED ITALIAN UNIFICATION?

1. "In the name of God and of Italy I dedicate myself to make Italy one free, independent, republican nation." This was the heart of the oath, or promise, that young Italians took when they joined the *Young Italy* society. This society began during the Metternich era (1815–48). At that time, neither Italy nor Germany was a united nation.

2. Yet the Italian people had good reasons for becoming united. They spoke the same language and read the same books. They followed the same customs and had the same history. They were all of the same nationality. In ancient times, Italy had been the center of the great Roman Empire. But the fall of the Roman Empire, in the 5th century, brought an end to the unity of the people on the Italian peninsula. Starting in the Middle Ages, the Italian peninsula was broken up into many small states. These states were each ruled by a prince or other noble ruler. Most of them were related to the Bourbons of France or the Hapsburgs of Austria. These princes and nobles did not want Italy to be unified. If it were, they would lose their land and power.

3. Austria was against a unified Italy. It controlled the Italian states of Lombardy and Venetia in northern Italy. Naturally, it did not want to lose these two states. Also, Austria knew that a united Italian nation would be a strong and dangerous neighbor. The land owned by the Catholic Church was another problem. The pope owned the land called the Papal States. This land was in the middle of the Italian peninsula. Italy could never become unified as long as the Catholic Church claimed this land.

HOW DID MAZZINI AND CAVOUR STIR NATIONALISM IN ITALY?

4. Thus the word *Italy* in the early 19th century was not the name of a country. It was only a geographic expression: a word referring to an area of land. The only truly independent Italian kingdom in the early 19th century was Sardinia. The kingdom of Sardinia was also called the kingdom of Piedmont. This small nation became the center around which the new Italian nation was to be built. But united Italy, like ancient Rome, was not built in a day. It took much planning and fighting to build a united Italian nation.

Giuseppe Mazzini, Camillo Cavour, Giuseppe Garibaldi. What role did each man play in the unification of Italy?

5. The spark of modern Italian nationalism was lit during the French Revolution and the Napoleonic era. Napoleon I conquered many of the Italian states. This helped to fan the flames of Italian patriotism. Napoleon also removed many of the ruling princes. The Congress of Vienna returned the Italian princes to their lands. But Italian nationalism continued to grow. Metternich's system of spies and force could not stop it.

6. Revolts against the Metternich System broke out in different parts of the Italian peninsula. All of them were put down by Austrian armies. Italian patriots began to form secret societies, such as the *Carbonari*. Then, in 1831, a fiery young Italian named Giuseppe Mazzini set up the *Young Italy* society. Its members took an oath to spread the idea of Italian unity. The Young Italy society stirred the spirit of Italian nationalism with its speeches, pamphlets, and parades.

7. Mazzini led a revolution of the Italian states in 1848. It was put down by Austrian and French troops. Then Count Camillo Cavour became the leader of the movement for Italian unification. Cavour was the prime minister of the kingdom of Sardinia, the independent Italian state. He realized that Austria was the chief block to Italian unity. So Cavour got Napoleon III of France to join Sardinia in a war against Austria.

HOW WAS ITALY FINALLY UNIFIED?

8. In the Austro-Sardinian War of 1859, the Austrians were badly defeated. As a result of the war, Sardinia took the Italian state of Lombardy from Austria. This was the first step in uniting Italy. Soon after the war, revolutions ended Austrian rule in the states of Tuscany, Parma, and Modena. These states then voted by a *plebiscite* (PLEB-ih-site) to become part of Sardinia. A plebiscite is a vote by the people. It is usually held to decide to what government they want to belong.

9. Then a revolt began in southern Italy, in the kingdom of the Two Sicilies. This revolt was helped by an invasion of about 1,000 patriotic Italians. These men, called the Red Shirts, were led by Giuseppe Garibaldi. The Red Shirts had little trouble in gaining control of Sicily. Again a plebiscite was held. The people in the kingdom of the Two Sicilies also voted to join Sardinia.

The Red Shirts of Italy. How did they help Italian unification?

10. To gain the Papal States, Prime Minister Cavour, of Sardinia, sent an army there in 1860. The Sardinian army took control of the entire area except the city of Rome. The Papal States were then joined to Sardinia. Thus, a single Italian nation was created. It extended from the island of Sicily, in the south, to Sardinia (Piedmont), in the north. Victor Emmanuel II, who had been king of Sardinia, became king of a united Italy in 1861. Three men were mainly responsible for uniting Italy: Cavour was the "mind" of Italian unification; Mazzini was the "soul"; and Garibaldi was the "sword."

11. But not all of Italy was unified yet. A few areas had not become part of the new Italian nation. Austria still controlled the northern states of Venetia, Trieste (tree-EST), and Trentino. The pope still held the city of Rome, guarded by French troops. To gain Venetia, Italy joined Prussia in the Seven Weeks' War against Austria. Austria was quickly defeated. Italy was given Venetia, in 1866. But it was not until the end of World War I that Italy gained Trieste and Trentino from Austria.

12. Italy gained Rome during the Franco-Prussian War of 1870–71. The French troops were forced to withdraw from Rome in order to fight Prussia. The Italian army entered Rome and took it without a fight. In a plebiscite, the people of Rome voted to join the Italian nation. Rome became the capital of Italy. Thus, by 1871 Italy became a unified nation through revolutions, wars, and plebiscites.

Garibaldi welcomes Victor Emmanuel II as the king of a unified Italy. Why was Garibaldi called the "sword" of unification?

Testing Your Vocabulary _____

Choose the best answer.

1. A *plebiscite*, like those held in the Italian states, meant
   a. a plan for unification of a country.
   b. a vote by the people of a particular area on some important issue.
   c. an oath taken by soldiers.
2. Italy is geographically a *peninsula* because
   a. it is surrounded by water on three sides.
   b. it is surrounded by water on all sides.
   c. all of its coastline is on the Mediterranean Sea.

3. The *unification* of Italy in the 19th century meant
   a. forming a democratic government.
   b. making one nation out of many states.
   c. building a strong army to defend the nation.
4. Napoleon I helped to *fan the flames* of Italian patriotism. This means that he
   a. burned the city of Rome.
   b. stirred up the nationalist feelings of the Italians.
   c. put down revolts by force.

Understanding What You Have Read _____

1. The purpose of paragraphs 2 and 3 is to describe
   a. the aims of Mazzini's Young Italy Society.
   b. blocks to Italian unification.
   c. wars for Italian unification.
   d. the glory of ancient Rome.
2. In what paragraphs do you find facts about
   a. Garibaldi and the Red Shirts?
   b. Napoleon I in Italy?
   c. Italy's gaining Trieste and Trentino?
   d. the results of the Austro-Sardinian War?
3. The French withdrew their troops from Rome in 1871 because
   a. Cavour asked Napoleon III to withdraw them.
   b. the French wanted to see Italy unified.
   c. the French were fighting a war with Prussia.
4. Italy joined Prussia in the Seven Weeks' War against Austria because it
   a. wanted to gain the state of Venetia.

   b. had promised to help France.
   c. hoped to get the Papal States.

5. Austria was against Italian unification because
   a. Austria would lose power to the pope.
   b. Austria controlled some Italian states.
   c. some Italian states were ruled by Prussian princes.

6. The pope was against Italian unification because
   a. it would end his control of the Papal States.
   b. Catholics would lose power in a united Italy.
   c. Cavour and the king of Sardinia were not Catholics.

7. Mazzini organized the Young Italy society because he wanted to
   a. become prime minister.
   b. protect the rights of the pope.
   c. unify the states of Italy into one nation.

Tell whether the following statements are true or false. If the statement is false, change the words in italics to make it true.

1. The Carbonari was a secret society of *Italian* patriots.

2. Italy is an *island*, with water on three sides.

3. Tuscany, Parma, and Modena were Italian states ruled by *France*.

4. Sicily is an island off the coast of *Italy*.

5. The independent state that led the movement for Italian unification was the *kingdom of the Two Sicilies*.

6. Cavour was the *"sword"* of Italian unification.

7. Italy won Trieste and Trentino from Austria at the end of *World War I*.

8. The Young Italy society was organized by *Garibaldi*.

9. The Red Shirts fought for Italian unification in the kingdom of *Piedmont*.

10. Italy became a unified nation at about the same time that the states of *Germany* were unified.

Developing Ideas and Skills

USING A MAP

Using the information in this chapter and this map, fill in the correct answers to the questions on page 361 in your notebook.

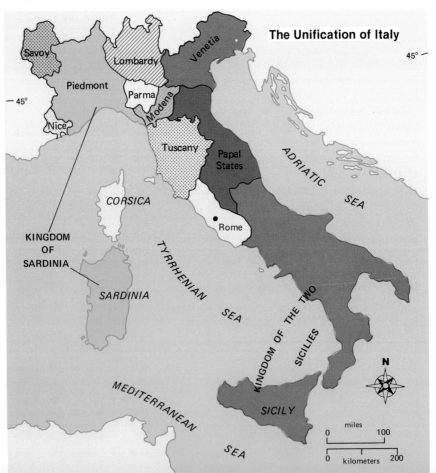

The Unification of Italy

1. Which lands were controlled by the pope?
2. Which Italian state was located farthest to the northwest?
3. Of which independent kingdom was Count Cavour prime minister?
4. Which area was invaded by Garibaldi and his Red Shirts?
5. Which island in the Tyrrhenian Sea was not Italian?
6. Which area took the lead in the unification of Italy?
7. From which city did the French withdraw troops during the Franco-Prussian War?

Using Original Sources

Before Italy became a united nation, Garibaldi led a volunteer army of Red Shirts in an invasion of Sicily and southern Italy. This was one of the steps by which Italy became united. Just before invading Sicily, Garibaldi issued the following announcement to the Italians.

Garibaldi's Announcement to the Italians

ITALIANS! The Sicilians are fighting against the enemies of Italy and for Italy. It is the duty of every Italian to help them with words, money, and arms, and above all in person. . . . Left to themselves, the brave Sicilians will have to fight not only the paid soldiers of the Bourbons but also those of Austria and the Priest of Rome. Let the inhabitants of the free provinces lift their voices in behalf of their struggling brethren and convince their brave youths to enter the conflict. . . .

The brave man finds an army everywhere. Listen not to the voice of cowards, but arm, and let us fight for our brethren, who will fight for us tomorrow. . . . To arms! Let me put an end, once and for all, to the miseries of so many centuries. Prove to the world that it is no lie that Roman blood inhabited this land.

G. Garibaldi

Complete the following outline.

1. All Italians could help win liberty with:
   a. words
   b. _____
   c. _____
   d. _____
2. The three enemies of Italian unification were:
   a. _____
   b. _____
   c. _____

AIM: How did the revolts of minority groups tear the Austrian empire apart?

CHAPTER 5

Nationalism Ends the Austrian Empire

HOW DID THE EMPEROR'S DIVIDE-AND-RULE POLICY WORK?

1. Two men once decided to do exercises to improve their health. In time, one man became strong and healthy. The other suffered a heart attack. Thus, the same plan, or idea, caused opposite results. So also, the spirit of nationalism brought opposite results in different parts of Europe. It led to the building up of small states into two strong nations: Italy and Germany. But the same spirit of nationalism broke apart the Austrian Empire. Austria was one of the oldest empires in Europe. This empire had been ruled by the Hapsburg family for hundreds of years.

2. Before the French Revolution, Austria was the center of the weak Holy Roman Empire. It included German states in the north and Italian states in the south. In 1806, Napoleon, by his military victories, ended the Holy Roman Empire. He separated the German and Italian states from Austria. He formed the German states into the Confederation of the Rhine.

3. During the next sixty years, the German states joined to form a united Germany. The Italian states joined to form a united Italy. But the Austrian Empire stayed under the Hapsburg emperors. The people of the Austrian Empire were of many different races and nationalities. These included Germans, Czechs, Poles, Romanians, Slovaks, Italians, Serbians, and Hungarians.

4. Many different nationalities lived in Austria. Yet the emperor was able to keep his empire together throughout the 19th century. He did so in two ways. First, he tried to make each nationality jealous of the others. Then they would not join together to throw off Hapsburg rule. This policy may be called a divide-and-rule policy. His second way was to put down by force all revolts of nationalities. The Congress of Vienna had made Austria one of the strongest powers in Europe. Prince Metternich, the emperor's chief minister, ruled Austria with an iron hand. By his methods he suppressed revolts all over Europe for 33 years.

HOW WAS AUSTRIA-HUNGARY FORMED?

5. Until 1848, Austrian power in central Europe was very great. In that year, uprisings started all over Europe. In the Austrian Empire, they took place in Vienna, in Hungary, and in other areas. The most serious uprising was the movement for self-government in Hungary. This was led by Louis Kossuth (kos-OOTH), a great Hungarian patriot. This revolt at first seemed successful. But it failed. Russia came to the aid of the Austrian Emperor Ferdinand I. The revolt was put down.

6. The first break in Austria's power came when it was badly defeated by Prussia in the Seven Weeks' War, in 1866. The Austrian emperor saw that this defeat might bring new uprisings in Austria. The Hungarians were the largest, strongest, and most troublesome minority group in the empire. So the emperor decided to give the Hungarians self-government before they started another uprising.

Many towns were sacked and burned during the 1848 uprisings.

Louis Kossuth urging the people to revolt against Austria. Why did the revolt fail?

7. An agreement was reached. In 1867, Austria and Hungary became separate but united nations. The Hungarians were given self-government. They were to have their own parliament and prime minister. Francis Joseph, the emperor of Austria, was to be the king of Hungary as well. The new name of the empire was Austria-Hungary. The system helped to keep peace in the empire for a while. But it did not fully satisfy the Hungarians. Nor did it settle the problems of other minority peoples in the empire. Minority groups in Hungary were as poorly treated by the Hungarians as they had been by the Austrians. Different national groups began to meet in secret to carry on the struggle for self-government and freedom.

HOW DID WORLD WAR I BEGIN?

8. In 1908, Austria-Hungary seized the Turkish state of Bosnia-Herzegovina (BOZ-nee-uh hur-tsuh-go-VEE-nuh) and made it part of the empire. More dissatisfied nationalities were thus added to the Austro-Hungarian Empire. The empire became like a pot of boiling water. Sooner or later it had to boil over. A shot

Joseph I, Emperor of Austria, enters Hungary to become king. How did this act achieve a temporary peace?

from an assassin's pistol finally led to the breakup of the empire. In 1914, a Serbian nationalist living in Austria-Hungary assassinated (murdered) the archduke Francis Ferdinand. He was to have been the next emperor of the Austro-Hungarian Empire.

9. Serbia, a small country, was blamed for the assassination. It was also blamed for causing revolts among Serbians living in Austria-Hungary. So Austria-Hungary declared war on Serbia. Russia came to Serbia's aid. Germany came to the aid of Austria-Hungary. Thus World War I began. During this war all the minorities under Austro-Hungarian rule tried to help defeat the emperor's armies. They hoped to gain their freedom. In 1918, the last year of the war, uprisings began among Czechs, Slavs, and even Hungarians.

10. The end of the war brought an end to the power of Austria-Hungary. Each nationality then began its own movement for freedom. By the treaties ending World War I, the huge Austro-Hungarian Empire was divided up. Each nationality became an independent nation or part of one.

11. Austria and Hungary were set up as two small, independent countries. The people of Czech nationality who had lived in Austria-Hungary became part of independent Czechoslovakia. The Polish people joined Poland. The Romanians joined independent Romania. The Croats (KROHTS) and Serbs joined Yugoslavia. Finally, the Italian states of Trieste and Trentino became part of Italy. Thus, the subject nationalities of the Austro-Hungarian Empire won their independence.

Testing Your Vocabulary

Choose the best answer.

1. The Archduke Francis Ferdinand was *assassinated.* He was
   a. overthrown.
   b. murdered.
   c. sent into exile.

2. During the 19th century, the Hungarians were one of the largest *minority* groups in the Austrian Empire. A minority is
   a. a smaller group that often starts revolutions.
   b. a nationality that wants independence.
   c. a group with a nationality different from that of most of the people in a country.

Understanding What You Have Read

1. A good title for paragraphs 9 through 11 is
   a. Problems of the Austrian Empire.
   b. History of the Austro-Hungarian Empire.
   c. How the Austrian Empire Was Ruled.
   d. Austro-Hungarian Nationalities Gain Freedom in World War I.

2. In which paragraphs do you find facts about
   a. the divide-and-rule policy?
   b. the assassination of Francis Ferdinand?
   c. the Confederation of the Rhine?
   d. the Seven Weeks' War with Prussia?

3. The Austro-Hungarian Empire fell apart mainly because of the
   a. imperialist ambitions of the emperor.
   b. death of Metternich.
   c. spirit of nationalism among minority groups.

4. Austria was called the empire of the Hapsburgs because
   a. it was once part of the Holy Roman Empire.
   b. it was the name of the Austrian capital.
   c. Hapsburg was the family name of the Austrian emperors.

5. Hungary was given a certain amount of self-government because it
   a. was the largest minority group in the Austrian Empire.
   b. was rich in coal and iron.
   c. had built a powerful army.

6. Austria-Hungary blamed Serbia for the assassination of Francis Ferdinand, in 1914, because
   a. Serbia had declared war on Austria-Hungary.
   b. Serbia wanted Austrian territory.
   c. the assassin was a Serbian nationalist.

7. The Holy Roman Empire came to an end during the Napoleonic era because
   a. the last emperor died without leaving a son to take the throne.
   b. Napoleon separated the German and Italian states from Austria.
   c. nationalist uprisings divided the empire.

Fill in the correct word or phrase in each of the following statements in your notebook. Do not write in this book.

1. An agreement gave self-government in the Austrian Empire to the _____.

2. The leader of the Hungarian nationalist movement was named _____.

3. The divide-and-rule policy was used by the emperor of _____.

4. The assassination of the Archduke Ferdinand in 1914 led to _____.

5. The territory of Bosnia-Herzegovina, which Austria took, had belonged to _____.

6. Austria put the blame for the assassination of the Archduke Ferdinand on the country of _____.

7. The name of the ruling family of Austria for hundreds of years was _____.

8. In World War I, the first nation to come to the aid of Serbia was _____.

9. The emperor of Austria who also became king of Hungary was _____.

10. After World War I, the Croats and Serbs of the old Austro-Hungarian Empire joined a new nation called _____.

Developing Ideas and Skills

TELLING FACT FROM OPINION

Can you tell the difference between a fact and an opinion? Read the following statements. Tell whether each is a fact or an opinion.

1. Without the union of Austria and Hungary, the Austrian Empire would have ended in 1867.

2. The Hapsburg family had ruled the Austrian Empire for hundreds of years.

3. A nation made up of many different races and nationalities will always be weak.

4. The Hapsburg emperors of Austria followed a policy of divide-and-rule.

5. The Hungarians were the largest and most troublesome minority in the Austrian Empire.

6. If the Hapsburg rulers had given self-government to all minority nationalities, the Austrian Empire would not have fallen apart.

7. World War I would never have started if the Austrian archduke had not been assassinated.

8. By the treaties ending World War I, the Austro-Hungarian Empire was divided into a number of independent nations.

9. Europe would be more peaceful today if the Austro-Hungarian Empire had not been broken up.

10. The Metternich System suppressed revolutions in Europe for more than thirty years.

AIM: How did Turkey change from a backward empire to a modern nation?

CHAPTER 6

Nationalism Ends the Turkish Empire

HOW DID TURKEY RULE THE BALKANS?

1. People looking for Turkey on a map of Europe might have trouble finding it. For only a tiny corner of Turkey is still part of Europe. Most of Turkey is outside Europe in the area called Asia Minor. We read little about Turkey today in our newspapers. But a century ago, it was one of the most important nations in the world. Then it was called the Turkish Empire, or Ottoman Empire. Its wars and revolutions affected the rest of Europe in many ways.

2. The spirit of nationalism was one reason for the fall of the Turkish Empire. Two centuries ago, Turkey's empire went as far east as Persia. It covered most of northern Africa. It also included all the land in southeast Europe to the Danube River. This huge area in southeast Europe is known as the Balkans. A large number of different nationalities lived in the Balkans. They included Greeks, Albanians, Romanians, Serbs, Croats, and Bulgarians.

3. These nationalities were different from their Turkish rulers. They had different histories. The Balkan people were mainly Christians. The Turks were Muslims. Because the people of the Balkans were so different from them, the Turkish rulers treated them cruelly and persecuted them. The Balkan nationalities had no voice in the Turkish government. They were

taxed heavily and unfairly. Sometimes the Turks would kill thousands of Christians within their empire.

4. The Balkan people had many reasons, therefore, for wanting to be free of Turkey. But gaining freedom took many years of bitter fighting. This was because nationalities in the Balkans were jealous of one another. So they

Serbia tried many times to gain independence from Turkey but was not successful until 1878. This picture shows skulls of Serbian patriots cemented into a monument tower in Nis, Serbia.

were never able to unite against Turkey. On the other hand, the large nations of Europe tried to get the Balkan people to revolt. Since most Europeans were Christians, they hoped to free the Christian Balkan people from their Muslim rulers. Of course, the large European nations also had selfish reasons for wanting the Balkan peoples to overthrow the Turks. They hoped that they could get some of Turkey's huge territory if a revolution took place.

5. The Greeks were the first of the Balkan peoples to win their independence. In 1821, when the Greeks began their revolt, England, France, and Russia came to their aid. These nations backed Greece because it was Christian and because of its ancient culture. After many years of fighting, the Turks finally agreed to give the Greek people independence. Greece became the first independent Balkan nation in

Lord Byron, a great English poet, fought as a freedom fighter for Greece. Much of his poetry shows his belief that people should be able to choose their own course in life.

1829. Half a century was to pass before any other nationalist group in the Balkans won its freedom.

HOW WAS THE TURKISH EMPIRE WEAKENED?

6. The great European nations disliked Turkish rule in the Balkans throughout the 19th century. At the same time, however, Russia, France, Great Britain, Germany, and Austria-Hungary were jealous of each other. They watched carefully to see that no one of them gained more than the others in Turkey. Turkey thus caused two problems for Europe. The first was the nationalist desire of the Balkan peoples to be independent. The second was the desire of European nations to gain territory from Turkey.

7. Russia's interest in the Balkans is a good example of these two problems. Russia wanted to help the Christians in the Balkans to gain independence. But it also hoped to get control of the Turkish straits called the Dardanelles. This was a narrow waterway leading from the Black Sea to the Mediterranean Sea. To control the Dardanelles, Russia had to take the Turkish city of Constantinople. Twice the Russians tried to do this through war. Twice they failed.

8. In the Crimean War (1853–56), Russia was defeated by Turkey. England, France, and Sardinia helped Turkey in this war. They did not want Russia to gain territory from Turkey. Twenty years later, Russia tried again. The Turks had killed many Christians in the Balkans. Russia used this as an excuse to declare war on Turkey once more. The Russo-Turkish War of 1877–78 ended in victory for Russia. But England, France, Germany, and Austria-Hungary were afraid of Russian gains. They said that the Balkans were an international problem. They demanded that all the European powers agree to any treaty about the Balkans.

9. Russia was forced to agree to a meeting

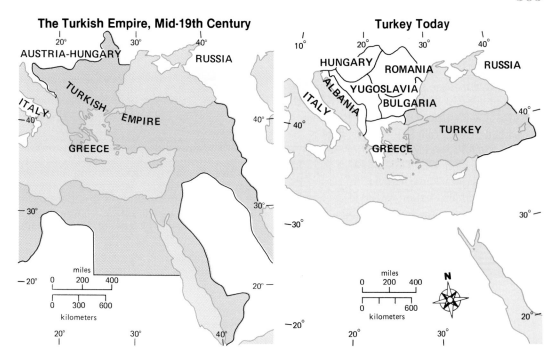

The Turkish Empire, Mid-19th Century

Turkey Today

of all the nations. At the Congress of Berlin, in 1878, the nations decided to set up three new independent Balkan nations: Serbia, Montenegro, and Romania. Bulgaria was another part of the Balkans. It was given self-government but stayed part of the Turkish Empire. It declared its full independence in 1908. The different countries then helped themselves to Turkish territory. Russia took some land. Austria-Hungary took control of Bosnia-Herzegovina, as you have read. Great Britain took the island of Cyprus.

HOW DID TURKEY FINALLY BECOME A REPUBLIC?

10. Having lost much of its territory to other nations, the Turkish Empire was badly weakened. Its government was dishonest and wasteful. Its people were poor and unhappy. Turkey became known as the "sick man of Europe." In 1908, a *Young Turk* group started a revolution in Turkey. It brought to an end the Turkish sultan's rule. But the new government of Turkey was not much better than the old.

11. Two Balkan Wars in 1912 and 1913 led to the loss of more Turkish land. When World War I began, in 1914, the city of Constantinople was almost all that was left of the old Turkish Empire in Europe. In less than one hundred years, the Turkish Balkans had been divided into six independent nations. They were Greece, Romania, Serbia, Montenegro, Bulgaria, and Albania.

12. Turkey entered World War I on the side of Germany. Defeat in the war was the final blow to Turkey. By the treaties ending the war, Turkey lost more of her land. France took control of Syria. Great Britain took control of Palestine, Transjordan, and Mesopotamia.

13. Turkey's disasters stirred up a new spirit of nationalism. In the midst of this nationalism, an age-old hatred blew up between the Turks and Armenians. Hundreds of thousands of Armenians were killed. In 1923, Turkey became a republic, and Mustapha Kemal Ataturk was elected president. Turks became proud of their new nation. Thus, nationalism made Turkey into a modern nation in the 20th century. However, nationalism among the people of the Balkans had ended the Turkish Empire of the 19th century.

Mustapha Kemal Ataturk. Among other reforms, he gave Turkish women their freedom and abolished the customs of the harem, the veil, and polygamy (practice of marriage to more than one wife or husband at the same time).

Testing Your Vocabulary

Choose the best answer.

1. The Russians hoped to gain control of the *straits* called the Dardanelles. A strait is
   a. a long trade route across a desert.
   b. a narrow waterway leading to the sea.
   c. an area of land on which churches are built.

2. An *international* meeting would include
   a. many different nations.
   b. many racial and religious groups.
   c. many generals and army officers.

Understanding What You Have Read

1. A good title for paragraphs 7 through 9 is
   a. The Young Turk Movement.
   b. The Importance of the Dardanelles.
   c. Religious Differences in the Turkish Empire.
   d. Russia's Dealings in the Balkans.
2. In which paragraphs do you find facts about
   a. the reasons why the Balkan people wanted independence?
   b. the nationalities living in the Turkish Empire?
   c. the land lost by Turkey after World War I?
   d. the Young Turk movement?
3. Russia was defeated in the Crimean War because
   a. the Russian armies were badly led.
   b. England, France, and Sardinia came to Turkey's aid.
   c. most of the fighting was in Turkey.

4. Many European countries supported the Greeks in their war for independence because
   a. they had signed a treaty promising to help the Greeks.
   b. they disliked the Turkish sultan.
   c. they wanted to help Christians living in Turkey.
5. Russia wanted to gain control of the city of Constantinople because it
   a. had many art treasures.
   b. was an excellent harbor.
   c. controlled the Dardanelles.
6. Russia's main reason for fighting the Turks in two wars in the 19th century was to
   a. protect the Greek Christians from persecution.
   b. get control of the Dardanelles.
   c. get Turkish territory in Africa.
7. At the end of World War I, Great Britain and France took Turkish territory because they wanted to
   a. gain more land.
   b. free the Christians in Turkey.
   c. keep peace in Asia Minor.

Developing Ideas and Skills

MAKING A CHART

In your notebook, fill in the items missing in the following chart on Nationalism in the Balkans.

Balkan Nation	Date of Independence	How Independence Was Won
Greece	_____	Revolt from Turkish Empire
Serbia	_____	Congress of Berlin
Montenegro	_____	_____
Romania	_____	_____
Bulgaria	_____	_____

Summary of Unit VIII

A few of the most important events and facts mentioned in this unit are listed below. Can you add any others?

1. Nationalism means love of one's country and loyalty to its ideals.
2. The ideas of modern nationalism began with the French Revolution and the Napoleonic era.
3. In the 19th and 20th centuries, the forces of nationalism unified some nations and destroyed others.
4. Germany became a unified nation in 1871 as a result of many wars.
5. The government of Germany before World War I was an autocracy under a kaiser.
6. Bismarck made Germany economically and militarily strong.
7. Italy became a united nation in 1871 through the leadership of Garibaldi, Mazzini, and Cavour.
8. The Austrian Empire in the 19th century was made up of many different nationalities.
9. At the end of World War I, the Austro-Hungarian Empire was broken up into many small nations.
10. The Turkish Empire was destroyed and divided by revolution and war in the 19th and 20th centuries.

Making Generalizations

For each of the following, make one accurate generalization based on the three factual statements given.

1. Factual statements:
   a. The spirit of nationalism weakened the once mighty Turkish Empire.
   b. The spirit of nationalism helped unite the many small German states.
   c. The desire of minorities for their own nation helped destroy the empire of Austria-Hungary.
   Generalization:
2. Factual statements:
   a. Bismarck wanted the Danes, French, and Poles in Germany to give up their language and customs.
   b. Austria-Hungary took Bosnia-Herzegovina without regard for the nationality of people who lived there.
   c. The Turkish Empire placed unfair taxes on the Balkan minorities.
   Generalization:

3. Factual statements:
   a. A single shot from an assassin's pistol led Europe into World War I.
   b. The Franco-Prussian War made it possible for the Italian army to capture Rome.
   c. Unrest among Balkan minorities in the Turkish Empire led to conflict between Russia and England.

   Generalization:

TURNING POINTS

Culture

The World: Flags

One way that people express feelings of nationalism is by honoring their country's flag. A nation's flag represents its land, people, government, and beliefs. The red flag of Turkey has a white crescent and a five-pointed star. These are the Muslim symbols for peace and life. More than 98 percent of Turkey's people are Muslims. Turkey's flag, then, represents important beliefs of its people.

Several nations with large Muslim populations have stars and crescents on their flags. Two examples are Mauritania and Pakistan. Some nations that have many Christian people, such as Iceland and New Zealand, have a cross on their flags. Stars, symbols of unity, are found on many flags. On the United States flag, the 50 stars stand for 50 states united under one government.

The ancient Egyptians were the first people to use flags. Egyptian soldiers attached long streamers to poles and carried them into battle. The armies of other early peoples, such as the Greeks, Assyrians, and Romans, also used flags. By the Middle Ages, flags were important symbols of power for many nobles in Europe. However, as nations began to develop in Europe, flags became symbols of national unity. They stood for all the people who belonged to a nation. The oldest national flag dates back to this period. It belongs to Denmark. Denmark's flag has been in use since the year 1219.

When a flag is designed, special thought is given to its colors. The flag of Kenya has stripes of three colors. The black stripe stands for the people of Kenya. The red represents their struggle for independence. The green stands for farming, which is the major occupation in Kenya.

Most countries have rules about how and when their flag should be flown and used. All nations want their flags treated with respect and dignity. A flag is one of the most important symbols that a nation has.

Critical Thinking

1. Based on what you have read here and in the last chapter, would you expect the flag of Greece to have a cross or a star and crescent? Explain.
2. National flags should be flown outdoors only in good weather. Why do you think this is so?

UNIT IX

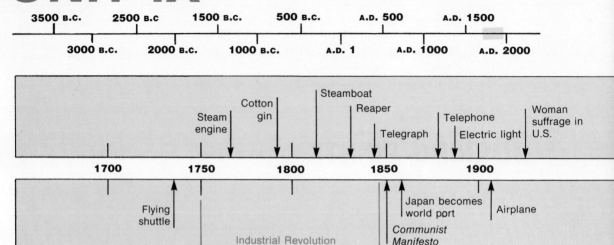

3500 B.C. 2500 B.C 1500 B.C. 500 B.C. A.D. 500 A.D. 1500

3000 B.C. 2000 B.C. 1000 B.C. A.D. 1 A.D. 1000 A.D. 2000

Steam engine

Cotton gin

Steamboat

Reaper

Telegraph

Telephone

Electric light

Woman suffrage in U.S.

1700   1750   1800   1850   1900

Flying shuttle

Industrial Revolution

Japan becomes world port

Communist Manifesto

Airplane

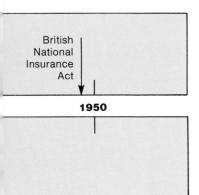

British
National
Insurance
Act

1950

What Changes in Industry, Science, and Culture Took Place?

A woman adjusts a spool of cotton thread in a textile factory in Santa Cruz, Bolivia.

375

AIM: What was the Industrial Revolution and why did it begin in England?

CHAPTER 1

Old Ways of Manufacturing Change

WHAT IS AN ECONOMIC REVOLUTION?

1. Two hundred years ago, it took a shoemaker two days to make one pair of shoes. Today, a shoe factory makes one pair of shoes per worker every half hour. What caused this change? It was the Industrial Revolution. The Industrial Revolution means the changes in the ways goods came to be made and the effects of

Ironworks factory in England in 1858. Why was the Industrial Revolution so important?

these changes. This change in manufacturing began in England about two hundred and fifty years ago. It has spread throughout the world. Before we study the Industrial Revolution, however, let us find out how people worked in Europe before it began.

2. Before the European discovery of America, the merchants of Europe traded with one another. After Columbus discovered the New World, the nations of Europe planted colonies in America and in Asia. European ships began to carry goods to these far-off places. They brought back to Europe raw cotton, tobacco, wood, spices, silks, gold, and silver.

3. Before Europe began to colonize the New World, most business was carried on by single merchants or partners. After colonization began, large amounts of money were needed to pay for ships and for the other costs of doing business with colonies. To raise the money, merchants and bankers formed *joint-stock companies*. These sold *shares* (part ownership) in the company to investors. An investor is a person who puts money into a company and shares in its profits or losses. Joint-stock companies were free-enterprise, capitalist businesses. In a free-enterprise system, people are free to start or share in a business and run it as they like. But they must obey laws and regulations for the good of society and the protection of their customers. Under capitalism, businesses are owned and run by private citizens, rather than governments. The European businesses that carried on trade with colonies made much money.

4. This worldwide growth of trade was known as the commercial revolution. It grew during the 17th and 18th centuries. It was the first of the great economic changes of modern times. (Do not confuse these revolutions which you are about to study with *political* revolutions. The American and French revolutions were political. In these, fighting and bloodshed brought changes in government.) The changes in trade of the 17th and 18th centuries caused an *economic* revolution. There was no fighting or bloodshed. There were no changes in government. Economic revolution means changes in ways of making goods, trading, or earning a living. Sometimes people who live through economic changes do not even realize they are doing so. But economic revolutions change people's lives as much as political revolutions do.

5. After America was discovered, English merchants shipped large amounts of textiles (woven goods) to their new colonies. These textiles had been woven by hand by English peasants. The peasants used very simple tools. They used a carding board and a spinning wheel to make thread. They used a hand loom to weave the cloth. They worked mainly at home. This system of manufacturing goods in homes is called the domestic system.

WHAT NEW MACHINES WERE INVENTED?

6. As the revolution in trade grew, so did the demand for textiles. But the handwork of the domestic system was too slow to fill the demand. English merchants found that they could not get enough thread or cloth. Soon, clever Englishmen started finding ways of making textiles faster. John Kay, for example, invented a flying shuttle in 1733. This machine

An artist's representation of the "domestic system" of work. How do you think the Industrial Revolution might change this scene?

wove cloth at a quick rate. But once cloth could be made faster, there was a greater demand for thread. James Hargreaves then invented a spinning jenny. This machine made many threads at one time. In 1769, Richard Arkwright invented a spinning machine called a water frame. The water frame did not have to be worked by people because it ran by water power.

James Hargreave's spinning jenny.

7. One invention led to another. In 1769, James Watt invented a steam engine. It could run any kind of machine. A few years later, Samuel Crompton invented a spinning mule. This was an improvement of the spinning jenny and water frame. Edward Cartwright invented the power loom, which used water power to weave cloth. These machines all increased the amount of thread that could be made and speeded up the weaving of cloth. They were all invented by Englishmen and used in England.

8. Once machines could make textiles faster, the need for raw cotton grew. This cotton came from the American colonies, where it was still cleaned by hand. This method was a slow one. In 1793, an American named Eli Whitney invented the cotton gin. It cleaned the cotton seeds out of the cotton fiber. Raw cotton could thus be prepared much faster. The sewing machine, invented in 1846 by Elias Howe, an American, was the last of the important textile machines to be invented.

9. These new machines were too large and too expensive to be used by families in the home. So businessmen set them up in large buildings. Such buildings are called *factories.* Then businessmen hired workers to come to the factories every day. The *factory system* of manufacturing goods in factories instead of at home began in England about 1750. The invention of textile machines and the spread of the factory system were among the changes known as the *Industrial Revolution.*

WHY DID THE INDUSTRIAL REVOLUTION BEGIN IN ENGLAND?

10. You may wonder why the Industrial Revolution began in England. Why didn't it begin in some other country? The answer is that in the 18th century, England had everything needed to start a new economic system. English merchants and business people had become rich

19th-century factory scene showing children doing the work. Why do you think the owners wanted to employ children?

from trade with the colonies. The capitalist system had worked very well during the commercial revolution. The English had learned how to form corporations to raise the money needed to buy the new machines and build the factories.

11. England also had the raw materials needed to supply factories. It had water power from streams and rivers. It had coal from its coal mines which could drive the steam engines. It had the workers for its factories. It had the ships to carry the finished goods. England had markets (places to sell its goods) in its American colonies and in its trading posts in India. For these reasons, the Industrial Revolution began in England. After 1800, the Industrial Revolution spread to the United States and to the countries of Western Europe.

12. Some inventors made textile machines. Others were working to improve transportation and communication. In the United States, Robert Fulton put Watt's steam engine on a boat. He had the engine turn a paddle wheel. The result was the first successful steamboat, in 1807. George Stephenson, an Englishman, put the steam engine on wheels. This was the first good steam locomotive. Steamboats and trains drawn by locomotives could now carry the products of factories quickly and cheaply. The first steamship to cross the Atlantic Ocean was called the *Great Western.*

13. The next step in the Industrial Revolution was to find ways of quickly letting people know what was going on. In 1844, Samuel F. B. Morse, an American, made an important invention in communications: the telegraph. By connecting any two places with electric wires, he could send messages almost as fast as one could wink an eye. In 1866, Cyrus W. Field, another American, laid the first telegraph line across the Atlantic Ocean. It was called the Atlantic Cable. It connected the United States and Europe by telegraph for the first time.

Testing Your Vocabulary

Choose the best answer.

1. An *economic* revolution is one that causes changes in
   a. government and politics.
   b. manufacturing, trade, and ways of earning a living.
   c. art, literature, and music.

2. The *domestic system* of manufacturing was a system in which most work was done
   a. in large factories and mills.
   b. in small shops.
   c. in the home.

Understanding What You Have Read

1. The main idea of paragraphs 5 through 7 is
   a. the Industrial Revolution began with many textile inventions.
   b. the Industrial Revolution had many causes.
   c. the Industrial Revolution had many results.
   d. Americans contributed to the Industrial Revolution.

2. In which paragraphs do you find facts about
   a. the beginning of the factory system?
   b. the kinds of goods sent to England by the colonies?
   c. the revolution in communication?
   d. the meaning of the domestic system?

3. Eli Whitney's cotton gin was important to the textile industry because it speeded up the
   a. spinning of cotton.
   b. weaving of cloth.
   c. cleaning of raw cotton.

4. One reason why the Industrial Revolution began in England was that
   a. the English people needed cotton cloth.
   b. English business people had money to pay for machines.
   c. the British needed money to fight the French.

5. The domestic system of manufacturing was slow because
   a. almost no machinery was used.

b. there were not enough raw materials.

c. sailing ships made transportation slow.

6. Edward Cartwright's invention of the power loom was important because it
   a. was the first invention in textile manufacturing.
   b. started the factory system in England.

c. speeded up the weaving of cloth.

7. The discovery of America was a step to the Industrial Revolution because
   a. new colonies provided goods and markets in which to trade.
   b. gold was discovered in the New World.
   c. European businessmen settled in the New World.

Tell whether the statements are true or false. If a statement is false, change the words in italics to make it true.

1. *James Watt* invented the steamboat.
2. The Industrial Revolution began *before* the discovery of America.
3. The telegraph was invented by an *American* scientist.
4. The Industrial Revolution began in the *United States*.
5. Early English inventors found that *water power* could run their machinery.
6. The American colonies provided England with *thread* to make textiles.
7. The factory system was part of the *French* Revolution.
8. Early textile machines were made by *French* inventors.
9. Before the Industrial Revolution began, textiles were made under the *domestic system*.
10. The French Revolution and the American Revolution were *economic* revolutions.

Developing Ideas and Skills

MAKING A CHART

Complete the following chart in your notebook.

Inventions of the Industrial Revolution			
Machine	**Inventor**	**Country**	**Result**
Flying shuttle	John Kay	England	Faster weaving of cloth
Spinning jenny	_____	_____	_____
Water frame	_____	_____	_____
Steam engine	_____	_____	_____
Spinning mule	_____	_____	_____
Power loom	_____	_____	_____
Cotton gin	_____	_____	_____

AIM: How did crop raising methods change during the Agricultural Revolution?

CHAPTER 2

Old Ways of Farming Change

Cyrus McCormick demonstrating his harvesting, or mechanical, reaper in 1831. This invention not only enabled farmers to cut grain faster but also reduced the number of workers needed for harvesting.

WHAT WAS FARMING LIKE IN THE EARLY 18TH CENTURY?

1. One-third of the world's people today go to bed hungry every night. In some countries, there is so little food that children get only one meal a day. In countries such as the United States and Canada, there is plenty of food. People have to go on diets in order not to get fat. Some countries grow more food than they can use. This extra food is called a *surplus*. Why do some countries grow more food than they need and others not enough? One important reason is that some countries have learned new ways of farming and use modern machines. These countries have had what we call an agricultural revolution. They use new methods of farming.

2. In the early 18th century, farming in Europe and America was done by hand and with simple tools. When George Washington was a young man, for example, farmers used tools very much like those used by ancient Egyptian farmers 3,000 years earlier. Wooden plows were used to break the soil. The plows were pulled by horses or cattle. Seeds were scattered or planted by hand. (Birds ate many of the seeds.) At harvest time, the crop was cut with a hand tool called a scythe (SYTH). The crop was then gathered by hand.

3. Without fertilizers, the same crop cannot be grown on the same farm land every year. If it is, the soil loses its richness. During the Middle Ages, this problem was solved by a three-field system of farming. One out of every three fields was left unplanted each year. The soil on the unused field would thus get back its fertility. But this was a wasteful method of farming since a large part of the land could not be used. Farmers, however, knew no other way to bring back life to the soil. Early methods of agriculture meant heavy work for the farmer. They also meant small crops for the market and small profits for the farmer.

4. In the 18th century, many English peasants left their farms for jobs in city factories. The Industrial Revolution had created many new jobs in factories. In addition, the Enclosure Acts were passed. These combined small farms into larger ones. One of their effects was to force British peasants to leave their farms and move to the cities. Since there were fewer farmers, less food was grown. England was faced with a serious problem. How could it grow enough food for all the people now living in the cities when there were fewer farm workers? Fortunately, the revolution in farming methods was beginning at about the same time as the Industrial Revolution. A number of agricultural machines were invented. New methods of farming were developed. These improvements made possible the raising of larger crops with fewer farm workers.

WHAT WERE THE NEW MACHINES THAT IMPROVED FARMING?

5. The first important improvement in farming in the 18th century was the invention of a seed drill by Jethro Tull. This machine planted seeds in rows. It slowly took the place of the old method of scattering seeds by hand. Then an English landowner, Viscount (VY-count) Townshend, developed a system of *crop rotation*. He found that by planting a different crop each year on the same piece of land the soil kept its fertility. Townshend's crop rotation system brought an end to the old three-field system. All farmland could now be farmed every year.

6. The old wooden plow was changed. Charles Newbold, an American, developed a cast-iron plow. This was stronger than the wooden plow. But like the wooden plow, the iron plow would break if it hit a large rock. In 1837, John Deere, another American, invented a tougher, steel plow. It could hit rocks and tree stumps without breaking. Later, a plow shaped like a wheel was invented. It was called a rotary plow. The rotary plow is used by modern farmers today.

7. Farmers raised cattle, sheep, hogs, and chickens as well as crops for food. A number of 19th-century scientists found ways of improving the *grade*, or quality, of farm animals. Robert Bakewell, an Englishman, used scientific methods to improve the quality of English sheep. Charles and Robert Colling improved the quality of English cattle. Improvements in farm animals meant that more meat was produced at a lower cost. Englishmen began to eat meat regularly at their meals.

8. An American named Cyrus McCormick invented the most important farm machine of the 19th century. This was the *reaper*, which McCormick invented in 1834. The reaper ended the cutting of wheat and other crops by hand. McCormick's first reaper was drawn by a horse or other animal. It could cut a crop ten times faster than a person could. With the reaper, farmers could cover ten times more land than they could with hand scythes.

WHAT NEW METHODS DO MODERN FARMERS USE?

9. The agricultural revolution, with its new farming machinery and new methods, began in the 18th century. It has continued to the present day. A modern farmer's barn is crowded with expensive machinery. A modern wheat farmer, for example, uses a huge rotary

gang plow to cut twenty rows in the soil at one time. The wheat seeds are planted with a seed drill twenty feet wide. The crop is later harvested with a *combine*. A combine is a machine that cuts the wheat and separates the wheat kernels from the grass.

10. Machines on modern farms are pulled by tractors instead of horses. Cattle or dairy farmers use a mowing machine to cut hay. They have baling machines to tie the hay into bales (bundles). A machine lifts the bales into the barn. Modern farmers even have automatic milking machines to milk the cows. The work of a modern farm, like that of a modern factory, is done mostly by machines.

11. Farming methods as well as machines have improved. A farmer now has several ways of fighting *erosion*, the wearing away of soil by heavy rains or winds. Today's farmers do not plow in straight lines all the time. If their farms are hilly, they plow in curves. This is called *contour* plowing. Contour plowing stops erosion. Farmers also use *strip cropping* to stop erosion. In strip cropping, the farmer plants a *row crop* near a *cover crop*. Such crops as corn and potatoes grow in rows and so are called row crops. Such crops as wheat and barley cover an entire field. They are called cover crops. Planting row crops and cover crops near each other keeps the soil from being washed away by rains. To keep winds and floods from wearing away soil, today's farmers also plant trees and grass. The roots of trees and grass hold the soil together and keep it from wearing away.

12. Farm crops can get diseases. In addition, insects like bugs and locusts can ruin a crop within a few days. Scientists have made chemicals that farmers spray on crops to protect them from insects and disease. Scientists have also developed chemical fertilizers. These chemicals can double the size of a farmer's crop. The agricultural revolution continues. New farm methods, new machinery, and new chemicals continue to bring larger harvests. The agricultural revolution has been going on for more than 200 years.

This picture shows land where soil erosion has taken place. How can farmers prevent this from happening?

A farmer practices contour plowing to prevent soil erosion. What other methods have been developed to increase farm production?

Testing Your Vocabulary

Choose the best answer.

1. A *surplus* of food is
   a. food that is used only as animal feed.
   b. food that is put in storage.
   c. more food than is needed.

2. To *rotate* crops means to
   a. scatter seeds by machine.
   b. plant different crops each year.
   c. plant large amounts of crops.

Understanding What You Have Read

1. A good title for paragraphs 2 and 3 is
   a. New Farm Machinery.
   b. Farming Before the Agricultural Revolution.
   c. Results of the Agricultural Revolution.
   d. Farm Crop Diseases.
2. In what paragraphs do you find facts about
   a. the development of crop rotation?
   b. machines used in modern wheat farming?
   c. scientific methods of improving animals?
   d. the invention of the reaper?
3. Modern farmers produce more crops than ever before because
   a. they have developed the three-field system.
   b. they use more farm workers.
   c. they use machinery and chemical fertilizers.
4. Wooden plows, used by farmers before the agricultural revolution, were not good because
   a. they did not cut deeply into the soil.

   b. they broke easily.
   c. they could be used to plow in a straight line only.
5. Cyrus McCormick's invention was important because
   a. it speeded up the cutting of farm crops.
   b. it improved the quality of farm animals.
   c. it ended the method of scattering seeds by hand.
6. The system of crop rotation helped farmers because it
   a. kept them from producing too much of one crop.
   b. could be used in the three-field system.
   c. kept the soil fertile while crops were raised on it.
7. The Enclosure Acts forced British peasants to leave their farms because the acts
   a. combined small farms into large ones.
   b. raised taxes on small farms.
   c. freed the serfs.

In your notebook, fill in the correct word or phrase for each of the following statements.

1. The system of leaving one-third of the land unused each year was called the _____.
2. The Englishmen Bakewell and Colling contributed to the agricultural revolu-

tion by improving the quality of _____.
3. John Deere helped farmers by developing the _____.
4. Wearing away of the soil by rain or

wind is called _____ .

5. Cyrus McCormick's machine for cutting wheat is called the _____ .

6. The modern system in which row crops are planted next to cover crops is called _____ .

7. Changing the crop grown each year on a piece of land is called _____ .

8. Plowing in curves to stop erosion is called _____ .

9. Jethro Tull invented the _____ .

10. The system of rotating crops in order to keep the soil fertile was developed by an English landowner named _____ .

Developing Ideas and Skills

WRITING AN OUTLINE

Complete this outline by filling in the blank spaces in your notebook.

The Agricultural Revolution

A. Farming before the agricultural revolution
   1. Wooden plows
   2.
   3.
   4.
B. Farming during the agricultural revolution
   1. Farm machinery
   2. Crop rotation
   3.
   4.
C. Farm machinery and inventors
   1. Seed drill—Jethro Tull
   2.
   3.

AIM: What newer improvements were made in the industrial system?

CHAPTER 3

A New Industrial Revolution Takes Place

HOW DID THE UNITED STATES BECOME A LEADER IN INDUSTRY?

1. Sometimes you walk into an elevator and an operator takes you to the floor you want. At other times you walk into an elevator and there is no operator. You push a button and the elevator goes to the floor you want. This is an example of *automation*. It means the use of machinery that works without people. Automation is part of the Industrial Revolution.

One of Thomas Edison's inventions was the phonograph. Compare this early machine to present-day models.

2. This revolution has been going on for more than two centuries. It began with John Kay's invention of the flying shuttle, in 1733. The first stage of the Industrial Revolution continued until the middle of the 19th century. It took place mainly in England. While the nations of Continental Europe were busy with the Napoleonic wars and with revolutions, England was developing its factory system. Soon England became known as the "workshop of the world" because it supplied foreign countries with goods. Then the Industrial Revolution and factory system spread to other countries. They reached the United States and the other countries of Europe.

3. The Industrial Revolution reached the United States about 1790. In that year, Samuel Slater built the first textile factory in America. During and after the War of 1812, American industries began to grow quickly. Since then, the building of factories in the United States has never stopped. The Industrial Revolution also spread slowly to France, Holland, and Belgium. England was the leader at the beginning. Later, the United States moved ahead.

4. Near the end of the 19th century, changes in manufacturing took place very quickly. These changes, from 1870 to the present, are often thought of as the *new* Industrial Revolution. There have been countless new inventions in the new Industrial Revolution. It would take a shelf of large books to list all the inventions in the United States in the last hundred years. But three of the most famous may be mentioned here. Alexander Graham Bell invented the telephone in 1876. Thomas Alva Edison invented the electric light in 1879. And the Wright brothers invented and flew the first airplane in 1903.

HOW DO MACHINE-MADE PRODUCTS AFFECT INDUSTRY?

5. Inventions changed the way in which business offices are run. The elevator, for example, was invented by Elisha Otis. Without elevators to carry people, there could be no skyscrapers. Christopher Sholes invented the typewriter, and Edmund Barbour invented the adding machine. These also improved business offices. Many inventors were working in America. But European inventors were also busy

developing new machines. An Englishman, Michael Faraday, built the first generator. This is a machine that produces electricity. Another Englishman, Sir Henry Bessemer developed a new method of making steel in 1856. Guglielmo Marconi, an Italian, invented the wireless telegraph in 1896. The wireless telegraph opened the way for the later inventions of radio and television.

6. New kinds of power for industry were found during the new Industrial Revolution. Earlier, the steam engine had been used in factories. It was also used for trains and ships. Now, new kinds of power were used. These were the electric motor, the gasoline engine, the diesel motor, and the jet engine. These new motors took the place of the old steam engines. Modern cars, airplanes, and locomotives are run by gasoline and diesel motors. Most factory machines today are run by electric motors.

7. You remember that the first inventions of the Industrial Revolution were mainly ma-

The first airplane flight at Kitty Hawk, North Carolina, December 17, 1903. Although the Wright brothers' airplane flew only a few seconds, it was an historic flight. Why?

Henry Ford began producing Model T cars on an assembly line. Why was this an important step in manufacturing?

chines for making cloth. In the new Industrial Revolution, machines were invented for use in almost all industries. Almost every product you can think of is made by machines today. The clothes you wear are made by machine. The pen you write with and the desk you sit at are machine-made. The book you are now reading was printed by a machine. It was bound in covers by machines. It is no wonder that our century has been called "the machine age."

IN WHAT WAYS IS THE NEW INDUSTRIAL REVOLUTION STILL GOING ON?

8. New methods of manufacturing goods were also developed during the new Industrial Revolution. One of these methods was *mass production*. Others were division of labor and the conveyor system. Mass production means the making of thousands of the same product. Division of labor means that each worker does only one particular job in making a product. No longer does a worker handle a product from start to finish. The conveyor system is a way of bringing materials on moving belts to workers at their work tables. The newest method in manufacturing is automation. We have seen that this means the use of machinery that works without people. It also means the use of machines to run other machines. The button-operated elevator mentioned before is an example of modern automation.

9. The new Industrial Revolution also brought changes in ways of doing business. Today, many businesses are corporations. A corporation is a company that exists almost like a person. The owners and workers may change, but the company lives on. Corporations may be owned by thousands of people who buy their stock. Corporations often control goods they manufacture from raw materials to their final sale to the customer. Modern businesses use advertising to sell the large amounts of goods they manufacture. Advertising on television and in magazines and newspapers is part of the usual way of selling goods today.

10. The first Industrial Revolution took place in England, the United States, and Western Europe. The new Industrial Revolution is worldwide. Germany and Italy became united nations in 1871. Then they also had a revolution in industry. Changes in industry came to Japan after 1853. It was then that Japan first opened its ports to world trade. Today, Japan is one of the great industrial nations of the world. After World War I, the Communist government of the Soviet Union began to build up Russian industries. Today the Soviet Union is also part of the new Industrial Revolution. After World War II, many countries in Asia and Latin America built modern factories. They also began to use new industrial methods. Today, the new Industrial Revolution affects the life and business of most countries in the world.

11. The new Industrial Revolution is not yet over. It is still going on around us every day. We have just started to use atomic power and rocket transportation. Rocket motors have already given us the power to explore the moon, the planets, and outer space. The time may not be far off when power from the atom will take the place of coal, oil, and gas. What new miracles of science will the new Industrial Revolution perform in the years to come?

388

Testing Your Vocabulary

Choose the best answer.

1. *Mass production* means
   a. the use of modern machines in textile making.
   b. the employment of many workers in a factory.
   c. the manufacture of large amounts of the same thing.
2. The *conveyor* system in modern factories refers to
   a. the use of telephones within the factory.
   b. the belt system of moving materials.
   c. the building of factories near railroad lines.
3. *Automation* in industry means
   a. the use of automatic machinery.
   b. restaurants without waiters.
   c. the use of atomic power.

Understanding What You Have Read

1. The main idea of paragraphs 4 through 6 is
   a. the Industrial Revolution reached Japan.
   b. the Machine Age had many results.
   c. many inventions brought on the new Industrial Revolution.
   d. the new Industrial Revolution began in the United States.
2. In which paragraphs do you find facts about
   a. possible future kinds of industrial power?
   b. mass production and division of labor?
   c. the first textile factory in the United States?
   d. the Industrial Revolution in the Soviet Union?
3. Modern businesses use advertising because it
   a. helps newspapers and television stations.
   b. encourages people to buy the large amount of goods being manufactured.
   c. brings a better quality of goods to customers.
4. The first Industrial Revolution did not affect Germany or Italy very much before 1871 because they
   a. were not yet unified nations.
   b. could not get the machines they needed.
   c. did not have the necessary raw materials.
5. During the 19th century, England was called the "workshop of the world" because
   a. it was the only country that had an industrial revolution.
   b. it set up factories in its colonies.
   c. its factories produced goods for other countries.
6. The Industrial Revolution did not reach the continent of Europe until after 1815 because
   a. no machines could be exported from England.
   b. the Metternich System would not allow the building of factories.
   c. the Napoleonic wars kept Europe from building up industry.
7. The first textile factory was built in the United States by
   a. Eli Whitney.

   b. Samuel Slater.

   c. Cyrus McCormick.

8. The American factory system began to grow after
   a. World War I.
   b. World War II.
   c. the War of 1812.

9. The wireless telegraph made possible the later invention of
   a. television.
   b. the automobile.
   c. the telephone.

10. The Bessemer process was a new method of making
    a. cloth.   b. steel.   c. paper.

11. Most factory machinery is driven by
    a. steam.
    b. gasoline.
    c. electricity.

12. Most large businesses today are
    a. partnerships.
    b. cooperatives.
    c. corporations.

13. Inventors who took the lead in developing new machines during the new Industrial Revolution were
    a. American. b. English. c. Russian.

14. Another name for the new Industrial Revolution is
    a. the space age.
    b. the machine age.
    c. the age of steam.

15. The first machine to generate electricity was built by
    a. Thomas Edison.
    b. Alexander Graham Bell.
    c. Michael Faraday.

16. The Asian country that had an industrial revolution in the late nineteenth century was
    a. China.   b. Japan.   c. India.

Developing Ideas and Skills

MAKING A CHART

Complete the following chart in your notebook.

Inventions of the New Industrial Revolution		
Invention	**Inventor**	**Country**
Telephone	_____	_____
Electric lamp	_____	_____
Airplane	_____	_____
Steelmaking	_____	_____
Wireless telegraph	_____	_____
Electric generator	_____	_____
Passenger elevator	_____	_____

AIM: What are some of the good and bad effects of the economic revolutions?

CHAPTER 4

The Industrial Revolution Brings Benefits and Problems

HOW HAS THE INDUSTRIAL REVOLUTION HELPED PEOPLE TO LIVE BETTER?

1. Who could claim a better life and more luxuries—an emperor of ancient Rome or a modern factory worker? One might answer, "The modern factory worker." He has a radio, a television set, an automobile, a telephone, electric lights, and hundreds of other luxuries. The emperor of Rome could not buy any of these things with all his wealth. On the average, a modern worker lives twice as long as a Roman citizen did two thousand years ago. Today, people live better than people have at any other time in the past. Their better life is the result of the industrial and agricultural revolutions.

2. Machines now do all the heavy work in factories and on farms. Because machines do the heavy work, there are now lighter factory jobs. Inventions such as washing machines and vacuum cleaners have made housework easier. People live longer today because of scientific and medical progress. New medicines and medical tools such as the X-ray machine have been developed. Modern hospital equipment is one result of the Industrial Revolution.

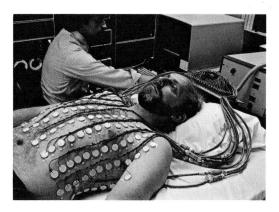

Modern medical equipment such as this electrocardiograph machine has helped diagnose disease early and aid in better treatment.

3. Because of the industrial and agricultural revolutions, more goods can be made faster. People have to work fewer hours a day. They often have more free time to enjoy and educate themselves. New inventions have brought new kinds of entertainment, such as movies, radio, and television. People can learn more. Newspapers, magazines, and books are so low in price that nearly everyone can buy them. People can attend good schools and col-

leges. They usually have the time to go to libraries and theaters.

WHAT ECONOMIC AND SOCIAL CHANGES HAS THE INDUSTRIAL REVOLUTION CAUSED?

4. As new machines in England began to take over much of people's work, some of them lost their jobs. This is called *unemployment*. Angry mobs burned factories and destroyed machines that had put them out of work. They blamed the new machines for hard times and unemployment. The history of the Industrial Revolution has shown, however, that unemployment caused by new machines lasts for a short time only. Then, new industries created by machines give rise to new jobs. In the end, there are more jobs than there were before. The Industrial Revolution puts an end to some jobs but creates many new jobs.

5. However, the Industrial Revolution has brought real problems. New poor workers moved to industrial cities. Soon crowded buildings and slums grew up. Men and women worked for long hours in factories at low wages. They often did not earn enough money. They had to send their young children to work in mines and factories. These bad labor conditions caused disease, misery, and crime. But in almost all industrial countries today young children are no longer allowed to work.

6. The Industrial Revolution also brought changes in social and economic classes. Before the Industrial Revolution there were peasants, skilled workers, and a few merchants and businesspeople. Today, there are two important economic groups. There is a class of working people and a class of business people, manufacturers, managers, and corporation owners. These two classes are known as *labor* and *management*. In modern times some workers join together in labor unions. These unions try to get better working conditions and higher wages

for their members. They sometimes go on strike, or refuse to work, in order to get what they want.

7. The lives of factory workers have been improved by laws passed by governments. Many people who moved to cities to work in factories wanted the right to vote. In most democratic countries, they received it. In addition, workers formed political labor parties in some countries. These labor parties often ran the government. Once workers could vote and get positions in government, they passed factory laws to protect themselves. These laws said that workers did not have to work more than a certain number of hours per week. They also must earn no less than a certain wage. In addition, governments passed laws to protect workers against sickness, old age, and unemployment.

Child abuse was common in 19th-century factories. Courageous social workers, concerned citizens, and skilled writers worked hard to get these abuses stopped and child labor laws passed.

Two new political ideas also grew out of the Industrial Revolution. These ideas were socialism and communism.

WHAT NEW PROBLEMS HAVE DEVELOPED?

8. In world affairs, the Industrial Revolution has had both good and bad effects. Industrial nations need supplies of raw materials. They need coal, oil, iron ore, timber, copper, and rubber. In the 19th century, such nations searched for colonies in foreign lands that had these needed materials. A nation's policy to use its power to control a foreign land is called *imperialism*. Great Britain, France, Germany, and other industrial countries were imperialistic when they searched for colonies. Sometimes, two industrial nations would fight over a valuable colony. Thus, industrialism could lead to imperialism, and imperialism to war.

9. Modern weapons of war are also unfortunate results of the Industrial Revolution. The airplane was a wonderful invention. But in wartime, it is used to bomb cities. New weapons of great destruction, such as guided missiles and hydrogen bombs, have been invented. The Industrial Revolution has also been the cause of a serious world problem—pollution. Factories have dirtied the air we breathe. They have polluted our rivers and lakes. Dangerous new

This view along the Rhine in the late 19th century shows the air pollution created by factories.

chemicals have poisoned the soil in which our food is grown.

10. The Industrial Revolution has, however, brought the people of different countries closer to one another. Today, the people of North America can watch a German television show. We can speak to someone in Italy on the telephone, or watch a Japanese movie. We can travel to any part of the world in 24 hours. In one day, a traveler can have breakfast in New York City, lunch in England, and late dinner in Turkey. Because people are closer today, they may learn to understand one another better. Better understanding would help keep peace.

Testing Your Vocabulary

Choose the best answer.

1. *Management* in industry refers to
   a. people who work on assembly lines.
   b. factory working conditions.
   c. people who run a business.

2. The rapid growth of large cities during the Industrial Revolution created *slums*. These are
   a. neighborhoods with many libraries.

b. areas with unclean and overcrowded buildings.
c. areas where merchants live.
3. A *raw material* is

a. an item needed to make another product.
b. a poorly made product.
c. a factory-made article of clothing.

Understanding What You Have Read _____

1. A good title for paragraphs 2 and 3 is
   a. The Rise of Socialism and Communism.
   b. Benefits of the Industrial Revolution.
   c. Growth of Labor Unions.
   d. Causes of Imperialism.
2. In which paragraphs do you find facts about
   a. the war weapons resulting from the Industrial Revolution?
   b. the causes of imperialism?
   c. unemployment caused by machines?
   d. laws passed to protect factory workers?
3. The Industrial Revolution has improved living conditions by
   a. creating jobs for young children.
   b. giving people more and better goods and services.
   c. making labor strikes possible.
4. On the average, people live twice as long today as they did two hundred years ago because they
   a. work harder.
   b. have more money to spend.
   c. have more and better medical services.
5. Imperialism grew out of the Industrial Revolution because nations wanted colonies in foreign lands that would
   a. give them needed raw materials.
   b. give them people for their armies.
   c. make them seem more important.
6. Wars are more deadly today than they were in the past because
   a. there are more independent nations to start wars.
   b. there is greater need for colonies.
   c. the Industrial Revolution has created more destructive weapons of war.
7. Today, we know more than before about people in other parts of the world mainly because
   a. there are better conditions in factories.
   b. government officials make visits to foreign countries.
   c. modern methods of transportation and communication have been developed.

Developing Ideas and Skills _____

WRITING AN OUTLINE

Complete the outline on page 395 in your notebook.

Results of the Industrial Revolution

A. Economic Results
   1. better living conditions
   2. possible unemployment
   3. _____
B. Social Results
   1. growth of cities
   2. _____
   3. _____
C. _____
   1. workers get right to vote
   2. _____
   3. _____

Using Source Materials

Mills, mines, and factories have been polluting our surroundings since the Industrial Revolution began. The great English novelist Charles Dickens described an industrial town in his novel *Hard Times*. He called it Coketown. Read Dickens's description (adapted) of it; then answer the questions that follow.

It was a town of red brick, or of brick that would have been red if the smoke and ashes had allowed it. But as matters stood it was a town of unnatural red and black like the painted face of a savage.

It was a town of machinery and tall chimneys. Out of them interminable serpents [endlessly long snakes] of smoke trailed themselves for ever and ever, and never got coiled.

It had a black canal in it, and a river that ran purple with ill-smelling dye. There were vast piles of building full of windows. In them, there was a rattling and a trembling all day long. The piston of the steam-engine worked monotonously [boringly without change] up and down, like the head of an elephant in a state of melancholy [sad] madness. Coketown contained several large streets all very like one another. And there were many small streets still more like one another. These were inhabited by people equally like one another. They all went in and out at the same hours, with the same sound upon the pavements. They did the same work. To them, every day was the same as yesterday and tomorrow. Every year was the counterpart [same thing] of the last and the next year.

1. Point out three signs of industrial pollution mentioned in this description.
2. Why might Dickens have compared the steam-engine piston to the head of a sad, crazy elephant?
3. Reread the description of the people; then decide what one word best describes their way of life.
4. What else can you say about the lives of these people?

AIM: Why were labor unions formed in industrial countries?

CHAPTER 5

Working Conditions Are Improved

HOW DID LABOR UNIONS GROW?

1. Early in the 19th century, some English factory workers lost their jobs. They were fired because their employers bought new machinery that did the job they had done. The workers became angry. They broke into the factories and smashed the new machines. Since those early days of the Industrial Revolution, workers have learned to use different methods. They no longer start riots against machines. Instead, they join labor unions. A labor union is a group of workers who together try to get management to give them better pay, shorter hours, and improved working conditions. They try to get these things by *collective bargaining*. This means that employers sit down with union leaders to talk over worker demands. If bargaining fails, unions may go on strike, or use other methods.

2. It was natural for labor unions to begin in England since the Industrial Revolution and the factory system had begun there. Yet it was not easy to set up the first labor unions. The British were afraid that labor unions might some day cause mob violence. Parliament therefore passed the Combination Laws, in 1800. These laws said that labor unions must not be formed and that labor strikes were

crimes. It was 25 years before Parliament ended these laws. After 1825, many labor unions with growing numbers of members appeared. As British labor unions grew stronger, they were able to get Parliament to pass laws to improve conditions in factories and mines.

3. In 1901, the labor unions of England formed the British Labour party. Now, labor unions would not have to beg Parliament to pass factory laws. They would elect their own members to Parliament. After a few elections, the Labour party became the largest, or majority, party in Parliament. It was then able to choose the prime minister and run the government. The Labour party brought many changes in the lives of the people of Great Britain. The system of insurance for old age, sickness, and unemployment, for example, was passed through the work of the Labour party. The Labour party also put a large part of the medical system under government control.

4. The British government tries to take care of its citizens throughout their lives. This is the aim of its system of medicine and social insurance. Because of this, Great Britain is sometimes called a *welfare state*. In a welfare state, a person's health and other basic needs are looked after by the government. But such benefits are costly. People living in a welfare state must pay high taxes to support it. The British Labour party also believes that industries should be *nationalized*—owned and operated by the government. When the Labour party has run the British government, it has passed laws that have given the government ownership of such industries as electric power, coal, railroads, gas, airlines, and radio broadcasting.

5. In most nations of Western Europe, the history of labor unions is about the same as in England. Labor unions were made legal in France, Italy, and Germany in the late 19th century. The unions in these countries also formed labor parties. Today, almost every country in Western Europe has labor unions and labor parties. In countries without democratic governments, labor unions are not allowed to exist or are given no power. In Communist dictatorships, workers may join labor groups. But these groups may not legally strike for higher wages. Among countries with Communist dictatorships are the Soviet Union, Red China, Poland, Hungary, and Cuba. In 1980, people in Poland organized a workers' movement free of Communist control. They demanded more freedom in their factories, as well as in their country. In 1982, the movement was halted by military force.

Polish Solidarity members strike against their Communist government. What has been the result of their efforts?

HOW WERE WORKING CONDITIONS CHANGED?

6. In the early years of the Industrial Revolution, there were no labor laws. Six-year-old children worked in factories for 14 hours a day. Eight-year-old children worked in coal mines. Sometimes, the child workers were whipped to keep them from falling asleep on the job. Women were hired to drag coal carts from the mines. Such actions are forbidden by law today in most countries. But it took more than one hundred years to get laws passed to protect workers in factories and mines.

A young girl is shown working in a cotton mill in 1909. Why do you think it took so long for laws to be passed that protected factory workers?

7. The fight for laws to protect workers started in England. It was there that the Industrial Revolution and the labor-union movement began. At first, the government of England would not pass laws to improve factory working conditions. This was an example of economic policy known as *laissez-faire* (LES-say-fair). These French words mean "allow to do." The idea is that government should not interfere in economic and business matters. Conditions in British factories and mines became so bad, however, that they had to be improved. Reformers such as Lord Shaftesbury said that slaves in ancient Rome had been treated better than factory workers in England were.

8. Slowly the British Parliament began to change its laissez-faire policy. In 1833, the first important factory law was passed. It said that children under 9 years of age must not work in textile factories. Children aged 13 to 18 were not to work more than 12 hours a day. Compared with modern factory laws, this law might seem a poor one. But it was a first step in factory reform. Later, Parliament passed other laws to protect workers. One law said that children under the age of 10 and women must not work in mines. A few years later, a law was passed that said that women and children must not work more than 10 hours a day.

9. After the Industrial Revolution reached the United States and other countries of Europe, these countries also passed labor laws. The laws lowered the number of hours a person had to work per week. They limited child labor, and improved working conditions. Today, almost all industrial nations have labor laws for workers in factories and mines. Most do not allow children to work at all in them. The work week for men and women has been shortened to 44 hours or less. Most factory laws now also have safety rules to prevent accidents and fires. Other laws require that workrooms and restrooms be kept clean.

WHY WERE SOCIAL INSURANCE LAWS PASSED?

10. During the early years of the Industrial Revolution, workers were thought of as just workers. They were protected by factory laws. These laws protected workers while they were on the job. They did not protect them when they were sick or unemployed. They did not help them when they were too old to work. During the new Industrial Revolution, labor unions and social reformers asked for new kinds of laws to protect workers when they were out of work, sick, or too old to work. Such laws are called social-insurance laws.

11. It was Germany, not England, that passed the first social insurance laws. In 1883, the German government passed the first sick-

In the days before social-insurance laws were passed, conditions for the old or sick were very bad. Read the caption on this picture and explain its meaning.

THE POOR MAN'S FRIEND.

ness insurance law in history. The law said that workers would get some payment when they were sick and could not work. One year later, Germany passed a law that said that workers were to be paid if hurt on the job. Later, Germany passed laws protecting older people and unemployed workers.

12. Great Britain was not far behind Germany in passing social-insurance laws. Most of them were passed when the Labour party was in power. After World War II, the Labour party came to power in England. Led by it, Parliament passed the National Insurance Act, in 1946. This law set up the most complete system of social insurance in the world. It included insurance for sickness, unemployment, old age, and widowhood. It gave maternity insurance to mothers. It paid for complete hospital, medical,

and dental care for all British citizens. It even paid funeral expenses.

13. Today, the idea of social insurance has become widespread. France, Italy, Belgium, Denmark, Australia, and many other nations have insurance laws for workers. The United States was one of the last major nations to set up a system of social insurance. In 1935, Congress passed the Social Security Act. This law gave old-age pensions and payments to the widows and children of workers who had died. It also set up a system of unemployment insurance, run by the states. In 1965, Congress passed the National Health Insurance Law. It gives medical and hospital insurance to retired workers in the United States. Since 1968, the Canadian government has provided complete medical and hospital insurance for all Canadians.

Testing Your Vocabulary

Choose the best answer.

1. In the United States *collective bargaining* between employers and workers is required by law. This means employers must
   a. give workers a raise in wages every year.
   b. settle labor conflicts before there are strikes.
   c. talk over workers' demands with union leaders.

2. Great Britain has *nationalized* certain industries. These industries
   a. are operated by the government.
   b. sell their products to other nations.
   c. have labor unions.

3. Lord Shaftesbury was called a *reformer* because he wanted to
   a. build more factories.
   b. improve working conditions.
   c. help inventors and scientists.

Understanding What You Have Read

1. A good title for paragraphs 8 and 9 is
   a. Germany's Early Laws
   b. Growth of Factory and Labor Laws
   c. Women and Children Workers
   d. Social Insurance in Great Britain
2. In which paragraphs do you find facts

about
   a. the meaning of *laissez-faire?*
   b. British Combination Laws?
   c. labor unions in Communist countries?
   d. the meaning of *welfare state?*

3. Early British factory and mine laws were passed by Parliament because
   a. there was a need for more workers.
   b. Parliament followed a policy of laissez-faire.
   c. working conditions were terrible.
4. Social insurance laws were passed by modern industrial nations to give workers
   a. old-age and unemployment insurance.
   b. fire and life insurance.
   c. the right to join unions.
5. Great Britain is called a welfare state today because
   a. it has passed factory laws.
   b. both of its political parties are run by labor unions.

c. the government runs medical and insurance programs for all citizens.

6. Labor unions have grown in many countries because
   a. the Industrial Revolution has brought about a large class of workers.
   b. housing conditions in cities are terrible.
   c. the Combination Laws were passed.
7. Parliament passed the British social insurance laws when
   a. Great Britain became the largest industrial nation in the world.
   b. the Labour party became very powerful.
   c. insurance companies began to favor such a policy.

Tell whether the following statements are true or false. If a statement is false, change the words in italics to make it true.

1. The modern labor union movement, like the Industrial Revolution, began in *England*.
2. The *Combination Laws* of England made labor unions unlawful.
3. The strike is a method used by *management*.
4. In *1801*, the British Labour party was formed.
5. *Great Britain* has been called a welfare state.
6. The first nation to pass laws regulating

factory conditions was the *United States*.
7. A policy of no government interference with business is called *laissez-faire*.
8. Lord Shaftesbury was an *Italian* social reformer.
9. The right to strike today is illegal in the Soviet Union, Red China, and *France*.
10. The *United States* was one of the last major industrial nations to set up a system of social insurance.

Developing Ideas and Skills

USING A TIME LINE

List the items below in your notebook. Tell when each happened by using the letters A, B, or C from the time line at the top of page 401.

1. British Labour party set up.
2. Combination laws passed in England.
3. First social-insurance laws passed in Germany.
4. First major factory law passed in England.
5. Social Security Act passed by the United States Congress.

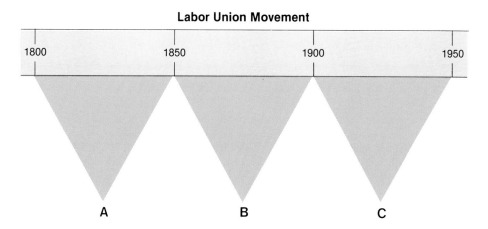

Labor Union Movement

1800   1850   1900   1950

A   B   C

Using Original Sources

The following passage was written by a committee studying labor conditions in British factories in 1832. Read it and see if you can answer the questions that follow:

Working Conditions in English Factories, 1832

It appears in evidence before this committee that the labor in mills and factories undergone by children and young persons of both sexes is rarely less than fourteen hours a day, including the time allowed for meals; and that, in many instances it greatly exceeds that term, and extends sometimes to eighteen or twenty hours, or upwards . . .

It is in evidence that the children and young persons employed in factories have often been roused from their lethargy (tiredness) . . . by constant whippings, beatings, or other means of a like nature.

Choose the correct answer for each of the following questions:

1. In which century did these conditions exist in England?
   a. 17th
   b. 18th
   c. 19th

2. How were the children kept from falling asleep on the job?
   a. rest periods
   b. whippings
   c. rewards

3. These conditions refer to child workers in
   a. factories.
   b. mines.
   c. stores.

4. How long did children usually work each day in British factories in 1832?
   a. eight hours or more
   b. twelve hours or more
   c. fourteen hours or more

AIM: How do the economic systems of cooperatives, socialism, and communism differ?

CHAPTER 6

New Economic Ideas Are Born

WHAT WERE THE BENEFITS OF THE COOPERATIVE SYSTEM?

1. Many people in North America today live in *co-op* apartment buildings. These people actually buy an apartment in the building. They become part owners of the building. When they wish to move, they sell their apartment to other people. Some people buy their groceries in a co-op store. Some farmers are members of farm co-ops. The word *co-op* means a cooperative business. In a cooperative, the customers own the business. The idea of cooperatives grew out of the Industrial Revolution.

2. Business people and landlords are in business to make a profit. When people form a co-op, they put an end to the profits of landlords or business people. In a co-op, a group of workers, farmers, or customers join together and start their own business. This may be a grocery store, an apartment house, or a grain elevator that stores wheat. A manager is hired to run the business. He is paid a certain salary. At the end of the year, the extra money made by the co-op is divided among the members.

3. The idea of cooperatives began in England. In 1844, a group of textile workers in the town of Rochdale set up a cooperative grocery store. They hired a manager to run the store. They bought all of their groceries there. At the end of the year, they divided the extra money. In this way, they earned and saved a great deal of money that would ordinarily have gone as profits to someone else. The Rochdale store was so successful that workers in other English towns copied the idea. Rochdale stores soon appeared all over England.

Adam Smith has been called the founder of modern economics. He believed in a laissez-faire economy.

4. Cooperatives were set up to manufacture goods and build houses. They bought farm machinery and sold farm crops. The cooperative movement spread to other countries in Europe and countries in North America. Today, co-ops do a great deal of business in Great Britain, Denmark, Sweden, and elsewhere. In the United States, the cooperative movement has been most successful among farmers. After World War II, cooperative apartments became popular in large American cities.

WHAT IS SOCIALISM AND HOW DID IT DEVELOP?

5. The cooperative movement was only one of many new ideas that grew out of the Industrial Revolution. *Socialism* was another. Socialism is the idea that a government or community should own and control industry, industrial wealth, and land. There should be no private profits. The early socialists believed that all the evils of the Industrial Revolution would be ended if there were no business people trying to make profits. Socialism would bring higher wages and shorter hours. Every worker would have a job, and there would be no strikes. There was, however, one main trouble with socialism: Believing that working hard would not bring more money, many people would not try to work hard. Nor would they have a reason to start new industries or invent new machines. Many people believed that socialism would end progress.

6. Socialist ideas became popular early in the 19th century. Such men as Claude Saint-Simon (san-see-MON) and Charles Fourier (FOO-ree-ay) of France and Robert Owen in England wrote about socialism. These men were called *utopian* (yoo-TOH-pee-un) socialists. They thought a perfect world, called a utopia, could be built on socialist ideas. Robert

New Lamark, Manchester, England. Robert Owen established a co-operative community factory village in 1814. Why did his utopian societies not succeed?

Owen tried to start small utopian villages based on socialist ideas. Such efforts usually failed because they were unrealistic.

7. In the middle of the 19th century, a new kind of socialism appeared. It was developed by Karl Marx, of Germany, and was called Marxian socialism. Karl Marx and his friend Friedrich Engels put their ideas in a pamphlet called *The Communist Manifesto,* in 1848. Later, Marx also wrote a famous work, *Das Kapital.* Marx pointed out that in an industry the worker and business people both got paid for their work. After they are paid, some money is left over. Marx called this money *surplus value.* The surplus value, said Marx, is usually taken as profits by the owners—*capitalists,* as he called them. The workers received no share of the surplus value. Marx called the workers the *proletariat* (proh-leh-TAIR-ee-at).

8. To get a share of the surplus value, said Marx, workers all over the world must unite against the capitalists. Throughout history, he said, the proletariat and capitalists have fought a *class struggle* for the surplus value. The capi-

Karl Marx. How did his ideas differ from those of Robert Owen?

talists usually won. Another of Marx's ideas was that events are caused by economic forces. Thus, the main ideas of Marxian socialism are these four: 1. the surplus-value idea, 2. the class struggle, 3. the need for unity of the proletariat all over the world, and 4. the economic nature of history.

9. Karl Marx's ideas spread. They led to the growth of socialist parties in Europe and North America. In England, the socialist party called itself the Labour party. As you have already learned, the Labour party ran the British government for many years after World War II. It set up a kind of socialism called the welfare state in England. In the United States, the So-cialist party has never been strong. The most votes it has ever received in a presidential election was about one million, in 1920. In Canada, the Socialist party is much stronger.

HOW DOES COMMUNISM DIFFER FROM SOCIALISM?

10. Early in the 20th century European socialist parties split into two groups. One group wanted to achieve socialist goals slowly and by peaceful methods. It hoped to do this by winning elections and passing socialist laws. Another group wanted to set up socialist governments quickly. This group favored revolution and bloodshed, if necessary. They became known as Communists. In Russia, the Communists were first called Bolsheviks.

11. In 1917, the Russian Revolution began. The czar was overthrown. The Communists in Russia were led by Vladimir Lenin and Leon Trotsky. They seized control of the government and set up a Communist dictatorship now known as the Soviet Union. The government took for itself all the people's property and ended private profits. For more than 25 years the Soviet Union was the only Communist country in the world. After World War II, Communist governments were set up in Poland, Romania, Hungary, Bulgaria, Yugoslavia, Albania, East Germany, and Czechoslovakia. Today, there are also Communist governments in China, North Korea, Vietnam, and Cuba.

12. Some Western European countries, such as France and Italy, have Communist parties. But they have never grown strong enough to take over the governments of these countries. In the United States, there are relatively few Communists. The Communist party of Canada is a legal political organization and puts forth candidates in all elections. Some of the new nations of Asia and Africa also have Communist parties. Most of these are small.

Testing Your Vocabulary

Choose the best answers.

1. A dictatorship of the *proletariat* means rule by
   a. the Communist party.
   b. the working class.
   c. the aristocracy.
2. There are often arguments between workers and *capitalists*. A capitalist is
   a. a person who owns a business and makes a profit from it.
   b. a supervisor in a factory who treats workers cruelly.
   c. a person who believes in socialist ideas.
3. Early socialist villages were called *utopias*. A utopia is
   a. an ancient civilization.
   b. an imaginary, perfect world.
   c. a secret society.

Understanding What You Have Read

1. A good title for paragraphs 7 and 8 is
   a. The Cooperative Movement
   b. The Socialist Movement
   c. Marxian Socialism
   d. The Social Reform Movement
2. In which paragraphs do you find facts about
   a. the Rochdale stores?
   b. the difference between socialists and communists?
   c. *The Communist Manifesto?*
   d. utopian socialists?
3. The cooperative movement began because customers wanted to
   a. improve housing conditions.
   b. give ownership of stores to the government.
   c. keep for themselves the profits of the business owner.
4. Socialism favors government ownership of industries because
   a. this would end private profits.
   b. this would take power from the Communists.
   c. this would mean an end to child labor.
5. The cooperative movement has not developed in Communist countries because
   a. cooperatives are based on socialist ideas.
   b. the government owns all industries and business.
   c. the population of Communist countries is too small.

Using Original Sources

One of the new ideas of the 19th century was communism. In 1848, the same year that many European countries were torn by revolutions, Karl Marx and Friedrich Engels published a statement of Communist ideas. This statement was called the Manifesto of the Communist party. Here are some of the ideas it contained. When you have read the selection, answer the questions that follow.

The Communist Manifesto

. . . The history of all . . . society is the history of class struggles. Free man and slave, patrician and plebeian, lord and serf, guild-master and journeyman—in a word, oppressor and oppressed—stood in constant opposition to one another. . . . Of all the classes that stand face to face with the bourgeoisie today, the proletariat alone is a really revolutionary class. . . . The Communists openly declare that their ends can be attained only by the forcible overthrow of all existing social conditions. Let the ruling classes tremble at a Communistic revolution. The proletarians have nothing to lose but their chains. They have a world to win. *Workingmen of all countries, unite!*

1. What groups of people might feel threatened by this manifesto? Why?
2. Are there social classes in the United States today? If so, what are they? Are they at war with each other, as Marx suggests classes normally are?
3. Does communism lead to peaceful or violent solutions to social problems?
4. Does Marx seem interested in revolution in Europe or throughout the world?

TURNING POINTS

Technology

Asia: Capitalism in Japan

It is the view of most Communists that workers are treated badly in the capitalist system. An excellent argument against this opinion is made by looking at Japan.

Capitalism is the economic system of Japan. Many Japanese employers are very concerned about the well-being of their workers. Their companies are run like large families. They provide many benefits, including child care and exercise gyms. They organize vacations and provide housing at low rates. To increase the feeling of team spirit, friendships among workers are encouraged. The employees take pride in their company. Some work their entire lives for one firm.

Akio Morita is the chairman and co-founder of one such company. In 1946, Morita borrowed $500 from his parents and began a small electronics business with a partner. Their company built the first transistor radios. Morita's company grew steadily over the years. Today, it is one of the largest electronic companies in the world. It produces many kinds of electronic appliances, such as calculators and television sets.

Akio Morita has helped Japan to become a leading industrial nation. He had done this by creating a company that treats its workers fairly and provides them with a satisfying means of making a living.

Critical Thinking

1. How do you think most Japanese workers feel about their employers?
2. What do you think Morita's view of communism might be?

AIM: How has modern science changed people's ideas about themselves and the world?

CHAPTER 7

An Age of Science Begins

WHO CONTRIBUTES TO MODERN SCIENCE?

1. We may speak of English literature, German music, French art. But we do not usually speak of English chemistry, German biology, or French astronomy. Science is universal. It does not stop at a country's borders. Scientists of many nations are in touch with one another through meetings and reports. They are always discussing their work and problems.

2. The making of the first atomic bomb is a good example of this. The bomb was not the invention of Americans only. It was the result of ideas and experiments by many scientists in many countries. They included Marie Curie, of France; Niels Bohr, of Denmark; Enrico Fermi, of Italy; Lise Meitner and Albert Einstein, of Germany; and J. Robert Oppenheimer, of the United States.

3. The atomic bomb and space travel are new products of science. Their development, however, was based on the work of earlier scientists. Much of modern science is based on theories developed in the last 150 years. They include the germ theory, the atomic theory, the theory of evolution, the theory of generating electricity, and the theory of relativity.

Madame Curie in her laboratory. She and her husband, Pierre, discovered radium.

Albert Einstein. Besides his contributions to atomic physics, Einstein developed the theory of relativity.

WHAT SCIENTIFIC DISCOVERIES WERE MADE IN THE 19TH CENTURY?

4. In medicine, the past century has brought many new cures. Robert Koch, a German, discovered the germ that caused tuberculosis. Emil Von Behring, another German, developed a drug that cured diphtheria. Walter Reed, an American, discovered that yellow fever was carried by certain mosquitoes.

5. More recently, Alexander Fleming, an Englishman, discovered penicillin (pen-i-SIL-in). Selman Waksman, an American, discovered streptomycin (strep-toh-MY-sin). Both drugs cure many kinds of sicknesses. Jonas Salk developed a vaccine against polio. The work of all of these scientists was based on the findings of Louis Pasteur, of France. Pasteur, a 19th-century scientist, first proved that many diseases were caused by germs or bacteria. His work led to other medical discoveries.

6. Thomas Dalton's atomic theory began a new era in chemistry. Dalton said that all chemicals are made up of very small units called atoms. Dmitri Mendeleev, a Russian, made use of Dalton's atomic theory. He drew up a chart of chemical elements. With this chart scientists were able to tell what new elements would be found and discover how chemicals worked. An important later result of Dalton's work was the making of the atomic and hydrogen bombs. It also led to the use of atomic energy to generate electricity and to run ships.

7. Many of our modern machines are run by electric motors. Refrigerators, washing machines, and vacuum cleaners, for example, use electric motors. Motors work by getting electrical power through wires. The electricity is made by generators. The electric generator developed from the work of Michael Faraday, an English scientist. Faraday was the first to generate an electric current. His idea is the basis of all electric generators.

8. Other scientists have also helped to develop electric power. Luigi Galvani, an Italian scientist, discovered that electric current will flow through a wire. Alessandro Volta, another Italian, built the first electric cell. André Ampère, a Frenchman, and Georg Ohm, a German, added to our knowledge of electricity. These scientists developed some of the basic laws of electric currents.

WHAT NEW SCIENTIFIC THEORIES GAINED ACCEPTANCE?

9. Which scientists made possible the modern exploration of space? The first was an Englishman named Sir Isaac Newton. More than two hundred years ago, he developed the

Sir Isaac Newton. How did his discovery of gravitation open the door for space exploration?

theory of gravitation. In the 20th century, Albert Einstein, a German scientist, developed the theory of relativity. This is one of the most important theories of modern science. It has helped explain time, space, and the universe. Einstein's relativity theory gave scientists an explanation for the movements of the planets and stars. It was also connected with the making of the first atomic bomb.

10. Louis Pasteur was a pioneer in medicine. Thomas Dalton started modern chemistry. Charles Darwin, an Englishman, founded mod-

ern biology. In 1859, Darwin published his famous work *The Origin of Species.* In this book he described his theory of evolution. Darwin wrote that over a period of millions of years, human beings developed from lower animals. He also put forth the idea of the "survival of the fittest." This means that some animals were able to change as conditions changed. Others, such as dinosaurs, could not change and died out. The fittest animals were those who could change and therefore live. Darwin's theory angered many people. They said that it was an attack on religion and the Bible.

11. Darwin's theory affected science. It also affected ideas of government and business. The idea of laissez-faire was popular in business in the 19th century. This theory said that the government should not interfere with business. Business leaders argued in favor of laissez-faire. They said that business success was also the result of "survival of the fittest." The smartest—fittest—business people made profits and survived in business. The worst—the unfit—made no profits and thus were forced out of business. Government should not have to interfere in business: people who ran their businesses poorly would be forced out automatically. Darwin's scientific theory was made into a business theory. The idea of "survival of the fittest" was also used by dictators as an excuse for fighting wars. Adolf Hitler, for example, was sure that Germany would win World War II. He said that the German people were a "master race" and were the "fittest to survive."

Testing Your Vocabulary _____

Choose the best answer.

1. A *theory* in science is
   a. a foolish suggestion.
   b. a proven law.
   c. an idea that tries to explain a set of facts.

2. If an animal was able to *survive* an ice age, it
   a. changed into a different animal.
   b. lived through the ice age.
   c. migrated, or moved, to another area.

Understanding What You Have Read

1. A good title for paragraphs 4 and 5 is
   a. Space Exploration.
   b. Building the Atomic Bomb.
   c. Science and War.
   d. Progress in Medicine.
2. In which paragraphs do you find facts about
   a. Einstein's theory of relativity?
   b. Darwin's evolution theory?
   c. Dalton's atomic theory?
   d. Pasteur's germ theory?
3. Success in fighting disease is the result of Louis Pasteur's
   a. opening of the first medical laboratory in France.
   b. finding a cure for tuberculosis.
   c. discovery that germs cause disease.
4. Darwin's theory of evolution was used by some business leaders to defend
   a. the search for colonies.
   b. socialist ideas.
   c. a laissez-faire policy.
5. Almost every modern use of electricity is based on the work of Michael Faraday, who
   a. invented the electric motor.
   b. discovered how to generate electricity.
   c. invented the electric cell.
6. Science can be called a universal subject because
   a. scientific discoveries are based on the work of people of many countries.
   b. science is discussed at the United Nations.
   c. one scientist may lecture at universities of many countries.

Developing Ideas and Skills

UNDERSTANDING A DRAWING

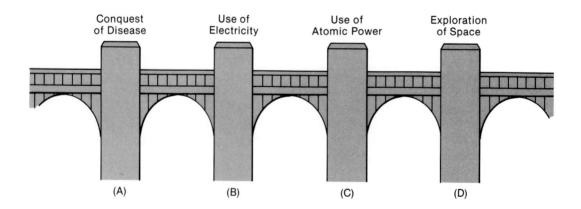

Conquest of Disease (A)   Use of Electricity (B)   Use of Atomic Power (C)   Exploration of Space (D)

1. A good title for this picture would be
   a. Building a Bridge.
   b. Modern Methods of Travel.
   c. Development of Modern Science.
2. On which of the four poles of the bridge would the following people belong:

a. Albert Einstein
b. Thomas Dalton
c. Louis Pasteur
d. Michael Faraday
e. Jonas Salk

TURNING POINTS

Technology

North America: Lewis Latimer

Lewis Latimer was born in Massachusetts on September 4, 1848. His father had been a slave. Six years before Lewis's birth, he became a free man.

As a young man, Latimer became interested in electricity. His experiments led to important developments in the incandescent lamp. This was an early version of the electric light bulb. His inventions made various parts of electric lamps connect better and last longer. He also found ways for one lamp in a group of lamps to work separately. Before that, if one lamp went out, every lamp went out. He was asked to put in lighting systems in Philadelphia and in Canada. In order to instruct the workers in Canada, he learned French. In 1881, he went to England to teach his methods to the workers in a lighting company in London.

In 1884, Thomas Edison heard about Latimer's achievements. He asked him to come work for his company. Latimer's knowledge and skills helped Edison to get many of his inventions patented. In 1890 Latimer, who had become an expert on electric lighting, wrote a book on the subject.

Latimer's interests extended into other areas as well. In 1925, he published a book of poetry entitled *Poems of Love and Life*. Latimer died in 1928. The Edison Pioneers, a group of scientists, wrote that they had a wonderful "memory at having been associated with [Latimer] in a great work for all people."

Critical Thinking

1. It has been said of Latimer that he was "a man of many talents." Explain.
2. There is a school that is named after Lewis Latimer. Explain why he deserves this honor.

AIM: How did social and cultural movements affect the course of history in the 19th century?

CHAPTER 8

Social and Cultural Progress Continues

WHAT RIGHTS DID WOMEN WANT?

1. Before the Industrial Revolution, men and women worked in their homes. This was called the domestic system (see p. 377). But when the Industrial Revolution and the factory system began, they took many men and women out of their homes. People began to work in factories, mines, offices, and shops. For the first time, many women began to earn their own money. They had become part of a nation's labor force. They were wage earners.

2. With this new freedom to work outside the home, some women began to ask questions: Why did the money a married woman earned belong to her husband? Why couldn't married women own property or make business contracts? Why were there no colleges for women? Why didn't women have the right to vote? During the 18th and early 19th centuries, women had no rights in these areas. A few women, called *feminists*, began to ask these questions. Feminists are those who want women to have the same rights as men. Thus the women's-rights movement grew in part out of the Industrial Revolution.

3. One of the first to say that women should have the same rights as men was Mary Wollstonecraft, an Englishwoman. In 1792, she published a declaration called a *Vindication of the Rights of Women.* In it she said women should attend the same schools as men. They should also have the right to go into business. John Stuart Mill, also from England, said it was unfair to refuse women the same rights that men had. He wrote an essay called *The Subjection of Women* (1861). Mill said that women should have the same chances to go into business as men. Women should also be given the right to vote.

4. During the 19th and the early 20th century, feminists in many countries began to fight for these rights. In Great Britain, the Pankhurst sisters—Emmeline and Christabel—led the crusade to give women the right to vote. This was called women's suffrage (*suffrage* means *right to vote*). In the United States, the fight for equal rights was led by Susan B. Anthony and Elizabeth Cady Stanton. Other early feminist leaders included Fredericka Bremer, in Sweden, Maria Deraismes (de-RAME), in France, and Nellie McClung, in Canada. An international Woman Suffrage Alliance was organized in 1888.

Mary Wollstonecraft published *Vindication of the Rights of Women* in 1792. Why might it be said that she was ahead of her time?

5. The feminist crusade finally brought results. During the 19th century, laws increasing women's rights were passed in most European countries and in the United States. Women were allowed to own property. They could also keep the wages they earned. They could go into business and make contracts. Special schools and colleges for women were opened. Women were also admitted to men's universities. New Zealand gave women the right to vote in 1893, and Australia followed soon after, in 1902. Norway was the first independent nation to give women the vote, in 1907. Finally, after World War I, the United States (1920), Great Britain (1928), and most countries in Europe also gave women the right to vote. Women in Japan did not get the vote until after World War II.

HOW DID LITERATURE REFLECT EUROPEAN LIFE?

6. Writers, artists, composers, and scholars are affected by the events around them. Many composers and writers of the 19th century were touched by the spirit of nationalism. Others were affected by the evils of the Industrial Revolution. Some were affected by the spread of imperialism. On the other hand, these creative people had an effect upon the age in which they lived. The music of Frédéric Chopin, for example, helped to stir up the spirit of nationalism in Poland.

7. In England, some writers showed how the factory system had changed people's lives. Charles Dickens did this in such novels as *Oliver Twist*. George Eliot (her real name was Mary Ann Evans) did the same in her novel *Silas Marner*. In her poem *Cry of the Children*, Elizabeth Barrett Browning described the evils of child labor. And William Blake wrote poems

The drawing shows Charles Dickens surrounded by many of the characters he created.

about the problems connected with industrialism. Rudyard Kipling wrote *The White Man's Burden* and other poems and stories about life in the British colonies. Kipling was in favor of British imperialism. He was known as "the poet of the British Empire."

8. George Bernard Shaw, a British playwright, believed in the new ideas of British socialism, and many of his plays show this. In France, Victor Hugo, in *Les Misérables*, and Honoré de Balzac, in *Le Pére Goriot*, showed what life was like in their country during the Industrial Revolution. Émile Zola became famous for his stories about the poor. He also criticized the dishonesty in the French army and government.

9. In 19th-century Russia, the czarist government controlled the work of all writers. In spite of this, great Russian authors wrote important novels. Among them are *Crime and Punishment,* by Fyodor Dostoevsky (FEE-uh-dor dus-toi-EV-skee), *Fathers and Sons,* by Ivan Turgenev, and *War and Peace,* by Leo Tolstoy.

HOW DID COMPOSERS AND ARTISTS EXPRESS THEIR IDEAS?

10. History affected some of those who wrote music in Europe. Some composers used music to show their political ideas. In the 19th century, many were touched by the spirit of nationalism. Franz Liszt's *Hungarian Rhapsodies* showed his love for his native country, Hungary. In his *Slavonic Dances*, Anton Dvořák (DVOR-zhak) used musical themes from the part of Czechoslovakia from which he came. Many of the works of Peter Tchaikovsky show his love for Russia. His *Overture of 1812* is a powerful description in music of Napoleon's invasion of Russia in 1812 and his defeat by the Russians.

11. Ludwig van Beethoven (BAY-toh-ven) was one of the world's greatest composers. Beethoven was a German who believed in demo-

Ludwig van Beethoven. Explain how his music reflected his political ideas.

cratic ideas. His works, such as the *Eroica* symphony, express his belief in human freedom and the dignity of human life. Richard Wagner (VAG-ner), another German composer, became world famous for such operas as *The Ring of the Nibelungen*. These operas were often based on old German legends and stories. Wagner's music stirred German nationalism very deeply. Other important German composers of the 19th century were Felix Mendelssohn and Johannes Brahms. Many of the operas of the Italian composer Giuseppe Verdi were nationalistic in spirit. Verdi himself took part in the movement for Italian unification.

12. The great painters of France have made the French people very proud. They feel that France has been the world leader in modern art. In the 19th century some great artists followed a style called *impressionism*. The impressionists tried to capture in paint visual impressions that come and go in an instant. The greatest of these were Edouard Manet, Claude Monet, and Paul Cezanne. Sculptors also raised French art to great heights. Rodin (roh-DAN) was France's most important sculptor. His statue *The Thinker* is one of the world's best-known works of art.

13. Nations are proud of their composers, artists, and writers. This pride is part of the spirit of nationalism in all countries. Germans are proud of their composers. The English are proud of their poets. The Russians are proud of their great novelists. The French are proud of their great painters. The works of creative men and women enrich the lives of all people.

Rouen Cathedral, by Claude Monet. Why do you think this painting is called impressionistic?

Testing Your Vocabulary

Choose the best answer.

1. During the 19th century a popular form of music was *opera*. This is
   a. a combination of music and art.
   b. a symphony in four parts.
   c. a drama set to music in which all the dialogue is sung.
2. A *legend* is
   a. a map.
   b. a story from the past.
   c. a hero.
3. A *feminist* is a person who
   a. thinks a woman's place is in the home.
   b. wants women to have the same rights as men.
   c. writes about women.

Understanding What You Have Read

1. A good title for paragraphs 7 and 8 is
   a. Cultural Developments in Modern Europe.
   b. The Development of European Music.
   c. Art in Modern Europe.
   d. Writers of the 19th Century.

2. In which paragraphs do you find facts about
   a. Russian writers?
   b. French impressionistic painting?
   c. German composers and their works?
   d. writers who were in favor of women's rights?

3. The movement for women's rights grew in part out of the
   a. domestic system.
   b. Industrial Revolution.
   c. Russian Revolution.

4. Emile Zola, the French novelist, became well known for his
   a. poetry about the Industrial Revolution.
   b. socialist ideas.
   c. criticism of the French army and government.

5. Rudyard Kipling was called the "poet of the British Empire" because of his
   a. poems about life in British colonies.
   b. criticism of British imperialism.
   c. travels in British colonies.

6. Richard Wagner's operas stirred German nationalism because they were based on
   a. Germany country life.
   b. old German legends and stories.
   c. lives of German military heroes.

7. Nineteenth-century Russian writers are most famous for their
   a. poems
   b. novels
   c. operas

Match the names in Column I with the artistic and literary works in Column II.

Column I	Column II
1. Mary Wollstonecraft	a. *The Eroica*
2. Ludwig van Beethoven	b. *The Overture of 1812*
3. Charles Dickens	c. *Oliver Twist*
4. Victor Hugo	d. *Slavonic Dances*
5. Franz Liszt	e. *War and Peace*
6. Leo Tolstoy	f. *Vindication of the Rights of Women*
7. Fydor Dostoevsky	g. *Hungarian Rhapsodies*
8. Peter Tchaikovsky	h. *Les Misérables*
	i. *William Tell*
	j. *Crime and Punishment*

Summary of Unit IX

A few of the most important events, facts, and ideas of this unit are listed on page 417. What others can you add?

1. The Industrial Revolution began in England with the invention of textile machinery.
2. The agricultural revolution changed and improved methods of farming.
3. The new Industrial Revolution introduced new machines, new sources of power, and new methods of manufacturing.
4. Industrial progress caused hardships but it also brought benefits to workers, farmers, and consumers.
5. Labor unions were formed in the 19th century to help improve labor conditions, raise wages, and lower working hours.
6. New ideas such as socialism, communism, and the cooperative movement were results of evils of the Industrial Revolution.
7. The feminist movement, as well as European literature, art, and music, was affected by nationalism and the Industrial Revolution.

Making Generalizations

For each of the following series of factual statements, make one accurate generalization.

1. Factual statements:
   a. After the factory system began, workers started to form labor unions to improve their working conditions.
   b. In the 19th century, factory workers in several European countries turned to political parties to pass social legislation.
   c. The socialist ideas of Karl Marx grew out of the poverty of European cities created by the factory system.
   Generalization:

2. Factual statements:
   a. Women became wage earners during the Industrial Revolution.
   b. Mary Wollstonecraft and John Stuart Mill wrote essays on equal rights for women.
   c. During the early 19th century, the wages of married women workers belonged to their husbands.
   Generalization:

3. Factual statements:
   a. The assembly line brought less-expensive products but created many dull jobs.
   b. Industrial growth led to new business forms, such as corporations, but encouraged some unfair business practices.
   c. The Industrial Revolution made new methods of transportation possible, but this also produced more destructive war equipment.
   Generalization:

UNIT X

3500 B.C.   2500 B.C.   1500 B.C.   500 B.C.   A.D. 500   A.D. 1500

3000 B.C.   2000 B.C.   1000 B.C.   A.D. 1   A.D. 1000   A.D. 2000

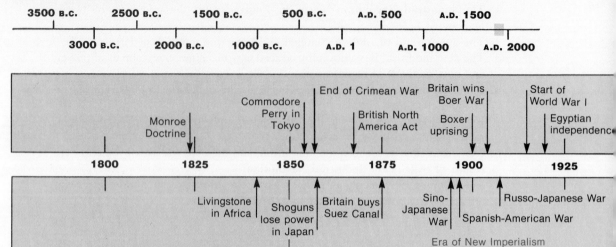

Monroe Doctrine

Commodore Perry in Tokyo

End of Crimean War

British North America Act

Britain wins Boer War

Boxer uprising

Start of World War I

Egyptian independence

1800   1825   1850   1875   1900   1925

Livingstone in Africa

Shoguns lose power in Japan

Britain buys Suez Canal

Sino-Japanese War

Spanish-American War

Russo-Japanese War

Era of New Imperialism

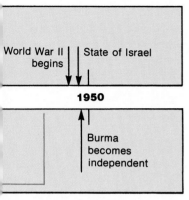

World War II begins | State of Israel

1950

Burma becomes independent

How Did a Race for Colonies Lead to World War I?

The Ginza is an active section of Tokyo that attracts people from all over the city.

AIM: Why did a new race for colonies begin in the 19th century?

CHAPTER 1

Nations Again Seek Colonies

WHY HAD IMPERIALISM DECLINED?

1. Some people like to buy large homes. When they own them, however, they find they are very expensive to run. The nations of Western Europe built large empires in the 17th and 18th centuries. They looked for colonies in the New World and Asia. But when the great nations finally got their empires, they often found that they were more trouble than they were worth. Great Britain and France found, for example, that they needed large navies to protect their colonies. All imperialist countries needed large armies to fight their rivals in long and costly wars. Large armies and navies were expensive. To pay for them, taxes had to be raised at home and in the colonies.

2. The colonies themselves often caused trouble for the parent countries. When colonies grew strong, they often tried to end the laws and taxes that the controlling country had forced upon them. Sometimes they rebelled. England's colonies in America in 1776 started a revolution, for example. They finally gained their freedom. The long war was very costly for England. In 1822, Brazil gained its independence from Portugal. Most of Spain's colonies in America also rebelled and won freedom.

3. The United States announced the Monroe Doctrine in 1823. The Doctrine said that European countries must no longer look for colonies in the Americas. This meant that all the money spent in building colonies in the New World had been wasted. All the wars fought to keep them were also wasted efforts. There were other reasons why imperialism began to fade at the beginning of the 19th century. The Industrial Revolution and the growth of factories became more important to some nations than owning colonies. There were wars and revolutions in Europe. These also kept Europeans from thinking about gaining new colonies.

4. The rise of Napoleon Bonaparte in France kept all of Europe busy defending itself. After the fall of Napoleon, revolutions broke out in many countries of Europe, in 1830 and 1848. With so much trouble at home, the nations of Europe were too busy to think about colonies or empires. Thus, for a number of reasons the spirit of imperialism and the desire for new colonies faded during the first half of the 19th century.

WHY DID IMPERIALISM RETURN?

5. Imperialism, however, did not die out completely in Europe. In the middle of the 19th century, the desire for empires suddenly burst forth again with new strength. Once more, the nations of Europe began a race for colonies. For almost a hundred years, from 1850 to the end of World War II, in 1945, the nations of Europe and Japan took part in a new race for colonies. This period is known as the time of the *new* imperialism. What caused this new upsurge of imperialism?

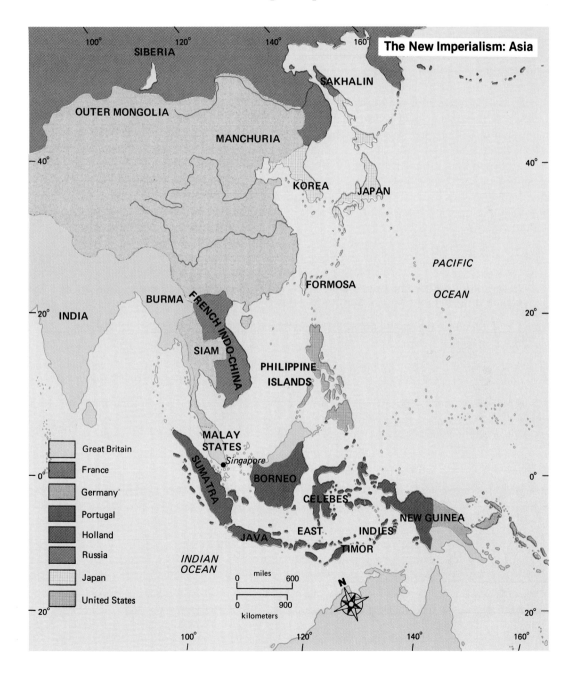

The New Imperialism: Asia

6. The Industrial Revolution was one of the reasons for the new imperialism, as it had been for the old. Business people and factory owners wanted their nations to get new colonies. Colonies would be good for business. They offered raw materials—copper, tin, oil, and rubber—that industry needed. Manufactured goods could, in turn, be sold in the colonies for added profit. Business people, therefore, wanted their nations to look for new colonies.

7. Another reason for the rebirth of imperialism was the strong spirit of nationalism in many countries. Many people believed that colonies added to the importance of their country. France's defeat in the Franco-Prussian War, for example, led the French to want new colonies. This would be one way of bringing back the glory that the French had felt before the defeat of their country.

8. Germany and Italy became unified nations in 1871. Proud of themselves, they soon wanted to become great powers. At the same time, Japan was becoming a modern nation. It, too, hoped to become a world power. Germany, Italy, and Japan thus entered the race for colonies in the second half of the 19th century. They felt that gaining colonies all over the globe would make them great powers.

WHY WERE NATIONS RIVALS FOR COLONIES?

9. Naturally, Italy, Germany, France, Great Britain, Russia, and Japan became rivals. Very often, more than one country wanted the same colony. This led to crises that almost caused wars. Colonial rivalries were among the causes of World War I and World War II.

During the Chinese–Japanese War, 1894–1895, Japan forced China to give up its claims in Korea and to give Taiwan to Japan.

10. The Industrial Revolution and nationalism were not the only reasons for imperialism. The nations of Europe and Japan wanted colonies for military and naval bases. Such bases would be important in time of war. If the population of countries grew too fast, people could go to the colonies. Finally, missionaries wanted to spread Christianity to all parts of the world. They also wanted to educate Asian and African peoples in the ways of the modern world. The English poet Rudyard Kipling expressed this idea. He believed that it was "the white man's burden," or responsibility, to help Asians and Africans in this way.

11. In their new search for colonies, the great powers used different ways of gaining territories. Sometimes they sent an army and took control by force. At other times the local ruler of an area, such as a sultan or maharajah, would allow a great power to run his territory for him. The local ruler would keep his throne. But he would have no real power. He would be a puppet ruler. In such a territory, a foreign government had greater control than the local government. A land ruled in this way was called a *protectorate.* Sometimes a foreign nation was given special rights to carry on business and trade in a territory. The territory was then called a *sphere of influence.*

12. During the first period of imperialism, in the 17th and 18th centuries, most colonies were in North and South America. Most of these colonies later won their independence. During the age of new imperialism, beginning

A memorial in Calcutta, India, built to Queen Victoria, who ruled England from 1837 to 1901.

in the middle of the 19th century, the great powers gained colonies in Asia and Africa. When the First World War began, in 1914, most of Africa and Asia had already been divided. The countries had become colonies, protectorates, and spheres of influence held by the great nations of the world.

Testing Your Vocabulary

Choose the best answer.

1. Among the people who went to colonies were *missionaries.* Missionaries are people who
   a. claim new land for their ruler or country.
   b. set up trading posts in colonies.
   c. try to spread their particular religious faith.

2. Colonies were *markets* for foreign countries. In this sentence, *market* means
   a. a grocery store.
   b. a place where goods are bought and sold.
   c. a raw material.

Understanding What You Have Read _____

1. A good title for paragraphs 6 through 8 is
   a. Causes of the New Imperialism.
   b. Revolutions in English and Spanish Colonies.
   c. Types of Imperialist Control.
   d. Imperialism in the Early 19th Century.
2. In which paragraphs do you find facts about
   a. the Monroe Doctrine?
   b. the Franco-Prussian War?
   c. the meaning of the word *protectorate?*
   d. Napoleon's effect on imperialism?
3. The desire to gain colonial empires faded in the early 19th century because
   a. business people were more interested in building factories than in gaining colonies.
   b. the Metternich System did not allow imperialism.
   c. the fur trade died out.
4. Rudyard Kipling, the English poet, wrote that colonial empires were the "white man's burden." He meant that
   a. colonies brought little profit to the controlling country.
   b. white people had a responsibility to educate people in colonies.
   c. rivalries over colonies led to war.
5. A sphere of influence is a form of colonial control in which a foreign government
   a. protected its citizens in colonies.
   b. taxed the natives in a colony.
   c. had trading rights in a colony.
6. Imperialism returned after 1850 because

a. colonies could provide men for European armies.
   b. colonies meant raw materials and markets for manufactured goods.
   c. colonies were ruled by foreign governments.
7. The Monroe Doctrine helped to protect the independence of the countries in
   a. Asia.
   b. Africa.
   c. Latin America.
8. In 1822, Brazil gained its independence from
   a. Spain.
   b. Portugal.
   c. Great Britain.
9. One of the major causes of imperialism after 1850 was the
   a. French Revolution.
   b. Industrial Revolution.
   c. American Revolution.
10. The group that usually wanted colonies was
    a. farmers.
    b. factory workers.
    c. people in business.
11. Colonial rivalries and imperialism were causes of
    a. World War I.
    b. the Franco-Prussian War.
    c. the American Civil War.
12. The country in Asia that joined the race for colonies was
    a. China.
    b. Japan.
    c. India.
13. Italy and Germany began to search for colonies
    a. after they were unified.

b. before they were unified.

c. before the Napoleonic wars.

14. A colony in which the local leader remained as a puppet ruler was called a
   a. sphere.
   b. territory.
   c. protectorate.

15. A sphere of influence in an area gave to the foreign power who had it

a. control of the government.

b. special trading rights.

c. the right to collect taxes.

16. During the period of new imperialism, the great powers looked for new colonies in
   a. Asia and Africa.
   b. North and South America.
   c. Australia and New Zealand.

Developing Ideas and Skills

INTERPRETING A POEM

Writers often get their ideas from events that happen during their lifetimes. Such an author was Rudyard Kipling. He is often thought of as the poet of British imperialism. One of his famous poems is "The White Man's Burden," written in 1899. The last three lines of the stanza printed here speak of the colonial peoples as inferior to white Europeans. Kipling is expressing a common imperialist attitude of his day. Read the following stanza of the poem; then answer the questions that follow.

Take up the White Man's burden—
Send forth the best ye breed—
Go bind your sons to exile
To serve your captives' need;
To wait in heavy harness
On fluttered folk and wild—
Your new-caught sullen peoples,
Half devil and half child.

1. When Kipling wrote "the white man's burden" he meant
   a. long hours of work in British factories.
   b. the duty of a parent country to help people in its colonies.
   c. heavy taxes paid by the English people.

2. According to the poem, Kipling believed that most people who lived in colonies were

a. friendly and loyal to the parent country.

b. useful in time of war.

c. savage and uncivilized.

3. The line "to wait in heavy harness" means
   a. to be eager to leave home to work in foreign lands.
   b. to serve, or work for, like a work animal.
   c. to bind in chains.

MAKING A CHART

Fill in the missing blanks of these charts in your notebook.

Why the First Phase of Imperialism Faded, from 1800 to 1850
1. Interest in factory building
2.
3.
4.

Why New Imperialism Developed, from 1850 to 1945
1. Need for markets and raw materials
2.
3.
4.

CHAPTER 2

Africa Is Explored and Divided

WHY WERE EARLY EXPLORERS NOT INTERESTED IN AFRICA?

1. After the discovery of America by Columbus, most Europeans became interested in exploring and settling the New World. They did not care about Africa, although it was much closer to them. Europeans saw Niagara Falls, in North America, almost 200 years before they saw Victoria Falls, in Africa. For hundreds of years, Europeans called Africa the "dark continent." They knew little about it. No European had explored the middle of Africa. In fact, no one knew where in Africa the Nile River began.

2. Portuguese explorers had explored the coast of Africa in the 15th century. They had not really been interested in Africa, however. Rather, they were looking for a way to sail around it. They wanted to reach India, China, and the East Indies Spice Islands. Africa was like a huge roadblock standing in the way of trade with the East.

3. The voyage around Africa from Europe to India was a long one. Sailing ships had to stop along the African coast to get fresh water and food. Because of this, a group of Dutch businessmen decided it would be a good idea to set up a colony in Africa. These men formed the Dutch East India Company. In 1652, one of

their ships landed some settlers at Cape Town, on the southern tip of Africa. Cape Town was the first important European settlement in Africa south of the Sahara Desert. It was set up at about the same time that some of the North American colonies were being settled.

4. The weather in South Africa was pleasant and the soil good for farming. As a result, more Dutch settlers came to Cape Town. These early colonists from Holland were called Boers (BOHRS), which means *farmers*. Settlers also came to Cape Town from France and England. The French and English settlers came to escape persecution or hard times in Europe. Except for the Dutch colony in South Africa, no important settlements were made by Europeans in Africa for almost 200 years.

WHY WAS THE SLAVE TRADE STARTED?

5. One group of Europeans remained busy in Africa, however: the slave traders. During the 16th century, European ships' captains, looking for profits, brought a few black slaves from Africa to the American colonies. This was the beginning of the trade that brought millions of Africans to the New World as slaves. Black African rulers and Arab slave merchants cap-

Jan van Riebeeck arrived in Cape Town in 1652 with colonists. He built Cape Town as a supply base for Dutch East India Company ships.

tured and chained the future slaves. Then European traders stopped their ships along the African coast. They bought the victims and shipped them to the New World.

6. The voyage to America was long. Hundreds of thousands of Africans died of hunger, thirst, sickness, and beatings. Fewer than half of them lived through the trip. Those who did live were sold as slaves to plantation owners in the American colonies and the West Indies. In two centuries of slave trading, more than 15 million people were brought from Africa to the Western Hemisphere.

7. European merchants ran the African slave trade and had begun a settlement at Cape Town. Yet they knew very little about the central part of Africa. Near the end of the 18th century, Europeans began to become interested in this area. They wanted to know what life was like there. In 1796 and again in 1805, a Scotsman named Mungo Park explored West Africa. He died during his last journey. Richard Lander, an Englishman, explored West Africa in 1830.

WHY WERE STANLEY AND LIVINGSTONE IMPORTANT?

8. In East Africa, European explorers tried to find the source of the Nile. It is the longest river in the world. James Bruce, a Scotsman, explored Ethiopia in 1768. He followed one branch of the Nile from its beginning in Ethiopia to its meeting with a branch in the Sudan. A Scottish missionary, David Livingstone, went to central Africa in the 1840's. At first, Livingstone concerned himself with trying to stop the slave trade. He also wanted to bring Christianity to the Africans. Later, he became interested in exploring the area and learning its geography. In 1856, he discovered a great African waterfall. He named it Victoria Falls, in honor of Queen Victoria of Great Britain.

9. Dr. Livingstone lived among the Africans for thirty years, teaching them and preaching to them. For years, nothing was heard of him back home. Was he lost? Had he died? The editor of a New York newspaper was curious. He decided to send a reporter to Africa to find out what had happened to Dr. Livingstone. The newspaperman was named Henry Stanley. Stanley suffered months of hardships and danger. At last, he found Livingstone living in the heart of Africa. When they met, Stanley greeted the missionary with the famous words: "Dr. Livingstone, I presume?"

HOW DID EUROPEAN NATIONS DIVIDE AFRICA?

10. After this famous meeting, both Stanley and Livingstone explored the Congo area of Central Africa. Livingstone died in Africa among the people who loved him. Stanley later wrote books and articles about the land and people of central Africa. Soon other explorers and missionaries went to central Africa. Richard Burton, an Englishman, tried to find the source of the Nile River. But it was John Speke, another English explorer, who finally discovered it: Ripon Falls. Here the waters of Lake Victoria start to flow down the Nile valley. They finally reach the Mediterranean Sea, 4,000 miles away.

11. Soon, the nations of Europe began to claim different parts of Africa as colonies. France already owned Algeria. It took a large part of the Sahara Desert region. France also took Morocco and Tunis, in North Africa, and the island of Madagascar, off the east coast. Great Britain had taken Cape Town in South Africa from the Dutch by a treaty of the Congress of Vienna, 1814–15. Many explorers of Africa had been Englishmen and Scotsmen. Therefore, Great Britain claimed the largest share of Africa. It added Nigeria, the Gold Coast, Kenya, and Uganda to its growing empire. It claimed Egypt as a protectorate. With Egypt it shared control of the Sudan, the area south of Egypt.

12. King Leopold II, of Belgium, took the rich Congo region as his colony. Angola, Mozambique, and Guinea were claimed by the Portuguese. Germany and Italy, the two newer nations of Europe, also entered the race for African colonies. Germany took southwest Africa and East Africa. Italy took Libya, Somaliland, and Eritrea. Within 75 years, almost all of the continent of Africa was divided like a huge pie. (See map page 430.)

13. The coming of Europeans to Africa was not taken peacefully by all people. Africans often tried to drive the Europeans from their territory. Cetewayo, for example, the African ruler of the Zulus of South Africa, tried to drive the British from his land. He did not succeed. Other rebellions by the people of Africa also failed. The Africans showed courage and bravery. But they did not have the weapons to match those of the invaders.

Henry Stanley greeting David Livingstone. Why do you think it was important for Europeans to learn the geography of Africa?

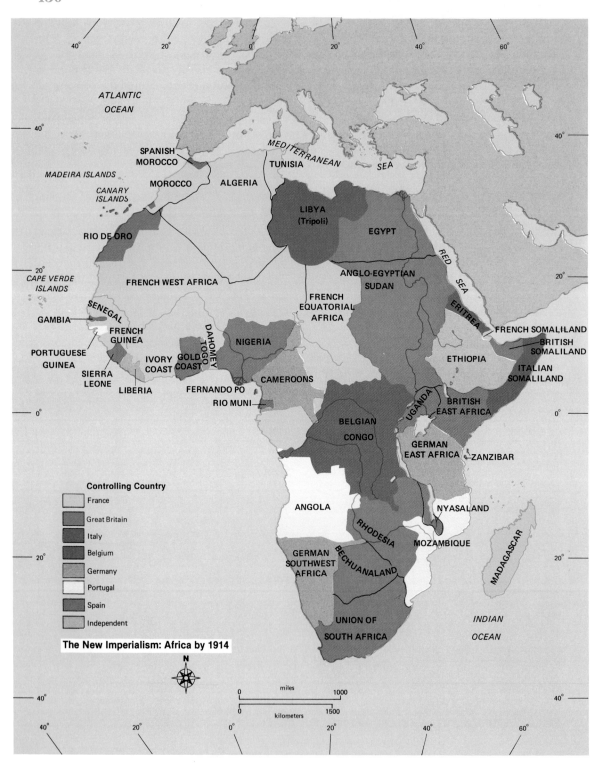

ATLANTIC
OCEAN

MADEIRA ISLANDS

CANARY
ISLANDS

CAPE VERDE
ISLANDS

SPANISH
MOROCCO

MOROCCO

RIO DE ORO

FRENCH WEST AFRICA

SENEGAL

GAMBIA

FRENCH
GUINEA

PORTUGUESE
GUINEA

SIERRA
LEONE

LIBERIA

IVORY
COAST

GOLD
COAST

DAHOMEY
TOGO

FERNANDO PO

RIO MUNI

MEDITERRANEAN

SEA

TUNISIA

ALGERIA

LIBYA
(Tripoli)

EGYPT

ANGLO-EGYPTIAN
SUDAN

FRENCH
EQUATORIAL
AFRICA

NIGERIA

CAMEROONS

BELGIAN
CONGO

RED
SEA

ERITREA

FRENCH SOMALILAND

BRITISH
SOMALILAND

ETHIOPIA

ITALIAN
SOMALILAND

UGANDA

BRITISH
EAST AFRICA

GERMAN
EAST AFRICA

ZANZIBAR

ANGOLA

GERMAN
SOUTHWEST
AFRICA

RHODESIA

BECHUANALAND

NYASALAND

MOZAMBIQUE

MADAGASCAR

UNION OF
SOUTH AFRICA

INDIAN
OCEAN

Controlling Country

France

Great Britain

Italy

Belgium

Germany

Portugal

Spain

Independent

The New Imperialism: Africa by 1914

N

miles
0   1000

0   1500
kilometers

Testing Your Vocabulary

Choose the best answer.

1. The Boers settled in South Africa. A *Boer* is a
   a. French merchant.
   b. Dutch farmer.
   c. English miner.

2. Black slaves were sold to plantation owners in the American colonies. A *plantation* is
   a. a large farm which uses many workers.
   b. the home of a nobleman and his family.
   c. a small farm where cotton and tobacco are raised.

3. Many explorers tried to find the source of the Nile. The *source* of a river is
   a. the beginning of the river.
   b. the end of the river, where it reaches the sea.
   c. the widest part of the river.

4. Great Britain claimed Egypt as a protectorate. A *protectorate* is
   a. a colony that has been set up for trading purposes.
   b. a military alliance between two nations.
   c. an area controlled by a foreign power.

Understanding What You Have Read

1. A good title for paragraphs 7 through 10 is
   a. Colonial Conflicts in Africa.
   b. European Settlements in Africa.
   c. Exploration of the Nile River.
   d. Exploration of Central Africa.

2. In which paragraphs do you find facts about
   a. the discovery of the source of the Nile River?
   b. the number of African slaves brought to America?
   c. the beginning of the Cape Town settlement?
   d. the exploration of West Africa?

3. The Dutch set up a colony at Cape Town because they wanted to
   a. mine for gold and diamonds.
   b. keep the British out of South Africa.
   c. have a stop-off place for ships sailing to India.

4. Early Portuguese navigators explored the coasts of Africa because they were looking for

   a. a route to India and the Spice Islands.
   b. places to set up colonies.
   c. slaves to bring to America.

5. David Livingstone went to Central Africa in order to
   a. add to Great Britain's empire.
   b. bring the Christian faith to the Africans.
   c. find the source of the Nile River.

6. One reason why Europeans were not interested in Africa for a long time was that
   a. they did not want to end the slave trade.
   b. they felt they could not build factories in Africa.
   c. they were busy exploring and settling the New World.

7. British and French settlers came to live in Cape Town because they wanted to
   a. escape from hard times at home.
   b. search for gold and silver.
   c. find the source of the Nile River.

Match the items in the second column with the names in the first column.

Column I	Column II
1. Henry Stanley	a. explored Ethiopia
2. David Livingstone	b. discovered Victoria Falls
3. Mungo Park	c. discovered Cape Town
4. James Bruce	d. American reporter who explored central Africa
5. Boers	e. king who claimed Belgian Congo
6. Leopold II	f. explored West Africa
7. John Speke	g. explored Madagascar
	h. found source of Nile River
	i. settlers of Cape Town

TURNING POINTS

Culture

Africa: The Arts of Africa

When Europeans explored Africa, they met people whose lives differed from their own. The beliefs and customs followed by the various African peoples were different from those of Europe. The art forms of the Africans reflected their particular beliefs and traditions. As a result, the art of Africa was unlike any the Europeans had ever seen before.

European travelers and scientists began to gather examples of African masks, statues, and ceremonial objects that they had found. In the late 1880s, a few were displayed in European museums. The Europeans were curious about the African art, but they did not really understand it. It was unfamiliar to them. They did not realize that the Africans were using styles that grew out of their own cultures.

By the early 1900s, a number of European artists had seen some of the African art. It had a strong effect on them. These European artists were looking for ways to express their feelings about civilization and nature. They felt that the Industrial Revolution had taken people too far away from nature. African art seemed to be a strong form of expression that was close to the basic things of life. To the European artists, African art was a new and fascinating way of looking at the world.

Some Europeans began collecting African art. By 1914, artists such as Pablo Picasso, Georges Braque, and Henri Matisse had filled their studio shelves with works from Africa. Some of the works of these European artists owe their inspiration to these earlier pieces of art from Africa.

Critical Thinking

1. Compare Pablo Picasso's attitude toward African art with the attitude of some late 19th-century Europeans.
2. Much of traditional African art was religious in nature. Which parts of the text above support this idea?

AIM: How did imperialism change the history of China?

CHAPTER 3

China Is Divided by Others

WHY DID CHINA REPEL FOREIGNERS?

1. This is one of the stories that American school children read in the 19th century:

> A Chinese emperor asked an artist to paint a picture of a battle. When the picture was finished, the emperor did not like it. He called for a slave and killed the slave with a sword. The emperor then turned to the artist and said: "This is what blood looks like. Now go back and paint the picture again."

The events in this story never actually happened. But they show what strange ideas Europeans and Americans had about the people of Asia. In the early 19th century, people knew almost as little about China as they did about Africa.

2. China was closed to foreigners. European nations had taken colonies in other parts of Asia, however. Great Britain controlled large parts of India and Ceylon. Holland ruled the rich East Indies islands of Java, Sumatra, and others. Spain ruled the Philippine Islands. But at the beginning of the 19th century, China and Japan had not yet been touched by European imperialism.

3. Since 1644, China had been governed by one family, called the Manchu dynasty. By the 19th century, the Manchu rulers had become weak. Their officials were greedy and dishonest. They did not build or repair roads, bridges, or canals. Food shortages and floods made life hard for the Chinese peasants. A number of times the people tried to overthrow their Manchu rulers. But the emperor hired foreign generals to put down these revolts.

4. The Manchu emperors kept foreign traders and missionaries out of China. They allowed foreign ships to stop at only one Chinese seaport, the port of Canton. One of the chief products that Europe sold to China was opium. Opium is a dangerous habit-forming drug. English merchants sold large amounts of it to China. When a Manchu emperor tried to stop the opium trade, Great Britain declared war on China. The British easily won this First Opium War (1839–42), as it is called. As a result, China was forced to give Hong Kong to Great Britain as a colony. In addition, China had to open four more of its ports to foreign merchants and traders.

Once China's ports were open to foreigners, many countries built factories near the port cities. These factories are in Canton. Why do you think Europeans wanted to build factories in China?

WHICH NATIONS DIVIDED CHINA?

5. The First Opium War led to other wars between European nations and China. In all of these wars, China was easily defeated. The swords of the emperor's soldiers were no match for European rifles and cannon. After each defeat, China was forced to give up a little more of its land. China was slowly carved into areas controlled by Europeans—spheres of influence. In the Second Opium War (1857–60), against Great Britain and France, China was again defeated. It was forced to open more ports to foreign traders. In addition, it had to agree to give special rights to foreigners in China.

6. Japan, a neighbor of China, also took part in the dividing of China. In 1894–95, Japan and China fought the Sino-Japanese War. China lost. As a result, Japan took the island of Formosa from China. Japan also gained the right to trade at more Chinese ports. China also lost Korea, which became independent for a few years. But it was taken by Japan in 1910. As China grew weaker, other European nations began to want special rights in China. The Manchu emperors were too weak to stop them. The Manchus continued to rule in China. But they had little power against the European and Japanese invaders.

7. Germany gained control of the Shantung Peninsula. France took control of south China. The British held on to a large area north and west of Hong Kong. Russia took Port Arthur and Manchuria, in North China. After Japan defeated Russia in the Russo-Japanese War (1904–05), Japan took over Russia's sphere of influence in north China. Just as Africa was divided into colonies, so China was divided into spheres of influence. In other regions of Asia, the French annexed Indo-China. The British, who controlled India, took Burma, and the Japanese seized Korea. (See map, page 437.)

8. The United States tried to stop the dividing up of China. It announced an Open-Door Policy, in 1899. This meant that it wanted all nations to have the same trading rights in China. The United States wanted the open-door policy to keep China from being further divided and wanted to hold on to its own share of Chinese trade. The United States also had imperialistic aims. As a result of its victory in the Spanish-American War (1898), the United States took the Philippine Islands and Puerto Rico from Spain. Europe, as well as Japan, refused to follow the open-door policy, and China remained divided. As China lost battle after battle, imperialist nations grabbed more and more of its land. Hatred for foreigners grew among the Chinese people. In 1900, a Chinese secret society called the Boxers was formed. The Boxers tried to drive all foreigners out of China. This movement is known as the *Boxer Rebellion*. European, Japanese, and American military forces, however, quickly put down the rebellion.

Chinese soldiers during the Boxer Rebellion. What in the picture supports the statement that the Chinese soldiers were no match for the military forces of Europe and Japan?

WHY WAS CHINA SO WEAK?

9. China was one of the oldest and largest kingdoms in the world. Why, then, was it so easily divided by foreign imperialists? There were many reasons. The Manchu government was weak. The people wanted to keep their old customs and ways of doing things. They refused to use Western methods of farming and manufacturing. Chinese education was based on the teachings of their ancient wise men, such as Confucius. There was no education in such modern subjects as chemistry, mathematics, engineering and agriculture. The Chinese army was not a modern fighting force, and the Chinese had no navy. China in the 19th century was an undeveloped nation.

10. As their country was being torn apart, many Chinese people began to realize that China had to become modern. If it did not, it would be destroyed. A Chinese patriot named Dr. Sun Yat Sen set up a party called the Kuomintang (kwo-min-TANG). Dr. Sun wanted to end the Manchu dynasty, and to make China democratic and modern. The Kuomintang began a revolution in China in 1911. The Manchu dynasty was at last overthrown. China became a republic. But when World War I began, the Republic of China was still divided into foreign spheres of influence.

When foreigners were captured, the Boxers tried them and often killed them. How was the Boxer Rebellion finally ended?

Testing Your Vocabulary

Choose the best answer.

1. During the 19th century China was ruled by one dynasty. A *dynasty* is
   a. an absolute king or emperor.
   b. an elected king or queen.
   c. a long line of rulers from the same family.
2. China was divided into spheres of influence by foreign nations. A *sphere of influence* is
   a. the right to collect taxes in an area.
   b. the right to run the government in an area.
   c. an area in which special trading rights are given to a foreign power.

Understanding What You Have Read

1. A good title for paragraphs 3 and 4 is
   a. China under the Manchu Emperors.
   b. United States' Interests in Asia.
   c. Japanese Imperialism.
   d. The Division of China.
2. In which paragraphs do you find facts about
   a. the Boxer Rebellion?
   b. the Sino-Japanese War?
   c. the revolution in China?
   d. the First Opium War?
3. The Open-Door Policy was announced by the United States in order to
   a. protect its interests in Japan.
   b. give all nations equal trading rights in China.
   c. protect the Philippine Islands from imperialist control.
4. The purpose of the Boxer rebellion was to
   a. open more Chinese ports to foreign trade.
   b. drive all foreigners out of China.
   c. set up a dictatorship in China.
5. The imperialist nations of Europe were interested in China mainly because they
   a. could fight Japan from China's mainland.
   b. wanted to trade with China.
   c. could set up military bases in China.
6. Sun Yat Sen formed the Kuomintang in order to
   a. overthrow the Manchu dynasty.
   b. drive European missionaries out of China.
   c. end the dishonesty of the Chinese government.
7. China, under the Manchu emperors, was defeated by foreign invaders because
   a. its population was small.
   b. it depended upon foreign countries for food supplies.
   c. its army was weak and lacked modern weapons.

Fill in the correct word or phrase for each of the following.

1. The Chinese uprising against foreigners in 1900 was known as the _____.
2. China's Oriental neighbor that took part in dividing China was _____.
3. The leader of the Kuomintang was _____.

4. In 1910, Korea was taken by _____.

5. Parts of China in which foreigners had special trading rights were called _____.

6. At the end of the First Opium War, China gave Hong Kong to _____.

7. The dynasty of Chinese emperors in the 19th century was one family called _____.

8. As a result of the Sino-Japanese War, Japan received the island of _____.

9. The United States' plan to give equal trading rights to all nations in China was called _____.

10. The victor in the Russo-Japanese War was _____.

Developing Ideas and Skills

USING A MAP

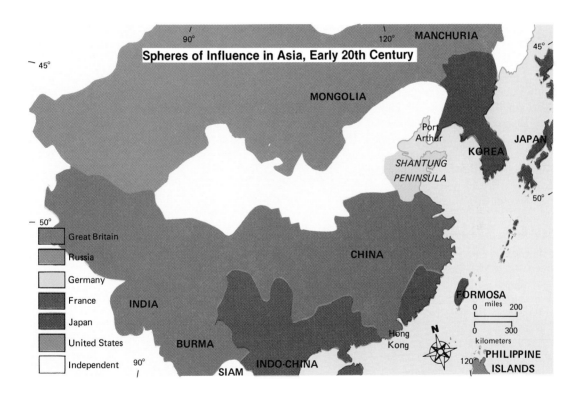

Spheres of Influence in Asia, Early 20th Century

Study this map. Then tell the name of the country controlling each of the areas listed below.

1. Manchuria
2. Indo-China
3. Korea

4. the Philippine Islands
5. Hong Kong
6. the Shantung Peninsula

AIM: How did Japan change its government, its economic system, and its way of life in less than fifty years?

CHAPTER 4

Japan Becomes a World Power

WHY WAS JAPAN UNDEVELOPED?

1. At the beginning of the 19th century, China and Japan were very much alike. Both were ruled by emperors. Both had a feudal economic system. Neither allowed foreigners to enter its borders. A century passed. One of the two countries, China, was carved into pieces by imperialist nations. The other country, Japan, became a world power. Why?

2. A little more than a century ago, the people of Japan lived as the Europeans of the Middle Ages had lived. They were ruled by an emperor called the Mikado (mik-KAH-doh). He had once been the absolute ruler of the country. The Japanese people worshipped him as a god. Worship of the emperor was part of the *Shinto* religion of the Japanese people. As the years passed, the emperor lost all of his power. The government of Japan was run by military dictators called *shoguns.*

3. Before the 19th century, the people of Japan lived under a system of feudalism. Japanese feudal lords lived on their manors. They often fought one another for land and power. The fighting class in Japan was called the *samurai* (SAM-uh-ry). They were like the knights of medieval Europe. They followed a

strict code of bravery, loyalty, and honor called *Bushido* (boo-SHEE-doh). European knights had followed a code called chivalry. Japanese peasants worked on the land of the feudal lords.

Emperor Meiji entering Tokyo Castle in 1868. Japan progressed from a feudal state to an industrial and military power during his rule.

This Samurai armor is made of steel, silk, and bronze. Describe the role of the Samurai.

4. The Japanese had welcomed foreigners to their land before the 16th century. They allowed European missionaries to convert some of their people to Christianity. In 1616, however, the Japanese rulers feared that Christianity would destroy Shintoism and Buddhism. These were the two important religions of the Japanese people. So the rulers ordered that foreigners should no longer be allowed to enter Japan. Japanese were no longer allowed to leave Japan. This "closed-door" policy lasted for more than 200 years.

HOW DID JAPAN BECOME MODERNIZED?

5. An American visitor who was to change Japanese history arrived in Tokyo harbor in 1853. He was Commodore Matthew C. Perry, of the United States Navy. Commodore Perry commanded four American warships. He had been sent by the United States government to try to persuade the Japanese to open their ports to American ships and trade. But the shogun, or military ruler of Japan, refused. Before leaving, Perry left a number of gifts for the Japanese emperor. These gifts included guns, a sewing machine, and a model of a railroad.

6. Perry said that he would return, and hoped the Japanese would change their minds at that time. He returned the next year. The shogun had changed his mind. Perhaps he realized that Japan could not stay apart from the modern world forever. Japan and the United States signed a treaty of trade. This agreement opened the ports of Japan to foreign merchants and ships. Other nations also signed trade treaties with the Japanese. Before long, the harbors of Japan were busy with the ships of many nations. Japan had been "opened" to the rest of the world.

7. The opening of Japanese ports to world trade was the first step in the changing of Japan. Within fifty years, the Japanese changed their whole way of life. In 1858, they took away the power of the shoguns. The emperor once more became the ruler of the country. The Japanese began to import and copy the factory machines of Europe and the United States. They built factories, steel mills, and railroads. Before long, they had their own industrial revolution.

8. The Japanese set up a modern public-school system. They even began to copy the clothes worn by Europeans. To make sure that Japan was not divided as China had been, the

Commodore Perry arriving in Japan. Why was this an important event?

Japanese formed a national army. It was trained like the powerful army of Prussia. The Japanese built a large navy modeled after the British fleet. Almost overnight, Japan became a modern nation. But the Japanese did not give up their Shinto religion or the worship of their emperor.

WHY DID JAPAN WANT MORE LAND?

9. Like the nations of Europe, Japan soon began to look for colonies. It began a war with China and won easily. By the treaty ending this Sino-Japanese War (1894–95), Japan took the island of Formosa from China. It also gained a sphere of influence in another part of China: Korea. In 1910, Japan took complete control of Korea. Japan became so powerful in Asia that in 1902 Great Britain decided to become its ally.

10. Shortly after the war with China, Japan fought another war. This war was against Russia. The Japanese won this Russo-Japanese War (1904–05). The war ended when President Theodore Roosevelt, of the United States, asked both countries to sign a treaty of peace. By the Treaty of Portsmouth, the Japanese gained Port Arthur in China. It also took for itself Russia's old sphere of influence in Manchuria, a part of north China. Thus Japan became a world power and took its place with other great powers as an imperialist nation. Few nations in world history have ever changed as fast or as completely as did Japan.

11. In World War I (1914–18), Japan joined the side of the Allies. As a result of the Allied victory in the war, Japan gained control of some German islands in the Pacific Ocean. The military leaders of Japan were not satisfied, however. They wanted to conquer China. In 1931, Japan started another war with China. Many nations protested, but took no action. The Japanese armies did not stop. They took control of part of north China. The Japanese hoped to seize all of Southeast Asia, as well. But while Japan was fighting China, World War II started in Europe.

12. Japan's hope of getting all of China and Southeast Asia led it to attack the United States fleet at Pearl Harbor, Hawaii, in 1941. This unexpected attack brought the United States into World War II. As we shall see, during the war Japan overran eastern China. It also captured the Philippine Islands, Malaya, and Java. In the end, however, Japan and its allies, Germany and Italy, were defeated. At the end of the war, in 1945, Japan lost all the land it had conquered. It also lost all of its old colonies, including Formosa and Korea. Thus, the dream of a great Japanese empire in Asia came to an end. Since then, Japan has become one of the great industrial powers of the world.

Present-day Japanese worker in a camera factory. Japan has become one of the leading manufacturing countries in the world. Name at least three products in your home or school that were made in Japan.

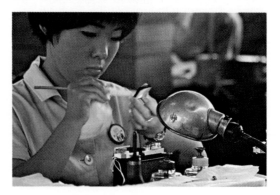

440

Testing Your Vocabulary

Choose the best answer.

1. Up to 1853, Japan followed a policy of *isolation.* This meant it
   a. allowed foreign merchants but not missionaries to enter its borders.
   b. tried to get colonies.
   c. had nothing to do with other countries.

2. The *Sino*-Japanese War ended in 1895. The word *Sino* means
   a. Russian   b. Chinese   c. British

Understanding What You Have Read

1. The main idea of paragraphs 7 and 8 is that
   a. Japan began to build factories.
   b. imperialist nations carved up Japan.
   c. Japan had a system of feudalism.
   d. Japan turned itself into a modern nation.

2. In which paragraphs do you find facts about
   a. the Sino-Japanese War?
   b. the Samurai?
   c. the opening of Japan?
   d. the Treaty of Portsmouth?

3. Unlike China, Japan was not divided into spheres of influence by foreign powers because
   a. Japan quickly became modern.
   b. the samurai were a powerful military force.
   c. Japan was an island kingdom.

4. Great Britain signed a treaty of alliance with Japan in 1902 because
   a. Japan promised special trading rights to the British.

   b. Great Britain was against American policy in Japan.
   c. Japan had become a world power.

5. Japan kept foreigners out in the 17th century because
   a. it feared it would be divided by imperialist nations.
   b. it feared Christianity would destroy Shintoism and Buddhism.
   c. foreigners tried to overthrow the Mikado.

6. The Japanese opened their ports to Western trade in 1853 because
   a. they needed imported food for their large population.
   b. the power of the shoguns came to an end.
   c. Commodore Perry showed them it would be a good idea.

7. Japan went to war with China in 1894 because Japan
   a. wanted trading rights in China.
   b. wanted to spread Shintoism in China.
   c. had become an imperialist nation.

In your notebook, fill in the correct word or phrase for each of the following statements.

1. The emperor of Japan, before modern times, was called the _____ .

2. The United States entered World War II when the Japanese bombed the American base at _____ .

3. The early military dictators of Japan were called _____ .

4. The Russo-Japanese War came to an end through the efforts of American President _____ .

5. The religion of Japan, which included worship of the emperor, was called _____ .

6. The old military class in Japan was called the _____ .

7. The United States naval commander who opened the ports of Japan to American trade was _____ .

8. The navy of modern Japan was modeled after the navy of _____ .

9. The strict code of loyalty, bravery, and honor of the early Japanese military class was called _____ .

10. At the end of the Sino-Japanese War, Japan took from China the island of _____ .

Developing Ideas and Skills

WRITING AN OUTLINE

Using the information in this chapter, complete the following outline in your notebook.

How Japan Became a Westernized Nation

I Economic Changes
  A. Ports opened to world trade
  B.
  C.

II
  A. Power of the shoguns ended
  B. Emperor became real ruler once more

III Military Changes
  A.
  B.

IV Cultural Changes
  A.
  B.

Using Original Sources

Read the passage on page 443, then answer the questions that follow:

Laws of Japan in 1634

1. Japanese ships shall not be sent abroad.
2. No Japanese shall be sent abroad. Anyone breaking this law shall suffer the penalty of death. . . .
3. All Japanese living abroad shall be put to death when they return home.
4. All Christians shall be examined by official examiners.
5. Informers against Christians shall be rewarded.
6. The arrival of foreign ships must be reported to Edo [Tokyo] and watch kept over them.
7. Those who spread Christianity shall be jailed. . . .
8. Everything shall be done in order to see that when a Christian dies none of his children or grandchildren will live on, and anyone not following this order shall be put to death. . . .
9. The samurai shall not buy goods on board foreign ships directly from foreigners.

Choose the correct answer for each of the following statements.

1. With these laws, the Japanese were following a policy of
   a. feudalism.
   b. isolation.
   c. imperialism.
2. Japanese living in foreign countries who returned home were to be
   a. honored.
   b. put in jail.
   c. killed.
3. Christian missionaries in Japan were to be
   a. jailed.
   b. sent home.
   c. given religious freedom.
4. The Japanese were not permitted to
   a. move to large cities.
   b. visit other countries.
   c. learn new languages.
5. These laws were obeyed by the Japanese before the visit of
   a. Commodore Perry.
   b. Admiral Dewey.
   c. President Theodore Roosevelt.

AIM: How did the British nation gain its colonies and rule its vast empire and commonwealth?

CHAPTER 5

Great Britain Builds an Empire

HOW DID BRITAIN DEFEAT ITS RIVALS?

1. "The sun never sets on the British Empire." This was the boast of many English people in the 19th and early 20th centuries. It meant that Great Britain owned colonies in all parts of the world. When it was nighttime in the colonies of one part of the world, the sun was shining over British territory in another part. Great Britain had colonies on every continent. At one time, almost one-fourth of the land on earth was part of the British empire. The oceans were dotted with islands held by the British. How did Great Britain build this vast empire, the largest in area in all history? And why did this huge empire finally come to an end?

2. Great Britain began building its empire in the 16th century. This was after the discovery of the New World. With each passing century, it defeated a different colonial rival. It toppled Spain in the 16th century by defeating the Spanish Armada. It defeated the Netherlands (Holland) in the 17th century. It beat the French in the 18th and 19th centuries. Britain's large navy gave it control of the world's oceans. With this navy, the British set up colonies all

over the world. Great Britain became known as "mistress of the seas." Thus, Great Britain became ruler of a world empire.

3. The British were at war with the Netherlands in the 17th century. The British seized the Dutch colonies of New Amsterdam and Delaware, in America. In the 18th century, the British took Gibraltar from Spain. Gibraltar guarded the western entrance to the Mediterranean Sea. Great Britain also defeated the French in the French and Indian War (1756–63). In Europe this conflict was called the Seven Years' War. At the end of this war, the British took colonies from France. Among them were Canada and different trading posts in India. English explorers of the 18th century also added colonies to the empire. Captain James Cook, for example, explored the coasts of Australia and New Zealand. He claimed them for Great Britain.

4. The British Empire was lessened somewhat when the thirteen American colonies won their independence, in 1783. But the British went right on adding to their empire. During the first half of the 19th century, the desire for colonies seemed to be dying in other great nations of Europe. They were busy with wars and revolutions at home. But Great Britain man-

Britain took over control of India in 1858. This picture shows Indian musicians playing for the English. From the picture, how are the two cultures different? How are they alike?

aged to get new colonies with almost every peace treaty.

5. During the Napoleonic era (1799–1815), the French conquered most of Western Europe. This included the Netherlands, Spain, and Denmark. Great Britain also went to war with France. Britain used its navy to capture some of France's colonies in the West Indies. The British also took such Dutch colonies as Ceylon, near India, and Cape Colony, in South Africa. From Spain the British took Trinidad.

WHY DID BRITAIN LOOK FOR COLONIES IN AFRICA AND ASIA?

6. The race for colonies in Africa and Asia began in the middle of the 19th century. Great Britain was among the leaders. In Asia, the British took Hong Kong from China and seized control of Burma. In Africa, they took Egypt, Nigeria, the Gold Coast, Kenya, Uganda, Rhodesia, and other areas. Great Britain's most important possession in Africa, however, was the narrow waterway called the Suez Canal. This canal had been built by a French company. Yet the British eventually took control of the Suez Canal.

7. Great Britain gained control of the Canal when the ruler of Egypt needed money. He owned most of the stock in the Suez Canal Company. Because he needed money, he offered to sell his stock to the British. Benjamin Disraeli was prime minister of Great Britain at the time. He accepted the Egyptian offer. In 1875, Great Britain bought control of the Suez Canal. To the British the canal was the "key to India." It shortened the travel distance to India by 5,000 miles. Great Britain kept control of the Suez Canal for almost a century.

8. Building the empire was not easy. It took many wars over many centuries. India was almost lost, for example, when the Sepoy (SEE-poy) mutiny took place, in 1857. The Sepoys were Indians serving as soldiers in the British army in India. These soldiers, who were Hindus and Muslims, felt that their religious beliefs were not being respected. Because of this they rebelled. Thousands of British in India were murdered during the uprising. But the Sepoy mutiny was finally put down and India remained a part of the British Empire. In 1899, the Dutch Boers in South Africa tried to win independence. The Boer War was finally won by the British in 1902. Great Britain kept control of this wealthy colony, also.

9. Why were the British so successful in getting and keeping colonies? There were many reasons. Great Britain had the largest and most powerful navy in the world. It controlled the seas leading to its colonies. The British carefully trained all officials sent to govern the colonies. They tried to develop the natural resources and industries of their colonies. They built railroads and opened mines. They set up schools and hospitals.

WHY WAS THE COMMONWEALTH FORMED?

10. The British government persuaded its own people to settle its colonies. Many English people settled in Canada, Australia, New Zealand, and South Africa. Most important in

building their empire, the British learned how to compromise. When its colonies asked for some self-government, the British government gave it. The British had learned a lesson when they lost the thirteen American colonies.

11. In the 19th century, Canada began to seek self-government. To satisfy the Canadians, the British thought up a new plan for governing. Under this plan, a colony could become a dominion. A colony that became a dominion remained in the British Empire. But the dominion could govern itself. In 1867, Parliament passed the British North America Act. This law made Canada the first self-governing dominion in the British Empire. In later years, Australia, New Zealand, the Union of South Africa, India, Pakistan, Ceylon, and other areas became dominions. They also received the right of self-government.

12. Today there is nothing left of the British Empire. What happened to these many colonies and dominions that the British had once ruled? After World War I, Parliament passed a law called the Statute of Westminster (1931). By this law, Great Britain gave all its dominions almost complete independence. Great Britain and its old dominions set up a loose union called the Commonwealth of Nations. Today, members of the Commonwealth are bound to one another through cultural and economic ties. But they are politically independent.

13. After World War II, nationalism and the desire for independence spread among the colonial peoples of the world. Great Britain and other imperialist nations were forced to give independence to almost all of their colonies. Great Britain gave independence to Burma in 1948, to Ghana in 1957, to Cyprus in 1959, to Nigeria in 1960, and to others at other times. Thus, the largest empire of all time came to an end after World War II. Many of Great Britain's former colonies joined the Commonwealth. These included India, Pakistan, Sri Lanka (formerly Ceylon), Ghana, Kenya, and Sierra Leone. Today, there are 46 independent states in the Commonwealth.

The fathers of the Canadian Federation. How did Canada's connection with Great Britain change during the 19th century?

Indira Ghandi speaking before the Commonwealth. Mrs. Ghandi was the first woman prime minister of India. She served from 1966 to 1977 and from 1980 until her death in 1984.

Testing Your Vocabulary

Choose the best answer.

1. Canada became the first British dominion. As the word is used here, a *dominion* is
   a. a colony given representation in the British Parliament.
   b. a colony ruled by a governor.
   c. a self-governing territory that remains linked to Great Britain.
2. The British Commonwealth of Nations was formed under the Statute of Westminster. A *statute* is
   a. a law passed by a parliament or congress.
   b. a monument made of stone.
   c. a kind of church.
3. A *mutiny* is
   a. a plague.
   b. a person who is unable to speak.
   c. a rebellion against a person or group in command.

Understanding What You Have Read

1. The main idea of paragraphs 9 through 11 is that
   a. the British Empire came to an end.
   b. Great Britain set up a Commonwealth of Nations.
   c. the British Empire grew in the 18th century.
   d. there were many reasons for British success in building an empire.
2. In which paragraphs do you find facts about
   a. Captain Cook's explorations of Australia and New Zealand?
   b. the Sepoy mutiny?
   c. the Statute of Westminster?
   d. the buying of the Suez Canal?
3. One of the reasons why Great Britain was successful in building a large empire was that it
   a. appointed local people to govern the colonies.
   b. ruled its colonies with absolute power.
   c. controlled the seas with its navy.
4. Canada sought to separate itself from Great Britain because
   a. British taxes were too high.
   b. Canada wanted more self-government.
   c. Great Britain would not allow freedom of speech and press.
5. Great Britain lost most of its empire after World War II mainly because
   a. its navy was defeated during the war.
   b. nationalism brought demands for independence in the colonies.
   c. Communist ideas were spread in British colonies.
6. The Sepoy mutiny began because
   a. Hindu and Muslim soldiers in the British army became angry.
   b. British taxes on tea and newspapers caused unrest.
   c. there were no Indian representatives in the British Parliament.
7. The British bought the Suez Canal from the ruler of Egypt because the canal
   a. was the shortest water route to India.
   b. was near Constantinople.
   c. gave Britain control of all Mediterranean lands.

Answer true or false. If a statement is false, change the words in italics to make it true.

1. At its largest, the *British Empire* covered one-fourth of the earth's land.
2. The explorations of Captain James Cook gave Great Britain its claims to *Canada* and New Zealand.
3. The Sepoy mutiny was an army revolt against the British in *South Africa*.
4. *Canada* was the first British colony to become a dominion.
5. The British thought of the *Suez Canal* as the "key to India."
6. Great Britain's success in building an empire was due mainly to the power of its *army*.

Developing Ideas and Skills

USING A MAP

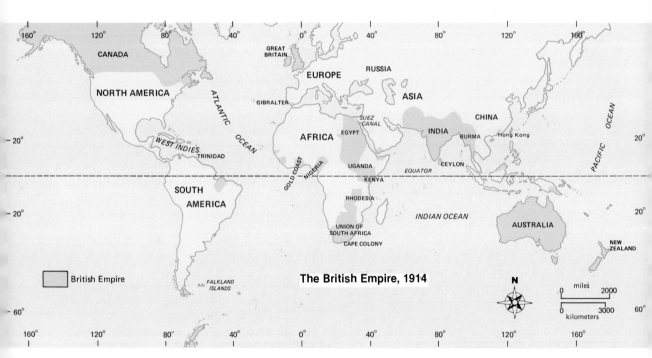

The British Empire, 1914

Using the information on the map, decide which of the following statements are true and which are false.

1. The British Empire included little of northern Asia.
2. Nearly all of the Empire was north of the equator.
3. Great Britain held more land in Africa than in South America.
4. The largest part of the Empire south of the equator was South Africa.
5. The largest part of the Empire in Asia was India.

AIM: Why are the countries of the Middle East so important today?

CHAPTER 6

Rivals in the Middle East

WHY IS THE MIDDLE EAST IMPORTANT?

1. We often read and hear about events in the Middle East. What exactly is the Middle East? It is the area between North Africa and India. Today, it includes such large nations as Turkey, Egypt, Saudi Arabia, and Iran. A number of small countries—Syria, Lebanon, Jordan, Kuwait, and Israel—are also part of the Middle East. In the 19th century, the Middle East was made up of only the Turkish Empire, Persia, and Egypt.

2. The early civilizations of ancient Egypt and Babylon were located in what is now the Middle East. Three great religions had their beginnings in the Middle East. Judaism and Christianity started in ancient Palestine (this is now the nation of Israel). Islam, the religion of Muhammad, began in Arabia. The Middle East was truly a "cradle of civilization." Today, most of the people in the Middle East are Muslims, followers of the religion of Islam.

3. A large part of the Middle East is a desert of sand and rocks. Only small areas are good for farming. But in the past the great powers of Europe wanted to control the Middle East. One of the important reasons was that the Suez Canal was located there. The Suez Canal

was built by Ferdinand de Lesseps and a French company. It was opened in 1869. It connects the Mediterranean Sea and the Red Sea. After it was opened, ships sailing from Europe to Asia no longer had to sail around the African continent.

4. Whichever country controlled the Suez Canal controlled the main water route to India, China, Japan, and Australia. In 1875, Benjamin Disraeli, the British prime minister, bought control of the Suez Canal from the ruler of Egypt. For almost a century, the Suez Canal was controlled by Great Britain. It was Great Britain's main link to India. In order to protect their ownership of the canal, the British tried to gain control of the countries around it. They used armed force to make Egypt a protectorate. From 1881 to 1922, Great Britain had military control over Egypt. Although the Egyptian ruler stayed in office, he had little power.

WHY IS THE MIDDLE EAST CALLED THE "CROSSROADS OF THE WORLD"?

5. A second reason for the importance of the Middle East was its geographic location. The Middle East was like the hub of a wheel.

A ship goes through the Suez Canal. Why is this such an important channel?

Three continents met there: Europe, Africa and Asia. Because of this, the Middle East has often been called "the crossroads of the world." Turkey was the largest empire in the Middle East in the 19th century. Its borders went from the Balkans, in Europe, to Persia, in the east. Turkey also controlled Egypt. The Turkish Empire was often the cause of fighting among the great powers of Europe.

6. In the 20th century, the Middle East became important for a third reason: oil. This valuable natural resource is found under the desert sands of Arabia, Iraq, Iran, and Kuwait (koo-WAYT). Oil is used to run automobiles, airplanes, ships and machines. It is also used to heat buildings and to make electricity. Many nations of Europe were eager to control the Middle East's large supply of oil. They tried to seize control of the weak countries of the Middle East. For many years, Great Britain controlled as protectorates the oil-rich countries of Iraq, Arabia, and Kuwait.

7. Russia, as well as Great Britain, was interested in the Middle East. Russia had few harbors that were free of ice during the winter months. Most of its ice-free ports were in the

south, on the Black Sea. To get out of the Black Sea and into the Mediterranean Sea, Russian ships had to pass through a narrow body of water, called the Dardanelles, or Turkish Strait. The Dardanelles was as important to the Russians as the Suez Canal was to the British.

8. For many years during the 19th century, Russia tried to get control of the Dardanelles. The Russians were mainly Christians. They were interested in protecting the Christian Slavic people of the Balkans from the Turkish Muslim rulers. Mainly for these reasons, Russia fought the Crimean War (1853–56) with Turkey. Great Britain and France feared Russia's power in the Middle East. They came to Turkey's aid. Russia lost the war.

Describe how this picture shows a blending of old and new cultures in the Middle East.

HOW DID THE MIDDLE EAST COUNTRIES GAIN THEIR INDEPENDENCE?

9. Twenty years later, Russia and Turkey fought the Russo-Turkish War. This time Russia won. The Congress of Berlin met after the war (1878). England, France, and Germany did not allow Russia to gain what it wanted in the Middle East. The Dardanelles stayed under Turkish control. By the early 20th century, Germany, not Russia, became Britain's most dangerous rival. Great Britain and Russia became more friendly. In 1907, they divided Persia (which is today called Iran) into spheres of influence. This meant that the British and the Russians gave themselves special trading and other economic rights in different areas of Persia.

10. Germany had become a united nation in 1871. It was a latecomer in the race for colonies. But it soon became interested in the Middle East. German businessmen drew up a plan to build a great railroad. It would connect the two key cities of Germany and Turkey: Berlin and Baghdad. Turkey agreed to the plan. Great Britain was against it. The British were afraid that the Germans would become powerful in the Middle East. Germany might threaten British control of the Suez Canal. The Berlin-to-Baghdad railroad project was stopped when World War I began.

11. Great Britain, France, and their allies defeated Germany, Turkey, and *their* allies in World War I. At the end of the war, Turkey lost a large part of its empire. Great Britain was given control of Palestine and Jordan. France was given control of Syria and Lebanon. After World War I, European imperialism began to decline. People in the colonies began to demand political freedom. Great Britain was forced to give Egypt independence in 1922. Ten years later, Great Britain lost control of Iraq.

12. Imperialism in the Middle East finally came to an end with World War II. France gave independence to Syria and Lebanon in 1944. Two years later, Jordan became an independent Arab state. Palestine was freed from British control. Part of this territory became the state of Israel, in 1948. In 1956, Egypt seized the Suez Canal. This ended British control of it. Kuwait became independent of Great Britain in 1961. Thus, after a century of European control, the Middle East was independent. The spirit of colonial nationalism had put an end to European imperialism.

Testing Your Vocabulary

Choose the best answer.

1. The Dardanelles is called a *strait* because it is
   a. a narrow waterway connecting two large bodies of water.
   b. a body of water that does not curve or turn.
   c. a body of water surrounded by land on three sides.

2. The oil of the Middle East is a *natural resource*. This phrase means that the Middle Eastern oil is
   a. manufactured.
   b. found in or on the land.
   c. used in industry.

Understanding What You Have Read

1. A good title for paragraphs 7 through 9 is
   a. The Importance of the Dardanelles.
   b. The Russo-Turkish War.
   c. Russian Interest in the Middle East.
   d. Christians and Muslims.
2. In which paragraphs do you find facts about
   a. Middle East oil?
   b. Great Britain's buying of the Suez Canal?
   c. the beginning of the state of Israel?
   d. the Berlin-to-Baghdad railroad?
3. Russia wanted to control the Dardanelles in order to
   a. weaken Turkey.
   b. help the Balkan people gain their independence.
   c. give Russian ships an outlet to the Mediterranean Sea.
4. The Suez Canal was important to Europe because it
   a. brought about more trade with South America.
   b. lessened the distance to Asia by 5,000 miles.
   c. was a warm-water port.
5. In the 20th century, European nations became interested in the Middle East mainly because of its
   a. oil.
   b. coal and iron ore.
   c. gold and silver.
6. The Suez Canal came under British control because the British
   a. took it from the French at the end of a war.
   b. bought control of it from an Egyptian ruler.
   c. gave Syria to France in return for it.
7. The Middle East is called the "crossroads of the world" because
   a. three continents meet there.
   b. ancient caravan routes crossed there.
   c. it was the cradle of ancient civilizations.

Developing Ideas and Skills

USING A MAP

Examine both maps on page 453 carefully. Then answer the questions below.

1. List five nations of the Middle East today that did not exist in 1815.
   1. _____
   2. _____
   3. _____
   4. _____
   5. _____
2. The modern name for Persia is _____.
3. Three countries that border the Persian Gulf today are _____, _____, and _____.
4. The nation bordering the Black Sea on the east is _____.

The Middle East, Past and Present

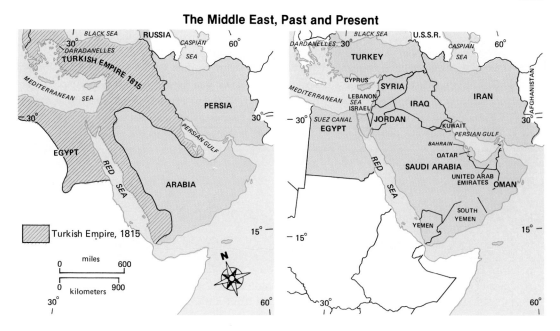

Using Original Sources

After World War I, the leaders of Turkey wanted to make Turkey a great modern nation. They wanted to change the laws, the calendar, the holidays, and even the clothes people wore. One of the biggest battles was to get Turkish men to stop wearing the fez—a hat with a red tassel and no brim. The description below is how one writer told the story of the "battle of the fez." Why do you think a hat could be so important?

The Battle of the Fez

Turkey's enemies were the turban, the fez, and the women's veil. These enemies must be destroyed. In Turkey the battle of the hats was on. The turban and the fez were more than head coverings to the people. They were part of their Islamic religion. But most men made the change because Turks were used to taking orders. Now the people saw that Allah did not kill those who took off the fez. But they saw that the government was ready to punish those who wore it. So they thought the government must be stronger than Allah.

Mustafa Kemal Ataturk, the Turkish leader, set an example. He had his picture taken in a full dress suit. The picture was shown everywhere in Turkey. It was printed on postage stamps. He was telling his people: "A good Turk wears European clothes. The fez and the veil belong to the dead past."

1. Why did the writer call the fez and the veil "the enemies" of Turkey?
2. What methods were used to get people to change their customs?
3. How do Mustafa Kemal Ataturk's efforts compare with Peter the Great's attempts to change the habits and customs of the Russian people?
4. What was the strongest force in the lives of the Turkish people before the government of Mustafa Kemal Ataturk? Do you think it will remain a strong force?
5. Do you agree with his efforts to get Turks to replace their traditional styles of dress with European styles? Why or why not?

TURNING POINTS

Culture

The Middle East: The Nightingale of the Nile

It happened all over the Middle East. At 10 P.M., on the first Thursday of each month, people stopped what they were doing. Traffic in the busy city of Cairo would stop. Coffee shops in Casablanca would become crowded with impatient customers. Farmers in the desert would turn on their radios. Everyone was eager to hear the monthly radio concert given by a woman named Um Kalthoum. Loved by millions, she was nicknamed "Star of the East." Some called her "Nightingale of the Nile." Um Kalthoum was a living legend.

Kalthoum was born in 1898. She came from a family of poor farmers. They lived in a village on the Nile delta. She began her career at the age of seven, singing religious songs. She sang from five to ten hours at a time, and was paid about seven cents a performance. In her twenties, Kalthoum began singing romantic songs. Soon, her concerts were attracting vast audiences.

Kalthoum sang political songs, battle hymns, and nationalistic songs. But she was mostly known for her love songs. Her personality was strong. Her singing affected everyone who listened to her. She stood alone on the stage, accompanied by a small orchestra. She sang for hours at a time. As she sang, she swayed back and forth and waved a silk scarf that she always held in one hand. In 1953, Kalthoum was stricken with a throat disease. Doctors would not dare treat her; they were afraid of damaging her voice. The United States offered Kalthoum treatment at an American hospital. It was successful, and she continued to sing for many more years.

When Kalthoum died in 1975, the entire Arab world mourned. For more than 50 years her voice had inspired people throughout the Middle East. To the Arabs, Kalthoum was more than a singer. She had expressed the values and feelings that were close to them. Five Arab countries had awarded her medals. Egypt's King Farouk had given her his country's highest civilian award. Kalthoum's fans in Egypt liked to say: "In the Middle East, only two things never change. The other one is the pyramids."

Critical Thinking

1. Why did Kalthoum's fans speak of her and the pyramids at the same time?
2. Why does an entertainer like Kalthoum become so popular? Explain.

AIM: What caused the nations of Europe to go to war in 1914?

CHAPTER 7

The First World War Begins

It has been said that World War I was a war fought in the trenches. How does this picture support that statement?

HOW DID IMPERIALISM AND NATIONALISM LEAD TO WAR?

1. Nations are like people. Often people will become angry with each other. But they will hide their anger for a long time. Then a

little thing happens, and their anger explodes. In the years before 1914, the nations of Europe had been growing angry with one another. But they hid their anger until the explosion of World War I. Some of the countries had agreed to help each other in case of a war. Thus Germany, Austria-Hungary, and Italy agreed to join together if any one of them fought a war. They called their agreement the Triple Alliance. Great Britain, France, and Russia were afraid of the Triple Alliance. They formed their own group and called it the Triple Entente (on-TONT). The French word *entente* means agreement.

2. One reason why some countries of Europe were angry with one another was that they wanted the same colonies. You will recall that European nations had been in a race for colonies in Africa and Asia. It sometimes happened that two countries wanted the same territory. Germany and France, for example, both wanted to control Morocco, in north Africa. France finally took Morocco as one of its colonies in 1911. But Germany was ready to start a war over this. Great Britain, however, promised to help France if a war started. Germany then decided that it would not be a good idea to begin a war. But the Germans did not forgive the French. As you have learned, the race by nations for colonies is called *imperialism*.

3. Nations wanted colonies because colonies helped their trade. Businesses could sell their manufactured goods and invest their money in the colonies. They could also get raw materials such as rubber, copper, and tin from the colonies. People were proud of their country if it owned colonies. As you have learned, this feeling of pride in one's nation is called nationalism. Keeping a nation strong meant that large armies and navies were needed to protect it. Of course, armies and navies could also be used to seize and hold colonies. Running a government on military ideals and wanting large armies and navies is called *militarism*.

4. People of many races and nationalities lived in some European countries. In Austria-Hungary, for example, lived Serbs, Italians, Romanians, and others. These different nationalities were called minorities because they were small groups. Naturally, they wanted to be able to follow their own customs. The Italians in

Austria-Hungary wanted to speak Italian and follow the customs of Italy. The Serbs wanted to live like the people of Serbia (which is part of Yugoslavia today). Turkey also had many minority groups, such as Romanians, Bulgarians, Serbs, and Albanians. They wanted to be free of Turkish rule. The desire of minorities to be independent, or to belong to a country of their own people, is also a form of nationalism.

5. Some countries wanted to get back territory they had lost in earlier wars. France, for example, had lost Alsace-Lorraine (AL-sass lor-RAYN) to Germany at the end of the Franco-Prussian War, in 1871. For many years, the French dreamed of getting back Alsace-Lorraine. The countries of Europe also had conflicts over a part of southeast Europe called the Balkans. In this area were some countries that were independent, such as Serbia, Romania, and Bulgaria. But there were other Balkan lands that were under the rule of Turkey.

WHY WERE THE BALKANS CALLED A "POWDER KEG"?

6. The big countries of Europe were interested in the Balkans for different reasons. Russia wanted an outlet from the Black Sea to the Mediterranean Sea. This outlet, called the Dardanelles, was controlled by Turkey. Germany wanted to build a railroad through the Balkans, from Berlin, in Germany, to Baghdad, in Turkey. This project was called the Berlin-to-Baghdad Railway. Great Britain was interested in the Balkans because of their nearness to the Suez Canal. It was afraid of losing control of the canal. Finally, Austria-Hungary was interested in the Balkans because they touched its own borders.

7. In 1908, Austria-Hungary seized a part of Turkish territory in the Balkans called Bosnia-Herzegovina. This action almost led to war in Europe. In 1912, a number of Balkan countries, with the backing of Russia, declared war

The Balkans at the Outset of World War I

☐ The Balkans

their minority groups. But they did not get into a big war. In June 1914, however, an event took place that finally made them go to war. Archduke Francis Ferdinand was to be the next emperor of Austria-Hungary. He was shot by a Serbian patriot. This happened in a small town in Austria-Hungary: Sarajevo (sa-ra-YAY-vo).

9. Ordinarily, an event like this would not have such important results. But the countries of Europe were already angry with one another over many things. Austria-Hungary used the murder of the archduke as an excuse for declaring war on Serbia. Austria-Hungary never expected that its war with Serbia would lead to a world war. But events moved very fast. As soon as Austria-Hungary declared war, Russia came to Serbia's aid. Then Germany came to the aid of Austria-Hungary. France came to the aid of Russia, and Great Britain came to the aid of France. Soon, most of the countries of Europe had taken sides and World War I began. About half of Europe was at war with the other half.

10. During the war, Austria-Hungary, Germany, Bulgaria, and Turkey were called the Central Powers. The Central Powers were fighting against Serbia, Russia, Great Britain,

on Turkey. Turkey was defeated in the First Balkan War. Then arguments began among the rival Balkan countries. They argued about dividing the Turkish territory. This led to a Second Balkan War, in 1913. In this war Bulgaria was defeated. During each of these wars, some of the great powers in Europe backed one side while some backed the other. It seemed that the Balkans might explode at any time into a world war. For this reason, the Balkans were called the "powder keg" of Europe.

HOW DID WORLD WAR I BEGIN?

8. The forces of imperialism, militarism, nationalism, and rival alliances were present at the same time in Europe in the early 20th century. The big countries argued with one another over colonies. They argued over the size of their armies and navies. They argued over

Archduke Francis Ferdinand and his wife one hour before the shot that killed him and started World War I.

and France. These countries were called the Allied Powers. Although Italy had been a member of the Triple Alliance, it did not join the fighting when the war began. In 1915, Italy entered the war on the side of the Allied Powers. The Allies had promised to give Italy more territory at the end of the war than the Central Powers had. Thus, the assassination of the archduke was the spark that started the first great World War. But the deeper causes of the war were imperialism, militarism, and the alliances among the great powers.

Testing Your Vocabulary

Choose the best answer.

1. Before World War I, the nations of Europe followed a policy of *militarism.* This meant
   a. they appointed soldiers to run their governments.
   b. they formed alliances in which they agreed to give one another different kinds of weapons.
   c. they ran their governments on military ideals and they had large armies and navies.
2. Before World War I, minority nationalities lived in Austria-Hungary and Turkey. A *minority* is a
   a. part of a country's population with a nationality different from most of the people.
   b. political party that loses an election.
   c. persecuted race or nationality.
3. Great Britain, France, and Russia formed the Triple Entente. An *entente* is
   a. a secret treaty.
   b. an agreement.
   c. a trade policy.

Understanding What You Have Read

1. A good title for paragraphs 2 and 3 is
   a. Germany versus France.
   b. Militarism as a Cause of War.
   c. Trouble in the Balkans.
   d. The Great Powers' Desire for Colonies.
2. In which paragraphs do you find facts about
   a. the assassination of the Archduke Ferdinand?
   b. the Berlin-to-Baghdad Railway?
   c. German and French rivalry for Morocco?
   d. the nations called the Central Powers?
3. Germany was interested in the Balkans because it wanted to
   a. get an outlet to the Mediterranean Sea.
   b. build the Berlin-to-Baghdad Railway.
   c. protect German minorities in the Balkans.
4. Before World War I, the French hoped to get Alsace-Lorraine from Germany because this land
   a. had once been part of France.
   b. would be a natural boundary between France and Italy.
   c. was a good farming region.
5. Before World War I, the Balkans were called the "powder keg of Europe" because
   a. conflict between nations in this area

could lead to a world war.

b. Turkey persecuted the Christian minorities in the Balkans.

c. Austria-Hungary hoped to seize the area.

6. Russia always wanted an outlet from the Black Sea because

   a. most Russian rivers emptied into the Black Sea.

   b. the area near the Black Sea was fertile.

   c. most of Russia's northern harbors were too icy to be used in the winter.

7. Germany almost declared war on France in 1911 because

   a. both nations wanted control of Morocco.

   b. they were economic rivals in China.

   c. both nations wanted Alsace-Lorraine.

Developing Ideas and Skills

UNDERSTANDING A CARTOON

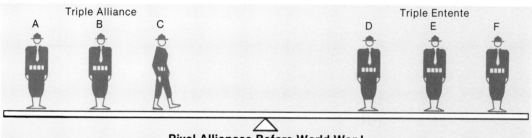

Triple Alliance

A   B   C

Triple Entente

D   E   F

Rival Alliances Before World War I

In your notebook, write which countries the figures A, B, C, D, E, and F stand for. Why is one of the figures shown facing the other group?

MAKING A CHART

Complete, in your notebook, the following chart:

Balkan Rivalries Before World War I	
Nation	Interest in the Balkans
Russia	
Germany	
Great Britain	
Austria-Hungary	
Turkey	

Using Original Sources

As German power grew in the years before World War I, France and Russia each feared that it might be left alone to fight against Germany. So, they entered into an agreement. Part of the agreement follows. Read it; then answer the questions below.

France and Russia Form an Alliance

France and Russia, led by a common desire to preserve peace, and to prepare for a defensive war brought against either of them by an attack by the forces of the Triple Alliance, have agreed upon the following:

1. If France is attacked by Germany, or by Italy supported by Germany, Russia shall use all her available forces to fight Germany. If Russia is attacked by Germany, or by Austria supported by Germany, France shall use all her available forces to fight Germany.

2. In case the forces of the Triple Alliance or one of the Powers that are a part of it should be mobilized, France and Russia shall mobilize all their forces (at the same time) and shall transport them as near to the frontiers as possible.

3. The forces available which must be employed against Germany shall be for France, 1,300,000 men; for Russia, from 700,000 to 800,000 men. These forces shall begin complete action with all speed so that Germany will have to fight at the same time in the east and in the west.

4. France and Russia shall not conclude peace separately.

5. All the clauses listed above shall be kept absolutely secret.

1. Why might Germany fear a war with either France or Russia if she knew of this agreement?

2. Why might France and Russia have wanted the agreement kept secret?

3. Why might it have been decided that, in the event of war, neither France nor Russia would make peace separately?

4. Why did France and Russia, in the event of war, want to force Germany to fight in the east and west at the same time?

5. Review the events mentioned in paragraph 9. Did France and Russia stick to their agreement?

CHAPTER 8

The First World War Is Fought

WHERE WAS THE WAR FOUGHT?

1. For four years, 1914–18, the Allied Powers and the Central Powers fought World War I. Almost every large nation and many of the smaller nations of Europe took sides in the war. In 1915, Italy joined the Allies when it declared war on Austria-Hungary. Greece came into the war on the side of the Allied Powers in 1917. Japan had a military alliance with Great Britain. It also joined the Allies.

2. At the beginning of the war, Germany invaded Belgium and France in the west and Russia in the east. In four years of fighting on the western front, the Germans could not capture Paris, the capital of France. Heavy fighting also went on between Austria-Hungary, Bulgaria, and Turkey (on one side) and Italy, Serbia, Romania, and Greece (on the other). During the war, many new kinds of weapons were used for the first time: armored tanks, airplanes, giant cannon, submarines, and poison gas. Fighting from long narrow ditches, called trenches, became a common way of doing battle.

3. It was against the Russians that Germany won its greatest victories in the war. The Russian army was poorly trained and badly

equipped. It was badly defeated in a number of major battles. In the middle of these defeats, a revolution started inside Russia in 1917 (see Unit 11, Chapter 2). The Russian government was taken over by a group called Bolsheviks. (This group later became the Communists.) Then the czar of Russia and his family were murdered. The new government of Russia signed a peace treaty with Germany and dropped out of the war. The Russian Revolution, as we shall see, was a turning point in world history.

WHY DID THE UNITED STATES ENTER THE WAR?

4. During most of the war years, the British navy controlled the oceans. Great Britain used its fleet to blockade the coast of Germany. The Germans tried to break the British blockade with submarine warfare. German submarines sank ships of any nation going to France or Great Britain. This was a serious threat to the Allies during the war. But in the end, Germany's policy of unrestricted submarine warfare led to its own defeat.

5. For three years the United States was

Fighter planes such as the one on the left introduced air warfare. The picture on the right shows Manfred von Richthofen, called the Red Baron, who shot down 80 Allied planes during World War I.

neutral in the war, joining neither side. In 1915, German submarines sank the British ship *Lusitania*. More than 100 Americans who were on

This picture shows a German submarine sinking an American freighter. Why do you think Germany's policy of unrestricted submarine warfare led to its own defeat?

board lost their lives. In 1917, President Woodrow Wilson asked Congress to declare war on Germany. One of his reasons was that "the world must be made safe for democracy."

6. Later, President Wilson wrote his famous Fourteen Points. This was a list of the war aims of the United States. Among these aims was the granting of equal rights to minorities and different nationality groups in Europe when the war was over. Wilson also wanted to stop secret treaties. He proposed that the number of weapons a country owned be reduced. He also wanted to guarantee freedom of the seas to all nations and to set up a world peace organization.

7. The entry of the United States into the war gave the Allied Powers the extra strength needed to win the war. Within a short time, American troops and war supplies began to reach the European battle fronts. More than one million American soldiers landed in Europe to help the Allies. One year after the United States entered the war, Germany, Bulgaria,

The sinking of the *Lusitania*. Why did the sinking of this British ship cause the United States to enter World War I?

Austria-Hungary and Turkey surrendered. It was 1918, and the First World War was over.

HOW WERE EMPIRES DIVIDED AND NEW NATIONS FORMED?

8. World War I cost over ten million lives. Statesmen wanted to make sure that such a war would not happen again. The leaders of the victorious allies met at Versailles, near Paris, in 1919. They held a conference and drew up a treaty of peace, the Versailles Treaty. They hoped that this treaty and later ones would end war forever. As we shall see, they failed.

9. Under the Versailles Treaty, Alsace-Lorraine was taken from Germany and returned to France. The Allies then divided Germany into two parts. They separated East and West Germany by a strip of land called the Polish Corridor. For damages caused in the war, Germany had to pay a large sum of money, called reparations (the word *reparations* means *payment for damages.*)

10. The Allies then divided all of Germany's colonies among themselves. The largest share went to Great Britain and its dominions. Great Britain took German East Africa (now part of Tanzania). The Union of South Africa took German Southwest Africa (called Namibia today). Australia and New Zealand got Germany's Pacific Islands south of the Equator. Japan was given the German Pacific Islands north of the Equator. The United States took nothing.

11. The Versailles Treaty and other treaties after the war created a number of new nations in Europe. Poland had not been a nation for more than a century. It was now made into an independent nation again from land taken from Germany, Austria-Hungary, and Russia. Czechoslovakia was formed from land taken from Austria-Hungary. The Austro-Hungarian Empire was broken up into many small pieces. Austria and Hungary were set up as two separate countries. Other parts of the former Austro-Hungarian Empire were given to Italy, Romania, and Serbia (Serbia became Yugoslavia).

463

Vittorio Orlando, premier of Italy; David Lloyd George, prime minister of Great Britain; Georges Clemenceau, premier of France; and Woodrow Wilson, President of the United States. They decided the terms of the Versailles Treaty.

12. Turkey was also punished. Almost all of its land in the Balkans was taken from it. The land was divided among Romania, Greece and Yugoslavia. Turkey's Middle East lands were also taken. Turkish Palestine, Transjordan (modern Jordan), and Mesopotamia (modern Iraq) were put under the rule of Great Britain. Turkish Syria and Lebanon were given to France.

13. Russia had dropped out of the war in 1917. It set up a Communist government. Because of this, the Allies treated Russia as if it were one of the defeated powers. Finland, Estonia, Latvia, and Lithuania were taken from Russia. They were set up as independent nations. Thus, by the time World War I was over, three great empires had come to an end. They were the empires of the Romanov rulers of Russia, the Hapsburg rulers of Austria-Hungary, and the Hohenzollern rulers of Germany.

14. After the war, a world peace organization was formed. It was called the League of Nations. Its purpose was to prevent future wars. Although it was one of President Wilson's ideas, the United States did not join it. The United States had decided to stay out of European political affairs as much as possible. This was called a policy of isolation.

Testing Your Vocabulary

Choose the best answer.

1. When Great Britain set up a naval *blockade* of Germany, it
   a. sank all German ships as soon as its navy spotted them.
   b. put warships outside of all German ports.
   c. stopped all ships from going to or from Germany.

2. When the United States decided to be *neutral* at the beginning of World War I, it
   a. did not enter the war or take sides in the fighting.
   b. was, in reality, practicing imperialism.
   c. did not trade with either side.

Understanding What You Have Read

1. The main idea of paragraphs 4 and 5 is that
   a. Germany won victories on the eastern front.
   b. Germany and Great Britain fought to control the seas.
   c. Germany used submarines in World War I.

d. fighting took place on many fronts during World War I.

2. In which paragraphs do you find facts about
   a. the League of Nations?
   b. the Bolshevik Revolution in Russia?
   c. the sinking of the *Lusitania*?
   d. President Wilson's Fourteen Points?

3. The war turned in favor of the Allies in 1917 because
   a. the Russian Revolution took Russia out of the war.
   b. the United States entered the war.
   c. the Italians surrendered on the southern front.

4. Germany used unrestricted submarine warfare during World War I because it
   a. wanted to invade England.
   b. wanted to punish the United States for helping Great Britain.
   c. wanted to stop ships from reaching Great Britain and France.

5. The United States entered the war in 1917 mainly because of the
   a. German policy of unrestricted submarine warfare.
   b. lies about the United States made up by the Allies.
   c. blockade set up by Great Britain.

6. The Russian Revolution of 1917 was an important event because it
   a. brought Japan into the war.
   b. led to the defeat of the Allied forces in Europe.
   c. set up a Communist dictatorship in Russia.

7. President Wilson announced his Fourteen Points because he
   a. thought they would help the Allies win the war.
   b. hoped they would keep the United States out of the war.
   c. wanted the world to know why the United States was fighting.

In each group listed below, one item does NOT belong with the others. In your notebook, write the one that does not belong.

1. Wilson's Fourteen Points:
   a. fewer weapons
   b. world peace organization
   c. colonies for the Allies

2. the Central Powers:
   a. Germany   c. Austria-Hungary
   b. Spain   d. Bulgaria

3. new weapons used in World War I:
   a. Armored tanks   c. ships
   b. airplanes   d. submarines

4. the Allied Powers:
   a. Greece   c. Sweden
   b. Great Britain   d. France

5. entered war in 1914:
   a. France   c. United States
   b. Russia   d. Turkey

6. new nations of Europe after World War I:

   a. Poland   c. Greece
   b. Czechoslovakia d. Hungary

7. new nations carved out of Russia after World War I:
   a. Bulgaria   c. Latvia
   b. Estonia   d. Lithuania

8. neutral nations during all of World War I:
   a. Spain   c. Switzerland
   b. United States   d. Denmark

9. lands taken from Turkey after World War I:
   a. Palestine   c. Lebanon
   b. Syria   d. Finland

10. ruling families that came to an end after World War I:
    a. Hapsburg   c. Hohenzollern
    b. Windsor   d. Romanov

Developing Ideas and Skills

USING A MAP

Europe before and after World War I

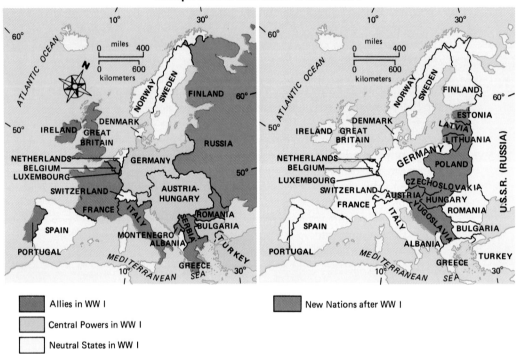

☐ Allies in WW I

☐ Central Powers in WW I

☐ Neutral States in WW I

☐ New Nations after WW I

1. Which nations were the Allied Powers in World War I? Copy the letters and complete the list in your notebook.
   a. _____ b. _____ c. _____ d. _____ e. _____
   f. _____ g. _____ h. _____
2. Which nations were the Central Powers in World War I?
   a. _____ b. _____ c. _____ d. _____
3. What new nations appeared on the map of Europe after World War I?
   a. _____ b. _____ c. _____ d. _____ e. _____
   f. _____ g. _____ h. _____
4. What nations disappeared from the map of Europe after World War I?
   a. _____ b. _____ c. _____

Summary of Unit X

1. The Industrial Revolution and colonial revolts brought a slowdown of imperialism during the early 19th century.
2. Central Africa was explored in the 19th century by such men as Mungo Park, David Livingstone, Henry Stanley, and John Speke.
3. European imperialist nations divided China into spheres of influence in the 19th century.
4. Japan became a modern world power by copying European economic, political, and military ideas.
5. The British empire, the largest in history, had colonies all over the world.
6. The imperialist nations of Europe tried to divide the Turkish empire. In other areas of the Middle East they set up colonies.
7. The basic causes of World War I were nationalism, imperialism, militarism, and rival alliances.
8. World War I was fought between the Central Powers and the Allied Powers.
9. The United States entered World War I in 1917 mainly because of Germany's policy of unrestricted submarine warfare.
10. At the end of World War I, Germany lost all its colonies. The Austro-Hungarian and Turkish empires were divided up into many countries.

Making Generalizations

After each generalization and supporting statement below, provide two additional supporting statements from your reading of Unit X.

A. Generalization: Geography often plays an important role in the history of a people.
   1. The jungles and deserts in the interior of Africa kept that continent from being explored by Europeans for centuries.
   2.
   3.
B. Generalization: Changes in one part of the world often have effects in many other parts of the world.
   1. The Industrial Revolution in Europe encouraged European nations to explore, colonize, and use the resources of Africa and Asia.
   2.
   3.
C. Generalization: Although European nations brought industries, education, and better health programs to their colonies, they caused them harm as well.
   1. Some European companies used Africans as slaves in their mines.
   2.
   3.

UNIT XI

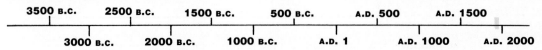

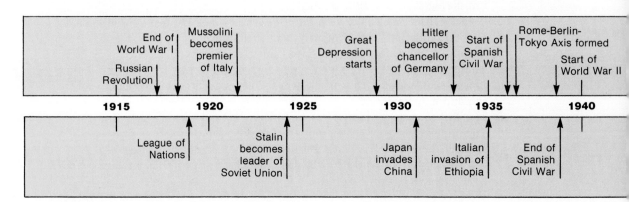

3500 B.C.	2500 B.C.	1500 B.C.	500 B.C.	A.D. 500	A.D. 1500
3000 B.C.	2000 B.C.	1000 B.C.	A.D. 1	A.D. 1000	A.D. 2000

End of World War I

Russian Revolution

Mussolini becomes premier of Italy

Great Depression starts

Hitler becomes chancellor of Germany

Start of Spanish Civil War

Rome-Berlin-Tokyo Axis formed

Start of World War II

1915	1920	1925	1930	1935	1940

League of Nations

Stalin becomes leader of Soviet Union

Japan invades China

Italian invasion of Ethiopia

End of Spanish Civil War

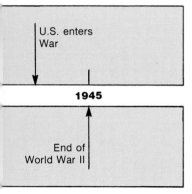

U.S. enters
War

1945

End of
World War II

How Did One World War Lead to Another?

Aboard a U.S. battleship in Tokyo Bay, representatives from Japan prepare to sign the surrender documents that formally end World War II.

469

AIM: Why did the movements for world peace fail after World War I?

CHAPTER 1

The Search for Peace

WHAT PEACE EFFORTS HAD BEEN MADE IN EARLIER TIMES?

1. For centuries men have looked for ways to keep peace. But wars have always come. People have suffered and nations have been destroyed. After the Napoleonic wars, for example, the nations of Europe met at the Congress of Vienna. They set up a Quadruple Alliance that was to keep peace in Europe. The Alliance put down democratic and nationalist revolts. As we have already learned, the Quadruple Alliance failed to keep peace.

2. In 1898, a peace effort was made. Czar Nicholas II, of Russia, invited the nations of the world to a meeting. He wanted them to discuss ways of keeping the world at peace. In the following year, delegates of many nations came to this first Hague Conference, in Holland. They set up an international court called the Hague Court. The purpose of this court was to settle arguments brought to it by any nation. It was the first court in modern times set up to settle disputes among nations.

3. A second Hague Conference was held in 1907. At this conference, new rules of international law for peace and war were agreed upon. In addition, wealthy men gave millions of dollars to world peace organizations. Among them were Andrew Carnegie, of the United States, and Alfred Nobel, of Sweden. Nobel set

up a fund to give a prize to the person who did most for world peace each year. Other prizes in science and literature were also set up. These annual awards are known as the Nobel Prizes. In spite of all these peace efforts, the nations of Europe went to war in 1914.

HOW DID NATIONS SEARCH FOR PEACE AFTER WORLD WAR I?

4. After World War I, a new world organization was formed in 1919. It was called the League of Nations. A new World Court was also set up to settle arguments among nations. For about ten years, the League of Nations was able to settle a number of small conflicts. But the League could not keep the peace when conflicts involved Germany, Italy, or Japan.

5. Many leaders in Europe and the United States believed that wars sometimes start because nations get into arms races. Each country tries to have the largest army or navy. Such an arms race is a form of militarism. Militarism was one of the causes of World War I. In 1921, President Warren G. Harding, of the United States, called a conference of the great naval powers in Washington, D.C. He wanted them to talk about ways to stop the building of more battleships. Since memories of the last war were still fresh, this Washington Conference was a great success. The great naval powers

President Harding at the Washington Conference in 1921. Why was this conference important?

agreed to cut the sizes of their battle fleets for ten years. This was called a "Ten-Year Naval Holiday." The nations signing this treaty were the United States, Great Britain, Japan, France, and Italy.

6. World War I had left bitter feeling between France and Germany. Leaders of both countries tried to find a way to end this hatred. They met in 1925 and drew up a number of agreements, called the Locarno Pacts. Under these agreements, the big powers of Europe agreed that the boundary between France and Germany set after the war would remain. The same was true of the boundary between Belgium and Germany. One year later, Germany joined the League of Nations. For a time it seemed that Europe would remain at peace.

7. Many Americans did not think that the United States should take part in the peacetime affairs of Europe. This view was called *isolationism*. Because of its policy of isolation, the United States never joined the League of Nations. But the United States was just as interested as other nations in putting an end to war. Most Americans knew that if another European war started, they would probably be forced into

the fighting again. In 1928, the United States and France joined to take a big step toward world peace. They drew up a treaty called the Pact of Paris, or the Kellogg-Briand Pact.

8. Under the Kellogg-Briand Pact, nations promised never to go to war in order to settle their problems. The United States, France, and almost every other nation in the world signed the Kellogg-Briand Pact. Germany, Italy, and Japan also signed this treaty. Yet eleven years later, World War II began. The great powers had signed many agreements to keep peace. They had a League of Nations and a World Court to settle their arguments. How did it happen that they became involved in another world war?

WHAT NEW THREATS OF WAR APPEARED?

9. The change from a peace movement to a war movement began about 1929. This was the year in which a worldwide economic depression began. The Depression caused hardships for people in all countries. The people of Germany, especially, faced many problems. In Germany, paper money had little value. Jobs were hard to get. Also, Germany had to pay war damages. This brought the nation close to economic ruin. Many people were also beginning to worry about the spread of communism. In Russia, the Communists had taken control of the government. Communist parties were growing larger in countries with heavy unemployment, such as Germany and Italy.

10. After World War I, most of the world's colonies were owned by Great Britain and France. Nations such as Germany, Italy, and Japan began to seek what they thought of as a fair share of colonies. Naturally, Great Britain and France would not give away any of their colonies. Thus, Germany, Italy, and Japan formed a military alliance, in 1937. It was called the Rome-Berlin-Tokyo Axis.

This painting by Howard Taft Lorenz is called *Dismissal.* **How does it reflect the Great Depression of 1929?**

11. In many countries of Europe, democratic governments began to give way to dictatorships. In Italy, Benito Mussolini and his Black Shirt followers set up a dictatorship. In Spain, a civil war (1936–39) ended in victory for Francisco Franco and his armies. They set up a dictatorship in Spain. The government of Japan also fell into the hands of military leaders. They favored going to war to get more colonies for Japan.

12. In Germany, Adolf Hitler formed a Nazi party. Its members were called Brown Shirts. Hitler promised the German people that he would break the Versailles Treaty. He said he would bring back the military power that Germany had once had. Hitler blamed Germany's defeat in World War I on traitors at home. He convinced many Germans that the only way to bring Germany back to greatness was to make him leader. In 1933, Adolf Hitler became dictator of Germany. From that moment, Europe was on the road to a second world war. Six years after Hitler came to power in Germany, World War II started in Europe.

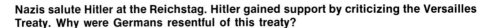

Nazis salute Hitler at the Reichstag. Hitler gained support by criticizing the Versailles Treaty. Why were Germans resentful of this treaty?

Testing Your Vocabulary _____

Choose the best answer.

1. After World War I, the United States followed a policy of *isolationism*. This meant that it
   a. would not let any European nation interfere in the affairs of the Western Hemisphere.
   b. would not trade with Communist Russia.
   c. would not take part in the affairs of Europe.

2. After 1933, Hitler established a *dictatorship* in Germany. The dictatorship was
   a. absolute rule by the Nazi party.
   b. absolute rule by one person.
   c. government ownership of all industries.

Understanding What You Have Read _____

1. The main idea of paragraphs 6 through 8 is that
   a. there were bitter feelings between Germany and France.
   b. the United States changed its foreign policy.
   c. efforts to keep peace followed World War I.
   d. dictatorships rose in Europe after World War I.

2. In which paragraphs do you find facts about
   a. the Rome-Berlin-Tokyo Axis?
   b. the Ten-Year Naval Holiday?
   c. Hitler's rise to power?
   d. the first Hague Conference?

3. The Hague Court was set up in 1899 in order to
   a. force Germany to pay for war damages.
   b. keep the United States out of European affairs.
   c. settle arguments between nations.

4. President Harding, of the United States, called a conference in Washington in 1921 because he hoped to
   a. stop a war between Japan and China.
   b. stop the naval arms race.
   c. reduce the size of land armies and air forces.

5. The United States did not join the League of Nations because
   a. the United States was following a policy of isolationism.
   b. the United States had not received any colonies at the end of World War I.
   c. the Soviet Union was a member.

6. The movements to keep peace and to reduce arms came to an end after 1929 partly because
   a. the Spanish Civil War began.
   b. a Communist revolution took place in Russia.
   c. military dictatorships rose in Germany and Japan.

Correctly match the names in the first column with the items in the second column.

1. Francisco Franco	a. first Hague Conference
2. Adolf Hitler	b. Black Shirts
3. Benito Mussolini	c. Nobel Peace Prize
4. Alfred Nobel	d. dictator of Soviet Union
5. Czar Nicholas II	e. Brown Shirts
	f. Spanish Civil War

1. Locarno Pacts	a. Ten-Year Naval Holiday
2. Kellogg-Briand Pact	b. end use of war to settle disputes
3. World Court	c. French-German boundary treaties
4. Congress of Vienna	d. international law to settle disputes
5. Washington Conference	e. United Nations
	f. Quadruple Alliance

Developing Ideas and Skills

USING A TIME LINE

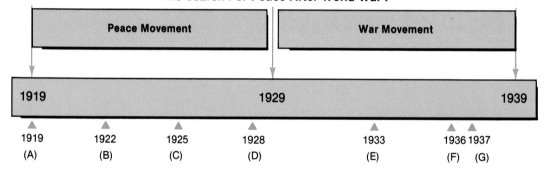

The Search For Peace After World War I

Tell when the following events took place by filling in the correct letter from the time line in your notebook.

1. Hitler's dictatorship began_____
2. Kellogg-Briand Pact signed_____
3. Washington Naval Arms Conference held_____
4. Spanish Civil War began_____
5. League of Nations formed_____
6. Locarno Pacts signed_____
7. Rome-Berlin-Tokyo Axis formed_____

CHAPTER 2

Revolution in Russia

HOW DID COMMUNIST IDEAS DEVELOP?

1. The Soviet Union has many names. Sometimes it is called Soviet Russia and sometimes the Soviet Union. (The word *soviet* means a law-making assembly.) On maps it is labeled the U.S.S.R. Its full name is the Union of Soviet Socialist Republics. It has this name because the country is made up of 15 republics. A republic in the Soviet Union is like a state in the United States. It is one of the parts that together make up the whole country. The largest of these re-

publics is the Russian Soviet Federal Socialist Republic.

2. The Communist revolution began in Russia in 1917, near the end of World War I. At that time, few people thought that communism would become a threat to democratic nations. Today, some form of Communist economic and political system can be found in almost one-fourth of the world. And about one-third of the world's people live under Communist governments. By the 1950s many non-Communist nations of the world had come to regard the Soviet Union and Communist China as threats to their security.

The Soviet Union Today

3. The ideas of modern communism began in the middle of the 19th century. Karl Marx and Friedrich Engels wrote a revolutionary booklet called *The Communist Manifesto* (page 406). This booklet called on the workers of the world to unite. It urged them to overthrow the capitalist system by revolution. According to Marx and Engels, history is the story of the struggle between capital and labor. Under capitalism, they wrote, most workers received only enough money to keep themselves and their families alive. The only way to change this was to set up a Communist system. Under communism, a government would own all property. It would run all businesses, industries, and farms.

4. These ideas became known as Marxian, or Marxist, socialism. They were later explained in more detail by Karl Marx in his famous work *Das Kapital.* Marxian socialism is called communism today. It did not have many followers in the 19th century. In the early 20th century, however, Marxian socialist parties began to appear in many countries of Europe. In time, a split developed among the Marxist parties. One group, called Socialists, wanted to make slow, peaceful changes through laws. Another group, called Communists, believed violent revolution was the only way to end capitalism. Instead of changing the system by changing the laws, the Communists believed in overthrowing capitalist governments with violence, if necessary.

Russian peasants before the revolution. Why do you think the ideas of Communism sounded good to many of the Russian peasants?

HOW DID THE SOVIET UNION DEVELOP?

5. In Czarist Russia, before World War I, the Communists were called *Bolsheviks.* Their party was outlawed. Their leaders were put in prison when caught. Then World War I began. During this war, the Russian people suffered great hardships because there was not enough food. The Russian armies lost many battles to the Germans. As a result, strikes and riots broke out in many Russian cities. Crowds shouted for "Peace and Bread." The Russian Revolution had begun.

6. In March 1917, Czar Nicholas II found himself faced with a revolution. He abdicated (gave up) his ruling power. At first, a democratic form of government was set up. But in November 1917, the Bolsheviks, led by Vladimir Lenin and Leon Trotsky seized control of the government. The Communists, as they were now called, were only a small group of revolutionaries. In gaining control, they used violence and terror against those who opposed them. From November 1917, to the present day, the Communists have been in power in Russia.

7. The Communist party quickly changed the political and economic system of Russia. A dictatorship was set up. In a dictatorship, nearly unlimited ruling power is held by one person. All land, factories, mines, railroads, banks, and other property were taken over by the government. This ended private ownership of property in Russia. No private citizen was allowed to run any business for profit. The farms were owned and run by the government. They were worked by peasant workers paid by the government. The factories and mines were also owned and run by the government. Capitalism was ended. And so, Czarist Russia became Communist Russia.

8. Thousands of Russians were against the Communist government. Many of them were put in prison, sent to forced labor camps in Siberia, or murdered by those in power. World

The Russian people took to street fighting in revolt against Czar Nicholas II. Compare the reasons for the Russian Revolution with the reasons of the people of France at the time of the French Revolution.

War I and the Russian Revolution had helped to destroy the Russian economy. Communist reforms were unable to solve the problems. Food crops were poor. Many people were starving. The Communist party, however, remained master of the nation. When Lenin died, in 1924, Joseph Stalin took his place as dictator. Stalin was a harsh ruler. He destroyed those he thought were enemies of communism. He also plotted the murder of Communist leaders he believed were against him. Stalin remained in power until his death, in 1953.

During the October revolution, the Bolsheviks stormed the Winter Palace in Petrograd (now Leningrad), which was the headquarters of the provisional government.

HOW DID COMMUNISTS RULE RUSSIA?

9. In order to develop farming and industry in the Soviet Union, the Communist leaders drew up plans for the future. These were called Five-Year plans. They listed the amount of coal to be mined and the amount of steel to be manufactured. They planned the number of tractors to be built and the amount of wheat to be grown over five-year periods. When one Five-Year Plan ended, a new Five-Year Plan was begun. The industries of the Soviet Union were expected to grow. Soviet farms, however, often did not raise enough food for all the people. In recent years, the Soviet Union has had to purchase large amounts of wheat from the United States and other countries.

10. The Five-Year plans also called for the manufacture of war equipment, such as guns, tanks, and airplanes. When World War II began, in 1939, few people had realized that the Soviet Union had become one of the most powerful nations in the world. The Soviet Union had usually been unfriendly toward and suspicious of other countries. Soviet leaders knew that the countries of Western Europe and the United States were against the Communist dictatorship. The United States, for example, did not send an ambassador to the Soviet Union until 1933. This was sixteen years after the Russian Revolution.

11. The Soviet Union under Stalin and Nazi Germany under Hitler had always been unfriendly toward each other. Hitler's armies invaded the Soviet Union in 1941. (The bitter Russian winter forced the Nazis to retreat.) After World War II, Communist governments were set up in Poland, Czechoslovakia, Romania, Hungary, and Bulgaria. Thus, most of Eastern Europe became Communist. Today, the Soviet Union and Communist China are rivals for the leadership of the Communist world.

Testing Your Vocabulary

Choose the best answer.

1. In 1917, Czar Nicholas II *abdicated* his power. This meant that he
   a. agreed to share political power with the revolutionaries.
   b. gave political control to the Communists.
   c. gave up, or resigned, his crown and his power.

2. Karl Marx attacked capitalism. *Capitalism* is
   a. an involved system of social-insurance laws.
   b. an economic system based on private business and profits.
   c. government ownership of important industries.

Understanding What You Have Read _____

1. A good title for paragraphs 7 through 9 is
   a. Soviet Foreign Policies.
   b. The Beginnings of European Communism.
   c. The New Soviet Political and Economic System.
   d. Lenin and Trotsky.
2. The Russian Revolution began because
   a. Russian armies were defeated and Russians at home were short of food.
   b. the Communists were the largest political party in Russia.
   c. the Czar put in prison those who were against him.
3. The Communists gained control of the Russian government in 1917 because they
   a. controlled the Russian armies and most of the weapons.
   b. promised the people a democratic government.
   c. used violence and terror against their enemies.
4. The purpose of the Five-Year plans was to
   a. plan Communist revolutions in other countries.
   b. set up goals for all Soviet industries and agriculture.
   c. manufacture enough goods for all Soviet families.
5. The Five-Year plans of the Soviet Union resulted in
   a. huge agricultural surpluses, which have been sold to the U.S.
   b. a sharp drop in production in some key industries.
   c. too little farm production to meet the needs of the Soviet people.

Developing Ideas and Skills _____

TELLING FACT FROM OPINION

Can you tell the difference between a fact and an opinion? In your notebook write **F** if the statement is a fact; **O** if it is an opinion.

1. The Communist system of government in the Soviet Union is a dictatorship.
2. The world cannot exist half Communist and half non-Communist.
3. Life under the Communists is no different from life under the czars.
4. The Soviet Union had Five-Year plans to help improve industry.
5. Marx and Engels wrote *The Communist Manifesto*.
6. The Bolsheviks seized control of the Russian government by violence and terror.
7. Factories and farms in the Soviet Union are owned by the government.
8. Most Soviet people want a more democratic form of government.
9. History is based on the struggle between capital and labor.
10. Statements by Soviet leaders are always based on lies.

Using Original Sources

Joseph Stalin was the leader of the Soviet Union from 1924 to 1953. Under his dictatorship, Russia became a world power. The name *Stalin* means *steel* in Russian. It was not the name he was born with. He adopted it as a young man. Can you see anything in the following selection that suggests why he selected this name for himself?

Joseph Stalin

When Stalin came to power, he didn't even speak proper Russian—at least he didn't speak it with a proper accent. . . . He was without originality in the intellectual sense. He had no personal charm, no oratorical [public-speaking] gifts.

. . . This was a man dominated . . . by vanity and love of power, coupled with the keenest sense of his own inferiority and a burning jealousy for qualities in others which he did not possess. He had certain well-known characteristics of the Caucasian mountain race to which his father is said to have belonged . . . touchiness . . . , an inability ever to forget an insult or a slight, but great patience in selecting and preparing the moment to settle the score. He is said once to have observed that there was nothing sweeter in life than to bide the proper moment for revenge, to insert the knife, to turn it around, and go home for a good night's sleep. At the same time, let us note, he was a man with the most extraordinary talent for political tactics and intrigue, a [supreme] actor. . . . He was a master, in particular, of the art of playing people and forces against each other, for his own benefit. . . .

1. What qualities do you think Stalin had that made it possible for him to hold power in the Soviet Union for 29 years?
2. What were some of the weaknesses in his character?
3. Did these weaknesses interfere with his rise to power? Give reasons for your answer.
4. How do you think Stalin's belonging to a race of mountain people may have affected the way he ruled?
5. What problems would leaders of free-world nations face when trying to make agreements with a dictator like Stalin?

AIM: How does communism differ from democratic capitalism?

CHAPTER 3

Communists Rule the Soviet Union

WHY DO SOVIET CITIZENS HAVE FEW RIGHTS?

1. "We are a democratic country!" That is what the dictators of the Soviet Union are always saying. To prove it, they point to the Soviet constitution. Under the constitution of the U.S.S.R., every man and woman has the right to vote. Elections are held often. An elected body called the Supreme Soviet passes laws. A president is elected. In all of these ways, the Soviet Union is like the United States. Why, then, is the Soviet Union a dictatorship and not a democracy?

2. A house may be dirty on the inside. But if the outside is neatly painted, a person may easily be fooled into thinking it is a beautiful home throughout. The Soviet constitution is like new paint on an old house. If we read this constitution, we believe that the Soviet Union is democratic. But if we watch how the Soviet government works, we find that it is really an absolute dictatorship. Everyone in the Soviet Union, for example, has the right to vote. But all the candidates in an election are members of the same party—the Communist party.

3. Thus, the Russian people can vote. But they have no real choice in an election. The

Lenin addressing a crowd. Notice that Joseph Stalin and Leon Trotsky are on the platform behind Lenin.

winner will always be a member of the Communist party. The reason for this is that the

Communist party is the only political party allowed to exist in the Soviet Union. Those who oppose the party are often punished for doing so.

4. For a government to be a democracy, the people must have civil liberties. Civil liberties include freedom of speech, freedom of the press, and freedom of religion. They include the right to a trial by jury. The people of the Soviet Union do not have civil liberties. Many people who have spoken out against the government have been arrested and sent to prison. But a few have managed to survive and keep their freedom in spite of the government. Of those who have spoken out against the evils of the Soviet government, one of the best known is the Russian writer Alexander Solzhenitsyn (sol-zheh-NEE-tsin).

5. Trials in the Soviet Union are usually held in secret. Accused people are often forced to confess. The government tries to keep people

Alexander Solzhenitsyn. What are civil liberties and why do democratic governments prize them so highly?

from practicing their religion. In recent years, Jews and other religious groups in the Soviet Union have had little religious freedom. The government has also made it very difficult for Jews to leave the country. By taking away religious freedom and the power of the religious leaders, the Communists have added to their own power.

6. The Soviet constitution says that women in the Soviet Union have exactly the same rights as men. They have the right to the same education and the same jobs as men. As a result, Soviet women are doctors, lawyers, dentists and engineers. They are also street cleaners, truck drivers, construction workers, and farm workers. Soviet women also have the right to vote and hold government jobs. However, few Russian women are ever chosen or elected to important government positions.

HOW DOES ONE-PARTY RULE WORK?

7. The Communists took control of Russia in 1917. Since then, the Communist party has been the only legal political party in the Soviet Union. The party decides who shall run in the elections. It decides what laws shall be passed. It controls the army. It controls the regular police force and the secret police. The Communist party decides which radio and television programs are to be broadcast. It decides which books, newspapers, and magazines may be printed. It decides what movies may be shown. The Communist party and its leaders are the real government of the Soviet Union.

8. The Soviet constitution, however, does not say anything about the Communist party. Thus, there are really two parts to the Soviet government: one part that *seems* to be powerful and another part that really is. The part of the government that seems to be powerful is described in the constitution. The part that really is powerful is the Communist party.

9. The Soviet constitution says that a president is to be elected. The president has very little power, however. The constitution also says there is to be an elected lawmaking parliament of two houses. This parliament is called the Supreme Soviet. The members of the Supreme Soviet are chosen by the people in local areas called soviets.

10. The Supreme Soviet usually meets twice a year. It votes on laws suggested by the Supreme Soviet Presidium. All members of this Presidium are important Communist party leaders. They suggest the laws that the Communist party wants. When a vote is taken in the Supreme Soviet, all the delegates usually vote in favor of it. In addition to passing laws, the Supreme Soviet chooses a cabinet. The cabinet is called the Council of Ministers. The chairman, or head of the Soviet Council of Ministers, is the *premier*. The premier is always an important member of the Communist party.

WHO HOLDS THE REAL POWER?

11. The real power in the Soviet government is not in the Supreme Soviet (the lawmaking body). It is not the president, or the Council of Ministers (cabinet). The real power is in the Communist party. Every important job in the government is held by a Communist party member. Yet, only 5% of the Russian people are members of the party. The Communist party has ruled the Soviet Union for more than half a century. It is powerful because it controls the Soviet army and the secret police.

12. Although the Soviet Communist party is small in number, it is well organized. Its members must obey party leaders. In almost every Soviet factory, office, and school, and on almost every farm, there is a small group of Communist party members. These groups elect delegates to higher party groups. The highest group is called the All-Union Party Congress. The Party Congress selects the party *Politburo*.

13. The Politburo is a small group of the top Communist party leaders. The general secretary is the top leader of the Communist party. He is the real ruler of the Soviet Union. Sometimes he is also chosen to be premier. In the past, the general secretary of the Communist party could order any law to be passed. He could have any person arrested. He was the absolute dictator of the U.S.S.R. Today, the general secretary no longer has absolute power.

14. When the general secretary dies, a struggle may take place for his job. After Joseph Stalin's death, in 1953, Communist party leaders fought to decide who would be the next general secretary. It was not until 1958 that one man, Nikita Khrushchev (nih-KEE-tuh KRUS-chev) finally gained control of the party. Only a few men have ruled the Soviet Union since the Russian Revolution. The most important dictators have been Vladimir I. Lenin (1917–24), Joseph Stalin (1929–53), Nikita Khrushchev (1958–64), and Leonid Brezhnev (1964–82). Yuri Andropov was in control from 1982 to 1984. After he died, Mikhail Gorbachev took over.

Joseph Stalin, general secretary of the Communist party. How does the role of the general secretary differ from the role of the prime minister of England?

Testing Your Vocabulary

Choose the best answer.

1. People in the Soviet Union do not have civil liberties. *Civil liberties* are
   a. political parties.
   b. insurance for unemployment and illness.
   c. personal freedoms.

2. The Soviet Union is a dictatorship. *Dictatorship* means
   a. absolute rule by one person or by a small group acting together.
   b. rule by a legislature.
   c. rule by the secret police.

Understanding What You Have Read

1. A good title for paragraphs 4 and 5 is
   a. The Soviet Secret Police.
   b. The Soviet Constitution.
   c. The Communist Party in the Soviet Union.
   d. Civil Liberties in the Soviet Union.
2. In which paragraphs do you find facts about
   a. the job of the Supreme Soviet?
   b. freedom of religion in the Soviet Union?
   c. the power of the general secretary of the Communist party?
   d. the percentage of people who belong to the Communist party?
3. The Soviet government is a dictatorship in that
   a. every voter must pay a tax.
   b. voters have no real choice when they vote.
   c. the secret ballot is not used.
4. Women in the Soviet Union
   a. cannot vote in elections.
   b. may not run for public office.
   c. have the right to be doctors, lawyers, and engineers.
5. The Supreme Soviet votes *yes* on almost all laws because
   a. the Communist party leaders order the laws to be passed.
   b. the laws are carefully planned.
   c. most of the members cannot read.

Developing Ideas and Skills

UNDERSTANDING DIAGRAMS

Using the diagrams on page 485 and the chapter for information, complete the following statements in your notebook.

1. The Council of Ministers is chosen by the _____.
2. Local election districts that choose delegates to the Supreme Soviet are called _____.
3. The Communist party leader in the Soviet Union is called the _____.
4. When Communist party delegates from all parts of the Soviet Union meet, the group they form is called the _____.
5. The group of people chosen by the All-Union Party Congress to decide policies and plans is known as the _____.

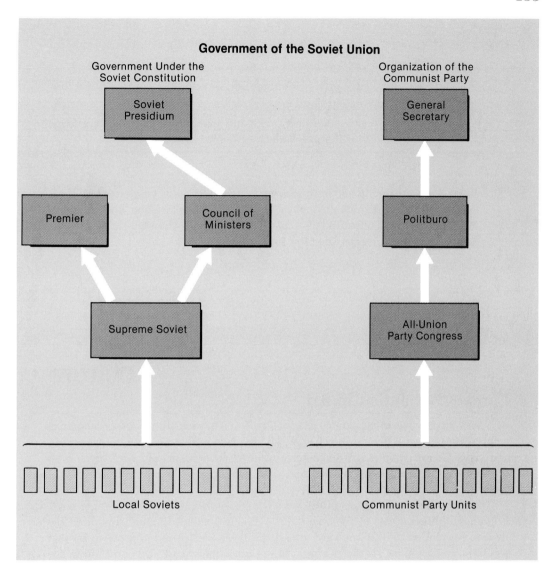

Government of the Soviet Union

Government Under the
Soviet Constitution

Organization of the
Communist Party

Soviet
Presidium

General
Secretary

Premier

Council of
Ministers

Politburo

Supreme Soviet

All-Union
Party Congress

Local Soviets

Communist Party Units

Using Original Sources

    The Soviet constitution was drawn up in 1936 and amended in 1960. It lists many rights of citizens. The only trouble with these rights is that they are not upheld. For example, Soviet citizens have the right to freedom of speech and freedom of the press. But they cannot use these rights to criticize the government. They cannot object to anything on which the Soviet leaders decide. Read the articles (sections) from the Soviet constitution on page 486; and then answer the questions that follow.

> ## The Soviet Constitution
>
> Article 121.   All citizens have the right to free education.
> Article 122.   Women in the U.S.S.R. have equal rights with men in all matters.
> . . . .
> Article 124.   All citizens have freedom of religion.
> Article 125.   All citizens of the U.S.S.R. are guaranteed freedom of speech, freedom of the press, and freedom of assembly.

1. What rights are mentioned in the Soviet constitution that are not mentioned in the United States constitution?
2. Is there any difference between freedom of religion as guaranteed by the United States constitution and the same freedom as guaranteed by the Soviet constitution?

TURNING POINTS

Culture

Europe: Revolution in Art

Art reflects what is happening in a society. In many ways the *avant-garde* movement in Russian art reflected the changes taking place in that country between 1910 and 1930. *Avant garde* is a French term used to describe people who break with tradition. At the time, many Russian artists were caught up in the new political ideas of the revolution. They were trying different ways to express themselves.

Some of the leading artists of this period were women. One was Liubov Popova. Like most Russian artists of the *avant garde*, Popova believed in and supported the Russian Revolution. In the years just after 1917, these artists tried to produce art that would mean something to the people. They wanted their work to contribute to the new society.

By the 1920s, the Communist government of the Soviet Union began to object to this art. It put limits on the artists' freedom to experiment. By 1934, their works were banned. Recently there has been interest in the art of the Russian *avant garde*. In the mid-1980s, major exhibits of this art were held in Europe and the United States.

Critical Thinking

1. Why was the Russian Revolution a turning point for Russian artists?
2. Why might freedom of expression in art be a threat to a Communist government?

AIM: How did Mussolini rule Italy?

CHAPTER 4

Italy Becomes a Fascist State

WHAT EVENTS BROUGHT ABOUT FASCISM IN ITALY?

1. Before World War I, Italy had joined Austria-Hungary in the Triple Alliance. However, she wanted a certain strip of land that belonged to Austria. On this land lived many Italians under Austro-Hungarian rule. When World War I began, therefore, Italy decided not to take sides. In 1915, however, the Allies offered to give Italy the piece of Austrian land Italy wanted. Italy then decided to join the Allies in the war.

2. The Allies signed a secret treaty promising Italy this land. Italy then declared war on Austria-Hungary and Germany, in 1915. When World War I was over, Italy was given the Austrian territory it wanted. But after the war, Italy was in almost as poor a condition as defeated Germany. Thousands of Italians could not find jobs. Factories were closing. Strikes were common. Food prices were high. Inflation was lowering the value of Italian money. These problems grew worse each year.

3. The democratic government of Italy did not seem to be able to do anything to improve conditions. Many people were becoming interested in communist ideas. Communism

had spread to Italy from Russia. Some Italian workers and peasants were calling for a Communist revolution in Italy. Another group, called Fascists (FASH-ists), said they were going to save Italy from being taken over by the Communists. Under fascism, the state and the nation are all-important. Fascist governments are run by dictators who try to control every part of a nation's life. The Fascist party in Italy was set up in 1921. It soon gained many followers. Men who had fought in World War I and who now could not find jobs, and other unemployed workers, were especially interested in fascism. Benito Mussolini, who had once been a newspaper writer, became the leader of the Fascist party.

4. Fascist party members wore black shirts. They held parades, and started street fights with Communists and Socialists. For a time, it seemed that there would be a civil war in Italy. In 1922, Mussolini felt that he had gained enough followers. He ordered his Black Shirts to march on Rome, the capital of Italy. His plan was to take over the government—by force, if necessary. But force was not needed. The weak king of Italy was afraid of Mussolini's growing power. The king made him prime minister. Thus, Mussolini became dictator without a shot being fired.

Mussolini and his black-shirted Fascists ready to march on Rome in 1922. How is fascism like communism? How is it different?

Benito Mussolini. Were civil liberties important to him? Why or why not?

HOW DID MUSSOLINI RULE ITALY?

5. As head of the Italian government, Mussolini made himself absolute dictator. He called himself *Il Duce*. This means *the leader*. Mussolini did not want a democratic government. He felt that democratic governments were dishonést and weak. Italy, he said, would become great once more under his leadership. He promised to bring back to Italy the power and glory of the ancient Roman Empire. The Mediterranean Sea, he said, would become "an Italian lake." It would be controlled by Italy alone. Mussolini also promised to make Italy's military power great again. And he said he would get more colonies for Italy.

6. All political parties except the Fascist party were outlawed. The secret police arrested all who spoke out against the government. Labor unions were ended. Strikes were outlawed. Books, newspapers, and radio broadcasts were controlled. Even the schools came under

Fascist control. The Fascists decided what should be taught in schools and colleges. Beginning at the age of eight, children were put into Fascist youth groups. They were given military training. Mussolini set up a large army. He ordered industries to manufacture arms for the new Italian army.

7. Mussolini took away the freedoms and civil liberties of the Italian people. But he tried to give them something in return. His war industries, road building, and other public improvements gave jobs to the unemployed. Street fighting and riots between rival political parties ended. The nation was run well. Although free speech, a free press, and free elections had been ended in Italy, Mussolini could boast that the Italian trains now ran on time. In addition, many Italians took new pride in the Italian army and navy. Mussolini's idea of bringing back the glory of ancient Rome brought a new spirit of nationalism to Italians.

8. Most Italians were Catholic and loyal to the pope. Mussolini, therefore, tried to settle an old argument with the Catholic Church. He wanted to get the pope on his side. When Italy had become unified, in 1870, it had taken large areas of land from the Church. These lands had been made part of the new Italian nation. They were called the Papal States. From that time on, the popes remained in a small area in Rome called the Vatican. They were sometimes called "prisoners of the Vatican."

9. To improve relations with the Church, Mussolini signed the Lateran Treaty with the pope in 1929. Under this treaty, the Catholic Church was given a sum of money to pay for the lands taken away. The lands inside Rome that the pope still owned were made into an independent state. It is called Vatican City. Mussolini also gave the Catholic Church control over marriage, divorce, and religious education in Italy.

HOW DID ITALY'S POWER GROW?

10. Life seemed to be going well in Italy. Then a worldwide economic depression began in 1929. Joblessness and poverty struck Italy as they did other nations of the world. Mussolini tried to keep the Italian people from thinking about their troubles. He talked of building a new empire. He spoke about getting new colonies for Italy. He called Italy a "have-not" nation because it had so few natural resources and so few colonies. Mussolini wanted France to give Tunisia, in North Africa, to Italy. He wanted Great Britain to give the island of Malta to Italy. Following the example of Adolf Hitler, in Germany, Mussolini said that the Italians were a superior race. He started a policy of persecuting Jews. He kept them out of schools and important government jobs. The Italian people in general did not like this anti-Jewish policy.

11. Mussolini then started to build his new Italian empire. In 1935, he ordered his army to invade Ethiopia, in Africa. Ethiopia was an underdeveloped country. The Italian army had little trouble in defeating it. The following year, Mussolini sent Italian troops to Spain. He ordered them to help the Fascist army of Francisco Franco in the Spanish Civil War. In 1936, Mussolini formed an alliance with Germany. This alliance was called the Rome-Berlin Axis.

12. Soon after World War II began, Italy joined Germany against France, Great Britain, and the Soviet Union. During the war, the Italian armies were driven out of Africa. Italy itself was invaded. The Italian people suffered while the war went on around them. Faced with defeat, they surrendered to the Allies in 1943. Mussolini was captured by anti-Fascist Italians and killed. Thus ended the life of Il Duce and the Fascist era in Italy.

Hitler and Mussolini after their alliance. Compare the promises of both men. How were they alike? How different?

Testing Your Vocabulary _____

Choose the best answer.

1. The *Fascist* type of government set up by Mussolini was
   a. a republic.
   b. a Communist system.
   c. a dictatorship.

2. Italy suffered from the Great Depression that began in 1929. A *depression* is
   a. a world war
   b. a time of serious economic troubles
   c. a strike by many unions at once

Understanding What You Have Read _____

1. The main idea of paragraphs 3 and 4 is that
   a. the Fascists marched on Rome.
   b. Mussolini rose to power in Italy.
   c. Italy suffered during World War II.
   d. Communists threatened Italy after World War I.

2. In which paragraphs do you find facts about
   a. the "march on Rome"?
   b. the Lateran Treaty?
   c. the invasion of Ethiopia?
   d. the Fascist control of schools?

3. Italy joined the Allies during World War I because it
   a. had a military alliance with them.
   b. was an enemy of Germany.
   c. was offered certain Austrian lands at the end of the war.

4. Mussolini became dictator of Italy without the use of force because
   a. the king in Rome was afraid of Mussolini's power.
   b. he controlled the Italian army.
   c. he had the support of Adolf Hitler.

5. Mussolini arranged the Lateran Treaty with the pope because
   a. he wanted the pope's support for his military plans.
   b. most Italians were loyal members of the Catholic Church.
   c. he wanted to return to the pope land taken from the Church by Italy in 1860.

6. Italy conquered Ethiopia without difficulty because
   a. Italy received help from Germany.
   b. Mussolini had the support of the pope.
   c. Ethiopia was an underdeveloped country.

7. Mussolini gave military aid to Francisco Franco in the Spanish Civil War because
   a. Franco was a Fascist.
   b. Mussolini hoped to get Spanish aid in his Ethiopian invasion.
   c. Mussolini had joined a military alliance with France.

Fill in the correct word or phrase in each of the following:

1. The "march on Rome" was led by
_____ .

2. Before World War I, Italy joined Austria-Hungary and Germany in a military union called _____ .

3. A Fascist government was set up in Spain by _____ .

4. The military alliance between Hitler and Mussolini was called the _____ .

5. The body of water that Mussolini wanted to be called an "Italian lake"

was the _____ .

6. The political party to which the Black Shirts belonged was the _____ .

7. The country in Africa conquered by the Italian Fascists was _____ .

8. The Lateran Treaty was arranged between the Italian government and _____ .

9. The religion practiced by most Italians is _____ .

10. The part of Rome that is ruled by the pope is called _____ .

Developing Ideas and Skills _____

USING A TIME LINE

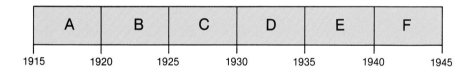

A	B	C	D	E	F

1915   1920   1925   1930   1935   1940   1945

List the events below in your notebook. After each, write the letter of the time period in which the event took place.

1. the Fascist party is set up in Italy
2. Mussolini's Black Shirts march on Rome

3. the Lateran Treaty is signed
4. the Rome-Berlin Axis is formed
5. Italy surrenders to the Allies

AIM: How did Adolf Hitler become absolute dictator in Germany?

CHAPTER 5

The Nazis Seize Power

WHAT HAPPENED IN GERMANY AFTER WORLD WAR I?

1. The long history of Europe is filled with stories of great achievements. But it also has its stories of cruelty and horror. No story in the 6,000-year history of civilization, however, is filled with such cruelty and slaughter as the story of the rule of Adolf Hitler. Hitler led Germany from 1933 until 1945. Through his ideas and actions, Adolf Hitler caused the death of more than 25 million people. Who was this half-mad leader? Who was this man who brought so much sorrow to so many and changed the course of world history?

2. Adolf Hitler, who became dictator of Germany, was born in Austria. During World War I, he served in the German army as a corporal. When the war was over, he got involved in German politics. He started the Nazi party in 1920. (The word *Nazi* is a shortened form of the German words for National Socialist German Workers' Party.) His party members wore brown shirts and armbands with symbols called swastikas (卐). They held parades and meetings. They often got into street fights with Communists and other political opponents.

3. Germany had been completely defeated in World War I. The kaiser had fled the country. The German people set up a democratic form of government known as the Weimar Republic. This government lasted from 1919, when the Versailles Treaty was signed, to 1933. Then Adolf Hitler became dictator. After World War I, Germany suffered from unemployment and labor strikes. The government printed so much paper money that it became almost worthless. Prices rose and rose, while purchasing power fell. This inflation brought much suffering. The Weimar government seemed helpless to solve the country's problems. The German people were restless and unhappy. In 1923, Hitler and his Nazi followers decided to overthrow the democratic government in Germany. They planned to seize power for themselves.

Paul von Hindenburg was president of Germany from 1925 until his death in 1934. He appointed Hitler chancellor in 1933 and Hitler became ruler of Germany after von Hindenburg's death.

HOW DID HITLER BECOME DICTATOR?

4. Hitler's first plan failed. He and some of his followers were sent to prison for their part in the revolt. While in prison, Hitler wrote a book, *Mein Kampf (My Battle)*. In it, he explained his plan to make Germany a great nation again. To understand what happened in Hitler's Germany between the two World Wars, and why it happened, we must look at the ideas in *Mein Kampf.*

5. Hitler said that the Germans were a master race. All other races and nationalities, such as the French, the Russians, and Jews, were inferior. Because Germans were the master race, Hitler wrote that Germany should conquer the whole world. War was noble. Fighting for one's country was the finest way of proving one's manhood.

6. To conquer the world, Hitler said, Germany must build the strongest military force. By using armed force and spreading lies about his enemies, Hitler felt he could destroy all democratic countries. He called democracy the government of stupid and inferior people. Hitler believed that he was the only man who could lead Germany to world conquest.

7. When Hitler was freed from prison, Germany's democratic government had begun to solve some of its problems. In 1929, however, the worldwide Great Depression began. Germany was again faced with not enough food, heavy taxes, and unemployment. This was Hitler's second chance, and he took it. In speech after speech, Hitler said that all of Germany's problems had been caused by Communists, Jews, and the Versailles Treaty. Germany, he said, had not lost World War I because of defeat on the battlefield. It had lost because of traitors at home. Of course, this explanation was false, but many Germans wanted to believe it.

8. Hitler promised the German people that he and his Nazi party would find jobs for all. He said he would bring back good economic

This poster urges Germans not to buy from Jews. Why is Hitler's persecution of the Jews often considered one of the world's greatest examples of discrimination?

times. He promised to destroy the Communists and the Jews. He would tear up the Versailles Treaty and end German payment for war damages. He would get back the colonies Germany had lost. Finally, he swore to make Germany a great nation once more. Hitler won followers by touching German nationalistic pride. By stirring up hatred against Jews and by spreading lies, he gained more followers. Soon, the Nazi party became one of the largest political parties in Germany.

9. In the last free election in Germany before World War II, Hitler's Nazi party won about 40% of the votes. Though not a majority, this was more votes than any other party received. The other political parties were unable to unite against the Nazis. As a result, Hitler made himself a dictator.

HOW DID HITLER AND THE NAZIS GAIN COMPLETE POWER?

10. The Germany Hitler ruled became known as the Third Reich (RYK). "Reich" means *empire* or *state*. The first Reich, said the Nazis, had been the Holy Roman Empire (962–1806). The second Reich had been the German empire under the kaisers (1871–1918). Hitler boasted that his Third Reich would last for a thousand years. It lasted only twelve years. But in that short time, Hitler changed the history of Germany and the world.

11. Looking back at Hitler's rule, people ask, "Why did it happen?" There are several reasons. During the Great Depression of 1929–33, Germany, like many other countries, was in terrible economic condition. Hitler promised jobs and higher wages to all. Many German workers thus became Hitler's followers. German business leaders and property owners were afraid of the Communist party. They feared it would gain control in Germany as it had in Russia. Hitler promised to destroy all Communists in Germany. Thus, many people in business and many property owners became followers of Hitler's Nazi party.

12. Hitler appealed to national pride. He promised to make Germany a great power, as it had been in the old days. He also said that he would rebuild the army and navy. These promises brought old soldiers and many university students to Hitler's side.

13. Hitler used two important weapons to gain power. One was violence. The other was propaganda, or the effective spreading of ideas, both true and false, to get what he wanted. Hitler organized his Nazi party followers into Brown Shirt squads. These squads broke up meetings of other political parties and beat up the speakers. They used violence to silence anyone who spoke out against the Nazis. Finally,

Hitler had an amazing gift for speech-making. He made people think what he wanted them to think. In speech after speech, he used lies and promises to win over his listeners. When he told the Germans that they were superior to other people, millions of them believed him. By such methods, Hitler became the absolute dictator of Germany.

This poster declares that "youth serves the Fuhrer" and urges all those who have reached the age of ten to join the Hitler Youth.

Testing Your Vocabulary ⎯⎯⎯⎯⎯⎯⎯⎯⎯⎯⎯⎯

Choose the best answer.

1. One of Hitler's methods for getting power was *propaganda*. This means
   a. making speeches.
   b. telling lies.
   c. spreading any ideas effectively to get what one wants.

2. After World War I Germany suffered from *inflation*. This means
   a. unemployment was high.
   b. taxes were high.
   c. prices went up while the value of money fell.

Understanding What You Have Read _____

1. A good title for paragraphs 2, 3, and 4 is
   a. The Nazi Military Buildup of Germany.
   b. The Fall of the Weimar Republic.
   c. Nazi Political Ideas.
   d. Hitler's Early Political Career.
2. In which paragraphs do you find facts about
   a. Hitler's becoming dictator?
   b. Hitler's "master-race" idea?
   c. the Brown Shirt squads?
   d. the setting up of the Weimar Republic?
3. The Weimar Republic, set up in Germany after World War I, was weak because
   a. the Versailles Treaty allowed it only a small army.
   b. it could not handle unemployment, strikes, and inflation.
   c. it had no written constitution.
4. Adolf Hitler was put in prison in 1924 because he
   a. organized the Nazi party.
   b. plotted to burn down government buildings.
   c. tried to overthrow the German democratic republic.
5. According to Hitler's *Mein Kampf*, Germany lost World War I because
   a. traitors at home worked against Germany.
   b. the German generals made too many mistakes.
   c. the United States entered the war.
6. Hitler wanted Germany to conquer all of Europe because he believed that
   a. it was the only way to stop the spread of communism.
   b. the Germans were a master race.
   c. it would end unemployment in Europe.
7. Some of the business leaders in Germany helped Hitler and the Nazi party because they
   a. believed in a policy of imperialism.
   b. were afraid of the spread of communism.
   c. wanted to end unemployment in Europe.

Tell whether you *agree* or *disagree* with each of the following statements. If you disagree, change the words in italics to make a statement with which you agree.

1. Hitler promised to disregard the terms of the *Versailles Treaty*.
2. War veterans, army officers, and university students *opposed* the Nazi party.
3. The *swastika* was the chief symbol of the Nazi party in Germany.
4. The Communists in Germany *favored* the rise of the Nazi party.
5. The government of Germany after World War I was called the *Berlin Republic*.
6. Hitler was a German *general* in World War I.
7. The *Black Shirts* were members of the German Nazi party.
8. *Das Kapital* was Adolf Hitler's book.
9. In the last free election in Germany before World War II the Nazi party won about *70%* of the votes.
10. The new Germany under Hitler became known as the *Second Reich*.

Developing Ideas and Skills

WRITING AN OUTLINE

Complete the following outline in your notebook by filling in the blanks with the items below.

The Nazis

A. Nazi Political Ideas
1. Absolute rule by the dictator
2. _____
3. Ignore the Versailles Treaty
B. Nazi Methods
1. Appeal to spirit of nationalism

2. _____
3. _____
C. Why People Supported Nazism
1. Promise of jobs for all
2. _____
3. _____

Use of violence and terror
Master-race theory
Fear of communism

False propaganda
Desire for German military power

Using Original Sources

Before Adolf Hitler became dictator of Germany, he was arrested for trying to overthrow the government. While in jail, he wrote a book called *Mein Kampf* (*My Battle*) in which he presented his ideas. These paragraphs are taken from his book. Read them and answer the questions that follow on page 497.

[Nazi Ideas]

One blood demands one Reich. Never will the German nation have the moral right to enter into colonial politics until, at least, it includes its own sons within a single state. . . . From the tears of war the daily bread of future generations will grow. . . .

All who are not of good race in this world are worthless straw. . . . No boy and no girl must leave school without having been led to a full and complete understanding of the need and importance of blood purity. . . .

Oppressed territories are led back to the bosom of a common Reich, not by flaming protests, but by a mighty sword. To make this sword is the responsibility of a country's internal political leadership.

Choose the correct answer.

1. By "one blood" Hitler meant
   a. a battle in a war.
   b. people of the same race.
   c. persecuted people.
2. Hitler wanted the schools to teach children that
   a. there would be another war.
   b. all people are born equal.
   c. the German race was better than other races.

3. Hitler planned to win territory by
   a. armed force
   b. complaining to the League of Nations.
   c. making speeches.
4. The responsibility of Germany's leader, according to Hitler, was to
   a. make swords.
   b. build up Germany militarily.
   c. run the schools.

AIM: What kind of government did the Nazis set up in Germany?

CHAPTER 6

Hitler Rules Germany

HOW WERE THE GERMAN PEOPLE CONTROLLED?

1. Germany had always been looked upon as a nation of educated and intelligent people. Germans were world-famous for their music, art, poetry, and science. Yet they let Adolf Hitler, a power-hungry madman, become their dictator. They let him lead them into World War II. Today, we wonder how such a thing could have happened. Yet it did indeed happen. Millions of people died in concentration camps and on battlefields as a result.

2. When Adolf Hitler and the Nazi party came to power, in 1933, every part of German life changed. Germany was changed from a democracy to an absolute dictatorship. Hitler became "der Führer," or leader. All laws were really made by him. The Reichstag, or lawmaking body, did not meet often. When it did meet, it merely approved what Hitler had ordered. Hitler's government was an absolute dictatorship. It was also an example of *totalitarianism*—strict and total rule by a single governing power or political party.

3. The swastika became the new symbol of Germany. The Nazis became the only legal political party. Leaders of all other parties went into hiding. Those who were caught were arrested. They were sent to concentration camps or put to death. Elections were held. But only members of the Nazi party could run for office. Anyone who dared to vote against the Nazi party was arrested, beaten, and imprisoned. Those who did not come out to vote for the Nazis were in danger of arrest.

4. Workers in Germany found jobs during Hitler's rule. The Nazis ended unemployment. They built huge factories to manufacture guns,

Hitler being cheered by the German people. What did he promise them?

Hitler speaks to his Storm Troops at Nurnberg. Shortly after this, Hitler moved to take over Czechoslovakia.

cannon, tanks, warplanes, bombs, and other war materials. But in return, the workers lost their freedom. Hitler's government took control over much of their lives. The Nazis did away with all labor unions. Strikes were forbidden. Hours of labor, wages, and working conditions were all decided by government order. Of course, the best jobs were always given to loyal Nazi party members. Spies were planted in all factories. Workers who complained or who said anything against Hitler were arrested and imprisoned.

5. Businessmen loyal to Hitler continued to own and run their factories and businesses. But they lost their freedom, too. The government told them what to manufacture. They were told what prices to charge. The government decided how much should be produced and how much profit the owner could gain.

Banks and trade were under Nazi control. Factories and stores owned by Jews and anti-Nazi Germans were taken away from them and given to loyal Nazi party members. No payment was made when such property was taken away from people. The Nazis took complete control of the economic life of Germany.

HOW DID THE NAZIS RULE?

6. Hitler protected his dictatorship by two methods: terror and propaganda. His rule of terror was run by the Gestapo, or secret police. Heinrich Himmler, one of Hitler's advisers, was the feared head of the Gestapo. People who had opposed the Nazis lived in terror from day to day. At any moment, the Gestapo might enter their homes and seize them. The Gestapo could arrest anyone at any time and for any reason. Those arrested were given no trial. They were tortured until they made false confessions. Then they were executed or sent to concentration camps. Thousands of innocent Germans—Jews, Protestants, and Catholics—disappeared forever. Because its secret police was so powerful, Germany became known as a police state.

7. A man named Joseph Goebbels carried out Hitler's policy of propaganda. Goebbels used what is called "the big-lie method." This means that if a lie is repeated often enough, no matter how unbelievable it may be, many people will begin to believe it. To carry out Goebbel's "big-lie method," every source of information in Germany was put under his control. He controlled all books, magazines, newspapers, and radio stations.

8. During Hitler's rule, people did not say "Good morning" or "Hello" to one another. Instead, they said, "Heil Hitler"(Hail Hitler). People who did not use these words were suspected of not being loyal. Every teacher had to be a Nazi party member. Every class began and ended with "Heil Hitler." Children were taught that Germans were a master race and that Jews

A Jewish family trying to flee Nazi Germany with a few of their belongings.

Germany, the Nazis destroyed their stores and homes. They burned their synagogues. Jews were not allowed to be doctors or lawyers. Nor were they allowed any rights that other citizens had. Many of the world's most talented writers, musicians, and scientists, such as Albert Einstein, had to flee from Germany.

HOW DID HITLER PREPARE TO CONQUER THE WORLD?

11. To carry out his plan of conquest in Europe, Hitler built great numbers of tanks, warplanes, and cannon. Most industries were made ready to produce even more supplies when war began. Super-highways were built to

The poster urges German women to join together in Nazism and says that German girls belong to "us"—the Nazi party.

were the special enemies of Germany. They were taught that war was noble, and that Germany would conquer the world.

9. The role of women in Nazi Germany was made clear by a slogan: "Children, Church, and Cooking." German women were expected to take care of the home, be religious, and raise strong children for the Nazi party and the army. Running the government and business of the country were jobs only for men. Children were taught to obey Hitler without question. Their first loyalty was not to their parents. It was to Hitler and Germany. They were even taught to report their parents to the secret police if the parents said anything against Hitler or the Nazis.

10. The persecution of the Jews was useful to the Nazis. It meant that they had a "scapegoat," or a group to blame for Germany's past failures. In persecuting the Jewish citizens of

move troops and war materials to any place in Germany quickly and easily. The Versailles Treaty had forbidden Germany to build up its war supplies. But Hitler went ahead and did so despite the Treaty.

12. The Nazis set up a network of spies. Dressed as German tourists, these spies found out the military secrets of neighboring coun-tries. Other German spies helped to form Nazi parties in Austria, Czechoslovakia, Poland, France, and elsewhere. These foreign Nazi par-ties were backed by Germany. It was their job to spread disorder. This would weaken Ger-many's neighbors. After six years of careful preparation, Hitler and Nazi Germany were at last ready for war.

Testing Your Vocabulary

Choose the best answer.

1. The Nazi government was *totalitarian.* This means that
   a. the government controlled every part of life.
   b. it totally destroyed all foreign ene-mies.
   c. it was run by only the wealthiest citi-zens.
2. One of Hitler's policies was to persecute the Jews. To *persecute* means to
   a. send people out of the country.
   b. make slaves of people of a different race.
   c. treat people badly because of their religion, race, or beliefs.
3. The Nazis used the Jews as *scape-goats* by
   a. falsely blaming them for Germany's failures.
   b. employing them as spies.
   c. forcing them to produce war mate-rials.

Understanding What You Have Read

1. The main idea of paragraphs 4 and 5 is that
   a. the Nazis controlled Germany's eco-nomic life.
   b. the Nazis used propaganda.
   c. the Nazis controlled education.
   d. the Nazis did not allow labor strikes.
2. In which paragraph do you find facts about
   a. the power of the Reichstag under Hitler?
   b. Goebbels and German propaganda?
   c. the persecution of Jews in Germany?
   d. German secret police?
3. Germany under Hitler was a police state in that
   a. the Nazis controlled the government.
   b. the secret police had great power.
   c. concentration camps were used.
4. The Nazis took control of all newspa-pers because
   a. newspapers were controlled by Com-munists.
   b. newspapers were owned by Jews.
   c. the Nazis wanted to use newspapers for propaganda.
5. During Nazi rule in Germany, women were expected to
   a. volunteer for military service.
   b. stay home and take care of the family.
   c. take the place of men in factories.

6. Almost every worker had a job in Germany under Hitler because
  a. many workers were employed in making war materials.
  b. the unemployed were sent to overseas colonies.
  c. foreign trade increased.
7. The Nazis built super-highways in Germany mainly because
  a. German roads had not been repaired under the Weimar Republic.
  b. they wanted to get Germans to buy automobiles.
  c. good roads made possible the quick movement of German troops and weapons.

Fill in the correct word or phrase for each of the following:

1. The German secret police was called the _____ .
2. Because the secret police were given such great power, Nazi Germany was known as a _____ .
3. Places where large numbers of Jews and the enemies of Nazism were confined were called _____ .
4. The common greeting among people in Nazi Germany was _____ .
5. The man who was known as "der Führer" was _____ .
6. The man who headed the secret police in Nazi Germany was _____ .
7. Many property owners in Germany supported Hitler because they were afraid of the _____ .
8. The man who ran Nazi propaganda was _____ .
9. The religious group that suffered most under Nazi rule was the _____ .
10. The only legal political party in Germany under Hitler was the _____ .

Developing Ideas and Skills

UNDERSTANDING A DIAGRAM

Using the information from the diagram on page 503 and this chapter, write in your notebook the word or words that will correctly complete the following sentences.

1. All news on radios and in newspapers was censored by the _____ .
2. Imprisonment without trial was a method used by the _____ .
3. All power in the government of Nazi Germany was in the hands of the _____ .
4. The orders of the dictator were carried out mainly by the _____ .
5. This diagram is of a type of government known as a _____ .

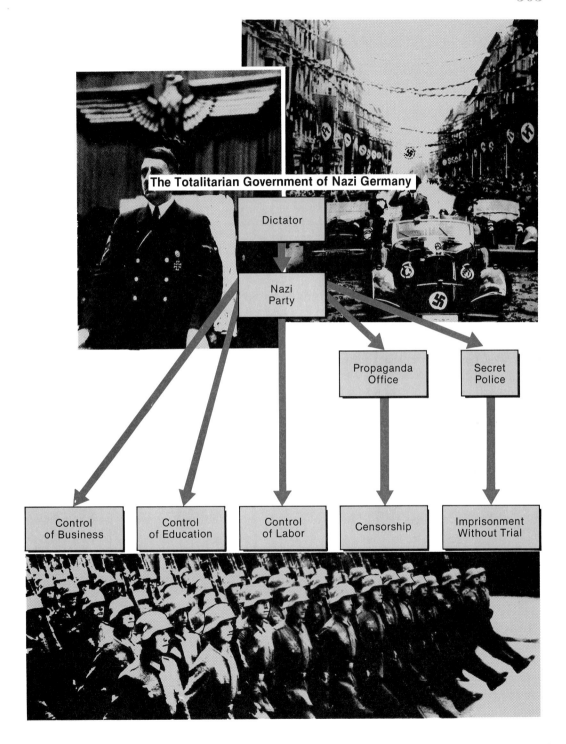

The Totalitarian Government of Nazi Germany

Dictator

Nazi Party

Propaganda Office

Secret Police

Control of Business

Control of Education

Control of Labor

Censorship

Imprisonment Without Trial

AIM: What events led to the outbreak of World War II?

CHAPTER 7

Dictators Seek New Conquests

WHY DID JAPAN INVADE CHINA?

1. At New Year's, people often make resolutions. They plan to do or not to do certain things in the coming year. These resolutions are sometimes forgotten a week later. Nations also make resolutions. After World War I, for example, the different countries set up the League of Nations in order to prevent future wars. In 1928, under the Kellogg-Briand Pact, almost every nation on earth agreed never to go to war again. Eleven years later, most of the world's nations were fighting World War II. What happened to their resolutions never to go to war? Why did the nations forget so quickly the terrible lesson of the First World War?

2. An early sign that war would come again was the rise of the military government of Japan. The Japanese people had become strongly nationalistic. They had great pride in their army and navy. But Japan was a small island. It was crowded with many people. It needed raw materials and markets in which to sell its manufactured goods. The military group in Japan believed that both of these problems could be solved. They planned to get control of nearby China. China was a large nation, rich in natural resources. It was governed by weak

leaders and torn by fighting between rival war lords.

3. At the Washington Conference of 1921–22, Japan, along with other nations, had promised not to invade China's territory. In 1928, Japan had signed the Kellogg-Briand Pact. By this treaty it promised never to go to war to settle conflicts. But the Japanese government came under the control of a nationalist and militarist party. In spite of its promises, Japan invaded China in 1931. The Japanese quickly conquered the northern part of China, called Manchuria.

4. Both the League of Nations and the United States spoke out against the Japanese invasion. But these protests did not stop Japan. Instead, it left the League of Nations. Then, in 1937, Japan invaded China a second time. This time it took most of the Chinese east coast. Fighting between the Japanese and Chinese was still going on in 1939 when World War II began in Europe.

WHAT OTHER LAWLESS ACTS OCCURRED?

5. The spirit of lawless conquest also appeared in Europe. The Italian Fascist government of Mussolini wanted colonies. In 1935, the

Italian army invaded Ethiopia, an under-developed country in Africa. Italy's aim was to take it as a colony. The Italians used modern bombing planes. The Ethiopians often fought with spears. Of course, Italy easily conquered Ethiopia. The League of Nations opposed the Italian invasion of Ethiopia. So Italy, like Japan, left the League of Nations. Italy's invasion of Ethiopia could not be stopped.

6. A third act of lawlessness was the Spanish Civil War. It began in 1936. Two rival groups went to war. The Loyalists represented the elected republican government of Spain. The rebels, under Francisco Franco, wanted to set up a Fascist government. They said they wanted to protect Spain from communism. Nazi Germany and Fascist Italy sent arms and troops to help Franco's forces. Communist Russia helped the Loyalists. Thus, the Spanish Civil War became a kind of little world war, in which the great powers took sides. Franco's armies finally won. Franco became head of the Spanish government. Spain, like Italy and Germany, became a Fascist dictatorship. Spain remained neutral during World War II. Franco's dictatorship in Spain lasted for 36 years. When he died, in 1975, the dictatorship came to an end.

Ethiopia mobilized to stop Mussolini, but their weapons were no match for the Italians.

This painting by Pablo Picasso, called *Guernica*, expresses the artist's feelings about the needless German bombing of the town of Guernica during the civil war in Spain. How would you describe the feelings expressed in the painting?

7. The climax in the drama of world lawlessness was played by Nazi Germany. Germany left the League of Nations in 1933. Hitler then ordered the German armies to march into the Rhineland. This was an area between France and Germany. German troops had been forbidden by the Treaty of Versailles to enter the Rhineland. But they did so anyway. Great Britain and France protested this breaking of the Versailles Treaty. But they did nothing to stop the Nazis.

HOW DID HITLER GAIN MORE LAND?

8. In 1938, the German armies marched into Austria. They took control of that country. Again there were protests. But no nation was willing to take up arms against Germany. In fact, each time the Nazi armies marched into another territory, Hitler promised that it was his last move. "I want peace," he told the world as his armies invaded each neighboring nation. Early in 1938, Hitler took another step in his plan to conquer Europe. He demanded to be given a part of Czechoslovakia called the Sudetenland. This was an area where a large number

of Germans lived. But the Sudetenland had never belonged to Germany. Hitler, however, demanded that it be given to Germany. Otherwise, he would take it by force.

9. Czechoslovakia prepared for war. It looked to Great Britain and France for help. But neither was willing to take the risk of helping Czechoslovakia. Instead, the prime ministers of Great Britain and France held a conference with Hitler. They agreed to let Germany take the Sudetenland. This agreement is known as the Munich Pact. After signing the Munich Pact, Hitler again said, "This is the last territorial demand I have to make in Europe." Six months later, he seized all of Czechoslovakia.

10. Again and again Hitler broke his promises. Finally, the nations of Europe realized that Hitler did not plan to stop until he controlled all of Europe. France and the Soviet Union had formed an alliance against Nazi Germany in 1935. They had agreed to help each other if either one was attacked by Germany. Italy, Japan, and Germany had formed their own military alliance. It was called the Rome-Berlin-Tokyo Axis. After the Germans took Czechoslovakia, Great Britain and France formed a new military alliance. Then, Germany and the Soviet Union signed a Nazi-Soviet pact.

11. Europe was again divided as it was before World War I. The League of Nations had failed. The conditions for a new world war were present. The people of the world now waited. Any new crisis would take the great powers into World War II. It came on the morning of September 1, 1939: Germany invaded Poland.

Neville Chamberlain, prime minister of Great Britain, and others talking with Hitler at the Munich Conference. Why do you think the allies gave in to Hitler's demands?

Testing Your Vocabulary

Choose the best answer.

1. Almost all nations signed the Kellogg-Briand *Pact*. A pact is
   a. an agreement between nations.
   b. a declaration of war.
   c. a government policy.
2. Germany, Italy, and Japan formed an *alliance* called the Rome-Berlin-Tokyo Axis. An alliance is
   a. a form of government.
   b. a promise not to declare war.
   c. an agreement among nations to join together or help each other.
3. The nations all made *resolutions* to keep the peace. A resolution is
   a. a written agreement.
   b. a decision to do or not to do a certain thing in the future.
   c. an official government policy that includes the ideas of militarism and imperialism.

Understanding What You Have Read

1. The main idea of paragraphs 7 through 9 is
   a. lawlessness among many nations broke out in the 1930's.
   b. Germany invaded its neighbors.
   c. the League of Nations could not stop war.
   d. European nations formed alliances before World War II.
2. In which paragraph do you find facts about
   a. the Spanish Civil War?
   b. the Rome-Berlin-Tokyo Axis?
   c. Japan's invasion of Manchuria?
   d. Italy's invasion of Ethiopia?
3. In 1931 and 1937 Japan invaded China because
   a. the Chinese army threatened Japanese security.
   b. Communists had taken control of the Chinese government.
   c. Japan wanted colonies for markets and raw materials.
4. Italy left the League of Nations because
   a. the League protested the Italian invasion of Ethiopia.
   b. the League did not stop the Japanese invasion of China.
   c. the United States had not joined the League.
5. In 1936, Great Britain and France protested the sending of German troops into the Rhineland because
   a. the Rhineland was French territory.
   b. the League of Nations objected to this warlike action.
   c. it broke a part of the Versailles Treaty.
6. The Spanish Civil War can be thought of as a little world war because
   a. France and Great Britain entered it in order to bring peace.
   b. the League of Nations sent an army into Spain.
   c. some of the great powers who were later to fight in World War II sent military forces to Spain.
7. The United States protested the Japanese invasion of China because Japan broke
   a. the United States "Open Door" policy.
   b. the Versailles Treaty.
   c. the Kellogg-Briand Pact.

Choose the item that does not belong with the others in each group.

1. Lands taken by Germany before World War II:
   a. Austria
   b. Czechoslovakia
   c. Bulgaria
2. Actions by Great Britain and France to stop Hitler:
   a. threatened war when Hitler took Austria
   b. signed Munich Pact
   c. protested Hitler's invasion of Austria
3. Countries allied *with* Germany before World War II:
   a. Spain
   b. Italy
   c. Japan
4. Countries allied *against* Germany before World War II:
   a. France
   b. Great Britain
   c. Italy
5. Actions by Italy before World War II:
   a. invaded Ethiopia
   b. formed an alliance with Germany

c. signed treaty with Soviet Union
6. Countries that sent troops to fight in Spanish Civil War:
   a. Italy
   b. Soviet Union
   c. Great Britain
7. Actions by Hitler before World War II:
   a. seized Austria
   b. invaded Italy
   c. sent troops to Spain
8. Left League of Nations before World War II:
   a. Germany
   b. Japan
   c. France
9. Dictators in Europe before World War II:
   a. Nikita Khrushchev
   b. Benito Mussolini
   c. Francisco Franco
10. Hitler's violations of the Versailles Treaty:
    a. rebuilt German army
    b. invaded Spain
    c. marched troops into Rhineland

Developing Ideas and Skills

USING A TIME LINE

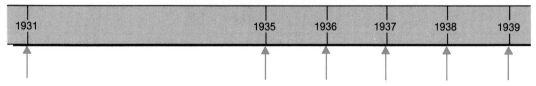

Crises Leading to World War II

1931   1935   1936   1937   1938   1939

Match the events below with the dates on the time line.

a. beginning of Spanish Civil War
b. German conquest of Czechoslovakia
c. first Japanese invasion of China

d. second Japanese invasion of China
e. Italian invasion of Ethiopia
f. German takeover of Austria

AIM: How did the Allied nations defeat the Axis Powers?

CHAPTER 8

The Globe Is Torn by World War II

WHAT WERE GERMANY'S EARLY VICTORIES?

1. It seems that nations do not learn from experience. World War I began in 1914. World War II began only 25 years later, in 1939. The basic causes of both world wars were about the same. They were militarism, imperialism, and nationalism. Imperialistic Germany, Italy, and Japan wanted colonies. Militarism showed itself in the race to build larger armies and navies. Nationalism was the force behind Hitler's idea that the Germans were a master race.

2. Nazi Germany invaded one country after another. It was only a matter of time before a general war would begin. In 1939 Hitler signed a Nazi-Soviet Pact with Stalin. His aim was to protect Germany from a surprise attack by the Soviet Union. Stalin was dictator of the Soviet Union. Hitler now felt he would not be attacked by the Soviets. He turned his attention to other nations—ones he felt he could defeat. He demanded that Poland give Germany certain rights in Poland and give Germany the city of Danzig. Poland refused. On September 1, 1939, the Nazi army invaded Poland. Two days later, Great Britain and France declared war on Germany. The Second World War was on.

3. The Nazi forces quickly overcame the weak Polish army. Within a month, Poland was forced to surrender. The leading citizens and most of the Jews of Poland were executed by the Nazis. After their victory in Poland, the Nazi armies turned west. Without warning, they attacked and conquered Denmark and Norway. Then they invaded the Netherlands, Belgium, and Luxembourg. Hitler's armies were on the march. No one could stop them.

4. At last, Germany was ready to try to conquer France. The French believed they had strong defenses. But their land was overrun by Nazi forces. In 1940, Paris was conquered. Then Mussolini, the dictator of Italy, joined Hitler. Italy declared war on the Allies. Soon afterward, France surrendered. German troops moved into France to police the nation. A puppet French government, which would do as the Nazis wanted, was set up in the town of Vichy. Meanwhile, many Frenchmen fled to England. From there, they plotted to drive the Nazis out of France.

5. England was Hitler's last important undefeated enemy in Western Europe. Hitler ordered the bombing of English cities by around-the-clock air raids. Week after week, the German air force bombed the cities of

This scene of London in 1941 shows the destruction of the city. Explain how it also shows the courage of the British people.

Great Britain. The small British Royal Air Force fought back bravely. In the Battle of Britain, England nearly fell. But its air force held out. Finally, Hitler realized that he would not be able to invade Great Britain.

WHY DID THE U.S. ENTER THE WAR?

6. France was defeated. England was damaged. But the United States still remained neutral. Most Americans, however, feared a Nazi victory. As a result, the United States passed laws making it easy to supply Great Britain and its allies with arms and supplies.

7. Meanwhile, Japan was seizing territory in Asia. The United States grew worried about continuing Japanese conquests in Asia. The United States also felt that Japanese conquests would hurt American trade. The United States tried to persuade Japan to stop its imperialist actions. In 1941, Japanese delegates came to Washington, D.C., to discuss these matters. On December 7, 1941, while these discussions were in progress, Americans heard terrible news on the radio. Without warning, Japanese planes had attacked the American naval base at Pearl Harbor, in Hawaii. The next day, Congress declared war on Japan. Germany and Italy, Japan's allies, then declared war on the United States.

8. By the time the United States entered the war, Germany had stopped its air bombardment of England. Instead, Hitler had turned his armies eastward. The Nazis invaded the Soviet Union. For a while it appeared that Germany would conquer the nation that it had promised not to invade.

The Japanese attack on Pearl Harbor in 1941. Why was this attack a unique event in history for Americans?

WHY DID AXIS
POWERS SURRENDER?

9. The Russians retreated but did not surrender. Then Hitler's forces were slowed by snow and the very cold Russian winter. What had happened to Napoleon's armies in Russia more than a century earlier happened to Hitler's armies now. The turning point of the invasion of Russia came at the Battle of Stalingrad, in 1942. Here the advance of the Nazi armies was finally stopped. The Germans were forced into a slow retreat out of Russia.

10. While German and Soviet armies battled in Russia, the United States began sending forces overseas. American troops landed in North Africa in 1942. Along with British forces they defeated the German and Italian armies in North Africa. An American army invaded southern Italy. In 1943, Italy surrendered. But the German armies continued to fight in Italy.

11. American, British, and Canadian forces opened a second fighting front in Western Europe in 1944. A large Allied army landed on the coast of Normandy, in France. Helped by the French "underground," or secret fighters, against Germany's occupying forces, the Allies pushed back the Germans. They freed the city of Paris. The Allies then invaded Germany from the west. At the same time, the Soviet armies began to push into Germany on the east. The two armed forces continued their advances until they met in Germany. Faced with total defeat, Hitler killed himself. On May 8, 1945, the Nazi armies surrendered.

Normandy Beach at night. Visitors to the area today can still see the wreckage of ships that took part in the invasion.

12. The victory in Europe was not total victory for the Allies. They still had a war to fight against the Japanese. During the early fighting against Japan, the American navy and marines held back Japanese advances in Asia. The Battle of the Coral Sea and the Battle of Midway were important victories for the United States Navy. American marines then began a slow and bloody struggle. Their aim was to drive the Japanese out of the Pacific islands they had seized in the first year of the war.

13. The Battle of the Islands started with the famous American victory at Guadalcanal, in 1942. It included the American recapture of the Philippine Islands in 1945. It ended with the capture of Okinawa in 1945. On August 6, 1945, an American plane dropped the first atomic bomb on the Japanese city of Hiroshima. The bomb destroyed the city and killed more than 75,000 people. Two days later, the Soviet Union declared war on Japan as it had promised to do. On August 9, the Americans dropped a second atomic bomb. Their target was Nagasaki. On August 10, 1945, the Japanese surrendered. The most terrible war in human history was over.

World War II: Areas of Japanese Control

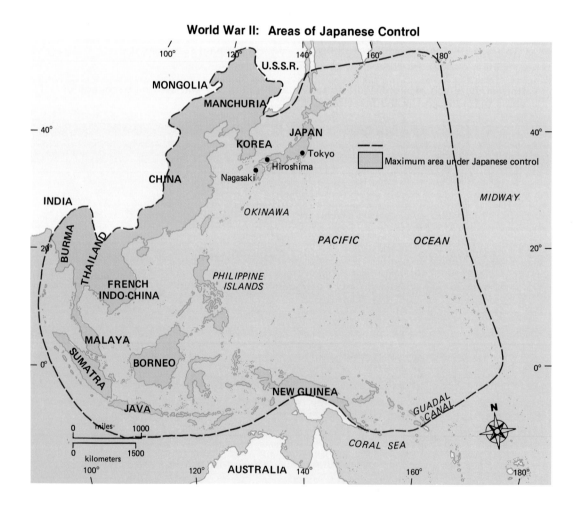

Testing Your Vocabulary _____

Choose the best answer.

1. The French underground helped drive the Germans out of France near the end of the war. The *underground* was
   a. a secret system of transportation.
   b. a secret fighting force.
   c. a secret propaganda system.

2. During the first two years of World War II, the United States remained *neutral.* This meant that it
   a. helped both sides.
   b. stopped trading with both sides.
   c. did not take sides.

Understanding What You Have Read _____

1. A good title for paragraphs 12 and 13 is
   a. The United States' War with Japan.
   b. Nazi Victories.
   c. Causes of World War II.
   d. Defeat of the Nazi Forces.
2. In which paragraph do you find facts about
   a. the Nazi defeat of Poland?
   b. the Battle of Guadalcanal?
   c. the Battle of Britain?
   d. the Nazi conquest of France?
3. Adolf Hitler started World War II when Nazi forces
   a. invaded France.
   b. invaded Poland.
   c. broke the Versailles Treaty.
4. The United States did not declare war on Germany at the beginning of World War II because it

a. feared a sneak attack by Japan.
b. was following a policy of neutrality.
c. was not a member of the League of Nations.

5. The Japanese attacked Pearl Harbor, in 1941, because
   a. the United States refused to discuss problems of trade with Japan.
   b. the Japanese feared that Germany would declare war on Japan.
   c. the Japanese wanted to destroy the United States Pacific fleet.
6. The Battle of Stalingrad was a turning point in World War II because
   a. it stopped the further advance of Germany into the Soviet Union.
   b. it caused Italy to surrender.
   c. it caused the United States to enter the war.

Developing Ideas and Skills _____

USING A MAP

Match the letters on the map with the following items:

1. African front
2. Eastern front in the Soviet Union
3. Second front in France
4. Southern front in Italy
5. Air battle over Great Britain

Using Original Sources

Less than a year after World War II began, Adolf Hitler and his Nazi armies had overrun most of Western Europe. As Great Britain waited for Germany's next move, Prime Minister Winston Churchill spoke these words to the British House of Commons in 1941.

[Their Finest Hour]

I expect that the Battle of Britain is about to begin. Upon this battle depends the survival of Christian civilization. Upon it depends our own British life and the long continuity of our institutions and Empire. The whole fury and might of the enemy must seem to be turned on us. Hitler knows that he will have to break us in this island or lose the war. If we can stand up to him, all Europe may be free and the life of the world may move forward into broad swift uplands. But if we fail, then the whole world, including the United States, will sink in the abyss [pit] of a new Dark Age. Let us therefore brace ourselves to our duties, and so bear ourselves that, if the British Empire and its Commonwealth last for a thousand years, men will still say, "This was their finest hour."

1. What was the purpose of this speech? (Which sentence most directly expresses Churchill's purpose?)
2. What did Churchill mean by "the abyss of a new Dark Age"? Why would the whole world be affected?
3. When he spoke of the possibility of the whole world's sinking into a new Dark Age, he used the phrase "including the United States." Why did he make special mention of the United States?
4. What did Churchill probably mean by the phrase "their finest hour"?
5. Was this speech a form of propaganda?

TURNING POINTS

Government

Europe: Raoul Wallenberg

As World War II came to an end in Europe, people became aware of a terrible situation. The Germans were killing large groups of innocent people. Their main target was the Jews. In 1944, the Germans' plan was to destroy the 900,000 Jews in Hungary.

Some countries in Europe were not involved in the war. The United States asked one of those nations, Sweden, for help in rescuing the Hungarian Jews. As a result, Sweden sent some representatives to Budapest, the capital of Hungary. A young man named Raoul Wallenberg was asked to go. He was from one of the richest families in Sweden. He spoke German and had been in Budapest many times before on business.

Wallenberg worked very hard to carry out his assignment. He gave Swedish passports to 20,000 Budapest Jews so that they could escape from the Nazis. Wallenberg also set up 32 houses under Swedish protection where Jews would be safe. He arranged for homeless people to receive food and medical supplies. He even pulled people from lines as the Nazis were taking them away. Sometimes he tricked Nazi guards so that captured Jews could go free. He risked his own life again and again.

Because of Wallenberg's bravery, 90,000 Jewish people were saved. His own story does not have a happy ending. On January 17, 1945, he disappeared. Some people believe he was either killed or captured by the Russians. No one knows for sure.

Critical Thinking

1. Why were countries such as Sweden asked for help in the rescue mission?
2. Write a definition of what you think a hero is. Based on what you know about Raoul Wallenberg, does he fit your definition of a hero?

AIM: What happened to the Axis Powers—Germany, Italy and Japan—after their defeat in World War II?

CHAPTER 9

The Effects of the War

Happy soldiers hold up a paper announcing Japan's surrender. Why was this victory celebrated all over the world?

WHAT WERE THE RESULTS OF THE WAR?

1. People are never the same after a big war. World War II was the biggest war in history. More than 20 million people were killed. Many of them were not soldiers. They were people who died in bombed cities or were mur-dered in Nazi extermination camps. Six million Jews were killed by Nazi firing squads or in the gas chambers of extermination camps. The Nazi attempt to destroy all Jews is called the *Holocaust*.

2. Only at the end of World War II did the rest of the world really learn how cruel the Nazis had been. Allied armies entering Germany reached many of the extermination camps. Here they saw sights they could hardly believe. Thousands of Jews and other prisoners were so starved that they looked like living skeletons. Gas chambers were found. Dead bodies were still piled up in them. The bodies of thousands of people were stacked like pieces of wood. The commanders of the extermination camps had not had time to bury their victims before the Allied forces arrived.

3. The war ended the dictatorships in Germany, Italy, and Japan. Mussolini was killed by his own people before the war ended. Hitler killed himself just before the city of Berlin fell to the Soviet armies. Twenty-two top Nazi leaders were captured and put on trial. They were charged with inhuman cruelty, violation of international law, and crimes against humanity. At these trials, held in the German city of Nuremberg, ten of the Nazi leaders were sentenced to death. The others were given long jail terms. In Japan, Tojo, the wartime prime minister, as well as other Japanese leaders, was tried for war crimes and hanged.

Inmates of an extermination camp greet the Allied soldiers who arrive to free them at the end of the war.

WHAT DISAGREEMENTS AROSE AMONG THE ALLIES?

4. Most wars end with the signing of peace treaties. World War I, for example, ended with the Versailles Treaty. But no general treaty was signed at the end of World War II. The nations had been able to unite for war. But they were not able to unite for peace. The United States, the Soviet Union, and Great Britain had been united while fighting their common enemy. As soon as Germany and Italy had been defeated, the Allied powers could not agree on what to do with Germany.

5. During the last year of the war, the Allies held two important meetings. They met first at Yalta, in the Soviet Union, in February 1945. At this meeting, the Allies agreed on a plan for dividing Germany. The Allies met again in July 1945, at Potsdam, Germany, to try to work out more lasting plans.

6. At the Yalta Conference, the Allied leaders decided to split up Germany. Part of Germany was given to Poland and part to the Soviet Union. The rest of Germany was divided into four military zones. The United States, the Soviet Union, Great Britain, and France were each to control a different zone. The city of Berlin was inside the Soviet zone. Berlin was also divided into four sections. The United States, the Soviet Union, Great Britain, and France were again each to control a zone of Berlin. Since Berlin was inside the Soviet zone, the United States, Great Britain, and France were given the right to reach their sections of the city through a narrow strip of land in the Soviet zone.

7. Thus, Germany and its capital city were split into military zones. The division was supposed to last only until a permanent treaty could be written. The Allies, however, could not agree on a treaty. As a result, many of the temporary plans decided upon at Yalta are still in effect today. Germany today is divided into Communist East Germany and democratic West Germany. The city of Berlin is still divided. One part is a Communist section. The other part is a free section.

8. Estonia, Latvia, and Lithuania had been independent countries before the war. In the last year of the war, the Soviet armies had driven the Germans out of these countries. The Russians made them part of the Soviet Union without asking the Allies. The Russians also held onto parts of Romania, Poland, and East Prussia.

9. Before World War II began, Germany had seized control of Austria and Czechoslovakia. During the war, Germany seized other countries in Eastern Europe. These included Romania, Bulgaria, and Hungary. In the last year of the war, the Soviet armies drove the German forces out of all of these countries.

Why was the Yalta Conference so important? In what ways were the results of the conference disappointing?

HOW WERE AXIS LANDS DIVIDED?

10. The three Allied war leaders were Franklin D. Roosevelt, of the United States; Winston Churchill, of Great Britain; and Joseph Stalin, of the Soviet Union. They made plans for the future of Eastern Europe. At Yalta, the So- viet Union promised to let the people of East- ern Europe decide on their own form of gov- ernment. When the war was over, however, the Soviet Union failed to keep its promise. It did not allow free elections. Instead, the Soviet Union set up Communist governments in all of these countries. They kept these new govern- ments in power by sending Soviet armies to police the nations. Thus, at the end of the war, almost all the countries of Eastern Europe were under the control of the Communists. And they still are today.

11. After Italy was defeated in World War II, its people ended their dictatorship. They set up a democratic republic. Italy lost all of its colonies. They were put under the control of the United Nations. Later, the United Nations granted independence to these former Italian colonies.

12. Defeat also brought changes to Japan. It had to give up all of the Asian territories it had seized during the war. These included part of China, the Philippine Islands, Malaya, and Indonesia. Japan also lost Korea and the large island of Formosa. It lost all of its small islands in the Pacific Ocean. The United States was given control of most of these small Pacific is- lands by the United Nations. After the war, the emperor of Japan remained in office, but he lost all his power. The Japanese people set up a democratic government, somewhat like that of Great Britain.

Testing Your Vocabulary _____

Choose the best answer.

1. The Yalta and Potsdam agreements were supposed to be *temporary.* This means they were to last
   a. permanently.
   b. for a short time.
   c. until the fighting stopped.
2. The Nazi leaders were accused of break- ing *international law.* This refers to
   a. laws that have been passed by the United Nations.
   b. laws that have to do with conduct in wartime only.
   c. laws that govern the relations be- tween nations.

Understanding What You Have Read

1. A good title for paragraphs 6 and 7 is
   a. Nazi War Crimes.
   b. The Division of Germany.
   c. Communism in the Nations of Eastern Europe.
   d. Japan after World War II.
2. In which paragraph do you find facts about
   a. the Nuremberg Trials?
   b. the decisions made at the Yalta Conference?
   c. what happened to Estonia, Latvia, and Lithuania at the end of the war?
   d. Italy after World War II?
3. Adolf Hitler was not tried for war crimes because he
   a. killed himself.
   b. escaped to Switzerland.
   c. died in battle.
4. The countries of Eastern Europe are under Communist governments today because
   a. they wanted to trade with the Soviet Union.
   b. the people voted for the Communist Party.
   c. Soviet armies put Communist governments in power.
5. After World War II, no permanent treaty was written by the Allies for Germany because
   a. Germany refused to sign any treaty.
   b. Germany had no colonies.
   c. the Allied Powers could not agree on a treaty.
6. The Allied Powers met at the Yalta and Potsdam conferences because they had to decide on plans for
   a. setting up a new League of Nations.
   b. an invasion of Japan.
   c. the control of Germany after its defeat.
7. Berlin is a divided city today because
   a. the Germans voted for the division.
   b. the Allies divided the city after World War II.
   c. half the people in the city are German and half are Russian.

Tell whether these statements are true or false. If a statement is false, change the words in italics to make it true.

1. *Italy* and Japan lost all of their colonies at the end of the Second World War.
2. Germany was divided into *two* military zones at the end of World War II.
3. The German city that was divided into four parts is *Versailles*.
4. The city of Berlin lies within the *French*-controlled zone of Germany.
5. The war put an end to the Nazi dictatorship in *Germany*.
6. The Soviet Union set up Communist governments in most countries of *Western* Europe.
7. About *six million* people were killed as a result of World War II.
8. Concentration camps were set up by the *Italians*.
9. The Yalta and Potsdam agreements included plans for the division of *Japan*.
10. *Mussolini*, the wartime prime minister of Japan, was tried for war crimes and hanged.

Developing Ideas and Skills

USING MAPS

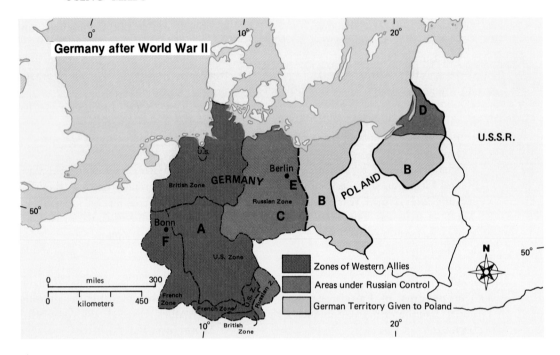

Germany after World War II

Match the letters on the map with the following items:

1. Area of Germany controlled by the Soviet Union.
2. Area of Germany controlled by Western Allies.
3. City controlled by four Allied Powers.
4. German territory given to Poland.
5. German territory taken by the Soviet Union.

Which of the following could also be a good title for this map?

1. Germany Divided.
2. Germany Reunited.
3. Communism in Modern Germany.

Summary of Unit XI

The following are key facts of Unit XI. What others might be added?

1. After World War I, the great powers set up a League of Nations to keep world peace, but it failed.

2. The Russian Revolution of 1917 ended Czarist rule and led to a communist form of government.

3. The government of the Soviet Union is run by the Communist party and by a dictator who is the party leader.

4. Mussolini established a fascist form of dictatorship in Italy in 1922.

5. Hitler and his Nazi party set up a dictatorship in Germany that lasted from 1933 to 1945.

6. The Nazi dictatorship in Germany planned to ignore the Versailles Treaty and conquer all of Europe.

7. The Spanish Civil War (1936–39) was called a "little world war" because many of the great powers sent help to the opposing sides in the war.

8. Before World War II, Japan seized part of China; Italy conquered Ethiopia; and Germany seized Austria and Czechoslovakia.

9. In World War II, the Axis Powers were Germany, Italy, and Japan. They were defeated by the Allied forces of Great Britain, France, the Soviet Union, the United States, and China.

10. The end of World War II brought changes to the governments of Germany, Italy, and Japan.

Making Generalizations

For each generalization below, provide two additional supporting statements from your reading of Unit XI.

1. Generalization: Unsettled conditions in a country often make it easier for strong leaders to come to power.
   a. The hardships suffered by the Russian people during the First World War helped make it possible for the Bolsheviks to seize control.
   b.
   c.

2. Generalization: The results of one war are often the causes of another war.
   a. The German people wanted revenge for having to pay high war damages after World War I.
   b.
   c.

3. Generalization: Extreme nationalistic feelings can lead to war.
   a. The Japanese leaders felt that Japan should control most of the land and raw materials of Southeast Asia.
   b.
   c.

4. Generalization: Dictatorships tend to deny citizens their rights.
   a. Adolph Hitler persecuted and killed millions of Jews living in Europe.
   b.
   c.

UNIT XII

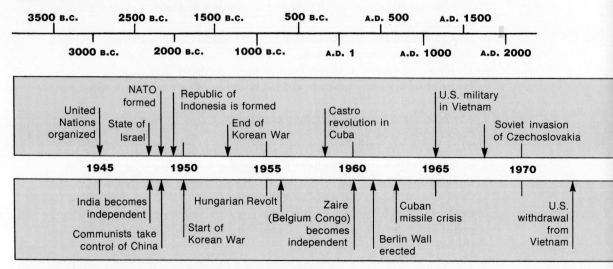

| 3500 B.C. | | 2500 B.C. | | 1500 B.C. | | 500 B.C. | | A.D. 500 | | A.D. 1500 | |

| | 3000 B.C. | | 2000 B.C. | | 1000 B.C. | | A.D. 1 | | A.D. 1000 | | A.D. 2000 |

United
Nations
organized

NATO
formed

State of
Israel

Republic of
Indonesia is formed

End of
Korean War

Castro
revolution in
Cuba

U.S. military
in Vietnam

Soviet invasion
of Czechoslovakia

1945   **1950**   **1955**   **1960**   **1965**   **1970**

India becomes
independent

Communists take
control of China

Start of
Korean War

Hungarian Revolt

Zaire
(Belgium Congo)
becomes
independent

Cuban
missile crisis

Berlin Wall
erected

U.S.
withdrawal
from
Vietnam

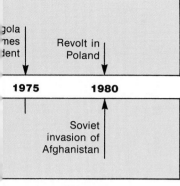

gola	Revolt in
nes	Poland
dent	

1975   **1980**

Soviet
invasion of
Afghanistan

How Was the World Changed after World War II?

SUB CONTRACTORS

PIONEER PLUMBERS LIMITED
P.O. BOX 42636 NAIROBI

RELIABLE ELECTRICAL ENGINEERS LTD.
P.O. BOX 41489 NAIROBI

PIONEER PLUMBERS LIMITED
P.O. BOX 42636 NAIROBI

LISTO LIMITED
P.O. BOX 30328 NAIROBI

RICO STEEL FABRICATORS LTD.
P.O. BOX 32138 NAIROBI

RICO STEEL FABRICATORS LTD.
P.O. Box 32138 NAIROBI

Construction workers in Kenya put up a new building in the growing city of Nairobi.

523

AIM: How does the United Nations try to settle world crises?

CHAPTER 1

The United Nations Tries to Keep Peace

WHY WAS THE UNITED NATIONS FORMED?

1. The United States entered World War I in 1917 to make the world safe for democracy. Twenty years later there was less democracy in the world than there had been before the war. Yet in 1941 the United States entered a second World War. What were American aims in this second world conflict?

2. President Woodrow Wilson had given reasons for America's involvement in World War I. They were called the Fourteen Points. Before the United States entered World War II, President Franklin D. Roosevelt had asked Congress to lend money to the countries fighting Nazi Germany. He gave four important reasons for this. They were to gain freedom of speech, freedom of worship, freedom from want, and freedom from fear for all. These goals were called the Four Freedoms. After the United States entered World War II, President Roosevelt and Prime Minister Winston Churchill, of Great Britain, listed the war aims of the Allies in the Atlantic Charter.

3. The Fourteen Points of 1918 and the Atlantic Charter of 1941 were very much alike. Both stated that all people should have the right to choose their own governments. Both stated that countries should reduce their arms

The United Nations buildings in New York City. Give one reason the United Nations has been more successful than the League of Nations.

and weapons in peacetime. Both called for freedom of the seas and greater freedom in world trade. Finally, the Fourteen Points and the Atlantic Charter both said that disputes among nations should be settled by a world peace organization.

4. The League of Nations was the peace organization formed after World War I. As we have learned, the League was a failure. During World War II, the most deadly weapon ever created by man—the atomic bomb—was developed and used. If ever the people of the world saw the need for peace, it was at the end of World War II. Near the end of it, delegates from fifty nations met in San Francisco, in 1945. Here they drew up a charter for the United Nations. Later, New York City was made the permanent home of the organization. Today, there are more than 150 nations in the U.N.

HOW DOES THE
UNITED NATIONS WORK?

5. The United Nations is made up of two main parts. They are a General Assembly and a Security Council. All member nations have delegates in the General Assembly. Its most important work is to discuss problems of world peace. It offers suggestions to the Security Council. More important than the General Assembly is the Security Council. It has only 15 members. Five nations are permanent members. They are the United States, Great Britain, the Soviet Union, France, and, since 1971, the People's Republic of China (Communist China). There are ten nonpermanent members. They are elected by the General Assembly for two-year terms. Each of the Security Council members has one vote. If any one of the five permanent members votes against (vetoes) any decision, it cannot be passed. The two main responsibilities of the Security Council are to try to settle disputes among nations and to stop wars.

6. In addition to the General Assembly and Security Council, the United Nations also has a number of special agencies. Each has a special purpose. The Secretariat does the office work of the United Nations. It is run by a person called the Secretary General. The U.N. also has an International Court of Justice, called the World Court. It hears cases involving treaties and other agreements among nations.

7. The most successful United Nations agency has been the Economic and Social Council (E.C.O.S.O.C.). This agency has many branches or divisions. Each does a different kind of work. The World Health Organization (W.H.O.), for example, fights disease epidemics all over the world. The International Labor Organization (I.L.O.) tries to improve working conditions in countries where laborers work long hours for low wages. The Food and Agriculture Organization (F.A.O.) tries to improve farming methods in developing countries. The United Nations Educational, Scientific and Cultural Organization (U.N.E.S.C.O.) tries to get scientists and writers of different countries to work together.

8. Since the signing of the U.N. charter, in 1945, more than 100 new nations have been admitted to the U.N. They are mainly the new countries of Africa and Southeast Asia. Formerly, they had been colonies of Great Britain, France, Belgium, Italy and the Netherlands. Many of these developing countries are called, together, the "Third World." At first, these new member nations usually voted with the United States in the U.N. The United States gave them foreign aid, such as loans and gifts of food, machinery, and money. However, this changed for two reasons: the United States began to reduce its foreign aid, and the United States almost always voted to support Israel in the U.N.

9. Meanwhile, the Arab nations of the Middle East had begun to grow rich from higher oil prices. They threatened to cut off all oil supplies to countries that did not vote against Israel in the U.N. Such threats often

worked. Many Third World countries, as well as European nations, began to vote on the side of the Arabs and the Soviet Union. Such votes were usually against Israel and the United States.

WHAT CRISES DID THE U.N. TRY TO SETTLE?

10. The control of nuclear weapons was one of the first problems that came before the United Nations. All nations realized that the use of nuclear weapons in wartime could destroy the world and all its people. The U.N. set up an Atomic Energy Commission to study the problem. But members of the U.N. could not reach any agreement. The main reason was the rivalry between the United States and the Soviet Union. Meanwhile, other nations—such as France and China—learned how to make nuclear bombs. Now, the danger of a future war with such weapons hangs over the head of all humankind.

11. Since the U.N. was founded, there have been many times when the peace of the world has been in danger. There have been crises in the Middle East, India, Korea, Zaire, Vietnam, and many other places. In each crisis the United Nations tried to settle the dispute. Sometimes it succeeded. Many times it failed. Here are some examples of its successes and failures.

12. In 1947, the U.N. was faced with a war between India and Pakistan. Both nations had been carved out of the British colony of India soon after World War II. The war began because of a dispute over who owned the rich region of Kashmir (kazh-MEER). Indian troops seized most of Kashmir, but the fighting continued. The U.N. tried to stop the war but failed. Finally, in 1966, the two countries stopped fighting each other.

13. Another crisis developed on the islands of the East Indies. The Dutch had owned and ruled these islands for more than 300 years. During World War II, the Japanese had captured the islands. After the war, the Dutch tried to get back control of the East Indies. However, the people of the islands began a revolt in 1947. The U.N. voted that the islands should be given their independence. The Dutch finally agreed. In 1949, the new nation was named the Republic of Indonesia.

14. Palestine also became a major problem for the U.N. Palestine had been under British rule since the end of World War I. During and after World War II, thousands of Jews fled from Europe to Palestine. After a struggle with Jewish rebels, the British finally gave up their control of Palestine. In 1948, the Jews set up the independent nation of Israel. It was approved by the U.N. and recognized by the United States. But the Arabs in and around Palestine did not want a Jewish state. Five times war broke out between Israel and the neighboring Arab nations. In the first outbreak, a U.N. truce team was led by an American, Dr. Ralph Bunche. It succeeded in getting both sides to stop fighting. In later wars, the U.N. again tried to arrange a cease-fire. But it was unable to bring about a lasting peace.

Dr. Ralph Bunche (center left) conferring with Arab leaders in an attempt to keep peace.

15. One of the greatest challenges to the United Nations was the Korean War. After World War II, Korea had been divided in half by Russian and American troops. The Russians set up a Communist government in North Korea. In South Korea, American troops pulled out after elections were held. In 1950, a Communist-led North Korean army invaded South Korea. The United Nations Security Council decided that North Korea was the aggressor. The U.N. voted to send United Nations fighting forces to Korea. It placed the United States in charge of them. The United States supplied the most men and equipment. But more than a dozen United Nations members sent troops and gave assistance. The fighting finally ended in a truce in 1953.

Israeli troops move into Syria in the 1967 war between Israel and the Arabs. Why do both Arabs and Jews want to control Palestine?

Testing Your Vocabulary

Choose the best answer.

1. The U.N. Charter set up a General Assembly and Security Council. A *charter* is a
   a. law passed by Congress.
   b. constitution.
   c. decision agreed upon by many nations.

2. When local wars start, the United Nations usually sends a truce team to the troubled area. A *truce* is
   a. economic help.
   b. a charter.
   c. a temporary stop in fighting.

Understanding What You Have Read

1. A good title for paragraphs 6 and 7 is
   a. The Crisis in Palestine.
   b. Special Agencies of the U.N.
   c. The United Nations Security Council.
   d. How the United Nations Works.

2. In which paragraphs do you find facts about
   a. the United Nations Secretariat?
   b. the Korean War?

   c. ideas in the Atlantic Charter?
   d. members of the Security Council?

3. The job of the U.N. Secretariat is to
   a. do the U.N. office work.
   b. help trade among nations.
   c. settle disputes among nations.

4. The U.N. Security Council's power to act is limited because
   a. the Security Council has fifteen members only.

b. the Security Council does not include Communist China.

c. any permanent member can veto a decision.

5. The Arabs did not want the state of Israel to exist, mainly because

a. they did not want a Jewish state on land where they lived.

b. the Jews seized the land without paying the Arabs.

c. Israel is near the Suez Canal.

6. India and Pakistan have disagreed for many years about

a. the ownership of Kashmir.

b. the rights of Muslims to visit holy places in India.

c. control of the waters of the Ganges River.

7. The Dutch granted independence to Indonesia in 1949 because

a. the Dutch forces in Indonesia were defeated in war.

b. the United Nations voted for Indonesian independence.

c. most of Indonesia's natural resources have been used up.

8. The permanent home of the U.N. is in

a. Paris.

b. Geneva.

c. New York City.

9. The Fourteen Points were announced by

a. Franklin D. Roosevelt.

b. Woodrow Wilson.

c. Winston Churchill.

10. The U.N. agency that fights disease epidemics throughout the world is

a. U.N.E.S.C.O.

b. I.L.O.

c. W.H.O.

11. The part of the U.N. in which all member nations are represented is the

a. Security Council.

b. General Assembly.

c. Secretariat.

12. Before its independence, Pakistan was controlled by

a. India.

b. Great Britain.

c. China.

13. The United Nations Security Council voted that the Netherlands grant independence to

a. Vietnam.

b. Korea.

c. Indonesia.

14. Before Israel became independent, Palestine was controlled by

a. Great Britain.

b. France.

c. Egypt.

15. The United Nations formed an armed force to fight in

a. Vietnam.

b. Korea.

c. Pakistan.

16. India and Pakistan each claimed the right to own

a. Ceylon.

b. Burma.

c. Kashmir.

17. The United Nations was first organized at the end of

a. World War II.

b. World War I.

c. the Korean War.

Using Original Sources

U.N.E.S.C.O., the United Nations Educational, Scientific, and Cultural Organization, has been one of the most successful U.N. agencies. U.N.E.S.C.O. has its own constitution, or charter. Part of it is printed on page 529.

Charter of UNESCO

. . . Since wars begin in the minds of men it is in the minds of men that the defenses of peace must be constructed; that ignorance of each other's ways and lives has been a common cause throughout the history of mankind of that suspicion and mistrust between the peoples of the world . . . that the great and terrible war which has now ended was a war made possible by the denial of the democratic principles of the dignity, equality, and mutual respect of men and by the propagation [spread] in their place through ignorance and prejudice of the doctrine of the inequality of men and races; that the wide diffusion [spread] of culture and the education of humanity for justice and liberty and peace are indispensable [necessary] to the dignity of man. . . .

Tell whether the following statements are true or false. If a statement is false, change the words in italics to make it true.

According to the Charter of UNESCO:

1. *Wars* begin in the minds of men and here must the defenses of peace be built.
2. *Low living standards* have been a common cause throughout history of mistrust among peoples of the world.
3. One of the causes of *World War I* was the idea that men and races are unequal.
4. All men in all countries should have justice, *liberty*, and peace.
5. The defenses of peace must be constructed *on all national borders.*

Developing Ideas and Skills

USING A MAP

Study the map on page 530 and answer the following questions.

1. Which of these crises involved the United States-Communist rivalry?
   a. the Arab-Israeli Crisis
   b. the Kashmir Crisis
   c. the Korean Crisis
   d. the Indonesian Crisis
2. Which of these crises is still with us today?
   a. the Arab-Israeli Crisis
   b. the Kashmir Crisis
   c. the Korean Crisis
   d. the Indonesian Crisis

In your notebook, match the letters on the map with the crises listed below:

1. Arab-Israeli Crisis
2. Kashmir Crisis
3. Korean Crisis
4. Indonesian Crisis

Some World Crises and The United Nations

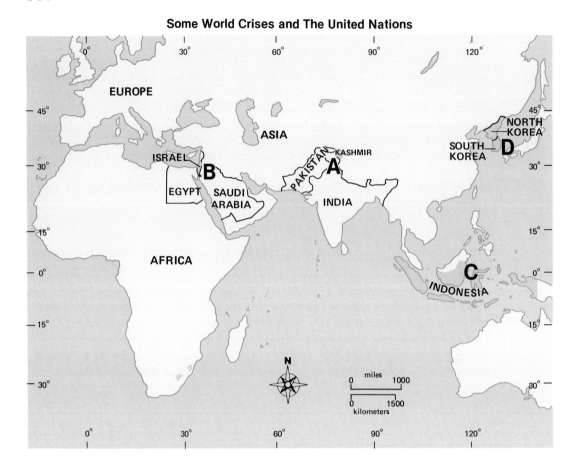

AIM: How did most colonies become independent nations after World War II?

CHAPTER 2

Imperialism Is Weakened

WHAT CAUSED THE NEW NATIONALISM?

1. Have you heard of Zambia, Tanzania, Malawi, or Zimbabwe? These are new independent nations on the map of the world today. When World War II ended, there were about 50 independent nations on earth. Today there are more than three times that number. From where did all of these new nations come? Almost all of them were former colonies. They were owned by Great Britain, France, Italy, the United States, Belgium, and the Netherlands.

2. After World War II, the local leaders of these colonies began to ask for independence. They wanted freedom for their people. They said they would rather be ruled by themselves than be governed by foreigners. Their slogans were "Asia for the Asians," "Africa for the Africans." The same spirit of nationalism that had swept over Europe in the 19th and early 20th centuries now swept over the colonies in Asia and Africa.

3. This new wave of nationalism after World War II was the result of a number of things. The war had been fought in many of these colonies. Local hopes for independence had, as a result, been stirred up. During the war many colonial leaders had fought against the Axis powers. After the war, these men became the leaders of nationalist movements for independence. In addition, the Atlantic Charter was drawn up during the war. It said that all people had the right to choose their own government.

4. Unfriendly relations between the Soviet Union and the United States are called the Cold War. The cold war helped bring on the new nationalism. The Soviet Union tried to spread Communist ideas in colonies. It told colonial people that the Western nations wanted to control them. Giving freedom to colonies, therefore, was one way Western nations could work against Communist propaganda. Finally, people in the free nations of the world began to see that colonialism was not democratic.

HOW DID COLONIAL EMPIRES END?

5. The colonies of the British Empire were among the first to gain independence. In India, a great leader, Mahatma Gandhi, worked for freedom from Great Britain for almost forty years. In 1947, Great Britain granted independence to the people of India. The country was divided into two independent nations: India and Pakistan. This was because in India most

Mahatma Gandhi. What was the main purpose of his leadership?

World War II. A long and bitter civil war in Indo-China forced the French to leave that area. Indo-China was divided into three independent nations: Laos, Cambodia (now called Kampuchea), and Vietnam. In North and Central Africa, the large French empire was divided into a number of independent nations. These included Morocco, Tunis, Chad, Guinea, Dahomey (now called Benin), Mali, Mauritania, Senegal, Malagasy (now called Madagascar), and others. In the French colony of Algeria, however, there were a large number of French citizens, as well as Arabs. At first, the French refused to grant independence to this African territory. But after a long and costly war, France was forced to grant independence to Algeria.

8. Other empires met the same fate as the British and French empires. The East Indies islands had been owned by the Dutch for more than 300 years. The native people rebelled and won their independence in 1949. The East In-

Prime Minister David Ben Gurion proclaiming Israel's independence in 1948. The portrait behind him is that of Theodor Herzl, who began the movement that led to the establishment of an independent homeland for the Jews.

people are Hindus. In Pakistan most people are Muslims. In 1971, East Pakistan broke away from Pakistan to form another new nation, called Bangladesh.

6. Great Britain gave most of its other colonies their freedom. In Asia, it gave independence to Ceylon (now called Sri Lanka), Burma, and Malaya (now Malaysia). In Africa, it gave independence to Ghana, Nigeria, Kenya, Southern Rhodesia (now Zimbabwe), Tanzania, Northern Rhodesia (now Zambia), Malawi, the Sudan, and other colonies. In the Middle East, the Jews of Palestine fought for independence against the British and Arabs. They set up the independent nation of Israel in 1948.

7. The French also lost their empire after

dies became the Republic of Indonesia. In 1946, one year after World War II, the United States gave independence to the Philippine Islands. The Belgian Congo in Africa won its freedom in 1960 after a century of Belgian rule. It became the Democratic Republic of the Congo, and is now called Zaire. In 1962, two smaller Belgian territories in Africa, called Rwanda and Burundi, also became independent.

9. Italy and Japan had been defeated in World War II. Japan was forced to give Manchuria and the island of Formosa (now Taiwan) back to China. Korea also was freed, but by 1948 it was permanently divided. Italy lost all of its colonies in Africa. Ethiopia, which Italy had conquered in 1936, was given its freedom. Emperor Haile Selassie, its former ruler, returned to his throne. Other Italian colonies were given to the United Nations as trusteeships. Later, they also were given independence. Libya, for example, was freed from Italian rule by the Allied victory in North Africa during World War II. In 1951, Libya became an independent Arab nation. Somalia was formed by joining lands once owned by Italy and Great Britain. Somalia became independent in 1960.

WHY DO NEW NATIONS HAVE PROBLEMS?

10. Portugal was the last European nation with a large colonial empire. Angola and Mozambique, the last Portuguese colonies in Africa, were originally set up as trading posts more than 400 years ago. They are both little-developed areas in southern Africa. In both these colonies, nationalist movements for independence began. Other independent nations of Africa demanded that Portugal get out of Africa. The United Nations was asked to help the independence movement. In 1975, Portugal was forced to give up both of these colonies. They became independent nations. After World War I, the Republic of South Africa had been given control of German Southwest Africa.

Today it is called Namibia. Because of fighting by colonial rebels, called *guerrillas*, and pressure from the United Nations, the Republic of South Africa has promised to give Namibia its independence.

11. Independence has made the new nations very proud. Many of them have changed their names. For example, the Belgian Congo, as it was once called, is now called Zaire. British Tanganyika is Tanzania. Rhodesia is now Zimbabwe. And the island of Ceylon is now Sri Lanka. But name-changing has not solved their problems. Many of the new countries have a difficult time remaining free. Rival local leaders try to seize power from one another. Revolts and civil wars are frequent. Many of the people are uneducated. Progress has been made in some of the new nations, but democracy cannot work where large numbers of people cannot read or write. Communist propaganda has added to the unrest in some of the new nations.

These Burmese students are studying to be scientists. Why do the new independent countries place great importance on education?

12. Most of the new nations are also weak economically. They do not have the money to develop their natural resources. They do not have the engineers needed to build railroads, factories, or power plants. Now that they are independent, they can no longer trade freely with their former parent countries. They must, instead, pay tariffs, like all independent nations. They must also find markets to sell their goods. The United States has tried to help many of these developing nations with money loans and gifts. It also sends Peace Corps workers to any nation that asks for them. Peace Corps workers are teachers, nurses, and other trained people.

Testing Your Vocabulary

Choose the best answer.

1. *Colonialism* came to an end after World War II. Colonialism means
   a. defeating native revolts in colonies.
   b. economic development of backward areas.
   c. control of colonies by stronger nations.
2. The United States and the Soviet Union are engaged in a *cold war*. A cold war is a war in which
   a. battles are fought in the winter months only.
   b. there are unfriendly relations but no military action.
   c. the two sides do not trade with each other.

Understanding What You Have Read

1. A good title for paragraphs 2, 3, and 4 is
   a. The End of the British Empire.
   b. The End of World Empires.
   c. Reasons for the New Nationalism.
   d. The New Map of Africa.
2. In which paragraphs do you find facts about
   a. a result of the cold war?
   b. the Portuguese empire?
   c. the division of India into two countries?
   d. civil war in Indo-China?
3. The number of independent nations more than doubled after World War II because
   a. all German colonies were given their independence.
   b. the imperialist movement grew stronger.
   c. colonies became independent.
4. The division of British India into India and Pakistan was based on
   a. differences in weather.
   b. differences in language and customs.
   c. differences in religion.
5. After World War II, France was unwilling to grant independence to Algeria because
   a. many French lived in Algeria.
   b. Algeria is located very close to France.
   c. the people of Algeria did not want independence.
6. France gave independence to Algeria and Indo-China because
   a. the United Nations insisted.
   b. it lost long and costly wars to the nationalist forces in those areas.

c. the Soviet Union threatened war.

7. After World War II, Japan gave up Korea, Manchuria, and the island of Formosa because it
   a. could not put down the revolutions in these areas.
   b. lost these colonies after its defeat in World War II.
   c. wanted to have friendly relations with China.

Tell which of the three choices does not belong with the others.

1. Colonies that once belonged to France
   a. Algeria
   b. Ethiopia
   c. Madagascar
2. Why imperialism ended after World War II
   a. new nationalism
   b. the cold war
   c. the Russian Revolution
3. Colonies that once belonged to Great Britain
   a. Indonesia   b. India   c. Pakistan
4. Former Portuguese colonies
   a. Angola b. Mozambique c. Ghana
5. Countries created out of French Indo-China
   a. Laos   b. Nigeria   c. Vietnam
6. Colonies that once belonged to Belgium
   a. Egypt
   b. Belgian Congo
   c. Rwanda
7. Problems of the new nations of Africa
   a. shortage of engineers
   b. lack of teachers
   c. lack of natural resources
8. Colonies that once belonged to Japan
   a. Siberia   b. Formosa   c. Korea
9. Colonies that once belonged to Italy
   a. Libya   b. Ethiopia   c. Nigeria
10. New nations in Asia
   a. Indonesia
   b. Ghana
   c. Philippine Republic

Developing Ideas and Skills

USING MAPS

Use the two maps on Page 536 to answer the following questions.

1. All of the following African countries were once colonies EXCEPT
   a. Nigeria
   b. Egypt
   c. Libya
2. The greatest number of European colonizing nations were in
   a. Africa
   b. India
   c. Southeast Asia
3. Since World War II, the greatest number of new country names would appear on a map of
   a. the islands of Southeast Asia
   b. continental Asia
   c. Africa
4. Vietnam was once a part of
   a. Burma
   b. the Dutch East Indies
   c. French Indo-China
5. Ceylon is now known as
   a. Malaysia
   b. Sri Lanka
   c. Bangladesh

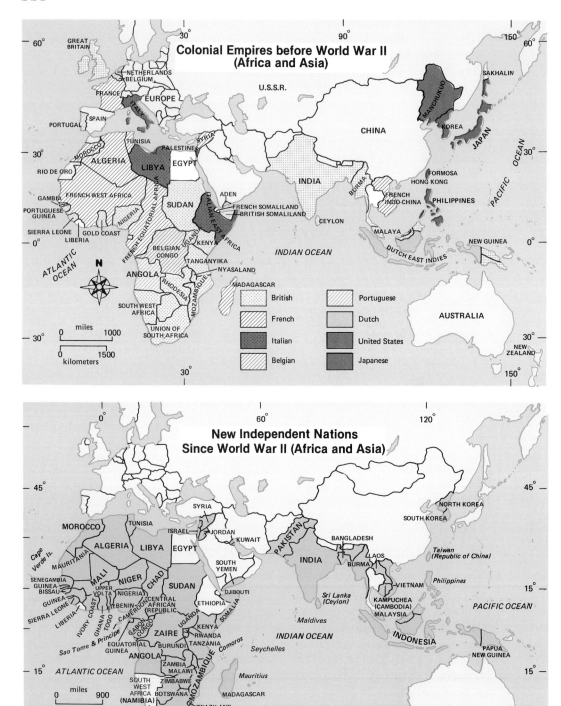

Colonial Empires before World War II (Africa and Asia)

British · French · Italian · Belgian · Portuguese · Dutch · United States · Japanese

New Independent Nations Since World War II (Africa and Asia)

New independent nations since WWII

AIM: What problems face the new African nations today?

CHAPTER 3

New African Nations Emerge

WHAT EVENTS LED TO NATIONALIST MOVEMENTS?

1. Africa, with about 550 million people, is a continent of newly independent nations. Americans and Europeans once knew little about Africa. Today we know a great deal about it. We know also that what happens in Africa will deeply affect future world history.

2. Africa is divided into two parts. In North Africa, along the coast of the Mediterranean Sea, live mainly Arabs and Berbers. They are Muslims. South of the Sahara most of the people are blacks. Some of them are Muslims.

3. Before World War II, most of Africa south of the Sahara Desert was divided into colonies, owned by European nations. After the war, some black African leaders began to look ahead to African independence. They wanted their people to be free of European control. Many Africans had helped the Allies win the war. They had defended European freedom and now wanted their own. At first, Great Britain, France, and Belgium tried to stop this movement. They imprisoned many African leaders. Some Europeans claimed that the Africans were not ready for independence.

4. The nationalist movement could not be stopped, however. Gradually, colony after colony in Africa gained independence. Thirty

King Sobhuza II announced the independence of Swaziland in September of 1968.

years after World War II, there were more than forty new nations in Africa south of the Sahara. These free nations included Ghana, Guinea, Dahomey, Kenya, Mali, Senegal, Zaire, Niger, Zambia, and many others. In North Africa, Morocco, Algeria, Tunisia, and Libya also became free and independent.

HOW HAVE THE NEW AFRICAN NATIONS TRIED TO SOLVE THEIR PROBLEMS?

5. Independence solved some problems for the people of Africa. It also brought new responsibilities and challenges. The most important challenge is to set up strong and long-lasting governments. In some of the African nations, there have been civil wars and military dictatorships. One of the most serious civil wars took place in the Republic of the Congo (Zaire) from 1961 to 1963. This trouble was settled with the help of a United Nations military force. A civil war in Nigeria (1967–69) also caused terrible bloodshed, starvation, and destruction.

6. In Uganda, Idi Amin, a military leader, seized control of the government in 1971. He proclaimed himself dictator. During his eight-year rule, thousands of his own people were murdered. Finally, he was driven out of the country. In Libya, Muammar el-Quaddafi seized power and made himself dictator. Military leaders have also seized power in other countries of Africa.

7. European nations have lost control of almost all of Africa. They still try, however, to keep the favor of the new African governments. The Soviet Union tries to spread communism in Africa. It does this by using propaganda and by lending money. It also sends experts and engineers to Africa. It gives free scholarships to young Africans to study in the Soviet Union. The United States and some nations of Europe use the same methods. But they want the new

nations of Africa to follow the democratic way. Aid from foreign countries helps the new nations of Africa. But at the same time it causes serious problems. The Africans want the foreign aid, but they do not want foreign nations to tell them how to run their governments.

8. Some new nations of Africa also have economic problems. They export only one or two crops. Ghana, for example, grows cacao beans, from which chocolate is made. Gambia and Senegal depend on peanuts. Madagascar depends on its vanilla beans. The main export of Sudan is cotton. "One-crop" countries can get into serious economic trouble. If the world price of their crop falls, or if they have a bad harvest, the country and its people suffer. For this reason, many African nations are trying to develop new industries. They do not want to depend too much upon a single crop or on one source of income.

9. A few countries of Africa are rich in oil and minerals. They are fortunate because minerals and oil are wanted all over the world. Zaire is rich in copper ore, diamonds, and uranium. Ghana and Guinea are rich in aluminum ore. Nigeria is rich in oil. In North Africa, such countries as Algeria and Libya have rich deposits of oil. The Republic of South Africa has rich deposits of diamonds, gold, iron ore, and other minerals. By about 1975, nearly three-fourths of the world's gold and diamonds were mined in Africa.

WHICH PROBLEMS HOLD BACK THE PROGRESS OF AFRICANS?

10. In Africa there are many different ethnic groups. An ethnic group is a society or a people that share a common culture. Their history, religion, and customs are the same or similar. Ethnic groups have their own languages and dialects. When the Europeans divided Africa, some ethnic groups were separated. Countries were formed of people who spoke

African, Asian, and Latin American students attend the Patrice Lumumba Friendship of Peoples University in Moscow. Why does the Soviet Union encourage foreign students to study in Moscow?

many hundreds of languages and dialects. These differences in language among ethnic groups can create problems. It sometimes becomes difficult for a government leader to unite a country where many different languages are spoken. The most common languages among black Africans south of the Sahara Desert are Zulu in South Africa, Swahili in East Africa, and Hausa in West Africa.

11. The Republic of South Africa, at the southern tip of the continent, is the richest country in Africa. It also presents the most serious problem for the blacks of Africa. In the Republic of South Africa there are about 23 million black people. There are also 4.7 million whites, most of whom are called Afrikaners, 2.7 million people of mixed ancestry, and almost one million Asians. Yet the government and industry are run by whites only. The white government follows a strict policy of separating the white people and the African blacks. It is called a policy of apartheid (uh-PART-hyt).

12. Under apartheid, the blacks are forced to live in separate areas from whites. They have little chance to make their lives better. They cannot vote or hold office. They cannot go to white schools or colleges. Naturally, blacks all over Africa resent the government of the Afrikaners. In addition, the Republic of South Africa has failed to give independence to Southwest Africa. This is the last large area in Africa still held as a colony. Today this region is called Namibia. It is a land rich in minerals. Ninety percent of the people are nonwhites. In 1966, the United Nations ordered the Republic of South Africa to give this land its independence. The South Africans promised to do so. But as yet they have not.

13. Rhodesia, as it was called in the past, is another important country in southern Africa. Here, too, live many more blacks than whites. In 1965, the white minority declared Rhodesia independent of Great Britain. In the new government, blacks had almost no voice. For many

539

What do these pictures suggest about the difference in way of life between blacks and whites under apartheid?

years, black guerrillas fought against Rhodesia's white government. Finally, in 1979, the white leaders agreed to let blacks take control of the government. Elections were held. A black leader became prime minister. The name of the country is now Zimbabwe.

Testing Your Vocabulary

Choose the best answer.

1. The *ancestry* of many people in Africa is mixed. *Ancestry* means
   a. one's profession.
   b. the line of descent through parents, grandparents, and others.
   c. one's race or religion.

2. The people of Africa speak many dialects and languages. A *dialect* is
   a. slang.
   b. a variety or different form of a language.
   c. any language similar to English.

Understanding What You Have Read

1. The main idea of paragraphs 3 and 4 is that
   a. there are many population groups in Africa.
   b. civil wars broke out in Africa before World War II.
   c. African nationalism grew after World War II.
   d. the people of North Africa gained their freedom.

2. In which paragraphs do you find facts about
   a. the "one-crop" system of farming?
   b. language problems in Africa?
   c. Africa's mineral resources?
   d. civil war in the Republic of the Congo?
3. The Soviet Union gives economic help to some new African nations in order to
   a. get new colonies.
   b. develop Africa's mineral resources.
   c. help spread communism in Africa.
4. The African continent has two main parts because
   a. the north is industrial and the south is agricultural.
   b. the Sahara Desert separates the people of the north from the south.
   c. the people of the east coast believe in apartheid, but those of the west coast do not.
5. Some African nations still face the challenge of
   a. building strong and long-lasting governments.
   b. developing one-crop economies.
   c. discovering minerals such as gold and diamonds.
6. Zaire is one of the most important new nations of Africa because it
   a. is very large.
   b. has excellent harbors.
   c. has rich mineral resources.
7. The Republic of South Africa follows an apartheid policy because it wants to
   a. raise the national standard of living.
   b. keep government control in the hands of whites.
   c. remain friendly with the United States.

Complete the following statements with the correct word or phrase.

1. Africa is divided into two geographic parts by the _____.
2. The religion of the Arabs in North Africa is _____.
3. The last large area in Africa still held as a colony is _____.
4. Ghana depends mainly on its crop of _____.
5. Societies or peoples with a similar history, religion, and customs are called _____.
6. The African nation that depends mainly on its export of cotton is _____.
7. The policy of the Republic of South Africa by which blacks are separated from whites is called _____.
8. The African country in which a white minority government declared independence is _____.
9. The most common language of the blacks of East Africa is _____.
10. Rich African oil deposits have been found in Algeria and _____.

Developing Ideas and Skills

USING A MAP

Using the information on the map on page 542, answer the questions at the bottom of page 542 in your notebook.

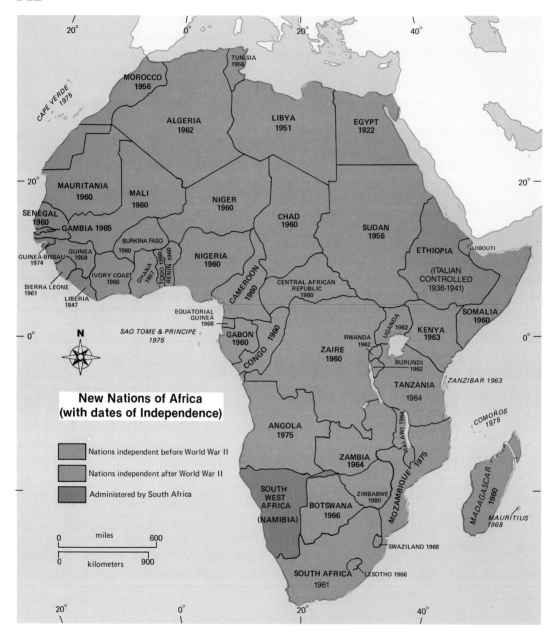

**New Nations of Africa
(with dates of Independence)**

Nations independent before World War II

Nations independent after World War II

Administered by South Africa

TUNISIA 1956
MOROCCO 1956
CAPE VERDE 1975
ALGERIA 1962
LIBYA 1951
EGYPT 1922
MAURITANIA 1960
MALI 1960
NIGER 1960
SENEGAL 1960
GAMBIA 1965
GUINEA-BISSAU 1974
GUINEA 1958
BURKINA FASO 1960
CHAD 1960
SUDAN 1956
ETHIOPIA
DJIBOUTI
NIGERIA 1960
IVORY COAST 1960
GHANA 1957
TOGO 1960
BENIN 1960
SIERRA LEONE 1961
LIBERIA 1847
CAMEROON 1960
CENTRAL AFRICAN REPUBLIC 1960
(ITALIAN CONTROLLED 1936-1941)
SOMALIA 1960
EQUATORIAL GUINEA 1968
SAO TOME & PRINCIPE 1975
GABON 1960
CONGO 1960
RWANDA 1962
UGANDA 1962
KENYA 1963
ZAIRE 1960
BURUNDI 1962
SAO TOME & PRINCIPE
TANZANIA 1964
ZANZIBAR 1963
ANGOLA 1975
MALAWI 1964
COMOROS 1975
ZAMBIA 1964
MOZAMBIQUE 1975
SOUTH WEST AFRICA (NAMIBIA)
BOTSWANA 1966
ZIMBABWE 1980
MADAGASCAR 1960
MAURITIUS 1968
SWAZILAND 1968
SOUTH AFRICA 1961
LESOTHO 1966

N

miles 0 — 600
kilometers 0 — 900

1. Which nations in Africa were independent before World War II?
a. ___ b. ___ c. ___

2. Six nations that gained their independence in the 1950s are: a. ___ b. ___ c. ___ d. ___ e. ___ f. ___

AIM: How are Africans of today changing their ways of living?

CHAPTER 4

New African Nations Try to Solve Problems

HOW IS THE CONTINENT OF AFRICA DIVIDED?

1. The continent of Africa takes up about 20 percent of the earth's land area. It only has about 11 percent of the world's population. But this population continues to grow steadily. In almost every part of Africa, black people are in the majority. In fact, about 98 percent of the people in Africa are of African origin. About two percent are of European or other ancestry.

2. There are many different ethnic groups on the continent. They speak more than 800 different languages. The Ibo are a group of Africans who live in eastern Nigeria. Their language has many dialects, but they all share common values. In the culture of the Ibo there is a stress on democracy and the importance of the individual. The Sudanese are another African group. They live on broad land south of the Sahara. Their art and sculpture are well known. Many museums have displayed their work.

3. The Bantu-speaking peoples are the largest group of black Africans. They live mainly in central and southern Africa. They speak many different languages. In fact, there are over 500 Bantu languages. Often, Bantu groups living in *kraals* (villages) on different sides of the same river speak different languages. In South Africa, there are four main groups of Bantu-speaking peoples. Though these groups may differ in their languages, they are united in their opposition to apartheid.

4. Many white Africans believe that the blacks should be kept in a lower social position than they. In response, some black African leaders feel that white people should have no part in ruling Africa. There is a third group, however, of both blacks and whites. They think that the two groups can work together as equals.

HOW IS AFRICA TRYING TO UNIFY?

5. The new nations of Africa, like all new nations, are faced with challenges. They seek to create strong governments and to build trade. They want to develop natural resources and to build new industries. They seek to improve education, to provide better health care, and to raise living standards. They also want to train more engineers, teachers, doctors, nurses, and chemists. To meet these challenges, African nations have sought help from one another.

The National Library of Nigeria received support from the Ford Foundation to help in the development of Nigeria's cultural and educational life.

Experts in advanced technology from one African country go to train workers in other nations. Also, the United Nations and other countries of the world have provided aid to Africa. A major international concern is to find ways to help Africa provide enough food for its people.

6. Cooperation among the peoples of Africa is not new. Even before World War II, representatives of African nations met. They talked about ways of ending colonialism and imperialism in Africa. In 1945, the sixth Pan African Congress set as its goal freedom and self-government for all of Africa. Twenty years later, this goal was reached by most of the peoples of Africa.

7. In 1963, delegates from almost all the African nations met in Ethiopia. They formed a group called the Organization of African Unity

(O.A.U.). This group is like the United Nations except that only African nations are members. The aim of the Organization of African Unity is to have African nations work together. Its goal is better education, less disease, and more trade and industry. The Organization of African Unity also tries to stop wars and settle boundary disputes between member nations. In 1968, nine nations organized the West African Regional Group to help bring economic unity to the area.

8. The United Nations helps African nations solve their problems. It sends experts from such agencies as the World Health Organization (W.H.O.) and the Food and Agriculture Organization (F.A.O.). The United States has sent trained people to Africa through its Peace Corps. The Soviet Union and Israel send help to those African nations that ask for it. They take help from many foreign nations. But the Africans do not want these countries to gain control of their governments. Having won political independence, they do not want to lose their economic independence.

9. On the North American continent there are three nations: Canada, the United States, and Mexico. On the African continent today there are 54 nations. Many of the nations face similar economic and social problems. The most serious problem is the shortage of food. Across the whole African continent, south of the Sahara, is a region called the Sahel. Millions of blacks live there. Drought, or lack of rain, often occurs in this region. When this happens, wells run dry, crops dry up, cattle die, and people starve.

10. Since World War II, drought and starvation have hit Somalia, Senegal, Ethiopia, Gambia, Uganda, Chad, Mali, and many other African nations. If a country is large, the people of one section can help the people of another. But if a country is small, a drought or crop failure becomes a national disaster. The whole country starves. This is a problem that faces the Organization of African Unity and the new na-

tions of Africa. Each one wants to remain independent. Nevertheless, they need to cooperate with one another in time of need.

HOW IS AFRICA CHANGING?

11. Along with its problems, Africa has its success stories. The Ivory Coast is one of them. This nation has had the same president since its independence from France in 1960. Its economy depends mostly on agriculture. It produces a range of crops to avoid the problems of a "one-crop" country. It is one of the largest exporters of cacao beans. Coffee, bananas, and timber are among the other products that are exported. Diamonds are exported too. Industry is growing in the Ivory Coast. Its factories make chemicals, textiles, and many other products. The French still hold positions in the industry and trade of the Ivory Coast. However, educational programs are bringing more and more Ivorians into these positions.

12. The Ivory Coast began changing its school system in the 1970s. As in other African nations, Ivorian schools were once run by Europeans. Most black people did not have a chance to enter these schools. They also were not taught things that would prepare them for jobs. New school systems throughout Africa are trying to solve these problems. The schools provide both academic and technical training. They also stress the importance of African cultures and languages.

13. While Africa is changing, Africans are becoming more aware of their own history and culture. Research centers are making new discoveries about Africa's past. For years, Western artists used ideas from Africa for their art, music, and dance. From African themes have come much of jazz and modern dance. Today, African artists and performers are becoming known. In the past, mostly European authors wrote about Africa. Today, African writers such as Chinua Achebe and Ngugi wa Thiongo are exploring the themes and ideas of their land.

These photographs show a changed Africa. The picture on the left shows a university graduation in Zambia and the photo on the right shows modern buildings in Kenya.

Testing Your Vocabulary

Choose the best answer.

1. *Kraals* are found in Africa south of the Sahara Desert. A kraal is a
   a. cooking pot made of clay.
   b. kind of village.
   c. tribal chief.
2. The African nations that suffer from *drought*
   a. do not have enough rain.
   b. depend on one crop to keep their economy going.
   c. do not have enough factories to make textiles.

Understanding What You Have Read

1. The main idea of paragraphs 2 and 3 is that
   a. African culture is changing.
   b. European art and music show African influence.
   c. different groups of people live in Africa.
   d. the United Nations gives help to African nations.

2. In which paragraphs do you find facts about
   a. the Bantus of Africa?
   b. African influence on jazz and modern dance?
   c. the forming of the Organization of African Unity?
   d. the number of languages spoken in Africa?

3. The French used to hold most of the important jobs in the Ivory Coast. Today,
   a. there are fewer jobs than before in the Ivory Coast.
   b. the French have all of the jobs.
   c. the Ivorians hold more of the jobs.

4. More and more, African writers are
   a. writing about European culture.
   b. writing about African subjects.
   c. studying in foreign universities.

5. The Organization of African Unity was formed mainly to
   a. unite African nations in case of war.
   b. help African nations work together.
   c. take the place of the United Nations.

6. African culture has influenced modern
   a. architecture and literature.
   b. science and mathematics.
   c. art, music, and dance

7. Everything in Africa is changing very rapidly today because
   a. African nations are developing their industries, trade, and resources.
   b. there are no longer any ethnic groups in Africa.
   c. the climate has been changing.

8. Since the Ivory Coast became independent, it has had
   a. a one-crop economy.
   b. the same president.
   c. an industrial economy.

9. The Organization of African Unity hopes to
   a. drive all whites out of Africa.
   b. bring independence to all of Africa.
   c. irrigate the Sahara Desert.
10. Unlike the colonial school systems, new school programs in Africa try to teach
    a. the importance of African culture.
    b. many European languages.
    c. traditional methods of farming.
11. The new nations of Africa have received help from
    a. Argentina and Brazil.
    b. Switzerland and Romania.
    c. the United States and the Soviet Union.
12. In Africa, the majority of people are of
    a. African origin.

b. European ancestry.
c. Bantu origin.
13. The largest group of blacks in Africa speak
    a. Ibo languages.
    b. Senegalese languages.
    c. Bantu languages.
14. One of the United Nations agencies that helps the new nations of Africa is the
    a. World Health Organization.
    b. Peace Corps.
    c. Organization of African Unity.
15. All of the following were set up after World War II EXCEPT the
    a. Organization of African Unity.
    b. Pan African Congress.
    c. Food and Agriculture Organization.

Using Original Sources

During the 19th century, European patriots wanted unity and independence for their national groups. In the 20th century, black African patriots led a drive for independence from foreign rule. One of these black leaders was Nnamdi Azikiwe. Here are some of the reasons he gave why Nigeria should be independent. After reading this passage, answer the questions below.

An African Leader Speaks Out

There exists in colonial lands a rule which has a stranglehold on the country's economy. I regard the idea of imperialism as a crime against humanity, because it enables any part of the human race which is armed with modern scientific knowledge to rule over less fortunate sections of mankind, simply because the latter are unable to resist the force which supports such rule.

We demand the right to take over responsibility for the government of our country. We demand the right to be free to make mistakes and learn from our experience.

1. According to Nnamdi Azikiwe, why was Europe able to colonize so much of Africa?
2. Why is Azikiwe so opposed to imperialism?
3. If you were an African leader, would you prefer the freedom of self-rule for your people or the protection of being under colonial rule? Explain.
4. Are there any advantages in remaining under the colonial control of a nation like Great Britain?

Developing Ideas and Skills

USING A CHART

Africa: An Overview of Some Underdeveloped Countries (1985 est.)				
Country	Population (in millions)	Life Expectancy	Literacy (percentage of population that can read and write)	Income per person (in dollars)
		male female		
Egypt	44.2	55.9 58.4	41.9	730
Ethiopia	42.0	39.4 42.6	15.0	120
Kenya	19.5	53.7 58.2	47.1	355
Zaire	30.1	45.0 48.0	57.9	171
Chad	4.4	41.5 43.9	17.8	125
Ghana	12.2	49.1 52.5	31	400
Liberia	1.9	54.5 56.2	24	520
Niger	6.0	43.1 46.1	9.8	330
Nigeria	91.4	48.3 51.7	34	775
Zambia	5.6	49.1 52.5	68.6	473
United States	236.1	71.6 76.3	95.5	15,670

1. Which of the African countries in this chart probably has the most developed educational system?
2. Which of the four items—population, life expectancy, literacy, income—do you think gives the clearest idea of how well or badly the people live? (Give reasons for your opinion.)
3. Which of the four items tells you the least about how well or badly the people live? (Give reasons for your opinion.)
4. Why do you think the chart includes facts on the United States?
5. If you were making a chart to show the differences between one country and another, what other items might you include in your chart?

AIM: How have European nations helped one another to improve trade?

CHAPTER 5

Europe Unites Economically

HOW DID WORLD WAR II HURT EUROPE?

1. How does a rich man feel if he suddenly loses his money? Not very well! The nations of Western Europe probably felt the same way after World War II. Western Europe had been one of the richest and most industrialized areas of the world before the war. After the war, it found that it had lost most of its business life. It would take many years to rebuild its industries, its farms, and its trade. The war had been a serious blow to the economic life of Western Europe.

2. The United States helped Europe to recover. Shortly after the war, Congress passed a European Recovery Plan. Its purpose was to help rebuild the economic life of Europe and stop the spread of communism. Under the plan, the United States gave food, money, equipment, and tools to European nations. Billions of American dollars were spent to put Europe back on its feet again. Former enemies, such as Germany and Italy, were included in the program. The European Recovery Plan succeeded. Within a short time, the factories of Western Europe were operating again.

3. The second blow to Europe was its loss of colonies after the war. Great Britain, France, Belgium, Italy, and the Netherlands saw their colonial empires quickly disappear. One colony after another gained its independence. Each lost colony meant lost markets and lost raw materials to its former controlling country.

4. A third economic problem faced Western Europe after the war. The nations again began to charge high tariffs, or taxes, on goods coming from other countries. Tariffs resulted in a reduction in foreign trade. The small nations of Western Europe had a hard time trying to sell their goods. They had trouble getting the raw materials they needed. It was hard to find places to sell their manufactured goods and farm products. To some people in Europe, the economic future looked very dark indeed.

HOW DID EUROPEAN NATIONS COOPERATE?

5. Most European leaders did not give up hope. They asked: "Is there any way we nations of Western Europe can bring back the business

Compare these photos of Hamburg, Germany, in 1945 and Hamburg today. Why was European recovery after World War II so difficult?

and trade we once had?" They saw that the answer was: "Not if each nation works alone." The only hope, said some statesmen, was to learn to work together. France must forget its hatreds and work with its old enemy, Germany. Italy must learn to get along with France. The other countries of Western Europe must learn to do the same. The nations of Europe must forget that they had fought each other and had been rivals for trade. They must begin to work together.

6. The first step in European economic cooperation was taken in 1949. A number of nations met to talk over their common economic problems. The group included Great Britain, France, Italy, West Germany, Greece, Turkey, and eight smaller European countries. These nations set up a Council of Europe. This council was to plan ways in which the nations could work together in both business and government. These countries were to try to set up a United States of Europe. This was not to be a single nation. It was to be more like a confederation of nations.

7. Rebuilding the steel industry was one of the most serious economic problems of Western Europe. Both iron ore and coal are needed to make steel. France was rich in iron ore. Germany and Belgium were rich in coal. Yet the sale of these raw materials from one nation to another was held up by tariffs among the nations. Robert Schuman, a French foreign minister, thought of a way to solve this problem. Let

the countries end their tariffs on coal, iron ore, and steel, he said. Then every nation would be able to manufacture or buy steel. Everyone would benefit. Six nations agreed to the Schuman Plan, as it was called. They were France, West Germany, Italy, and the Benelux (BEN-a-lux) countries of Belgium, the Netherlands, and Luxembourg. From the start, the Schuman Plan was a great success.

8. Five years later the Plan had expanded to include some farm products. It was hoped that the tariffs on other farm and factory products would be ended later. These six cooperating nations became known as the European Common Market. Never before in the history of Western Europe had there been such cooperation among the nations. The European Common Market was a success. Within a few years, the member nations had regained their economic health. Factories were busy. Employment was high. And trade was thriving.

HOW HAS ECONOMIC UNION PROVED HELPFUL?

9. The success of the European Common Market led other European nations to form another economic organization in 1959. This second union was called the European Free Trade Association. It was formed under the leadership of Great Britain. Seven nations who were not members of the Common Market

550

This Englishwoman chose an unusual way to demonstrate her support for the Common Market.

united to try to lower tariffs among themselves. The members of the European Free Trade As-sociation were Great Britain, Sweden, Norway, Denmark, Portugal, Austria, and Switzerland. They were sometimes known as the Outer Seven. Except for Great Britain, these nations did not have large factory industries or large amounts of key raw materials. For these reasons, the European Free Trade Association was not as successful as the Common Market. In 1973, Great Britain, Ireland, and Denmark joined the European Common Market. In 1981, Greece joined too, raising the number of members to ten. Spain and Portugal became members in January 1986, raising the total to twelve.

10. All members of the European Common Market have some form of democratic government. This has made possible political as well as economic cooperation. All members of the Common Market are now also members of the European Parliament and the European Court of Justice. The existence of these organizations shows that the democratic nations of Europe are seriously striving for greater harmony and cooperation.

11. There are also plans for yet more economic cooperation in the years ahead. Today, a traveler in Europe must change the kind of money he uses each time he goes from one country to another. There is a plan to have one kind of money for all of Western Europe. This plan, however, has not yet been approved. Through these and similar plans for cooperation, the nations of Western Europe hope to remain great industrial centers of the world. So far their efforts seem to be successful.

Testing Your Vocabulary

Choose the best answer.

1. The European Common Market brought about *economic cooperation* among the member nations. Economic cooperation means

   a. working together on matters of business and trade.
   b. forming military alliances.
   c. giving up colonies.

2. The European Common Market ended individual country's *tariffs* on many products. Tariffs are
   a. laws to stop spying.
   b. taxes on imported goods.
   c. plans to increase manufacturing.

Understanding What You Have Read _____

1. The main idea of paragraphs 4 and 5 is that
   a. tariffs hurt trade.
   b. the United States sent economic aid to Europe.
   c. European leaders hoped for lower taxes.
   d. there was a need for cooperation among European nations after World War II.
2. In which paragraphs do you find facts about
   a. the European Recovery Plan?
   b. the Schuman Plan?
   c. the European Common Market?
   d. the European Parliament?
3. Robert Schuman proposed his European iron and steel plan because
   a. some European nations had iron ore whereas others had coal.
   b. he wanted to improve relations between France and Germany.
   c. the United States promised to support the plan.
4. Fourteen nations decided to set up a Council of Europe in 1949 because
   a. they wanted a military alliance to stop communism.
   b. the United States wanted them to become allies.
   c. they saw the need for economic and political cooperation.
5. The European Common Market was more successful than the European Trade Association because it
   a. included a larger number of member nations.
   b. had one form of money for all of its member nations.
   c. had key raw materials and large factory industries.
6. Western Europe quickly rebuilt its economic life after World War II because
   a. the Common Market was set up shortly after the war.
   b. the United States gave large amounts of economic aid.
   c. Great Britain gave economic aid to France and West Germany.
7. One reason why the United States helped its former enemies Germany and Italy after the war was because the United States wanted to
   a. stop the spread of communism.
   b. form an alliance with the Soviet Union.
   c. get former German and Italian colonies.

Tell whether the following statements are true or false. If a statement is false, change the words in italics to make it true.

1. The main raw materials needed to make steel are iron ore and *copper*.
2. Today, the European Common Market has *eight* members.
3. Before the European Common Market was formed, trade among nations was restricted by high *tariffs*.
4. The nations of Europe lost their colonies after *World War I*.
5. The Benelux nations include Belgium,

the Netherlands, and *Luxembourg*.
6. The European Recovery Plan was drawn up by the *United States*.
7. The plan to cut tariffs in Europe was first proposed by *Robert Schuman*, of France.
8. *Poland* was one of the last nations admitted to the European Common Market.
9. All member nations of the European Common Market are in Western Europe except *Greece*.
10. All member nations of the European Common Market have some form of *democratic* government which makes political cooperation possible.

Developing Ideas and Skills

USING A CHART

The World's Great Economic Powers (during a recent year)				
	European Common Market**	United States	Soviet Union	Japan
Area (square miles)	640,593	3,623,420	8,649,490	147,470
Population (millions)	273	236	272	119
Gross National Product* ($ billions)	$2,217	$3,701	$706	$1,200
Exports ($ billions)	$621	$218	$62	149
Automobile Production	9,328,000	7,770,000	1,300,000	7,150,000

*Gross National Product means the value of all final goods and services produced in a nation during a year. **Except for Spain and Portugal

Using the information in this chart, choose the best answer for each of the questions below.

1. The European Common Market is the largest economic power in terms of
   a. gross national product and population.
   b. automobile production and exports.
   c. area and automobile production.
2. The economic unit with the highest Gross National Product is
   a. the Soviet Union.
   b. the European Common Market.
   c. the United States.
3. The Soviet Union leads the United States in

   a. population and automobile production.
   b. area and population.
   c. gross national product and exports.
4. The gross national product of the European Common Market is larger than that of
   a. Japan and the Soviet Union combined.
   b. the United States and Japan combined.
   c. the United States and the Soviet Union combined.

AIM: Why did communism spread so rapidly after World War II?

CHAPTER 6

Communism Spreads in Europe and Asia

HOW DID COMMUNISM SPREAD TO EASTERN EUROPE?

1. Before World War II, the Soviet Union was the only Communist country in the world. Today, one-third of the world's people live under Communist governments. The spread of communism since the end of World War II has troubled the free nations who believe in democracy. Growing Communist power has caused a "cold war" between the free nations and the Communist nations. It has also led to dangerous "hot wars" in Korea and Vietnam.

2. The free nations fought the Second World War to end dictatorships in Nazi Germany, Fascist Italy, and militarist Japan. But after the war, equally dangerous Communist dictatorships arose in many countries. Why did communism spread after World War II? During the war, the United States, the Soviet Union, and the other Allies all fought the same enemy: Nazi Germany. Thus the United States sided with the Communists in Russia in order to defeat the Nazis in Germany.

3. In the last year of the war, Russian forces drove the Nazi armies out of the Soviet Union. The Nazis were also driven out of the countries of Eastern Europe. These include Po-

land, Romania, Bulgaria, Hungary, and Czechoslovakia. Each of these countries set up a Communist form of government. They were aided by the Soviet Union and backed by its army. The United States and the Allied powers were unable to prevent this. In Yugoslavia, Marshal Tito set up a Communist government. In Albania, the Communist party won a major election after the war. It also set up a Communist government.

4. Three years after the war, seven countries of Eastern Europe were Communist. They have remained so to the present time. The Soviet Union has a great deal of power in all of these countries, except Yugoslavia and Albania. In Yugoslavia, the government under Marshal Tito (TEE-toh) refused to take orders from Moscow. Since 1978, Albania has had nothing to do with most other Communist countries. In 1956, the Hungarians tried to throw off Soviet control, but failed. Czechoslovakia tried, in 1968, to lessen Soviet control by peaceful means. It also failed. And in the 1980s, organized labor in Poland was in revolt against Poland's Soviet-dominated government. You recall that the Allies and the Soviet Union could not agree on a treaty for Germany. Because of this, the Soviet Union was able to set up a Communist government in East Germany: the German Democratic Republic. Thus, as a result of World War II, most of Eastern Europe is ruled by Communist dictatorships.

HOW DID THE COMMUNISTS WIN CONTROL IN CHINA?

5. The spread of Communist ideas in Asia started before World War II. Small Communist movements began in China, Burma, the Dutch East Indies, and even in the American-owned Philippine Islands. Only in China did the Communists succeed in taking over the government. The struggle between Communist and Nationalist (non-Communist) forces in China started in 1927. At that time Communist leaders began to win over the poor peasants by promising them food and land.

6. The Communist Chinese forces grew in strength. They became a serious threat to the Nationalist Chinese government of Chiang Kai-shek (CHANG-KY-SHEK). Soon a civil war broke out. For ten years (1927–37) the civil war raged between the Nationalist and Communist armies in China. Neither side could win a clear-cut victory. The Nationalist government of Chiang Kai-shek was weakened by its many selfish and dishonest leaders.

7. The Japanese invaded China in 1937. The civil war was still going on. The Nationalist and Communist Chinese called a truce. They united to fight the Japanese invaders. The Japanese were finally driven out of China at the end of World War II. As soon as this happened, the civil war between the Nationalists and Communists began once more in China.

8. The United States gave aid to the Nationalists. Yet year by year the Nationalists under Chiang Kai-shek grew weaker. At last the well-organized Communist army defeated the Nationalists. In 1949, Chiang-Kai-shek and his Nationalist army fled to the island of Formosa (now Taiwan). A Communist nation, the People's Republic of China, was formed on main-

Chiang Kai-shek. Name at least one factor that weakened the Nationalist government of China.

land China under Mao Zedong. Today, China has over a billion people. This is more than four times the population of the United States.

WHICH NATIONS ARE COMMUNIST TODAY?

9. Six other nations have also become Communist. These are North Korea, Vietnam, Cambodia (now Kampuchea), Cuba, Laos, and Afghanistan. At the end of World War II, Korea was taken from the Japanese. American and Soviet armies moved in. In North Korea, the Russians formed a Communist government. In South Korea, the United States helped the people set up a pro-American government. In 1950, a North Korean army invaded South Korea. This invasion was stopped by the United States and other United Nations members. They sent armies to drive out the Communist invaders. This action was called the Korean War, of 1950–53.

10. After World War II, the people of Indo-China rebelled against their French rulers. After years of fighting, the French were de-

Mao Zedong controlled China's artistic, intellectual, and agricultural policies as well as its military and industrial plans.

feated, in 1954. At a Geneva conference, the French agreed to divide Indo-China into three independent countries. These were Cambodia (Kampuchea), Laos, and Vietnam. The Communists were given control of North Vietnam. Elections to unite Vietnam were never held. The Communists, helped by China, began a civil war to win control of South Vietnam. The United States sent an army to fight the Communists. Neither side could win a final victory. In 1973, the United States withdrew the last of its forces. Two years later, South Vietnam fell to the Communists. Cambodian Communists won control of their government in the same year. Laos was taken over by Communists in 1975.

11. The island of Cuba is only 90 miles from the United States. A revolution in Cuba in 1958 forced the dictator, Fulgencio Batista, to leave the island. Fidel Castro, the leader of the revolution, took control of the government.

The new government began to take away private property from its owners. Land and industries were taken over by it. In 1961, Castro declared Cuba to be a Communist state. Cuba thus became the first nation in the Americas to have a Communist form of government.

12. When the Communists took control of China, in 1949, they were friendly with the Soviet Union. Beginning in 1960, however, conflicts began to divide the Chinese and Soviet leaders. The Chinese believed that Communists should try to bring about Communist revolutions in all countries. The Russian leaders wanted to use their strength to build up their own country. The Chinese and Russians also had boundary disputes. These arguments brought about a deep split between Communist

Fidel Castro during the revolution against Batista. Name one change made by Castro after he took control of the government.

China and Communist Russia. But both of these nations remain rivals of the United States.

13. The Soviet Union and Cuba have continued to spread the influence of communism. They have aimed their propaganda at the so-called Third World countries. These include many of the new nations in Africa created since World War II. It also includes developing nations in Latin America, the Middle East, and Asia. Cuba has sent arms and troops to help Communist guerrilla forces in other countries. Cuban military forces were sent to help Communist guerrillas in Central America and in Africa. Soviet military forces invaded Afghani-

stan in 1980. There they set up a pro-Soviet, Communist government.

14. The United States fears that communism may spread to the Philippines. For 20 years, President Ferdinand Marcos had run the government. It had become more and more like a dictatorship. Then, in 1986, the widely popular Corazon Aquino became President. Even some military leaders supported Aquino because Marcos's rule had been so corrupt and harsh. The United States welcomes the idea of a democracy under Mrs. Aquino. But they fear that the Communist-led New People's Army may try to seize control of the government.

Testing Your Vocabulary

Choose the best answer.

1. Cuba is the first Communist country in the *Americas*. The word *Americas* refers to the nations of
   a. South America.
   b. North America.
   c. the Western Hemisphere.

2. *Eastern Europe* today is made up of many Communist countries. Eastern Europe refers to the part of Europe
   a. east of the Soviet Union.
   b. west of the Soviet Union.
   c. east of China.

Understanding What You Have Read

1. A good title for paragraphs 9 and 10 is
   a. Causes of the Spread of Communism.
   b. The Wars in Korea and Vietnam.
   c. Communism in China.
   d. Communism in Eastern Europe.
2. In which paragraphs do you find facts about
   a. the population of China?
   b. Yugoslavia's attitude toward the Soviet Union?
   c. the defeat of Nationalist China?
   d. communism in Cuba?
3. Poland, Czechoslovakia, and Bulgaria became Communist countries because
   a. the Nazis did not try to conquer these

   countries.
   b. Soviet armies overran them while fighting the Nazi forces during World War II.
   c. the people in these countries voted in free elections for a Communist form of government.
4. Yugoslavia is not friendly with the Soviet Union today because it
   a. does not have a Communist form of government.
   b. does not have a border on the Soviet Union.
   c. has refused to take orders from Moscow.

5. The Communist movement in China had its beginnings before World War II because
   a. the Communists promised the peasants bread and land.
   b. the Japanese invaded China.
   c. Chiang Kai-shek led a rebellion against the government.
6. The Chinese Nationalists were defeated by the Communists partly because
   a. many of the Nationalists were selfish and dishonest.
   b. the United States would not aid the Nationalists.
   c. the Soviet Union supported the Communists.
7. North Korea failed to defeat South Korea in 1950 because
   a. the Chinese Communists did not support the North Koreans.
   b. the United Nations cut off aid to North Korea.
   c. the United Nations sent a military force to help South Korea.

Test your sense of time. Arrange the items in each group in the order in which they took place.

A. Group I
   1. civil war starts in Vietnam
   2. United States sends military forces to Vietnam
   3. Indo-China is divided

B. Group II
   1. Communist government set up in Poland
   2. Communist government set up in the Soviet Union
   3. Communist government set up in Cuba

C. Group III
   1. Korean War
   2. World War II
   3. war in Vietnam

D. Group IV
   1. Marshal Tito sets up a Communist government in Yugoslavia
   2. Mao Zedong takes control of Communist China
   3. Fidel Castro takes control of Cuba

Developing Ideas and Skills

USING A MAP

Study the map on page 559. Then answer the following questions.

1. The largest land area that is Communist controlled is in
   a. Asia
   b. Europe
   c. the Americas
2. The Communist country farthest from other Communist countries is
   a. Vietnam
   b. Cuba
   c. East Germany

List in your notebook under the headings "Asia," "Europe," and "The Americas" the communist nations of the world today.

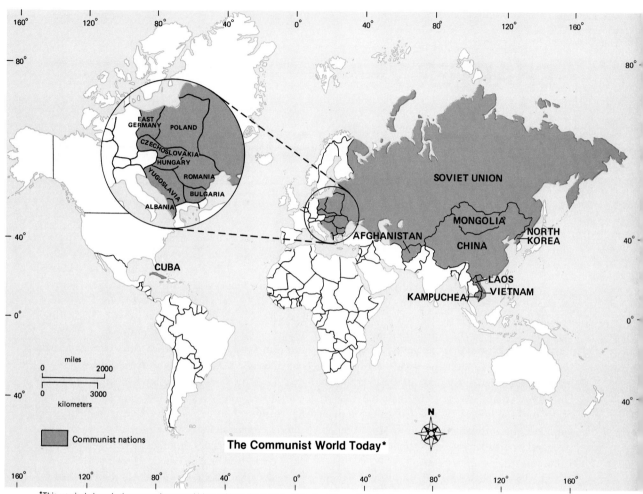

EAST
GERMANY
POLAND
CZECHOSLOVAKIA
HUNGARY
YUGOSLAVIA
ROMANIA
BULGARIA
ALBANIA

SOVIET UNION

MONGOLIA

NORTH
KOREA

AFGHANISTAN

CHINA

CUBA

LAOS
VIETNAM
KAMPUCHEA

miles
0   2000

0   3000
kilometers

N

Communist nations

The Communist World Today*

*This map includes only those countries most widely considered Communist. Other countries, not included, have ties to the Soviet Union or China, or have governments in which Communist influence is strong.

AIM: How did the United States meet the challenge of communism?

CHAPTER 7

A World Divided

HOW DID COMMUNIST POWER GROW?

1. A nation is called a great power if it has great strength, wealth, and size. When World War II began, there were a number of great powers. These were Great Britain, France, Italy, Japan, Germany, the Soviet Union, and the United States. After the war, the European nations and Japan lost most of their colonies. Only two great powers remained: the United States and the Soviet Union. The other nations were still important. But in military strength, size, and wealth they were far behind the Soviet Union and the United States.

2. As we have learned, the Soviet Union set up Communist governments in many countries after the war. Among these countries were Poland, Romania, Bulgaria, and other nations of Eastern Europe. Soviet leaders also helped the Chinese Communists defeat the Nationalist Chinese. Only one great power was left to oppose the Soviet Union: the United States.

3. The Communists found many people who were willing to listen to their propaganda after World War II. In Europe, factories and farms had been destroyed. Millions of workers had no jobs. There was poverty and hunger in many countries. To starving men and women, the Communist promise of "bread" was more important than a promise of "liberty." In

France, Italy, and Germany, Communist parties grew quickly. There was a chance that all of Europe might become Communist. Many American leaders saw this as a danger. They feared that their victory in World War II would be wasted if Communist dictatorships took the place of Nazi and Fascist dictatorships. Communism seemed a dangerous threat to American ideas of democracy and freedom.

4. After the war, the Soviet Union spread communism in two ways. One was by force, or aggression. Another was to destroy non-Communist governments by propaganda. How could the spread of communism be stopped? In the years after World War II, the United States used three methods to keep communism from spreading. These were: economic help, military alliances, and military force.

WHAT U.S. ACTIONS AIDED EUROPE?

5. One of the first American leaders to see the growing threat of world communism was President Harry S. Truman. In 1947, he announced a plan that became known as the Truman Doctrine. Under this plan, the United States promised to give food, machinery, and supplies to all free nations that were threatened by communism. The Truman Doctrine was soon

LULL

What do you think is meant by the title of this cartoon? Why do you think the artist used a spider's web to join the military alliances representing the two super powers?

expanded by the Marshall Plan. Finally, it became known as the European Recovery Program.

6. Under this program, billions of dollars in food, farm and factory machinery, and arms were sent to France, Italy, West Germany, and a number of other nations in Western Europe. The European Recovery Program was successful. Business in Western Europe showed new life. Millions of people returned to work. The spread of communism was stopped in Western Europe, Greece, and Turkey. Could it be stopped in the rest of the world?

7. In 1949, President Truman and the United States Congress drew up another plan. It became known as the Point Four Program. Under this plan, the United States provided help to poor and developing nations in Asia, Africa, and Latin America. The United States gave money and tools to the poor nations to improve farming methods and to develop their resources. It gave money to build factories, power plants, hospitals, and schools. The goal

was to improve living conditions and raise the standards of living in poor countries.

8. It was hoped that this would stop the spread of communism in developing countries. Dozens of foreign nations received a share of American aid under the Point Four Program. These included India, Pakistan, Iran, Jordan, the Philippines, Indonesia, and many others. In the 20 years after World War II, the United States spent more than one hundred billion dollars to help foreign countries. It was the price paid to stop the spread of communism.

9. President John F. Kennedy believed that the giving of American money and supplies was not enough to make foreign countries turn away from communism. President Kennedy had another idea. Under his plan young American men and women could go to less-developed countries as members of a Peace Corps. Many countries asked for these volunteers. Young Americans joined the Peace Corps to work in other countries as teachers, nurses, farm experts, and engineers.

A Peace Corp volunteer works in Zambia, Africa.

WHY WERE MILITARY ALLIANCES FORMED?

10. American aid helped limit the effects of Communist propaganda in poor countries. But there was another danger. If Communists could not take control of a country by revolution, they might still try to do so by a military invasion. A military union, or alliance, of free countries seemed the best way to meet this threat. The United States took the lead in forming such alliances. The United States and the republics of Latin America signed the Rio Pact, in 1947. By this treaty they agreed to fight together if any nation in Latin America were attacked.

11. Two years later, in 1949, the North Atlantic Treaty Organization (NATO) was formed by fourteen nations. Its purpose was to stop any Communist military force in Europe. The members promised to help one another if any one of them were attacked by an enemy power. The enemy they all had in mind was, of

Former NATO leaders from left to right: Lieutenant General Paul Ely, France; General Omar Bradley, United States; Lord A.N. Fedder, Great Britain; Lieutenant General W.D. Crittenburger, U.S. deputy representative.

course, the Soviet Union. Today, NATO members include the United States, Canada, Great Britain, Denmark, West Germany, Greece, Turkey, Italy, and eight other nations. In 1966, France withdrew its armed forces from NATO. However, it is still a member of NATO.

12. A third military alliance was formed by the United States in 1954. Its purpose was to protect the nations of Southeast Asia. This organization was called the Southeast Asia Treaty Organization (SEATO). It included Australia, New Zealand, Pakistan, the Philippine Republic, Thailand, France, Great Britain, and the United States. Great Britain also organized a Central Treaty Organization (CENTO), in 1959. CENTO included Great Britain, Turkey, Iran, and Pakistan.

13. Because of these alliances, the Soviet Union formed one of its own. It set up a military organization with its Communist allies in Central Europe. This was known as the Warsaw Pact. Thus the United States and its allies formed one world. The Soviet Union and *its* allies formed a second, or Communist, world. Some nations did not join either the Warsaw Pact or any of the free-world alliances. These were called the Third World or neutralist nations. They did not take sides. The neutralist or Third World nations included India, Burma, Indonesia and most of the new nations of Africa. After the Vietnam War (1975), SEATO and CENTO came to an end.

Testing Your Vocabulary

Choose the best answer.

1. The United States and the Soviet Union are called *great powers* because they
   a. won in World War II.
   b. have the largest populations in the world.
   c. have the most resources and the strongest military forces.

2. The Soviet Union spread communism by *aggression*. To do something by aggression means to
   a. use force.
   b. use peaceful methods.
   c. use only propaganda.

Understanding What You Have Read

1. A good title for paragraphs 10 through 12 is
   a. The Threat of Communist Invasion.
   b. United States Foreign Aid Program.
   c. Military Alliances Against Communism.
   d. The Signing of the Rio Pact.

2. In which paragraphs do you find facts about
   a. the Peace Corps?
   b. the purpose of Truman's Point Four Program?
   c. the Southeast Asia Treaty Organization?
   d. the Third World nations?

3. The Truman Doctrine was announced

in 1947 because the United States wanted to
a. stop the spread of communism.
b. keep Europe out of the affairs of Latin America.
c. help the Nationalist Chinese fight the Chinese Communists.

4. The North Atlantic Treaty Organization (NATO) was formed because the United States wanted to
a. allow free trade among member nations.
b. keep peace among member nations.
c. protect member nations from Communist attack.

5. India and Indonesia are called neutralist nations today because they
a. did not fight in World War II.
b. refuse to join American or Soviet military alliances.
c. refuse to accept American or Soviet economic help.

6. President Kennedy suggested the setting up of a Peace Corps because he
a. wanted young American men and women to work in less-developed countries.
b. planned to form an army to fight communism.
c. hoped the Corps would help the United Nations.

7. After World War II, many people in Europe began to accept the ideas of communism because
a. Communists promised freedom and independence.
b. Communists promised food and jobs.
c. the United States would not give Europeans economic help.

8. The American president who started the United States foreign aid program was
a. John F. Kennedy.
b. Franklin D. Roosevelt.
c. Harry S. Truman.

9. The United States's military alliance with nations of Asia was the
a. North Atlantic Treaty Organization.
b. Southeast Asia Treaty Organization.
c. Rio Pact.

10. Members of the Central Treaty Organization included Great Britain, Turkey, and
a. Pakistan. b. Egypt. c. India.

11. The Rio Pact was an American military alliance with the nations of
a. Europe. b. Latin America.
c. Africa.

12. President John F. Kennedy set up the
a. North Atlantic Treaty Organization.
b. Peace Corps.
c. Marshall Plan.

13. The Soviet military alliance of Communist nations is called the
a. Moscow Pact. b. Berlin Pact.
c. Warsaw Pact.

14. Communist propaganda in developing poor countries usually promised to give the people
a. food. b. colonies. c. freedom.

Developing Ideas and Skills

WRITING AN OUTLINE

Complete the following outline in your notebook.

Stopping the Spread of Communism

    I. Why communism was spreading after World War II
       A. Factories and farms destroyed
       B.
       C.
   II. Economic help to stop the spread of communism
       A. Truman Doctrine
       B.
       C.
       D.
  III. Military alliances to stop communism
       A. Rio Pact
       B. North Atlantic Treaty Organization
       C.

TURNING POINTS

Government

Africa: Jomo Kenyatta

After World War II, many Africans began to think about independence from their European rulers. In the country of Kenya, many people wanted independence from Britain. One of the leaders in the movement for self-government was Jomo Kenyatta.

Jomo Kenyatta was a member of the Kikuyu. These people are an ethnic group who live in central Kenya. Most Kikuyu of Kenyatta's time were very poor. Kenyatta organized the Kikuyu and other Kenyans into a political party. The party worked to bring unity to the different peoples of Kenya. It also demanded the right to vote. The party wanted better living conditions for the Africans of Kenya.

Unfortunately, a few members of the party began committing secret acts of terrorism. The British accused Kenyatta of being the leader. Kenyatta, who argued that he was innocent, was sent to jail. He remained imprisoned from 1953 to 1961.

Kenya finally gained its indepenence in 1963. Jomo Kenyatta became its first prime minister. In 1964 his title was changed to president. His policy was called *Harambee*. In the Swahili language that means "Let us all pull together." Kenyatta's government worked to develop new businesses, to increase trade, and to improve education. Kenyatta served as his nation's leader until his death in 1978.

Critical Thinking

1. Why would a colonial power disapprove of a person like Kenyatta?
2. Why do you think it was important for Kenyatta to unify the people of Kenya?

AIM: How has the Cold War between the United States and the Soviet Union been fought?

CHAPTER 8

The Cold War

The Berlin Wall divides East and West Berlin. Why has it become a dramatic symbol of the Cold War?

WHAT IS THE COLD WAR?

1. What is the difference between a "cold war" and a "hot war"? In a cold war there are no military battles or bombings. A cold war is fought with name-calling, propaganda, spies, and *subversion*. Any plot to overthrow or ruin a government is an example of subversion. A cold war has been going on in the world for more than three decades. On one side are the free nations of the world, led by the United States. On the other side are the Communist nations, who generally follow the lead of the Soviet Union.

2. During World War II, the United States and the Soviet Union fought together to defeat Nazi Germany. Once the war was over, however, the two nations became bitter rivals. Hardly a year has passed since the end of the war without some kind of crisis between the two nations. Why did two nations that had previously been allies later become such enemies? There are many reasons.

3. The United States and the Soviet Union have different systems of government and business. The Soviet Union is a dictatorship. The American government is a democracy. Under the Soviet Communist system, the government runs and owns all businesses, factories, and farms. The American economic system is different. It is based largely on *private enterprise*—people running their own businesses. They are allowed to make profits for themselves. Their private property is protected. These political and economic differences are part of the reason for rivalry between the two nations.

4. After World War II, the United States and the Soviet Union could not agree on a treaty for Germany. They finally divided Germany into two separate nations. In West Germany, free elections were held. The people set up a democratic government. It is called the Federal Republic of Germany. In East Germany, however, the Soviet Union set up a Communist government. It is called the German Democratic Republic.

5. In the United Nations, the Soviet Union and the United States became leaders of two rival groups. The Communist nations generally followed the lead of the Soviet Union. Many of the non-Communist nations generally followed the lead of the United States. In almost every world crisis that came before the United Nations, the Communist and non-Communist nations seemed to be on opposite sides. There was also a third group of nations in the U.N.: the non-aligned countries. These nations tried to be neutral in the cold war. They did not support either side. Today, the nonaligned nations include India, Pakistan, Indonesia, Kenya, Nigeria, Egypt, and many others.

WHAT CRISES HAVE MARKED THE COLD WAR?

6. The Berlin crisis of 1948–49 is a good example of a cold-war conflict. At the end of World War II, the Allies agreed to divide the city of Berlin into four parts. But the Soviet leaders tried to force the Allies out of the city. They blockaded, or cut off, roads leading to the Allied part of Berlin. The United States, in turn, used hundreds of planes in a great airlift to supply Berlin with food. Thus, the Communist blockade failed. In this crisis no shots were fired. Yet the outbreak of a new world war was a real possibility. In 1961, the Communists built a wall between the Communist and non-Communist sections of Berlin. This wall has become a symbol of the cold-war hostility between the Communist and the free world.

7. Another crisis developed in 1983. A Korean Air Lines passenger plane was shot down over Soviet airspace. All 269 people on the Korean plane died. A U.S. congressman and 59 other Americans were among those killed. The Soviets claim the Korean plane was on a spy mission. But President Reagan called the Soviet shooting an "act of violence." He protested to the United Nations. He closed two Soviet airlines offices. No war broke out, but cold war tensions became worse.

8. The cold war has been going on for many years. Any civil war in some small country might find the two great powers trying to help the opposing sides. This happened during the civil wars in Zaire (the Republic of the Congo in 1961 and during the Vietnam War and the Arab-Israeli Wars of 1956, 1967, and 1973. It happened when the Soviet Union invaded Afghanistan in 1979–80. It also happened during the civil war in Angola in 1975–78.

9. The nuclear arms and missile race is another reason for the cold war. For many years the United States and the Soviet Union could not agree on a plan to control the testing and buildup of atomic weapons and missiles. Finally, in 1963, the two nations signed a nuclear-test-ban treaty. This agreement did not stop the manufacture of nuclear weapons; it only stopped the testing of these weapons above ground. In 1985, President Reagan and Soviet leader Gorbachev held a summit meeting. They discussed arms control and nuclear testing. They did not reach any real agreement. Meanwhile, more nations have learned how to make atomic bombs and the missiles to deliver them. The world continues to live under a threat of nuclear destruction.

WHAT METHODS ARE USED IN THE COLD WAR?

10. The Communists have said in the past that they hope to destroy democracy and capitalism all over the world. One Soviet dictator,

The Hungarian revolt of 1956 was an attempt by the Hungarian people to resist Communist domination of their country.

Nikita Khrushchev, referring to the United States, declared: "We will bury you." The goal of the Soviet Union is to make the whole world Communist. Fortunately, this desire, and American opposition to it, have not led to a third world war. Instead, the two sides have so far kept their battles within the limits of the cold war.

11. The Soviet Union and Cuba have sent their agents to other countries to encourage Communist movements. These agents have come to the new nations of Asia and Africa and the older nations of Latin America. They have stirred up strikes, riots, and even killings. Guerrillas have been given weapons. Terrorist bombings have been encouraged. When a country has been weakened by these methods, then the chances for a Communist takeover are increased. Poverty has also led people in many developing countries to accept Communist ideas.

12. The cold war is in part a battle of ideas of how people should live and be governed. Both sides can claim some victories in the cold war. Sometimes the relations between the United States and the Soviet Union become more friendly for a short time. This easing of tensions is called *detente* (day-TANT). But then a new crisis occurs and the cold war starts up again.

13. Communist China has played a strange role in the cold war. For many years, the United States voted against admitting the People's Republic of China to the U.N. In 1971, the United States dropped its objections. China was admitted. But China and the Soviet Union continued a quarrel that began years before.

The Soviets invaded Czechoslovakia in order to enforce Communist rule in that country.

They argued over Communist policies. They argued over the boundary between Siberia and China. They also clashed over policies in Southeast Asia. These arguments led to threats of war by both sides. Thus, the two largest Communist nations, China and the Soviet Union, became enemies. Meanwhile, relations between the United States and China became more friendly. American presidents visited China. Trade agreements were signed. China was opened to American tourists. An era of improved relations began between the two nations. Thus, as the cold war continues, nations seek new friends and challenge old enemies.

Testing Your Vocabulary

Choose the best answer.

1. When one nation tries to destroy another by *subversion* it
   a. plots to overthrow the lawful government.
   b. organizes a military force.
   c. tries to win elections.

2. The Soviet Union blockaded all the roads leading to Berlin. To *blockade* means to
   a. destroy.
   b. rebuild.
   c. cut off.

Understanding What You Have Read

1. The main idea of paragraph 4 is
   a. Communist China is not a member of the United Nations.
   b. the cold war began in 1949.
   c. the United States and Soviet Union could not agree on a treaty for Germany.
   d. a nuclear-test-ban treaty has been signed.
2. In which paragraphs do you find facts about
   a. the Berlin Blockade?
   b. the meaning of a cold war?
   c. the nuclear-test-ban treaty?
   d. the division of Germany?
3. The nuclear-test-ban treaty between the Soviet Union and the United States was important because it stopped the
   a. manufacture of nuclear weapons.
   b. wartime use of nuclear weapons.
   c. testing of nuclear weapons above ground.

4. In the Berlin crisis of 1948–49, the Soviet Union
   a. gave up its share of Berlin.
   b. built a wall separating East and West Berlin.
   c. blocked routes by which the United States reached the Allied section of Berlin.
5. In 1983, the United States protested to the United Nations because
   a. two Soviet airline offices were shut down in the United States.
   b. the Soviets shot down a Korean Air Lines passenger plane.
   c. a Korean Air Lines passenger plane landed in the U.S.S.R. without asking permission.
6. One issue that China and the Soviet Union quarreled about was the
   a. admission of China to the United Nations.

b. civil war in Zaire.

c. boundary between Siberia and China.

7. The basic reason why there is a cold war between the Communist nations and the democratic nations is that the Communists

a. fear the military power of the United States.

b. do not like the United States' system of military alliances.

c. want to destroy capitalism and democracy and replace them with communism.

Using Original Sources

In 1962, the Soviet Union placed nuclear missiles in Cuba. The crisis that developed is an example of how a cold war can come close to becoming a "shooting war." The missiles were a threat to the United States. President John F. Kennedy ordered a naval blockade around Cuba on October 23, 1962. The Soviet Union withdrew the missiles when the United States pledged not to attack Cuba. Here is President Kennedy's statement. After reading it, answer the questions that follow.

The Cuban Missile Crisis

. . . Within the past week . . . evidence has established the fact that a series of offensive missile sites is now in preparation on that imprisoned island [Cuba]. The purpose of these bases can be none other than to provide a nuclear strike . . . against the Western Hemisphere.

. . . Each of these missiles . . . is capable of striking Washington, D.C., the Panama Canal, Mexico City, or any other city in the southeastern part of the United States and Central America. . . .

The [change] of Cuba into an important strategic base . . . is a threat to the peace and security of all the Americas. . . .

Nuclear weapons are so destructive and ballistic missiles are so swift that any possibility of their use . . . may well be regarded as a definite threat to peace.

. . . I want to say a few words to the captive people of Cuba. I speak to you as a friend . . . and I have watched with sorrow how your revolution was betrayed— and how your fatherland fell under foreign domination.

Now your leaders are no longer Cuban leaders inspired by Cuban ideals. They are puppets and agents of an international conspiracy which has turned Cuba against your friends and neighbors in the Americas and turned it into the first Latin American country to have these weapons on its soil. These new weapons are not in your interest.

. . . I have no doubt that most Cubans today look forward to the time when they will be truly free—free from foreign domination. Free to choose their own leaders. Free to select their own system. Free to own their own land. Free to speak and write and worship without fear. . . .

1. Why do you think President Kennedy called Cuba an "imprisoned island"?

2. Why did President Kennedy think that the presence of nuclear weapons would be a threat to American security?

3. What is a *puppet*, as President Kennedy used the word? Why did he call Cuban leaders puppets?

4. Many felt that President Kennedy's action in blockading Cuba brought the United States to the edge of war. From this speech, why did President Kennedy believe the blockade was necessary?

TURNING POINTS

Government

Asia: Indira Gandhi

India gained its independence from Britain in 1947. As a new nation, India faced many challenges. It needed to develop its industry and to raise the living standards of its people. It also had to find a way for its many different groups to live in peace.

The first prime minister of the new nation was Jawaharlal Nehru. He did not want India to become involved in the cold war. He did not want his nation to take sides. Nehru remained in office until his death in 1964. During that time, he was often assisted by his daughter, Indira Gandhi. Years before, Indira Gandhi and her husband had fought for India's independence. As a result, the British had jailed them both for 13 months. Under her father's leadership, she was the minister of information and broadcasting. In 1966, Mrs. Gandhi became the prime minister of India.

When Indira Gandhi took office, India was still struggling with problems. Many people did not have jobs. There was not enough food for everyone to eat. Trouble along India's borders kept breaking out. In addition, various groups within India were still fighting among themselves.

Mrs. Gandhi's strength as a leader was tested again and again. As prime minister, she continued to work hard to solve the nation's problems. She took measures to control prices and to protect small farmers. Mrs. Gandhi served two terms as her country's leader—from 1966 to 1977 and from 1980 until her death. In 1984, Prime Minister Gandhi was assassinated. Her son, Rajiv, took her place.

Critical Thinking

1. What do you think was the British attitude toward Indira Gandhi in the 1940s?
2. What generalizations could you make about Indira Gandhi's character?

AIM: How did the Cold War turn into shooting wars in Korea and Vietnam?

CHAPTER 9

Two Wars Are Fought

HOW DID THE KOREAN WAR GROW OUT OF THE COLD WAR?

1. The cold war between the nations of the free world and the nations of the Communist world has been fought mainly with propaganda. But twice since the end of World War II, the cold war turned into a "hot," or shooting, war. Most of the arguments between the United States and the Soviet Union were about problems in Europe. Therefore, you might expect a shooting war to have started in Europe. But none did. Rather, two shooting wars took place in Asia. The first began in Korea and the second in Vietnam. Why did these wars start? And why did they take place in Asia and not in Europe?

2. Before World War II, Japan owned the land near northern China called Korea. After Japan lost the war, Soviet troops went into North Korea. American troops went into South Korea. It was agreed at the time that the Koreans would vote for their new government. But the Soviet Union did not let the North Koreans vote in this election. As a result, two governments were set up: a democratic government in South Korea and a Communist government in North Korea. Both Soviet and American troops then left Korea.

3. Suddenly in 1950, a North Korean Communist army invaded South Korea. The people of South Korea were not prepared to stop the invaders. President Truman wanted to stop this Communist invasion. The United States asked the United Nations to do something to stop the war. The U.N. Security Council acted at once. It said that North Korea was the aggressor. It ordered the North Korean army to leave South Korea. When the North Korean Communists did not leave, President Truman ordered American forces to help South Korea. On the same day, the U.N. Security Council voted to send a United Nations military force to South Korea.

4. Fifteen member nations of the U.N., including Great Britain, Australia, Turkey, and the Philippine Republic, sent soldiers to Korea. But most of the fighting forces in Korea were Americans. So the job of turning back the North Korean Communists fell mainly on the United States. The U.N. forces, led by American General Douglas MacArthur, drove the North Korean army out of South Korea. When the North Korean troops were driven close to the Chinese border, China sent a large force into the war.

5. The war in Korea lasted for two more years. Finally, in 1953, the two sides agreed to an armistice—a stopping of fighting. Under the armistice agreement, the boundary line between North and South Korea was to be about

An American infantry regiment guards a hill during the Korean War. How did the conflict end?

the same as it had been when the fighting first started.

HOW DID THE VIETNAM WAR BEGIN?

6. The United States has used military force to try to stop the Communists in Southeast Asia. This area was once known as Indo-China. It had been ruled by the French. After World War II, the people of Indo-China revolted against the French. In 1954, the French were defeated. They were forced to give up control of the area. Indo-China was divided into three free nations. They were Laos, Cambodia (present-day Kampuchea), and Vietnam. Soon a crisis developed in Vietnam.

7. By the Geneva agreements that ended French control, a Communist government was established in North Vietnam and a non-Communist government in the south. Elections were

to be held in 1956 to unite the country. But these elections never took place. Some South Vietnamese Communists, called the Vietcong, wanted to have a Communist government in South Vietnam. Aided by the North Vietnamese, the Vietcong used guerrilla fighters to try to overthrow the government of South Vietnam. Guerrillas are small bands of soldiers who make sudden raids. The South Vietnamese government could not stop the Communists. It seemed that the Communists might soon win.

8. At first, the United States sent only supplies and military advisers to help South Vietnam. But this did not stop the Communists. They were getting supplies and support from the Soviet Union and from China. Finally, in 1965, the United States sent a large military force into South Vietnam. American soldiers and marines began to go into the jungles in search of the Vietcong. American war planes began bombing military targets in North Vietnam.

Search-and-destroy missions were conducted by infantry platoons dropped by helicopter during the war in Vietnam.

Captured Vietnamese soldiers, some of whom are still young boys, wait to be taken to prisoner-of-war camps.

HOW DID THE VIETNAM WAR END?

9. In spite of South Vietnamese and United States efforts to stop the Communist Vietcong, the war continued. The United States did not want to invade North Vietnam, because China might then enter the war. This might have led to a third world war. In 1968, the United States and North Vietnam began talks in Paris to see if the war could be ended.

10. The people of the world were sharply divided in their opinions on the war. One side said that the United States had promised to help countries, such as Vietnam, that were threatened by a Communist takeover. They also believed that communism must be stopped in Vietnam. Otherwise, it would spread to other countries of Asia. Others argued that the United States should not be a policeman for the whole world. They said it was the job of the United Nations, and not of the United States, to end such wars. They also said that the Vietnam War could lead to a war with China or even to World War III.

11. A peace settlement was finally reached in 1973. The United States then removed the last of its forces from Vietnam. But fighting continued. Two years later, the Communists overran South Vietnam and set up a Communist government. In that same year, Cambodian Communists, called the Khmer Rouge (KMEER ROOJ), captured the government and killed several million people. The American effort to stop communism in Southeast Asia failed.

Testing Your Vocabulary

Choose the best answer.

1. At first, the Communists in Vietnam were mainly guerrilla fighters. *Guerrillas* are people who
   a. are specially trained to fight in jungles.
   b. fight at night only.
   c. fight in small bands and make sudden raids.
2. The U.N. called North Korea the *aggressor* in the Korean War because North Korea
   a. started the war by an invasion.
   b. won the war.
   c. took territory after winning the war.
3. An armistice ended the Korean War. An *armistice* means
   a. total victory by one side in a war.
   b. both sides stop fighting.
   c. one side surrenders.

Understanding What You Have Read

1. A good title for paragraph 10 is
   a. The Cause of the Korean War.
   b. World Opinion About the Vietnam War.
   c. The French in Indo-China.
   d. The U.N. and the Korean War.
2. In which paragraphs do you find facts about
   a. the end of the Korean War?
   b. the division of Indo-China into Laos, Cambodia, and Vietnam?
   c. the Communist invasion of South Korea?
   d. the meaning of the word *guerrillas?*
3. President Truman first sent the United States Army into Korea in order to
   a. follow the orders of the United Nations Security Council
   b. stop the spread of communism.
   c. hold back an invasion by the Soviet Union.
4. North Korea is governed by Communists because
   a. North Koreans voted for a Communist government.
   b. Communist China seized the territory after World War II.
   c. the Soviet Union set up a Communist government there after World War II.
5. The French lost control of Indo-China because
   a. the people revolted against French rule and won.
   b. the French were defeated by Germany in World War II.
   c. the United Nations divided Indo-China into three independent countries.
6. Some people were against American involvement in the war in Vietnam because
   a. the United Nations opposed American interference in Vietnam.
   b. they believed that the United States was trying to be an international policeman.
   c. the government of South Vietnam did not want American help.
7. In the Vietnam War the United States did not invade North Vietnam, chiefly because
   a. the United Nations opposed it.

b. the United States Army was not large enough for such an invasion.

c. it might have led to a war with Communist China.

Tell whether each of the following statements is fact or opinion.

1. The Korean War ended with an armistice.
2. The United States should not have sent troops to Vietnam.
3. The United Nations called North Korea the aggressor in the Korean War.
4. General Douglas MacArthur led the American forces during the Korean War.
5. Most Americans favored the United States' role in the war in Vietnam.

6. Communist China helped North Korea during the Korean War.
7. The Communists won control of South Vietnam in 1975.
8. After World War II, a rebellion started in Indo-China because the French did not govern well.
9. In 1975, Cambodia was taken over by Communists called the Khmer Rouge.
10. In 1954, Indo-China was divided into Laos, Cambodia, and Vietnam.

Developing Ideas and Skills

USING A MAP

Using information from this chapter, answer these questions in your notebook.

1. Which countries in eastern Asia have Communist governments today?
   a. North Korea   e.
   b.   f.
   c.   g.
   d.
2. Which countries were once part of French Indo-China?
   a. Laos
   b.
   c.
3. Which *two* pairs of countries in eastern Asia have been the scene of wars between Communists and non-Communists since World War II?
   a.
   b.

Summary of Unit XII

1. The United Nations was formed after World War II to try to preserve world peace.
2. The United Nations has been able to solve a few world crises, but it has failed to solve many others.
3. After World War II, almost all of the colonial empires of the world came to an end.
4. Africa has become a continent of many free nations.
5. The new nations of Africa were faced with many problems after they became independent.
6. The nations of Western Europe recovered from the economic damage of World War II partly by forming the Common Market.
7. After World War II, communism spread to many countries in Europe and Asia.
8. The spread of communism divided the world into rival alliances of free nations and Communist nations.
9. The cold war between the United States and the Soviet Union led to a number of world crises.
10. The Korean War and the Vietnam War were fought mainly because of the efforts of Communists to extend their control in Asia.

UNIT XIII

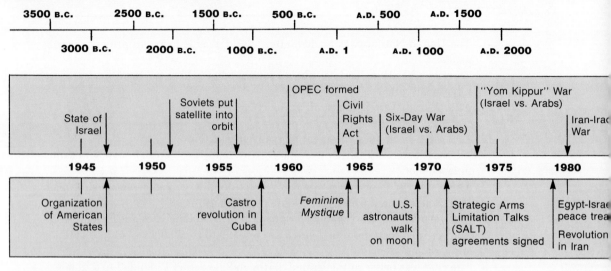

3500 B.C.		2500 B.C.		1500 B.C.		500 B.C.		A.D. 500		A.D. 1500
	3000 B.C.		2000 B.C.		1000 B.C.		A.D. 1		A.D. 1000		A.D. 2000

OPEC formed

"Yom Kippur" War
(Israel vs. Arabs)

Soviets put
satellite into
orbit

Civil
Rights
Act

Six-Day War
(Israel vs. Arabs)

State of
Israel

Iran-Iraq
War

| 1945 | 1950 | 1955 | 1960 | 1965 | 1970 | 1975 | 1980 |

Organization
of American
States

Castro
revolution in
Cuba

*Feminine
Mystique*

U.S.
astronauts
walk
on moon

Strategic Arms
Limitation Talks
(SALT)
agreements signed

Egypt-Israel
peace treaty

Revolution
in Iran

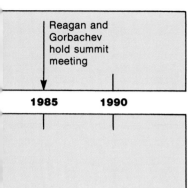

Reagan and
Gorbachev
hold summit
meeting

1985   **1990**

What Important Problems Face the World Today?

The people who came to Los Angeles for the
1984 Olympic Games were greeted with a
grand opening ceremony.

AIM: How did the Middle East become a center of political unrest?

CHAPTER 1

The Middle East Is Torn by Crises and Wars

WHY IS OIL A KEY NATURAL RESOURCE?

1. Every family that owns a car knows that gasoline has become very expensive. Sometimes it also becomes very scarce. Then long lines form at gas stations. What causes this scarcity and these high prices? The answer often is: trouble in the Middle East. You will recall that after World War II, European colonial empires fell apart. Instead of colonies, the Middle East, like other parts of the world, became a region of free nations.

2. Some of the new Middle East nations were Israel, Syria, Lebanon, Jordan, Iraq, Saudi Arabia, Egypt, and Kuwait. But independence did not bring peace to the Middle East. The region has been torn by revolutions, civil wars, local wars, assassinations, and terriorism. Many political leaders warned that the troubles in the Middle East could lead to a third world war. Why?

3. One of the most important reasons is oil. Oil is the most common source of energy used in the world today. It is necessary for all industrialized societies. The Middle East is one

During the gas shortages of the 70's, filling stations would put signs such as this one on the last car in the line they would be able to supply with gasoline.

of the richest oil regions in the world. More than half of the world's oil supply comes from there. When this supply of oil is cut off or reduced, serious problems develop all over the world.

4. In 1960, a number of Middle East nations joined other oil-producing countries to form a world oil *monopoly.* It is called the Organization of Petroleum Exporting Countries, or OPEC. Such a worldwide monopoly to control the supply and price of a product is known as a *cartel.* The Middle East members of OPEC are Iran, Iraq, Saudi Arabia, Kuwait, Qatar, and the United Arab Emirates. The other members are Libya, Nigeria, Venezuela, Algeria, Indonesia, Ecuador, and Gabon.

OPEC representatives meeting to determine a price for oil. What is a cartel? Do you think a worldwide monopoly on oil is good or bad? Give reasons for your answer.

HOW HAS OIL MADE THE MIDDLE EAST IMPORTANT?

5. The members of OPEC meet each year. In the 1970s, they raised the price of their oil. Whatever price they asked, the rest of the world paid. As a result, the oil-producing nations earned billions of dollars each year. Their rulers became very rich. Some of this vast wealth has been used to raise the standards of living in OPEC countries. Education, housing, and medical services have been improved. But much of the wealth has also been used to buy war planes, tanks, and guns. These weapons have been needed for protection against revolutions at home and possible wars with neighboring countries.

6. Middle East oil is also one of the causes of the cold war between the Soviet Union and the United States. Control of Middle East oil supplies would be a great advantage if international conflicts developed. Therefore, the Soviet Union and the United States have tried to find friends in the Middle East. But Arab allies tend to change their loyalties from one crisis to another. In most Middle East conflicts, the

United States and the Soviet Union are usually on opposite sides.

7. By the 1980s, however, new sources of oil were found in other parts of the world. The increased production of oil led to an oversupply. In addition, people learned to make do with less oil. When the price of oil was high, people began to buy smaller cars that used less fuel. Other sources of energy were developed. As a result, the price of oil meant lower prices for users of oil. But for the oil-producing countries of the Middle East, it means less money to raise the living standards of their people.

WHY HAS ISRAEL FOUGHT FOUR WARS?

8. Before World War II, one small area of the Middle East was called Palestine. Here, the democratic Jewish state of Israel was founded in 1948. When this happened, a war began be-

tween the Arabs and Jews in Israel. Thousands of Palestinian Arabs fled from Israel. Thousands of Jews fled Arab lands to Israel. The Palestinian Arabs became refugees in nearby Jordan, Syria, and Lebanon. After the war, the refugees wanted to return. But the Israelis would not let them come back. Some of the refugees formed the Palestine Liberation Organization (P.L.O.). Its aim has been to destroy Israel and form an independent Arab Palestinian nation. The P.L.O. has made many guerrilla raids and terrorist attacks on Israeli towns and settlements. An Arab League of Middle East countries has supported the P.L.O.

Yasir Arafat became chairman of the P.L.O. in 1969. What is the aim of this organization?

9. Soon after the new nation of Israel was born, the neighboring Arab nations tried to destroy it. Between 1948 and 1973, Israel fought four wars with its Arab neighbors. Israel's survival depended on the outcome. Israel was able to defeat its enemies. It captured the Sinai Peninsula from Egypt and a strip of land from Syria. Israel also seized the land on the west bank of the Jordan River. All of the city of Jerusalem came under the control of Israel. This city is sacred to three different religious groups—Jews, Christians, and Muslims.

10. Having failed to defeat Israel, the Arab League declared an economic boycott of it. They stopped all trade with it. The Suez Canal was closed to Israeli ships. In 1979, however, Israel signed a peace treaty with Egypt. This was done largely through the efforts of Jimmy Carter, the President of the United States. Under the treaty, Israel agreed to return the Sinai Peninsula to Egypt. Other Arab nations called Egypt a traitor to the cause of Arab nationalism. President Anwar Sadat of Egypt, who had signed the treaty, was assassinated in 1981. His successor pledged to keep the terms of the treaty. But no other Arab nations have signed treaties with Israel.

WHY DID A CIVIL WAR START IN LEBANON?

11. Another crisis in the Middle East was a civil war in Lebanon. Lebanon is a small Arab nation directly north of Israel. For many years, Lebanon was a democratic republic. Its people had a high standard of living. They followed Western customs and ideas. Its capital, Beirut, was known as "the Paris of the Middle East." According to a 1932 census, about half of Lebanon's people were Christians. Today the Muslims outnumber the Christians. After 1948, there were also thousands of Palestinian refugees in Lebanon.

12. For a time, Lebanon's mix of Chris-

Anwar Sadat of Egypt, President Jimmy Carter of the United States, and Prime Minister Menachem Begin of Israel met at Camp David in 1978. Name at least one provision of the peace treaty they signed the following year.

tian, Muslim, and Palestinian Arabs lived in peace. But in 1975, civil war broke out between the different groups. The fighting was bitter. Syria sent a military force to try to restore peace. But the war continued. In addition, P.L.O. guerrillas in Lebanon attacked settlements in northern Israel. In 1982, Israel invaded Lebanon. Israeli troops swept north to Beirut. Israeli planes bombarded the city, forcing the P.L.O. to withdraw. Lebanese Christian troops entered P.L.O. refugee camps south of the city and killed hundreds of civilians. In 1985, Israel withdrew its forces. Lebanon remained divided into warring groups.

Testing Your Vocabulary

Choose the best answer.

1. Many oil-producing nations formed a cartel called OPEC. A *cartel* is
   a. a large corporation.
   b. an international monopoly to control prices and supply.
   c. a peace-keeping organization.

2. When the Arab League declared an economic *boycott* of Israel, what began was
   a. the beginning of high tariffs.
   b. a declaration or war.
   c. a refusal by the Arab League to trade or do business.

Understanding What You Have Read _____

1. A good title for paragraph 8 is
   a. Israel and the P.L.O.
   b. Arab Influence in the United Nations.
   c. Israeli Wars with the Arabs.
   d. How OPEC Was Organized.

2. In which paragraph do you find facts about
   a. the Palestine Liberation Organization?
   b. the "Paris of the Middle East"?
   c. the city of Jerusalem?
   d. the Organization of Petroleum Exporting Countries?

3. One reason for conflict between Israel and the P.L.O. is that
   a. both want the same land.
   b. Israel has always been friendly with all other Arab groups.
   c. both need to control the Suez Canal.

4. OPEC was formed in order to
   a. cut waste in the use of oil.
   b. search for more oil.
   c. control the world price and supply of oil.

5. One reason why the Soviet Union and the United States have been rivals in the Middle East is that
   a. the Middle East is rich in oil.
   b. Arab countries have large standing armies.
   c. both nations want to control the city of Jerusalem.

6. A civil war in Lebanon started because of rivalry between
   a. Jews and Arabs.
   b. landowners and the nobility.
   c. Christian Arabs and Muslim Arabs.

7. Arab countries have a great deal of power in the United Nations because they
   a. control an important natural resource.
   b. have large populations.
   c. are heavily armed.

Tell which one of the three choices does not belong with the others in the group.

1. Members of the Organization of Petroleum Exporting Countries:
   a. Iran   b. Iraq   c. Israel
2. Middle East countries:
   a. Venezuela
   b. Saudi Arabia
   c. Syria
3. Countries that have been openly hostile to Israel:
   a. Syria   b. Greece   c. Jordan
4. Supporters of the Palestine Liberation Organization:
   a. the United States   b. Iraq   c. Syria
5. Rival groups in Lebanon:
   a. Christian Arabs   b. Muslim Arabs
   c. Jewish Arabs

6. Religious groups to whom Jerusalem is sacred:
   a. Buddhists   b. Jews   c. Christians
7. Nations that have not signed a peace treaty with Israel:
   a. Soviet Union   b. Egypt   c. Syria
8. Nations that have controlled the Sinai Peninsula:
   a. Iraq   b. Israel   c. Egypt
9. African members of OPEC:
   a. Libya   b. Nigeria   c. Egypt
10. Causes of turmoil in the Middle East:
   a. wars against Israel
   b. rivalry between the United States and China
   c. civil war in Lebanon

Developing Ideas and Skills

USING A MAP

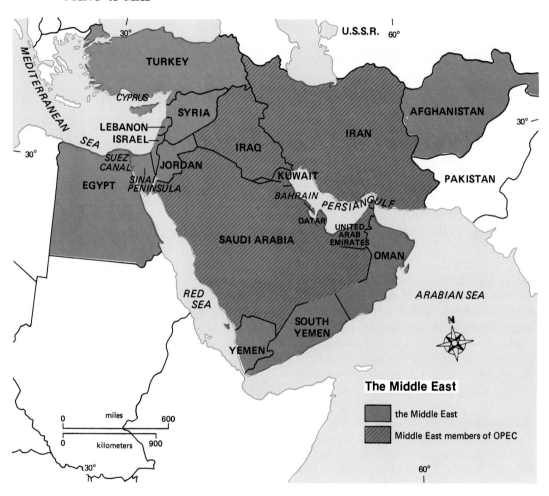

Answer the following questions using this map and the information in this chapter.

1. Explain why the location of the Suez Canal makes it such an important waterway for many nations.
2. Why do you think the Sinai Peninsula plays an important role in the relations between Egypt and Israel?
3. Name at least two nations of the Middle East that are not members of the Organization of Petroleum Exporting Coun-

tries (OPEC).
4. The Soviet Union invaded Afghanistan in 1979. How did Afghanistan's geographic location contribute to the Soviet Union's decision to invade the small country?
5. How does this map help to explain why the Middle East has often been a scene of wars and crises?

AIM: Why are there so many hostile rivalries in the Middle East?

CHAPTER 2

The Middle East Is Divided Against Itself

HOW DID A REVOLUTION IN IRAN CAUSE A WORLD CRISIS?

1. Almost three thousand years ago, Persia was one of the great empires of the ancient world. Today, it is called Iran. It is one of the larger countries in the Middle East and has huge deposits of oil. In 1941, Muhammad Reza Pahlevi (REE-zuh PAH-lev-ee) became ruler of the country. Using Iran's vast oil wealth, he tried to modernize the country. Steel mills, nuclear power plants, modern housing, and modern communications systems were built. The United States bought much of Iran's oil. The Shah bought warplanes and other armaments from the United States. In return, the United States gave him its support.

2. In spite of the Shah's reforms, many Iranians opposed his rule. Some opposed his plans to introduce Western ideas and customs. Others were angered over corruption in the government. His secret police force, called SAVAK, was noted for its cruelty. It was hated and feared. In 1979, a revolution started in Iran. It was led by Ayatollah Khomeini (eye-yah-TOH-luh koh-MAY-nee), an Islamic religious leader. The Shah was forced to flee from his country.

The former Shah of Iran. Why did many Iranians want to end his rule?

Ayatollah Khomeini. How is his rule of Iran different from the Shah's?

3. Khomeini wanted to restore the old customs of Iran. He wanted women to wear veils when in public. He opposed listening to Western music and the drinking of alcoholic liquor. He wanted his people to follow strictly the teachings of the Koran, the holy book of Islam. However, not all the revolutionists in Iran wanted to follow the strict rules of the Ayatollah.

4. Soon after the flight of the Shah, Iranian revolutionists raided the American embassy in Teheran, the capital of Iran. They seized more than fifty American embassy workers and held them as hostages for more than a year. Some Americans favored the use of military force to free the hostages. Others feared such force

might stop the flow of oil from the Middle East. It could also have led to another world war. Fortunately, the hostages were finally released early in 1981. Iran, however, continued to be torn by rival groups. The orthodox Muslims wanted to enforce the Ayatollah's anti-Western ideas. The liberal Muslims favored keeping Western customs. A third group, called the Majahedeen, wanted to set up a Communist government.

WHY DID THE SOVIET UNION INVADE AFGHANISTAN?

5. East of Iran is a country of herdsmen, nomads, and farmers. (Nomads are wandering people or tribes.) This poor, landlocked nation is called Afghanistan. The Soviet Union is directly north of it. In 1979, while the United States was busy trying to free its hostages in Iran, the Soviet Union invaded Afghanistan. Soviet military forces began to wage a bitter war against guerrilla fighters in the Afghan mountains. A pro-Soviet Communist government took control of the country.

How did Americans feel about the Iranian seizure of U.S. Embassy workers?

---

6. This invasion of a free Middle East country was a surprise. It was a new world crisis. Soviet control of Afghanistan brought the Russians one step closer to the oil-rich region of the Middle East. If a war started, the United States feared that the Soviet Union would be able to cut off American oil supplies from the Middle East.

7. The United States protested the invasion of Afghanistan. It ordered an embargo (a stoppage of trade) on all grain shipments to the Soviet Union. The United States also refused to send American athletes to the Moscow Olympic games in 1980. Furthermore, a planned agreement with the Soviet Union to limit strategic armaments was dropped by the United States. The United States took these steps to show that it opposed the Soviet invasion. But Soviet troops, tanks, and planes did not leave Afghanistan. The cold war between the two great powers had worsened.

HOW HAVE RIVALRIES WITHIN THE MUSLIM WORLD CAUSED UNREST?

8. The Arab-Israeli wars have caused much of the unrest in the Middle East. But the region has also been torn by rivalries and jealousies among the Muslim nations themselves. Most of the people of the Middle East and North Africa are believers in Islam, the Muslim faith. However, there are Arab Muslims and non-Arab Muslims. For example, the people of Syria, Egypt, and Saudi Arabia are Arab Muslims. But the people of Turkey and Iran are almost all non-Arab Muslims.

9. There are also two rival Muslim sects: the *Sunni* Muslims and the *Shiite* Muslims. In Egypt, Syria, Turkey, and Saudi Arabia most of the people are Sunni Muslims. In Iran, almost all are Shiite Muslims. The majority of Muslims in Iraq and Lebanon are also Shiite. These two sects are of the same Muslim faith. But some of

their religious beliefs are different. They are also rivals for political power in many of the nations of the Middle East.

10. Finally, there are the orthodox Muslims and the liberal Muslims. The orthodox believe strictly in the teachings of the Koran. They want women to keep their faces covered with veils. Men and women, they believe, should not mix in public places such as beaches or swimming pools. They also forbid gambling and the use of alcoholic drinks. Liberal Muslims, on the other hand, accept a Western style of dress for women. They copy Western social customs. They listen to Western music and watch Western films and television programs. Often, the rivalry between these two groups of Muslims breaks out into violence. The Muslim Brotherhood, a small group of orthodox Muslims, has used terrorist methods against liberal Muslims.

11. In 1945, the Arab nations of the Middle East and Africa formed an Arab League. Its purpose was to have the Arab nations work together. They have usually been united on one subject—hostility to Israel. They organized the economic boycott of Israel. Only Egypt has signed a peace treaty with Israel. On other issues the Arab countries are often divided among themselves. Their rivalries often lead to threats of war. A good example of the turmoil in the Arab world is the rivalry between Iran and Iraq. Both countries are rich in oil. But the people of Iran are mainly non-Arab Shiite Muslims. The people of Iraq, on the other hand, are mainly Arab Muslims and a majority are also Shiites. The Iraqi government is run by Sunni and Shiite Muslims.

12. A boundary dispute in 1980 led to a war between Iran and Iraq. While the revolution was going on in Iran, the armed forces of Iraq invaded the country. Oil shipments from both countries were halted by the fighting. Other Arab nations began to take sides. Syria supported Iran. Jordan supported Iraq. An inter-Arab war threatened to break out. The

Soviet Union and the United States remained neutral. Both feared that one or the other might try to increase its influence in the Middle East. Both had eyes on the oil riches of the Arab world. Thus, the Middle East moves from one crisis to another.

Testing Your Vocabulary

Choose the best answer.

1. The United States began an *embargo* on grain. This meant that the United States
   a. refused to import foreign grain.
   b. raised the tariff on grain.
   c. raised the price of grain.
   d. stopped the export of grain.

2. Afghanistan is a country of farmers, nomads, and herdsmen. *Nomads* are
   a. foreign immigrants.
   b. wandering people or tribes.
   c. guerrilla fighters.
   d. businessmen and bankers.

Understanding What You Have Read

1. A good title for paragraphs 2 and 3 would be
   a. The Beginning of the Revolution in Iran.
   b. Ayatollah Khomeini and Islam.
   c. The Seizure of American Hostages.
   d. The Invasion of Afghanistan.
2. In which paragraphs do you find facts about
   a. the Iranian secret police?
   b. the war between Iran and Iraq?
   c. the difference between orthodox and liberal Muslims?
   d. the United States grain embargo against the Soviet Union?
3. One of the reasons for the revolution in Iran was
   a. fear of a Soviet invasion.
   b. the military power of the Ayatollah Khomeini.
   c. public fear and hatred of the SAVAK.
4. The United States opposed the Soviet invasion of Afghanistan because
   a. it was a threat to America's Middle East oil supplies.
   b. Afghanistan was a United States ally.
   c. Afghanistan had valuable mineral resources.
5. The Ayatollah Khomeini wanted to restore traditional customs in Iran because
   a. he followed the teachings of the Koran strictly.
   b. he wanted to establish a dictatorship.
   c. almost all Iranians favored such a policy.
6. The 1980 war between Iran and Iraq began because of an argument over
   a. trade and tariffs.
   b. the American hostages.
   c. boundaries.
7. The main purpose of the Arab League was to
   a. get Arab nations to work together
   b. continue the war with Israel
   c. control the oil supplies of the Middle East

Match the items in Column I with their meanings in Column II.

Column I	Column II
1. SAVAK	a. orthodox Muslim terrorists
2. Ayatollah Khomeini	b. association of Arab nations
3. Reza Pahlevi	c. Iranian secret police
4. Muslim Brotherhood	d. bible of Islam
5. Majahedeen	e. former ruler of Iran
6. Koran	f. Muslim religious sects
7. Arab League	g. ruler of Afghanistan
8. Sunni and Shiite	h. Middle East Communist group
	i. Islamic religious leader

Developing Ideas and Skills

USING A CHART

According to oil experts, there is a large amount of oil still in the ground all over the world. This oil is called "proven oil reserves." In the following chart are the countries that have the largest known oil reserves. Each drawn barrel stands for 10 billion barrels of oil.

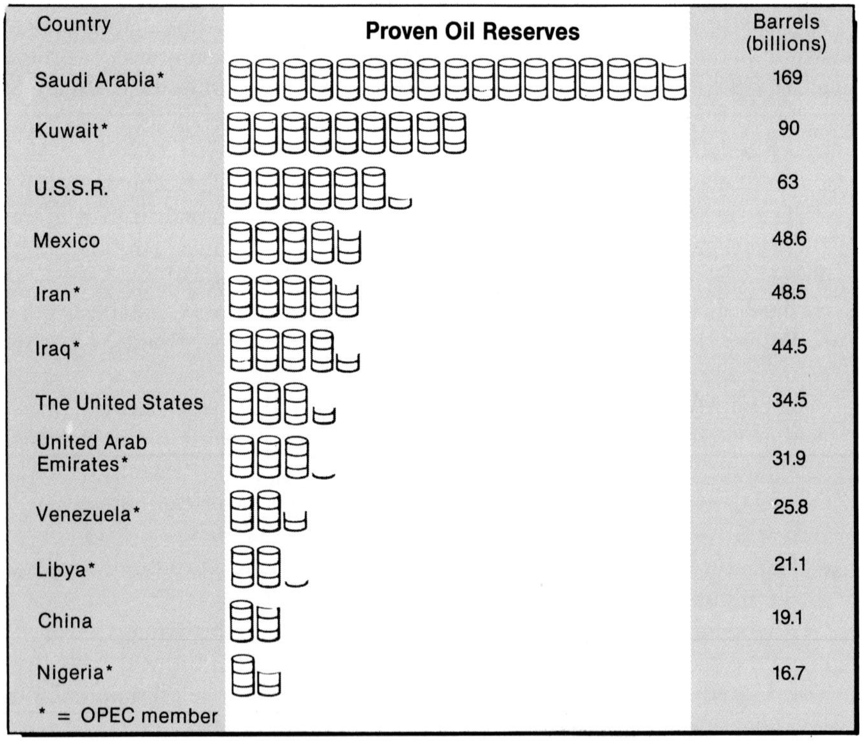

Country	Proven Oil Reserves	Barrels (billions)
Saudi Arabia*		169
Kuwait*		90
U.S.S.R.		63
Mexico		48.6
Iran*		48.5
Iraq*		44.5
The United States		34.5
United Arab Emirates*		31.9
Venezuela*		25.8
Libya*		21.1
China		19.1
Nigeria*		16.7
* = OPEC member		

Using the information in this chart, answer the following questions:

1. Does Saudi Arabia by itself have more proven oil reserves than the countries on this chart that are *not* members of OPEC?

2. Does the United States have more proven oil reserves than every other country in the Americas?

3. Does this chart suggest that a geographically large country will always have greater oil reserves than a geographically small country. (You might wish to refer to the map of the world near the end of the book.)

4. Why is the Soviet Union eager to gain more influence in the Middle East?

5. Why has the United States tried to establish more friendly relations with Mexico in recent years?

AIM: What problems have faced the countries of Latin America?

CHAPTER 3

Latin America Tries to Move Ahead

WHAT KIND OF NEIGHBORS HAVE THE UNITED STATES AND THE COUNTRIES OF LATIN AMERICA BEEN?

1. In many American cities today you will hear people say "buenos dias" instead of "good morning" and "adios" instead of "goodbye." Signs in their store windows say "bodega" instead of "grocer" and "carniceria" instead of "butcher." These are people of Spanish origin. There are almost 17 million of them in the United States. They live in large numbers in such American cities as New York, Los Angeles, Houston, and Miami. Many have come to the United States since the end of World War II. Most have not come from Spain. Rather, they have come from the countries of South and Central America, from Mexico, and from the Caribbean islands. This whole region is known as Latin America.

2. During the late 19th century, Africa and Asia were divided into colonies by European nations. But Europe was kept out of Latin America by the Monroe Doctrine (1823). The United States acted like the policeman of the Western Hemisphere. But the United States fol-

What was the purpose of the Monroe Doctrine? In what ways was it like imperialism? In what ways was it different?

Latin America

lowed its own kind of imperialism in Latin America. The United States won a victory in the Spanish-American War (1898). After the war, it took the islands of Puerto Rico and Cuba from Spain. Later Cuba was given its independence but Puerto Rico remained part of the United States.

3. During a revolution in Panama in 1903 the United States helped the rebels win their independence from Colombia. Panama then gave the United States the right to build the Panama Canal. For many years, American business companies had large investments in Latin America. Whenever these businesses were in danger, the United States sent marines to protect them. In the early 20th century, United States marines were sent into several countries of Latin America. This kind of American impe-

rialism was called "dollar diplomacy." Naturally, it did not make the United States popular with the people of Latin America.

4. After Franklin D. Roosevelt was elected president of the United States (1933), he decided on a new plan for Latin America. He called it the Good Neighbor Policy. The United States gave up dollar diplomacy. It promised not to interfere in the internal affairs of Latin America. In 1948, twenty Latin American republics and the United States formed the Organization of American States (O.A.S.). Its main aim was to have the members help one another in case of an attack by a foreign power. Disputes among the Latin American member nations were to be settled peacefully. Also, the O.A.S. was to encourage trade, friendship, and cultural ties among the members.

Theodore Roosevelt and the Rough Riders charge up San Juan Hill in 1898. Why has the Spanish-American War been called by some America's imperialistic war?

WHY DO LATIN AMERICAN GOVERNMENTS CHANGE SO OFTEN?

5. For more than 150 years almost all of Latin America has been independent. Yet many of the countries have not been able to set up long-lasting governments. There have been many revolutions and military dictatorships. Sometimes a dictator is overthrown by a popular revolt. For example, in Haiti the Duvalier family ran a dictatorship for 28 years. Their rule was corrupt and cruel. They used torture to control the public. They became very wealthy while Haiti remained the poorest nation in the Americas. Many Haitian people left the country for the United States. Then in 1986, the Duvaliers were driven from Haiti. The new government may not last. But the Haitian people have a new sense of power. They are demanding jobs and other changes. They want to avoid a new dictatorship.

Eva and Juan Peron. Peron was dictator of Argentina from 1946 to 1955, and again from 1973 to 1974. Eva Peron shared power with him and was one of the most important figures in Argentine politics.

594

6. Since the end of World War II, however, some of the governments of Latin America have been more stable than governments in the past. But a new problem has developed. Some of the revolutions are led by Marxist guerrillas. Their goal is to set up communist dictatorships in Latin America. That is what happened in Cuba in 1957 under Fidel Castro. The United States considers such communist dictatorships a threat to its own security.

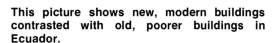

This picture shows new, modern buildings contrasted with old, poorer buildings in Ecuador.

WHAT ECONOMIC PROBLEMS FACE LATIN AMERICA?

7. A tourist visiting such countries as Mexico, Brazil, Peru, or Haiti will see modern hotels, fine restaurants, and beautiful boulevards. But behind the modern buildings there are often crowded slums. Here people live in tin shacks or in huts. This picture of poverty behind a front of riches is found in many large cities of Latin America.

8. Yet many countries in Latin America are rich in natural resources. Mexico and Venezuela have vast reserves of oil and natural gas. Copper is found in Chile, Bolivia, and Peru. Bauxite, from which aluminum is made, is found in Jamaica, Haiti, and Guyana. In the past, many of these resources were owned and run by United States companies. The profits naturally went to American stockholders. After World War I, however, many of these resources were taken over by the governments of Latin America. They planned to use the profits to reduce poverty, illiteracy, and disease. However, improvements have come very slowly.

9. One of the reasons for the slowness of progress has been the shortage of trained people. Latin America does not have enough trained engineers, technicians, doctors, or teachers. Another reason has been the rapidly growing population. Latin America has one of the highest birth rates in the world. There are never enough jobs for those who want to work.

Political leaders in Latin America have tried to raise living standards and provide jobs. They have tried to improve housing conditions and provide good medical service. But they cannot keep up with the rapidly growing population.

10. Poverty in rural or farm areas is often worse than in cities. Socialist governments in Mexico, Chile, and Venezuela have tried to break up the large landholdings of the rich. Plots of land have been given to the landless peasants. But this has created a new problem: modern machinery and modern farming methods cannot be used profitably on small pieces of farmland. In much of Latin America, 90% of the land is still owned by only 10% of the people. In rural areas and in cities, there is a large gap between the very rich and the very poor.

11. The United States has tried to give some help to Latin America. In 1961, the United States announced a plan called the Alliance for Progress. This set up a program by which the United States gave money to Latin American countries to try to reduce poverty. To encourage trade with one another, six Latin American countries formed the Andean Common Market, in 1969. This group included Venezuela, Colombia, Ecuador, Peru, Bolivia, and Chile. Its main aim was to encourage the growth of industries in the member countries by lowering tariffs (taxes on imports). It also aimed to make them less dependent on trade with the United States and Europe.

595

rich
t has

a. manufactured goods, such as automobiles and television sets.
b. farm products, such as coffee and sugar.

c. raw materials, such as oil, iron ore, and copper.

2. There is poverty in the rural areas of Latin America. The *rural* areas are the
   a. city slums.
   b. mining areas.
   c. farming regions.

Understanding What You Have Read _____

1. The main idea of paragraph 10 is that
   a. Latin America has a shortage of engineers and doctors.
   b. too few people own too much land.
   c. the population grows too fast.
2. In which paragraphs do you find facts about
   a. poverty in farm areas?
   b. patterns of government in Latin America?
   c. natural resources in Latin America?
   d. population growth in Latin America?
3. The United States was able to build the Panama Canal because
   a. Colombia gave its permission.
   b. the countries of Latin America wanted it.
   c. Panama broke away from Colombia.
4. The Organization of American States (O.A.S.) was formed in 1948 to
   a. protect Latin America from foreign attack.

   b. keep the United States out of Latin America.
   c. raise the price of oil.
5. The United States followed a policy of "dollar diplomacy" in Latin America in order to
   a. keep out Communist guerrillas.
   b. support democratic governments.
   c. protect American business interests.
6. In some countries of Latin America, governments are overthrown by a popular revolt. This is what happened in Haiti because the Duvaliers
   a. were corrupt and cruel leaders who kept Haitians poor and fearful.
   b. tried to bring land reform to Haiti.
   c. started programs for the poor.
7. One of the causes of unemployment in Latin America has been the
   a. rapid growth of the population.
   b. poor climate.
   c. lack of good farmland.

AIM: What have been the United States's relations with Mexico, Cuba, and Puerto Rico?

CHAPTER 4

The United States and Some of Its Neighbors

WHY IS MEXICO AN IMPORTANT NEIGHBOR TO THE UNITED STATES?

1. Mexico is the United States's closest Latin American neighbor. The two countries share a two-thousand-mile border. Mexico is the third-largest country in Latin America and the second-largest in population. Only Brazil has more people. Before World War I, Mexico had many revolutions and was ruled by different military dictators. One dictator, Porfirio Diaz ruled for thirty years.

2. Since the end of World War I, however, there have been no revolutions or military dictators in Mexico. The Mexican constitution of 1917 set up a democratic republic. Mexico has a president and a legislature. The president holds office for six years. He is not allowed to run for a second term. However, one political party has controlled the Mexican government for more than fifty years. Since 1970, everyone in Mexico over the age of eighteen has the right to vote.

3. Soon after the new constitution was written, the Mexican government began to break up the vast estates of the wealthy land-owners. Some of the land was divided into small farms. These were given to poor farmers who owned no land. The government also took over ownership of all oil resources and railroads. Today, the Mexican government also owns all electric-power and telephone companies. Thus, Mexico has a partly Socialist government.

4. Many of Mexico's presidents have tried to improve the lives of their people. Mexico set up a large-scale program of social security for its people. It also passed special laws to protect workers and improve education. Other laws aimed to improve housing and health services. But in past years, many of the social programs could not be carried out because the government did not have enough money.

5. Since 1972, however, vast deposits of oil and gas have been found in southeast Mexico. It is now estimated that Mexico has the fourth-largest oil reserves in the world. Much of the oil and gas is sold to foreign countries, including the United States. Mexico is now using this new wealth to carry out its old social programs. It has begun to raise the standard of living of some of its people. In 1940, Mexicans lived, on the average, to the age of 39. Today, life expectancy in Mexico is close to 70 years.

This photo shows the burning of excess gas at an oil well in Mexico. How has the discovery of oil affected Mexico?

With its new wealth, Mexico has also begun to rebuild its railroads and to start steel mills and other new industries. It has encouraged the growth of the tourist industry. Visitors from the United States and other countries spend millions of dollars in Mexico each year as tourists.

6. Mexico still has many problems. The population grows quickly. In the cities, there are more people than there are jobs. In farm areas, most of the people are very poor. Crops suffer because of a lack of adequate rainfall. In 1983, under President Miguel de la Madrid Hurtado, a financial crisis hit Mexico. This crisis was partly due to a drop in world oil prices. It was also partly due to Mexico's high foreign debt (over $89 billion), which the government could not pay. These economic problems have caused thousands of Mexicans to migrate illegally to work on American farms and in factories. They are often treated poorly. Many of their children do not attend school. The workers must accept low pay. This makes it harder for American farm workers to get higher wages from their employers.

SHOULD PUERTO RICO BECOME THE FIFTY-FIRST STATE?

7. After the Spanish American War (1898), the United States took the islands of Cuba and Puerto Rico from Spain. Cuba was given its independence. But Puerto Rico remained a part of the United States. In 1917, Puerto Ricans were made citizens of the United States. They can enter the United States freely. They pay taxes to Puerto Rico, but not to the United States. Puerto Rico is not a state. It has its own constitution and its own government.

8. In 1952, the United States Congress made Puerto Rico a free commonwealth under the protection of the United States. Since then, there have been three rival political groups on the island. One group wants Puerto Rico to remain a commonwealth. Another group wants it to be added to the United States as a fifty-first state. A third group wants Puerto Rico to become an independent country. Some members of this last group are known as the Armed Forces for National Liberation (F.A.L.N.) and the Macheteros. They have used terrorist methods to try to gain Puerto Rican independence. In recent Puerto Rican elections, however, a majority of the people voted to keep the island a commonwealth.

WHY IS CUBA A THREAT TO THE UNITED STATES?

9. Cuba was given complete independence by the United States in 1934. But the United States has kept an important naval base on the island at Guantanamo Bay. In 1952, Fulgencio Batista set up a harsh and corrupt dictatorship in Cuba. Seven years later, a revolution movement led by Fidel Castro forced Batista to flee from the island. At first, many Americans favored Castro. But then, to the surprise of many Americans, Castro set up a Communist government in Cuba. More than half a million

This photo, released in November of 1962, was taken by U.S. reconnaissance planes. It shows a missile base in San Cristobal, Cuba.

Cubans fled the country to escape living under communism. Many came to the United States.

10. After Castro's Communist government seized American property on the island, the United States broke relations with Cuba. The United States declared an embargo, or trade stoppage, on almost all exports to the island. Cuba became very friendly with the Soviet Union. In 1961, a number of Cuban exiles with United States help tried to overthrow Castro's government. They launched an invasion, but it failed. It is known as the Bay of Pigs invasion. One year later, the United States demanded that the Soviet Union remove its missiles from Cuba, or else risk war. The Russians removed their missiles in return for an American pledge not to invade Cuba.

11. Cuba under Castro has become a center for Communist propaganda in Latin America. The Russians have also sent advisers to Cuba to help in their efforts to spread communism. Cuba, in turn, has sent advisers and guerrilla fighters to help Communist revolutionary movements in Latin America. Cuban soldiers have also fought in Africa. Americans now fear that any new revolution in Latin America may end up as another Communist dictatorship. A new Communist victory in Latin America is viewed by most Americans as a threat to American security.

12. Fears about new Communist dictatorships have led to conflicts with other close neighbors. The Caribbean island of Grenada had been controlled by Britain since 1783. In 1974, Grenada became independent. Five years later, a revolution took place under the leadership of Maurice Bishop. He established a socialist government that was anti-American. He also brought Cuban military advisors to Grenada. In 1983, Bishop was overthrown by a group within his own government. The United States feared the new group would be even more anti-American than Bishop's government had been. With the support of five Caribbean nations, American troops invaded Grenada in 1983. The invasion enabled a new government to be formed. This government opposes Communism and receives American aid.

13. Problems have also arisen in the Central American country of Nicaragua. For 45 years, Anastasio Somoza Garcia and his sons ruled Nicaragua. They helped improve the economy. But people accused them of brutality and corruption. In 1979, rebel forces began a civil war. These forces were called Sandinistas. They were named after a popular general who was killed by Somoza. The Sandinistas won control of the government.

14. At first, most people supported the Sandinistas. But after a few years, several groups opposed them. In 1981, the United States stopped giving aid to Nicaragua. It claimed that Nicaragua was using aid from Cuba and the Soviet Union to arm rebels in El Salvador. It claimed that Nicaragua was stirring up revolutions throughout Latin America. The United States condemned the Sandinistas. It said Nicaragua was becoming a Communist dictatorship. Some Nicaraguans who opposed the Sandinistas began a civil war. These Nicaraguans are called "contras." The United States supports the contras and gives them aid. It believes the contras will rid Nicaragua of Communist influence and restore democracy.

Testing Your Vocabulary

Choose the best answer.

1. Many Mexicans *migrate* in search of jobs. To migrate is to
   a. start an uprising.
   b. move from one place to another.
   c. ask for unemployment insurance.
2. Puerto Rico today is called a free *commonwealth*. This means that Puerto Rico is
   a. a state.
   b. a self-governing country under the protection of the United States.
   c. an independent nation.

Understanding What You Have Read

1. The main subject of paragraphs 9 and 10 is
   a. the reasons for the revolution in Cuba.
   b. the meaning of social reforms in Mexico.
   c. the relationship between Cuba and the United States.
   d. how Puerto Rico is governed.
2. In which paragraphs do you find facts about
   a. the Mexican Constitution?
   b. the Puerto Rican movement for independence?
   c. the invasion in Grenada?
   d. the discovery of new oil resources in Mexico?
3. Mexico today is a partly Socialist nation because
   a. it has a democratic constitution.
   b. the government owns many businesses and industries.
   c. the president can be elected for one term only.
4. Mexico has been able to start new programs to improve education, housing, and medical services because of
   a. wealth from the sale of grain.
   b. new wealth from the sale of oil and gas.
   c. loans from the United States.
5. Puerto Ricans may enter the United States freely because
   a. Puerto Ricans are citizens of the United States.
   b. Puerto Rico is a United States colony.
   c. Puerto Rico is a state.
6. Many people have fled from Cuba because of
   a. the lack of jobs.
   b. the shortages of food.
   c. the Communist government.
7. Cuba can be considered a threat to the security of the United States because
   a. Soviet missiles are located in Cuba.
   b. Cubans have helped revolutionary groups in Asia.
   c. Cuba and the Soviet Union are closely allied.

In your notebook fill in the best word or phrase for each of the following statements.

1. Miguel de la Madrid Hurtado is the president of _____.
2. One of Mexico's most important natural resources is _____.
3. The United States acquired Puerto Rico and Cuba as the result of a war with _____.
4. The present dictator of Cuba is named _____.
5. The attempt that failed to overthrow the Communist government of Cuba in 1961 is known as the _____.
6. An American naval base is located at Guantanamo Bay, on the island of _____.
7. The president of Mexico is allowed to hold office for one term of _____ years.
8. The dictator of Cuba who was overthrown by the Castro revolution was _____.
9. The Latin American nation with the largest population is _____.
10. The F.A.L.N. and the Macheteros are revolutionary terrorists seeking independence for _____.

Developing Ideas and Skills _____

UNDERSTANDING A CARTOON

Study this cartoon carefully. Then choose the best answer for each of the following questions:

1. The people behind the doors are probably
   a. Americans.   b. Russians.
   c. Cubans.
2. The wall and doors mean that
   a. Cubans like privacy.
   b. no one may leave Cuba.
   c. Cuba is an island.
3. A good title for this cartoon might be
   a. Sun and Fun in Cuba
   b. Walls Do Not a Prison Make
   c. Trouble in "Paradise"

4. The cartoonist drew the sign "Workers' Tropical Paradise" to suggest that
   a. Cuba is truly a good place for workers.
   b. Cuba has a warm and pleasant climate.
   c. Cuba is not the paradise for workers that it pretends to be.
5. "We want out" is the cry of
   a. Cuban refugees in the United States.
   b. people in Cuban prisons.
   c. the working people of Cuba.

AIM: How have art, music, and literature changed in the 20th century?

CHAPTER 5

A Cultural Revolution Begins

WHY DO PEOPLE HAVE MORE LEISURE?

1. A century ago people worked long hours in factories. Farmers worked from sunrise to sunset. There was little time for rest or play. Only the rich could afford vacations. Today this has changed. In industrial countries all over the world, factory laborers work fewer hours during the week. With modern machinery, farmers can do as much in an hour as they once did in a day. Now, many people have more leisure time than ever before.

2. The increase in people's spare time is part of the modern world's cultural revolution. More people now have time to enjoy good music, art, and literature. In addition, modern inventions have lowered the cost of enjoying these pleasures. A century ago, only the rich could enjoy going to the opera or attending a fine concert. Today, millions of people can enjoy music on phonographs, tape recorders, and radios. They can also watch and hear the greatest performers in movies and on television. The inventions of the modern world have brought the artistic treasures of the performing arts into millions of homes.

3. New methods of printing and selling books have led to a book-reading revolution. Thanks to mass production and modern ways of distribution, paperback books and magazines are available almost everywhere. Hundreds of millions of paperback books are now sold in Europe and America. Today, anyone can build a home library. For the cost of an ice cream soda, a person can buy a copy of Shakespeare's *Hamlet* or Homer's *Odyssey*.

4. Today, people can use their free time to visit museums and attend shows and concerts. Millions now have the time to walk through art museums. They can see the treasures of the world's great painters and sculptors. They can even buy copies of the works of great artists at low prices. Many large cities in Europe, Asia, and America have built their own centers of culture. They have orchestras, opera companies, and art museums. A century ago most people spent their days off at home. The pleasures open to them did not go beyond what their homes and small communities could offer. Today, they can attend concerts, dance performances, operas, and plays.

The Metropolitan Opera House, New York. Why is this a good example of cultural exchange?

HOW ARE DIFFERENT CULTURES OF THE WORLD MIXING?

5. The spread of culture to all people is one part of the modern cultural revolution. A second part is the mixing of cultures of different parts of the world. Today, teenagers in Japan listen to records made in the United States. People in India go to movies made in Italy and Germany. If you walk into an American art museum, you will probably find examples of African sculpture and Chinese and Mexican paintings.

6. Television also has led to cultural mixing. Television programs that Americans see in one year are shown in Europe, Africa, and Asia the next year. Americans, on the other hand, can sit home and see on television a dance from Java, an opera from Germany, or an orchestra from Brazil. They can see a bullfight from Spain, or perhaps the Olympic Games from Montreal, Tokyo, or Rome.

7. Modern art, music, and literature are always changing. Some of these changes are difficult to understand. A person who looks at a modern painting or sculpture will often feel that it does not make sense. Modern music may sound strange and unmusical. If a person reads a book written in a modernistic style, he or she

may have trouble understanding it. Even today's movies are sometimes hard to understand.

8. In the past, many scientists and inventors have been called fools because they seemed to have strange ideas. Yet they opened new roads in science. It is much the same with many modern artists, musicians, and writers. They have new and different ideas. They are opening new artistic roads. Modern art, music, and literature have not been created by fools. They have something new to say about our world.

Bird in Space, **a bronze sculpture by Constantin Brancusi from the collection of the Museum of Modern Art, New York. Why do you think this sculpture has been called "a monument to aviation"?**

604

WHAT NEW IDEAS MARK MODERN CULTURAL MOVEMENTS?

9. In modern music, composers have tried out new combinations of sounds and tones. The Austrian composer Arnold Schönberg was one of the first to use unusual musical tones. He is sometimes called the "father of modern music." The Russian composer Igor Stravinsky used many of Schönberg's ideas. Stravinsky wrote such great works as *The Firebird* and *The Rite of Spring*. They have both beauty and great power. Other modern composers have also brought new ideas to music. Olivier Messiaen was very influential in the 1950s. John Cage began to develop new forms of music in the 1930s and still composes today. Benjamin Britten combined both old and new kinds of music to create modern operas. Steve Reich also uses some traditional and modern ideas to create a form of music called "minimalism".

10. Among modern artists, Pablo Picasso is probably the most famous 20th century painter. He is perhaps most well known for a kind of painting called cubism. Jackson Pollack and Willem de Kooning both had a great impact on a kind of painting called abstract expressionism. Alberto Giacometti became a major European sculptor after World War II. Alexander Calder and Louise Nevelson are

The Persistance of Memory, by Salvadore Dali from the collection of the Museum of Modern Art, New York. In what ways does this painting show the difference between modern art and the art of past ages?

important modern sculptors of today.

11. Sigmund Freud (FROYD), though not an artist, greatly affected much modern art and literature. He was the Austrian doctor who started the modern science of psycho-analysis. Freud believed that memories and feelings buried in people's minds can trouble their lives. Freud's method of exploring the depths of the mind inspired writers such as Eugene O'Neill and Virginia Woolf. Psychological themes and many other ideas have influenced other 20th century writers. The most important writers and poets in the first part of the century included James Joyce, T. S. Eliot, and Albert Camus (KAH-moo). In more recent decades, the list has included James Baldwin, Pablo Neruda, Gabriel Garcia Marquez, and Kawabata Yasunari.

Testing Your Vocabulary _____

Choose the best answer.

1. Sigmund Freud developed the modern science of *psychoanalysis*. This is a study of
   a. space travel.
   b. criminals.
   c. the mind.

2. When we speak of a *cultural* revolution we mean a revolution in
   a. government and politics.
   b. art, music, and writing.
   c. manufacturing methods.

Understanding What You Have Read_____

1. A good title for paragraphs 9 and 10 is
   a. The Mass Production of Books.
   b. Modern Music and Art.
   c. The Electronic Age.
   d. The Mixing of World Cultures.
2. In which paragraphs do you find facts about
   a. the paintings of Picasso?
   b. the book-reading revolution?
   c. the music of Stravinsky?
   d. the influence of Sigmund Freud?
3. People in industrial countries have more leisure time today because
   a. there is less demand for workers.
   b. the use of machinery means people work fewer hours.
   c. people own more automobiles.
4. Millions of paperback books are availa-

ble today because
   a. of mass-production.
   b. more people are writing books.
   c. paperback books are easy to carry.
5. The mixing of cultures has been speeded up by television because
   a. some countries can sell TV sets to others.
   b. we can know the weather conditions around the world.
   c. we learn about different societies from programs of other countries.
6. Sigmund Freud had an important effect on modern writing because of his studies about
   a. history and economics.
   b. the planets and stars.
   c. the workings of the mind.

Developing Ideas and Skills

TELLING FACT FROM OPINION

Tell whether each of the following statements is a fact or an opinion.

1. Modern composers are experimenting with new combinations of sounds.
2. More books are being printed today than a century ago.
3. Worldwide television will lead to greater friendship and understanding among nations.
4. Workers in industrial countries have more leisure time today.
5. Modern painters are really trying to confuse the public.
6. Freud's discoveries affected modern writers and painters.
7. Most of the great writers of the 20th century are Americans.
8. Foreign-made movies are better than American-made films.
9. The modern art, literature, and music we call masterpieces today will still be masterpieces a hundred years from now.
10. Many of today's movies cannot be understood.

TURNING POINTS

Technology

The World: The Live Aid Concert

On July 13, 1985, an audience of a billion and a half people watched a concert. It was called the Live Aid Concert. It was held to help people in Ethiopia, the Sudan, and some other parts of Africa. The people there were badly in need of food. Through the use of television, viewers in 152 countries became part of a single community. For 16 hours, people saw and heard musicians playing from stages in London and Philadelphia. Most important, the audience was made aware of a major global problem: many people on Earth were starving.

Technology had made the world aware of the emergency in Africa. Television had beamed pictures of hungry children and adults to every corner of the planet. During the Live Aid Concert, people were asked to give money to help. Millions of dollars were sent.

When President Abraham Lincoln was assassinated, it was months before all the people in America knew about it. Today we learn the news—from wherever it happens—almost as quickly as it takes place. Mass communication has made faraway parts of the world seem closer. It has created what one writer has called "the global village." It enables us to share our cultures. It makes it possible to bring attention to problems and to take steps to solve them.

Critical Thinking

1. How can mass communication help to improve world conditions?
2. Is "global village" a good description of the world? Why or why not?

AIM: How have scientific discoveries of the 20th century changed our lives?

CHAPTER 6

The World Enters a New Age of Progress

WHAT NEW ACCOMPLISHMENTS IN SPACE HAVE BEEN MADE?

1. In 1969, people all over the world read one of the most amazing headlines ever to appear in newspapers: ASTRONAUTS WALK ON THE MOON. This achievement was only one of hundreds made by scientists since the end of World War II. Scientific achievements since that time have been so great and numerous that the modern age can be thought of as the era of the scientific revolution.

2. Learning about space is only one way in which our knowledge of the universe has grown. We have also learned new things in biology, medicine, and chemistry. We have learned how to use nuclear power for peaceful purposes. We are now learning how to use the power of the sun. We are beginning to develop methods to use the ocean waters for drinking and for the irrigation of farmlands.

3. The exploration of space is the most exciting of scientific developments. It began during World War II, when the Germans developed advanced rockets. After the war, Soviet scientists continued rocket experiments. In 1957, they surprised the world by putting a satellite into orbit around the earth. American sci-

This painting shows a space shuttle orbiter vehicle paying a visit to a space-operation center in Earth orbit. Scientists think this could be a reality in the not too distant future.

entists quickly joined the race to develop missiles and to explore space.

4. Russia and the United States have developed missiles that can travel thousands of miles and can carry atomic or hydrogen bombs to any place on earth. Nations with such weapons have the ability to destroy each other within minutes.

5. Four years after the first satellite was sent into space, a spaceship carrying a man was sent into orbit around the earth. In 1965, an astronaut left his spaceship for the first time and floated in space. Spaceships carrying scientific instruments have been sent to Venus, Mars, and Saturn. In 1969, two American astronauts landed on the moon. In 1981, the United States launched the first reusable spacecraft, known as a shuttle. In 1986, a shuttle blew up a few seconds after takeoff. Tragically, the seven astronauts aboard were killed.

HOW DID THE NUCLEAR AGE BEGIN?

6. The exploration of space for peaceful purposes began with wartime rocket experiments. In the same way, the peacetime use of nuclear energy began with the use of the atomic bomb in World War II. The atom can give off large amounts of heat and power. Scientists have learned to use this heat and power to meet our energy needs. The atom has also been used in the field of medicine. Doctors have learned to use radioactive atoms to study the workings of the human body.

7. The use of nuclear energy, however, carries many dangers. Nuclear reactors give off dangerous radiation. In 1979, a small amount of radiation leaked from a nuclear power plant in Three Mile Island in Pennsylvania. In 1986, a serious accident occurred in the town of Chernobyl in the Soviet Union. Another problem is where to dump nuclear wastes. Radioactive matter continues to give off dangerous ra-

diation for a long time. Finally, there is the threat of nuclear weapons in war. A third world war fought with nuclear weapons would quickly destroy most of life on earth.

8. You have probably gone to a supermarket whose door opened as you stepped up to it. Most of us have at some time switched on our television sets and seen a show broadcast from Europe. These are only two of many examples of the practical uses of *electronics*. Electronic machines can do the work of hundreds of workers in one minute. Computers can send a missile to its target thousands of miles away.

This photo is magnified many times to show micro-computer circuitry going through the eye of a needle.

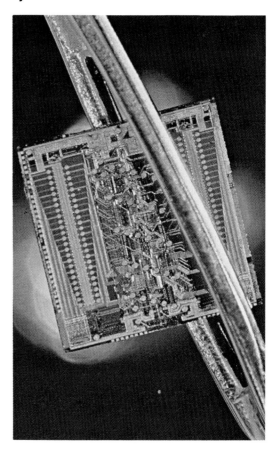

They can steer spaceships to the moon and keep track of all the operations of a large corporation.

9. Today, large factories are run by only a few people who use computerized robots. It is now possible to put manufacturing instructions on cards or tapes. When they are fed into a computer, they start the factory machinery. They feed raw materials, package a finished product, and send out bills. This use of computers and robots is the newest form of *automation.*

WHAT ARE SOME OF THE NEWEST MEDICAL DISCOVERIES?

10. We live in an atomic age. We live in an age of space exploration. We are also living in an age of medical wonders. Hundreds of new drugs have been developed to conquer disease. The drug penicillin was discovered in 1929 by Dr. Alexander Fleming. Dr. Charles R. Drew, a black scientist, developed a method of saving blood for long periods of time. The use of penicillin and blood banks saved thousands of wounded soldiers from death during World War II. Near the end of the war, Dr. Selman Waksman developed the drug streptomycin. This drug cures tuberculosis, among other diseases.

11. After the war, medical scientists developed new drugs to treat arthritis. Drugs for the treatment of mental disorders have also been developed. Probably the best known medical discovery of our time is the polio vaccine (vak-SEEN), by Dr. Jonas Salk. The vaccine was improved by Dr. Albert Sabin. Only forty years ago, many children were crippled by polio. Through the use of the vaccine, few people get polio today.

12. New medical technology is changing the way we live and how long we live. Organ transplants prolong the lives of people with damaged hearts, livers, and other body organs. Artificial hearts, while still experimental, are

Dr. Jonas Salk. Why can polio vaccine be called the "best known medical discovery of our time"?

being used to lengthen lives. Heart "pacemakers" help regulate the function of a weak heart. Dialysis (die-AL-uh-sis) machines do the work of damaged kidneys by taking out wastes from the blood.

13. In many areas, there is a shortage of fresh water. Scientists believe that in the next half century, millions of people will be using ocean water from which the salt has been removed. Millions of acres of desert land will be irrigated with this water. Changing saltwater to fresh water will thus help solve a very serious problem: the need for more food.

14. Modern scientists have made other important discoveries to improve farming. In 1970, Dr. Norman E. Borlaug, of the United States, won the Nobel Peace Prize for developing a new kind of wheat seed. His seeds greatly increased the amount of wheat a farmer could grow. Rice seeds that produce almost twice as much food as before have also been developed. And new methods of controlling insects and plant diseases are now used in many countries. These modern improvements in farming have been called the Green Revolution.

15. Thus, scientific discoveries can be used for peace and for war. Space satellites, nuclear power, and electronic machines can be dangerous military weapons. We live in a world where science can give us enough food, protection from disease, and machines that do heavy work. The great question for modern people is this: Will new scientific knowledge be used to harm or to help the people of the world?

Testing Your Vocabulary

Choose the best answer.

1. Atomic reactors give power to make electricity. A *reactor* is a machine that
   a. can bomb cities.
   b. uses the atom's energy to change water to steam power.
   c. changes steam power into electricity.
2. Automation has greatly increased the production of goods. *Automation* means the
   a. building of large factories.
   b. improvement of farming methods.
   c. use of labor-saving devices such as computers, robots, and other electronic machines.

Understanding What You Have Read

1. The main idea of paragraph 8 is that
   a. people can travel in space
   b. electronics has changed our way of living.
   c. modern medicines have cured many diseases.
   d. factories are now run by only a few workers.
2. In which paragraphs do you find facts about
   a. the discovery of polio vaccine?
   b. changing salt water to fresh water?
   c. computers?
   d. missiles?
3. The development of rocket bombs during World War II led to the
   a. building of nuclear submarines.
   b. rebuilding of the bombed cities of Great Britain.
   c. exploration of space.
4. Atoms are used in medicine because they
   a. cure tuberculosis.
   b. can help in the study of the human body.
   c. bring dead things back to life.
5. The modern science of electronics is important because it
   a. is used in radio, television, and industry.
   b. is used in the making of atomic bombs.
   c. helps improve farm crops.
6. Achievements in medicine since the end

of World War II have been mainly in
a. discovering new kinds of bacteria.
b. the invention of new medical equipment.
c. new drugs and medical technology

7. The need to change ocean water to fresh water cheaply is an important world problem today because
a. rainfall throughout the world has dropped since World War II.
b. atomic explosions have dried up sources of fresh water.
c. there is much dry land that must be irrigated.

Tell whether the statements are true or false. If a statement is false, change the words in italics to make it true.

1. The first man-made satellite was sent around the earth by the *United States.*
2. Ocean water is changed into fresh water by removing its *bacteria.*
3. The automatic opening of doors is an achievement of *atomic* science.
4. Dr. Alexander Fleming discovered the drug *streptomycin.*
5. Water can be changed into steam by *reactors.*
6. Blood can be cleaned of wastes through the use of a *dialysis machine.*
7. Polio has been conquered by the vaccine developed by *Dr. Jonas Salk.*
8. Weapons that strike targets thousands of miles away are called *satellites.*

Developing Ideas and Skills

UNDERSTANDING A CARTOON

1. What future scientific developments might be added to fill the empty steps of this cartoon?
2. Make up a title for this cartoon.

Using Original Sources

Although he was pope for only five years (1958–1963), Pope John XXIII was one of the most popular in the long history of the Catholic Church. Two months before he died, he prepared a public letter in which he listed the things that people must do to live in peace. It was a message for people of all religions, all races and all colors. He called it *Pacem in Terris* which is Latin for *Peace on Earth*. Among its many parts were the following. After reading the selection, answer the questions below.

Pacem in Terris

Every man has the right to life . . . to food, clothing, shelter, rest, medical care. . . . A human being also has the right to security in cases of sickness, inability to work, widowhood, old age, unemployment.

Every human being has the right to respect for his person . . . the right to freedom in searching for the truth. . . . Natural law also gives man the right to share in the benefits of culture and therefore the right to a basic education.

Every human being has the right to honor God according to the dictates of an upright conscience.

Human beings have . . . the right to work.

In human society . . . racial discrimination can in no way be justified. . . . If a man becomes conscious of his rights, he must become equally aware of his duties.

Justice . . . right reason and humanity urgently demand that . . . nuclear weapons should be banned.

All human beings . . . are living members of a universal family of mankind.

1. What rights did Pope John XXIII feel belonged to every human being?

2. Did John XXIII list any rights that you feel are not basic to human beings? Are there any that you would add to this list?

3. How do you think Pope John would have looked on the United States Declaration of Independence? The Bill of Rights? The Soviet Constitution?

4. What are some rights Pope John mentions that many governments have granted to their people only in the last 50 years?

5. What do you think Pope John's attitude would have been toward the ideas of Adolf Hitler? the use of the atom bomb? United States civil-rights laws? public schools? social security laws?

AIM: How did the Women's Liberation Movement affect modern women?

CHAPTER 7

A Feminist Revolution Gains More Rights for Women

HOW HAVE WOMEN BROADENED THEIR ROLES?

1. The American Declaration of Independence says that all *men* are created equal. Does this include women? During the 19th and early 20th centuries women did not have the same rights as men. Only after years of feminist campaigns were laws passed in the United States and many other countries to widen women's rights. These laws finally gave married women the right to own property. It gave them the right to sign contracts and to keep the money they earned. Women also won the right to get the same education as men. But it was not until 1917 that a woman, Jeanette Rankin, was elected to the United States Congress. Finally, after World War I, women were granted the right to vote. In spite of all these gains, women were still denied some rights.

2. During World War II, thousands of women in Europe and the United States took jobs in factories. They also joined noncombat volunteer units in the armed forces. When the war was over, however, most women returned

Jeanette Rankin, the first woman elected to Congress. Do research and find at least three other women who have been members of Congress.

to their roles as mothers and homemakers. Regardless of their wartime efforts, it was still the tradition that a woman's place was in the home. It was their duty to raise children and take care of the home and family. Politics and business were not for them.

3. There were, of course, some women who continued to work because they needed the money or because they enjoyed working. They usually held jobs as secretaries, waitresses, nurses, and teachers. But on the job, women were like "second-class" citizens. They often did not get the same wages as men for the same work. They were rarely considered for promotions. One reason for this was that many working women kept their jobs only until they married. Then they left their careers to become wives and mothers.

4. There were many jobs that were not open to women. They could not become police officers, fire fighters, coal miners or airline pilots. They were not allowed to become ministers, priests, or rabbis. Except in the Soviet Union, one rarely heard of women doctors. Few women became lawyers, dentists, mayors, or judges. Women were hardly ever directors of banks, presidents of corporations or managers of factories. One woman writer who protested against this situation was the French author Simone de Beauvoir. In her book *The Second Sex* (1949), she wrote that women's rights were still unequal to men's. She claimed this was because most women did not object to the unfairness they met with.

This 1920s photo shows a woman doing a job that in the past was done mainly by men. What other jobs can you name that are now open to both men and women?

WHAT DID THE NEW FEMINISM ACHIEVE?

5. Beginning in the 1960s, a new movement for equal rights for women began in the United States. It soon spread to other countries and it became known as the Women's Rights Movement. One of the writers who helped to start this new movement was the American feminist Betty Friedan. In her book *The Feminine Mystique* (1963) she urged women to do something about changing their roles. She told them to demand the right to hold any job and enter any profession. Through her efforts, the National Organization for Women (NOW) was formed in the United States. Similar associations were also organized in many other countries.

6. The new feminist campaign soon brought results. The United States Congress passed the Equal Pay Act (1963) requiring equal pay to men and women who did the same work. In 1964, Congress also passed the famous Civil Rights Act. Among other things, it forbade almost all discrimination based on sex. It forbade discrimination against women in hiring or firing. Women were to have the same rights as men in wages, promotions, sick leaves, and other conditions of employment. In Great Britain, an Equal Pay Act was passed in 1970. Similar laws were also passed in other countries of Western Europe.

7. Universities began to admit more women to their medical and law schools. In many cities, women joined the police and fire departments. Women were admitted to all United States military academies. They became regular officers when they graduated. Almost every large corporation in the United States chose at least one woman for its board of directors. Women also entered politics in larger numbers than in the past. In many countries, including the United States, they were elected mayors, governors, and members of law-making bodies. Many were appointed judges, cabinet members, and heads of government agencies. In

1981, Sandra Day O'Connor became the first woman justice of the United States Supreme Court. In 1975, the French government established a new cabinet position—Secretary of State for the Condition of Women. France was the first nation in the world to establish such a cabinet post.

8. In some countries women have risen to the highest levels of political power. Golda Meir (my-EER) became prime minister of Israel. Indira Gandhi was elected prime minister of India. Women also became prime ministers of Sri Lanka (Ceylon) and of Norway. In 1979, Margaret Thatcher was chosen the first woman prime minister in Great Britain's history. And in 1986, Corazon Aquino became the president of the Philippines. Her presidency ended 21 years of rule by Ferdinand Marcos.

9. Women have also begun to take their proper place in international affairs. In 1967, the United Nations adopted a Declaration of Women's Rights. This document urged all nations to end sex discrimination in voting, inheriting property, education, employment, and many other areas of life. In 1953, Vijaya Lakshmi Pandit, a woman, was elected president of the United Nations General Assembly. One of the most dramatic rises of a woman in international affairs can be seen in the career of Simone Veil. As a teenager during World War II, she had been imprisoned in a Nazi concentration camp. After the war, she was elected to the French Chamber of Deputies. In 1979, she was elected president of the Parliament of Europe. This is the political arm of the European Common Market.

WHAT OPPOSITION HAS THE WOMEN'S LIBERATION MOVEMENT FACED?

10. Women won many victories in the modern Women's Rights Movement. However, there were also some defeats. Many women as well as men have opposed the new ideas of feminism. They fear the destruction of the traditional ties that keep families together. They worry about protection on the job. The United Nations' Declaration of Women's Rights was not approved by many nations in the Middle East, Latin America, and Africa. In the United States, a proposed Equal Rights Amendment to the Constitution has not been approved by the necessary three-fourths of the states.

11. In Islamic countries, orthodox Muslims oppose equal rights for women. Some members of other orthodox religious faiths also oppose the new demands of women. In Latin American countries, there is a strong tradition of *machismo*. According to this tradition, the man is the master of the family. The Women's Rights Movement has not yet changed this Hispanic tradition. Finally, in many countries where families have barely enough to eat, equal rights for women have not yet become a major issue.

This picture shows the traditional dress of women in Islamic countries. Do you think that such a style of dress can fit with new roles for women?

Testing Your Vocabulary

Choose the best answer.

1. The modern Women's Rights Movement started in the 1960s. In this sentence the word *rights* means
   a. freedom from slavery.
   b. freedom from unfair treatment.
   c. equal educational opportunities.

2. There is a strong tradition of *machismo* in Latin American countries. *Machismo* means
   a. respecting women's rights.
   b. male control of the family.
   c. male openness to new ideas.

Understanding What You Have Read

1. A good title for paragraphs 6, 7, and 8 would be
   a. Opponents of Feminism.
   b. Recent Feminist Gains.
   c. Women in International Affairs.

2. In which paragraphs do you find facts about
   a. women who became prime ministers?
   b. the Civil Rights Act of 1964?
   c. the National Organization for Women?
   d. admission of women to military academies?

3. Betty Friedan's book *The Feminine Mystique* is important because it
   a. inspired the Women's Liberation Movement in the United States.
   b. increased the number of women in Congress.
   c. encouraged women to be mothers and homemakers.

4. Discrimination against women in employment is illegal in the United States today because of
   a. the Equal Rights Amendment.
   b. the Civil Rights Act of 1964.
   c. the Declaration of Independence.

5. The United Nations' Declaration of Women's Rights was not approved unanimously because it was opposed by
   a. American women's organizations.
   b. the U.S. Congress.
   c. orthodox Muslims in Middle Eastern countries.

6. The proposed Equal Rights Amendment in the United States is not a part of the Constitution because
   a. Congress failed to pass it.
   b. the president vetoed it.
   c. the required number of states has failed to pass it.

7. Between 1939 and 1945 thousands of women in Europe and the United States took jobs in factories because of
   a. new civil rights laws.
   b. the Vietnam War.
   c. World War II.

Match the names in Column A with the identifications in Column B.

<table>
<tr><td colspan="2" align="center">Column A</td><td colspan="2" align="center">Column B</td></tr>
<tr><td>1.</td><td>Corazon Aquino</td><td>a.</td><td>prime minister of Israel</td></tr>
<tr><td>2.</td><td>Margaret Thatcher</td><td>b.</td><td>president, U.N. General Assembly</td></tr>
<tr><td>3.</td><td>Jeanette Rankin</td><td>c.</td><td>author of The Feminine Mystique</td></tr>
<tr><td>4.</td><td>Golda Meir</td><td>d.</td><td>prime minister of Canada</td></tr>
<tr><td>5.</td><td>Indira Gandhi</td><td>e.</td><td>president of the Philippines</td></tr>
<tr><td>6.</td><td>Vijaya Lakshmi Pandit</td><td>f.</td><td>author of The Second Sex</td></tr>
<tr><td>7.</td><td>Betty Friedan</td><td>g.</td><td>prime minister of Great Britain</td></tr>
<tr><td>8.</td><td>Simone de Beauvoir</td><td>h.</td><td>first United States Congresswoman</td></tr>
<tr><td></td><td></td><td>i.</td><td>prime minister of India</td></tr>
</table>

Using Original Sources

In the United States, the Women's Liberation Movement succeeded in getting Congress to pass an important Civil Rights Act and a proposed Equal Rights Amendment. The Civil Rights Act is the law of the land. The Equal Rights Amendment, however, still requires the approval of three-fourths of the states.

The Civil Rights Act of 1964—Section VII

It shall be unlawful for an employer "to fail or refuse to hire or discharge any individual or otherwise to discriminate against any individual with respect to his compensation [salary], terms, conditions, or privileges of employment because of such individual's race, color, religion, sex, or national origin."

The Equal Rights Amendment

Equality of rights under the law shall not be denied or abridged [cut short, lessen] by the United States or by any State on account of sex.

1. What employment rights were guaranteed to women under the Civil Rights Act of 1964?
2. Does the Civil Rights Act guarantee women the same rights as men in job promotions and sick leaves?
3. What difference is there between the Civil Rights Act of 1964, Section VII, and the proposed Equal Rights Amendment?

AIM: What are the most serious problems that call for world action today?

CHAPTER 8

Problems Facing Today's World

IS THE COLD WAR STILL GOING ON?

1. Since the end of World War II, the non-Communist nations of the world, led by the United States, and the Communist nations, led by the Soviet Union, have been locked in a cold war of threats, propaganda, and mistrust. Rival military alliances have been formed. A nuclear-arms race has been going on. Two bitter wars—the Korean War (1950–52) and the Vietnam War (1964–75)—have been fought. The cold war has not helped either the non-Communist world or the Communist world. The threat of a nuclear war has created a balance of terror on earth.

2. Every few years the two rival world powers try to end the cold war. They begin to talk of working together. A few agreements to control nuclear weapons are discussed. Plans are made to increase trade and cultural exchanges between Communist and non-Communist nations. But then a new crisis develops and the plans and discussions become meaningless.

3. In 1962, for example, the United States told the Soviet Union to take its missiles out of Cuba. Our government claimed that they were a threat to the United States. The Soviet Union

claimed that American weapons in Turkey were a threat to the Soviet Union. Again, in 1980, the United States condemned the Soviet

How does this cartoon show the cold-war struggle between the United States and the Soviet Union?

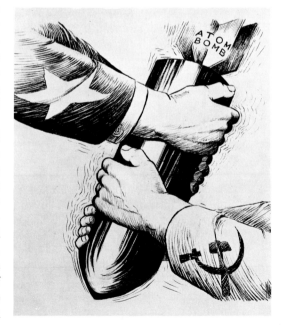

Union's invasion of Afghanistan. The Soviet Union then claimed that the United States was interfering in Poland. Thus, the cold-war disputes and crises begin again. Rivalry between the United States and the Soviet Union is one of the most serious problems facing the world today. Such rivalry can develop into a war.

WHERE ARE THE WORLD'S TROUBLE SPOTS TODAY?

4. There are many trouble spots all over the world. Two of them are the Middle East and Central America. In the Middle East, there have already been battles in Israel, Egypt, Syria, Jordan, Iraq, and Lebanon. There is concern over hostile acts carried out from Libya. In Central America, tensions have increased between Nicaragua and the United States.

5. The Vietnam War in Southeast Asia came to an end in 1975. But there is continued danger that civil war may break out again in that part of the world. Elsewhere in Asia, China and the Soviet Union look upon each other as threats. They have often argued over their common boundary along Siberia. They also differ over how communism should be spread.

6. Africa, with its many new, independent nations and its racial struggles, is also a possible source of world conflict. In several of the new African nations, military leaders have set up dictatorships. In such new independent countries as Angola, Mozambique, and Guinea Bissau (formerly Portuguese Guinea), rival groups have fought civil wars for control of the new governments. In some cases, as in Angola and Zaire, other countries have sent aid or troops to one side or the other. Such actions by outsiders could lead to a larger conflict. In South Africa, harsh racial apartheid laws have made second-class citizens of the black people. In Uganda, on the other hand, a black dictator, Idi Amin, followed a policy of "Africa for the (black) Africans." He forced thousands of non-

blacks to leave his country. But he also killed about 300,000 black Ugandans. Finally, a civil war and an invasion by Tanzanian troops forced him to flee.

TERRORISM BECOMES A WORLD PROBLEM

7. One of the frightening developments of the late 20th century has been the rise of worldwide terrorism. Terrorism means killings, bombings, and kidnappings by small groups of people. They commit these acts to protest against their political enemies or to gain attention for their own cause. Often, the people hurt by terrorists have nothing to do with politics. Terrorism is not a new idea. You will recall that World War I began when a terrorist assassinated Archduke Francis Ferdinand of Austria-Hungary. But terrorism has never been as widespread as it has been in recent years.

8. Since the end of World War II, terrorist groups have been active in many countries all

This is President Reagan, Press Secretary James Brady, D.C. Policeman Thomas K. Delahanty (officer on the right) seconds before the president was shot by a gunman concealed behind officer Delahanty.

over the world. There are the Red Brigades in Italy and the Baader-Meinhof Gang in West Germany. In Iran and Iraq, there is the Moslem Brotherhood, and in the Philippine Republic there is the Third Force. The French terrorists are called Cagoulards (hooded ones). In Turkey, the terrorists are known as the People's Liberation Army. In the United States, a small group called the Weathermen carried on terrorist activities in the 1960s to protest American involvement in the Vietnam War. In 1986, Libyan terrorists threatened American interests.

9. Some of the terrorist groups are left-wing Communists or right-wing Fascists. Others are nationalist groups seeking independence for a country or a region. Such nationalist terrorist groups usually think of themselves as champions of freedom. This group includes the Irish Republican Army (I.R.A.), which wants Northern Ireland to be politically independent of Great Britain. It also includes the E.T.A., which seeks independence for the Basques in northern Spain. There is also the Breton Liberation Front, which seeks independence from France for the Bretons, a people who live in a region of northwest France called Brittany. Among the best-known nationalist terrorist groups is the Palestine Liberation Organization. The P.L.O. seeks an independent nation for Palestinian Arabs. The F.A.L.N. and the Macheteros want Puerto Rico to be independent of the United States.

10. Terrorist gangs have been responsible for many crimes and atrocities. They were responsible for the assassination of Italian, Syrian, and Turkish prime ministers. They murdered Israeli Olympic athletes and the Catholic Archbishop of El Salvador. They have hijacked passenger airplanes and bombed or machine-gunned police stations, buses, and railroad and airline terminals. They have killed great numbers of innocent people. Yet they have rarely achieved their goals. Unfortunately, it is extremely hard to catch terrorists before they have caused destruction and suffering.

WHAT OTHER PROBLEMS MUST BE SOLVED?

11. There is an ancient story about a fierce monster with many heads. When one of its heads was cut off, two heads grew in its place. It seems that our world today is like that monster. As soon as one problem seems to be solved, two new ones show up in its place. Modern science learned how to kill harmful insects with DDT. But the DDT also killed birds and fishes. Farmers used new chemical fertilizers to raise bigger crops. But the fertilizers poisoned rivers and lakes. And automobile manufacturers learned how to build millions of cars each year. Automobiles, however, dirty the air we breathe.

12. Many of the new problems, such as the ones mentioned, are problems of pollution. Pollution means that our air, water, and land are made unfit for living beings. It is a worldwide problem. It affects such widely scattered cities as Venice, Tokyo, Hamburg, Los Angeles, and Moscow. It includes such widely separated waters as Lake Erie, in the United States; Lake Baikal, in Siberia; the Ganges River, in India; and the Rhine River, in Germany. Now that we have done so much to make life easier for ourselves, we must find ways to keep the earth clean and healthful.

This bird was a victim of oil pollution. Why is pollution a world-wide problem?

13. In the past 10 years, the prices of most things have gone up sharply. A hot dog that cost 20 cents a few years ago costs one dollar today. This sudden rise in prices is called *inflation*. It causes hardships for most people, especially those with fixed incomes. It makes it difficult for merchants and manufacturers to run their businesses. Merchants who buy from and sell to foreign countries are never sure from day to day how much they will have to pay for imports or how much they will get for their exported goods. Today, inflation is a worldwide problem.

14. Is there a limit to the number of people who can live on our planet? Scientists have discovered that when they put two mice in a cage, they get along well. When twenty mice are put in the same cage, they begin to fight each other. The space is too small for so many. Is the population of our earth reaching the same limit? In 1850, there were one billion people on earth. Today, there are more than 4.8

Programs such as CARE have helped to provide food for the starving children in India.

Mother Theresa won the Nobel Peace Prize for her work with the poor and homeless of India. She has worked to give them not only food but also self-respect and dignity.

billion people. If the same rate of growth continues, the population of the earth will be more than 8 billion people by the year 2025.

15. Is there enough land on which to raise food for so many people? Are we making the best use of the land that can be cultivated? Only seven countries in the world (the United States, Canada, Argentina, Australia, New Zealand, Thailand, and Ireland) now produce more food than their people need. One-third of the world's people live in 50 hungry nations in Asia, Africa, and South America. These nations produce far less food than their people need. Ten thousand people die of starvation each week in these hunger-ridden parts of the world. In some nations of Africa, governments have fallen from power because of a shortage of food. Much of the world's social and political unrest is due to widespread hunger.

16. Despite these problems, however, there is cause for hope in today's world. The leaders of the United States and the Soviet Union are aware that in a nuclear war there cannot be winners—only losers. Modern medicine is gradually ridding the world of diseases that once killed millions of people. Agricultural scientists are steadily increasing the amount of food that can be produced. The problem facing the world is to see that these gains benefit all the world's people.

Testing Your Vocabulary

Choose the best answer.

1. *Inflation* eats away the incomes of retired people. In this sentence, inflation refers to
   a. the rising price of goods.
   b. low interest rates on bank deposits.
   c. shortages of food and fuel.

2. Because of *pollution* our air and water are filled with harmful wastes. In this sentence *pollution* means to
   a. make pure and healthful.
   b. manufacture poisons.
   c. make unclean and impure.

Understanding What You Have Read

1. The main idea of paragraph 3 is that
   a. the cold war has continued and could grow into a "hot" war.
   b. terrorism has spread to many coun tries.
   c. the bitterness of the cold war h eased in the 1970s.
   d. the Soviet Union invaded Afghar stan.

2. In which paragraph do you find fac about
   a. worldwide inflation?
   b. countries that cannot grow enou food for their people?
   c. the disagreements between Ch and the Soviet Union?
   d. problems in using some chemical tilizers?

3. The cold war is a serious world prob because it
   a. could lead to a nuclear war.
   b. always benefits the Soviet U

6. Some recent scientific improvements have been compared to the monsters of myth that grew two heads when one had been cut off because
   a. pollution is a problem in more than one place in the world.
   b. a scientific discovery may solve one problem, yet create two new ones.
   c. both clean air and water are needs of all people.

7. There is a concern about the steady rise in the world's birth rate because
   a. the amount of food raised cannot be increased.
   b. one-third of the world's people do not have proper schools.
   c. overpopulation causes serious problems.

Tell whether these statements are true or false. If a statement is false, change the words in italics to make it true.

1. The Basques are people who live in northern *Italy.*
2. The I.R.A. is a group that seeks to free *Northern Ireland* from Great Britain.
3. The South African policy of keeping blacks and whites apart is called *terrorism.*
4. Threats and propaganda have been used in the cold war between *China* and the United States.
5. The group that seeks to establish a separate nation for Palestinian Arabs is called the *P.L.O.*
6. The Macheteros are a group of *Italian* terrorists responsible for many assassinations.
7. The problem of unclean air and water is called *inflation.*
8. An American group that protested United States participation in the Vietnam War was called the *Weathermen.*
9. The United States and the Soviet Union have often discussed a ban on the testing of *nuclear-powered submarines.*
10. The Muslim Brotherhood is active in Iraq and *Greece.*

Making Generalizations

For each of the following sets of statements, make one reasonable generalization based on the three factual statements given.

1. Factual statements:
   a. The ancient Greeks made slaves of those who were not Greek.
   b. In the Middle Ages, Jews were not allowed in occupations reserved for Christians.
   c. In the 20th century, black people are still not allowed the same rights as whites in South Africa.

   Generalization:

2. Factual statements:
   a. Indonesia gained its freedom from the Dutch in 1949.
   b. India and Pakistan became independent in 1947.
   c. There have been over 50 new nations in Africa since World War II.

   Generalization:

3. Factual statements:
   a. Phonographs, radios, and tape recorders bring music and information into homes around the world.
   b. Many Americans rely on television for their news and entertainment.
   c. Paperback books have made good reading available to millions of people throughout the world.

   Generalization:

Developing Ideas and Skills

REASONING FROM HEADLINES

The following are groups of headlines that appeared in newspapers in several large cities of our country in recent years. As you read each group of headlines, see if you can determine what problem mentioned in Chapter 8 the group is connected with. After each group, there are questions to guide you in gaining more information about the world problem that is touched on.

1. PORTUGAL LEAVES ANGOLA AS CIVIL WAR GOES ON.
   RHODESIANS SAY, "IT'S OUR COUNTRY."
   MOZAMBIQUE—FREE AFTER 470 YEARS.
   SOVIET INFLUENCE IN AFRICA—A DANGEROUS GAME.
   CONGRESS SAYS U.S.—STAY OUT OF ANGOLA.
   a. How many different problems in Africa do these headlines refer to?
   b. Why do you think Soviet influence in Africa is called "a dangerous game"?

2. FERTILIZER FOR YOUR LAWN OR FOOD FOR INDIA?
   WILL THE SOVIET UNION EVER FEED ITSELF?
   FAMINE SPREADS IN BANGLADESH.
   GARBAGE IS MONEY FOR THE POOR IN INDONESIA.
   BURUNDI—THE POOREST PLACE ON EARTH.
   a. On what continents are the places in the headlines located?
   b. What problem is presented in the first headline?
   c. From what you have learned, why do you think the Soviet Union must often buy grain from other countries to feed her people?

3. INDIA CONDUCTS FIRST TEST OF A NUCLEAR BOMB.
   CHINA ANNOUNCES NUCLEAR BLAST.
   DOES ISRAEL HAVE A NUCLEAR BOMB?
   U.S. AND SOVIET TALK INSPECTION OF NUCLEAR BLASTS.
   a. What do the headlines tell us about the spread of nuclear weapons?
   b. Why might the United States and the Soviet Union be more willing now to make treaties concerning nuclear explosions?
   c. India and China announced that their tests were for peaceful purposes only. Do you think nuclear power can be limited to peaceful uses only? Explain.

4. GREECE TRIES TO PROTECT ANCIENT BUILDINGS FROM POLLUTION.
   PAPER PLANT DISCHARGES WASTES INTO LAKE BAIKAL.

AIR POLLUTION—ONE OF TOKYO'S WORST PROBLEMS.
U.S. COST TO CLEAN ENVIRONMENT—284 BILLION.
IN BELGRADE, THEY'D WALK A MILE FOR CLEAN AIR.

a. How many kinds of pollution are mentioned in these headlines?
b. What might you infer about the extent of pollution in the world from the headlines? How many different places are mentioned?
c. Why do you think Greece is particularly concerned about its buildings?
d. What problem in controlling pollution is implied in these headlines?
e. Why do you think it is not enough to rely on headlines to gain information about a problem or event?

Reviewing Chapter 8

Each of us has opinions about events taking place in our neighborhood, our country, and our world. We approve of some; we do not like others. All of us react to events according to our likes and dislikes. Some things are important to us; others are less important. We react according to the *values* we have.

Values are those matters or ideas on which we place great importance. We may value peace so much that we could never think of going to war with anyone. Nations have values, too. In a democracy, the people can determine their country's values. In a dictatorship, the ruler or rulers decide what is important for the country—what actions it shall take.

The information in this chapter gives you some opportunities to examine your own values and thos. of your nation, too.

Explore som   ²es by answering the following questions.

Do you believe th   .mportan.   try to help a weaker, friendly nation if it is threatened or attacked by a larger, unfrien.,   n? Would you risk war to provide this help? When would you want your nation to help other peoples? In what way should it help? When would you not offer such help?

Do you believe that all people have a right to enough food, clothing, and shelter to live comfortably? Is this one of your values? Would you eat less and spend less if it meant more food for a starving person thousands of miles away? If you had a lawn or garden, would you give up fertilizer so that farmers in Pakistan might grow more food?

Do you believe that all nations should have nuclear weapons? None of them? Only some of them? Do you believe that the spread of nuclear weapons is a threat to peace in the world? Would you want your country to reduce or get rid of its nuclear weapons completely?

Do you do anything to cause pollution in your environment? If your family's automobile polluted the air, would you be willing to do without it? If the cost of some things you like had to be increased so that the producer could pay to prevent pollution by his plant, would you be willing to pay the higher prices? Would you want to eliminate "throwaway" packages because they are part of the huge garbage-removal problem?

AIM: What kinds of relationships link the lands and cultures of the World?

CHAPTER 9

A World of Connections Between Peoples

WHAT ARE CULTURAL DIFFERENCES?

1. "Let's eat out!" Many families today like to celebrate by going out to eat. But at which restaurant? There are so many kinds from which to choose. There are French, Greek, and German restaurants. There are Russian tea rooms and English chop houses. There are Italian restaurants that serve pizza and Mexican restaurants that serve tacos. There are eating places that serve Southern-fried chicken and hamburgers. There are also Chinese, Japanese, and Indian restaurants. Each serves a different kind of food.

2. These various eating places are really examples of different kinds of cultures. Food, of course, is not the only thing that makes one culture different from another. People in different regions of the world also speak different languages. They dress differently and hold different religious beliefs. They enjoy different kinds of dancing, music, art, literature, and drama. They have different traditions and social customs. They have their own ways of celebrating birthdays and weddings, and of mourning at funerals. People all over the globe live in different ways. These various ways of living are cultural differences.

3. These cultural differences have been an important force in world history. From the beginning of civilization, the world has been affected by the exchange of ideas, goods, and knowledge between different cultures. When people from different parts of the globe make contact, each group gets something from the other. Both become richer because they have learned from each other. The mixing of cultures is one of the forces in the progress of civilization. It has helped to bring humankind from the Stone Age to the world of today.

The 1980 Winter Olympics. How do activities such as the Olympics help strengthen global ties?

WHAT ARE SOME EARLY EXAMPLES OF CULTURAL CONTACTS AND EXCHANGE?

4. The past provides many examples of cultures coming together where both benefitted. The ancient Greeks learned about the cultures of Egypt, Syria, Persia, and India through the conquests of Alexander the Great. Alexander wanted to combine the culture of Greece with the cultures of the lands he conquered to form a vast empire with a single great culture. He founded many cities, such as Alexandria, in Egypt, and Antioch, in Syria. These cities were adorned with temples, theatres, and other buildings based on Greek models. The Greek language and style of dress and other Greek customs influenced the educated class there.

5. On the other hand, Alexander encouraged the Greeks to copy many customs, ideas, and styles of art of the lands they entered. The merging of Greek ideas and Oriental customs created a new culture, called Hellenistic. The Hellenistic Age produced many great works of art. It encouraged trade among Greece, Persia, and Syria. Some of the greatest minds the world has ever known lived during this period. Among them were Archimedes, in physics; Galen, in medicine; Ptolemy, in astronomy; Euclid, in geometry; Epicurus, in philosophy; and many more.

6. Another example of contact between cultures is seen in the travels of Marco Polo, during the 13th century. Marco Polo, his father, and his uncle—all merchants—traveled by caravan from Venice to China. Their journey took $3\frac{1}{2}$ years. Marco Polo stayed in China for 17 years as the guest of the emperor, the Kublai Khan. While there, he told the emperor many things about the people and customs of his native land. He taught the Chinese how to build a war machine called a catapult. It could hurl a stone weighing 300 pounds through the air.

7. When Marco Polo returned home, he wrote a book describing the wonders he had

Marco Polo represents an early example of cultural exchange between Europe and China. Can you name other, later examples? Why do you think it is important to study cultural exchange?

seen. He described strange marriage and religious customs. He told of the tea and spices the people used. He explained how the Chinese made porcelain and silk and described what they ate and wore. He also described a new material that did not burn (asbestos) and another that did (coal). His book alerted Europeans to the value of trade with the people of Asia. It gave Europeans one of their first introductions to civilizations and cultures different from their own. It also led indirectly to the discovery of America almost two centuries later.

HOW DID EUROPEAN AND AMERICAN INDIAN CULTURES MEET?

8. The settlement of the New World is another vivid example of the meeting of entirely different cultures. European explorers, settlers, and missionaries found strange new cultures in the Americas. The Spanish found the rich civilization of the Incas in Peru and of the Aztecs and Mayans in Mexico. The English and the French found many of the Indian tribes of North America still living in a less developed culture. From Europeans, the Indians learned how to ride horses and use firearms. They also learned the uses of the wheel and the superiority of metal tools to stone tools.

9. From the Indians the Europeans learned to plant corn, tomatoes, pumpkins, peanuts, and white and sweet potatoes. They learned that chestnuts, strawberries, blackberries and crab apples could be eaten. They learned how to tap maple syrup from trees, to use turkeys as food, and to eat chocolate. Never before had Europeans tasted any of these things. More than half of the world's farm products grown today come from plants first found and used by the Indians in America.

HOW DID JAPANESE AND WESTERN CULTURES MEET?

10. A more recent example of a link between different cultures is seen in the history of Japan. Before the middle of the 19th century, the rulers of Japan did not permit any foreigners or traders to come to their land. It was a crime for a citizen of Japan to travel abroad. For many centuries, this policy kept Japan isolated from the rest of the world. While the United States and the nations of Europe were becoming modern industrial nations, the people of Japan were still living under a feudal system.

11. In 1853, Commodore Matthew C. Perry of the United States arrived in Tokyo harbor with four warships. He had been sent to persuade the Japanese to start trading with the United States. When the Japanese saw smoke pouring from the stacks of Perry's warships, they were terrified. They ran to their temples to pray for their lives. Perry gave the Japanese

emperor many gifts, including a sewing machine, a toy railroad, and a telegraph machine. The Japanese had never seen any of these things before. They finally agreed to end their isolation. They rapidly began to copy the ways of the West. Within fifty years, Japan became a modern nation with factories, railroads, power plants, and warships.

12. Japanese culture, in turn, influenced Europeans and Americans. For the first time, Japanese customs and traditions became known to the Western world. Western women began to decorate their homes with Japanese vases, screens, paintings, wallpaper, and other ornaments. Japanese ideas entered Western art, literature, and music. Gilbert and Sullivan's comic opera *The Mikado* (1885) and Puccini's opera *Madame Butterfly* (1904) are just two among many examples of Western works of art inspired by Japanese culture. Today, Americans and Europeans use Japanese radios, recorders, television sets, computers, cameras, automobiles, and scores of other products. Thus, Western industrial culture has changed Japan and Japanese culture has enriched the West.

WHY IS OURS A WORLD OF INTERCONNECTING CULTURES?

13. Before the beginning of the modern era, the world was made up of separate pockets of different cultures. Contacts between people of different cultures occurred, but they were not everyday events. There were many reasons for this. Methods of travel and communication were slow. Natural barriers such as deserts, mountains, and oceans kept people apart and unknown to each other. Also, ancient people were usually afraid of foreigners, who had strange customs and spoke odd-sounding languages.

14. In ancient times, one way by which people of different cultures met and mixed was war. The conquests of Alexander the Great are

How does this picture show cultural contact and exchange? What is good about such an exchange? What is not good about such an exchange?

an example. Another way was by merchants and travelers, such as Marco Polo. Missionaries and explorers also bridged different cultures. In those early days, the time needed to travel by sailboat or caravan was measured in months and years. But in the modern era all this has changed.

15. Our modern means of communication—telephone, radio, and television—require no time at all. Steamships, trains, trucks, buses, automobiles, and jet airplanes are very much faster means of travel than the methods early people had. The shift from very slow to very rapid travel and communication has shrunk the size of the world. As a result, cultures and peoples interconnect more rapidly than ever before. Also, the kinds of interconnections are greater in number than ever before.

16. Our planet is no longer a measureless globe of unknown regions and strange people. Contacts between different world cultures continue all the time. For example, ballet dancers from the Soviet Union perform in New York City. Tourists from South America take vacations in Miami Beach. Japanese businessmen have offices in New Jersey. American engineers drill for oil in Indonesia and Saudi Arabia. American jazz musicians perform in Nigeria. The Chinese government sends an art exhibit to Washington, D.C. Mexican folk dancers perform in Canada. Today the audience for sports, art, music, drama and the dance spans the entire globe.

17. Through these global exchanges and contacts people can learn to appreciate and respect the traditions and ideas of others. In ancient times, people of a different culture were usually held to be inferior. Foreigners were considered dangerous. Today, civilized people have come to respect and appreciate men and women whose customs, religion, language, and ideas are different from their own. They know that different cultural groups have much to offer to enrich their lives. The globe is now increasingly crisscrossed with connections among the lands and peoples of the world. Because of these connections, our planet seems smaller than it did to our ancestors. In the past, many people never traveled more than a few miles from the farm or village where they were born. Today, people in countries with developed systems of travel can soar over oceans and continents in a few hours. In our world, no land is unknown territory.

Testing Your Vocabulary

Choose the best answer.

1. There are people of many different cultures all over the world. A *culture* means a group of
   a. raw materials, crops, and industries.
   b. ideas, traditions, beliefs, customs, and language.
   c. governments, laws, and treaties.
2. For centuries the Japanese remained *isolated* from the rest of the world. This means that they

a. lived under a feudal system and an emperor.
b. believed their culture was best.
c. had few contacts with anyone else.

3. Marco Polo traveled across Asia by *caravan*. A caravan is
   a. people traveling together on land with wagons and pack animals.
   b. a fleet of sailing ships.
   c. an invading army or military force.

Understanding What You Have Read

1. In which paragraphs do you find facts about
   a. the culture of American Indians?
   b. modern methods of travel and communication?
   c. the culture of the Hellenistic Age?
   d. the ending of Japanese isolation?
2. A good title for paragraph 16 is
   a. War: One Way that Cultures Meet and Mix.
   b. Barriers Between Peoples of Different Cultures.
   c. Cultural Connections.
3. Commodore Perry was sent to Japan in order to
   a. persuade the Japanese to start trading with the United States.
   b. conquer Japan and make it a colony.
   c. give the Japanese emperor gifts from the United States.
4. Contacts and connections between different cultures have been an important force in world history because they
   a. led to the writing of travel books.

b. encouraged the exchange of ideas, knowledge, and goods.
c. helped the tourist industry.

5. In ancient times people were afraid of foreigners because foreigners
   a. tried to start revolutions.
   b. carried disease and caused epidemics.
   c. had strange customs and spoke different languages.
6. Many Indian tribes in North America were considered to be less developed than Europeans because they
   a. used stones to make their tomahawks and other tools.
   b. lived in caves carved out of rock.
   c. made carvings and sculptures in stones.
7. When historians say that the earth is getting smaller they mean
   a. the oceans are drying up.
   b. it takes less time to travel and communicate than it used to.
   c. this is the age of space exploration.

Developing Ideas and Skills

USING A TIME LINE.

Tell when the events listed below took place by filling in the correct letter from the time line. Write the answers in your notebook.

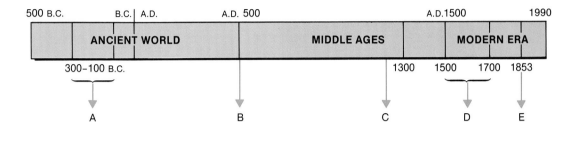

1. the isolation of Japan ends   _____
2. the Hellenistic Age   _____
3. European exploration and settlement of the New World   _____
4. the travels of Marco Polo   _____

Summary of Unit XIII

1. Middle East crises have been caused by rivalry for oil, wars with Israel, and civil wars.
2. The United States' policy toward Latin America has changed since 1933.
3. Mexico has a stable government and is rich in oil and natural gas resources.
4. The United States views Soviet influence in Cuba and Nicaragua as a threat to American security.

5. Many changes in Western art, literature, and music have occurred during the 20th century.
6. New scientific discoveries have changed the lives of most people.
7. Nuclear power is a valuable source of energy, but its use involves many dangers.
8. Since 1960, a feminist revolution has gained more rights for women.
9. The cold war, pollution, and famine are key problems in the world today.
10. The use of terrorism as a political device has become a serious problem in many countries.
11. Modern means of transportation and communication have made the world a vast network of connections and relationships.

TURNING POINTS

Technology

The World: Food Production

Throughout the world, people eat great varieties of foods. One reason is cultural. People from different cultures have different food habits. Another reason is location. The food that people eat often depends on where they live. In wealthy countries, people can produce or import all the food they need or want. Other countries are not as fortunate. Sometimes their farmers cannot produce enough food. In many cases, they cannot afford to buy it from other nations.

Many of the nations that do not have enough food are located near the tropics. Their soils are poor. Their climates are not suitable for large-scale farming. Sometimes these nations are hit by natural disasters such as droughts or floods. Wars and other problems can also affect their food production.

To increase food production, scientists and farmers work together to develop new crops and to improve those that exist. For instance, in the 1960s new kinds of wheat and rice were introduced. These plants had stronger stalks and produced more grains. As a result, countries such as India, Pakistan, China, and Thailand were able to grow more food.

Today, researchers are working to improve such crops as cassava and maize. These foods are popular in Africa. Crops that are high in protein are also being developed. Plants are a cheaper source of protein than is meat. Some of these plants are soybeans, coconuts, cottonseed, and peanuts. Scientists are trying to raise plants that need less water and fertilizer. They also want to grow plants that are tasty, more nutritious, and not easily destroyed by insects. Scientists are trying to find ways to produce enough food for all the people of the world.

Critical Thinking

1. Why would plants that need less water help to increase the world's food production?
2. Would a snack of some peanuts and coconut be good for you? Explain.

The World

International Boundaries

kilometers
miles

636

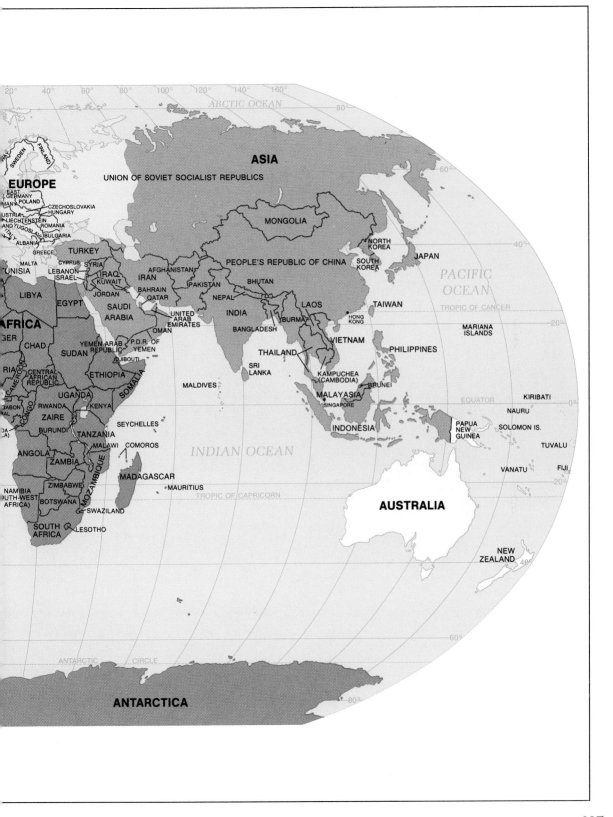

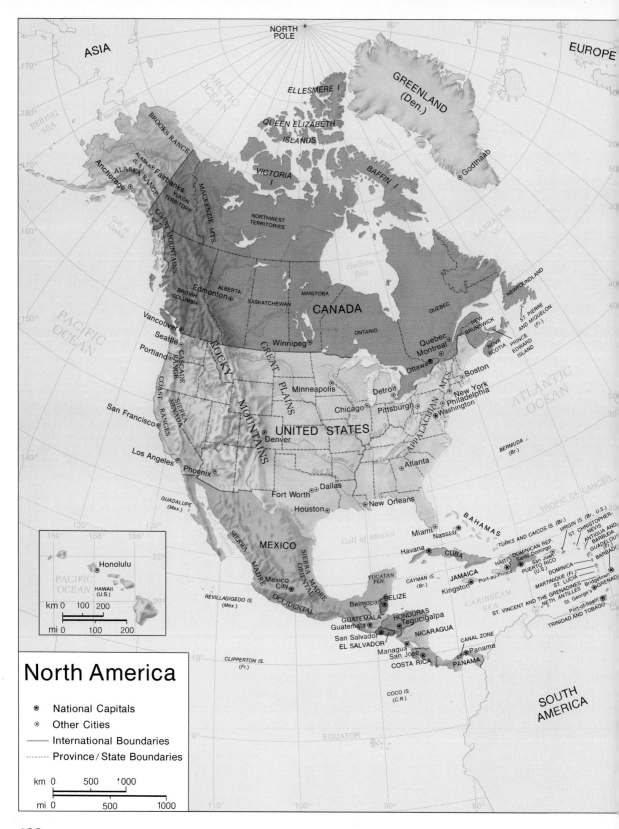

North America

- ⊛ National Capitals
- ⊙ Other Cities
- ——— International Boundaries
- --------- Province/State Boundaries

km 0   500   1000
mi 0   500   1000

638

ASIA

EUROPE

NORTH POLE

ARCTIC OCEAN

BERING SEA

BEAUFORT SEA

ELLESMERE I

GREENLAND (Den.)

QUEEN ELIZABETH ISLANDS

BROOKS RANGE

Godthaab

VICTORIA I

BAFFIN I

Davis Strait

Anchorage

ALASKA (U.S.)

Fairbanks

ALASKA RANGE

YUKON TERRITORY

MACKENZIE MTS.

NORTHWEST TERRITORIES

LABRADOR SEA

Gulf of Alaska

COAST MOUNTAINS

Hudson Bay

NEWFOUNDLAND

Edmonton

ALBERTA

BRITISH COLUMBIA

SASKATCHEWAN

MANITOBA

CANADA

QUEBEC

ST. PIERRE AND MIQUELON (Fr.)

Vancouver

ROCKY MOUNTAINS

ONTARIO

NEW BRUNSWICK

NOVA SCOTIA

PRINCE EDWARD ISLAND

PACIFIC OCEAN

Winnipeg

Seattle

CASCADE RANGE

GREAT PLAINS

Quebec

Montreal

Portland

Ottawa

Boston

SIERRA NEVADA

Minneapolis

Detroit

APPALACHIAN MTS.

New York

San Francisco

COAST RANGES

Chicago

Pittsburgh

Philadelphia

Washington

ATLANTIC OCEAN

UNITED STATES

Denver

Los Angeles

Phoenix

Atlanta

BERMUDA (Br.)

GUADALUPE (Mex.)

Fort Worth

Dallas

New Orleans

TROPIC OF CANCER

Houston

MEXICO

SIERRA MADRE ORIENTAL

Miami

Nassau

BAHAMAS

TURKS AND CAICOS IS. (Br.)

VIRGIN IS. (Br., U.S.)

ST. CHRISTOPHER-NEVIS

ANTIGUA AND BARBUDA

GUADELOUPE (Fr.)

Havana

CUBA

HAITI

DOMINICAN REP.

Santo Domingo

PUERTO RICO (U.S.)

San Juan

DOMINICA

BARBADOS

REVILLAGIGEDO IS. (Mex.)

YUCATAN PEN.

CAYMAN IS. (Br.)

JAMAICA

Kingston

Port-au-Prince

MARTINIQUE (Fr.)

ST. LUCIA

Bridgetown

SIERRA MADRE OCCIDENTAL

Mexico City

BELIZE

Belmopan

ST. VINCENT AND THE GRENADINES

NETH. ANTILLES

St. George's

GRENADA

Port-of-Spain

CARIBBEAN SEA

CLIPPERTON IS. (Fr.)

GUATEMALA

Guatemala

HONDURAS

Tegucigalpa

TRINIDAD AND TOBAGO

San Salvador

EL SALVADOR

NICARAGUA

Managua

CANAL ZONE

San José

COSTA RICA

Panama

PANAMA

COCO IS. (C.R.)

EQUATOR

SOUTH AMERICA

HAWAII (U.S.)

Honolulu

PACIFIC OCEAN

km 0   100   200
mi 0   100   200

CENTRAL
AMERICA

CARIBBEAN SEA

Barranquilla
Maracaibo
Caracas

GUYANA
Georgetown
SURINAME
Paramaribo
FRENCH GUIANA
Cayenne

Medellín
VENEZUELA

MALPELO
(Colombia)

Bogotá
LLANOS
GUIANA
HIGHLANDS

Cali
COLOMBIA

GALÁPAGOS ISLANDS
(Ecuador)

Quito
ECUADOR
Guayaquil

SELVAS
Negro R.

EQUATOR

Belém
ROCAS
(Brazil)

Iquitos
Amazon R.
Manaus

FERNANDO DE
NORONHA
(Brazil)

AMAZON BASIN

Recife

PERU
ANDES

Madeira R.

BRAZIL

Callao
Lima
Cuzco

MOUNTAINS

PACIFIC
OCEAN

La Paz

MATO
GROSSO
PLATEAU

Salvador

Brasília

BOLIVIA
Sucre

BRAZILIAN HIGHLANDS

Belo
Horizonte

TROPIC OF CAPRICORN

CHACO

Antofagasta

SAN FÉLIX
(Chile)
SAN AMBROSIO
(Chile)

GRAN

PARAGUAY

São
Paulo
Rio de
Janeiro

Tucumán
Asunción

JUAN
FERNÁNDEZ
(Chile)

Córdoba

ARGENTINA

Valparaíso
Santiago

Porto
Alegre

URUGUAY

ATLANTIC
OCEAN

Buenos Aires

PAMPAS

Montevideo

CHILE
ANDES
MOUNTAINS

Bahía
Blanca

Valdivia

PATAGONIA

South America

⊛ National Capitals
⊙ Other Cities
—— International Boundaries

FALKLAND ISLANDS (MALVINAS)
(U.K.—claimed by Argentina)

Strait of
Magellan

SOUTH GEORGIA
(Falkland Is.)

CAPE
HORN

km 0   350   700

mi 0   350   700

639

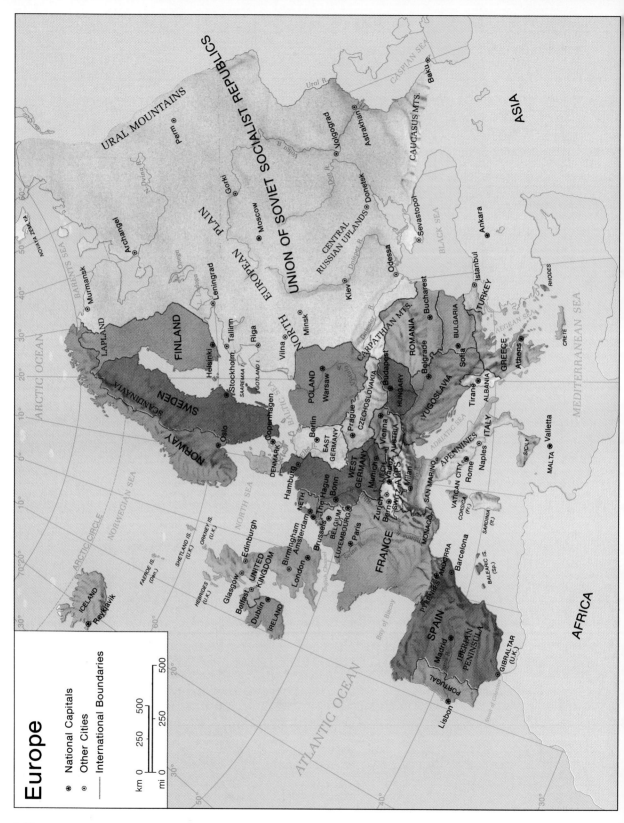

Europe

- ⊛ National Capitals
- ⊙ Other Cities
- —— International Boundaries

km 0   250   500
mi 0   250   500

ARCTIC OCEAN

NORWEGIAN SEA

BARENTS SEA

URAL MOUNTAINS

NOVAYA ZEMLYA

Archangel

Murmansk

Perm

Gorki

Moscow

EUROPEAN PLAIN

UNION OF SOVIET SOCIALIST REPUBLICS

CENTRAL RUSSIAN UPLANDS

Volgograd

Astrakhan

CASPIAN SEA

Baku

ASIA

CAUCASUS MTS.

Donetsk

Sevastopol

BLACK SEA

Odessa

Kiev

Minsk

Leningrad

Vilna

Riga

Tallinn

Helsinki

FINLAND

LAPLAND

SCANDINAVIA

SWEDEN

NORWAY

Stockholm

Oslo

Copenhagen

DENMARK

GOTLAND I.

SAAREMAA I.

BALTIC SEA

NORTH SEA

POLAND

Warsaw

Berlin

EAST GERMANY

Hamburg

WEST GERMANY

Bonn

Prague

CZECHOSLOVAKIA

Budapest

HUNGARY

Vienna

AUSTRIA

LIECH.

Munich

SWITZ.

Zurich

Bern

Vaduz

ALPS

Milan

CARPATHIAN MTS.

ROMANIA

Bucharest

Belgrade

YUGOSLAVIA

BULGARIA

Sofia

Tirane

ALBANIA

GREECE

Athens

ADRIATIC SEA

AEGEAN SEA

Istanbul

Ankara

TURKEY

RHODES

CRETE

MEDITERRANEAN SEA

ITALY

APENNINES

Rome

Naples

SAN MARINO

VATICAN CITY

MONACO

CORSICA (Fr.)

SARDINIA (It.)

SICILY

MALTA

Valletta

FRANCE

Paris

LUXEMBOURG

BELGIUM

Brussels

NETH.

The Hague

Amsterdam

Seine R.

Bay of Biscay

PYRENEES

ANDORRA

Barcelona

SPAIN

Madrid

IBERIAN PENINSULA

PORTUGAL

Lisbon

GIBRALTAR (U.K.)

BALEARIC IS. (Sp.)

Strait of Gibraltar

AFRICA

ATLANTIC OCEAN

ICELAND

Reykjavik

FAEROE IS. (Den.)

SHETLAND IS. (U.K.)

ORKNEY IS. (U.K.)

HEBRIDES (U.K.)

Edinburgh

Glasgow

UNITED KINGDOM

Belfast

Dublin

IRELAND

Birmingham

London

English Channel

ARCTIC CIRCLE

640

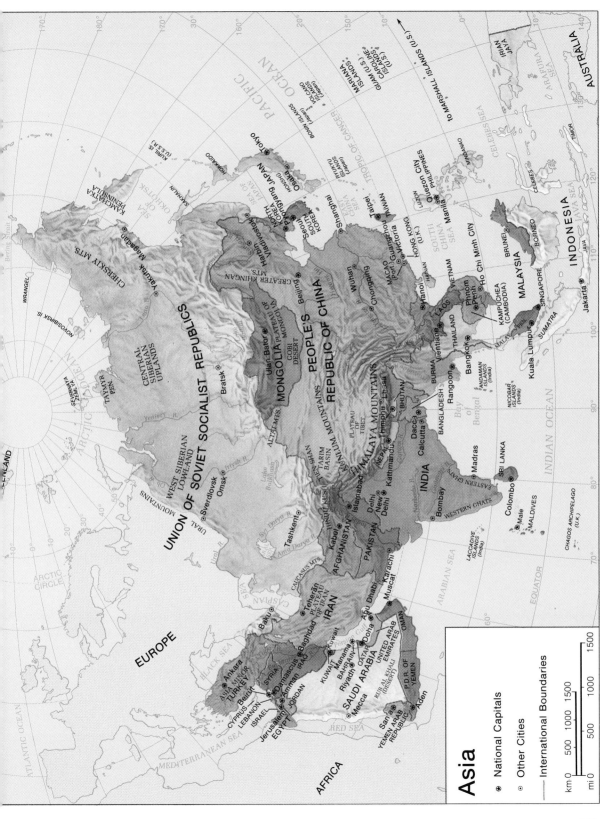

Asia

- ⊛ National Capitals
- ⊙ Other Cities
- —— International Boundaries

km 0   500   1000 1500
mi 0   500   1000 1500

641

Africa

⊛ National Capitals

⊙ Other Cities

— International Boundaries

km 0   500   1000

mi 0   500   1000

EUROPE

ATLANTIC OCEAN

MEDITERRANEAN SEA

ASIA

Tangier ⊙   Tunis
⊛ Algiers
⊙ Rabat Oran ⊙
Casablanca ⊙   TUNISIA
MADEIRA ISLANDS (Port.)
⊙ Tripoli
Benghazi ⊙   Alexandria ⊙
Suez Canal
CANARY ISLANDS (Sp.)
Cairo ⊛
MOROCCO
ALGERIA   **LIBYA**   **EGYPT**
LIBYAN DESERT
El Aaiun ⊙   Luxor ⊙
TROPIC OF CANCER   AHAGGAR MOUNTAINS   *Lake Nasser*
MAURITANIA
to CAPE VERDE ISLANDS (Port.)
⊛ Nouakchott   S A H A R A   **NIGER**   TIBESTI MOUNTAINS   **SUDAN**   Port ⊙ Sudan
Timbuktu ⊙   *Niger R.*   Khartoum ⊛   Asmara ⊙
Dakar ⊛   **MALI** ⊙ Gao   **CHAD**   Al Ubayyid ⊙
Banjul ⊛ SENEGAL Bamako ⊛ Niamey ⊛   DJIBOUTI ⊛ Djibouti ⊙
GAMBIA   ⊙ Ouagadougou   N'Djamena ⊛   *Gulf of Aden* *SOCOTRA (P.D.R.Y.)*
Bissau ⊛ GUINEA BISSAU BURKINA FASO Kano ⊙   **ETHIOPIA**
GUINEA   ⊛ Conakry   BENIN   **CENTRAL AFRICAN REPUBLIC**   Addis ⊛ Ababa
Freetown ⊛ SIERRA LEONE   **NIGERIA**   *White Nile R.*   ETHIOPIAN HIGHLANDS
Monrovia ⊛ LIBERIA IVORY COAST GHANA Lagos ⊙   Bangui ⊛   Mogadishu ⊙
Abidjan ⊙ Accra ⊛ Porto-Novo ⊛   **CAMEROON**   **SOMALIA**
Lomé ⊛   Lomé Malabo ⊛   Yaounde ⊛   *Zaïre R.*   Kisangani ⊙   Kampala ⊛ **UGANDA**
Gulf of Guinea EQUATORIAL GUINEA   **CONGO** RWANDA   *Lake Victoria* **KENYA**
SÃO TOMÉ AND PRÍNCIPE São ⊛ Tomé Libreville ⊛   **ZAIRE** ⊛ Kigali Nairobi ⊛
EQUATOR   GABON CONGO   BASIN   BURUNDI Mombasa ⊙
Brazzaville ⊛ ⊙ Kinshasa   Bujumbura ⊛ **TANZANIA**
CABINDA (Angola)   Dar es Salaam ⊙
⊙ Luanda   *INDIAN OCEAN*
ASCENSION (St. Helena)   Lubumbashi ⊙   *ALDABRA ISLANDS*
Lobito ⊙ **ANGOLA** **ZAMBIA** *Lake Nyasa* MALAWI Moroni ⊙ **COMOROS**
ATLANTIC OCEAN   Lusaka ⊛ Lilongwe ⊛
ST. HELENA (U.K.)   Harare ⊛ **MOZAMBIQUE** **MADAGASCAR**
NAMIB DESERT **ZIMBABWE**   Antananarivo ⊛
TROPIC OF CAPRICORN NAMIBIA (S.W. AFRICA)   *REUNION (Fr.)*
Windhoek ⊛   **BOTSWANA**   *Mozambique Channel*
WALVIS BAY (S. Afr.) KALAHARI DESERT Gaborone ⊛ Maputo ⊛
Pretoria ⊛ Mbabane ⊛ SWAZILAND
Johannesburg ⊙   Maseru ⊛
Bloemfontein ⊙   **SOUTH AFRICA** Durban ⊙
LESOTHO
DRAKENSBERG
Cape Town ⊛
CAPE OF GOOD HOPE

642

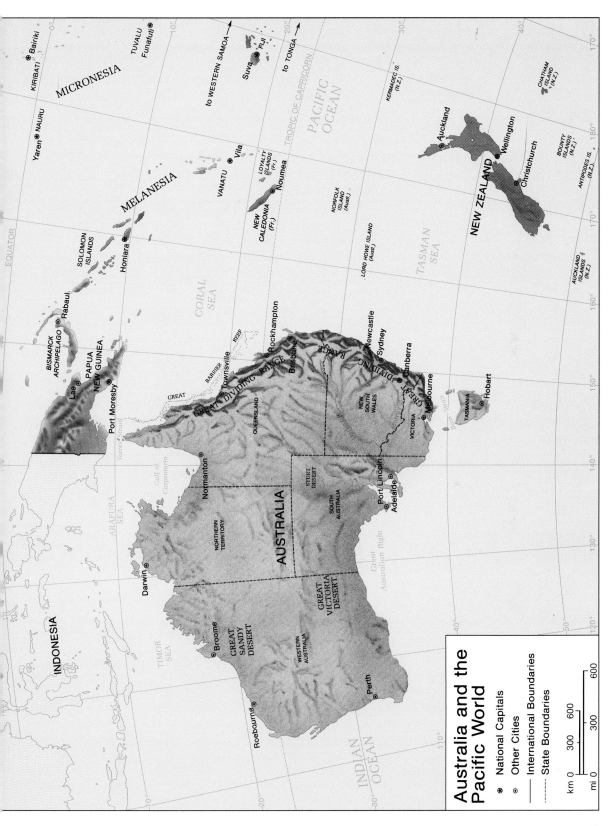

Australia and the Pacific World

* ⊛ National Capitals
* ⊙ Other Cities
* —— International Boundaries
* ----- State Boundaries

km 0   300   600
mi 0   300   600

GLOSSARY

abdication   (ab-di-KAY-shun) The act of a king or monarch when he gives up his power and right to rule.

Afrikaners   (af-ri-KAHN-erz) Members of the white ruling class of the Republic of South Africa.

Age of Reason   The period in history when people began to question their beliefs and began to depend on their ability to figure out the causes of events.

aggressor   (a-GRESS-or) Any country that attacks another country.

agriculture   (AG-ri-kul-cher) Relating to farming and crops.

alliance   (a-LYE-ans) An agreement among nations to act together and to help one another.

ally   (AL-lye) A friend or companion; a country on the same side in a war.

Alsace-Lorraine   (Al-sase lo-RAIN) The territory between Germany and France which is often claimed by both countries.

Angles   (ANG-els) Members of a barbarian tribe that settled in Britain and mixed with the Saxons.

anthropologist   (an-throe-POL-o-jist) A scientist who studies how people live with one another.

apartheid   (a-PAR-tite) The policy of the South African government of keeping black people in an inferior position to whites and forcing them to live separately.

apprentice   (a-PREN-tis) A young man who ran errands for a master craftsman as a way of beginning to learn a trade.

aqueduct   (AK-we-dukt) A channel built to carry water over long distances.

archaeologist   (ark-e-AHL-o-jist) A scientist who studies ancient ruins and other remains.

aristocrat   (a-RIS-to-krat) A person of noble birth; a member of a superior class.

assassination   (a-sass-i-NAY-shun) Murder of an important leader for political reasons.

astronomer   (a-STRON-o-mer) A scientist who studies the heavens.

Atlantic Charter   The war aims listed by Franklin D. Roosevelt and Winston Churchill **during** World War II.

autocracy   (aw-TOK-ra-see) A government controlled by one person.

automation   (aw-toe-MAY-shun) The use of electronic devices to run machines.

Axis Powers   (AK-sis POW-ers) Germany, Italy, and Japan during World War II when **they** formed a military alliance; also called the Rome-Berlin-Tokyo Axis.

Balance of Power   A means of keeping peace by making sure that no nation or group of **nations** becomes so powerful that it can dominate others.

Balkans   (BALL-kanz) The countries located on the Balkan Peninsula, in the southeastern part of Europe.

ballot   (BAL-ot) A sheet of paper used to cast a vote; the list of candidates in an election; or the vote itself.

Benelux   (BEN-e-luks) The combined countries of Belgium, the Netherlands, and Luxembourg.

Berbers   (BER-berz) The Muslims of North Africa.

Bill of Rights   The first ten amendments to the Constitution of the United States, which lists the rights of citizens; also, any document listing the civil rights of people in a democracy.

644

blockade	(blah-KADE) A barrier of ships or soldiers whose purpose is to stop the movement of supplies into or out of a country.
Boers	(BO-erz) Colonists from Holland who settled in South Africa as farmers in the nineteenth century.
Bolsheviks	(BOLE-shi-viks) The original members of the Communist Party in Russia.
Bosnia-Herzegovina	(BOZ-nee-a hertz-e-go-VEE-na) Balkan territory taken by Austria-Hungary before World War II.
Boxers	(BOK-serz) A group of Chinese who tried to drive foreigners out of China in the late nineteenth century.
boycott	(BOI-kot) An organized effort to avoid doing business with an individual, group, nation, etc.
Buddhism	(BOO-dizm) A religion started by Gautama Buddha.
Bundesrat	(BOON-des-raht) The upper house of the German parliament.
bushido	(boo-SHEE-doe) The code of behavior of Japanese warriors (samurai), based on bravery, loyalty, and honor.
Byzantine	(BIZ-an-teen) The Eastern Roman Empire, centered in ancient Constantinople, once called Byzantium.
cabinet	(KAB-i-net) A group of people, or a council, who advise the ruler of a country.
caliph	(KAY-lif) A ruler within the Muslim empire.
capitalism	(KAP-i-tal-izm) An economic system based on free enterprise and private profit.
caravan	(KAR-a-van) A group of travelers, especially desert travelers.
Carbonari	(kar-bo-NAHR-ee) An Italian secret society of the nineteenth century whose purpose was to unify Italy.
cartel	(car-TEL) An internationally organized group controlling prices or production in some field of business.
caste system	(KAST SIS-tem) An ancient practice in India by which people are born into a social class and cannot move out of it.
catacombs	(KAT-a-kohmz) Underground cemeteries where Christians hid from persecution by Roman emperors.
Cavaliers	(KAV-a-LEERZ) Nobles and landowners who sided with Charles I of England in the English Civil War.
Catholic	(KATH-o-lik) A member of the Roman Catholic Church.
censorship	(SEN-sor-ship) Suppression by the government of printed or spoken ideas that it does not want people to learn of.
century	(SEN-chu-ree) A period of one hundred years.
chancellor	(CHAN-sel-or) A government official: may be either the highest person in a government, as in the German empire, or a lower official, as in the British cabinet.
charter	(CHAR-ter) A document that describes the organization or aims of a political body (such as the United Nations) or business corporation.
Chartists	(CHAR-tists) English reformers of the nineteenth century who wanted better social and working conditions for the lower classes.
chivalry	(SHIV-al-ree) The rules of behavior for knights.
Christianity	(kris-chee-AN-i-tee) The religion of the followers of Christ.

city-state	A town or city that is independent, as in ancient Greece.
Civilization	(siv-ih-lih-ZAY-shun) An advanced state of society.
civil liberties	(SIV-il LIB-er-teez) Rights of people living in a democracy, such as freedom of speech, assembly, and religion.
civil war	A war fought between groups of the same country.
classical	(KLAS-ik-kul) Characteristic of ancient Greece and Rome; of an artistic or literary style characterized by simplicity, balance, dignity, and emotional restraint.
clergy	(KLER-jee) Those trained to carry out the functions of a church, such as priests and monks.
climate	(KLI-mat) The generally present weather conditions of a region.
cold war	War of words and propaganda between the Soviet Union and the United States after World War II.
collective bargaining	(kol-LEK-tiv BAR-gen-ing) Discussion between labor unions and management to reach agreement on wages and working conditions for employees.
colonialism	(ko-LOE-nee-al-izm) A national policy of owning and governing less powerful nations.
colony	(KAHL-o-nee) A land and people owned and governed by a more powerful nation.
Combination Laws	(kom-bi-NAY-shun LAWZ) Nineteenth-century British laws forbidding labor strikes and unions.
Continental System	(kon-ti-NENT-al SIS-tim) Napoleon's plan to prevent European nations from trading with England.
Common Market	Agreement made after World War II among six nations of Western Europe that they will not have tariffs on the goods they import from one another.
Commonwealth of Nations	Loose organization of former British dominions and colonies that are now independent nations.
communications	(kom-yoon-i-KAY-shunz) The sending and receiving of messages and other information.
communism	(KOM-yoon-izm) An economic system based on government ownership of all industry.
compensation	(kom-pen-SAY-shun) Payment for damages or losses.
congress	(KON-gress) A meeting of political leaders or a body of lawmakers, such as the U.S. Congress
conservative	(kon-SERV-a-tiv) Tending to preserve existing conditions and ways and to rely on the wisdom of the past.
constitution	(kon-sti-TOO-shun) A system of principles by which a nation or any group of people is governed.
contour plowing	(KON-toor PLOW-ing) Plowing soil in curves rather than in straight rows as a way of preventing soil erosion.
conveyor system	(kon-VAY-er SIS-tem) Use of moving belts to bring material to workers in factories.
cooperative	(ko-OP-er-a-tive) A business owned by the same people who buy from it; also called a co-op.

corporation	(kor-por-RAY-shun) A business company whose identity remains the same regardless of changes in the ownerships or work force.
council	(KOWN-sil) An assembly of people chosen to give advice or make laws.
Creoles	(KREE-ohlz) People of European descent born in Latin America; people of Spanish and black or French and black ancestry; people of French ancestry born in Louisiana.
crop rotation	(KROP ro-TAY-shun) Method of farming by which a different crop is planted on a piece of land each year.
Crusades	(kroo-SADES) Expeditions by Christians during the Middle Ages to take back the Holy Land from the Turks.
culture	(KUL-chur) The features or way of life of a civilization; also the expression of that way of life through music, literature, painting, sculpture, and architecture.
cuneiform	(kew-NEE-a-form) Wedge-shaped markings in clay; a system of writing in ancient Mesopotamia.
czars	(ZARZ) Rulers of Russia before the Russian Revolution overthrew the monarchy in 1917.
Dardanelles	(dar-da-NELZ) Narrow body of water belonging to Turkey which separates Europe from Asia Minor.
Dark Ages	The period from about A.D. 500 to A.D. 1000 in Europe.
democracy	(de-MOK-ra-se) A government ruled by the people or by people who represent them.
dialect	(DYE-a-lekt) A way of speaking a language that is somewhat different from the standard way.
dictatorship	(dik-TAY-tor-ship) A government in which one person rules a nation with absolute power.
diet	(DYE-et) A meeting to make decisions on religious or political matters.
divine right	(di-VINE RITE) The belief that the right to rule is granted by God, not by the people.
doctor	(DOK-tor) One who continues study in a special field.
doctrine	(DOK-trin) A rule or policy followed by a government or political leader.
Domestic System	(do-MES-tik SIS-tem) The practice, before the Industrial Revolution began, of making goods in the home.
dominion	(do-MIN-yun) A self-governing territory that recognizes the British king or queen as ruler.
duma	(DOO-ma) The first Russian parliament called together by Czar Nicholas II after the revolution of 1905.
dynasty	(DYE-nas-tee) A long line of rulers from the same family.
East India Company	A group of people who organized settlements in the New World.
economic	(ek-o-NOM-ik) Having to do with earning a living and buying and selling.
ECOSOC	Abbreviation for United Nations Economic and Social Council, an agency of the United Nations.
embargo	(em-BAR-go) A government order preventing merchant ships from entering or leaving ports.

émigrés	(EM-i-grayz) French nobles who left their country during the French Revolution to get help for the aristocracy.
emperor	(EM-per-or) Supreme ruler of an empire.
Enclosure Acts	(en-KLOE-zher AKTS) British laws of the eighteenth century that combined small farms to make large ones and thus forced peasants to leave their lands.
enlightened despot	(en-LITE-end DES-pot) An autocrat who showed interest in the common people.
erosion	(e-ROE-zhun) The wearing away of soil by wind, rain, or flood.
estate	(es-TATE) A large piece of land.
Estates-General	(es-TATES JEN-er-al) The lawmaking body of France before the French Revolution.
ethnic group	(ETH-nik GROOP) A society or people that share a common culture.
evolution	(ev-o-LOO-shun) Any slow development; also, a theory developed by Charles Darwin that human beings developed from lower forms of animal life.
excommunicate	(eks-ka-MEW-ni-kate) To cut off from the Church.
exile	(EKS-ile) To banish a person from his or her country.
extermination camp	(ex-ter-mi-NAY-shun KAMP) A place where Nazis imprisoned and killed millions of people during World War II.
fair	An event at which merchants met to sell their goods.
fallow	(FAL-oh) Not used for growing crops.
fascism	(FASH-izm) A form of government of which the head is a dictator and which is highly militaristic, nationalistic, and intolerant of opposition.
feminism	(FEM-in-izm) An organized movement to gain for women social and political rights equal to those of men.
Fertile Crescent	(FUR-til KRES-sent) A half-circle of fertile land in the area of the Tigris and Euphrates Rivers.
fertilizer	(FER-til-eye-zer) Natural or man-made material used to make the soil more productive.
feudalism	(FEW-dal-izm) The social and economic system of the Middle Ages in which serfs worked the land for the lords.
Führer	(FEW-rer) Leader (in German); title given to Adolf Hitler, dictator of Germany.
fief	(FEEF) A piece of land under the feudal system.
fossil	(FOSS-il) Remains or trace of an ancient animal or plant.
Four Freedoms	U.S. aims for all people, as announced by Franklin D. Roosevelt before World War II: freedom of speech, freedom of worship, freedom from want, and freedom from fear.
Fourteen Points	List of U.S. war aims drawn up by President Wilson during World War I.
Franks	Members of a barbarian tribe that took control of Gaul (now the country of France).
Gaul	(GALL) The ancient Roman name for the land that is today chiefly France.
generation	(jen-er-RAY-shun) A group of people born at about the same time; also, a period of about thirty years.

geologist	(jee-AHL-o-jist) One who studies the history of the earth and its structural changes.
gestapo	(gess-TOP-oh) Secret police in Germany during the rule of Hitler and the Nazis.
Glorious Revolution	The change in monarchs in England in 1688 accomplished without any bloodshed.
Golden Age	The period of prosperity and great culture in a people's history.
Gothic	(GOTH-ik) A style of architecture which produced large buildings with towers and pointed arches.
glacier	(GLAY-sher) A large mass of ice.
guerrillas	(guh-RIL-ahz) Small bands of fighters, not part of a regular army, who fight wars or revolutions.
guild	(GILD) An organization of businessmen or skilled workers.
guillotine	(GILL-a-teen) A machine to behead persons by means of a heavy falling blade.
habeas corpus	(HAY-bee-us KOR-pus) (Latin: "have the body") A court-issued order intended to protect a person from illegal imprisonment.
Hapsburg	(HAPS-burg) Family name of rulers of the Austrian and Austro-Hungarian empires.
Hausa	(HOW-zah) A language spoken in West Africa.
Hegira	(huh-JYE-ruh) The flight of Muhammad from Mecca to Medina in A.D. 622.
helot	(HEE-lot) Slave in ancient Sparta.
heresy	(HERR-e-see) Stating beliefs which differ from the official teachings of the Church.
hieroglyphics	(hie-roe-GLIF-iks) An ancient Egyptian system of writing in which a picture or symbol stands for a word.
Hinduism	(HIN-doo-izm) The major religion of India.
Hohenzollern	(HOE-en-zoll-ern) Family name of rulers of Prussia and the German empire.
Holocaust	(HOL-uh-cost) The organized killing of 6 million Jews by the Nazis during World War II.
Huguenot	(Hew-go-not) French Protestant.
humanist	(HEW-man-ist) A person who studies literature, the arts, philosophy, etc., as distinguished from pure theology.
Huns	(HUNZ) Members of a fierce, barbarian tribe from Central Asia.
icon	(EYE-kon) A picture of a saint, usually painted on a wood or ivory surface.
Il Duce	(ILL DEW-che) Benito Mussolini's title when he was dictator of Italy; means "the leader" in Italian.
imperialism	(im-PEER-ee-al-izm) A national policy of taking control of less powerful nations.
Impressionism	(im-PRESH-uh-nizm) A style of painting that aims to show impressions, rather than objective reality.
independence	(in-de-PEN-dens) Freedom from control by a person or nation.
indulgence	(in-DULL-jens) A pardon for sin granted to a person who has made a sacrifice.
inflation	(in-FLAY-shun) A rise in prices and salaries that lessens the purchasing power of money.

Inner Six	The western European nations of France, Luxembourg, the Netherlands, Belgium, West Germany, and Italy, who are members of the Common Market.
Inquisition	(in-kwuh-ZISH-un) An inquiry, or investigation, to find out if a teaching is in keeping with the teachings of the Church.
interdict	(IN-ter-dikt) In the Roman Catholic Church, a punishment by which Church members are for a time cut off from full participation in rites and sacraments.
international law	(in-ter-NAH-shun-al LAW) Rules which are accepted by most independent nations and which govern their acts toward one another in time of war and peace.
intolerance	(in-TAHL-er-ans) Disrespect for the beliefs of others.
investiture	(in-VESS-tuh-chur) The power to place Church officials in office.
Iron Chancellor	(EYE-urn CHAN-sel-or) The informal title given to Otto von Bismarck of Germany.
Islam	(ISS-lam) The religion of the followers of Muhammad.
isolation	(eye-so-LAY-shun) A government's policy of not getting involved in the affairs of other nations.
Jesuit	(JEZ-oo-it) An order of priests of the Catholic Church founded by Ignatius Loyola in 1534.
journeyman	(JUR-nee-man) One working to become a master craftsman.
kaiser	(KYE-zer) Title of emperor of the German empire until 1918.
knight	(NITE) A soldier who lived by the code of chivalry.
Koran	(ko-RAN) The holy book of Islam.
kraal	(KRAL) A small village in Africa, usually surrounded by a stockade.
kremlin	(KREM-lin) A fort in old Russia; today, the headquarters of the Soviet government.
Kuomintang	(kwo-min-TANG) Chinese political party that aimed to make China a democracy and a republic.
laissez-faire	(LES-say FAIR) (French: "allow to act") A government's policy of not trying to control business or industry.
legion	(LEE-jun) A group of 3000 to 6000 soldiers in the ancient Roman army.
Legislative Assembly	(LEG-is-lay-tiv a-SEM-blee) the lawmaking body of France established by the Constitution of 1792.
legislature	(LEJ-is-lay-chur) The branch of government that makes laws, such as a parliament or congress.
legitimacy	le-JIT-i-ma-see) The legal right of a monarch or government to rule a nation.
liberal	(LIB-e-ral) Favoring change and reform; open-minded or tolerant.
Lombards	(LOM-bards) An ancient Germanic tribe that moved into northern Italy.
Loyalists	(LOY-al-ists) People who supported the elected republican government of Spain during the Spanish Civil War.
Machine Age	The industrial era, when much is made and run by machines.

Magna Carta	(MAG-na KAR-ta) The first written document that limited the power of British monarchs, signed in 1215.
majority	(ma-JOR-i-tee) More than half of any number; usually refers to election results or legislative votes.
management	(MAN-aj-ment) People who run businesses, as distinguished from workers.
mandates	(MAN-dates) Countries taken from defeated countries by the League of Nations and given to its members at the end of World War I.
manor	(MAN-er) The land and mansion owned by a lord in the Middle Ages.
Marshall Plan	U.S. plan to give economic aid to war-torn nations of Europe after World War II.
Marxian Socialism	(MARK-see-an SO-shal-izm) An economic, political, and social system based on the ideas of Karl Marx.
mass production	Manufacture of large numbers of the same article.
master	A skilled craftsman of the Middle Ages.
mercantilism	(MER-kan-til-izm) Economic system based on the idea that a country's wealth is measured by the amount of gold and silver it has.
mestizos	(mes-TEE-zos) People of Latin America who are part European and part Indian.
Metternich System	(MET-er-nik SIS-tem) System of spies, censorship, and force used by Prince Metternich of Austria to put down democratic ideas.
Middle East	A region made up of countries of south and southwest Asia and northeast Africa.
Middle Ages	The period from about A.D. 500 to 1500.
middle class	Merchants, bankers, lawyers, etc.; people who are neither very rich nor very poor.
mikado	(mi-KAH-do) Title of an emperor of Japan.
militarism	(MILL-i-tar-izm) National policy of building up the army and navy.
minister	(MIN-is-ter) In a monarchy, an adviser to the king or queen.
ministerial responsibility	(min-i-STEER-ee-al re-spon-si-BILL-i-tee) Legal requirement of a prime minister and the cabinet to follow the wishes of the parliament or other law-making body.
minority	(my-NOR-i-tee) A group differing by race, religion, or ethnic background from the majority of a population.
mirs	(MEERZ) Lands bought by groups of Russian peasants from nobles during the rule of Czar Alexander II.
missionary	(MISH-un-eh-ree) A religious person who goes to distant lands in order to convert people to his faith.
monastery	(MON-as-ter-ee) A place where monks live away from the rest of the world.
Mongols	(MON-goles) A people of Central Asia who conquered large parts of Asia and Europe in the Middle Ages.
monks	(MUNKS) Persons who, for religious reasons, live away from the rest of the world in a monastery.
monotheism	(MON-o-thee-izm) Belief in one god.
Monroe Doctrine	The U.S. policy of opposing European colonies in the Western Hemisphere.
Moors	(MOORZ) North African followers of Muhammad.
mosaic	(mo-ZAY-ik) Small colored pieces of stone arranged to form a picture or pattern.
mosque	(MOSK) Muslim place of worship.

Munich Pact   (MEW-nik PAKT) A treaty signed before World War II in which Great Britain and France agreed to let the Nazis take part of Czechoslovakia.

Muslim   (MUZ-lim) A believer in, or follower of, Islam.

National Assembly   (NAH-shun-al ah-SEMB-lee) The lawmaking body of France that grew out of the Estates General.

nationalism   (NASH-un-nal-izm) Devotion to the interests of one's own nation.

nationality   (nash-un-AL-i-tee) Membership, especially by birth, in a particular nation.

nationalize   (NASH-un-al-ize) The taking over by a government of privately owned property, factories, or raw materials, to be used for public operations and purposes.

NATO   (NAY-toe) Abbreviated name for the North Atlantic Treaty Organization, an alliance of the United States and several European nations.

navigator   (NAV-i-gay-ter) One skilled at guiding a ship or airplane.

Nazis   (NOT-seez) Adolf Hitler's followers.

neutral   (NOO-tral) A nation or person that does not take sides in a war or dispute.

neutrality   (noo-TRAL-i-tee) A country's policy of not taking sides in a war or dispute.

noble   One who has a title or belongs to the upper class by birth.

nomad   (NOH-mad) A wandering person.

Normans   (NOR-manz) People from northern Europe who conquered the west coast of France in the tenth century.

nuclear weapons   (NOO-klee-ur WEP-uns) Explosives using the power of atoms.

obelisk   (OB-e-lisk) A stone shaft ending in a pyramidal tip.

Open Door Policy   American plan to give all nations equal trading rights in China.

OPEC   (OH-pec) The short form of the name Organization of Petroleum Exporting Countries.

oracle   (OR-uh-kul) One who tells the future.

Ottoman empire   (OT-toe-man EM-pire) Another name for the Turkish empire when it was under the rule of the Ottomans.

Ostrogoths   (OSS-tro-goths) A barbarian tribe that moved into Italy in the 5th century.

Outer Seven   The seven European nations that are members of the European Free Trade Association.

pact   (PAKT) An agreement or treaty, especially one between nations.

page   A boy attendant; a youth being trained for knighthood.

Papal States   (PAY-pal STATES) Lands in central Italy formerly owned by the Catholic Church.

papyrus   (pa-PYE-rus) A plant growing along the Nile River from which the Egyptians made a form of paper.

parchment   (PARCH-ment) Fine paper made from the skins of calves or sheep.

parliament   (PAR-li-ment) The chief lawmaking body in Great Britain and other countries.

party bloc   (PAR-tee BLOK) A number of political parties that vote as one group.

patricians   (pa-TRISH-unz) Wealthy landowners in ancient Rome.

Peace Corps	(PEASE KOR) A U.S. organization of volunteers sent to underdeveloped countries to help as teachers, nurses, and farm experts.
peasant	(PEZ-ent) A person of low social rank, usually from a farming or rural community.
peninsula	(pen-INS-yew-la) Any piece of land surrounded on three sides by water.
persecution	(per-se-KEW-shun) Harsh and unjust treatment of a person or group.
petition	(pe-TISH-un) A request; a list of persons who ask a leader or ruler to do something.
pharaoh	(FAY-roe) A ruler of the kingdom of Egypt.
philosopher	(fil-OSS-o-fer) One who studies and thinks about life and the reasons for people's actions.
plague	(PLAYG) A deadly contagious disease or sickness, such as the Black Death of the fourteenth century.
plebeians	(ple-BEE-anz) Poorer people of Rome who had few rights.
plebiscite	(PLEB-i-site) A vote by the people to decide which country they prefer to be ruled by or what kind of government they want.
P.L.O.	The initials of the Palestine Liberation Organization.
Point Four Program	U.S. plan to give economic and military aid to foreign countries in order to stop the spread of Communism.
police state	A dictatorship in which secret police deny all civil liberties and civil rights.
Polish Corridor	(POH-lish KOR-id-or) A strip of land dividing East and West Germany after World War I.
politburo	(PO-lit-BEW-ro) A small group of top Communist Party leaders.
political	(po-LIT-i-kal) Having to do with government matters, such as elections, parties, rulers, and laws.
pope	The spiritual leader of the Roman Catholic Church.
predestination	(PRE-des-tin-AY-shun) The belief that a person does not control the course of his own life since it has already been planned by God.
prehistoric	(pre-his-TOR-ik) Before written history.
premier	(preem-YEER) One of the chief officials, or leaders, of a government.
president	The chief officer or leader of a republic.
Presidium	(pre-SID-ee-um) The highest and most powerful agency of the Soviet government.
prime minister	The chief officer, or leader, of a government, as in Great Britain.
proletariat	(pro-le-TAIR-ee-at) The term used by Karl Marx for the working class in a capitalist society.
propaganda	(prop-a-GAN-da) The systematic spreading of ideas to influence the thinking of people.
prosperity	(pros-PER-i-tee) A state of economic well-being.
protectorate	(pro-TEK-to-ret) A colony whose political and military power is controlled by a foreign government.
Protestants	(PROT-es-tants) A member of any of the Christian bodies that separated from the Roman Catholic Church during the Reformation.
puppet government	(PUP-it GUV-ern-ment) A government without power and controlled by another government or secret ruler.

Puritan	(PURE-i-tuhn) A 16th-century English Protestant demanding strictness in religious matters and conduct.
Quadruple Alliance	(kwa-DROO-pul al-LYE-ans) Agreement among Prussia, Great Britain, Austria, and Russia to put down revolutions in Europe after the Napoleonic Era.
radical	(RAD-i-kal) A political party or person that favors fundamental, revolutionary changes in government.
Reformation	(ref-or-MAY-shun) The 16th-century religious movement which led to the beginning of the Protestant religions.
reign	(RANE) The time during which a monarch rules.
Reign of Terror	The period during the French Revolution when the king, the queen, and many nobles were executed.
Reichstag	(RYSHE-tag) The lower house of the German parliament.
Renaissance	REN-a-sans) The period from the 14th- to the 17th-century when a great rebirth of art, literature, and learning occurred in Europe.
reparations	(rep-a-RAY-shunz) The compensation that a nation defeated in war pays a victorious nation for damages or losses suffered during the war.
republic	(re-PUB-lik) A form of government in which the leaders are elected.
Restoration	(res-tor-AY-shun) The period in English history following the return of the monarchy when Charles II came to the throne.
revolution	(rev-o-LOO-shun) An uprising against a ruler or government.
Romanov	(ROE-man-off) Family name of the last czars in Russia.
rotten boroughs	(ROT-en BUHR-ohz) Small British election districts before 1832 which had many votes.
Roundheads	(ROWND-HEDS) Puritans and small landowners who cut their hair short to show they opposed the "long-hairs" of the court of the King of England.
Russification	(russ-i-fi-KAY-shun) Czarist policy to make all people in Russia speak, dress, and act like Russians.
samurai	(SAM-ur-rye) The former fighting class in Japan.
Sanskrit	(SAN-skrit) Early Hindu language.
satellite	(SAT-e-lite) Any object that circles the earth or another planet.
satire	(SAT-ire) A type of literature that pokes fun at foolishness in life, people, or governments.
Saxons	(SAK-sunz) A barbarian tribe that crossed into Britain and settled there.
scapegoat	(SKAPE-gote) A person or group on whom others blame their troubles.
Schuman Plan	(SHOO-man PLAN) A six-nation European tariff union for free trade in iron, coal, and steel.
sculptor	(SKULP-ter) An artist who makes statues.
SEATO	(SEE-toh) The abbreviated name for the Southeast Asia Treaty Organization.
Secretariat	(SEK-ri-TER-ee-at) The agency that does the office and organization work for the United Nations.
Secretary General	(SEK-rih-ter-ee GEN-er-al) The elected head of the United Nations and director of the Secretariat.

separation of powers	Division of the powers of government so that no one person or group may gain all the power.
serf	A farm peasant who owed his or her loyalty to a noble during the Middle Ages.
Sepoy Mutiny	(SEE-poy MEW-ti-nee) An uprising of Hindu and Muslim soldiers serving in the British army in India in 1857.
shadoof	(sha-DOOF) A system of buckets and poles used by Egyptians to take water from the Nile in order to irrigate nearby fields.
Shinto	(SHIN-toh) Japanese religion based on worship of the emperor.
Shoguns	(SHOW-guns) Military dictators who ran the government of Japan before the government was modernized.
Slavs	(SLAHVZ) Race of people spread widely over Eastern Europe.
slum	A crowded, unclean, and unsanitary area of a city.
smuggling	(SMUG-ling) Bringing goods into a country illegally.
social	(SO-shal) Relating to the activities of people living in groups.
social insurance	(SO-shul in-SUR-ince) Laws providing for payments to people who can't work because of sickness, old age, or accidents.
socialism	(SO-shal-izm) An economic system based on government ownership of industry and the abolition of private profits.
soviet	(SO-vee-et) Any local election district in the Soviet Union.
sphere of influence	Those territories in which the political and economic interests of a certain nation have full control.
squire	(SKWIRE) During the Middle Ages, a boy who trained to become a knight by carrying and caring for the weapons of his lord.
statute	(STA-choot) Any law passed by a legislature.
stockholder	(STOK-hold-er) One who owns a share in a business and receives part of its profits.
Stone Age	The stage of cultural development when a society's tools and weapons are made of stone, wood, and bone; the dawn of human history in Europe, Africa, and Asia.
strait	STRATE) A narrow body of water separating two large areas of land.
strip cropping	(STRIP KROP-ing) Planting rows of "cover" crops between rows of harvest crops in order to stop soil erosion.
subversion	(sub-VER-zhun) Any attempt to overthrow a lawful government or institution.
Sudetenland	(soo-DAY-ten-LAND) The part of Czechoslovakia seized by Nazi Germany before World War II.
Sultan	(SULL-ten) The title of the ruler of Turkey before it became a republic.
suppression	(sup-PRE-shun) Putting down rebellions or ideas by force.
surplus	(SIR-plus) Any goods that are left over after all needs for those goods are filled.
surplus value	The difference between the wages workers receive and the value of the goods or services they create.
Swahili	(swa-HEE-lee) The language spoken by many people of East Africa.
swastika	(SWAS-ti-ka) The symbol used by the Nazi Party in Germany under Adolf Hitler's dictatorship.
tapestry	(TAP-is-tree) A design or picture woven with thread, often used as a wall hanging.

tariff	(TAIR-if) A tax on goods brought into a country.
tariff union	(TA-rif YOON-yun) An agreement among nations to lower or end taxes on goods sent from one country to the other.
terrorism	(TER-or-izm) Killings, bombings, kidnappings, etc., for political purposes.
textiles	(TEK-styles) Woven materials made from natural or synthetic fibers.
theses	(THEE-seez) Ideas or principles stated; also, topics for discussion.
Third Reich	(THIRD RISHE) The dictatorship of Adolf Hitler in Nazi Germany.
three-field system	A method of farming in which one-third of the land was unused each year.
tithe	(TITHE) A tax, usually one-tenth of one's income, paid to support the Church.
topography	(tah-POG-ra-fee) The surface features of a land area; the mapping or charting of these features.
totalitarianism	(toe-TAL-i-TER-ee-an-ism) Government by dictatorship, can be either communist, fascist, or military.
treason	(TREE-zun) Giving help or military secrets to an enemy country.
tribute	(TRIB-yoot) To pay for the right to do something; also, to show respect for.
Triple Entente	(TRIP-ul on-TONT) The military alliance of Great Britain, France, and Russia before World War I.
truce	(TROOS) A halt in fighting during a war.
Truce of God	The period from Thursday evening to Monday morning in the Middle Ages when the Church did not allow fighting.
trusteeship	(truss-TEE-ship) Any one of the colonies given by the United Nations to the Allied Powers after World War II.
underground	A system of secret fighters or spies in a conquered country.
UNESCO	(yoo-NES-koh) The abbreviated name for the United Nations Educational, Scientific, and Cultural Organization.
unification	(yew-ni-fi-KAY-shun) The joining of different territories to form one nation.
Utopian Socialism	(yew-TOE-pe-an SO-shal-izm) A theory of government based on a belief in an ideal society in which all property and industry are owned in common.
vassal	(VAS-el) One who owned a fief or piece of land in the Middle Ages.
Vatican	(VAT-i-kan) The area of Rome controlled by the pope as an independent state.
veto	(VEE-toe) The rejection of a bill or law.
viaduct	(VYE-a-dukt) A bridgelike structure used to support a road going over a valley.
Vikings	(VYE-kings) Fierce warriors from Norway who raided coastal settlements from England to the Mediterranean Sea.
Vinland	(VIN-land) The name given to the land discovered by Lief Ericson on the coast of North America.
Visigoths	(VIZ-i-goths) A barbarian tribe that invaded Rome in A.D. 410.
Warsaw Pact	(WAR-saw PAKT) The alliance of the Soviet Union and many of the Communist nations of Eastern Europe.
Weimar Republic	(VYE-mar re-PUB-lik) The government of Germany after World War I.
welfare state	A state in which the government pays for the well-being of the people.
ziggurats	(ZIG-oo-rats) Temples of Mesopotamia which have steep steps on the outside.

INDEX

——————— J ———————

PHOTO ACKNOWLEDGMENTS

The photographs included in this text, on the pages indicated below, appear by courtesy of the following:

Abbreviations:
E.P.A.: Editorial Photocolor Archives
F.P.G.: Freelance Photographers Guild

L.C.: Library of Congress
U.P.I.: United Press International
Bettmann: The Bettmann Archive

Page 3: Document Henri Lhote. 5: (upper) American Museum of Natural History, (lower) E.P.A., SEF. 9: Historical Pictures Service, Chicago. 10: The Granger Collection. 11: (upper) World Bank, (lower) Israel Office of Information. 16, 17: Bettmann. 18: (upper) L.C., (lower) The British Museum. 23: Bettmann. 24: L.C. 26: Oriental Institute, U. of Chicago. 29: Bettmann. 30: Israeli Embassy. 31: Bettmann. 37: Freer Gallery of Art. 38: E.P.A., SEF. 43: (upper) F.P.G., (lower) Freer Gallery of Art. 49: E.P.A., SEF. 50: Sekai Bunka. 51: Bettmann. 54: U.P.I. 55: The British Museum. 56: Republic of Zimbabwe Mission to the U.N. 60: The Granger Collection. 61: Photo Researchers, George Holton. 68: E.P.A./Tzvoras. 69: Bettmann. 70: American Museum of Photography. 75: Bettmann. 76: Historical Pictures Service, Chicago. 77: Metropolitan Museum of Art, Harris Brisbane Fund, 1950. 82: Metropolitan Museum of Art (all rights reserved), Purchase, 1890, Levi Hale Willard Bequest. 83: Bettmann. 84, 88: The Granger Collection. 89: (upper) The American Museum of Photography, (lower) Metropolitan Museum of Art, Rogers Fund, 1906. 93: Historical Pictures Service, Chicago. 94: Bettmann. 95: American Museum of Photography. 99: F.P.G. 100: Academy of Motion Picture Arts and Sciences. 101: E.P.A., Scala. 105: Alpha. 106, 107: Bettmann. 111: American Museum of Natural History. 110, 112: Bettmann. 117: (upper) Bettmann, (lower) E.P.A., Scala. 127, 128: Bettmann. 131: L.C. 133: (upper) Alpha, (lower) Lee Rosenberg. 137: The Granger Collection. 139, 143: Bettmann. 144: Coronet Instructional Media. 148: (right) Kay Reese & Associates, (left) Brown Brothers. 149: E.P.A., Scala. 153: Bettmann. 154: (upper left) L.C., (upper right) Bettmann, (lower) Giraudon-Paris. 157: E.P.A., Scala. 160: E.P.A., SEF. 165: Photo Researchers, Guy Gillette. 166: Bettmann. 172: Biblioteque Nationale. 180: French Information Service. 181: Alpha. 182: Bettmann. 186, 187: E.P.A., Scala. 188: Pitti Gallery, Florence, Italy. 189: E.P.A., Scala. 193: N.Y. Public Library. 194: Bettmann. 197: Alpha. 199: (left) Folger Shakespeare Library, (right) Bettmann. 202: Bettmann. 203: National Library of Medicine. 207: (upper) The Granger Collection, (lower) Bettmann. 212: L.C. 213: (upper) L.C., (lower) Bettmann. 218: The Granger Collection. 219: The British Museum. 220: Bettmann. 225: N.Y. Public Library. 226: L.C. 235: Bettmann. 236: (upper) Bettmann, (lower) The Folger Shakespeare Library. 241: The Louvre. 242: Photo Researchers, L. Sir. 245: Bettmann. 246: The Granger Collection. 247: Bettmann. 253: (upper) John and Mable Ringling Museum of Art, Sarasota, Florida; (lower) Bettmann. 254: N.Y. Public Library. 258: Bettmann. 259: (upper) Bettmann, (lower) Historical Pictures Service, Chicago. 262: European Art Color Slides, copyright Adelberg, Inc. 264: (upper) Bettmann, (lower) L.C. 271: (upper) Bettmann, (lower) L.C. 272: The Louvre. 276: L.C. 277: (upper) L.C., (lower) Valley Forge Historical Society. 280: Bettmann. 281: L.C. 286: The Louvre. 287, 288:

Bettmann. 290: Historical Pictures Service, Chicago. 293: The Louvre. 294: Musées royaux des Beaux-Arts de Belgique, Bruxelles. 297, 298, 299: The Louvre. 306: Bettmann. 307: The Granger Collection. 312, 313: Bettmann. 318: (right) The British Museum, (left) Historical Pictures Service, Chicago. 319: Bettmann. 323: Alpha. 324: L.C. 325: Black Star, Dennis Brack. 329: (left) Historical Pictures Service, Chicago, (right) L.C. 330: Gamma Liaison. 334: L.C. 335: The Granger Collection. 340: Kay Reese & Associates. 341: National Film Board of Canada. 346: Photoworld. 348: (left) Historical Pictures Service, Chicago, (right) The Granger Collection. 352: Historical Pictures Service, Chicago. 353: L.C. 355: Historical Pictures Service, Chicago. 357: L.C. 358: (upper) Bettmann, (lower) Historical Pictures Service, Chicago. 363: Historical Pictures Service, Chicago. 364: N.Y. Public Library. 367: Mladen Grcevic. 368: Historical Pictures Service, Chicago. 370: The Granger Collection. 376: British Museum. 377: (upper) Textile Museum, (lower) British Crown copyright, Science Museum, London. 378: Bettmann. 381: International Harvester Co. 383: U.S.D.A. 386: The Granger Collection. 387: NASA. 388: Ford Motor Co. 391: Black Star. 392: Bettmann. 393: The Granger Collection. 397: (left) Gamma Liaison, (right) National Archives. 398: Bettmann. 402: Historical Pictures Service, Chicago. 403: Bettmann. 404: Sovfoto. 407: Bettmann. 408: Wide World. 409: The Granger Collection. 413: (upper) L.C., (lower) Bettmann. 414: Austrian Information Service. 415: European Art Color Slides. 422: The Granger Collection. 423: Shostal Associates, Charles May. 428: The Granger Collection. 429: Bettmann. 434: Peabody Museum of Salem, Mark Sexton. 435: (upper) E.P.A., Snark; (lower) The Granger Collection. 438: E.P.A., Scala. 439: The Granger Collection. 440: (upper) L.C., (lower) Photo Researchers, Dr. Georg Gerster. 445: India Office Library. 446: (left) National Film Board of Canada, (right) Gamma Liaison. 450: (upper) World Bank, Ray Witlin; (lower) American Petroleum Institute. 455: L.C. 457: Bettmann. 462: (upper left) U.S. Dept. of the Navy, (upper right) L.C., (lower) Bettmann. 463: Historical Pictures Service, Chicago. 464: National Archives. 471: L.C. 472: (upper) National Museum of American Art (formerly Nat'l. Collection of Fine Arts), Smithsonian Institution, Howard Taft Lorenz, DISMISSAL, 1940, oil on canvas, 91.4 × 76.2 cm., 1971. 447.62. Transfer from Museum of Modern Art; (lower) Bettmann. 476: Sovfoto. 477: Sovfoto, Novosti. 481: Sovfoto. 482: Black Star, Dennis Brack. 483: Sovfoto, Novosti. 488: (left) The Granger Collection, (right) U.S. Dept. of the Army. 489: L.C. 492: Wide World. 493: U.P.I. 494, 498: L.C. 499: Wide World. 500: (upper) The Bettmann Archive, (lower) L. C. 505: (upper) European Art Color/© S.P.A.D.E.M., Paris/V.A.G.A., New York, 1981; (lower) Historical Pictures Service, Chicago. 506: U. P. I. 510: (upper) U. P. I., (lower) National Archives. 511: U. S. Dept. of the Army. 512: Leo de Wys. 516: U. S. Dept. of the Army. 517: The Bettmann Archive, 518: British War Museum. 524: United Nations. 526: Wide World. 527: Woodfin Camp, Tony Howorth. 532: (upper) The Granger Collection, (lower) Historical Pictures Service, Chicago. 533: United Nations. 537: James H. Pickerell Associates ©. 539: Sovfoto, Tass. 540: Photo Researchers—(right) Friedman, (left) Joe Scherschel. 544: Ford Foundation. 545: (right) World Bank, (left) Woodfin Camp, Marc and Evelyn Bernheim. 550: (right) Photo Researchers, Paolo Koch; (left) Wide World. 551: Wide World. 555: Black Star, Charles C. Lowe. 556: (upper) U.P.I., (lower) Black Star. 561: Historical Pictures Service, Chicago. 562: (upper) Peace Corps, (lower) Historical Pictures Service, Chicago. 566: Black Star, Scheler. 568: Black Star—(upper)

Harry Redl, (lower) Dennis Brack. 573, 574: U.S. Dept. of the Army. 580: Black Star, Dennis Brack. 581: Black Star, Sipa Press. 582: Black Star, James Nachtway. 583: U.P.I. 586: Black Star, Michael Setbonn. 587: (upper) Black Star, Sipa Press, (lower) Gamma Liaison, Alain Mingam. 592: Bettmann. 594: (upper) Bettmann, (lower) Wide World. 595: Lester A. Sebel. 599: Black Star, Bob Schalkwijk. 600: Wide World. 602: Flannery. 604: (upper) Shostal Associates, Eric Carle; (lower) Collection, the Museum of Modern Art, New York. *Bird in Space.* (1928?) Bronze (unique cast), 54″ high. 605: Collection, the Museum of Modern Art, New York. Salvadore Dali *The Persistence of Memory.* 1931. Oil on canvas, $9\frac{1}{2}″ \times 15″$. 608: NASA. 609: I.B.M. 610: March of Dimes. 614: L.C. 615: U.P.I. 617: Lee Rosenberg. 620: L.C. 621: U.P.I. 622: Black Star, Sipa Press. 623: (upper) Wide World, (lower) U.P.I. 628: Woodfin Camp, Wally McNamee. 629: The Granger Collection. 631: Woodfin Camp, Bob Davis.

Cover: Robert Frerck. Page XVIII: The Metropolitan Museum of Art, Rogers Fund. 66: Robert Frerck. 124: The Metropolitan Museum of Art, Rogers Fund. 178: The Granger Collection. 232: The Metropolitan Museum of Art, Rogers Fund. 268: Robert Frerck. 304: The Metropolitan Museum of Art, Bequest of Mrs. Martha T. Fiske Collord. 338: Robert Frerck, 374: Milton & Joan Mann. 418: Milton & Joan Mann. 468: American Heritage. 522: Jason Lauré. 578: Focus West.

ACKNOWLEDGMENTS FOR PRINTED MATTER

Herodotus Describes Trade on the Euphrates, p. 34
From *The Histories of Herodotus.* Reprinted by permission of J. M. Dent & Sons, Ltd., and E. P. Dutton & Co., Inc.

"To My Husband," by Hsu Shu, p. 48
From *The Penguin Book of Chinese Verse,* trans. Robert Kotewall and Norman L. Smith. Translation copyright © Norman L. Smith and Robert Kotewall, 1962. Reprinted by permission of Penguin Books, Ltd.

Thucydides on Writing History, p. 87
From *The Greek Historians,* ed. Francis B. Godolphin. Adapted and reprinted by permission of Random House, Inc. Copyright 1942 by Random House.

Pericles' Speech to the Athenians, p. 92
From *The Peloponnesian War.* Reprinted by permission of E. P. Dutton & Co., Inc. Copyright 1934.

Tacitus Describes the Germans, p. 115
From *The Complete Works of Tacitus.* The Macmillan Co., Ltd. (London), 1942.

A Crusader Describes the Middle East, p. 163
From *The Crusades,* by Harold Lamb. Reprinted by permission of Doubleday & Co., Inc. Copyright 1930 by Harold Lamb.

Marco Polo's Description of the Mongols, p. 169
From *The Travels of Marco Polo.* Reprinted by permission of E. P. Dutton & Co., Inc.

A Medieval Doctor's Advice, p. 184
From *University Records and Life in the Middle Ages.* Reprinted by permission of Columbia University Press. Copyright 1944.

Leonardo da Vinci Looks for Work, p. 195
From *The Renaissance,* by Will Durant. Reprinted by permission of Simon & Schuster, Inc. Copyright © 1953 by Will Durant.

Letter Sent by Joan of Arc to the English during the Siege of Orleans, p. 205
From *Proceedings of the Condemnation of Joan of Arc,* ed. P. Champion. Copyright 1920 by Librairie Honore Champion.

Charles I on Sunday Entertainment, p. 238
From *Readings in European History,* ed. James H. Robinson. Copyright 1906 by Ginn and Company.

Louis XIV: The Sun King, p. 244
From *Readings in European History,* ed. James H. Robinson. Copyright 1906 by Ginn and Company.

Bishop Brunet's Description of Peter the Great, p. 250
From *Readings in European History,* ed. James H. Robinson. Copyright 1906 by Ginn and Company.

British Troops Surrender at Yorktown, p. 279
From *The American Reader,* ed. Paul M. Angle. Copyright 1958 by Rand McNally, Inc.

Metternich's Note to Czar Alexander I, p. 315
From *Memoirs of Prince Metternich,* ed. Prince Richard Metternich; trans. Mrs. Alexander Napier. Copyright 1881 by Charles Scribner.

Debate over the Great Reform Bill, p. 321
From *Readings in European History,* eds. Leon Bernard and Theodore Hodges. Copyright 1961 by the Macmillan Publishing Company, Inc.

I Accuse, p. 332
From *Readings in European History Since 1814,* eds. Alexander Baltzly and Jonathan F. Scott. Copyright 1946 by F. S. Crofts, Inc.

Iron and Blood, p. 355
From *Readings in European History,* eds. Leon Bernard and Theodore Hodges. Copyright 1961 by the Macmillan Publishing Company, Inc.

Garibaldi's Announcement to the Italians, p. 361
From *The Campaign of Garibaldi in the Two Sicilies,* by Charles Stuart Forbes. Copyright 1861 by William Blackwood and Sons.

From *Hard Times,* p. 395
Hard Times, by Charles Dickens.

The Communist Manifesto, p. 406
From *Capital, the Communist Manifesto, and Other Writings,* by Karl Marx. Copyright 1932 by Random House, Inc.

Laws of Japan in 1634, p. 443
From *The Economic Aspects of the History of Civilization in Japan,* by Yosoburo Takekoshi. Copyright 1930 by George Allen and Unwin.

France and Russia Form an Alliance, p. 460
From *The Origins of the World War,* by Sidney B. Fay. Copyright 1943 by the Macmillan Publishing Company, Inc.

Joseph Stalin, p. 480
From *Russia and the West Under Lenin and Stalin,* by George Kennan. Copyright © 1961 by James Hotchkiss. Reprinted by permission of Little, Brown and Company, Inc., in association with the Atlantic Monthly Press.

From *Mein Kampf,* p. 496
Mein Kampf, by Adolf Hitler, trans. Ralph Manheim. Copyright 1943 by Houghton Mifflin, Inc.

Their Finest Hour, p. 514
From *The War Speeches of the Right Honorable Winston S. Churchill,* compiled by Charles Eade. Copyright 1953 by Houghton Mifflin.

Charter of UNESCO, p. 529
From *Readings in European History,* eds. Leon Bernard and Theodore Hodges. Copyright 1961 by the Macmillan Publishing Company, Inc.

An African Leader Speaks Out, p. 547
From *Zik: a Selection from the Speeches of Nnamdi Azikiwe.* Reprinted by permission of the Cambridge University Press. Copyright 1961.

The Cuban Missile Crisis, p. 570
From *The Public Papers of the Presidents of the United States: John F. Kennedy.* Copyright 1963 by the United States Government Printing Office.

Pacem in Terris, p. 613
From *Pacem in Terris: Encyclical Letter of Pope John XXIII.* Reprinted and adapted by permission of the Paulist/Newman Press. Copyright 1963 by the Missionary Society of St. Paul the Apostle in the State of New York.

The Civil Rights Act of 1964—Section VII, p. 619
From *A Bill of Rights Reader,* ed. Milton R. Konovitz. Copyright 1968 by the Cornell University Press.